Children and Adolescents with Learning Disabilities

Cecil D. Mercer

University of Florida

With contributions by Rex E. Schmid, Lynn Erb,
Ann R. Mercer, Bob Algozzine

Charles E. Merrill Publishing Co.
A Bell & Howell Company
Columbus   Toronto   London   Sydney

Published by
Charles E. Merrill Publishing Company
A Bell and Howell Company
Columbus, Ohio 43216

This book was set in Helvetica and Newtext.
The production editor was Jan Hall.
The cover was prepared by Will Chenoweth.

Copyright© 1979, by Bell & Howell Company. All rights reserved. No part of this book may be reproduced in any form, electronic or mechanical, including photocopy, recording, or any information storage and retrieval system, without permission in writing from the publisher.

Photo credits

Jeff Bates, p. 28; **Resource Teaching,** Charles E. Merrill 1978, pp. 17, 52, 56, 57, 62, 65, 75, 86, 185, 190, 198, 220, 226, 234 bottom, 265, 298, 308, 318, 320, 326, 327 top & bottom; 329, 333; **Values in the Classroom,** Charles E. Merrill 1977, pp. 20, 150, 296, 306, 332 right, 345; **Myron Cunningham,** pp. 25, 40, 81, 92, 156, 173, 178, 180, 186, 196, 200, 217 left, 228, 245, 249, 262, 324, 435, 441 top, 443, 444, 451; **Roger DeMuth,** *Instructor,* calendar on p. 405; **Valentine Dmitriev,** 336; **Celia Drake,** pp. 1, 18, 36, 149, 162, 165, 170, 187, 189, 204, 213, 215, 216 left & right, 219, 233, 234 top, 235, 254, 257, 259, 264, 267, 269, 272, 276, 277, 278, 280, 281, 284, 299, 304 left & right, 309, 310, 312, 316, 321, 322, 332 left, 380, 384, 385, 387, 398, 399, 401, 405, 410, 423, 426 top & bottom, 441 bottom, 458; **Julie Estadt,** p. 21; **Larry Hamill,** pp. 95, 102, 103, 105, 107, 108 top & bottom, 112, 115; **Jerry Harvey,** Children's Hospital, pp. 120, 126 left & right, 129, 132, 139, 140; **Eleanor Henry,** p. 167; **Tom Hutchinson,** Charles E. Merrill, cover, pp. 2, 24, 55, 70, 97, 99, 208, 217 right, 336, 338, 339, 340, 347, 368, 370, 371, 372, 373; **Cecil D. Mercer,** p. 393; **University of Southern California,** pp. 79, 109, 169, 362, 461.

Library of Congress Catalog Card Number: 78–70780

International Standard Book Number: 0–675–08272–2

Printed in the United States of America

2 3 4 5 6 7 8 9 10/ 85 84 83 82 81 80

It is with deep appreciation, love, and respect that I dedicate this book to my wife, Ann, who made extensive contributions to it. Throughout its preparation she maintained her roles of wife, mother, typist, editor, author, and friend in an admirable manner. A real heartfelt thanks, Ann.

Preface

The area of learning disabilities has experienced enormous growth during its short history. Interest and knowledge about it continue to expand rapidly. Children and adolescents with such disabilities are found across all ages, socioeconomic levels, and races with learning and behavior problems ranging from mild to severe. Professionals as well as parents now seek more knowledge about learning disabilities and effective methods for facilitating the academic and social-emotional growth of learning disabled individuals.

The purpose of this book is to provide *comprehensive* coverage of the learning disabilities field. Many theories and practices have emerged in a short time, and fortunately, many of them have been challenged and systematically investigated. Thus, some practices have been refined whereas others have diminished or increased in popularity. This book not only acquaints the reader with a wide range of theories and practices in learning disabilities, but its coverage allows the reader to develop his own perspective.

Section I, Foundations of Learning Disabilities, includes five chapters. Chapter 1 presents the history of learning disabilities within a broad framework of significant events in education, legislation, theoretical developments, and the formation of organizations. Chapter 2 discusses definitions, terms, and characteristics within four phases: the brain injured, minimal brain dysfunction, learning disabilities, and refinement of learning disabilities. Chapter 3 presents a comprehensive diagnostic process and highlights a five-step model. This section views the ability and skill approaches and their respective contributions within the context of the total diagnostic process. Chapter 4 describes parental adjustments to handicapped children and offers several different perspectives on the parent-teacher-child triad. Chapter 5 includes numerous medical aspects of learning disabilities and features such topics as drugs, megavitamin therapy, the Feingold diet, and patterning.

Section II, Specific Learning Disorders, includes five chapters. Chapter 6 describes the language disorders of learning disabled students in five areas: phonology, morphology, semantics, syntax, and pragmatics as well as an additional section on the *Illinois Test of Psycholinguistic Abilities* and the effectiveness of psycholinguistic teaching. Chapter 7 discusses reading problems: etiology, behavioral manifestations, tests, the development of reading, and reading approaches. Chapter 8 describes common arithmetic problems: etiology, characteristics, a skills hierarchy, tests, and selected teaching practices. Chapter 9 presents theories, related research, and practices in the perception and perceptual-motor areas, as well as implications for teaching. Chapter 10 offers a description of the social-emotional aspects of learning disabilities, highlighting etiology, behavioral characteristics, and curriculum suggestions.

Section III, Educational Services, includes four chapters. Chapter 11 describes the numerous service delivery models for learning disabled students. Chapter 12 presents early identification practices and extensively reviews early identification research. Early identification is discussed in terms of a multi-dimensional model; specific recommendations are offered. Moreover, it features early intervention approaches and related research. Chapter 13 focuses on an area of increasing concern, the learning disabled adolescent. Characteristics of these adolescents, secondary school practices, and specific recommendations are discussed. Chapter 14 focuses on teaching approaches, describing in detail several major instructional approaches and applied behavioral analysis. It offers five methods for organizing instruction and self-correcting materials; it presents instructional games appropriate for seatwork activities.

The book is primarily designed for use in introductory courses in learning disabilities. In addition to including theories, research, history, and characteristics, a representative sample of teaching methods is presented to provide the reader with some understanding and skills regarding educational and management practices. For teachers, these practices are only a beginning; for other professionals, they offer an overview of some teaching and management techniques that are often used with LD students.

The completion of this book was the result of the efforts of many people; however, several individuals deserve special acknowledgment for their exceptional contributions. I extend much appreciation to Dr. Rex E. Schmid, University of Florida, for his encouragement in the beginning stages of the book and for his contribution of Chapters 1, 5, and 13. Also, appreciation and thanks go to Dr. Lynn Erb and Dr. Bob Algozzine for writing selected chapters. Their contributions added needed expertise to Chapters 6 and 10. Special thanks go to Dr. Sara Tarver, University of Wisconsin, and Dr. James Ysseldyke, University of Minnesota, for their very helpful reviews of selected chapters and suggestions concerning the organization and format of the book. In addition, much gratitude goes to the reviewers, Dr. Thomas Stephens, Ohio State University, Dr. Judy Olson, Florida Technological University, and Dr. Colleen Blankenship, University of Illinois, for reading and critiquing the entire manuscript. Their constructive criticisms were invaluable. Thanks go to Dr. Myron A. Cunningham for his expert assistance with the photographs, and to Six Pence School for allowing us to take some of our pictures there. I am also especially grateful to Tom Hutchinson, special education editor, for encouragement and support, and to Jan Hall for her very skillful services as production editor.

Cecil D. Mercer

Contents

Section I: Foundations of learning disabilities   1

1   Historical perspectives   3
    Rex E. Schmid
2   Definitions, terms, and characteristics   37
3   Educational diagnosis   63
4   The family and learning disabilities   93
5   Medicine and learning disabilities   121
    Rex E. Schmid

Section II: Specific learning disorders   149

6   Language disabilities   151
    Lynn Erb, Cecil D. Mercer
7   Reading disabilities   197
    Ann R. Mercer, Cecil D. Mercer
8   Arithmetic disabilities   227
9   Perception and perceptual-motor disabilities   263
    Cecil D. Mercer, Ann R. Mercer

10	Social-emotional problems *Bob Algozzine*	297

Section III: Educational services for the learning disabled   317

11	Providing educational services	319
12	Early identification and intervention	337
13	The learning disabled adolescent *Rex E. Schmid*	381
14	Teaching children and adolescents	411

Appendix a	Tests	465
Appendix b	Films and filmstrips	469

Name index	473
Subject index	481

section I

Foundations of learning disabilities

1

Historical perspectives

There was once a very ignorant frog. One memorable spring morning, the frog was awakened by a messenger from the castle with a request that the frog present himself to the king that afternoon. Naturally, the frog was excited and puffed up with pride. After a meticulous grooming, the frog began his journey to the castle.

With each hop he speculated on why the king had summoned him. "Perhaps he wishes to congratulate me for my fine singing at twilight," he mused. "He's heard of my deeds and will make me chief protector of the pond," thought the frog, with the reward growing after each jump.

Upon arriving at the castle and being shown into the throne room, he leaped to the center of the floor and croaked, "Ah yes, my king, here is your Lord Chancellor of the Kingdom's Waterways."

With a nod to the guards, the king murmured, "Ah yes, here are my frog legs for dinner."

Had the ignorant frog been attentive to the past he would have known the king had a taste for fresh frog legs. How can we avoid repeating past mistakes? There are several reasons for examining the area of learning disabilities from a historical perspective. First, it provides an overview of an area in special education in which educational concepts, goals, and procedures are being vigorously generated, tested, and refined. Identification of evolutionary landmarks and milestones increases the chances of accurately assessing and interpreting contemporary events. Second, "You can't tell the players without a program." Without the advantage of what Frierson (1976) calls a "point of viewing," the people, agreements, disagreements, organizations, and alliances are incomprehensible. Third, unlike the ignorant frog, knowledge of history may keep us from jumping to conclusions.

In its brief history, the area of learning disabilities (LD) has had a growth rate unequaled by that of any other handicapping condition. Unknown to most educators prior to 1965, it was familiar to all special educators by 1970 and the term was used by a majority of all educators by 1975. *Learning disabilities* also has been regularly used—and misused—by the press, school boards, and legislators in the latter half of the 1970s.

To provide an overview of events, individuals, and time sequences relevant to the history of learning disabilities, Wiederholt's (1974) two-dimensional framework for examining the history of LD is expanded and modified. The categories of education, legislation/litigation, reinforcement theorists, and organizations are added. A discussion of selected events from each category is included to place learning disabilities in a perspective with other social and educational landmarks.

The content of this chapter is organized into a discussion of events and individuals drawn from three time periods: *genesis* (1647–1959), *birth* (1960–1969), and *growing pains* (1970—). Table 1.1 shows an *in toto* historical perspective of learning disabilities.

GENESIS PERIOD

Education

Education is a lifelong process of learning from the environment. The individual continually acquires knowledge, skills, attitudes, and appreciations of the society in which he lives (Good, 1958). "The major goal of educators in a democratic society should be to provide an opportunity for each individual to develop his abilities to their maximum potential and to prepare him to make his greatest contributions to society as a citizen" (Ikenberry, 1974, p. 230). Until the last half of the 19th century, this goal was given only lip service. Table 1.1 lists the landmarks in the evolution of American education toward implementing this goal for the handicapped.

In colonial America (1607–1787) three aims dominated education: religion, literacy, and a classical education. The varied attitudes of the colonists toward education led to three separate school patterns. The New England colonies evolved toward the Calvinist principle of compulsory, theologically centered education controlled by the state. The middle colonies established a system of parochial schools reflecting the many religious denominations settling in the region. The southern colonies transplanted the concept of selective education—the well-to-do received an excellent private education, while the poor were provided, at best, a meager schooling.

Education was not an obligation of the state. Families had to provide for their own, so the majority of Americans received only the rudiments of "readin', writin', and cipherin'." Education for the handicapped individual was relatively nonexistent and left to the discretion of the family.

Two events significantly influenced education during the emergence of the new nation (1787–1820). First, development of a nationwide school system lagged for nearly 50 years due to the social discordance following the American Revolution. Second, a decentralization precedent was set by the 10th Amend-

TABLE 1.1
Historical overview.

			Type of Disorder			
Period	Education	Legislation Litigation	Spoken Language	Written Language	Perceptual and Motor	Reinforcement Theorists	Organizations

GENESIS

Period	Education	Legislation Litigation	Spoken Language
1647		Old Deluder Satan Act	
1787		Northwest Ordinance	
1791		10th Amendment to Constitution	
1802	Philadelphia Sunday School organized		Gall
1817	Columbian Institute (Gallaudet College)		
1818	Lancastrian Schools		
1820	Common School Movement		
1821	First public high school		
1825			Bouillaud
1840		First compulsory education law	
1857		Columbian Institute funded by Congress	
1861			Broca

TABLE 1.1 cont.

			Type of Disorder			
Period	Education	Legislation Litigation	Spoken Language	Written Language	Perceptual and Motor	Reinforcement Theorists	Organizations
1862		Morrill Land Grant Act					
1864			Jackson				
1865	Beginning of hand training						
1873	First public kindergarten						
1874		Kalamazoo case					
1879		Education for blind					
1887			Bastian				
1896	John Dewey opens laboratory school						
1909							National Committee for Mental Hygiene
1911		Mandatory legislation for handicapped (N.J.)					
1912	Federal Children's Bureau organized						
1917		Smith-Hughes Act		Hinshelwood			
1918		Military Vocational Rehabilitation Act					

Year	Event	Person(s)
1919	Progressive Education Society organized	
1920	Civilian Vocational Rehabilitation Act	
1921		Fernald
1922	National Society for Crippled Children; International Council for the Education of Exceptional Children	
1926		Head
1928		Orton
1930	White House Conference on Child Health and Protection	
1931	Department of Special Education established in USOE	Thorndike
1932		Monroe
1935	Social Security Act	
1936		Gillingham & Stillman; Kirk; Goldstein
1939		Strauss & Werner
1944	G.I. Bill	
1946	Commission on Life Adjustment for Youth	
1947		Lehtinen

TABLE 1.1 cont.

Period	Education	Legislation Litigation	Spoken Language	Written Language	Perceptual and Motor	Reinforcement Theorists	Organizations
1949							United Cerebral Palsy Association
1950	"Baby boom"	National Science Foundation Act			Cruickshank		
1953			Osgood			Skinner	National Association for Retarded Children
1954	School integration movement	Cooperative Research Act					
1955			Myklebust		Kephart		
1956	Council on Basic Education			Spalding			
1957	Sputnik						Fund for Perceptually Handicapped Children; New York Association for Brain-Injured Children
1958		National Defense Education Act					
BIRTH							
1960			Wepman				
1961			Kirk				
1962		Institute of Child			Cruickshank	Haring & Phillips	

Type of Disorder spans Spoken Language, Written Language, Perceptual and Motor columns.

Year					
1963		Health and Human Development			
1964	War on Poverty		Doman & Delacato Frostig		Association for Children with Learning Disabilities
1965	Head Start	ESEA amendments			
1966		ESEA amendments			
1967		ESEA amendments; *Hobson v. Hansen*	Johnson & Myklebust	Lindsley Lovitt	
1968	Follow Through	Early Education Act for Handicapped; *Arreola v. Board of Education*			Division for Children with Learning Disabilities
1969		Children with Specific Learning Disabilities Act			

GROWING PAINS

1973	Mainstream movement			↑	
1974				│ Quay	↑
1975		PL 94-142		│	│ Ysseldyke & Salvia
1976				↓	│
1977	Secondary programming emphasis				↓
1978					↑ │ │ Contemporary problems │ ↓

Division on Career Development

ment to the Constitution (1791), which placed the responsibility for education on the individual states. Thus the quality and availability of education offered by the states varied widely. Some isolated experiments such as the Lancastrian Monitorial Schools and the Philadelphia Sunday School attempted to increase the number of children receiving an education during this period, but these were exceptions to the general pattern.

A general public education system (1820–1870) developed slowly. Decentralization continued to cause wide variations in program quality. Because educational traditions in the three sections of the country differed, few people agreed as to what should constitute a public school program. During this period, however, public attitudes, concerns, and opinions began to support the notion of taxation and legislation to establish a free, compulsory education system. Often called the *common school movement* (Church & Sedlak, 1976), education efforts of this period centered on three goals: (*a*) to provide a free elementary education to every white child living in the United States, (*b*) to create a trained education profession, and (*c*) to establish some form of state control over local schools. The third goal was important because achieving the first two was dependent on gaining some form of central control.

Toward the end of the common school movement in the 1860s, an educational concept with significant implications for the handicapped gained popular support. The educational focus shifted from the "three Rs" to providing educational programs designed to fit the needs of specific groups. By 1865, differential schooling (usually called *hand training*, which included manual training, vocational training, and industrial education) had become a responsibility of the schools. The importance of this concept for the handicapped was that society had begun to consider individual differences and support special programs. Also important were the establishment of a free elementary education program, trained teachers, and supervision from a central state agency.

The standardization of American education (1871–1939) was characterized by continued growth in number of schools, pupil attendance, and public insistence on schooling for all children. For the handicapped, several developments of significance occurred:

1. The "child-centered" education movement, with its focus on the individual, gained popular acceptance.
2. The proliferation of preschools and kindergartens provided the foundation for early intervention programs.
3. New directions in educational psychology exemplified by James, Hull, and Thorndike indicated an increasing concern for individual differences in children.
4. Fresh approaches to the philosophy of education by individuals such as Harris, Parker, and Dewey established the role of the school as preparing every child for a productive life.
5. The advent of World War I stimulated psychological and educational comparisons of Americans on a national scale, and injuries to soldiers promoted interest in the physiology and psychology of individual differences.
6. Of particular importance was the 1930 White House Conference on Child Health and Protection and the establishment in 1931 of the Department of Special Education in the U.S. Office of Education.

Two decades of complacency in general education (1940–1959) began with World War II. The concern for individual differences became muted as educators struggled with the "baby boom" that flooded the schools in the late 1940s and early 1950s. Viewed as custodial institutions, schools tried to keep America's youth busy and off the labor market (Church & Sedlak, 1976). The schools prepared children for life: not how to do a job, but how to get one; how to get along with the boss and other workers; and how to handle a family, childrearing, money and leisure time activities. This trend prompted the U.S. Office of

Education to establish in 1946 a Commission on Life Adjustment Education for Youth.

Some did challenge the complacency. Critics (Bell, 1949; Bestor, 1953; Conant, 1959; Hutchins, 1953; Rickover, 1959; Smith, 1949, 1954) questioned the efficacy of "life adjustment" education. In addition, the struggle to integrate segregated school systems was just beginning to grow into the intensity that would later include housing, jobs, and almost every aspect of society.

In the last 5 years of the 1950s, pressure for change mounted, although no one agreed on the specific changes needed. Cornerstones were laid for the turbulent 60s: general awareness of handicaps, parents publicly acknowledging the presence and needs of their exceptional children, the difficulty in obtaining education for the handicapped, and the desegregation movement.

Americans had prided themselves on their strength, wealth, and position after World War II. They were shocked when in October, 1957, the Soviets launched Sputnik I. The public severely criticized American education. They demanded reform. Educational philosphy and goals radically changed, and special education suddenly expanded.

Legislation and Litigation

Historical legislation on education illustrates that the current concern for the learning disabled was not only improbable prior to 1960, but perhaps impossible. It took 300 years to evolve the social and legislative climate necessary to provide the comprehensive services we take now for granted.

The roots of a free public education began in the Massachusetts colony with the Old Deluder Satan Act, which required all towns of over 50 households to support a school master. Little legislation of consequence followed until the Northwest Ordinance of 1787, which reserved one section of land in each township of 36 sections for the support of public schools. While it did not require that schools be built in the territory (Ohio, Indiana, Illinois, Michigan, Wisconsin, and part of Minnesota), it did stipulate that the rent or sale of the school section assist in financing schools.

But it was not until Rhode Island's compulsory education law was passed in 1840 (Aiello, 1976) that the exceptional child legally deserved an education. Gradually, other states adopted the Rhode Island model during the establishment and standardization of the general public education system (1820–1939). With the advent of compulsory education legislation, educators wondered what to do for the less able student.

In general, legislative patterns between 1820 and 1939 reflect a gradual change in social attitude toward acceptance of universal education. For the handicapped, some key federal and state legislation was approved. *Federal* legislation must be emphasized because it permits one to trace the role of the federal government from a minor contributor to a major force in American education. [For a complete review, see LaVor (1976).]

Early federal legislation of importance includes:

1. In 1857 the establishment of the Columbian Institute for the Instruction of the Deaf, Dumb, and Blind (changed to Gallaudet College in 1954).
2. In 1857, Congressional approval of federal aid for students at the Columbian Institute.
3. The Morrill Land Grant Act (1862), providing federal land to be used for the establishment of colleges in each state.
4. In 1879, Congressional authorization of federal monies to support the provision of materials to the blind.

Of the multitude of laws and court cases at the state level, two stand as landmarks. First, by 1870, private academies provided most secondary education, while the state provided elementary education. The public often vigorously objected to the use of tax money for high schools. In 1874, the Michigan Supreme Court ruled in the Kalamazoo case *(Stuart v. School District No. 1,* 1874) that state and local governments could tax citizens for the support of secondary education. With this decision, resistance to public secondary schools faded and the establishment of an elementary through secondary public school system was assured. Second, statutory provisions for permissive and/or mandatory education of the handicapped began in New Jersey in 1911 (Melcher, 1976) and was followed by other states (Minnesota in 1915; Wisconsin, Illinois, and New York in 1917) until the depression and World War II curtailed the expansion.

With the signing of the Military Rehabilitation Act on June 27, 1918, a 39-year period of federal inactivity in educational legislation ended. Approval for a similar vocational rehabilitation act for civilians followed two years later. These two federal acts provided counseling, job training and placement, and prosthetic devices for disabled persons. The Social Security Act of 1935 also provided income and rehabilitative services for several categories of disabled individuals. Significant federal legislation followed World War II, such as the G.I. Bill, the National Science Foundation Act, and the Cooperative Research Act (designed to foster cooperative research between institutions of higher learning and the federal government).

Despite the legislation mentioned, federal involvement with education from 1791 to 1957 ranged from negative to lukewarm. This reluctance to get involved retarded the growth of services for the handicapped. Sputnik catalyzed the idea of federal involvement, resulting in equality of services, adequate financial support, and properly trained school personnel.

Type of Disorder

An examination of the contributions to research, theory, and treatment strategies that helped shaped the learning disabilities field suggests the following:

1. The early theoretical foundation of learning disabilities lies primarily within three disorders: spoken language, written language, and perceptual and motor disorders.
2. Mostly physicians and psychologists researched disorder areas.
3. Prior to the late 1950s, researchers emphasized clinical investigations rather than practical application in the school.
4. The population investigated by these researchers evolved from brain-injured adults, to brain-injured children, to children of normal intelligence.

Investigators in all three areas focused on process disorders or designed interventions based on the concept of process deficit. *Process* refers to the series of biophysical and psychological changes that effect learning. Specific process areas investigated included auditory, visual, tactile, motor, vocal, feedback, closure, and memory. They assumed that process integrity related to appropriate responses and learning.

As should be expected, many investigators worked with the same concepts. In discussing the development of concepts and knowledge, Selye (1977) notes, "Usually some vague realization of the concept goes back so far in history and its authors are so numerous that by the time it is generally accepted, we can no longer identify the origins of the idea with any degree of precision" (p. ix). Only when an investigator arranges all the bits and pieces of a concept into a meaningful new pattern is he considered a discoverer. "In other words, here the discoverer is the scientist who discovered the subject not for the first time, but more than anyone else" (Selye, 1977, p. x).

Disorders of Spoken Language

Most investigators of spoken language disorders tended to focus on etiology, clinical treatment, and development of models. Specifically, the concepts of localized brain injury and hemispheric dominance received extensive attention. According to Wiederholt (1974), Franz Joseph Gall, a German physician, theorized in 1802 that head injuries were likely to result in mental disorders. Based on his work with brain-injured adults, Gall speculated that specific regions of the brain controlled certain mental activities. He advocated the controversial position that specific localized brain injury resulted in the loss of speech. His theories and the association of his name with phrenology eventually tarnished his reputation. Most considered him a discredited charlatan.

However, Gall's hypothesis of localization was accepted and defended by a well-respected member of the French medical establishment, John Baptiste Bouillaud. In the 1820s, Bouillaud worked to locate the faculty of speech in the frontal anterior lobes of the brain.

Forty years later, the idea surfaced again in France. During the 1860s, Pierre Paul Broca continued the work of Bouillaud. Unlike Bouillaud, however, Broca believed that movement and sensation were not located in separate areas of the brain, and that speech disorders were due to damage of the frontal convolutions of the brain. Broca contributed the hypothesis that the functions of the brain's left hemisphere differed from those of the right hemisphere.

Following Broca's idea, another researcher in the 1860s, John Hughlings Jackson, attempted to locate speech disorders in the cerebral cortex. Jackson proceeded to develop an entire classification and definition system for the components of the speech process.

The medical establishment was thrown into chaos. Many stoutly defended the older theories. Others contributed to the general discord (Bastian, 1887, 1898; Wernicke, 1908) by actually developing "models" to describe the speech process.

Much of this controversy was dampened by the consolidation of theory by Head (1926) which led to wide acceptance of several conclusions about disorders in spoken language.

1. Disorders in language could not be dichotomized as sensory or motor.
2. Motor correlates of language disabilities were not necessarily due to a disturbance in higher level brain processes.
3. Brain localization and hemisphere differentiation were valid concepts.
4. Loss of symbolic speech functions did not necessarily include a concomitant loss in mechanical aptitudes.

Theorists and researchers continued to investigate disorders of spoken language for the next two and one-half decades. Few discoveries or conjectures were accepted as milestones, however, until Charles Osgood postulated his communication model. Although he drew from the work of many investigators, Osgood was most influenced by the work of clinical neurologists who were seeking to develop a "schematic diagram" of the communication process (Osgood & Miron, 1963).

The Osgood model attempts to explain what happens within an individual between the presentation of an external stimulus and the individual's overt response to the stimulus. The model includes the three common elements of the language process: decoding, encoding, and association. *Decoding* refers to the perception of language, *encoding* refers to the use of language for the expression of ideas and concepts, and *association* refers to the process elicited by decoding and resulting in encoding. More discussion of Osgood's model is presented in Chapter 6.

A contemporary of Osgood, Helmer R. Myklebust, also contributed to the knowledge of spoken language disorders. Myklebust (1955) defined *language* as symbolic behavior (i.e., using words as symbols for expression ideas, feelings, and labeling objects). He later hypothesized five developmental stages of abstraction: sensation, perception, imagery, symbolization, and conceptualization (Myklebust, 1960). He thought that each stage related directly to experience and maintained that an unimpaired peripheral and central nervous system was prerequisite to the development of language. In addition, three basic psychological processes must be intact: identification, internalization, and assimilation. The first is the recognition of and identification with the human voice. In the second process the child relates personal experience to communication symbols. The third is the process by which experiences become related to produce abstractions.

Myklebust's (1960) theory of language included five development levels. In order of development, the levels include *inner language*—auditory symbolic experience; *auditory receptive language*—comprehending the spoken word; *auditory expressive language*—speaking; *visual receptive language*—reading; and *visual expressive language*—writing.

Unlike earlier investigators, Osgood and Myklebust focused on children with suspected brain damage rather than on brain-damaged adults. Their contemporaries in the other disorder areas also used this strategy.

Disorders of Written Language

Research on disorders in written language was recognized after 1900, with one or two investigators dominating the area. In 1917, a French physician, James Hinshelwood, presented the first well-accepted publication describing etiology and intervention techniques. He defined *word blindness* as a "condition in which, with normal vision and therefore seeing the letters and words distinctly, an individual is no longer able to interpret written or printed language" (p. 2). Such difficulty could be caused by a defect in an area of the brain storing visual memories of words and letters. The defect could be due to disease, injury at birth, or faulty development. He further theorized that the brain defect was localized in a specific portion of the left hemisphere.

To help a patient compensate for word blindness, Hinshelwood suggested a three-stage method of reading instruction. First, the teacher should teach the individual letters of the alphabet. He reasoned that the student would store the letters in the visual-memory part of the brain. Second, the student should learn words by spelling them aloud, thus appealing to auditory memory for recall of the whole word. Third, the learner would gradually acquire words for storage in the visual memory. Reading proficiency, Hinselwood believed, could be attained only through intensive practice and the development of the brain's visual memory.

Like the investigators of spoken language, who paired disorders of language with brain damage, Hinshelwood ascribed disorders of written language to defects in specific areas of the brain. Like other investigators, he relied on studies of adults with brain injury or disease and autopsy findings to validate his speculations.

In the late 1930s, Samuel T. Orton, a specialist in neurology and neuropathology, established himself as a dominant force in the field. His theories, established after a 10-year study of language acquisition disorders, influenced many investigators. He speculated that one side of the brain dominated the language processes (Orton, 1937). He thought that language-disabled children who had no demonstrable brain injury had failed to establish hemispheric dominance. The children examined by Orton displayed "mixtures of right and left sidedness, handedness, eyedness, and footedness" (Myers & Hammill, 1976, p. 258). Orton concluded that mixed or confused dominance interfered with language functions as well as motor functions and that treatment must remediate mixed dominance or establish dominance. Other aspects of Orton's theory were that a mixed dominant state of the brain could be transferred hereditarily, and that the location of a brain injury was more important than the amount of damage.

Little empirical evidence supports these notions. However, educators continue to use the practical remediation strategies Orton suggested. Why? First, Orton spoke little of practical applications. Second, Orton's theoretical position influenced several investigators who developed and publicized the practical adaptations. Third, these practical applications have been successful with children exhibiting written language problems. Among those influenced by Orton, who in turn influenced other investigators, were Marion Monroe, Anna Gillingham, Bessie Stillman, Samuel Kirk, Romalda Spalding, and Grace Fernald.

Monroe, Orton's research assistant at the Iowa State Psychopathic Hospital, helped test the efficacy of his theories for education. She published *Children Who Cannot Read* in 1932 and credited Orton for calling her attention to children with specific reading disabilities. She also described assessment tests (based on the "dominance" theory) and a teaching strategy called the *synthetic phonetic approach*. This approach begins with pictures mounted on cards from which the child identifies initial consonants and then vowels. Blending begins after a few elements are learned and gradually the child starts to read selected stories. The child repeats and drills considerably. The kinesthetic approach (learning via movement exercises, e.g., tracing a word) is used as needed. Monroe reported success using this method with children with serious reading disabilities who had difficulty making visual associations.

Gillingham and Stillman (1936) acknowledge Orton in their book on remedial reading procedures. Their approach focuses on developing language-pattern associations between the visual, auditory, and kinesthetic mechanisms in the dominant hemisphere. In building these associations *(linkage)*, a multisensory teaching approach is used. For example, the translation of visual symbols into sound (visual-auditory linkage) is taught by showing the child a phonogram printed on a card. Its name and sound are clearly pronounced by the teacher and repeated by the student.

These researchers felt that failure to establish any one of the linkages would result in a language disability. "We suppose that in individuals with perfect unilateral dominance all these linkages take care of themselves without special training. In the cases which we are considering, however, it is essential to establish each linkage with patient care, even into the thousandth repetition" (p. 36).

Concurrently, Kirk was experimenting with remedial techniques for written language disorders. As a result of his success in 1929 with a retarded delinquent boy, the Chicago Institute for Juvenile Research invited him to confer with Monroe. Following that conference, Monroe agreed to tutor Kirk in the diagnosis and remediation of severe cases of reading disabilities.

After completing his master's degree, he conducted research at the Wayne County Training School in Northville, Michigan, on the academic ability of the mentally retarded. Superintendent Robert Haskell established the research department and Thorleif G. Hegge directed it. Many other individuals who later played significant roles in the development and direction of special education and learning disabilities began there: Alfred Strauss, Heinz Werner, Sidney Bijou, Newell Kephart, Boyd McCandless, and William Cruickshank.

In 1936, some department researchers developed a system to teach phonetic reading (Hegge, Kirk, & Kirk, 1936). Orton, Monroe, and Fernald (Kirk, 1976) influenced the system, based on principles of learning from the Chicago school of functional psychology. *Remedial Reading Drills* (2nd ed.) (Hegge, Kirk, & Kirk, 1970) now contains the manual and drills for this system.

Two decades after the Kirk materials appeared, Spalding presented an approach to written language disability called *Unified Phonics Methods*. Acknowledging the influence of Orton, she claimed her approach was a

> highly successful method for teaching the basic techniques of the language-accurate speaking, spelling, writing, and reading, as one integrated subject. . . . The core of the method is a technique by which the child learns how to write down the sounds used in spoken English as they are combined into words. Thus, conversely, he can pronounce any printed word. Meaning is thoroughly taught hand-in-hand with the writing and by using new words in original sentences. It begins with correct pronunciation

of words and the writing of their component sounds in accordance with the rules of English spelling. By this means the saying, writing, reading and meaning of words are well learned and understood. After this initial grounding, a child in his reading recognizes words at a glance—very soon without any resort to pictures or any other aids except the use of phonics. (Spalding & Spalding, 1962, p. 8)

Beginning in 1921 with the establishment of the clinic school at the University of California, the work of Fernald influenced the development of many remedial reading programs. She focused on children's problems in reading and writing without speculating about process, dominance, or brain injury. Her techniques exemplify the VAKT (visual-auditory-kinesthetic-tactile) approach to reading instruction (Fernald, 1943). She divided reading problems into two general disability groups, total and partial. To Fernald, those with partial disability were more hampered because of bad habits interfering with learning.

Disorders of Perceptual and Motor Processes

While investigation of perceptual and motor processes related to learning did not gain momentum until after 1900, individuals within this area strongly influenced the learning disability movement. Why? Reasons might include

1. The establishment of a center encouraging investigation of motor and perceptual problems at the Wayne County Training School.
2. The attraction of many outstanding individuals to the center during and after the depression year.
3. The prolific work of the individuals investigating perceptual and motor problems.
4. The cumulative influence and interaction with other professionals by the perceptual-motor clique.
5. The large number of protégés who became influential in the area of learning disabilities.

Hallahan and Cruickshank (1973) suggest that the work of Kurt Goldstein (1936, 1939) helped provide the basis for perceptual-motor investigations. In his adult, brain-injured patients, he observed meticulosity, perseveration, figure-ground confusion, forced response to stimuli, and catastrophic reaction.

Goldstein's work stimulated Werner and Strauss to study brain-injured retarded children. These two German associate professors—Strauss, a neuropsychiatrist, and Werner, a developmental psychologist—had fled Germany during Hitler's rise to power. Strauss had worked 3 years (1933–1936) at the University of Barcelona, Spain, before accepting an invitation from Superintendent Haskell to become a research psychiatrist at the Wayne County Training School. Werner, after a brief stay in the Netherlands and short periods at Harvard and Michigan, also accepted Haskell's invitation to join the research staff. Together they designed and conducted a series of studies (Strauss & Werner, 1942; Werner & Strauss, 1939, 1940, 1941) to investigate brain-injured, mentally retarded children. Using the terms *exogenous* (mental retardation due to brain-injury resulting from factors outside the genetic structure) and *endogenous* (retardation due to inherited factors), they replicated Goldstein's results with brain-injured adults. These findings led to the identification of a subgroup of retarded children who exhibited unique characteristics. Prior to these findings researchers had thought retarded individuals a homogeneous group and provided a common treatment program. In a revolutionary statement, Strauss and Werner concluded that a standard institutional regimen was inappropriate for the exogenous group. Researchers such as Sarason (1949) hotly debated their position.

For the next 35 years, their landmark investigations, educational concepts, and interactions with young scholars continued to spark the learning disability movement. The works of Laura Lehtinen, Newell C. Kephart, and William M. Cruickshank expanded their theoretical positions.

Some theorists believe classrooms should be devoid of distractions.

Lehtinen, the education director of the Cove School for Brain-Injured Children in Racine, Wisconsin, collaborated with Strauss to develop teaching procedures. They believed that methods could be developed to relieve perceptual and conceptual disturbances and, thus, reduce symptomatic behavior disorders. In 1947, Strauss and Lehtinen coauthored *Psychopathology and Education of the Brain-Injured Child.* Prior to this book, few educators knew that brain-injured children existed. Strauss and Lehtinen held that in such children, various disorders in perception, concept formation, and mental organization seriously interfered with learning. They suggested two interventions: *(a)* manipulating and controlling the environment, and *(b)* teaching the child voluntary control. Specific recommendations included these ideas:

1. Brain-injured children should be taught in small groups.
2. Classrooms should be large and well lighted.
3. Visually stimulating material and decorations should be eliminated.
4. Windows should be covered.
5. Teachers should wear plain, unornamented clothes.
6. Daily routines should be established.
7. Instructional materials should be simple, with no distractions.
8. Lessons should be slow paced and proceed from simple to complex.

Like some investigators of written and spoken language disorders, Strauss and Lehtinen recommended the use of kinesthetic approaches to teaching. However, all activities attempt to develop visual-perceptual abilities.

Eight years after the publication of the Strauss and Lehtinen volume, Strauss and Kephart (1955) coauthored Volume II of *Psychopathology and Education of the Brain-Injured Child.* In this volume, they compare the research on brain-injured children of normal intelligence with the research on mentally retarded brain-injured children. Kephart (1960) later postulated perceptual-motor development as the basis for all learning. He held that because cognitive development is largely dependent upon perceptual-motor development, in an educational program perceptual information must be matched to motor information. Focusing on practical applications, Kephart developed an assessment scale and specific educational strategies. Chapter 9 further discusses Kephart's contributions.

William Cruickshank, one of the most influential individuals of the Wayne County Training School, first applied Werner and Strauss' findings. In a series of studies beginning with a doctoral dissertation by Jane Dolphin (1950) Cruickshank facilitated the transfer of research focus from exogenous retarded children to children with normal intelligence.

While perceptual and motor problems were being identified in both these populations, clinical evidence accumulated indicating that some nonretarded and noncerebral-palsied children also exhibited these problems. In the late 1950s, Cruickshank, Bentzen, Ratzeburg, and Tannhauser (1961) designed a project to study the educational methods suggested by Strauss and Lehtinen. All of the children in the study had normal or near-normal intelligence and exhibited the behavioral characteristics associated with brain-injury. Not all of the children, however, could be shown to have definite central nervous system impairment. Consequently, it was proposed that perceptual and perceptual-motor problems were not an exclusive function of mental retardation or definite brain injury (i.e., children of normal intelligence with learning problems were also found to exhibit perceptual-motor problems). Such children today are considered learning disabled whether or not brain injury is evident.

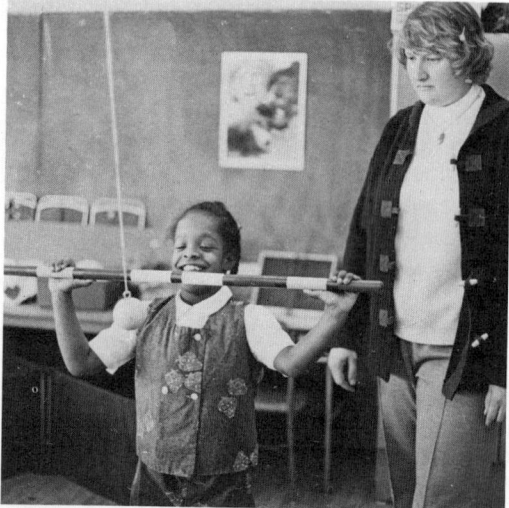

Perceptual-motor problems may accompany learning disabilities.

Considering this research, Cruickshank suggested that the grouping of such children for instruction should not simply be based on IQ. He also specified educational strategies such as reducing the amount of stimuli to which a child is exposed and increasing structure in programming.

Reinforcement Theorists

Animals persist in behaviors if a reward or reinforcement immediately follows the activity. Behavior modification applies this reinforcement theory to human beings (Lerner, 1976). Theorists in the area are a subgroup of the larger field of learning and behavior theory. When experimenting, they *(a)* determine a target behavior, *(b)* carefully and systematically observe and record the specific events that occur before and after the target behavior, and *(c)* manipulate these events to produce a desired change in the target behavior.

During the genesis period of learning disabilities, relatively little practical application of this theory to school children was attempted. However, two individuals, Thorndike and Skinner, made contributions that influenced later investigators to a significant degree.

Edward L. Thorndike, considered by some (Hilgard & Bower, 1966; Hill, 1963) to be the "father" of reinforcement theory, believed the connection formed between stimulus and response represented all learning. To him, animal (and human) learning occurs in accordance with three laws: *effect, readiness,* and *exercise.* In the law of effect, a connection becomes stronger or weaker depending on its consequences. A connection is strengthened when it is followed by a satisfying event. The law of readiness refers to the physiological basis for the law of effect. The law of exercise states that practice strengthens a connection. Thorndike later questioned the law of exercise and concluded that repetitions produce negligible strengthening of connections. The works of later investigators applying learning and reinforcement theory to education (Gagné, 1965; Homme, 1969; Skinner, 1963) reflect his influence.

B. F. Skinner (Hilgard & Bower, 1966; Hill, 1963; Mercer & Snell, 1977; Skinner, 1953, 1963) conducted most of his work with animals. He generated a theory of behavior that emphasized observable events. He defined two types of learned behavior: respondent and operant. Respondent behaviors, elicited by a stimulus occurring *prior* to the behavior, contrast with operant behaviors, those strengthened or weakened by consequences occurring *after* the behavior. According to Skinner, only a small part of human behavior is respondent. In his view, *reinforcement* receives an operational definition: the increased probability of a response, resulting from the application of a positive reinforcer or the removal of a negative reinforcer. Skinner rejected the "cause-effect" model and refused to consider "inner causes" to explain behavior. Instead, he described observable events, which occurred together in a particular order. For example, if a child refused to do schoolwork, Skinner would advocate finding events or objects that would increase the frequency of doing schoolwork. In application, the child might be rewarded every time he engaged in schoolwork. Skinner would not, however, attempt to determine the cause of the negative behaviors as functions of ego strength, poor self-concept, or other unobservable "inner" causative processes. His theories received attention from investigators in the 1960s and 1970s and resulted in a wide variety of applications to educational problems.

Organizations

Volunteer groups and professional organizations concerned with the handicapped have been part of our nation's history since colonization. In most cases a specific goal became a rallying point; on obtaining the goal or after a number of years, the organization faded away. Organizations prior to 1900 particularly fit this pattern. Exceptions consisted of professional groups having strong common interests or vocational ties.

As a result of changing attitudes about responsibility for the handicapped, such organizations became more numerous and better established after 1900. Some have had a lasting impact. The Mental Hygiene Movement, founded by Clifford Beers in 1909, strove to (a) protect the mental health of the public, (b) raise standards for care, (c) promote study of mental disorders, and (d) encourage and disseminate research (Deutsch, 1949). The National Society for Crippled Children, organized in 1921, attempted to aid crippled children and adults, educate the public, support research about the causes of crippling conditions, and finance the treatment of crippled children. In 1922, Elizabeth Farrell organized the International Council for the Education of Exceptional Children to promote adequate education for handicapped and gifted children (Lord, 1976). The original organization, consisting of 12 members, matured to the present organization, the Council for Exceptional Children, with over 900 local chapters.

In the late 1940s and early 1950s, the structure of these organizations changed. Operating with greater tenacity, political "savvy," and financial independence, they sparked public interest and mobilized support among legislators and administrators at the local, state, and federal levels. The organizations provided services unavailable from public agencies, preschools, day-care centers, summer camps, recreational programs, and small residential facilities. The United Cerebral Palsy Association (UCP) grew from a handful of local groups and organizations into a national organization in 1949. The UCP aggressively worked to promote research in cerebral palsy, educate the public, and increase employment opportunities for persons with cerebral palsy.

Representatives from 20 local parent groups met in 1950 to form the National Association of Parents and Friends of Retarded Children. In 1953 the organization became the National Association for Retarded Children and, more recently, the National Association for Retarded Citizens (NARC). Like the UCP, NARC militantly promotes the welfare of the mentally retarded of all ages. The UCP, NARC, and similar organizations successfully obtained services and legislation favorable to the handicapped by wielding political pressure and instituting litigation. They stimulated favorable responses from government bureaucracy, something professional organizations had been unable to do.

Taking their cue from groups like UCP and NARC, in the late 1950s parents of children with learning problems began to organize. In 1957, two of the earliest local groups were the Fund for Perceptually Handicapped Children (in Evanston, Illinois) and the New York Association for Brain-Injured Children (Lerner, 1976). Local groups such as these later coalesced into a strong national organization and increased their power as voters and pressure groups.

The UCP Association and NARC helped bring about legislation by making the government aware of the needs of the handicapped.

Summary: Genesis Period

By the 1950s, public attitudes toward education had advanced to the point that *(a)* most Americans agreed that education should be for all children, *(b)* a legal foundation had been established for providing such an education, *(c)* theories about learning disorders had been developed in three disability areas, *(d)* application of educational interventions based on these theories appeared effective, and *(e)* public pressure for increased services was reaching a critical point. The cumulative effect of these diverse trends and Sputnik produced a 10-year period of radical change in American society. During these years, learning disabilities first emerged.

BIRTH PERIOD

Education

To understand the 1960s and its educational innovations, one must examine several basic changes in American society. Educational complacency characterized the period before the late 1940s, but during the late 1940s and the 1950s, schools were expected to aid in the cold war against international communism. Sputnik had immediately focused attention, concern, and financial resources upon education.

With the waning of the cold war and American success in the space program, society's goals changed extraordinarily. Attention rapidly shifted from raising intellectual capacities for competing with the Soviets to the plight of the American poor and disadvantaged: Presidents Kennedy and Johnson declared a "war on poverty" in 1963 and 1964; the urban poor rioted massively in Harlem, Watts, and Detroit; youth rejected wholesale society's traditional values and committed revolutionary terrorist acts. Americans examined their conscience, took stock of their condition, and rose in awareness above "consumerism." They demanded that schools help the poor achieve justice. In response, educators promised the eradication of poverty and rushed to design new programs. Church and Sedlak (1976) see five main efforts: *(a)* compensatory education, *(b)* efforts to make the curriculum more relevant to the poor, *(c)* efforts to recruit more teachers from a "poverty" background, *(d)* racial integration programs, and *(e)* community control of schools.

In committing themselves to the war on poverty schools radically departed from custom. Traditional promises—to improve children's morals and skills, to make them better workers, to conform to American values, and to make them reasonably literate—were significant goals but vague and difficult to measure. The goals of the war on poverty, however, were primarily economic and subject to precise assessment. Thus educators unwittingly committed themselves to the nettlesome principle of accountability.

Society was in a receptive mood to develop educational programs for the disadvantaged of America. As such, it was a fertile time for special education. Federal and state governments poured money into programs. America seemed determined to make a new society

—a *great society*—one in which everyone shared the fruits of prosperity.

Legislation and Litigation

The proposals, rules, laws, and lawsuits that emerged in the 1960s reflect the ferment in American life. Most important was the abrupt change in federal involvement with education. Prior to 1957, the federal bureaucracy only reluctantly dealt with education; but during the 1960s the federal establishment became a pervasive force at all levels. Milestone federal legislation included the establishment of an Institute of Child Health and Human Development in 1962, the Elementary and Secondary Education Act amendments of 1965, 1966, and 1967, the Mental Retardation Act of 1967, the Handicapped Children's Early Education Assistance Act of 1968, and the Handicapped Elementary and Secondary Education Act amendments of 1969 (which included the Children with Specific Learning Disabilities Act).

Legislation now greatly influences the field of learning disabilities.

Two court cases of major importance occurred during this time. In 1967 Judge Skelly Wright *(Hobsen v. Hansen, 1967)* ruled that placing children into "curriculum tracks" on the basis of test scores was illegal. He felt this practice violated the equal protection clause of the Constitution because it used culture-biased tests. In 1968, plaintiffs in *Arreola v. Board of Education* sought to incorporate "due process" into the procedures for referring a child to special education (Ross, DeYoung, & Cohen, 1971). These two cases began a rash of litigation over special education procedures continuing into the 1970s. Such litigation is reviewed by Ross et al. (1971), Schmid, Moneypenny, and Johnston (1977), and Weintraub and Abeson (1974).

Type of Disorder

A continuous process of investigation, discovery, and testing founded the learning disabilities area. During the 1960s three developments were especially important:

1. As clinical investigations of learning problems shifted from a focus on brain-injured adults to children with normal intelligence and suspected brain injury, educators began to assume the responsibility for providing treatment to most of the children with learning problems.
2. The perceptual-motor point of view in research and education continued to gain strength. In some cases remedial training for perceptual-motor skills literally became the educational curriculum for children with learning problems.
3. The term *learning disabilities* was selected from a long list of competing terms (Clements, 1966) for inclusion in the 1969 Elementary and Secondary Education Act amendments (PL 91–230). This legislation at the federal level established the term for common use in education and research.

Disorders of Spoken Language

Wepman developed a model similar to Osgood's to explain spoken language disorders. Clinical experience and research with aphasics led Wepman and his colleagues (Wepman, Jones, Buck, & Van Pelt, 1960) to develop a schema of functional organization within the central nervous system. Unlike Osgood, Wepman included memory, internal and external feedback, and modes of transmission in his model.

Wepman postulated two processes in the central nervous system dealing with spoken language. The *transmission* process is divided into receptive and expressive modes. *Integration,* the second process, provides for the decoding and encoding of previously learned patterns to give meaning to the stimulus. The two processes operate at three levels: reflexive, perceptual, and conceptual. At the reflex level, elementary sensory responses occur, while at the perceptual level, nonmeaningful, imitative language activity occurs. At the conceptual level, symbolic activity necessary for concept formation takes place.

Stimuli transmitted by the two processes are received and stored in the memory as associations. Wepman emphasized the role of recall in spoken language with the memory bank interconnecting all stages of the perceptual and conceptual levels. While he does not discuss the role of feedback at length, he places importance on both internal and external feedback as affecting the accuracy and control of response modification. In his model, aphasia is an integrative deficit rather than a transmission problem. The modality aspects of transmission had direct application to teaching in that the child's strengths and weaknesses through visual, auditory, and tactile modes had to be evaluated for planning instruction. Wepman and Jones (1961) developed the *Language Modalities Test for Aphasia* in which items were classified in terms of modality. Thus, both Osgood and Wepman developed models of spoken language.

During this time, one of the most significant figures in learning disabilities outside of the perceptual-motor group was Samuel A. Kirk. His involvement with language disorders can be traced to his research with the mentally retarded in the 1950s (Kirk, 1976). In attempting to analyze and program for language problems in young mentally retarded children, he developed tests to isolate individual abilities and disabilities.

Kirk (1972) felt individual differences in ability had two meanings. First, there could be an *inter*individual difference (i.e., a comparison of one child's skills with another or with those of a group). Second, there could be *intra*individual differences (i.e., differences in ability within the individual child himself). Kirk observed that much school testing was of the first rather than the second type. Dissatisfied with his early attempts at construction of an intraindividual test and convinced that part of the problem was the lack of a theoretical framework, Kirk enrolled in a course taught by Osgood at the University of Illinois. Following experiments (conducted by Kirk's students) in test construction based on the Osgood model (McCarthy, 1957; Sievers, 1955), McCarthy and Kirk (1961) produced the *Illinois Test of Psycholinguistic Abilities (ITPA).* Unique among current tests, it assessed intraindividual differences and facilitated instruction. The *ITPA* has become a primary test in the area of learning disabilities and in some cases the constructs it measures have become synonymous with the use of psycholinguistics in learning disabilities.

Disorders of Written Language

Building on the work of Kirk, Monroe, Gillingham and Stillman, and Spalding, educators continued to develop teaching strategies. The work of Myklebust exemplifies the increasing focus on educational strategies during this period. His original work in the 1950s focused on disorders in spoken language; but by the 1960s, Myklebust broadened his theories to include disorders of auditory language, reading, written language, arithmetic, and nonverbal disorders of learning (Johnson & Myklebust, 1967). Myklebust (1965) considered written language to be humanity's culminating verbal achievement. Disorders of written language included dysgraphia, deficits in revisualization, and disorders of formulation and syntax. In dysgraphia, a child cannot initiate the motor patterns necessary for writing—even though he can read and speak. Revisualization involves visual memory problems in that while the child can speak, read, and copy, he cannot remember what words or letters look like. Disorders of formulation and syntax involve ideation. The child can read, spell, copy, and vocally express himself, but he cannot put ideas on paper.

Disorders of Perceptual and Motor Processes

Cruickshank, Doman and Delacato, and Frostig have made important contributions. William Cruickshank's first major report on the Montgomery County Project (Cruickshank, Bentzen, Ratzeburg, & Tannhauser, 1961) began a career focused on intervention strategies, following close to the theoretical foundations of Werner and Strauss. His highly structured lessons incorporated a multisensory approach in an environment of reduced stimuli. Among other things, he suggested specific procedures for increasing visual discrimination and eye-hand coordination, auditory training, motor training, a kinesthetic approach to writing, concrete and practical methods for arithmetic, and strategies for teaching reading.

Cruickshank also directed a year-long seminar of leaders in the area of learning disabilities to identify teaching competencies and procedures for preparing teachers (Cruickshank, 1966). Material from this seminar is still viable today.

Because of his theoretical orientation, the accepted term *learning disability* troubles Cruickshank:

> The appearance of the term *learning disabilities* in 1963 opened a Pandora's box which has resulted in confusion, the phenomenon of the instant specialist, inappropriate definitions of the problem, and a major attempt by many to bring within the definition issues which are far removed from the initial concepts of perceptual disability. (Cruickshank, 1976, p. 109)

As a result of his dissatisfaction, Cruickshank and his doctoral student, Daniel Hallahan, coauthored a historical overview, published in 1973 as *Psychoeducational Foundations of Learning Disabilities* (Hallahan & Cruickshank, 1973). A two-volume publication followed (Cruickshank & Hallahan, 1975) that presents a multidisciplinary perspective on the area of learning disabilities.

Carl Delacato, an educational psychologist, collaborated in the late 1950s with Glen Doman, a physical therapist, to construct a theory of neurological organization to guide treatment and education of brain-injured children. Doman and Delacato attempted to remediate learning problems by "repatterning" the brain. While the public accepted their treatment procedures, professionals strongly criticized them.

The basic premise of their theory and treatment (discussed further in Chapter 5) is that the neurological development of a human follows a sequential continuum. If the continuum is not followed, the individual will exhibit problems in mobility and communication. Treatment includes five major elements:

1. training activities to remediate damaged areas of the brain
2. external manipulation of body patterns to correspond with the brain's developmental level
3. imposition of hemispheric dominance and unilaterality
4. carbon dioxide therapy
5. stimulation of the senses to improve body awareness

Marianne Frostig has also contributed significantly to the area of learning disabilities. Her theories and treatments, derived from a unique set of experiences, resemble those of the Strauss and Werner clique. Born in Vienna, Frostig prepared for a career in social work at the University of Vienna. After marrying a neuropsychiatrist, she moved to Poland where her husband was director of a small psychiatric hospital and she was director of rehabilitation from 1932 to 1937. Like Werner and Strauss, the Frostigs fled the Nazis in 1938 and settled in the United States, where Marianne attended the New School for Social Research in New York. She taught elementary school children in California (1945–1947), received a MA from Claremont Graduate School in 1949, and a Ph.D. from the University of Southern California in 1955.

During the early 1950s, Frostig worked part-time with delinquents in Los Angeles. In testing, she noticed indications of perceptual deficits, especially disturbances in body image and spatial orientation, which she had seen earlier while working in Vienna and Poland. After reading Goldstein, Strauss and Lehtinen, and Werner, Frostig concluded that many of the children might be suffering from neurological dysfunction. Her further investigations led to the construction of the *Developmental Test of Visual Perception* (Frostig, Lefever, & Whittlesey, 1961; Frostig, Maslow, Lefever, & Whittlesey, 1964) and training materials for visual perceptual difficulties (Frostig & Horne, 1964). Chapter 9 further elaborates on her contributions.

Reinforcement Theorists

Theorists swiftly refined the practical application of theory proposed by earlier investigators. Most reinforcement theorists assumed that (a) behavior is modifiable, and modification occurs through learning; (b) the development, maintenance, and removal of behavior depends on environmental events or stimuli; and (c) a lawful, functional relationship exists between behavior and environmental events (Russ, 1972). While educators most often use behavior modification to eliminate children's unacceptable social behaviors, Hallahan and Kauffman[1] (1976) suggest that its growth in popularity was intimately related to the growth of the learning disabilities area, for three reasons:

---

[1] Hallahan and Kauffman consider the terms *behavior modification* and *applied behavior analysis* synonymous in this reference. Other investigators in special education do not.

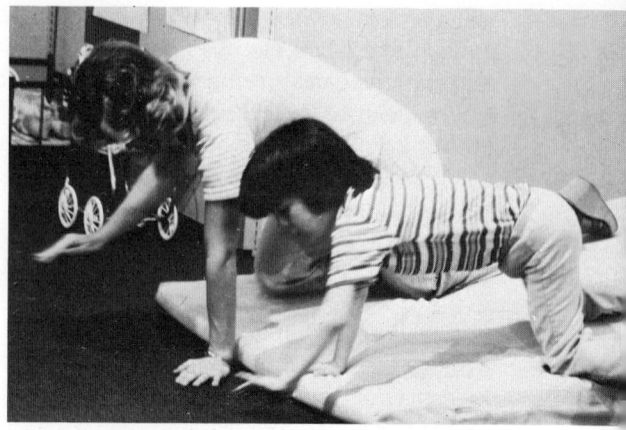

Some patterning activities involve crawling.

First, the application of applied behavior analysis to education can be viewed as an extension and elaboration of the highly structured, directive approach found by Strauss and Lehtinen (1947), Cruickshank et al. (1961), Zimmerman and Zimmerman (1962), Haring and Phillips (1962), and others to be successful with retarded, brain-injured, and emotionally disturbed children. Second, current methods of applied behavior analysis have had a profound influence on the development of educational methodology for all handicapped children. Third, the concern of applied behavior analysis for specification of abilities is congruent with the emphasis of the field of learning disabilities. (p. 14)

Behavior modification does aid the learning disabled child. In addition, it meets the demand for "accountability."

Of the many reinforcement theorists (Bandura, 1969; Becker, Thomas, & Carnine, 1969; Bijou, 1965; Ferster & DeMyer, 1962; Ullman & Krasner, 1965) working in the 1960s, three exemplify the development of the specialization in education: Norris Haring, Ogden R. Lindsley, and Thomas C. Lovitt. Like the Werner-Strauss dynasty in the area of perceptual-motor research, a cadre of professionals evolved who investigated the potential applications of behavior modification. This group centered primarily in midwestern universities and the University of Washington.

The group included Richard J. Whelan, Donald M. Baer, Wesley C. Becker, Sidney W. Bijou, Jay Birnbrauer, Florence Harris, R. Vance Hall, Todd R. Risley, and Montrose M. Wolf.

The professional development of Haring paralleled the transition of learning disabilities from a focus on clinical investigation to practical educational application. Studying under Cruickshank at Syracuse University, Haring became aware of the need for establishing scientific objectivity in education. The Montgomery County Project (Cruickshank et al., 1961) convinced Haring of three things:

> First, there is a serious lack of procedures, personnel, and facilities for identifying the causes of individual and developmental differences. Second, statistical data and group studies are inadequate as methods of evaluation for instructional program curriculum guides, and psychological and achievement tests. Finally, there is a dichotomy between the philosophy and practice of individual instruction. (Haring, 1974, p. 80)

With E. Lakin Phillips, he combined Cruickshank's structured environment and Skinner's work in operant conditioning to develop educational programs for emotionally disturbed children (Haring & Phillips, 1962; Phillips & Haring, 1959). As educational director of the Children's Rehabilitation Unit at the University of Kansas Medical Center, he decided to hire a behavioral scientist to develop procedures for measuring classroom behavior. He selected Lindsley, who had studied with Skinner at Harvard. Five years of work resulted in measurement procedures and educational methods more firmly rooted in learning research (Haring & Whelan, 1965; Lindsley, 1964; Whelan & Haring, 1966).

In 1965, Haring moved to the University of Washington in Seattle. As director of the Experimental Education Unit he formulated experimental techniques characterized by three factors: *(a)* focusing on observable and measurable behavior, *(b)* developing educational procedures based on operant conditioning, and *(c)* basing instructional decision on behavioral data.

Lindsley had successfully applied operant techniques to the rehabilitation of severely emotionally disturbed patients in Boston. After joining the staff at the University of Kansas, he developed a comprehensive set of measurement procedures, which, in final form, he called *precision teaching*. The system includes pinpointing behavior, counting and charting performance, and making instructional decisions based on performance data. Equally effective in the measurement of overt behavior and academic performance, it provides systematic procedures for analyzing behavior to make instructional decisions.

Lovitt's work highlights the use of reinforcement of theory in learning disabilities. A student of both Haring and Lindsley, he became interested in behavior modification when Haring asked that he read and report on every operant conditioning study—applied and basic—that had been published. From this literature review, Lovitt moved to investigate conjugate reinforcement with Lindsley.

After successfully completing a task, this student chooses a prize from the reinforcement board.

Moving to the University of Washington in 1966, Lovitt continued to investigate conjugate reinforcement at the Experimental Education Unit; but his primary assignment was to coordinate the program in learning disabilities. His struggle to reconcile the tenants of reinforcement theory and the "disorder" philosophy of learning disabilities (Lovitt, 1976) is representative of the problems faced by the early behaviorists. Since he was close to teachers struggling with problem learners, however, it seems natural that his interests focused on turning the methods of precision teaching and behavior modification toward learning disabilities and curriculum research (Haring & Lovitt, 1967; Lovitt, 1967, 1968, 1970).

Organizations

During the late 1950s and early 1960s many children were referred to special education because they were not learning. To their parents' frustration, the children were allowed to go to school but were not provided with adequate services because they were not diagnosed as blind, retarded, crippled, or one of the other recognized categories. Local associations of parents formed to organize classes and provide the services denied by the public schools. The number of local groups and state organizations grew quickly; by 1963, a national conference was planned to organize a national association.

Kirk and other interested professionals were invited to attend this conference. Several individuals approached him to help name the proposed organization. He urged against establishing another category of exceptionality and stated:

> Recently I have used the term "learning disabilities" to describe a group of children who have disorders in development, in language, speech, reading, and associated communication skills needed for social interaction. In this group I do not include children who have sensory handicaps such as blindness or deafness, because we have methods of managing and training the deaf and the blind. I also exclude from this group children who have generalized mental retardation. (Kirk, 1976, pp. 255–256)

After much debate, delegates decided to name the new group the *Association for Children with Learning Disabilities (ACLD)*. Given the social setting and the extent of parent involvement in education at the time, it seems fitting that the coining of the term *learning disabilities* occurred at a national conference of parent organizations.

In 1964, the ACLD was formally established. Four years later, the Division for Children with Learning Disabilities (DCLD) was organized as a professional division within the Council for Exceptional Children. Since that time, both groups have been active in securing services, resources, and favorable legislation to benefit the learning disabled child.

Summary: Birth Period

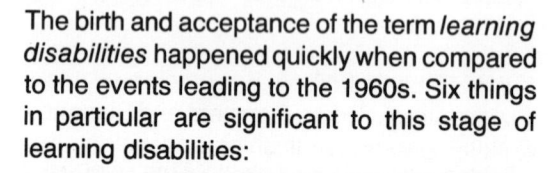

The birth and acceptance of the term *learning disabilities* happened quickly when compared to the events leading to the 1960s. Six things in particular are significant to this stage of learning disabilities:

1. Education had never been more popular with society—or better financed. All of America's disadvantaged (social, emotional, physical, intellectual) received aid. Extravagant promises were made and a profusion of programs were established.
2. Legislation and litigation reflected the mood of society; federal aid to education was massive and indiscriminate. The public demanded immediate change, regardless of the ability to deliver quality with the change.
3. In the investigation of disorders, theorists examining perception and perceptual-motor aspects of learning emerged as the most influential in the learning disability movement.
4. A label was coined and a definition was accepted to identify the movement and the

children it served. While the label and definition have been criticized, they represent a beginning in bringing order and direction to the study of learning disabled children.
5. The growth, refinement, and acceptance of reinforcement theory provided a useful tool for the treatment of learning disability problems. Conflict, however, has been generated between proponents of reinforcement techniques and advocates of "disorders" in the learning process.
6. The organization and strength of ACLD and DCLD provided an effective lobby for service, treatment, and financial aid to the learning disability movement. These groups (and others) have stimulated research, interdisciplinary cooperation, and legislation on a state and national level.

GROWING PAINS PERIOD

Serious growing pains became evident in the area of learning disabilities. The movement matured from a handful of interested individuals to thousands of people. The number of learning disabled children receiving special education services was unreported until 1969 when 120,000 children were identified (Kirk, 1972). Grant and Lind (1977) report that by spring, 1970, the public schools were serving 648,000 learning disabled children. This unprecedented growth generated problems of collecting reliable enrollment data, agreeing on conflicting theories of etiology, providing information dissemination, establishing logistical and funding procedures, and preparing an adequate number of competent teachers.

Education

Developments in education during the 1970s were generally extensions of the directions previously established. The trend toward viewing learning disabilities as an educational phenomenon strengthened; the educator assumed a dominant role (Larsen, 1978). In the late 1970s, education was assigned the responsibility for effective intervention and leadership. Concurrently, two other educational shifts of emphasis occurred: mainstreaming and secondary education.

Criticisms of segregating exceptional children rose during the 1960s (Dunn, 1968; Johnson, 1962) and focused on concern for children inadequately served or who could be better served in general education classrooms. Researchers (Deno, 1970; Lilly, 1970, 1971; Meisgeier & Perez, 1973; Molloy, 1974) began to insist that many exceptional children could function in the general classroom. Advocates of mainstreaming now feel certain that the needs of many learning disabled children can be met by placement in regular classrooms. Learning disability specialists, such as Cruickshank (1977), criticize this position and make reference to a lack of research validating efficacy, a general lack of training for and an unwillingness by regular classroom teachers to work with exceptional children, and the few school administrators willing to support mainstreaming.

The clear mandate from court decisions and federal legislation, however, defines the problem as *how* mainstreaming can be implemented, not *should* it be implemented. The application of the mainstream concept with learning disabled children will continue to generate disagreement and debate among professionals. It is further discussed in Chapter 11.

Because of the belief in early intervention and remediation, little attention was initially given to developing programs for the adolescent with learning problems. With the establishment of programs at the preschool and elementary levels and the requirement of Public Law 94–142 that *all* children receive a free appropriate education, attention is now evident in the increased number of publications regarding the secondary level learning disabled student (Goodman & Mann, 1976; Marsh, Gearheart, & Gearheart, 1978; Scranton & Downs, 1975; Strother, 1971).

Foundations of learning disabilities

Several questions, however, remain unresolved about secondary school programs:

1. Can the high school meet the needs of learning disabled adolescent within the present administrative organization (Clark, 1975; Harmer, 1977)?
2. How many adolescents have a learning disability?
3. Are learning problems of adolescents different in kind or degree from those of children?
4. Are successful teaching strategies for adolescents different from those for children? (Educational programs for the adolescent with learning disabilities are further discussed in Chapter 13.)

Legislation and Litigation

Many of the court cases initiated during the 1960s were litigated in the early 1970s. Most (*Diana v. California State Board of Education,* 1970, 1973; *Larry P. v. Riles,* 1972; *Mills v. Board of Education of the District of Columbia,* 1972; *Pennsylvania Association for Retarded Children v. Commonwealth of Pennsylvania,* 1972) were concerned with placement procedures and due process. Plaintiffs won the bulk of the cases (i.e., the education system *had* violated children's rights).

On November 29, 1975, President Ford signed a landmark piece of federal legislation culminating over 300 years of education evolution: the *Education for All Handicapped Children Act* (PL 94–142). It recognizes learning disabilities as a legally designated handicapping condition; insures the provision of a free, appropriate education to all handicapped children; establishes evaluation and assessment policy; guarantees the right to due process of law; and establishes a process for

Public Law 94–142 recognizes a learning disability as a handicap requiring educational assistance.

financial support of educational services. Its implications pertinent to learning disabilities are discussed (where appropriate) in each chapter of this text.

Type of Disorder and Reinforcement Theorists

The trend toward shifting the responsibility of managing the learning disabled to the education establishment and the popularization of behavioral strategies (Lovitt, 1978) generated a major debate between professionals espousing a disorder viewpoint and those holding a behavioral position (Smead, 1977). Quay (1973) and Ysseldyke and Salvia (1974) delineate the issue and discuss both positions. Essentially, the controversy centers on two different theoretical models.

One group of investigators advocates a process-training approach. In this approach the purpose of diagnosis is to identify process strengths and weaknesses in order to prescribe remediation for the abilities. The chief concern is to identify perceptual or psycholinguistic processes that are presumed to cause inadequate skill development. This group is composed primarily of individuals with a "type of disorder" viewpoint. The other group stresses skill training and suggests assessment of academic skill development and individualized instruction to help the child progress from his functioning level toward appropriate skill goals. These individuals reject training of processes that presumably underlie faulty skill development. The controversy continues (Hammill & Larsen, 1978; Lund, Foster, & McCall-Perez, 1978); it is further discussed in Chapters 3, 6, and 14.

Organizations

Most of the organizations previously discussed have continued to gain strength and influence the direction of the learning disabilities movement. One new organization, the Division on Career Development, became the 12th division of the Council for Exceptional Children in October, 1976. Its members are interested in the career development of exceptional children. While the organization has had little impact on the area of learning disabilities to date, it has the potential for valuable contributions to the educational programs and strategies for learning disabled adolescents.

Contemporary Problems

A review of the professional literature of the 1970s (Barsch, 1976; Bryan & Bryan, 1978; Cruickshank, 1976, 1977; Hallahan & Cruickshank 1973; Hallahan & Heins, 1976; Hallahan & Kauffman, 1976; Kirk, 1976, Lerner, 1976; Lovitt, 1976; McCarthy, 1976, Wallace & McLoughlin, 1975; Wiederholt, 1974) discloses seven contemporary and future problems of concern.

1. *Definition.* The search for an acceptable definition will continue to be a center of controversy among professionals. Issues yet to be resolved include references to central nervous system dysfunctions, exclusion of concomitant handicapping conditions, and "operationalizing" the definition. (Definitions and related issues are discussed in Chapter 2.)
2. *Research.* Research is the foundation of every discipline. Since the genesis and birth periods, research activity in learning disabilities has developed in three areas: *(a)* investigations of etiology and characteristics, *(b)* analysis of diagnostic/assessment instruments and procedures, and *(c)* development of teaching methods. Specific areas mentioned in the literature as needing more investigation include genetics, epidemiological and demographic studies, validation (and revalidation) of contemporary beliefs, teaching strategies, medical aspects (e.g., diets, vitamins, drugs), and development and refinement of "models." While studies in these and other areas are being conducted to establish an adequate research foundation, debate on many points will continue until definitive answers are found. (Included in

each chapter of this text is a review of the research relevant to the chapter topic.)
3. *Territorial rights.* Serious conflict has developed between learning disability professionals and those in the areas of language disorders and reading disabilities. Language and reading specialists feel their areas of expertise have been invaded by individuals with less training who claim to offer services of equal quality. The controversy has led to rivalry in budget allocations and certification requirements and has hampered development of comprehensive educational programs. (Aspects of this problem are discussed in Chapters 6 and 7.)
4. *Early identification and intervention.* A strong belief among learning disability specialists is that early identification and intervention are essential. They assume the effectiveness of early detection of a handicapping condition and immediate intervention. Implementation of the belief has been extensive and has been supported by state and federal legislation. Within the early childhood effort, however, are many unresolved questions: How valid are the identification or predictive instruments? What are the implications of diagnostic data for intervention? Does early identification outweigh potential negative effects of labeling? (These issues, critical to educators of the learning disabled, are discussed in Chapter 12.)
5. *Teacher preparation.* A continuing source of controversy concerns the discrepancies in programs for training teachers. A standard curriculum for teacher preparation has yet to be accepted and there is no quality control of training programs. Moreover, as with all areas in special education, specific competencies that should be required of teachers completing programs have not been delineated and accepted on a large scale. (In each chapter of this text, where appropriate, teacher preparation is related to the chapter topic.)
6. *Individualization.* Among others, Frierson (1976), Getman (1976), Lerner (1976), and Lovitt (1976) insist that practical application of individualization is urgently needed. In spite of legislative mandates, administrators too often organize programs for convenience. (The concept of individualization and implementation practices is discussed in Chapter 14.)
7. *Role of the federal government.* While a strong central authority can effectively implement needed programs and establish standards, it is also responsive to pressure groups. Consequently, the potential exists for policy and practices to be mandated contrary to the best interests of the area of learning disabilities. (Where appropriate in this text, the role of the federal government is related to each chapter topic.)

Summary: Growing Pains Period

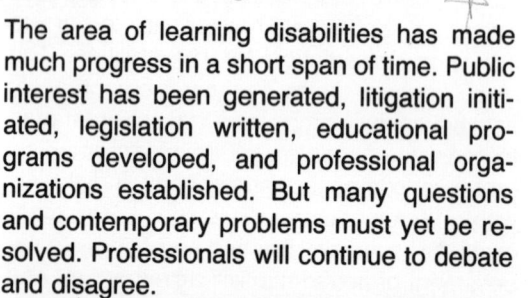

The area of learning disabilities has made much progress in a short span of time. Public interest has been generated, litigation initiated, legislation written, educational programs developed, and professional organizations established. But many questions and contemporary problems must yet be resolved. Professionals will continue to debate and disagree.

If this area continues to consolidate and refine, we should not assume it is stagnating. After the unprecedented growth, a period of research and stabilization appears necessary. While the 1980s may be a decade of equilibrium, the area of learning disabilities will likely continue with an activity level paralleling that of the 1970s.

REFERENCES

Aiello, B. Especially for special educators: A sense of our own history. *Exceptional Children,* 1976, *42,* 244–252.

Bandura, A. *Principles of behavior modification.* New York: Holt, Rinehart & Winston, 1969.

Barsch, R.H. Ray H. Barsch. In J.M. Kauffman & D.P. Hallahan (Eds.), *Teaching children with learning disabilities: Personal perspectives.* Columbus, Ohio: Charles E. Merrill, 1976.

Bastian, H.C. On different kinds of aphasia, with special reference to their classification and ultimate pathology. *British Medical Journal,* 1887, *2,* 931–990.

Bastian, H.C. *A treatise on aphasia and other speech defects.* London: Lewis, 1898.

Becker, W.C., Thomas, D.R., & Carnine, D. *Reducing behavior problems: An operant conditioning guide for teachers.* Urbana, Ill.: National Laboratory on Early Childhood Education, 1969.

Bell, B. *Crisis in education: A challenge to American complacency.* New York: Whittlesey House, 1949.

Bestor, A. *Educational wastelands: The retreat from learning in our public schools.* Urbana, Ill.: University of Illinois Press, 1953.

Bijou, S.W. Experimental studies of child behavior, normal and deviant. In L. Krasner & L.P. Ullman (Eds.), *Research in behavior modification.* New York: Holt, Rinehart & Winston, 1965.

Bryan, T.H., & Bryan, J.H. *Understanding learning disabilities* (2nd ed.). Port Washington, N.Y.: Alfred, 1978.

Church, R.L., & Sedlak, M.W. *Education in the United States.* New York: The Free Press, 1976.

Clark, G.M. Mainstreaming for the secondary educable mentally retarded: Is it defensible? *Focus on Exceptional Children,* 1975, *7*(2), 1–5.

Clements, S.D. *Minimal brain dysfunction in children* (NINDS Monograph No. 3, U.S. Public Health Service Publication No. 1415). Washington, D.C.: U.S. Government Printing Office, 1966.

Conant, J.B. *American high school today: A first report to interested citizens.* New York: McGraw-Hill, 1959.

Cruickshank, W.M. (Ed.). *The teacher of brain-injured children: A discussion of the bases for competency.* Syracuse: Syracuse University Press, 1966.

Cruickshank, W.M. William M. Cruickshank. In J.M. Kauffman & D.P. Hallahan (Eds.), *Teaching children with learning disabilities: Personal perspectives.* Columbus, Ohio: Charles E. Merrill, 1976.

Cruickshank, W.M. Myths and realities in learning disabilities. *Journal of Learning Disabilities,* 1977, *10,* 57–64.

Cruickshank, W.M., Bentzen, F.A., Ratzeburg, R.H., & Tannhauser, M.T. *A teaching method for brain-injured and hyperactive children.* Syracuse, N.Y.: Syracuse University Press, 1961.

Cruickshank, W.M., & Hallahan, D.P. (Eds.) *Perceptual and learning disabilities in children. Psychoeducational procedures* (Vol. 1). *Research and theory* (Vol. 2). Syracuse, N.Y.: Syracuse University Press, 1975.

Deno, E. Special education as developmental capital. *Exceptional Children,* 1970, *37,* 229–237.

Deutsch, A. *The mentally ill in America.* New York: Columbia University Press, 1949.

Diana v. California State Board of Education, Civil Action No. C–70–37 R.F.P. (N.D. Calif., Jan., 7, 1970 and June 18, 1973).

Dolphin, J.E. *A study of certain aspects of the psychopathology of children with cerebral palsy.* Unpublished doctoral dissertation, Syracuse University, 1950.

Dunn, L.M. Special education for the mildly retarded—Is much of it justified? *Exceptional Children,* 1968, *35,* 5–21.

Fernald, G.M. *Remedial techniques in basic school subjects.* New York: McGraw-Hill, 1943.

Ferster, C.B., & DeMyer, M.K. A method for the experimental analysis of the behavior of autistic children. *American Journal of Orthopsychiatry,* 1962, *32,* 89–98.

Frierson, E.C. Edward C. Frierson. In J.M. Kauffman & D.P. Hallahan (Eds.), *Teaching children with learning disabilities: Personal perspectives.* Columbus, Ohio: Charles E. Merrill, 1976.

Frostig, M., & Horne, D. *The Frostig program for the development of visual perception: Teacher's guide.* Chicago: Follett, 1964.

Frostig, M., Lefever, D.W., & Whittlesey, J.R.B. A developmental test of visual perception for evaluating normal and neurologically handicapped children. *Perceptual and Motor Skills,* 1961, *12,* 383–394.

Frostig, M., Maslow, P., Lefever, D.W., & Whittlesey, J.R.B. *The Marianne Frostig Developmental Test of Visual Perception: 1963 standardization.* Palo Alto: Consulting Psychologists Press, 1964.

Gagné, R.M. *The conditions of learning.* New York: Holt, Rinehart & Winston, 1965.

Getman, G. Gerald Getman. In J.M. Kauffman & D.P. Hallahan (Eds.), *Teaching children with learning disabilities: Personal perspectives.* Columbus, Ohio: Charles E. Merrill, 1976.

Gillingham, A., & Stillman, B. *Remedial work for reading, spelling and penmanship.* New York: Hackett & Wilhelms, 1936.

Goldstein, K. The modifications of behavior consequent to cerebral lesions. *Psychiatric Quarterly,* 1936, *10,* 586–610.

Goldstein, K. *The organism.* New York: American Book, 1939.

Good, C.V. *Dictionary of education.* New York: McGraw-Hill, 1958.

Goodman, L., & Mann, L. *Learning disabilities in the secondary school: Issues and practices.* New York: Grune & Stratton, 1976.

Grant, W.V., & Lind, C.G. *Digest of educational statistics: 1976 edition* (National Center for Education Statistics No. 77–401). Washington, D.C.: U.S. Government Printing Office, 1977.

Hallahan, D.P., & Cruickshank, W.M. *Psychoeducational foundations of learning disabilities.* Englewood Cliffs, N.J.: Prentice-Hall, 1973.

Hallahan, D.P., & Heins, E.D. Issues in learning disabilities. In J.M. Kauffman & D.P. Hallahan (Eds.), *Teaching children with learning disabilities: Personal perspectives.* Columbus, Ohio: Charles E. Merrill, 1976.

Hallahan, D.P., & Kauffman, J.M. *Introduction to learning disabilities: A psycho-behavioral approach.* Englewood Cliffs, N.J.: Prentice-Hall, 1976.

Hammill, D.D., & Larsen, S.C. The effectiveness of psycholinguistic training: A reaffirmation of position. *Exceptional Children,* 1978, *44,* 402–414.

Haring, N.G. Norris G. Haring. In J.M. Kauffman & C.D. Lewis (Eds.), *Teaching children with behavior disorders.* Columbus, Ohio: Charles E. Merrill, 1974.

Haring, N.G., & Lovitt, T.C. Operant methodology and educational technology in special education. In N.G. Haring & R.L. Schiefelbusch (Eds.), *Methods in special education.* New York: McGraw-Hill, 1967.

Haring, N.G., & Phillips, E.L. *Educating emotionally disturbed children.* New York: McGraw-Hill, 1962.

Haring, N.G., & Whelan, R.J. Experimental methods in education and management. In N.J. Long, W.C. Morse, & R.G. Newman (Eds.), *Conflict in the classroom.* Belmont, Calif.: Wadsworth, 1965.

Harmer, E.W. Veteran teachers and curriculum development. *Phi Delta Kappan,* 1977, *58,* 751–752.

Head, H. *Aphasia and kindred disorders of speech* (Vols. 1 & 2). Cambridge: Cambridge University Press, 1926.

Hegge, T.G., Kirk, S.A., & Kirk, W.D. *Remedial reading drills.* Ann Arbor, Mich.: George Wahr, 1936.

Hegge, T.G., Kirk, S.A., & Kirk, W.D. *Remedial reading drills* (2nd ed.). Ann Arbor, Mich.: George Wahr, 1970.

Hilgard, E., & Bower, G. *Theories of learning.* New York: Appleton-Century-Crofts, 1966.

Hill, W.F. *Learning: A survey of psychological interpretation.* San Francisco: Chandler, 1963.

Hinshelwood, J. *Congenital word blindness.* London: Lewis, 1917.

Hobson v. *Hansen,* 269 F. Supp. 401 (1967).

Homme, L.H. *How to use contingency contracting in the classroom.* Champaign, Ill.: Research Press, 1969.

Hutchins, R. *The conflict in education in a democratic society.* New York: Harper, 1953.

Ikenberry, O.S. *American education foundations: An introduction.* Columbus, Ohio: Charles E. Merrill, 1974.

Johnson, D., & Myklebust, H.R. *Learning disabilities: Educational principles and practices.* New York: Grune & Stratton, 1967.

Johnson, G.O. Special education for the mentally handicapped—A paradox. *Exceptional Children,* 1962, *2,* 62–69.

Kephart, N.C. *The slow learner in the classroom.* Columbus, Ohio: Charles E. Merrill, 1960.

Kirk, S.A. *Educating exceptional children* (2nd ed.). Boston: Houghton Mifflin, 1972.

Kirk, S.A. Samuel A. Kirk. In J.M. Kauffman & D.P. Hallahan (Eds.), *Teaching children with learning disabilities: Personal perspectives.* Columbus, Ohio: Charles E. Merrill, 1976.

Larry P. v. *Riles,* Civil Action No. 6–71–2270, 343 F. Supp. 1036 (N.D. Calif., 1972).

Larsen, S. Learning disabilities and the professional educator. *Learning Disability Quarterly,* 1978, *1,* 5–12.

LaVor, M.L. Federal legislation for exceptional persons: A history. In F.J. Weintraub, A. Abeson, J. Ballard, & M.L. LaVor (Eds.), *Public policy and the education of exceptional children.* Reston, Va.: The Council for Exceptional Children, 1976.

Lerner, J.W. *Children with learning disabilities* (2nd ed.). Boston: Houghton Mifflin, 1976.

Lilly, M.S. Special education: A teapot in a tempest. *Exceptional Children,* 1970, *37,* 43–49.

Lilly, M.S. A training based model for special education. *Exceptional Children,* 1971, *37,* 745–749.

Lindsley, O.R. Direct measurement and prosthesis of retarded behavior. *Journal of Education,* 1964, *147,* 62–81.

Lord, F.E. Great moments in the history of the Council for Exceptional Children. *Exceptional Children,* 1976, *43,* 6–9.

Lovitt, T.C. The use of conjugate reinforcement to evaluate the relative reinforcing effects of various narrative forms. *Journal of Experimental Child Psychology,* 1967, *5,* 164–171.

Lovitt, T.C. Free-operant assessment of musical preference. *Journal of Experimental Child Psychology,* 1968, *6,* 361–367.

Lovitt, T.C. Behavior modification: Where do we go from here? *Exceptional Children,* 1970, *37,* 157–167.

Lovitt, T.C. Thomas C. Lovitt. In J.M. Kauffman & D.P. Hallahan (Eds.), *Teaching children with learning disabilities: Personal perspectives.* Columbus, Ohio: Charles E. Merrill, 1976.

Lovitt, T.C. Learning disabilities. In N.G. Haring (Ed.), *Behavior of exceptional children: An introduction to special education* (2nd ed.). Columbus, Ohio: Charles E. Merrill, 1978.

Lund, K.A., Foster, G.E., & McCall-Perez, F. The effectiveness of psycholinguistic training: A reevaluation. *Exceptional Children,* 1978, *44,* 310–319.

Marsh, G.E., Gearheart, C.K., & Gearheart, B.R. *The learning disabled adolescent: Program alternatives in the secondary school.* Saint Louis, Mo.: C.V. Mosby, 1978.

McCarthy, J.J. Qualitative and quantitative differences in the language abilities of young cerebral palsied. Unpublished doctoral dissertation, University of Illinois, 1957.

McCarthy, J.J., & Kirk, S.A. *Illinois Test of Psycholinguistic Abilities: Experimental edition.* Urbana: Universtiy of Illinois, 1961.

McCarthy, J.M. Jeanne McRae McCarthy. In J.M. Kauffman & D.P. Hallahan (Eds.), *Teaching children with learning disabilities: Personal perspectives.* Columbus, Ohio: Charles E. Merrill, 1976.

Meisgeier, C.H., & Perez, F.I. An integrated behavioral-systems model of accountability for education. In N. Kreinberg & S.H.L. Chow (Eds.), *Configurations of change: The integration of mildly handicapped children into the regular classroom.* Sioux Falls, S.D.: Adapt Press, 1973.

Melcher, J.W. Law, litigation, and handicapped children. *Exceptional Children,* 1976, *43,* 126–130.

Mercer, C.D., & Snell, M.E. *Learning theory research in mental retardation: Implications for teaching.* Columbus, Ohio: Charles E. Merrill, 1977.

Mills v. Board of Education of the District of Columbia, 348 F. Supp. 866 (D.D.C., 1972).

Molloy, L. *One out of ten: School planning for the handicapped.* New York: Educational Facilities Laboratories, 1974.

Monroe, M. *Children who cannot read.* Chicago: University of Chicago Press, 1932.

Myers, P.I., & Hammill, D.D. *Methods for learning disorders* (2nd ed.). New York: John Wiley, 1976.

Myklebust, H.R. Training aphasic children. *Volta Review,* 1955, *57,* 149–157.

Myklebust, H.R. *The psychology of deafness.* New York: Grune & Stratton, 1960.

Myklebust, H.R. *Development and disorders of written language.* New York: Grune & Stratton, 1965.

Orton, S.T. *Reading, writing and speech problems in children.* New York: Norton, 1937.

Osgood, C.E., & Miron, M.S. *Approaches to the study of aphasia.* Urbana, Ill.: University of Illinois Press, 1963.

Pennsylvania Association for Retarded Children v. Commonwealth of Pennsylvania, F. Supp. 279 (E.D. Pa. 1972, Order, Injunction, and Consent Agreement).

Phillips, E.L., & Haring, N.G. Results from special techniques for teaching emotionally disturbed children. *Exceptional Children,* 1959, *26,* 64–67.

Quay, H.C. Special education: Assumptions, techniques, and evaluative criteria. *Exceptional Children,* 1973, *40,* 165–170.

Rickover, H.G. *Education and freedom.* New York: Dutton, 1959.

Ross, S.L., DeYoung, H.G., & Cohen, J.S. Confrontation: Special education placement and the law. *Exceptional Children,* 1971, *38,* 5–12.

Russ, D.F. A review of learning and behavior theory as it relates to emotional distrubance in children. In W.C. Rhodes & M.L. Tracy, *A study of child variance* (Vol. 1). Ann Arbor, Mich.: The University of Michigan Press, 1972.

Sarason, S.B. *Pshchological problems in mental deficiency.* New York: Harper, 1949.

Schmid, R.E., Moneypenny, J., & Johnston, R. *Contemporary issues in special education.* New York: McGraw-Hill, 1977.

Scranton, T., & Downs, M. Elementary and secondary learning disabilities programs in the U.S.: A survey. *Journal of Learning Disabilities,* 1975, *8,* 394–399.

Selye, H. Foreword. In B.B. Brown, *Stress and the art of biofeedback.* New York: Harper & Row, 1977.

Sievers, D.J. *Development and standardization of a test of psycholinguistic growth in preschool children.* Unpublished doctoral dissertation, University of Illinois, 1955.

Skinner, B.F. *Science and human behavior.* New York: Macmillan, 1953.

Skinner, B.F. Reflections on a decade of teaching machines. *Teacher's College Record,* 1963, *65,* 168–177.

Smead, V.S. Ability training and task analysis in diagnostic/prescriptive teaching. *The Journal of Special Education,* 1977, *11*(1). 113–125.

Smith, M. *And madly teach: A layman looks at public school education.* Chicago: H. Regnery, 1949.

Smith, M. *The diminished mind: A study of planned mediocrity in our public schools.* Chicago: H. Regnery, 1954.

Spalding, R.B., & Spalding, W.T. *The writing road to reading: A modern method of phonics for teaching children to read.* New York: Morrow, 1962.

Strauss, A.A., & Kephart, N.C. *Psychopathology and education of the brain-injured child: Progress in theory and clinic* (Vol. 2). New York: Grune & Stratton, 1955.

Strauss, A.A., & Lehtinen, L.E. *Psychopathology and education of the brain-injured child.* New York: Grune & Stratton, 1947.

Strauss, A.A., & Werner, H. Disorders of conceptual thinking in the brain-injured child. *Journal of Nervous and Mental Disease,* 1942, *96,* 153–172.

Strother, C.R. Who is he? In E. Schloss (Ed.), *The educator's enigma: The adolescent with learning disabilities.* San Rafael, Calif.: Academic Therapy Publications, 1971.

Stuart v. School District Number 1 of Village of Kalamazoo, 30 Michigan 69 (1874).

Ullman, L.P., & Krasner, L. *Case studies in behavior modification.* New York: Holt, Rinehart & Winston, 1965.

Wallace, G., & McLoughlin, J.A. *Learning disabilities: Concepts and characteristics.* Columbus, Ohio: Charles E. Merrill, 1975.

Weintraub, F.J., & Abeson, A. New education policies for the handicapped: The quiet revolution. *Phi Delta Kappan,* 1974, *55,* 526–529.

Wepman, J.M., & Jones, L.V. *The Language Modalities Test for Aphasia.* Chigaco: University of Chicago Education Industry Service, 1961.

Wepman, J.M., Jones, L.V., Buck, R.D., & Van Pelt, D. Studies in aphasia: Background and theoretical formulations. *Journal of Speech and Hearing Disorders,* 1960, *25.* 323–332.

Werner, H. *Comparative psychology of mental development.* New York: International Universities Press, 1948.

Werner, H., & Strauss, A.A. Types of visuo-motor activities in their relation to low and high performance ages. *Proceedings of the American Association of Mental Deficiency,* 1939, *44,* 163–168.

Werner, H., & Strauss, A.A. Causal factors in low performance. *American Journal of Mental Deficiency,* 1940, *45,* 213–218.

Werner, H., & Strauss, A.A. Pathology of figure-background relation in the child. *Journal of Abnormal and Social Psychology,* 1941, *36,* 236–248.

Wernicke, C. The symptom-complex of aphasia. In A. Church (Ed.), *Diseases of the nervous system.* New York: Appleton, 1908.

Whelan, R.J., & Haring, N.G. Modification and maintenance of behavior through systematic application of consequences. *Exceptional Children,* 1966, *32,* 281–289.

Wiederholt, J.L. Historical perspectives on the education of the learning disabled. In L. Mann & D. Sabatino (Eds.), *The second review of special education.* Philadelphia: Journal of Special Education Press, 1974.

Ysseldyke, J.E., & Salvia, J. Diagnostic-prescriptive teaching: Two models. *Exceptional Children,* 1974, *41,* 181–186.

Zimmerman, E.H., & Zimmerman, J. The alteration of behavior in a special classroom situation. *Journal of the Experimental Analysis of Behavior,* 1962, *5,* 59–60.

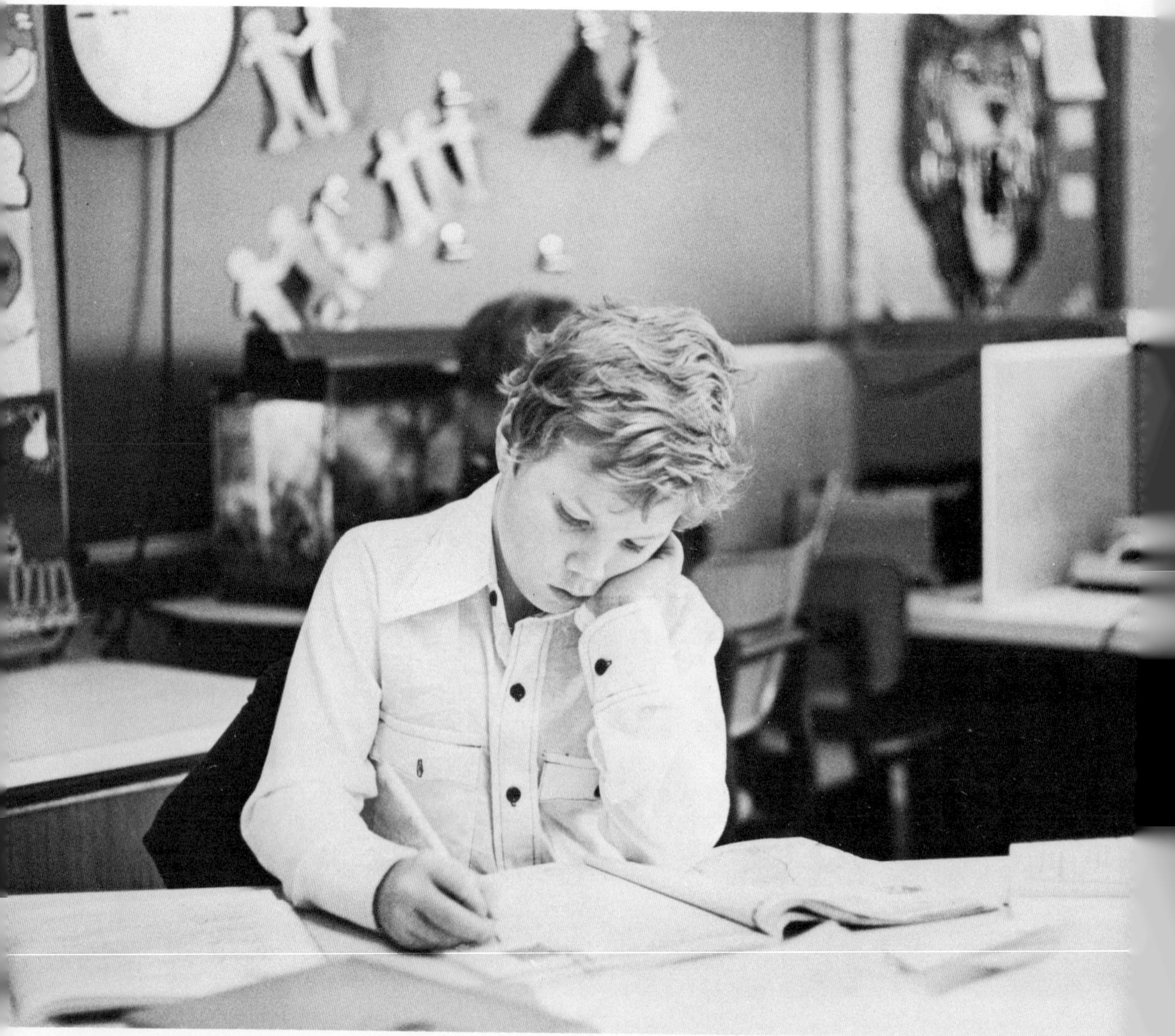

2

Definitions, terms, and characteristics

The term *learning disabilities* emerged from a need to identify and serve students who experience continuous school failure yet elude the traditional categories of exceptionality. Numerous disciplines contribute to the evolvement of this field: medicine, language, psychology, and education (Lerner, 1976). The generic nature of learning disabilities, the multi-disciplinary contributions, and high interest have combined to generate numerous terms and definitions. Cruickshank (1972) notes that more than 40 English terms have been used to refer to essentially the same child.

Numerous definitions naturally accompany the diversity in terminology and professional interests. Kass (1969) reports that in no other area of special education has so much effort been expended concerning the development of a definition. She presents 5 definitions of *learning disabilities* that evolved from 1962 to 1968 as the result of the efforts of various groups. Vaughn and Hodges (1973) used 10 established definitions in order to ascertain whether or not special education personnel could agree upon a definition of learning disabilities. Bryan and Bryan (1978) report that little agreement exists regarding the conditions that define a specific learning disability. They note that not enough research data are available to state with certainty the common characteristics of all such students.

The problem of definition has generated concern among legislators, lay persons, and professionals. They are asking penetrating questions. In a highly controversial article, Divoky (1974), a magazine editor, states, "The truth is that learning disabled are whomever the diagnosticians want them to be" (p. 21). Cruickshank (1972) states:

> It is my considered opinion, however, that of all aspects of the psychology of disability and special education, the field of learning disabilities is in the most critical phase. The field is at a point where it cannot continue as it has in the past decade without the expectancy of failure and without bringing down on the heads of children professional frustrations, political hostility, and parental antagonism. (p. 5)

Lovitt (1976) examines the problem of defining exceptional children and learning disabled children from a functional viewpoint. He notes that, unlike the classification system in special education, many such systems have greatly assisted other sciences (e.g., biology). Specifically, he states:

> In contrast, the system of classification we have used in special education has not served us well and might be likened to a grocer who chose to classify his stock according to color. In the white section he placed together the eggs, milk, flour, salt, bread, onions, paper towels, oysters, toothpaste, white wine, and vanilla ice cream. In the yellow, red, and blue sections the items were equally divergent. The purchaser could not shop for items according to any useful dimension. Furthermore, the grocer would have to design unusual shelves and storage spaces for each section—he would, for example, have to provide refrigeration units for all of the sections. (p. 300)

Unrest in the area may have saluatory implications if special education personnel confront the issues facing the area and embark on systematic efforts to resolve some of them. For example, investigation of the definition problem has received substantial impetus from the passage of the Education For All Handicapped Children Act of 1975 (PL 94-142). This law requires that a more precise definition be developed. Consequently, everyone involved is making an organized effort toward an improved terminology.

Even though an accepted definition has been elusive, school districts, clinics, and private schools throughout the nation have managed to develop and operate programs in the area. The development of these programs, in large part, has resulted because of the work of professionals and lay persons who were instrumental in defining and identifying these children during the past 25 years. In the next four sections of this chapter the major works concerning characteristics, terminology, and definitions are organized and presented according to four phases: *(a)* the Brain-Injured Phase, *(b)* the Minimal Brain Dysfunction Phase, *(c)* the Learning Disabilities Phase, and, currently, *(d)* the Refinement Phase.

BRAIN-INJURED PHASE

As noted in Chapter 1, the beginnings of the study of learning disabilities, in part, are readily traced to the works of Strauss and his colleagues. In the late 1930s and early 1940s, Strauss and Werner joined forces to study brain-injured retarded children. The culmination of their work is presented in the first volume of *Psychopathology and Education of the Brain-Injured Child* by Strauss and Lehtinen (1947). In this now classic volume they define *brain-injured child* as follows:

> The brain-injured child is the child who before, during or after birth has received an injury to or suffered an infection of the brain. As a result of such organic impairment, defects of the neuromotor system may be present or absent; however, such a child may show disturbances in perception, thinking, and emotional behavior, either separately or in combination. This disturbance can be demonstrated by specific tests. These disturbances prevent or impede a normal learning process. Special educational methods have been devised to remedy these specific handicaps. (p. 4)

Strauss and Lehtinen (1947) theorized that these brain injuries resulted from exogenous rather than endogenous factors. They used *exogenous* to refer to brain impairment resulting from an injury that occurred outside of the genetic structure (e.g., shortage of oxygen during birth, extremely high fever during infancy, or insult to head). *Endogenous* referred to inherited brain structures or patterns that resulted in learning impairments. Although both etiologies generated learning impairments, Strauss and his colleagues differentiated the characteristics of the two groups (i.e., endogenous retarded and exogenous retarded). They established seven criteria for classifying the exogenous retarded child. Four of the criteria, classified as behavior criteria, include

1. *Perceptual disorders.* When viewing a picture, a child with perceptual problems may see parts instead of wholes or confuse the background with the foreground. For example, a line drawing of a triangle may be viewed as three unrelated lines. Similarly, the child with figure-ground problems would have difficulty following words printed over a background of scenic landscapes.
2. *Perseveration.* Perseveration is the continuation of an activity once it has started; it is accompanied by difficulty changing to another activity. For example, a child may repeatedly color the same area and have difficulty switching to a new task.
3. *Conceptual or thinking disorders.* Problems associated with organizing material or thoughts.
4. *Behavioral disorders.* Uninhibited behavior, which may be manifested in hyperative, erratic, and/or explosive behavior patterns.

The remaining three criteria, classified as biological criteria, include

1. *Slight neurological signs.* Subtle neurological abnormalities. Numerous; some take the form of general clumsiness, confusion regarding dominance, awkward gait, and/or problems with fine motor tasks.
2. *A history of neurological impairment.* Evidence in medical records that suggests damage to the nervous system.
3. *No history of mental retardation.* This criterion excludes brain abnormalities due to endogenous or genetic factors.

Later, Strauss indicated that a diagnosis of brain injury could be determined by only using the behavioral criteria. Omitting the necessity of the biological criteria for determining brain injury lessened the pressure on diagnosticians for determining organic injury and made *brain injury* more of a pseudo-medical term.

Strauss and his colleagues based their research and descriptions on work with mentally retarded children. Their work prompted Cruickshank to initiate studies regarding the effects of brain injury on normal I.Q. children. He and his colleagues established that the perceptual problems described by Strauss were not unique to retarded children. Professionals and lay persons began to develop awareness of children at all IQ levels whose learning problems were primarily due to brain injury. Some of Cruickshank's writings include *A Teaching Method for Brain-Injured and Hyperactive Children* (Cruickshank, Bentzen,

Balance is sometimes a problem for the LD child.

Ratzeburg, & Tannhauser, 1961); *The Brain-Injured Child in Home, School and Community* (Cruickshank, 1967); and *The Preparation of Teachers of Brain-Injured Children* (Cruickshank, Junkala, & Paul, 1968).

However, many people objected to the term *brain injury*. Parents viewed the term as negative, as stressing a condition of permanence. Wortis (1956) stated that the term had little value as a means of classifying, describing, or teaching children. Stevens and Birch (1957) delineated four major objections. Specifically, they noted that *brain injured* is (a) cause-oriented and does not relate to the behavioral aspects of the condition, (b) associated with such a wide range of conditions (cerebral palsy, epilepsy) that it has little specific meaning, (c) not useful in planning teaching approaches, and (d) too broad, leading to oversimplification.

Stevens and Birch (1957) recommended that the term *Strauss syndrome* be used to replace *brain-injured*. Thus, *Strauss syndrome* now describes those who exhibit many or all of the following characteristics:

1. erratic and inappropriate behavior on mild provocation
2. increased motor activity disproportionate to the stimulus
3. poor organization of the behavior
4. distractibility of more than ordinary degree under ordinary conditions
5. persistent faulty perceptions
6. persistent hyperactivity
7. awkwardness and consistently poor motor performance (Stevens & Birch, 1957, p. 348)

MINIMAL BRAIN DYSFUNCTION PHASE

During the 1960s, a shift in terminology occurred with the introduction of the term *minimal brain dysfunction (MBD)*. This term brought in the concept of minimal or minor brain injury and linked it with learning problems. Brain injury may be presented on a continuum from severe to mild (see Table 2.1). Children with severe brain impairments such as cerebral palsy and epilepsy are readily identified, but children with minimal impairments are affected in more subtle ways. *MBD* is very similar to *brain injury* in that both terms focus on brain impairment; however, *MBD* popularized the position of minor brain injury or dysfunction. MBD was primarily advanced by Clements, the project director of Task Force I.

Task Force I: Characteristics

Task Force I (Clements, 1966) described some of the symptoms by which MBD indi-

TABLE 2.1

Classification guide to severe and minimal brain dysfunction.

Severe or Overt Manifestations	Borderline or Minimal Manifestations
Cerebral palsies	Impairment of coordination or fine motor skills
	Excessive clumsiness
	Minor tremor
Mental deficiency	Mild retardation
	Overactivity, distractibility, short attention span, tantrums, low tolerance for frustration
	Perseveration, difficulty in abstraction, dyscalculia
Blindness, deafness, and severe aphasia	Impaired memory for shapes or designs
	Impaired memory for letters or words (sound and configuration)
Epilepsies	Abnormal EEG without seizures

viduals could be identified. Due to the lack of useful literature concerning characteristics of MBD or LD individuals, this was a very difficult task. Characteristics presented by the Task Force I were primarily obtained through clinical observation rather than through precise measure (i.e., systematic measurement of a large and well-defined sample was not used). The 10 most frequently mentioned characteristics, presented in a rank order listing, include

1. *Hyperactivity.* Motor behavior that does not appear to be goal-oriented and is often disruptive.
2. *Perceptual-motor impairments.* Problems in coordinating auditory or visual input with a motor response (e.g., copying words or numerals).
3. *Emotional lability.* Wide swings in mood behavior that do not appear to be directly related to the situation.
4. *General orientation deficits.* Difficulty with various motor movements (e.g., clumsiness).
5. *Disorders of attention.* Short attention span and general distractibility (e.g., difficulty maintaining attention to relevant stimuli or tasks).
6. *Impulsivity.* Behavior without thinking of the consequences.
7. *Disorders of memory and thinking.* Difficulty in recalling information that should have been mastered; problems in comprehending abstract concepts.
8. *Specific learning disabilities.* Difficulty in academic skills: reading, arithmetic, writing, and/or spelling.
9. *Disorders of speech and hearing.* Difficulty in understanding or remembering spoken language, deficits in articulation, and difficulty in expressing oneself verbally using correct vocabulary and syntax.
10. *Equivocal neurological signs.* Irregular EEG patterns and "soft" neurological

signs (e.g., motor problems, perceptual problems, and uneven or delayed development in language and motor areas).

Task Force I: Definition

Task Force I concentrated on terminology and identification of minimal brain dysfunction in children. In Clements' (1966) report, *MBD* was defined as

> children of near average, average, or above average general intelligence with certain learning or behavioral disabilities ranging from mild to severe, which are associated with deviations of function of the central nervous system. These deviations may manifest themselves by various combinations of impairment in perception, conceptualization, language, memory, and control of attention, impulse, or motor function ... these aberrations may arise from genetic variations, biochemical irregularities, perinatal brain insults or other illnesses or injuries sustained during the years which are critical for the development and maturation of the central nervous system, or from unknown causes. (pp. 9–10)

Clements (1966) thus presented the first formal definition proposed at a national level (Bryan & Bryan, 1978). Although similar to the one proposed by Strauss and Lehtinen (1947), several differences appear noteworthy. Whereas he included only those children whose measured intelligence was near average, average, or above average, thus excluding children with low IQs, Strauss and Lehtinen placed no limitation on intelligence. In terms of behavioral manifestations, the *MBD* definition was expanded to include motor and language disorders.

Brain injury or central nervous system (CNS) impairment may result from many factors. During pregnancy, the RH factor, diseases such as rubella, and medication taken by the mother may result in brain injury. During the birth process, anoxia, prematurity, long, hard labor, and difficult delivery are possible causes. Other events and diseases causing it include encephalitis, meningitis, dehydration, extremely high fevers, and head injuries. Remember that these conditions *potentially* cause brain injury. Oftentimes a child's history will include some of these events, yet the child manifests no evidence of brain injury. Currently the determination of minor injury remains a difficult task. Pediatricians and neurologists still primarily depend on behavioral characteristics and case history to make the diagnosis.

The *MBD* definition, like that of *brain-injured,* was never widely accepted. Diagnosticians did not like the task of detecting minimal brain dysfunction. Moreover, special educators found that labels that connotated a medical etiology were not useful in planning educational interventions. Bryan and Bryan (1978) comment on the dilemma of detecting MBD in the following passage:

> The problem is that the educational diagnostician is limited to evaluation of intellectual and social behavior. The stronger the direct evidence for brain damage, such as seizures or paralysis, the less likely the diagnostic conclusion is to be "minimal" damage. The less direct the medical evidence, the more the reliance upon social and academic performance, and the more likely the diagnosis of "minimal brain dysfunction." By definition, the linkage of brain damage with learning disabilities through direct evidence becomes an impossibility. (p. 29)

McIntosh and Dunn (1973) comment on the characteristics and generic nature of the *MBD* definition. They state that "it would be difficult to find a child who did not possess some of the qualities listed by Clements. Thus the 'minimal brain dysfunction' label became somewhat of a catch-all" (p. 536).

Paralleling the creation of the MBD definition and accompanying characteristics was the introduction of a definition with a similar focus by Johnson and Myklebust (1967): "We refer to children as having a psychoneurological learning disability, meaning that behavior has been disturbed as a result of a dysfunction of the brain and that the problem is one of altered processes, not of a generalized incapacity to learn" (p. 8). As with the *MBD* definition, the Johnson and Myklebust definition was not widely accepted and was subject to many of the same criticisms regarding lack of specificity and medical-etiological emphasis.

Later, definitions without reference to organic etiology resolved the dilemma. In the next phase, (the learning disabilities phase), reliance on psychological and educational variables replaced the emphasis on CNS damage.

LEARNING DISABILITIES PHASE

The learning disability (LD) terminology began to appear on a small scale previous to and concurrently with the MBD terminology. Special educators sought terms with greater educational relevance (e.g., *educationally handicapped, language disordered, perceptually handicapped*). Kirk (1962) coined the term *learning disability* four years before Clements (1966) published his report using *MBD*. Bateman (1965) introduced a definition of *learning disorders* that added a new and important dimension. She included a discrepancy clause, which referred to the existence of a difference between estimated capacity and achievement. Her definition stated:

> children who have learning disorders are those who manifest an educationally significant discrepancy between their estimated intellectual potential and actual level of performance related to basic disorders in the learning process, which may or may not be accompanied by demonstrable central nervous system dysfunction, and which are not secondary to generalized mental retardation, educational or cultural deprivation, severe emotional disturbance, or sensory loss. (p. 220)

NACHC Definition

When the U.S. Office of Education (USOE) was given the responsibility of funding special education programs for children with learning disabilities, it became apparent that a definition acceptable to educators was needed for funding purposes. The National Advisory Committee on Handicapped Children (NACHC) was formulated in 1968 to develop an acceptable definition. Under Kirk's leadership, the committee submitted a definition that was incorporated into PL 91–230, the Learning Disabilities Act of 1969. This definition stated:

> Children with special learning disabilities exhibit a disorder in one or more of the basic psychological processes involved in understanding or in using spoken or written languages. These may be manifested in disorders of listening, thinking, talking, reading, writing, spelling or arithmetic. They include conditions which have been referred to as perceptual handicaps, brain injury, minimal brain dysfunction, dyslexia, developmental aphasia, etc. They do *not* include learning problems which are due primarily to visual, hearing or motor handicaps, to mental retardation, emotional disturbance or to environmental disadvantage. (USOE, 1968, p. 34)

This definition, referred to as the NACHC definition or the USOE definition, is now the major definition used in the United States. A compilation of two surveys of state departments of education conducted during the 1974–1975 period revealed that 62% of the 50 states used the NACHC definition or some variation of it (Mercer, Forgnone, & Wolking, 1976; Murphy, 1976). Due to its widespread and continued use, it is important to examine the NACHC definition thoroughly in order to understand many practices (identification, testing, programming) in the area of learning disabilities. Moreover, a close look at the NACHC definition makes one aware of modern definitional problems and helps provide a framework for comprehending future directions concerning the definition.

Process Component

The NACHC definition introduces the process factor in the following phrase: "exhibit a disorder in one or more of the basic psychological processes involved in understanding or in using spoken or written languages" (USOE,

1968, p. 34). Although process factors compose a major part of the NACHC definition, they represent a very nebulous area. Hammill (1974) feels doubtful that authorities can agree on the nature of the process component. However, if the intent of the process component in the definition is examined, perhaps it is possible to determine the general nature of process factors. On examination of the field it is reasonable to conclude that the process component is primarily interpreted within three contexts (i.e., perceptual-motor, psycholinguistic, and cognitive process) (see Table 2.2).

The perceptual-motor interpretation stresses that higher-level mental functioning depends on an adequate development of the motor and perceptual system. Visual, tactile, and haptic perception, as well as intersensory organization, are basic in this position. (Several perception and perceptual-motor approaches are presented in Chapter 9.)

The psycholinguistic interpretation of the process disorder is highlighted by the development and widespread use of the *Illinois Test of Psycholinguistic Abilities (ITPA)*. This position examines the reception, integration, and expressive abilities of a child by presenting stimuli in the auditory-vocal and visual-motor channels. When discussing this interpretation remember that the term is not used in the generic sense but is primarily limited to the *ITPA* (the Osgood model). (The psycholinguistic approach is presented in Chapter 6.)

The cognitive process interpretation focuses on attention and memory problems. Selective attention deficits, as well as short-term memory deficits, are viewed as basic psychological process problems that interfere with learning (Chalfant & Scheffelin, 1969; Dykman, Ackerman, Clements, & Peters, 1971; Hallahan, 1975).

For purposes of this examination, the inclusion of process factors refers to *(a)* perceptual-motor processes (visual perception, haptic perception, intersensory integration, etc.); *(b)* psycholinguistic processes (visual reception, auditory reception, verbal expression, etc.); and *(c)* cognitive processes (selective attention, visual discrimination, memory). The NACHC definition states that these processes interfere with the understanding and/or use of spoken and/or written language. Since language may include listening, talking, reading, and writing, it is easy to ascertain that any of the three process positions could interfere with language development.

Academic Component

The NACHC definition, like most other definitions, includes the academic component, saying, "These may be manifested in disorders of . . . reading, writing, spelling or arithmetic" (USOE, 1968, p. 34).

Exclusion Component

The exclusion component delineates characteristics of children that exclude them from being identified as learning disabled. The exclusion section of the NACHC definition eliminates visual handicaps, hearing handicaps, motor handicaps, mental retardation, emo-

TABLE 2.2

Interpretations of the psychological process disorder in the NACHC definition.

Process Positions[a]	Academic Disorder
1. Perceptual-Motor Process Deficit	Learning problems in reading, math, spelling, etc.
2. Psycholinguistic Process Deficit	
3. Cognitive Process Deficit	

[a]*An eclectic position may include one or more of these process positions.*

tional disturbance, and/or environmental disadvantage when they are the *primary* cause(s) of a learning problem. Embedded in the exclusion section of the NACHC definition is a consideration of physical factors. For example, this section mentions sensory and motor deficits: "They do not include learning problems which are due primarily to visual, hearing or motor handicaps" (USOE, 1968, p. 34). The use of *primarily* suggests that these disabilities may be included as characterizing a LD child when not the primary problem.

Neurological Component

The neurological component includes the consideration of central nervous system dysfunction. The NACHC definition includes this component in the statement, "They include conditions which have been referred to as . . . brain injury, minimal brain dysfunction, dyslexia" (USOE, 1968, p. 34). From this statement it is inferred that is *possible* for the LD child to have neurological deficits. Unlike earlier definitions, the NACHC broke away from the medically oriented position that the learning problems were directly due to some type of central nervous system dysfunction. The NACHC took the position that the determination of a CNS dysfunction was arbitrary and not germane to identifying a LD child.

Intelligence Component

The intelligence factor consists of the ability level or range of ability of the persons being identified. It is usually reported in terms of an intelligence quotient (IQ) derived from the administration of an intelligence test. In the NACHC definition this component is referred to in the exclusion section, which states that the learning disorder is not due primarily to mental retardation. Mercer, Forgnone, and Wolking (1976) report that 45% of 42 states surveyed exclude mental retardation from their definition of LD, whereas the remaining 55% do not delineate the IQ range. Due to the vagueness of the intelligence factor in the NACHC definition, it is plausible to conclude that the NACHC definition does not actually identify the intelligence level of learning disabled individuals.

Affective Component

Emotional disturbance and/or social maladjustment make up the affective component and include factors that primarily involve how an individual copes with the interpersonal environment. The NACHC definition only mentions this component in the exclusion section, which states, "They do *not* include learning problems which are due primarily to . . . emotional disturbance" (USOE, 1968, p. 34).

Although no major revisions of the definition of learning disabilities have occurred since the adoption of the NACHC definition in 1968, it has been criticized notably:

1. There is no mention of how severe the disability must be in order for the individual to qualify for services (McIntosh & Dunn, 1973).
2. It does not include the discrepancy clause introduced by Bateman in 1964.
3. It depends too heavily on exclusion to define its target population. In addition, many special educators claim that children from other areas of special education may exhibit a specific learning disability (Lerner, 1976).
4. The definition is too general and ambiguous (Hammill, 1974; McIntosh & Dunn, 1973).
5. It serves administrative rather than professional considerations (McIntosh & Dunn, 1973).
6. The term *basic psychological processes* lacks clarity.
7. The definition has not generated consistent incidence figures.

Since 1969, the NACHC definition has helped secure funds and develop programs. Skepticism grew during the 1973–1976 period and coupled with the requirements of PL 94–142 to define LD more concisely. A new phase thus emerges in the development of the LD definition, namely, the refinement phase.

REFINEMENT PHASE

Focusing on a search for a functional and operational definition, the refinement phase (Table 2.3) is highlighted by five major events and/or activities: *(a)* an analysis of components of LD definitions, *(b)* an operationalization of the components, *(c)* the passage of PL 94–142, *(d)* the proposed regulations of the 1976 *Federal Register,* and *(e)* the regulations of the 1977 *Federal Register.*

An Analysis of Components

One fruitful approach consists of delineating and analyzing the components included in widely used definitions. Mercer, Forgnone, and Wolking (1976) surveyed the LD definitions used in 42 states and listed 15 components included in the state definitions. Murphy (1976) surveyed the remaining 8 states; her data were compiled with the data from the Mercer et al. survey in order to complete the survey of all states. Table 2.4 lists the 15 components included in the definitions and the number and percentage of states that included each respective component.

Most of the components listed in Table 2.4, except "Miscellaneous," are discussed in the section regarding the NACHC definition. Out of this last category, most state definitions do not specifically mention motor-attention disorders. They are included under miscellaneous because a few state definitions specifically included one or both of them.

Attention Disorders

Deficits in attention are frequently attributed to these children (Clements, 1966; Hallahan, 1975; Ross, 1976). Specifically, they are unable to select relevant stimulus dimensions and maintain attention to these dimensions (i.e., they have poor selective attention).

TABLE 2.3

Major events in refinement phase.

Event	Emphasis
1. Analysis of components	Identifying the common components of an LD definition
2. Operationalization of the components	Determining specific diagnostic and assessment procedures for each component (e.g., Florida criteria)
3. Passage of PL 94–142 in 1975	Defining LD more precisely and recommending 2% prevalence
4. Proposed regulations of 1976 *Federal Register*	Identifying LD by using a formula to determine 50% discrepancy between ability and performance
5. Regulations of 1977 *Federal Register*	Dropping formula, endorsing the NACHC definition (USOE, 1968), and elaborating on procedures for evaluating specific learning disabilities

TABLE 2.4

Number of states and respective percentages of components included in state definitions.

Components	No. of States	Percentages
Definition		
NACHC only	13	26%
NACHC with variations	18	36%
Different	16	32%
None	3	6%
Intelligence		
Average and above	12	24%
Above mental retardation	9	18%
Not stated	29	58%
Process		
Process disorder	42	84%
Language disorder	41	82%
Academic		
Reading	37	74%
Writing	37	74%
Spelling	37	74%
Arithmetic	37	74%
Exclusion		
Visual impairment	34	68%
Auditory impairment	34	68%
Motor impairment	31	62%
Mental retardation	38	76%
Emotional disturbance	31	62%
Environmental disadvantaged	29	58%
Neurological Impairment		
Included	4	8%
Possible	31	62%
Not stated	15	30%
Affective		
Includes emotionally disturbed	5	10%
Includes socially maladjusted	7	14%
Miscellaneous		
Attention deficits	5	10%
Motor deficits	7	14%
Thinking deficits	34	68%
Discrepancy component	12	24%
Special education required	14	28%
Intraindividual differences	5	10%
Prevalence	2	4%
Chronological age	5	10%

Motor Disorders

These disorders involve both gross motor problems (uneven gait, clumsiness, poor balance) and fine motor problems (handwriting difficulty, problems using scissors, buttons) (Kephart, 1971; Cratty, 1971; Barsch, 1967).

Discrepancy Component

Many consider the discrepancy component, popularized by Bateman (1964), as the common denominator of learning disabilities. In this characteristic, a child's estimated ability differs greatly from her academic performance (see Figure 2.1). This factor, basic to the notion of underachievement, may be across one or all academic skill areas. (Problems regarding the use of the discrepancy component are featured in Chapter 3.)

Child's Educational Program Needs

What the child needs to learn determines the definition of learning disabilities. The need for special education with minimal consideration of other components serves as a criterion for defining children with learning disabilities in various definitions. The NACHC definition does not include the educational programming needs of children.

Intraindividual Differences

Gallagher (1966) initially advanced this factor when he proposed the concept of "developmental imbalances." Kirk, McCarthy, and Kirk (1968) popularized the notion with the *ITPA*. Some refer to it as the "scatter effect" on test profiles. For example, the child may score high in some skill areas and very low in others (i.e., low in auditory discrimination and high in visual discrimination). The scatter phenomenon directly influences remediation strategies in that some emphasize teaching to the deficits while others stress teaching to the strengths. Moreover, some people criticize the concept of intraindividual differences because of the reliability and validity problems of the tests used to determine individual strengths and weaknesses.

This component is often confused with the discrepancy component; however, estimated capacity and overachievement are not primary features of intraindividual differences.

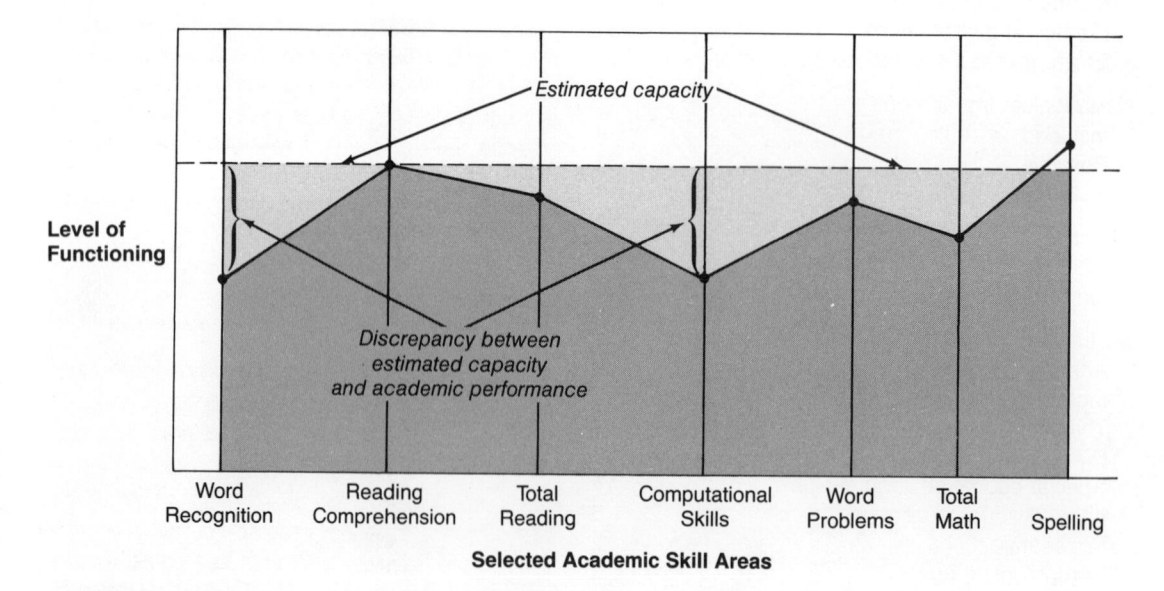

FIGURE 2.1.
Discrepancy component.

Definitions, terms, and characteristics

Prevalence

The number of children likely to be identified within an area of exceptionality becomes important in funding and planning programs. As noted by McIntosh and Dunn (1973), prevalence deserves consideration in defining exceptional children. The NACHC definition per se does not include it; however, the USOE suggests a 1–3% prevalence from the use of the NACHC statement.

Chronological Age

Chronological age may serve as a crucial parameter considering the emphasis on both early identification and secondary programming; but few definitions mention it, including the NACHC's.

In discussing the components, Mercer, Forgnone, and Wolking (1976) note that it is important to realize that many factors (e.g., prevalence, age) omitted in state definitions of learning disabilities are included in general special education guidelines. However, the survey data probably delineate the relative popularity of the various components in applied situations. For example, numerous investigators stress attention deficits, motor deficits, and/or uneven growth patterns, yet these factors tend to be excluded in state definitions. Are school personnel unable to deal with such characteristics in an operational or functional manner? If these are critical factors, special educators must detail how they can be used.

Chalfant and King (1976) examined definitions of learning disabilities and conclude that many can be made operational. They note that failure to identify and agree on the components that need to be operationalized has hindered the development of an operational definition. They consider these five factors to be essential components: *(a)* task failure, *(b)* exclusion factors, *(c)* physiological correlates, *(d)* discrepancy, and *(e)* psychological correlates. They also briefly outline operational procedures for each component.

Chalfant and King's (1976) task failure component is analogous to the academic component discussed earlier. Their exclusion factors closely parallel exclusion in the NACHC definition and their discrepancy component is similar to Bateman's (1964) discrepancy clause. Their physiological components include genetic variations, biochemical irregularities, perinatal brain insults, and illnesses and injuries affecting the maturation of the CNS. They note that the medical profession could operationalize this component. Finally, they stress the psychological process component, an area very difficult to operationalize. They divide it into attention, discrimination memory, sensory integration, concept formation, and problem solving. For each of these subprocesses they list tests and sets of questions that they regard as pertinent to operationalization. On this component's difficulty, they note that it is hard to measure directly and the diagnostician must depend on inferential testing (e.g., one infers that a child has an auditory memory problem because he performs poorly on a digit-span test). In their conclusion they stress the importance of clinical judgment in identification. Specifically, they state:

> When behavioral observations in the classroom, on the playground, and at home support test results, the determination of a disability can be made with greater confidence. On the other hand, if observation of the child's performance does not support the results of standardized tests, then further investigation into the child's problem is indicated. (p. 241)

Operationalizing the Components

Among other states, Washington, Iowa, and Florida have made extensive efforts to operationalize their definitions of learning disabilities. These states focus on quantifying the criteria for identification. Florida's procedures are presented in some detail because they may provide some direction in this task.

Via the leadership of Dennis Ehrhardt, former consultant in Specific Learning Disabilities, Florida State Department of Education, an operational definition is being field tested in many Florida school districts. Although the NACHC definition is used in Florida, the following criteria have been established on an experimental basis in an attempt to operationalize it.

Expectancy Age

The expectancy age (EA) formula (Harris, 1970), $EA = \frac{2MA + CA}{3}$, is used in the academic and process components of the Florida operational procedures to exclude the slow-learning child who, if based on chronological age, would be expected to score well below the norm. Thus, the child is theoretically being measured against her potential, not her age. Conversely, this procedure will identify the gifted child who is performing only at grade or age level.

Intelligence Component

The child with learning disabilities must obtain a score of not less than −2 standard deviations on an individual test of intelligence. This criterion thus excludes the child whose primary learning problem is due to mental retardation.

Physical Component

The child must have normal or near normal vision and auditory acuity and no evidence of a primary physical handicap. Specifically, she must demonstrate (a) visual acuity of at least 20/70 in the better eye with best correction or evidence that the student's inability to perform adequately on tasks that require visual processing is not due to poor visual acuity; (b) auditory acuity of no more than a 30 dB loss in the better ear unaided or evidence that the student's inability to perform adequately on tasks that require auditory processing or language is not due to poor auditory processing or language is not due to poor auditory acuity; and (c) that a physical impairment does not interfere with the student's ability to perform adequately on tasks measuring the basic psychological processes.

Academic Deficit Component

The determination of an academic deficit is based on a student's expectancy age. As measured by a standardized test, the resultant score would be in the lower 10th percentile in one or more of the following areas: reading, writing, arithmetic, spelling, and prerequisite skills. This criterion identifies those children who have disorders in academic areas. The figure 10% is used as a starting point since this is considered severe. Prerequisite skills do not mean process skills but rather preacademic skills such as recognizing letter names and understanding the right-left concept. Thus children with a specific learning disability can be identified prior to development of reading, writing, arithmetic, and spelling skills. In order to account for the effects of age on academic functioning in a more systematic way, the following criteria were used for the 1977–1978 school year. Based upon the student's EA, a score in an academic skill must fall within the range of (a) 85% EA or below for 3–6 years of school attendance, (b) 75% EA or below for 7–9 years of school attendance, or (c) 65% EA or below for 10 or more years of school attendance. For children in K–2, evidence must be presented of achievement substantially below expected level on preacademic tasks that require listening, thinking, or speaking.

Emotional-Social Component

No evidence of a severe emotional disturbance as based on test data or on the clinical judgment of a qualified psychologist should be found. This criterion thus excludes such disturbed children. This is perhaps one of the most difficult areas of exclusion since emotional overlays may accompany a learning disability.

Process Disorder Component

A process disorder is based on a student's EA, with a resultant score(s) of less than 70% EA or −2 standard deviations in one area, or 80% or −1.5 standard deviations in three or more areas that measure the following basic psychological processes: *(a)* visual, *(b)* auditory, *(c)* haptic, *(d)* receptive or expressive language, and *(e)* sensory integration. This criterion screens out the slow learner or culturally deprived youth who does *not* have a specific learning disability.

Here is one example of the Florida criteria for determining a process disorder:

Jane Thomas
CA = 8 years (96 months)
WISC Full Scale IQ = 90

1. Determining EA from IQ and CA

$$IQ = \frac{MA}{CA} \times 100, \text{ thus } 90 = \frac{MA}{96} \times 100;$$
$$100MA = 96 \times 90; 100MA = 8640;$$

MA = 86.4 (or 86 months)

$$EA = \frac{2MA + CA}{3}; EA = \frac{2(86) + 96}{3};$$
$$EA = \frac{268}{3};$$

EA = 89.3 months (or 7 years 5 months)

2. Process Disorder

To be judged as having a process disorder, the child must score 70% EA on one process area or 80% EA in three or more areas.

70% EA = 89 × .70 = 62 months
(or 5 years 2 months)

80% EA = 89 × .80 = 71 months
(or 5 years 11 months)

Therefore, the child would need *one* score on a process test of 5 years 2 months or lower (70% EA), or three scores above 5 years 2 months but at or lower than 5 years 11 months.

3. Academic Disorder

Since EA = 89 months (7 years 5 months), the examiner would use 7 years 5 months when looking up the percentile for the grade score that the child achieved. For example, if Jane achieved a 1.2 grade level on reading, this 1.2 score would be compared with the norms for 7 years 5 months. If the child's percentile using the expectancy age is at the 10th percentile or lower, she would have an academic disorder severe enough to be considered a severe learning disorder (SLD). With the 1977–1978 Florida criteria of 85% EA, an age score of 6 years 3 months results (89 × .85 = 6 years 3 months). Thus, to have a learning disability in academics, the child must be functioning at or below the grade level expected of a child 6 years 3 months old (e.g., approximately 1.3 grade level).

Recent legislation (PL 94–142) requires the following criteria to document evidence of previous educational adjustments and opportunities.

1. Evidence must exist that indicates that viable general educational alternatives have been attempted and found to be ineffective.
2. Evidence must exist that indicates the student's inability to improve his performance in deficit areas. Students will be excluded who demonstrate substantial improvement after mere exposure and repetition of the tasks.

These two criteria thus exclude children whose learning problems are primarily due to poor teaching and/or environmental disadvantage.

These and similar criteria have been used in Florida since 1973. In order to ascertain the reactions of practitioners to the operational criteria, Mercer, Lessen, and Algozzine (1977) surveyed 18 special education directors, 14 learning disabilities coordinators, 77 elementary level learning disabilities teachers, 35 secondary level learning disabilities teachers, 32 school psychologists, 30 speech clinicians, and 9 guidance counselors. The professional personnel reacted favorably. Although they generally favored the quantification of criteria

In this staff meeting, a teacher reports what she feels would be the best placement for a student.

in the Florida definition, they stressed the importance of staff communication in placing such children. They said that while some children may meet the operational criteria, placement in a learning disabilities program would not be best. At staff meetings much information (social history, teacher reports, psychological reports) is presented and decisions are made that insure that the best placement for the child is recommended. In this way, dependence on quantification scores is minimized when it conflicts with other observations.

Operational criteria coupled with the professional judgment of staffings generate an incidence figure of approximately 2% for learning disabilities in Florida. However, these problems hinder operationalization:

1. The difficulty of determining appropriate problem level (severity) of academic or process functioning for the different grade levels (e.g., first grade criteria must differ from ninth grade criteria).
2. The lack of adequate tests to assess the basic psychological processes and academic readiness skills.
3. The difficulty of determining capacity (MA) of a student for inclusion in the expectancy age formula. In order to obtain an estimate of capacity, an individual test of intelligence must be given. In many instances this task becomes a logistics problem. In addition, such test results are not always indicative of ability.
4. Difficulty of determining for primary children a cut-off score that qualifies them on the academic component.
5. Lack of valid tests for assessing the skills of minority groups.

Public Law 94–142 and the LD Definition

The USOE offers the most influential direction concerning the LD definition. At a national level, it disperses and monitors the expenditures of many federal monies in special education. With the passage of PL 94–142, it is charged with providing leadership and support to the very difficult task of defining SLD more precisely. It is faced with making crucial decisions in selecting, eliminating, or integrating the various positions on definition. Unfortunately this decision must be made without the benefit of research data, for none exists. Considering the varied causes, behavioral manifestations, and theories regarding LD, it is possible that Congress has requested something that cannot be done effectively at this time. Likewise, if this request were made of other categories of exceptionality (e.g., educable mental retardation and emotional disturbance), the question of effective accomplishment would emerge.

To begin this task Congress defined children with specific learning disabilities by using a definition (USOE, 1976) almost identical to NACHC's. The USOE reports that no legislative recommendations will be made regarding the definition until research indicates the types of changes that are needed. However, to begin the immediate task of defining SLD more precisely, the USOE is concentrating on *(a)* outlining the specific criteria for determining a particular disorder or condition, *(b)* determining appropriate diagnostic procedures, and *(c)* monitoring procedures for use in determining if states are following *(a)* and *(b)*.

1976 Federal Register

According to USOE (1976),

> At present, the only generally accepted manifestation of a specific learning disability is that there is a major discrepancy between expected achievement and ability which is not the result of other known and generally accepted handicapping conditions or circumstances. (p. 52404)

The issue of determining this discrepancy between achievement and ability is the major focus of the proposed rules included in the November, 1976, *Federal Register.* For example, proposed regulations require "that a child be achieving at or below 50 percent of his expected achievement level in order for a severe discrepancy to exist" (USOE, 1976, p. 52405). The regulations offer a formula for determining the severe discrepancy level:

$$CA\left(\frac{IQ}{300} + 0.17\right) - 2.5 = \text{severe discrepancy level}$$

This formula was designed to consider the interrelationship between ability, chronological age, previous educational experience, and level of discrepant achievement. The USOE requested feedback and received 982 reactions to the proposed formula. Due to the large number of negative reactions, the formula was not included in later regulations. In the March 1978 issue of the *Journal of Learning Disabilities* Danielson and Bauer report on the issues and varied reactions to the formula-based classification of LD children. The formula is no longer supported or used by the USOE.

1977 Federal Register

After 2 years of extensive efforts to improve on the definition of SLD, the USOE released the 1977 *Federal Register,* which includes the regulations for defining and identifying SLD students under PL 94–142. These regulations endorse a definition almost identical to the NACHC's:

> "Specific learning disability" means a disorder in one or more of the basic psychological processes involved in understanding or in using language, spoken or written, which may manifest itself in an imperfect ability to listen, think, speak, read, write, spell, or to do mathematical calculations. The term includes such conditions as perceptual handicaps, brain injury, minimal brain disfunction, dyslexia, and developmental aphasia. The term does not include children who have learning problems which are primarily the result of visual, hearing, or motor handicaps, of mental retardation, or emotional disturbance, or of environmental, cultural, or economic disadvantage. (USOE, 1977, p. 65083)

In addition, the regulations delete the formula and the 50% figure for determining a severe discrepancy.

Although formally unchanged in definition since 1968, SLD is now evaluated differently

(USOE, 1977) in the *Federal Register.* For example, people do not now use process disorder in identification. On the other hand, the discrepancy component, which is not specifically stated in the definition, is now the major factor in identification.

Evaluation procedures require the involvement of a multidisciplinary team. This team must include *(a)* the child's regular teacher or a qualified replacement if the child does not have a regular teacher, *(b)* for preschool children, an individual qualified by the state educational agency to teach a preschool child, and *(c)* at least one individual qualified to conduct individual diagnostic examinations of children (e.g., school psychologist, speech-language pathologist, learning disabilities specialist).

The *Federal Register* (USOE, 1977) outlines the criteria for determining learning disability:

> *A team may determine that a child has a specific learning disability if:*
>
> 1. The child does not achieve commensurate with his or her age and ability levels in one or more of the areas listed in [the] paragraph . . . [below] . . . this section, when provided with learning experiences appropriate for the child's age and ability levels; and
> 2. The team finds that a child has a severe discrepancy between achievement and intellectual ability in one or more of the following areas:
>
> Oral expression; listening comprehension; written expression; basic reading skill; reading comprehension; mathematics calculation; or mathematics reasoning.
>
> *The team may not identify a child as having a specific learning disability if the severe discrepancy between ability and achievement is primarily the result of:*
>
> 1. A visual, hearing, or motor handicap;
> 2. Mental retardation;
> 3. Emotional disturbance; or
> 4. Environmental, cultural or economic disadvantage. (p. 65083)

Additionally, observation is an important procedure.

> (a) At least one team member other than the child's regular teacher shall observe the child's academic performance in the regular classroom setting.
> (b) In the case of a child of less than school age or out of school, a team member shall observe the child in an environment appropriate for a child of that age. (USOE, 1977, p. 65083)

In preparing a written report of the results, the team must include documentation of the required criteria; this task reflects the continuing effort to define SLD in a more precise manner. Reactions to these evaluation procedures will doubtless stimulate new questions and offer additional procedures. For example, Senf (1978) questions the influence of the regulations on *(a)* research efforts across disciplines, *(b)* services to children whose learning problems are more complicated than a specific skill deficit (e.g., a hyperactive child or a child with allergies) and *(c)* who teaches the SLD student. Until reliable and valid diagnostic instruments are developed and solid research data are obtained regarding the common characteristics of SLD students, a widely accepted operational definition will remain elusive.

CHARACTERISTICS OF LEARNING DISABILITIES

General Characteristics

Since Clements's (1966) report on the 10 most frequently mentioned characteristics of LD individuals, very little systematic research has accrued regarding the incidence of selected characteristics. His list no longer presents an accurate description; for example, he ranks hyperactivity as the most frequent and academic difficulty as eighth. Since the 1977 *Federal Register* features discrepancy as primary, obviously academic learning problems are now the number one characteristic of LD individuals.

Detailed descriptions of characteristics are featured in numerous chapters (3–10, 12, and 13) of this text. This chapter presents a list of characteristics to provide a brief overview of contemporary thought. In reviewing the list, remember that the LD population is a heterogeneous group. Each student is unique and may exhibit difficulty in one area and not in another area. Also, the range of combinations is enormous. Moreover, examine characteristics with the perspective that the identifying behaviors must *persist over time*. Many students who are not LD exhibit selected behaviors for brief time periods (e.g., hyperactivity due to excitement over a field trip).

Rather than assigning characteristics, most teachers describe behaviors. For example,

Each child has unique problems and strengths.

"Max is constantly out of his seat during seatwork activities" and "Max fidgets at his desk" tell more about Max than saying that he is hyperactive. The label *hyperactive* infers a diagnosis and assigns a trait-type characteristic to the student. In essence, teachers can usually defend behavioral observations but have difficulty justifying a label. When reviewing the following list, consider individual differences, persistence of identifying behaviors, and the merits of behavioral descriptions.

Academic Learning Difficulty

Discrepancy means academic problems (USOE, 1977). Specifically, students may lack basic reading skill, reading comprehension, mathematics calculation, and mathematics reasoning. This difficulty, unifying all SLD students, is featured throughout this text but is specifically discussed in Chapters 7 and 8.

Language Disorders

Language problems, like academic problems, are part of the discrepancy component. Specifically, the 1977 *Federal Register* mentions deficient skills in oral expression, listening comprehension, and written expression. In addition, language disorders are featured in the first sentence of the SLD definition. Kirk, Kliebhan, and Lerner (1978) report that the study of how these disorders relate to learning problems (see Chapter 6) is receiving extensive attention from numerous disciplines (psycholinguistics, language pathology, linguistics, and language arts and communication). Vogel (1975) notes that research indicates that many children who do not read well suffer from underlying language problems. Because language skills and academic functioning are so closely related, confusion exists concerning the diagnostic and instructional roles of language clinicians and SLD specialists.

Perceptual Disorders

Although several leaders in LD stress perceptual problems, the concentration on perceptual disorders (inability to recognize, discrimi-

Foundations of learning disabilities

nate, and interpret sensation) has diminished in recent years. The 1977 *Federal Register* does not include perceptual disorders in the evaluation procedures of SLD. However, LD research history reflects a heavy emphasis on this problem. Cruickshank (1976) maintains that perception and neurological involvement are the key factors in defining learning disabilities. This position was evident in the national Project on the Classification of Exceptional Children under the direction of Nicholas Hobbs. In this project a committee examined the classification of LD and finally offered the following definition:

> *Specific learning disability*, as defined here, refers to those children of any age who demonstrate a substantial deficiency in a particular aspect of academic achievement because of perceptual or perceptual-motor handicaps, regardless of etiology or other contributing factors. The term *perceptual* as used here relates to those mental (neurological) processes through which the child acquires his basic alphabets of sounds and forms. (Wepman, Cruickshank, Deutsch, Morency, & Strother, 1975, p. 306)

In discussing the formulation of this definition, Cruickshank (1976) comments:

> Although the members of the committee came from different orientations and held differing points of view on some matters, we established unanimity in an astonishingly short time. There was no question as to the essential locus of the problem, i.e., neurological; and there was no hesitation to speak of this problem in terms of what it actually is, i.e., perceptual or perceptual-motor. (p. 113)

Chapter 9 presents a detailed discussion of perceptual disabilities and includes the reasons for the recent de-emphasis.

Motor Disorders

Myers and Hammill (1976) divide motor disabilities into four areas: hyperactivity, hypoactivity, incoordination, and perseveration. Students with motor problems may walk with an awkward gait or have difficulty throwing or catching a ball, skipping, or hopping. Others exhibit fine motor difficulties when cutting with scissors, buttoning, or zipping. Like perceptual disabilities, motor problems received substantial emphasis in research history but recently are being de-emphasized. For example, the 1977 *Federal Register* does not refer to them. Also, the SLD definition only mentions motor disabilities to the extent that basic psychological processes refer to them. (Chapters 5 and 9 cover motor disabilities and their recent de-emphasis.)

Social-Emotional Problems

Many LD learners do not develop in a normal social-emotional pattern. Frustrated with their learning difficulties, they act disruptively, acquiring negative feelings of self-worth. Effec-

Some LD students need help improving motor coordination.

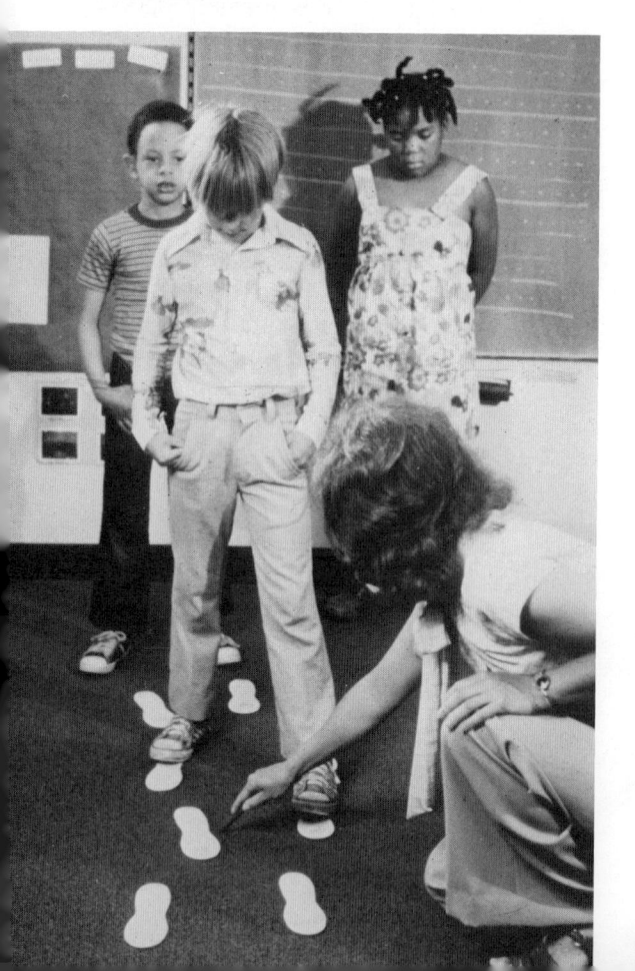

tive learning requires an emotional well-being and a positive attitude (Kirk, Kliebhan, and Lerner, 1978). Any plans must consider emotional problems.

Poor perception of social situations leads to a deficit in social skills. Such children seem insensitive to the needs of others. (Chapter 10 discusses further how social and emotional factors relate to learning disabilities.)

Memory Problems

Students who cannot store and retrieve previous sensations forget information soon after it is presented. They cannot recall math facts or remember words and directions. Frequently specific problems are discussed in terms of the input modality. For example, the student who cannot recall what she hears has difficulty in auditory memory. (Chapter 9 specifically addresses memory, and other content-area difficulties—reading, arithmetic, language—appearing throughout the text.)

Attention Problems

To succeed in school a student must be able to recognize and maintain thought on relevant classroom tasks. She must be able to shift attention to new tasks.

Students with this problem cannot screen out extraneous stimuli; a barrage of irrelevant, impinging stimuli attract them. Additional behaviors include short attention span, distractibility, and hypersensitivity.

LD and the Mildly Handicapped

Hallahan and Kauffman (1976) delineate the similarities in characteristics of learning disabled (LD), emotionally disturbed (ED), and educable mentally retarded (EMR) children. They propose a generic definition that stresses the identification of mildly handicapped children. Specifically they suggest, "If the term 'learning disabilities' is to continue to be used, that it be used to refer to learning problems found in children who have traditionally been classified as mildly handicapped, whether it be emotionally disturbed, mildly retarded, or learning disabled" (p. 28).

The Hallahan and Kauffman position generated studies regarding the respective characteristics of LD, ED, and EMR students and

Scotty needs to learn how not to be distracted by what's going on around him.

the relative merits of mixing the three groups for instruction. For example, Becker (1978) compared the three groups (LD, ED, EMR; N = 20 for each group) by using five problem-solving tasks (i.e., digit span, *Raven's Progressive Matrices, Matching Familiar Figures Test,* puzzle task, and the rod and frame test). On four of the five tasks, the groups significantly differed, especially in the problem-solving strategies and learning characteristics of children matched on CA. Becker summarizes the data:

> In light of the data presented in this study, one needs to closely examine the use of generic categories or labels such as those being used under the California Master Plan for Special Education. Before implementing generic programs, one needs to consider the effects of such a shift on the children being served, the teachers in the classroom, and the teacher trainers at the colleges and universities. The assumption of homogeneity or overlap of child characteristics argued by Hallahan and Kauffman, as well as the assumption of teacher competence, need to be critically evaluated with additional research. (p. 510)

INCIDENCE OF LEARNING DISABILITIES

Due to variations in terminology and definitions, estimates of accurate prevalence rates have no stable foundation. Estimates range from 1% to 30% of the school population (Lerner, 1976). If one includes mildly handicapped learners, the figure is likely to be close to but above 3%. If one includes children with severe specific learning disabilities, the figure may approximate 1.5%. Table 2.5 presents incidence studies and various committee recommendations.

At this point a comparison of incidence rates across studies or recommendations is not warranted. Committee recommendations must be tempered with regards for their respective interpretation differences; studies must be considered both in terms of such variances and the different groups of children

TABLE 2.5

Incidence of learning disabilities.

Study	Estimated Percentage
Kass & Myklebust (1969)	3.0–5.0%
Myklebust & Boshes (1969)	7.0–8.0%
Commission on Emotional and Learning Disorders in Children (1970)	1.6%
Meier (1971) (medical diagnosis)	4.7%
Special Study Institute for Specific Learning Disabilities (1975)	1.0–2.0%
COMMITTEE OR GROUP RECOMMENDATION	
McIntosh & Dunn (1973) (Strauss syndrome only)	1/5 of 1.0%
McIntosh & Dunn (1973) (MBD definition)	1.0–2.0+%
National Advisory Committee on Handicapped Children (USOE, 1968)	1.0–3.0%
Public Law 94–142 (USOE, 1976)	no more than 1/6 of 12%
Federal Register (USOE, 1977)	no figure provided

studied (e.g., children from low socioeconomic areas versus children from middle socioeconomic areas). Initially for PL 94–142 (USOE, 1976), for "count" purposes Congress stated "that children with specific learning disabilities may not constitute more than one-sixth of the children eligible to be counted as handicapped" (p. 52404). However, the 1977 *Federal Register* (USOE, 1977) removed the 2% "cap" on SLD.

Gearheart (1977) reports that with the passage of PL 94–142, LD is included in the general category of handicapped for the first time. This means that money will not be allocated for learning disabilities and for handicapped children separately but will be authorized for "handicapped," which includes all handicapped children. Some Congressional members feel that under this new funding pattern LD will receive more than its share of the funds and children with other handicaps will not receive enough.

CONCLUSION AND SUMMARY

Caution prevailed during the 1960s and 1970s regarding labels and classifications. The stigma attached to labels, the creation of low expectations of the labeled child by teachers and peers, and the uselessness of labels in planning instruction all influence the movement to abolish labels. At a recent conference, some participants wore buttons stating, "Label jars, not children."

Despite these influences, labels continue to exist. Proponents of labels point out their necessity in developing legislation and funding, in administration of special education programs, and in research. In support of labels, McCarthy (1971) states:

> The most important decision you will make is that of definition—because your definition will dictate for you the terminology to be used in your program, the prevalence figures, your selection criterion, the characteristics of your population, and the appropriate remedial procedures. (p. 14)

A classification system seems to be important and is, hopefully, evolving. This chapter traces the evolvement of the definition, characteristics, and terminology in learning disabilities through four phases (Brain-Injured, Minimal Brain Dysfunction, Learning Disabilities, and Refinement). These phases do not each represent a series of mutually exclusive events but overlap in time and thought. Although much activity exists regarding definition, the NACHC's remains the one most widely used. Likewise, the reader should note that the Refinement Phase is characterized by an examination of components of LD definitions and attempts to operationalize these components. The 1977 *Federal Register* emphasizes the discrepancy factor and presents evaluation procedures for identifying SLD individuals.

Contemporary characteristics of SLD students are presented as different from Clements's (1966) original 10 characteristics. Those discussed include *(a)* academic learning difficulty, *(b)* language disorders, *(c)* perceptual disorders, *(d)* motor disorders, *(e)* social-emotional problems, *(f)* memory problems, and *(g)* attention problems. The incidence figures vary greatly depending on the interpretation of the definition and the group of children studied. In addition, a specific prevalence figure is not recommended in the 1977 regulations.

Regarding the definition, it appears to be an active and exciting time in learning disabilities. Hopefully, the disenchantment with existing definitions and demands for a more precise definition will foster advancements in the area that will reduce its enigmatic state and help special educators deliver services to the child who, *in fact,* needs to be in a program for LD students.

REFERENCES

Barsch, R.H. *Achieving perceptual-motor efficiency* (Vol. 1). Seattle: Special Child, 1967.

Bateman, B.D. Learning disabilities—Yesterday, today, and tomorrow. *Exceptional Children,* 1964, *31,* 167.

Bateman, B.D. An educator's view of a diagnostic approach to learning disorders. In J. Hellmuth (Ed.), *Learning disorders* (Vol. 1). Seattle: Special Child, 1965.

Becker, L.D. Learning characteristics of educationally handicapped and retarded children. *Exceptional Children*, 1978, *44*, 502–511.

Bryan, T.H., & Bryan, J.H. *Understanding learning disabilities* (2nd ed.). Port Washington, N.Y.: Alfred, 1978.

Chalfant, J.C., & King, F.S. An approach to operationalizing the definition of learning disabilities. *Journal of Learning Disabilities*, 1976, *9*, 228–243.

Chalfant, J., & Scheffelin, M. *Central processing dysfunction in children: A review of research* (NINDS Monograph No. 9). Bethesda, Md.: U.S. Department of Health, Education, and Welfare, 1969.

Clements, S.D. *Minimal brain dysfunction in children* (NINDS Monograph No. 3, U.S. Public Health Service Publication No. 1415). Washington, D.C.: U.S. Government Printing Office, 1966.

Commission on Emotional and Learning Disorders in Children. *One million children*. Toronto, Ont.: Leonard Crainford, 1970.

Cratty, B. *Active learning: Games to enhance academic abilities*. Englewood Cliffs, N.J.: Prentice-Hall, 1971.

Cruickshank, W. *The brain-injured child in home, school and community*. Syracuse, N.Y.: Syracuse University Press, 1967.

Cruickshank, W.M. Some issues facing the field of learning disability. *Journal of Learning Disabilities*, 1972, *5*, 380–388.

Cruickshank, W.M. William M. Cruickshank. In J.M. Kauffman & D.P. Hallahan (Eds.), *Teaching children with learning disabilities: Personal perspectives*. Columbus, Ohio: Charles E. Merrill, 1976.

Cruickshank, W.M., Bentzen, F.A., Ratzeburg, R.H., & Tannhauser, M.T. *A teaching method for brain-injured and hyperactive children*. Syracuse, N.Y.: Syracuse University Press, 1961.

Cruickshank, W.M., Junkala, J.B., & Paul, J.L. *The preparation of teachers of brain-injured children*. Syracuse University Press, 1968.

Danielson, L.C., & Bauer, J.N. A formula-based classification of learning disabled children: An examination of the issues. *Journal of Learning Disabilities*, 1978, *11*, 163–176.

Divoky, D. Education's latest victim: The "LD" kid. *Learning*, 1974, *3*, 20–25.

Dykman, R.A., Ackerman, P.T., Clements, S.D., & Peters, J.E. Specific learning disabilities: An attentional deficit syndrome. In H.R. Myklebust (Ed.), *Progress in learning disabilities* (Vol. 2). New York: Grune & Stratton, 1971.

Gallagher, J.J. Children with developmental imbalances: A psychoeducational definition. In W.M. Cruickshank (Ed.), *The teacher of brain-injured children: A discussion of the bases for competency*. Syracuse: Syracuse University Press, 1966.

Gearheart, B.R. *Learning disabilities: Educational strategies* (2nd ed.). Saint Louis: C.V. Mosby, 1977.

Hallahan, D.P. Distractibility in the learning disabled child. In W.M. Cruickshank & D.P. Hallahan (Eds.), *Perceptual and learning disabilities in children. Research and theory* (Vol. 2). Syracuse: Syracuse University Press, 1975.

Hallahan, D.P. & Kauffman, J.M. *Introduction to learning disabilities: A psycho-behavioral approach*. Englewood Cliffs, N.J.: Prentice-Hall, 1976.

Hammill, D. Learning disabilities: A problem in definition. *Division for Children with Learning Disabilities Newsletter*, 1974, *4*(1), 28–31.

Harris, A.J. *How to increase reading ability* (5th ed). New York: David McKay, 1970.

Johnson, D., & Myklebust, H. *Learning disabilities: Educational principles and practices*. New York: Grune & Stratton, 1967.

Kass, C.E. Introduction to learning disabilities. *Seminars in Psychiatry*, 1969, *1*, 240–244.

Kass, C., & Myklebust, H. Learning disabilities: An educational definition. *Journal of Learning Disabilities*, 1969, *2*, 377–379.

Kephart, N.C. *The slow learner in the classroom* (2nd ed.). Columbus, Ohio: Charles E. Merrill, 1971.

Kirk, S.A. *Educating exceptional children*. Boston: Houghton Mifflin, 1962.

Kirk, S.A., Kliebhan, J.M., & Lerner, J.W. *Teaching reading to slow and disabled learners*. Boston: Houghton Mifflin, 1978.

Kirk, S.A., McCarthy, J.J., & Kirk, W.D. *The Illinois Test of Psycholinguistic Abilities*. Urbana: University of Illinois Press, 1968.

Lerner, J.W. *Children with learning disabilities* (2nd ed.) Boston: Houghton Mifflin, 1976.

Lovitt, T.C. Thomas C. Lovitt. In J.M. Kauffman & D.P. Hallahan (Eds.), *Teaching children with learning disabilities: Personal perspectives.* Columbus, Ohio: Charles E. Merrill, 1976.

McCarthy, J.M. Learning disabilities: Where have we been? Where are we going? In D.D. Hammill & N.R. Bartel (Eds.), *Educational perspectives in learning disabilities.* New York: Wiley, 1971.

McIntosh, D.K., & Dunn, L.M. Children with major specific learning disabilities. In L.M. Dunn (Ed.), *Exceptional children in the schools: Special education in transition* (2nd ed.). New York: Holt, Rinehart & Winston, 1973.

Meier, J.H. Prevalence and characteristics of learning disabilities found in second grade children. *Journal of Learning Disabilities,* 1971, *4,* 6–21.

Mercer, C.D., Forgnone, C., & Wolking, W.D. Definitions of learning disabilities used in the United States. *Journal of Learning Disabilities,* 1976, *9,* 376–386.

Mercer, C.D., Lessen, E.I., & Algozzine, B. *Toward an acceptable definition of learning disabilities.* Manuscript submitted for publication, 1977.

Murphy, M.L. *Idaho study of learning disabilities: Definition, eligibility criteria, and evaluation procedures.* Unpublished manuscript, State of Idaho Department of Education, 1976.

Myers, P.I., & Hammill, D.D. *Methods for learning disorders* (2nd ed.). New York: John Wiley & Sons, 1976.

Myklebust, H., & Boshes, B. *Minimal brain damage in children* (Final Report, U.S. Public Health Service Contract 108-65-142, U.S. Department of Health, Education, & Welfare). Evanston, Ill.: Northwestern University Publication, 1969.

Ross, A.O. *Psychological aspects of learning disabilities & reading disorders.* New York: McGraw-Hill, 1976.

Senf, G.M. Implications of the final procedures for evaluating specific learning disabilities. *Journal of Learning Disabilities,* 1978, *11,* 124–126.

Special study institute for specific learning disabilities: Proceedings. Tallahassee, Fl.: State of Florida Department of Education, 1975.

Stevens, G.D., & Birch, J.W. A proposal of clarification of the terminology and a description of brain-injured children. *Exceptional Children,* 1957, *23,* 346–349.

Strauss, A.A., & Lehtinen, L.E. *Psychopathology and education of the brain-injured child* (Vol. 1). New York: Grune & Stratton, 1947.

U.S. Office of Education. *First annual report of National Advisory Committee on Handicapped Children.* Washington, D.C.: U.S. Department of Health, Education, & Welfare, 1968.

U.S. Office of Education. Education of handicapped children: Assistance to states: Proposed rulemaking. *Federal Register,* 1976, *41,* 52404–52407.

U.S. Office of Education. Assistance to states for education of handicapped children: Procedures for evaluating specific learning disabilities. *Federal Register,* 1977, *42,* 65082–65085.

Vaughn, R.W., & Hodges, L. A statistical survey into a definition of learning disabilities: A search for acceptance. *Journal of Learning Disabilities,* 1973, *6,* 658–664.

Vogel, S.A. *Syntactic abilities in normal and dyslexic children.* Baltimore: University Park Press, 1975.

Wepman, J.M., Cruickshank, W.M., Deutsch, C.P., Morency, A., & Strother, C.R. Learning disabilities. In N. Hobbs (Ed.), *Issues in the classification of children* (Vol. 1). San Francisco: Jossey-Bass, 1975.

Wortis, J. A note on the concept of the "brain-injured" child. *American Journal of Mental Deficiency,* 1956, *61,* 204–206.

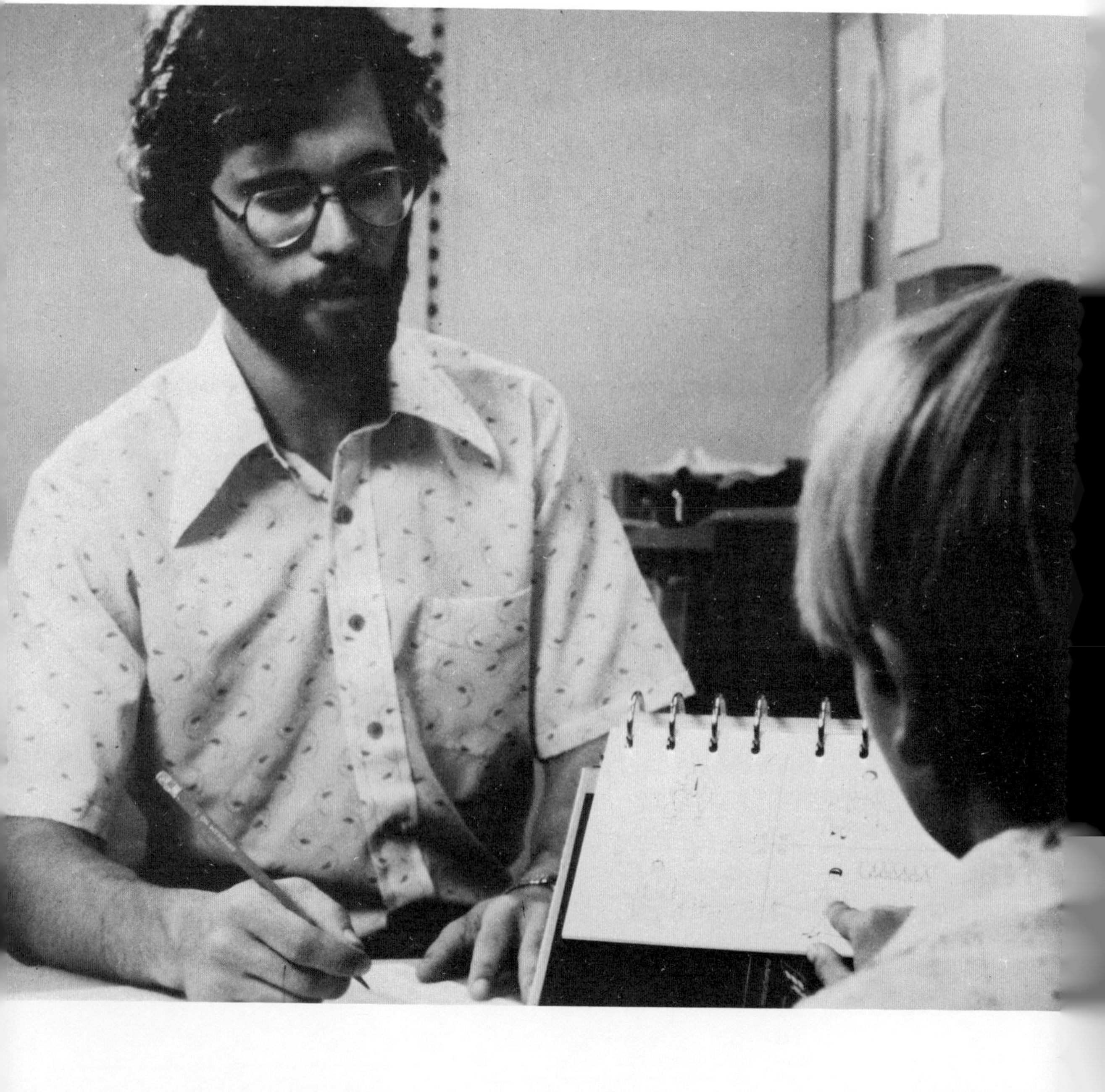

3

Educational diagnosis

To accurately identify emotionally disturbed individuals, Foster, Algozzine, and Kaufman (in press) developed the *Cat Test.* This simple yet novel test is easily administered by professionals, parents, and aides. It involves three simple steps: *(a)* place testee in empty room facing far wall, *(b)* place cat into center of room, close and latch door, and *(c)* after 10 minutes, open the door. Foster et al. note that the *Cat Test* allows fine discriminations between subsets of emotional disturbance. They offer the following guidelines for interpretation of results.

1. *Obsessive Compulsive*—four neat, meticulous piles of fur to be found in the corners of room—cat alive, but cold.
2. *Socialized Delinquent*—fur scattered randomly about room and on testee—cat alive, still cold.
3a. *Manic/Depressive (Manic Stage)*—pieces of cat scattered randomly about room—cat terminated.
3b. *Manic/Depressive (Depressive Stage)*—pieces of testee scattered randomly about room—emotional stability of cat suspect.
4. *Paranoid Reaction*—testee cowering in far corner of room—cat alive and sleeping in center of room.
5. *Psychopathology*—only evidence of cat is skin, wrapped loosely about testee's head—cat assumed terminated.
6. *Schizophrenic Reaction*—testee in center of room carrying on long existential discussion with cat—cat alive, but confused.
7. *Neurotic Reaction*—testee asking cat for advice about migraine headache—cat alive and still confused.
8. *Catatonic Reaction*—testee in corner of room with back arched, hair on end, hissing and refusing to acknowledge presence of cat—cat alive, confused and sexually aroused. (p. 2)

A sense of humor is helpful in the task of identification. It is a complex and controversial area, beset with problems. Although everyone wants accurate diagnosis, reliable and valid tests are still not available in many areas germane to identification (e.g., process disorders, adaptive behavior, and behavior disorders). PL 94–142 requires nondiscriminatory tests—which do not yet exist. Further, categorical definitions are vague and subject to many interpretations (e.g., the definition of LD). As a result, there is proliferation of tests aimed at identifying exceptional children, especially LD children.

In the last decade, the term *diagnosis* has changed or expanded markedly. Traditionally, it has been interpreted within a medical orientation as the determination of a condition (e.g., pneumonia or trainable mental retardation) that either requires a specific treatment or implies that no treatment exists to correct the problem. Moreover, the condition is viewed as a problem within the child (disease model).

Now *diagnosis* includes descriptions of behaviors that do not necessarily pinpoint a "condition." For example, it may refer to a description of reading behavior; in this context, a problem behavior is not viewed as caused by some dysfunction "within the child." Moreover, within this expanded context, treatment suggestions are numerous and focus on the manipulation of factors in the environment. This latter use of diagnosis is often used interchangeably with the terms *assessment* and *evaluation*.

In this chapter *diagnosis* is used in two ways. First, it refers to the process of identifying, placing, and teaching a student. Secondly, it refers to specific evaluation procedures that occur in the total diagnostic process (e.g., reading diagnosis). This chapter focuses on diagnostic practices in learning disabilities and covers *(a)* purposes of diagnosis, *(b)* diagnostic approaches, *(c)* the diagnostic process, *(d)* types of educational testing, and *(e)* issues and directions in diagnosis.

PURPOSES OF DIAGNOSIS

The *primary goal* of diagnosis is to gather and analyze pertinent information that directly aids teaching. In the school, this process serves three purposes: *(a)* screening, *(b)* identification and placement, and *(c)* instruction.

Screening, a quick process, detects individuals who *may be* learning disabled. Standardized tests are frequently used. After the teacher administers the test to groups of children, he compares individual scores to the norms. He may refer a child with a low score for further testing. Screening also uses observations of teachers and parents, checklists, behavior rating scales, and information in the child's history. Suspected pupils are referred for more intensive diagnosis. (See Chapters 11 and 12 for more detailed information concerning screening procedures.)

This teacher is administering a paper and pencil test to her class.

Through intensive diagnosis, students are actually identified as learning disabled. Thus, this phase identifies or labels the student who is LD and eliminates those pupils who do not qualify for an LD program. In most schools, a student must be identified as LD before he can be admitted into a special education program. Intensive diagnosis usually involves the administration of standardized tests by numerous professionals. Since a label results, diagnosis receives extensive attention and criticism. Before a label is assigned, diagnosticians must consider the reliability and validity of tests, the standardization group of tests, and observations of teachers. If identification and subsequent labeling do not lead to an educational placement (e.g., resource room, special class) where the child receives appropriate instruction, the identification process is not beneficial. A label may negatively affect the teacher's expectations of the child. Such a label would not be appropriate.

After placement, diagnostic information primarily serves to facilitate daily instruction. Unfortunately most information gathered from tests does not practically aid daily instruction. Thus, teachers usually perform an educational assessment to establish instructional objectives. They frequently rely on informal tests that feature criterion tasks (e.g., see vowels—say vowel sounds). After determining objectives, the teacher begins a teach-test-teach-test cycle (i.e., evaluation and teaching are a continuous process). (Chapter 14 relates this process in detail.)

DIAGNOSTIC APPROACHES

The ability training model and the skill model represent two fundamentally different approaches to the diagnostic prescriptive teaching process (Stephens, 1977). In the ability model, the psychoeducational focus is on identifying strengths and weaknesses in ability or process areas and in assessing levels of performance in academic areas. The skill model, representing a behavioral viewpoint, features assessment of specific academic skills and task analysis (analyzing the be-

Foundations of learning disabilities

havioral components and prerequisite skills of a task). Both approaches are used extensively but controversy exists regarding the relative merits of each. Examination of the models aids understanding of their uses and issues.

Ability Model

The ability model, based on the premise that the cause of the learning problem is within the individual, stresses the position that LD students suffer from impairments or dysfunctions in processes that are essential to learning. Perceptual-motor, visual perception, short attention span, and auditory perception are some of the process areas that are highlighted. The basic tenets include

1. The basis of the learning problem is within the child (e.g., in information processing).
2. These processes underlie academic functioning.
3. These processes can be identified and strengths and weaknesses can be assessed.
4. Valid and reliable instruments exist that assess the specified processes.
5. These processes can be remediated.
6. The student can benefit from teaching methods that are based on strengths and weaknesses identified in the process areas.

Some of the most commonly used tests for assessment of process or ability areas are

1. *Illinois Test of Psycholinguistic Abilities*
2. *Wepman Auditory Discrimination Test*
3. *Detroit Tests of Learning Aptitude*
4. *Frostig Developmental Test of Visual Perception*
5. *Developmental Test of Visual-Motor Integration*
6. Subtests of the *Wechsler Intelligence Scales for Children and Adults*
7. *(Slingerland) Screening Tests for Identifying Children with Specific Language Disability*

In addition to the process tests, a diagnostician administers academic tests. This assessment provides information that enables him to correlate academic problems to process disabilities. From the results of the psychological process and academic tests, he determines the student's specific strengths and weaknesses. With such knowledge, he can formulate an instructional prescription. Bannatyne (1968), Frostig (1967), Johnson and Myklebust (1967), and Kirk and Kirk (1971) promote this approach in their descriptions of diagnostic-prescriptive teaching. In addition, numerous books and programs contain extensive teaching activities for improving processing skills. Table 3.1 illustrates the diagnostic-prescriptive teaching technique via the ability model.

Research Concerning the Ability Model

Are the psychological processes used in the ability model correlated to academic achievement? Hammill and his colleagues (Hammill & Larsen, 1974; Larsen & Hammill, 1975; Newcomer & Hammill, 1976) extensively reviewed research regarding the relationship of auditory and visual abilities to academic areas. In a review concerning the relationship between auditory skills and reading, Hammill and Larsen (1974) report that when IQ is controlled in the studies, the correlation of auditory skills and reading is not supported. Larsen and Hammill (1975) report similarly that when controlling for CA and IQ, the relationship between visual perception and school learning is minimal.

In 1967 Bateman acknowledged a need for research to determine the effectiveness of process-oriented diagnosis in guiding teaching techniques. Newcomer and Hammill underscored this need in 1976. In a review of research studies on the effects of psycholinguistic training, they report that "the effect of such training on academic abilities is relatively unexplored at the present time" (p. 68). Arter and Jenkins (1977) reviewed 15 studies using the ability model to design reading instruction. In each study, modality strengths and weaknesses were assessed, materials that

TABLE 3.1

Example of a process-oriented teaching plan.

Process Disability	Observable Classroom Behavior	Teaching Technique
Visual-motor problems (auditory processing is good).	Confuses letters and words with similar configuration when writing.	*Strength:* Use phonetic reading approach to take advantage of auditory strengths.
	Reverses *b, d, p, g, u,* and *n* when writing.	*Weakness:* Provide the student with exercises to train visual-motor abilities

stressed modality teaching were used, and modality-instructional interactions were examined. In 14 of the studies, no interactions occurred. They questioned the validity of the modality model in its present form.

Ysseldyke (1973) reports that little support exists for the claim that instruction can be differentiated on the basis of diagnostic strengths and weaknesses. He further contends that methodological problems in the research center in two areas: *(a)* questionable validity and reliability of tests, and *(b)* constructs that are too factorily complex. Quay (1973), Ysseldyke and Salvia (1974), Haring and Bateman (1977), and Stephens (1977) severely criticize the ability model and recommend the use of the skill model.

The Skill Model

Primarily focusing on assessment of academic development, the skill model emphasizes direct instruction in either the terminal academic behavior or its immediate antecedents. Frequently a skill hierarchy is used in assessment and instruction. For example, the pupil is assessed in terms of a subject skill hierarchy and instruction begins at the lowest skill not mastered. The basic tenets include

1. The locus of the handicap is primarily outside the child (i.e., an experience deficit exists).
2. Behavior assessed is directly observable.
3. Test items should be similar to tasks demanded of the child in the classroom.
4. There is a hierarchy of skills and learners must sequentially pass through the steps.
5. There is a criterion of acceptable performance.
6. Direct skill instruction corrects inadequate responses.
7. Students can learn to generalize specific responses across conditions.

While the skill approach uses standardized academic achievement tests, the major assessment procedures are nonstandardized, consisting primarily of teacher-devised measures (informal), direct observations, and criterion-referenced tests (Stephens, 1977). After the initial assessment, the teacher measures pupil progress daily or continuously. He bases specific instructional prescriptions on the student's present level of functioning within a skill hierarchy. For example, a diagnostic report may consist of deficits pinpointed in specific skill areas. As illustrated in Table 3.2, the teacher translates these deficits into instructional objectives oftentimes specified in terms of rate or percent correct.

Research Concerning the Skill Model

Much research (Bijou, 1973; Haring & Phillips, 1972; Lovitt, 1973; Mann, 1971) supports the position that direct instruction of a specific skill results in improvement of that skill. The major

68 Foundations of learning disabilities

TABLE 3.2

Instructional objectives in terms of rate and percent correct.

	Entry Level	Objective	Instruction
Rate	See words—say words Correct: 40 Incorrect: 10 1 minute	See words—say words Correct: 75 Incorrect: 2 1 minute	Place words on Language Master cards and instruct student to listen to the word and then say it.
Percent Correct	See words—say words 20-word list Correct: 70% Incorrect: 30%	See words—say words 20-word list Correct: 100%	Same as above

premise of the skill approach, directive teaching, lacks valid criticism. When task analysis and skill hierarchies are used within the framework of the model, the critics attack. For example, reviews of studies (Resnick, 1973; White, 1973) provide no conclusive evidence regarding the validity of hierarchical orderings of specific skills. Lovitt (1974) suggests that further investigation may show that " 'sequences of learning' are mere superstitions" (p. 68). He feels research may reveal that "in some areas the various skills can be developed in almost any order" (p. 68).

More research is needed to validate mastery level criterion on specific tasks (Smead, 1977). Smead questions task analysis and skill hierarchies:

1. Do natural hierarchical sequences of learning skills exist?
2. Does the most efficient learning occur in small, carefully guided steps or in massive general experience?
3. Should child variables receive more attention?

To see the respective applications of the two models, we will now view them within the context of the primary purposes of diagnosis: *(a)* identification and placement, and *(b)* instruction and evaluation of instruction.

The Functions of the Ability and Skill Models

Identification and Placement

The orientation of the ability model lends itself to identification. Its emphasis on the problem being within the child is consistent with the classification (labeling) of disorders and exceptionalities. Identification usually requires the administration of various standardized tests and diagnostic exams (e.g., those testing intelligence, ability, process, personality, achievement, physical ability, and in some cases, neurology). Many of the tests require extensive training to administer, score, and interpret. Consequently, the professional team draws from the fields of medicine, psychology, language, education, and other health-related professions. A typical team consists of a neurologist, psychologist, physical therapist, speech clinician, and special educator. In public schools, a minimal team involves a school psychologist and an LD teacher. Also, PL 94–142 provides the parents with the right to function on any team.

The orientation of the skill model does not lend itself to student classification. It focuses on the tasks rather than on an impairment within the individual. Most testing is informal, conducted by the teacher for the purpose of identifying skill levels on academic tasks. Assessment within this model could contribute to identification if norms are established for the assessment tasks (e.g., performances in the lower 10th percentile or below a certain rate on a criterion task could qualify the child as having a learning deficit). For example, Magliocca, Rinaldi, Crew, and Kunzelmann (1977) used performances on classroom tasks to identify high-risk kindergarten children (see Chapter 12). Although this information may be useful for identification and placement, it is not implicit in the skill model.

Instruction and its Evaluation

The usefulness of diagnostic data gathered in the ability model remains an unsettled issue. How can valid and reliable tests be developed that differentially diagnose (identify) and provide information directly related to instruction? One of the first tests used for identification and instruction, the *ITPA*, now is being critically examined (Newcomer & Hammill, 1976). The *ITPA* was developed to correct or improve the underlying processes considered essential to academic learning. Moreover, it advocates using the student's strengths and weaknesses to plan instructional activities. Today's researchers question if these are valid practices.

In the ability model, the evaluation of instruction usually follows a pre–posttest format using standardized tests. The time interval between the pretest and the posttest varies, but it is usually in units of weeks or months. (Chapter 14 examines instructional approaches based on the ability model.)

Basic to the skill approach is the principle that assessment information should lead directly to designing daily instruction. Various instruments can evaluate the effectiveness of instruction: teacher-made devices, criterion-referenced tests, and charting. (Refer to Chapter 14 for a detailed review.)

Although the ability model emphasizes instruction, it is apparent that it is best suited for identification; the skill model, totally geared toward designing daily instructional activities, has little use for identification.

Smead (1977) claims that neither model fully covers the full spectrum of diagnostic-prescriptive teaching (see Chapter 14). She cautions against rejecting either model and supports further study in both, offering numerous suggestions for combining and examining various factors in each model:

1. Remediate the flaws in present ability instruments and reassess their efficacy. Place emphasis on establishing adequate reliability and construct validity. Measure improvement against actual school achievement-related dependent measures.
2. Rather than concentrating on single modalities, examine the relationship between modalities. According to Silverston and Deichman (1975), perceptual shifting, intersensory transfer, and modality preference appear to be fruitful areas for investigation.
3. Identify new aptitudes having ecological validity within a specific setting. Smead notes that Glaser (1972) promotes the identification of new aptitudes that capture the ongoing interaction between the learner and aspects of the educational setting.
4. Coordinate task analysis and ability training so each can provide essential information. In this arrangement the ability model provides the concern for individual differences and "because" statements, whereas task analysis offers a skill network and specific instructional objectives.
5. Base ability on observable behavior.
6. Pinpoint abilities that account for skill-acquisition problems on task-analytic, criterion-referenced tests. Develop remediation strategies.
7. Examine the influence of teacher and setting variables on the achievement of objectives. Keogh (1972) and McKee (1976) stress the need to consider environmental and situational variables in planning programs. Specifically, Keogh recommends an analysis of the interaction of child-by

Foundations of learning disabilities

task–by setting. Chart the progress of targeted behaviors.
8. Consider learner motivation, values, and attitudes in the combined approach.

Since administrative policies require identification of students within a classification framework before they can receive special education services, a combination ability-skill approach is essential to complete the diagnostic-prescriptive teaching process.

THE DIAGNOSTIC PROCESS

Identification, placement, instruction, and evaluation comprise the steps of the diagnostic process. It involves components from both the ability and skill model. As described by Kirk (1972), Bateman (1965), Smith (1974), and others, the following ideas are essential:

1. Determine if a learning disability exists.
2. Determine present levels of performance.
3. Analyze how the student learns.
4. Plan and begin instruction.
5. Evaluate the effects of instruction.

Determine If a Learning Disability Exists

The determination of a learning disability begins by examining the parameters that define learning disabilities. Numerous definitions exist; however, Mercer, Forgnone, and Wolking (1976) report that several components are included in the majority of definitions used by State Departments of Education: a process component, an academic achievement component, and an exclusion factor. A final component that many claim is the common characteristic of LD individuals is the discrepancy factor. Popularized by Bateman (1964), it refers to the existence of a discrepancy between a learner's estimated ability and what the child has learned. (See p. 43.) The use of these basic components as descriptors of a learning disability necessitates that diagnostic data be gathered in each area.

Exclusion Component

It may be helpful to start with the exclusion component in order to check a number of factors (e.g., hearing, seeing) that should be examined before an extensive examination is undertaken. If the practitioner uses the exclusion areas in the NACHC definition, the following criteria seem appropriate:

1. Exclusion of mental retardation, as evidenced by a score of not less than -2 standard deviations on an individual test of intelligence, with interpretation of a certified psychologist.
2. Exclusion of blind or partially sighted, as evidenced by visual acuity in the better eye

The classroom environment is integral to planning instruction.

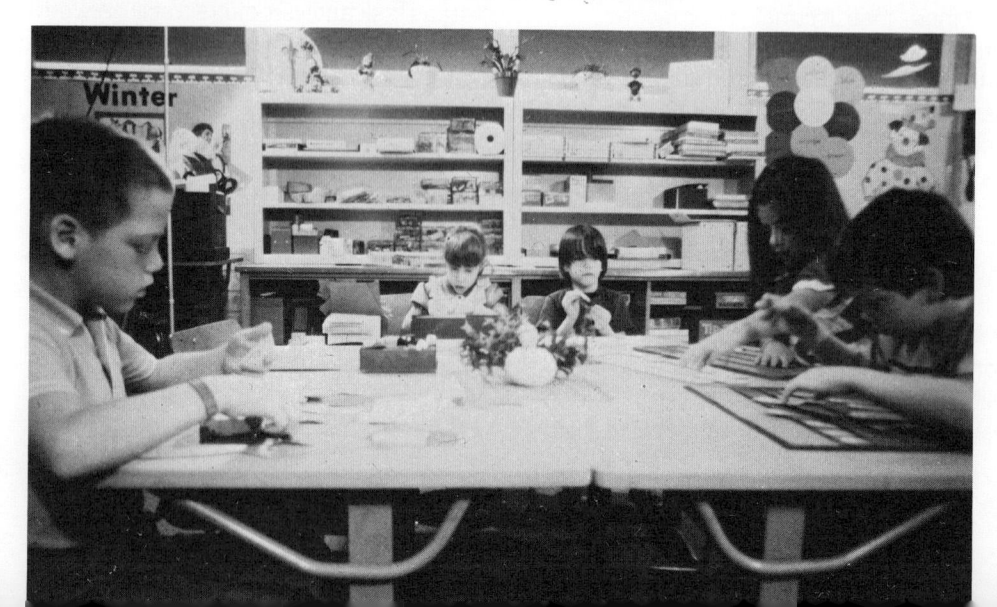

with best possible correction of 20/70 or better.
3. Exclusion of deaf or hard of hearing, as evidenced by auditory acuity of no more than a 30dB loss in the better ear unaided, and speech and language learned through normal channels.
4. Exclusion of physical handicap; no evidence of a primary physical handicap directly related to the child's deficit areas.
5. Exclusion of emotional disturbance of such a severe nature that a therapeutic-affective instructional program is needed.

Exclusion factors 2, 3, and 4 require a physical exam or a check of a recent medical record. Factors 1 and 5 require testing by a psychologist.

Academic Achievement Component

This component is covered by administering standardized achievement tests in the following areas: reading, writing, arithmetic, spelling, and preacademic skills. Selected achievement tests are listed in Appendix A. Generally these tests compare an individual's score with that of the standardization group of the test, thus identifying those below the norm. Scores are reported in a variety of ways (e.g., grade level, age level, percentile, stanine, and scale score).

According to the 1977 *Federal Register* (USOE, 1977), one must consider the pupil's educational experiences. For the pupil to be eligible for a SLD program, his learning problem must exist even when he is provided experiences appropriate for his age and ability level. In essence, the use of alternative educational strategies must be documented.

Process Component

The process component, highly criticized because of nebulous constructs and measurement problems, continues to be considered by many professionals. Mercer et al. (1976) report that the process factor is included in 83% of the LD definitions used by state departments of education. It is not, however, included in the 1977 *Federal Register* procedures for evaluating SLD. Standardized tests reveal diagnostic data about processing in the following areas:

1. *Visual:* perceptual (discrimination and closure), memory, association, reception.
2. *Auditory:* perception (discrimination and closure), memory, association, reception.
3. *Haptic:* tactile, kinesthetic.
4. *Sensory-integration:* visual-motor, auditory-motor, auditory-vocal, visual-auditory (vocal).

Test scores include age-equivalent scores, critical cut-off scores, scaled scores, and percentiles. Selected process tests are listed in Appendix A.

Discrepancy Component

To determine if a discrepancy exists between an individual's potential and level of learning, Lerner (1976) advocates posing these questions:

1. What is the individual's potential for learning? (What is his ability level or capability for learning?)
2. What is the individual's present achievement level? (What has he learned?)
3. What degree of discrepancy between potential and achievement is significant?

The assessment of an individual's potential is difficult because the various intelligence tests yield different measures and the relationship between IQ test scores and learning capacity is not well established. Many authorities now severely attack the concept of IQ and mental age as accurate indices of intelligence (Lerner, 1976). Furthermore, an individual's score on an IQ test may change from one administration to another and as a function of experience.

Standardized achievement tests usually determine an individual's present level. Due to measurement error, scores on these tests cannot always be interpreted as accurate.

Grade level and/or age also complicates the matter. For example, a 1-year discrepancy at 2nd grade for an 8 year old is more severe than a 1-year discrepancy at 10th grade for a 16 year old.

Despite these numerous difficulties, the practitioner must make decisions using the available quantitative data. Several techniques that incorporate the expectancy factor are used in quantifying learning disabilities: (a) the years-in-school method, (b) the mental grade method, (c) the learning quotient method, and (d) the Harris method.

a. Years-in-school method. For calculating grade expectancy, Bond and Tinker (1967) offer the following formula (in this formula, RE means *reading expectancy grade* and YIS means *years in school*):

$$RE = \frac{YIS \times IQ}{100} + 1.0$$

In addition to considering IQ, this formula gives considerable weight to the number of years the child has been in school.

Eleven-year-old Ann, with an IQ of 110, is in the middle of the 5th grade, thus accruing 5.5 years in school. Using this formula, her reading expectancy grade is 7.05.

$$RE = \frac{5.5 \times 110}{100} + 1.0 = 7.05$$

If Ann reads at 4.5 grade level, the discrepancy between her expectancy and achievement levels is 2.55 years.

b. Mental grade method. Using the student's mental age, Harris (1961) provides a very simple method to determine a student's RE. The examiner subtracts five years from the child's mental age:

$$RE = MA - 5$$

To determine if a discrepancy exists, a comparison is made between the student's RE and the present reading level. Ann is 11 years old and has an IQ of 110.

$$MA = \frac{IQ \times CA}{100}$$

Using the formula, Ann's reading expectancy grade is 7.1.

$$RE = MA - 5;$$

$$RE = \frac{110 \times 11}{100} - 5;$$

$$RE = 12.1 - 5 = 7.1$$

If Ann reads at 4.5 grade level, she has a 2.6-year discrepancy in reading.

c. Learning quotient method. Developed by Myklebust (1968), this method includes mental age, chronological age, and grade age (GA). In these formulae of several steps, LQ refers to *learning quotient* and AA to *achievement age.*

$$EA = \frac{MA + CA + GA}{3}$$

$$LQ = \frac{AA}{EA}$$

The learning quotient is thus the ratio between the present achievement age and expectancy age; a score of .89 or below classifies a child as learning disabled.

As measured by the *Wechsler Intelligence Scale for Children,* two types of MA, verbal and performance, are considered separately. Verbal MA is obtained by multiplying verbal IQ by CA and dividing by 100.

$$\text{Verbal MA} = \frac{\text{Verbal IQ} \times CA}{100}$$

The performance MA is obtained by multiplying performance IQ by CA and dividing by 100.

$$\text{Performance MA} = \frac{\text{Performance IQ} \times CA}{100}$$

To determine GA, add 5.2 to the present grade placement (grade + 5.2). To determine AA, add 5.2 to the present achievement level.

Ann is 11 years old, in grade 5.5, and has a WISC IQ of 110. Her verbal IQ is 120 and her performance IQ is 100. Her reading achievement grade level is 4.5, thus yielding an achievement age of 9.7.

EA with verbal IQ =

$$\frac{13.2 \text{ (MA)} + 11 \text{ (CA)} = 10.7 \text{ (GA)}}{3}$$

$$= 11.63$$

EA with performance MA =

$$\frac{11 \text{ (MA)} + 11 \text{ (CA)} + 10.7 \text{ (GA)}}{3}$$

$$= 10.9$$

EA with total score MA =

$$\frac{12.1 + 11 + 10.7}{3}$$

$$= 11.27$$

$$LQ = \frac{9.7 \text{ (AA)}}{11.27 \text{ (EA)}} = .86$$

Since Ann's LQ is below .89 (.79 with verbal MA, .89 with performance, and .86 with total score MA), she would be designated *learning disabled*. Using the verbal MA, her LQ suggests that Ann is learning 79% of what she is capable of learning; using the performance MA, 89%. Using the total score MA, the results indicate Ann is learning 86% of what she is capable of learning.

d. Harris method. Harris (1970) offers another technique for determining expectancy age. It includes both mental age and chronological age but gives priority to mental age.

$$EA = \frac{2MA + CA}{3}$$

Using the previous example of 11-year-old Ann,

$$EA = \frac{2(12.1) + 11}{3} = 11.73$$

As noted in Chapter 2, Florida uses the Harris method. In the state's criteria an achievement level of 70% EA or lower determines a significant discrepancy.

In addition to the problems mentioned earlier (p. 71) regarding the discrepancy factor, it is apparent that these methods of determining a discrepancy have certain flaws. For example, in examining discrepancy research, Salvia and Clark (1973) and Ysseldyke and Salvia (1974) report that difference scores between two tests are less reliable than each score separately. This lack of reliability prompted Salvia and Clark to note that a large percentage of children may exhibit discrepancies by chance alone. Also, the techniques fail with the preschool or primary grade child who has not yet learned to read. Although these methods have inherent flaws, they may help in making decisions.

Some practitioners examine the discrepancy factor by analyzing subskills of the child's mental functioning. An uneven pattern or extensive scatter may show learning disability. Caution must be exercised in using this approach because some research (Kaufman, 1976) suggests that normal children may exhibit scatter.

Summary

The determination of a learning disability is a complex and difficult task. Scores on the various instruments can only serve as guidelines. To date, *nothing can replace the clinical judgment of a diagnostician or team who examine the test data in light of other types of diagnostic information* (e.g., health, attendance, background, environment, language, motivation, classroom behavior, and psychodynamics). As noted in Chapter 2, the 1977 *Federal Register* requires that a multidisciplinary team determine the eligibility of pupils for SLD programs. In addition, each member must sign his agreement or disagreement with the staffing decision. Table 3.3 summarizes an eligibility staffing. Note where signatures are required. If a member disagrees with the decision, he must sign as such and explain his position.

Determine Present Levels of Performance

Since the identification of the learning disability is determined in the initial step, the remaining steps (see p. 70) focus on instruction

TABLE 3.3

Specific learning disabilities eligibility/staffing summary.

Name _____ D.O.B. _____ C.A. _____ E.A. _____ Date _____
School _____ Grade _____ Teacher _____
SLD Resource Teacher _____ Date of SLD Testing _____

Personnel Present: (initials indicate attendance at staffing)   SLD Teacher _____
  Principal _____   Curriculum Specialist _____   Counselor _____   Social Worker _____
  Psychologist _____   Classroom Teacher _____   Speech _____   Other _____

Prerequisites: Prior to referral a parent conference is held and behavior observations are noted. Documentation of alternative strategies attempted include: _____
_____

Criteria for eligibility: To receive SLD service the student must meet *all* of the following criteria.

1. Evidence of a disorder in one (1) or more of the basic psychological processes.
Meets criteria _____   Does not meet criteria _____
Specific Language Disability Tests _____
Detroit _____   ITPA _____   Other _____
Deficit areas: _____

2. Evidence of academic deficits.
Meets criteria _____   Does not meet criteria _____
PIAT _____   WRAT _____   Other _____

Prerequisite	Reading Recognition/Comprehension	Arithmetic	Other
_____	_____	_____	_____

3. Evidence that learning problems are not due primarily to other handicapping conditions.
Intellectual:
  Meets criteria _____   Does not meet criteria _____
  WISC–R V _____   P _____   FS _____   Stanford-Binet _____   Slosson _____   Other _____
Physical: (see health records for documentation)
  Auditory: Meets criteria _____   Does not meet criteria _____
  Visual: Meets criteria _____   Does not meet criteria _____
  Motor: Meets criteria _____   Does not meet criteria _____
Emotional:
Meets criteria _____   Does not meet criteria _____
Documentation _____

Diagnostic prescriptive summary: (Meets, does not meet) criteria for placement in the program for specific learning disabilities. _____

Signature: _____

The psychologist, principal, and speech therapist are included in this diagnostic team.

(what to teach and how to teach). The major purpose of this second step is to develop appropriate instructional objectives. Again, standardized tests may be helpful. The diagnostician must analyze performances to discover which specific skills the student has mastered. He must pinpoint the skills, saying, for example, "the child's understanding of place value in two-column addition problems." Some diagnostic tests *(Durrell Analysis of Reading Difficulty, Key Math Diagnostic Arithmetic Test)* assess in this manner. However, many diagnosticians rely on informal or teacher-made devices.

The areas of assessment may include personal-social, prevocational, and motor skills. The following model guides the determination of present levels:

1. Decide what behavior to assess.
2. Decide what evaluative activity can be used to measure the behavior directly.
3. Administer the evaluative device.
4. Record the student's performance level.
5. Determine a specific instructional objective.

Analyze How the Student Learns

Knowing *how* to teach the student greatly increases the *efficiency* of instruction. For example, the diagnostician noticed that Leon counted on his fingers while solving simple addition problems. Leon's teacher began to see improvement when he switched to the use of manipulative materials in Leon's math program. In addition, following each response to the diagnostician, Leon asked if he was correct. Self-correcting or programmed materials may also help his teacher. The key to obtaining this type of information is through direct

TABLE 3.4

Analysis of student learning form.

PART I: STIMULUS EVENTS

Instructional Setting

____ Large group
____ Small group
____ One to one
____ Peer teaching
____ Seatwork
____ Classroom
____ Resource room
____ Cubicle
____ Quiet area
____ Open area
____ Desk
____ Table
____ Other: _____

Mode of Input

____ Visual
____ Auditory
____ Tactile
____ Kinesthetic
____ Olfactory
____ Multisensory
____ Other: _____

Attributes of Materials

____ Colorful
____ Simple (uncluttered)
____ Complex
____ Few items
____ Relevant stimuli—highlighted
____ Many items
____ Single modality
____ Game format
____ Multimodality
____ Self-correcting
____ Verbal response
____ Motor response
____ Other: _____

Types of Instruction

____ Model and demonstration
____ Direct verbal instructions
____ Written instructions
____ Drill and practice
____ Game format
____ Questions
____ Direct application
____ Prompting
____ Cueing
____ Rate of presentation
   ____ Fast
   ____ Moderate
   ____ Slow
____ Other: _____

Types of Materials

____ Textbooks
____ Worksheets
____ Pictures
____ Chalkboard
____ Graphs
____ Flash cards
____ Manipulatives
____ Tape recorder
____ Other: _____

Type of Instructor

____ Teacher
____ Aide
____ Peer
____ Parent
____ Counselor
____ Nurse
____ Student teacher
____ Other: _____

TABLE 3.4 cont.

Evaluative Devices

___ Daily chart
___ Timings
___ Bar graph
___ Wall chart
___ Criterion tests (% correct)
___ Pre-post tests
___ Others: _____

COMMENTS:

---

observation and the use of sources that provide it (e.g., interviewing the parents, chatting with the student, reading cumulative files, using behavioral checklists). Quay (1968) suggests that educators must obtain information across three parameters fundamental to learning: stimulus input (antecedent events), response, and reinforcement (subsequent events).

Stimulus Events

Jobes and Hawthorne (1977) note that antecedent or stimulus events include a large number of stimulus materials, instructional methods, and classroom settings that "set the stage" for the student to respond. Since teachers determine many of the antecedent factors in the classroom (arranging student seating, grouping students, providing instructions, selecting materials), it is important to examine these events to understand how students learn best. Through observing and interacting with the student, the teacher can gather information concerning the student's preferences. The Analysis of Student Learning Form (Part I) in Table 3.4 includes a checklist of selected stimulus events to aid in such analysis. "Stimulus events" involve instructional setting, types of instruction, mode of input, types of materials, attributes of materials, type of instructor, and evaluative devices.

To illustrate the use of the checklist, consider the case of Harold Hyp, a student who has difficulty staying on task, is constantly out of his seat, and seldom completes an assignment. The teacher recommends the following:

For *instructional setting:*

   small group
   one to one
   some use of cubicle
   quiet work area
   uncluttered work area

For *types of instruction:*
  model and demonstration for skill acquisition
  drill and practice for skill maintenance
  game format
  cueing (color, arrows, etc.)
  moderate rate

For *mode of input:*
  multisensory as much as possible (e.g., Language Master, Fernald approach)

For *types of materials:*
  small chalkboard at desk
  manipulatives
  attractive worksheets that are not cluttered

For *attributes of materials:*
  simple
  few items
  highlight relevant stimuli
  self-correcting
  motor response (e.g., writing, push buttons)

For *type of instructor:*
  teacher
  peer

For *evaluative devices:*
  bar graph
  criterion tests

Mode of input has received much attention in learning disabilities. In the ability model diagnosticians and teachers usually administer various process tests to determine a student's modality preferences. If the test results indicate that the student performs better in the visual modality, instruction should stress visually oriented materials and techniques. Although commonly practiced, recent research (Arter & Jenkins, 1977) on this strategy points out dangers in determining modality preferences by existing tests. Ysseldyke and Salvia (1974) provide reliability data on many of the process tests being used *(ITPA, Developmental Test of Visual Perception, Bender Gestalt)* and point out that the reliability coefficients are too low for use in applied settings. Such low reliability coefficients should make educators extremely cautious (Logan, 1977).

What are the implications of these negative findings for diagnosticians and teachers? Should the emphasis on modality be disregarded? Although to disregard the modality preference factor appears premature, educators should not over-rely on the process tests for determining modality strengths and weaknesses. The modality factor holds much promise for helping teachers design optimal instructional programs. Using informal measures, the teacher may find that modality preference is task specific. Hayes (1975) offers an extensive list of "classroom clues" for determining modality strengths and weaknesses. For a student with an auditory learning problem and a visual preference some of the clues include:

1. tends to ignore verbal directions
2. needs questions and directions to be frequently repeated using different words
3. substitutes gestures for words
4. frequently looks to see what others are doing before following instructions
5. does poorly in phonics instruction
6. tends to describe things in terms of visual factors and omit auditory factors
7. prefers visual games to games that involve listening or speaking
8. substitutes words that are similar in sound or meaning for one another
9. has a limited vocabulary
10. has difficulty with rhymes and rote verbalizations (e.g., alphabet recitation)
11. does not appear as bright as test scores indicate
12. uses many *yes-no* responses and few complex sentences

For a student with a visual learning problem and an auditory preference, Hayes (1974) lists some of the following clues:

1. poorly attends to visual tasks
2. exhibits poor handwriting
3. frequently exhibits reversals, inversions, or omissions in writing

Educational diagnosis

4. prefers word games (riddles) to more visually oriented games (checkers)
5. does not remember reading material but remembers very well material discussed in class
6. frequently makes math errors as a result of inattention to signs, spacing problems with columns and rows, and confusion of similar numerals
7. reads below level expected for his ability
8. skips words or whole lines while reading and uses fingers to keep his place
9. tends to subvocalize while performing seatwork activities
10. seems brighter than test scores indicate
11. poorly organizes papers; his answers may be in the wrong place
12. makes spelling errors that make sense (i.e., word is spelled the way it sounds—*beem* for *beam*)

If a modality strength or weakness is suspected, numerous observations can be made in the classroom to validate or refute suspicions. Note that if a pupil has a visual learning problem, it does not necessarily mean that an auditory strength exists (or vice versa).

Response

Tasks usually require students to make a motor or verbal response or both. The Analysis of Student Learning Form (Part II) in Table 3.5, p. 80, illustrates some responses required in the classroom. Determining the type of response can be a crucial feature in designing instruction for a student. Some students function better if the response requires extensive motor involvement (e.g., write numerals, connect dots, push button, operate tape recorder, color items, arrange items on feltboard), whereas others function better with simple verbal responses (yes, no, nod). Finally, speed of responding deserves attention. If a student writes numerals slowly or talks rapidly without thinking, these response tendencies need to be considered in planning instruction.

Subsequent Events

Consequences influence behavior. Payne Polloway, Smith, and Payne (1977) report that consequences motivate students and manage their behavior. Frequently used positive consequences include social praise, special activities and privileges, evaluation marks, positive physical expression, awards, tokens, and tangibles (see Chapter 14). Numerous techniques exist that help the teacher determine what reinforces a student. The teacher can note free-time preferences for activities or objects. In reinforcement sampling, the student samples the object or activity before it is used as a possible reinforcer. Table 3.6, pp. 81–82, provides the teacher with a starting point for identifying reinforcing events.

For optimal use, timing, amount, and ratio of reinforcement deserve attention. Some students need immediate reinforcement to main-

Mike has a hard time paying attention to what's being said.

TABLE 3.5

Analysis of student learning form.

PART II: RESPONSE

Verbal

___ Short one word (e.g., *yes, no*)
___ Simple sentence
___ Complex sentence
___ Extensive dialogue
___ Soft
___ Loud
___ Rate
___ Other: ___

Verbal-Motor

___ Verbalize response while touching item
___ Operate hardware while verbalizing
___ Write and say answer
___ Sing and clap
___ Operate hand puppet
___ Other: ___

Motor

___ Point
___ Touch
___ Nod
___ Manuscript writing
___ Cursive writing
___ Write numerals
___ Copy work
___ Raise hand
___ Gross motor
___ Fine motor
___ Pencil holder
___ Rate
___ Other: ___

COMMENTS:

---

tain a target behavior, whereas others can tolerate a delay in reinforcement without decreasing the target behavior. Some students require a great deal of reinforcement only for certain changes. For instance, when the teacher is attempting to establish a new behavior, it is likely that much reinforcement will be needed. As the learning proceeds, reinforcement may be reduced.

In planning instruction, stimulus input, response modes, and subsequent events must be weighed in relation to each other. No teaching strategy is strictly a function of one of these factors. In considering how a student learns best, all three factors together will form instructional strategies that facilitate growth.

Plan and Begin Instruction

Once the teacher determines from the assessments *what* needs to be taught and *how* the student learns, he formulates and implements an instructional plan. This step, the crux of the diagnostic-teaching process, translates into the student's daily instruction. Not only does the program include specific instructional objectives; it recommends input, response, and subsequent events that foster optimal progress toward the specified goals.

Educational diagnosis 81

Hand puppets promote verbal and motor responses.

TABLE 3.6

Analysis of student learning form.

PART III: SUBSEQUENT EVENTS

Verbalizations

___ Good
___ Great
___ That's right
___ Fantastic
___ You're hot now
___ Nice work
___ Other: _____

Privileges

___ Leading group
___ Early dismissal
___ Listening to records
___ Free-time

___ Pass to library
___ Visit with friend
___ Interest center
___ Other: _____

Physical Approval

___ Smile
___ Raising eyebrows
___ Touch
___ Wink
___ Hug
___ Thumbs up
___ Move close to teacher
___ Handshake
___ Other: _____

82 Foundations of learning disabilities

TABLE 3.6 (cont.)

Evaluation Marks

____ A 1
____ Happy faces
____ Checks
____ Stars
____ Number correct
____ Letter grades
____ Rubber stamps
____ Other: ____

Awards

____ "Happy-grams"
____ Citations
____ Letters
____ Report cards
____ Others: ____

Tangibles

____ Candy
____ Trinkets
____ Toy
____ Cookie
____ Other: ____

Token Rewards

____ Points
____ Chips
____ Check marks
____ Tickets
____ Grades
____ Others: ____

Amount and Timing of Reinforcement

____ Continuous
____ Intermittent
____ Delayed
____ Immediate
____ Other: ____

COMMENTS:

(Chapter 14 details ways to plan and implement.)

Evaluate the Effects of Instruction

Measuring the progress of students has always interested educators. PL 94–142 demands teacher accountability. Teachers of learning disabled students must face the reality of highly variable performances from many of their students. They must know if a student is making adequate progress toward specified goals so that they can modify procedures.

Van Etten and Van Etten's (1976) measurement model aids the teacher in measuring progress. Their model makes use of frequency and directness, two primary dimensions of measurement. Under frequency, they discuss noncontinuous measurement and continuous measurement.

Historically teachers have measured in a noncontinuous manner. For example, measurement may occur at given intervals throughout the school year at the end of the year. Teachers measuring noncontinuously cannot modify daily instruction.

Educational diagnosis

In continuous measurement teachers record daily, precisely, the pupil's progress. Although modification on a daily basis is possible, some teachers find the data collection overwhelming.

Under directness, Van Etten and Van Etten (1976) discuss two types of measurement: indirect and direct. Indirect measurement refers to the sampling of behaviors that appear to be indicative of an ability or process. The measurement of intelligence is an indirect measure (i.e., behaviors that seem to be related to intelligence are sampled and levels of intelligence are inferred). Programs designed to develop specific learning processes (e.g., auditory and visual memory) frequently use this kind of measurement. Disadvantages include (a) the behaviors measured are not the exact behaviors taught, and (b) the inferred relationship between the measured behavior and the ability may be weak or nonexistent. Van Etten and Van Etten prefer indirect methods when the goal is to measure generalization or broad concepts of learning processes.

Direct measurement assesses learned skills. After teaching Dolch words, the teacher tests the student's recognition. In direct measurement he focuses on a specific skill (e.g., math facts sums to 9) and avoids inferences regarding abilities or processes.

Van Etten and Van Etten's model involves four measurement types. They note: "These four measurement types describe all of the procedures presently being used to measure pupil behavior and pupil change" (p. 471).

Today's system commonly applies Type I measurement (indirect and noncontinuous). Schools using Type I do not necessarily measure what is learned and infrequently administer tests of standardized achievement, aptitude, and IQ. Such measurement gives little direct value to the teacher. Primarily, administrators use it for labeling, placement, and grouping for instruction.

Type II measurement (indirect and continuous) continuously assesses what is not directly taught. For example, a teacher may measure daily recall on a digit span task while teaching recall of story content. Type II does not appear to be a very useful.

Type III (direct and noncontinuous), an integral part of classroom teaching, involves the teaching of a skill and then directly testing the student to see if the skill is mastered (e.g., giving a spelling test each Friday on the words studied during the week). Popular applications of Type III include the criterion test (see Chapter 14), skill checklists, review tests, and unit mastery tests.

The most sensitive measurement, Type IV (direct and continuous), records the student's response each time there is an opportunity for the response to occur. Type IV enables the teacher to examine the learning pattern and progress of the student on a daily basis. (Chapter 14 describes in a section of applied behavioral analysis the procedures used in direct and continuous measurement.)

Table 3.7, p. 84, lists the steps of the diagnostic process and the purpose/s and types of evaluation used at each step. Step 1 focuses on identification and placement, whereas Steps 2–5 concentrate on instruction. In addition, the diagnostic process uses two types of evaluation: formal and informal.

TYPES OF EDUCATIONAL TESTING

Logically, educational testing divides into two categories: formal and informal. Formal evaluation consists of administering standardized tests and primarily serves to document the existence of a learning problem and label handicapped students. Consequently, it is mainly used in Step 1 of the diagnostic process. Larsen (1977) notes that formal evaluation is used primarily as an administrative convenience to label handicapped learners and justify placement. Informal evaluation consists of using nonstandardized assessment devices and procedures to provide information that directly aids viable instructional programming. Consequently, teachers often evaluate in this method to gather information

TABLE 3.7

Steps in the diagnostic process.

Steps	Primary Purposes	Primary Type of Evaulation
1. Determine if a learning disability exists.	Label and place	Standardized tests, including intelligence, process, achievement Physical exam Documentation of use of alternative strategies
2. Determine present levels of performance.	Establish instructional objectives	Informal testing with focus on academic skills
3. Analyze how the student learns.	Establish *how* to teach the student	Informal assessment focusing on stimulus events, types of responses, subsequent events
4. Plan and begin instruction.	Establish an instructional program based on evaluation data	Assimilation of all data into an instructional program
5. Evaluate effects of instruction.	Assess effects of instruction and modify teaching accordingly; maintain teach–test–modify cycle	Informal assessment through the use of Type III (direct and noncontinuous) measurement (e.g., criterion testing) and Type IV (direct and continuous) measurement (e.g., charting)

required in Steps 2, 3, and 5 of the diagnostic process.

Formal Evaluation

Most formal evaluation (using standardized tests) is conducted outside the classroom by school psychologists, social workers, language clinicians, physical therapists, and/or medical personnel. On occasion a teacher who has extensive assessment training may evaluate pupils in this manner. Standardized tests gives reliability and validity data, which means that they compare a student's score with normative data collected on a regional or national level. Results are usually reported in terms of age scores, grade level, percentiles, stanines, or scaled scores and are used to determine if the student meets the specific criteria required for placement in a special education program. Available tests measure *(a)* intelligence, *(b)* perceptual, process, and/or psycholinguistic functioning, *(c)* academic achievement, and *(d)* social/emotional development. A list of selected standardized tests is included in Appendix A. *The Seventh Mental Measurements Yearbook* and *Reading Tests and Reviews* (Buros, 1972a, 1972b) critically analyze commercially available standardized tests. Books discussing specific tests include Fass (1976); Gearheart and Willenberg (1974); Hammill and Bartel, (1978); Salvia and Ysseldyke (1978); Stephens (1977); Wallace and Larsen (1978).

The examiner and/or teacher must be aware of the limitations of standardized tests and thoroughly familiar with the specific tests he is using. For example, limitations needing consideration include

1. The statistical validity and reliability of many tests used in learning disabilities are being seriously questioned (Lerner, 1976).
2. Scores on tests represent a very small sample of a student's behavior at a particular time and may not be indicative of the student's ability or skill level. For example, a student's motivation, attitude, and health at the time of the test can influence performance.
3. Researchers now question the relevance of many tests, specifically, ability tests. Also, test scores may not provide practical, useful information.
4. Many tests do not yield the level of specificity demanded for instructional programming. Item analysis often helps but it has limited value because many subtests have too few items (Stephens, 1977).
5. Many tests are normed on a "normal" population and then used with exceptional students.

On the other hand, an advantage of standardized tests includes objective results providing useful global information to document a student's achievement over a period of time. Also, the results often alert teachers to areas that need informal evaluation. Finally, norm-referenced measures do identify students for placement.

Informal Evaluation

Teachers conduct informal evaluation to obtain information directly related to instructional planning. According to Hammill and Bartel (1978), its goals are to "detect areas of weakness and strength; to verify, probe, or discard the conclusions and recommendations of the formal evaluation; to deduce the child's particular instructional and behavioral needs; and to formulate a remedial program for him" (p.7).

Numerous techniques available to the teacher include anecdotal records, rating scales, checklists, personality inventories, criterion tests, skill-probe sheets, attitude scales, and interviews with the parents. Stephens (1976) reports that such evaluation reveals four types of information: *(a)* academic skills and concepts, *(b)* sensory channel strengths and weaknesses, *(c)* social behavior, and *(d)* reinforcement system.

The informal assessment of academic skills is an integral part of the teacher's instructional program. For example, to check reading comprehension, the teacher asks Rico to read a passage from a basal reader and answer comprehension questions. He records the percentage of questions Rico answers cor-

Assessment can include informal classroom testing.

rectly and proceeds until Rico reaches his instructional level. A similar format is followed for math facts and spelling. The teacher may use probes to determine Rico's rate correct on academic tasks. (Examples of probes are presented in Chapter 14 in the applied behavior analysis section.)

Stephens (1977) has devised some informal procedures for determining sensory channel strengths and weaknesses. For example, to assess visual discrimination:

1. Select visual stimuli from an academic skill area in which the student has difficulty.
2. Set a criterion level below which visual discrimination will be considered inadequate.
3. Assign exercises to the student that will test accuracy of visual discrimination. These will vary depending upon the nature of the material and its level of difficulty.
4. Ask the student to repeat those items that were incorrectly seen and, if he repeats the errors, tell him the correct reponses.
5. Select instructional material to which he has not had prior exposure.
6. Again, test discriminations.
7. Ask him to repeat the items missed. (pp. 160–161)

Using these guidelines, Stephens offers the following example:

a. Ten pairs of words were typed on a paper. Andy was to write *D* if the words were different: made, made; fat, fat; sit, sat; cat, cat; dog, bog; fog, fog; car, car; ship, boat; ball, ball.
Criteria 9 (9 correct)
b. Test 1—Section D of *California Achievement Test,* Lower Primary Form W. Using the first 10 pictures and identifying the correct word from 3 given through visual clues only, he attempted 9 and refused to go further when the answer choices became more than one word.
Criteria 9 (9 correct)
c. Seven words were printed with four variations of spellings beneath each word, the same spelling was to be underlined. The following words were used; the word Andy chose is italicized: glad—*glab;* hen—*hen;* gate—*gate;* can—*can;* what—*want;* there—*there;* pear—*pear.* (p. 191)
Criteria 7 (5 correct)

The Analysis of Student Learning Form in this chapter presents a checklist format for the informal assessment of stimulus events, response preferences, and subsequent events.

The informal evaluation has several advantages. Namely, the person responsible for instruction performs the evaluation, so assessment will be only in relevant areas. Also, informal evaluation is specific.

The major disadvantage of informal assessment centers on the teacher's competency. He needs to know what specific skill areas warrant assessment, as well as which skills are related to terminal behaviors (reading, computing long division, taking turns in a game). (Chapters 6, 7, and 8 offer examples of informal evaluation devices.)

Guidelines for Test Administration

Teachers must follow good testing procedures. Several guidelines include

1. Select the target behavior for assessment.
2. Select or develop an instrument.
3. Become very familiar with the administration, interpretation, and psychometric qualities of the instrument.
4. Establish rapport with the student and administer the test or device.
5. Score and interpret the instrument with full consideration of the strengths and weaknesses of the instrument and other factors that influence test performance.
6. Make recommendations for placement and/or instruction.

ISSUES AND DIRECTIONS IN DIAGNOSIS

Generally, issues and developments in diagnosis greatly influence the current and emerging directions in learning disabilities. For example, identification, placement, and teacher accountability are directly tied to evaluation practices. With the advent of PL 94–142 and the demands for more viable and sensitive evaluation procedures, it is likely that evaluation will receive extensive attention and undergo rapid changes. Issues and directions warranting consideration are *(a)* development of reliable and valid tests, *(b)* development of nondiscriminatory tests, *(c)* the competency of teachers to evaluate, *(d)* the consideration of student-teacher-environment interactions, and *(e)* the development of a more precise definition of LD.

Development of Reliable and Valid Tests

In evaluation, an inordinate amount of time is often spent on an assessment generating very little instructionally relevant information (Larsen, 1977). For example, Larsen questions much test data because numerous tests are based on ill-defined psychological constructs *presumed* to underlie learning problems. Although an abundance of standardized commercial tests exists, the need for reliable and valid tests persists. Simultaneously these tests should provide instructionally relevant information.

Development of Nondiscriminatory Tests

The demand for nondiscriminatory tests by legislatures, parents, minority groups, and the courts pressures special educators and psychologists to develop tests sensitive to cultural differences. Mercer and Lewis (forthcoming) are refining a diagnostic system they refer to as a "System of Multi-Cultural Pluralistic Assessment" (SOMPA). It incorporates medical, social, and pluralistic models in an effort to assess developmental and learning potential levels across various cultures. Logan (1977) reports that "the SOMPA approach is a very ambitious undertaking that promises to provide a wealth of data not heretofore tapped" (p. 118).

Competency Level of Teachers Regarding Evaluation

Instruction and evaluation, inseparately meshed, require the teacher's continuous involvement in evaluation. As Gillespie and Sitko (1976) state:

> The teacher should be constantly modifying his/her program based on new information—every lesson can be part of the assessment procedure. . . . This is a radical departure from traditional diagnostic treatment procedures because it gives the teacher a central role in the diagnostic process. Furthermore, this view considers decision making or problem solving as an integral part of the development of instructional strategies. (p. 401)

Teachers must be competent evaluators. They need extensive preservice and inservice training to learn about selecting appropriate target behaviors, devising or choosing effective instruments, recording pupil progress, and modifying instructional strategies.

Examine Student-Teacher-Environment Interactions

Many educators now call for the systematic analysis of student-environment interactions (Haring & Bateman, 1977; Larsen, 1977; McKee, 1976; Smead, 1977). This type of evaluation permits the examiner to determine if an educational problem persists across settings. The examination of such factors as time of day, subject area, curricular approach, teacher interaction, and peer interaction should provide educators with valuable information when planning instructional programs. Much research has been conducted concerning how teachers and peers initiate or continue school problems as well as school progress. For example, Brophy and Good (1974) provide an excellent review of literature concerning characteristics of students and their effect on teacher behavior.

Development of a More Precise Definition

Accurate identification will remain a very difficult task as long as the definition is based on vague and imprecise constructs (e.g., process deficits and discrepancy between potential and achievement). Preciseness in this matter is an enormously complex task; its accomplishment depends on the sophistication of forthcoming assessment instruments. Bradley (1977) points out that until the issues of identification and labeling are resolved, special educators must continue to face a serious question. Specifically, she states:

> The real question then becomes, will the program or service that accrues to the handicapped child more than offset the possible negative effects of being labeled as handicapped in obtaining an education? Answering that question, child by child, is the ethical dilemma we face. (p. 146)

SUMMARY

This chapter discusses the purposes of diagnosis in terms of screening, identification and placement, instruction, and evaluation of the effects of instruction. The major diagnostic approaches are presented within the context of the ability model and the skill model. The total diagnostic process involves five steps:

1. Determine if a learning disability exists.
2. Determine present levels of performance.
3. Analyze how the student learns.
4. Plan and begin instruction.
5. Evaluate the effects of instruction.

Whereas step 1 stresses the ability model and primarily requires formal evaluation with the use of standardized tests, Steps 2–5 stress the skill model and informal evaluation using nonstandardized testing. Finally, issues and directions in diagnosis are discussed. Specific areas covered include: *(a)* development of reliable and valid tests, *(b)* development of nondiscriminatory tests, *(c)* the competency level of teachers regarding evaluation, *(d)* the consideration of student-teacher-environment interactions, and *(e)* the development of a more precise definition of learning disabilities.

REFERENCES

Arter, J.A., & Jenkins, J.R. Examining the benefits and prevalence of modality considerations in special education. *Journal of Special Education,* 1977, *11*(3), 281–297.

Bannatyne, A. Diagnostic and remedial techniques for use with dyslexic children. *Academic Therapy Quarterly,* 1968, *3,* 213–224.

Bateman, B.D. Learning disabilities—Yesterday, today, and tomorrow. *Exceptional Children,* 1964, *31,* 167.

Bateman, B.D. An educator's view of a diagnostic approach to learning disorders. In J. Hellmuth (Ed.), *Learning disorders* (Vol. 1). Seattle: Special Child, 1965.

Bateman, B. Three approaches to diagnosis and educational planning for children with learning disabilities. *Academic Therapy Quarterly,* 1967, *3,* 11–16.

Bijou, S. Behavior modification in teaching the retarded child. In C. Thoresen (Ed.), *Behavior modification in education* (The Seventy-Second Yearbook of the National Society for the Study of Education). Chicago: University of Chicago Press, 1973.

Bond, G., & Tinker, M. *Reading difficulties: Their diagnosis and correction* (2nd ed.). New York: Appleton-Century-Croft, 1967.

Bradley, C. State education agency considerations in identification of the handicapped. In R.D. Kneedler & S.G. Tarver (Eds.), *Changing perspectives in special education.* Columbus, Ohio: Charles E. Merrill, 1977.

Brophy, J., & Good, T. *Teacher-student relationships: Causes and consequences.* New York: Holt, Rinehart & Winston, 1974.

Buros, O. (Ed.). *Reading tests and reviews.* Highland Park, N.J.: Gryphon Press, 1972. (a)

Buros, O. (Ed.). *The seventh mental measurements yearbook.* Highland Park, N.J.: Gryphon Press, 1972. (b)

Fass, L.A. *Learning disabilities: A competency based approach.* Boston: Houghton Mifflin, 1976.

Foster, G., Algozzine, B., & Kaufman, J. A practical approach to personality testing at the elementary grade level: The Cat Test. *Journal of Irreproducible Results,* in press.

Frostig, M. Testing as a basis for educational therapy. *Journal of Special Education,* 1967, *2,* 15–34.

Gearheart, B.R., & Willenberg, E.P. *Application of pupil assessment information for the special education teacher* (2nd ed.). Denver: Love, 1974.

Gillespie, P., & Sitko, M. Training preservice teachers in diagnostic teaching. *Exceptional Children,* 1976, *42,* 401–402.

Glaser, R. Individuals and learning: The new aptitudes. *Educational Researcher,* 1972, *1,* 5–13.

Hammill, D.D., & Bartel, N.R. *Teaching children with learning and behavior problems* (2nd ed.). Boston: Allyn & Bacon, 1978.

Hammill, D., & Larsen, S. The relationship of selected auditory perceptual skills and reading ability. *Journal of Learning Disabilities,* 1974, *7,* 429–434.

Haring, N.G., & Batemen, B. *Teaching the learning disabled child.* Englewood Cliffs, N.J.: Prentice-Hall, 1977.

Haring, N.G., & Phillips, E. *Analysis and modification of classroom behavior.* Englewood Cliffs, N.J.: Prentice-Hall, 1972.

Harris, A.J. *How to increase reading ability* (5th ed.). New York: David McKay, 1970.

Harris, I. *Emotional blocks to learning.* New York: The Free Press, 1961.

Hayes, M.L. *The tuned-in, turned-on book about learning problems.* San Rafael, Calif.: Academic Therapy, 1974.

Hayes, M.L. *Somebody said learning disabilities.* San Rafael, Calif.: Academic Therapy, 1975.

Jobes, N., & Hawthorne, N. Informal assessment for the classroom. *Focus on Exceptional Children,* 1977, *9*(2), 1–16.

Johnson, D., & Myklebust, H. *Learning disabilities: Educational principles and practices.* New York: Grune & Stratton, 1967.

Kaufman, A. A new approach to interpretation of test scatter on WISC-R. *Journal of Learning Disabilities,* 1976, *9,* 160–168.

Keogh, B.K. Psychological evaluation of exceptional children: Old hangups and new directions. *Journal of School Psychology,* 1972, *10*(2), 141–145.

Kirk, S.A. *Educating exceptional children.* Boston: Houghton Mifflin, 1972.

Kirk, S.A., & Kirk, W.D. *Psycholinguistic learning disabilities: Diagnosis and remediation.* Urbana: University of Illinois Press, 1971.

Larsen, S.C. The educational evaluation of handicapped students. In R.D. Kneedler & S.G. Tarver (Eds.), *Changing perspectives in special education.* Columbus, Ohio: Charles E. Merrill, 1977.

Larsen, S., & Hammill, D. The relationship of selected visual-perceptual abilities to school learning. *Journal of Special Education,* 1975, *9*(3), 281–292.

Lerner, J.W. *Children with learning disabilities* (2nd ed.). Boston: Houghton Mifflin, 1976.

Logan, D.R. Diagnosis: Current and changing considerations. In R.D. Kneedler & S.G. Tarver (Eds.), *Changing perspectives in special education.* Columbus, Ohio: Charles E. Merrill, 1977.

Lovitt, T. Self-management projects with children with behavioral disabilities. *Journal of Learning Disabilities,* 1973, *6,* 138–147.

Lovitt, T.C. Applied behavior analysis and learning disabilities: Curriculum research recommendations. In S.G. Brainard (Ed.), *Learning disabilities: Issues and recommendations for re-*

search. Washington, D.C.: U.S. Department of Health, Education, & Welfare, 1974.

Magliocca, L.A., Rinaldi, R.T., Crew, J.L., & Kunzelmann, H.P. Early identification of handicapped children through a frequency sampling technique. *Exceptional Children,* 1977, *43,* 414–420.

Mann, L. Psychometric phrenology. *Journal of Special Education,* 1971, *5,* 3–14.

McKee, B.E. An interactional approach to learning disabilities. *Journal of Learning Disabilities,* 1976, *9,* 423–426.

Mercer, C.D., Forgnone, C., & Wolking, W.D. Definitions of learning disabilities used in the United States. *Journal of Learning Disabilities,* 1976, *9,* 376–386.

Mercer, J., & Lewis, J. *SOMPA: System of multicultural pluralistic assessment.* New York: Psychological Corporation, forthcoming.

Myklebust, H. Learning disabilities: Definition and overview. In H. Myklebust (Ed.), *Progress in learning disabilities* (Vol. 1). New York: Grune & Stratton, 1968.

Newcomer, P., & Hammill, D.D. *Psycholinguistics in the schools.* Columbus, Ohio: Charles E. Merrill, 1976.

Payne, J.S., Polloway, E.A., Smith, J.E., Jr., & Payne, R.A. *Strategies for teaching the mentally retarded.* Columbus, Ohio: Charles E. Merrill, 1977.

Quay, H.C. The facets of educational exceptionality: A conceptual framework for assessment, grouping and instruction. *Exceptional Children,* 1968, *35,* 25–31.

Quay, H.C. Special education: Assumptions, techniques, and evaluation criteria. *Exceptional Children,* 1973, *40,* 165–170.

Resnick, L.B. Hierarchies in children's learning: A symposium. *Instructional Science,* 1973, *2*(3), 311–349.

Salvia, J., & Clark, J. Use of deficits to identify the learning disabled. *Exceptional Children,* 1973, *39,* 305–308.

Salvia, J., & Ysseldyke, J. *Assessment in special and remedial education.* Boston: Houghton Mifflin, 78.

Silverston, R.A., & Deichman, J.W. Sense modality research and the acquisition of reading skills. *Review of Education Research,* 1975, *45,* 149–172.

Smead, V.S. Ability training and task analysis in diagnostic/prescriptive teaching. *The Journal of Special Education,* 1977, *11*(1), 113–125.

Smith, R.M. Clinical teaching: *Methods of instruction for the retarded* (2nd ed.). New York: McGraw-Hill, 1974.

Stephens, T. *Directive teaching of children with learning and behavioral handicaps* (2nd ed.). Columbus, Ohio: Charles E. Merrill, 1976.

Stephens, T.M. *Teaching skills to children with learning and behavior disorders.* Columbus, Ohio: Charles E. Merrill, 1977.

U.S. Office of Education. Education of handicapped children: Assistance to states: Proposed rulemaking. *Federal Register,* 1976, *41,* 52404–52407.

U.S. Office of Education. Assistance to states for education of handicapped children: Procedures for evaluating specific learning disabilities. *Federal Register,* 1977, *42,* 65082–65085.

Van Etten, C., & Van Etten, G. The measurement of pupil progress and selecting instructional materials. *Journal of Learning Disabilities,* 1976, *9,* 469–480.

Wallace, G., & Larsen, S.C. *Educational assessment of learning problems: Testing for teaching.* Boston: Allyn & Bacon, 1978.

White, R.T. Learning hierarchies. *Review of Educational Research,* 1973, *43,* 361–375.

Ysseldyke, J.E. Diagnostic-prescriptive teaching: The search for attitude-treatment interactions. In L. Mann & D. Sabatino (Eds.), *The first review of special education* (Vol. 1). Philadelphia: Journal of Special Education Press, 1973.

Ysseldyke, J.E., & Salvia, J. Diagnostic-prescriptive teaching: Two models. *Exceptional Children,* 1974, *41,* 181–185.

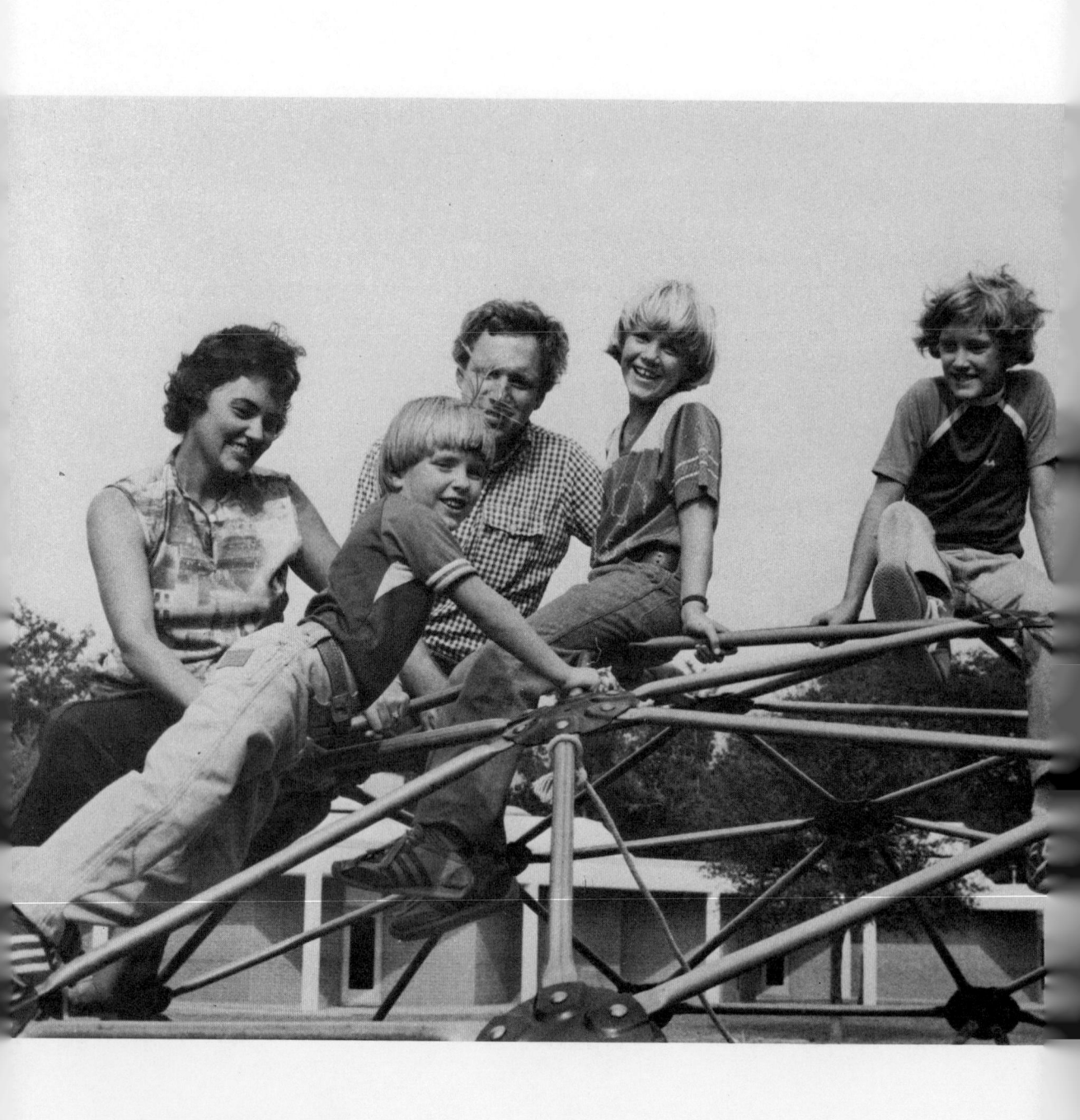

4

The family and learning disabilities

The history of learning disabilities documents the influence of parents in securing services for their children. Parents have formed organizations, started schools, and actively supported legislation. Moreover, parent involvement is a prominent feature of many contemporary educational programs. For example, Lillie (1976) states that "All across the country, parents are engaging in activities that range from listening to lectures . . . to making decisions about directions that child development programs should take" (p. 3). Parents of various educational and socioeconomic levels use their respective skills and resources for activities ranging from beginning private schools and securing grant monies to volunteering time to public school programs.

Conditions that continue to foster this increased concern are

1. Recent legislation (Public Law 94–142) insures that parents or a parent substitute will have the opportunity to participate in all phases of their child's educational program.
2. Parent groups are a major force in securing special programs, contacting other parents, and in stimulating special education legislation (Wallace & McLoughlin, 1975).
3. Media informs everyone about learning disabilities. Prime time television shows have focused on learning disabilities and popular magazines frequently feature articles about it.
4. The significant and positive impact of parents is receiving extensive documentation (Watson & Van Etten, 1976).
5. How handicapped children affect their families is becoming more understood (Robinson & Robinson, 1976).
6. Numerous books and materials assist parents to live with and educate their LD child.
7. Parent training programs are emerging (Lillie, 1976; McDowell, 1976).

These conditions indicate that parents and school personnel will be working more closely together. In this chapter, the reader will gain the knowledge and skills needed to work effectively with parents. For example, when working with parents, the teacher or counselor will want answers to numerous questions. What are the common reactions and defenses of such parents? How do you organize a parent conference? What are some ways of reporting the child's progress to the parent? Should parents teach school subjects to their child? Should parents screen and observe their child for learning and behavior problems? When is usually the best time for parents to work with their child? What are some management techniques that parents can use at home? What is the parents' role in prevention and in remediation? What are some activities and techniques that can help the parents and the child adjust at home? What are the rights of the child and the parents? What are some good resources (e.g., books, parent groups, periodicals, family physician, psychologist) for the parents? What are some ways of comparing teacher-parent attitudes toward the child?

This chapter furnishes information regarding these and other related questions. Parents of learning disabled children may also find this chapter helpful in adjusting and securing services for their child.

PARENTAL ADJUSTMENT

Barsch (1969) notes that "no parent is ever prepared to be the parent of a handicapped child" (p. 49). The parent primarily learns about the child through the experience of family living; professionals working with the parents must focus on these learning experiences. Our society offers a variety of services to support families with normal children: physicians, teachers, counselors, babysitters, recreation programs, and friends. These standard resources are not readily available to the family of a handicapped child. Families may thus turn to a specialist who is frequently a physician, counselor, teacher, or another parent of an LD child. The individual rendering help must be very conscious of his potential impact. According to Wolfensberger (1967), "Unless he approaches his task with awe and the willingness to be most cautious and circumspect with his counsel, he is not ready to work with parents" (p. 354).

Barsch (1968) examined the childrearing practices among parents of children with five different handicapping conditions. There were no significant differences among the parents; he cautions against stereotyping parents on the basis of their child's disability. Although the literature reports commonalities among parents concerning their reactions and adjustment problems to a handicapped child, each family must be treated in an individualized manner. Parents may share common problems and reactions; but the combinations of reactions that are possible, the intensity of the reaction, and the duration of the reaction are several of many factors that necessitate that each family be considered from an individualized point of view. In addition, there are some parents who may react or adjust in an exceptional manner.

A review of common adjustment problems helps the professional and/or the parent to better understand the unique matrix of reactions that may be present in a particular family situation.

Various authors have presented the successive stages of parental reaction to a handicapped child. The stages have ranged in number from three to six, and clinical intuition, rather than empirical data, has provided the rationale for the various schemes (Robinson & Robinson, 1976). Rosen (1955) offers a five-stage framework that is used to discuss the successive reactions of parents. In Rosen's schema the stages include *(a)* awareness of a problem, *(b)* recognition of the problem, *(c)* search for a cause, *(d)* search for a cure, and *(e)* acceptance of the child. In examining the stages, remember that the developmental pattern is not clear–cut and that different parents pass through them at various rates and within different time spans (Weiss & Weiss, 1976).

Awareness of a Problem

The wide range of characteristics used to describe LD children makes it difficult to establish a reliable diagnosis. Some children may exhibit significant problems in the first few months of infancy while the problems of others will not be manifested until they enter kindergarten or first grade. When the child displays early symptoms the mother is usually the first person to suspect there are problems. Brutten, Richardson, and Mangel (1973) list some of the usual behaviors or signs which deserve attention:

> Failure to sit by nine months; failure to walk without holding by 18 months to two years; failure to speak understandable single words by

Parents must adjust to their child's learning problems.

three years; any severe spasm or repeated blackouts; any sort of distant vacant look about the eyes or a lack of recognition and pleasure at familiar voices and faces; exceptional clumsiness with the hands; stumbling gait and much falling; prolonged drooling; unusual and marked emotional reactions; gusts of violent response to *trivial* occurrences; lack of laughter; failure to enjoy ritualized games such as peekaboo and pat-a-cake. (p. 58)

When a mother notices some of the early symptoms, she usually expresses her concerns to the father, the pediatrician, and/or the child's preschool or kindergarten teacher. At this beginning stage of awareness, one of the parents, relatives, and/or friends may individually or collectively deny that there is anything wrong. In addition, emotionally healthy parents frequently exhibit temporary denial to lessen the impact of the situation (Michaels & Schucman, 1962).

Weiss and Weiss (1976) describe their initial reaction: "Initially, we can recall the sense of shock through which we passed when we first became aware of our own child's difficulty in learning according to predictable norms" (p. 59). Parents approach this stage of problem awareness with difficulty; their initial concerns must be regarded very seriously. In an effort to recognize and cope with the problem, they usually seek and benefit from professional information and support.

Recognition of the Problem

Parents then must recognize the nature of the disability. This usually entails receiving and confronting a diagnosis of learning disabilties and its ramifications. Prior to finding out that their child is disabled, the parents have usually formulated an image of the child approximating the cultural stereotype of the "ideal" child. In their fantasy they expect great achievements by the child. Smith and Neisworth (1975) note that most parents want their child to surpass or at least attain their own level of sociocultural accomplishment. In addition, due to social pressures of middle class American society, the parents may be distressed if they do not produce such an offspring (Brutten, Richardson, & Mangel, 1973). At the diagnosis of a disability, the parents' worst fears are realized. Their future dreams, temporarily shattered, cause a discrepancy between expectations and reality that creates a major obstacle to their coping abilities. Common reactions include parental conflict, "doctor shopping," and the use of various defense mechanisms to reduce the anxiety generated by numerous aversive states (e.g., guilt, bewilderment, sorrow, anger, grief, and panic).

Parental Conflict

Each parent differs in perception and reaction to the problem; this situation leads to episodes of conflict. Mothers often try to persuade the father that professional help is needed. She assumes the major responsibility of raising the child and securing services. He accepts exclusion and involves himself in business or other outside activities (Kronick, 1969). She may resent his freedom and the fact that he does not share the burden. These tensions result in disagreements.

"Doctor Shopping"

Some parents react to the disability by questioning the accuracy of the diagnosis. A period of "doctor shopping" begins in which the child is rushed from one specialist to another in hopes of repudiating the original diagnosis. One must not confuse doctor shopping with the sound practice of validating a diagnosis. Learning disabilities, especially milder forms, are often very difficult to diagnose during the preschool years. This difficulty, coupled with the limited number of professionals knowledgeable in the field, provides the parents with valid reasons for seeking several evaluations. The parent should only be suspected of "doctor shopping" after several professionals render similar diagnoses and the parents continue to seek more diagnoses.

Defense Mechanisms

Parents will attempt in numerous ways to reduce anxiety. This situation is reinforcing and serves to maintain and/or increase the anxiety-reducing behaviors. These behaviors, frequently called *defense mechanisms,* may lead to distortions of reality and complicate the search for a cause. Moreover, they may interfere with the relationship between the parents and the child.

One of the most common and primitive defense mechanisms is *denial,* refusal to believe anything is wrong. Parents may claim that their child is very capable and insist on making unrealistic demands (e.g., piano lessons, little league, dancing lessons, spelling bees, oral reading). Also, they may overprotect the child, not allowing the child to participate in an activity he can do and enjoy. Unrealistic expectations and overprotection interfere with the child's optimum development. Unrealistic expectations often cause the child to feel frustrated and inadequate, whereas overprotection may cause the child to be overly dependent. Smith and Neisworth (1975) point out that denial becomes more difficult to maintain as the child grows older and is thrust into situations where comparison with other children increases. These comparisons make the reality of the situation too obvious, thus threatening the validity of denial.

Obviously, recognition of the problem is difficult. Shattered expectations, guilt, anger, parental conflict, pity, and many other aversive states form a kaleidoscope of feelings from which the unique responses of a set of parents emerge. These parental reactions may serve a healthy function in that they enable the parents to face the problem and its impact and emerge with thoughtfully considered attitudes. Solnit and Stark (1971) think that during this stage, in part, the parents could be mourning the loss of a fantasy child. Robinson and Robinson (1976) recommend that this period not be interrupted with reassurance and comfort from professionals too quickly, thus allowing the parents the time and opportunity to adjust to the problem. Once they face the issue and are confident of assistance, parents can begin to pick up the pieces and prepare to raise the child. In some situations the parents do not adjust and continue to use the defense mechanisms, inhibiting the child's optimum development.

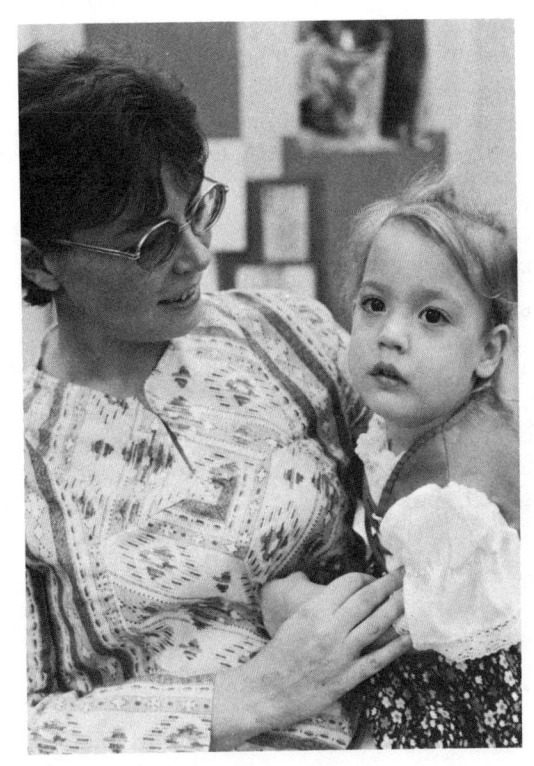

Good relationships foster growth.

Search for a Cause

According to Robinson and Robinson (1976), the search for a cause may spring from two types of motivation. First, some parents hope that the determination of etiology may lead to a cure or to prevention. Secondly, they may desire to diminish the heavy burden of responsibility and guilt. By asking, "Why did this happen to us?" they search the past for possible explanations. Are they being punished for an act of omission or commission? Did they neglect the child and allow him to injure himself? Is it due to drug usage, alcoholic intake, or sexual practices? These and many other "soul-searching" questions may be considered in the search for a cause.

Parents may end up highly frustrated, because in most cases, etiology is elusive. Diagnosis is usually based on behavioral manifestations, not on precise neurological or genetic findings. Moreover, parents encounter numerous varying theories: megavitamin (Cott, 1972), neurological organization (Delacato, 1959), maturational lag (Bender, 1957), minimal brain dysfunction (MBD) (Clements, 1966), genetic (Hallgren, 1950), food additive (Feingold, 1975), and environmental inadequacy (dyspedagogia) (Cohen, 1971). Of these, the two most widely espoused are the MBD and environmental inadequacy (dyspedagogia) (Cohen, 1971).

Frequently much time and money are devoted to seeking a cause when the child would benefit more if attention focused on his current status and planning helpful strategies. In essence, speculation about the cause of a learning disability can be time-consuming, costly, and result in very little useful information.

Search for a Cure

Many parents encounter specialized treatment recommendations originating from specific etiological viewpoints and latch on to them as a possible cure. Table 4.1 outlines some of the theories and their respective interventions.

Although not always paired with their respective theory, these treatments do represent common practices that are associated with theories. Teachers need to be aware of these various etiology-intervention approaches and their effects on children (see Chapter 5). Since many of these approaches are highly controversial, informed teachers can provide the parents with necessary knowledge and, perhaps, direction.

Acceptance of the Child

Although Rosen (1955) labels the final stage of parental adjustment *acceptance,* no explicit definition has emerged. Usually it is described in general terms. For example, Robinson and Robinson (1976) describe it as "a warm respect for the child as he is, appreciation of his assets, tolerance for his shortcom-

TABLE 4.1

Etiological theories and respective interventions.

Etiological Theory	Treatment
Megavitamin	Large doses of specific vitamins
Food Additives	Special diet
Maturational Lag	Tendency to say child will "outgrow" the problem without intensive intervention
Neurological Organization	Patterning exercises
Dyspedagogia (lack of good teaching)	Intense environmental manipulation to achieve growth in specified areas (directive teaching)
Minimal Brain Dysfunction	No one intervention procedure, although some assume it implies perceptual-motor training

ings, and active pleasure in relating to him" (p. 420). Wortis (1966) reports two indices of acceptance: *(a)* the mother maintains her usual acquaintances and continues with her normal activities, and *(b)* the parents meet the needs of both their normal children and the retarded child. To facilitate acceptance, Brutten, Richardson, and Mangel (1973) recommend involvement in outside interests and periodic employment of a baby-sitter. Some parents of LD children have benefitted by baby-sitting for each other's LD child. The independence boosts morale. Also, McWhirter (1976) finds that parents receive emotional support by meeting with other parents of LD children.

Weiss and Weiss (1976) discuss some characteristics of accepting parents:

> The most significant characteristic of these parents is that they treat their children as basically normal, emphasizing their strengths rather than becoming preoccupied with their weaknesses. They see these children as independent beings rather than extensions of themselves and thus do not treat each failure as a tragedy. These parents are usually successful human beings who are satisfied with their own lives and don't seem to need their child's successes to fill the void of a failing marriage, declining career, or their own loneliness. (p. 245)

Unlike acceptance, rejection is usually readily identified. Gallagher (1956) discusses it as a persistence of unrealistic negative values of the child, which casts a general negative tone in the parent-child relationship and may manifest itself in four ways: *(a)* under-expectations, *(b)* maintaining unrealistic goals, *(c)* escape, and *(d)* masking the rejection by espousing an exactly opposite viewpoint. Furthermore, Gallagher delineated between *primary rejection* and *secondary rejection.* Primary rejection emerges from an unchangeable condition (e.g., ability level) of the child, whereas secondary rejection springs from the child's behaviors. He postulates that most rejection is secondary and quite understandable. Anyone would have difficulty adjusting to the persistent and aversive behavior of some LD children. Weiss and

Oftentimes school personnel can help parents understand their child's learning disability.

Weiss (1976) vividly portray some of these behaviors:

> Let us describe just one small freckle-faced, blue-eyed boy who would run and never walk. He might bump into things as he went, breaking treasures, unmindful of the havoc he created. ... His face and hands were dirty most of the time, and mustard, ketchup, and chocolate stains often decorated his newly washed shirts.
>
> Could any mother communicate approval to this small tornado of arms and legs, screams and cries, torn pants and patches, chaos and disorder? (p. 242)

In cases of secondary rejection, one should not assume that the negative attitude of the parents is pervasive and that they will not be cooperative.

Most parents of handicapped children rely on trial and error strategies (Barsch, 1968). This technique, coupled with the multitude of parent-child adjustments, makes acceptance a difficult but hopefully obtainable goal. Silva (1969) reminds parents not to get caught up in coping with undesirable behavior to the extent that their children learn that "love is a reward rather than a constant factor" (p. 13).

PARENT COUNSELING AND TRAINING

Although the critical role of parents in their children's academic success was widely acknowledged as early as the 1920s (Schlossman, 1976), our society has done little to prepare people for parenting. This condition, combined with a society geared to the average (raising normal children), oftentimes places the parents of handicapped children in need of assistance.

Dembinski and Mauser (1977) conducted a survey of parent members of the Association of Children with Learning Disabilities to ascertain what parents most want from teachers, psychologists, and physicians. In general, their results indicate that parents:

1. Encourage the use of language that communicates free of jargon.
2. Recognize the importance of including both parents in conferences involving the child.
3. Seek reading material that may help them understand their child.
4. Feel they should receive copies of written reports involving their child.
5. Encourage interdisciplinary communication among professionals involved.
6. Want to receive relevant advice and information concerning management and teaching.
7. Want feedback on both academic and social behavior of their child.

As depicted in Rosen's (1955) five stages, adjustment is obviously complex. The many factors involved result in an infinite number of combinations of individual parent and family reactions. Parent counseling and/or parent training must be designed to insure flexibility in providing individualized treatment programs (Karnes & Zehrbach, 1972). McDowell (1976) classifies most parent counseling strategies under three headings: informational, psychotherapeutic, and parent training programs.

Informational Strategies

Informational programs provide parents with knowledge concerning specific handicapping conditions. For example, McWhirter (1976) provided parents of LD children with an informational program in which he conducted a series of six group sessions with 20 sets of parents. The content areas for the respective sessions included definitions, laterality and directionality, visual perception problems, auditory perception and discrimination problems, perceptual-motor issues, and a summary and review. Attendance for the sessions was excellent; parents commented favorably about the program's value.

Lillie (1976) reports that numerous programs now provide information on child-rearing practices and child development sequences. He feels that if teachers share educational goals and expectations with the parents, the school's activities will be consistent with those used at home.

Closer Look, a nationwide program, provides parents of handicapped children with information. Their message is "Take a Closer Look at your child to see if he needs special education." Specifically, Closer Look offers: *(a)* supportive reading materials that help parents learn about their handicapped child's condition; *(b)* suggestions for coping with the challenges of parenting a handicapped child; *(c)* referral to local associations or organizations; *(d)* a description of the respective state's special education law and due process steps; and *(e)* information about forming coalitions to change inadequate laws. In addition to supplying information, Closer Look services feature a personal reply to inquiries including problems that are difficult to solve. Send all inquiries to Closer Look, Box 1492, Washington, D.C. 20013.

Psychotherapeutic Strategies

Psychotherapeutic approaches concentrate on helping the parents understand their family's conflicts and concomitant emotional difficulties. They assist parents in dealing with their feelings. Abrams and Kaslow (1977) stress the need for differential treatment based on an examination of family dynamics and the child's problems. They suggest matching family dynamics with one of seven different treatment strategies:

1. *Educational intervention only.* For the child without emotional problems whose family is reasonably stable and happy.
2. *Individual therapy only.* For the child whose parents are essentially inaccessible (e.g., drug addicts, alcoholics, psychotics, or completely rejecting of the child).
3. *Parent group counseling.* For parents who get along well but would benefit from group sessions that focus on solving common problems (e.g., ACLD).
4. *Individual therapy plus tutoring.* For LD children who need systematic academic intervention and whose parents are "unreachable" (see #2).
5. *Concurrent therapy of child and parents with different therapists.* For families in which anxiety and feelings are so strained that it would not be beneficial to counsel the child and parents together.
6. *Concurrent therapy of child and parents with the same therapist.* When the parents and child can share the therapist without engaging in power and/or competitive struggles.
7. *Conjoint family therapy of child, parents, and siblings.* For families who can engage in problem solving in a mutually supportive environment.

McDowell (1976) notes that the psychotherapeutic approaches tend to place undue emphasis on the parents' role in creating emotional problems in their children. He indicates a need to examine the total environment.

Parent Training Programs

In the last decade, parent training programs blossomed. They assist parents in learning effective techniques for interacting with and managing the behavior of their children. McDowell (1976) identifies two types of programs: *(a)* communication, and *(b)* involvement. Communication approaches emphasize the establishment of direct communication between the parent and the child. Several professionals (Buscaglia, 1975; Kroth, 1975; McDowell, 1976) purport that the parent involvement strategy, with an emphasis on promoting positive parent-child relationships, is a major trend in parent counseling. The Parent Effectiveness Training Program, developed by Gordon (1970), is popular. It features active listening, "no lose" interactions, and problem ownership. However, it tends to create a child-directed rather than parent-directed home. He reasons that this comes from the program's strategy, which involves the parent redefining a position until she is put in a "lose" position.

Filial Therapy, developed by Guerney (1969), is another communications strategy. Based on the principles of play therapy, it encourages parents to open lines of communication and seek a better understanding of their children.

C-Group, an involvement strategy developed by Dinkmeyer and Carlson (1973), helps parents solve practical problems through collaboration, consultation, clarification, confrontation, concern and caring, confidentiality, and commitment to change. Parents present practical problems to the group and then commit themselves to attempting the solution suggested by the group. This approach's strengths are its action emphasis and involvement.

McDowell's involvement strategy (1974) is titled Managing Behavior: A Program for Parent Involvement. Designed to assist parents to acquire behavior management skills, it asks them to choose a target behavior, select a method of recording the behavior, and apply systematic consequences to the behavior in an effort to alter it.

Another such strategy is highlighted in the books *Teach Your Child to Talk* (Pushaw, Collins, Czuchna, Gill, O'Betts, & Stahl, 1969) and *Ways to Help Babies Grow and Learn* (Segner & Patterson, 1970). These authors provide parents with systematic experiences (activities) for obtaining optimal interaction with their child. The experiences may focus on a specific area of development (e.g., language) or on activities that are appropriate for a child at a certain developmental age.

HOME-BASED SERVICES AND ACTIVITIES

Numerous activities are available for parents to foster the social and academic growth of their child. Some of these activities are discussed within the areas of parent observation, home management, and parents as teachers. It is important that parent activities be determined according to the unique circumstances regarding family resources and characteristics.

After assistance, many parents are able to work effectively with their children.

Parent Observation

Since parents spend more time with their child in a wider variety of settings than teachers, physicians, and counselors, they can help by developing observational skills. Once parents confront the issue and are assured of some assistance, they can be very accurate judges of their child's level of development (Wolfensberger & Kurtz, 1971). They can record behaviors. In a study by Herbert & Baer (1972), three mothers counted the episodes of their attending to appropriate and inappropriate behavior. Two demonstrated an improvement in their child's behaviors. A 5-month follow-up indicated gains were maintained.

When a physician examines the child, he may seek information that can be gained via observation. For example, does the child play and/or get along with his brothers and sisters? Does he get along with other children? What types of games does he like to play? What are his eating and sleeping habits? What are some of the child's interests and fears? Parents can help answer such questions.

When the child reaches school age, the parent must become aware of any behaviors having educational significance. The teacher may give the parent a checklist to guide home observation. Not only can observation provide the teacher with valuable information, it also helps foster parental sensitivity regarding the child's strengths and weaknesses. Weiss and Weiss (1976) devised an extensive observational checklist to help parents decide if their child was experiencing learning problems. In addition to motivation, the checklist covers speaking, listening, reading, writing, and math skills. They acknowledge that a checklist cannot substitute for professional testing, but it can help parents direct their efforts in specific areas.

Home Management

At home, the LD child presents numerous management problems. After studying 18 children with learning problems, Wilson (1975) discovered that parental indulgence and infrequent punishment are associated with learning problems in some children. Compared with a control group of normal children, the children with learning problems in Wilson's study received less physical punishment and completed fewer household tasks. These findings are especially interesting in that characteristics such as hyperactivity, short attention span, clumsiness, emotional lability, and learning problems may separately or collectively contribute to behavior that is difficult to tolerate or manage. In addition, Doleys, Cartelli, and Doster (1976) found that mothers of LD children think their children have more behavioral and adjustment problems than do the mothers of normal children.

Many parents using systematic strategies can successfully manage their children. Weiss and Weiss (1976), parents of two children with learning problems, feel that parents

Home management starts with good communication.

need to deal with their own tension while interacting with the child.

> Our calm response often helped him to gain control of himself. If, on the other hand, we became embroiled in his frustrations and responded in anger, we only fed into his problems and made them worse. We found that our response acted as the "plunger" or the "pacifier" in feeding his poorly controlled emotions. (p. 73)

Brutten, Richardson, and Mangel (1973) stress the importance of providing LD youngsters with firmness, consistency, and clarity. In addition, Tomaro (1972) proposes patience and persistence. The establishment of routines can provide these essential factors. Hart and Jones (1968) share in detail the weekly and daily schedules used with a learning disabled boy named Hannah. Although briefly describing home management strategies generally helps to orient parents and/or teachers, the beginner needs more information to guide or implement a successful management plan immediately. A list of helpful sources follows.

Becker (1971)
Blackham & Silberman (1971)
Bradfield (1970)
Brown (1971)
Dardig & Heward (1976)
Deibert & Harmon (1970)
Hall (1970)
Hart & Jones (1968)
Patterson (1971)
Patterson & Gullion (1971)
Smith & Smith (1966)
Stephens (1977)
Vallett (1971)
Weiss & Weiss (1976)

Successful home management is essential for domestic peace. The experiences of other parents and the resources listed can greatly facilitate the accomplishment of a successful strategy.

Parents as Teachers

Parents transmit the customs, unique family habits, and traditions from generation to generation. Society expects parents to teach values and social skills. But should parents systematically teach their children academic skills?

Parent Tutoring–No!

Barsch (1969) finds parents often admit to having no patience in teaching their child. He presents numerous reasons for not using parents to teach academics:

1. Parents lack essential teaching skills.
2. The parent-child instructional session often results in frustration and tension for both members.
3. Most parents and children wish that academics could be accomplished during the school day.
4. Most teachers do not have the time to guide the parent.
5. When both the home and school stress academics, the child finds little rest.
6. Parents differ greatly in their competence as teachers.
7. Parents may feel guilty if they do not find the time to tutor their child regularly.

Barsch (1969) does admit that home tutoring is a common practice. In this vein he offers numerous principles that parents should adhere to as home teachers.

Barsch concludes:

> The parent conducts a curriculum called child rearing. The teacher conducts a curriculum called academics, language development, or perceptual training. Both seek to advance the learner to greater levels of complexity. A method must be found to profitably mesh the two "professional" disciplines. (p. 72)

Kronick (1969) also suggests that parents not tutor their children. She finds that most parents, anxious for their child to succeed, cause this anxiety to manifest itself in subjective reactions to the child's frustrations and behavior. One can imagine this hypothetical scene:

Tommy was learning to develop his reading skills at the end of the school year and his mother was quite anxious for him to continue to practice during the summer. When she read in the newspaper that the circus was coming to town, she bought a book about circus acts and suggested to Tommy that they read a section in the book every night. At first Tommy enthusiastically worked with his mother for 20 to 30 minutes every evening. However, soon he became frustrated with the book's difficult reading level. He continually made mistakes and guessed at words. Finally he couldn't stand it any longer.

"I don't like to read and I'm *not* going to do it!" he wailed.

Tommy's mother was annoyed and asked him to continue. "Just a little more, Tommy. You know we agreed to finish a section each night."

Tommy tried but again he mispronounced words and became quite impatient and irritated with himself. He hastily closed the book and put it down. "I can't do it," he said, miserable.

His mother responded angrily, "If you don't finish reading the book, I'm not going to take you to see the circus."

That did it. Tommy began to yell and cry. He had tried to please his mother and had worked hard to read material that was beyond his instructional level. Now he was being punished for trying.

Brutten, Richardson, and Mangel (1973) encourage parents to work side by side with their child in areas that intrigue her; for example, caring for pets, building models, going camping, playing games, and going fishing can be enjoyed by all. These activities help build self-respect and contribute immeasurably to the overall remedial program.

They also feel that parents should not be tutors, claiming that parents are too emotionally involved to teach their own children. "When the mother-child relationship, or the father-child, is converted to that of teacher-child, the child in effect no longer has a mother, or a father, but only one more mediocre teacher" (p. 127).

According to Lerner (1976), academic learning is an area of difficulty for an LD child and when she is tutored by her parents she is put in the position of constantly failing in front of the most meaningful adults in her life. Lerner maintains that the pressures and tensions of academic learning negatively inter-

During tutoring sessions, the parent must be aware of her child's frustration level.

fere with the parent-child relationship. She encourages parents to involve their children in domestic tasks and to concentrate on helping them develop good self-images.

Parent Tutoring–Yes!

Galloway and Galloway (1971) taught precision-teaching skills to parents. Parents identified specific behaviors (pinpoints) and measured progress in these behaviors. They selected a target behavior and the reinforcement strategy (consequation). Galloway and Galloway found that the parents began to understand their children's behavior; and this technique provided them with insights on how to change behavior. Parents effectively changed the academic skills of their children and their attitudes improved toward the child's handicap.

Kroth (1975) encourages teachers to demonstrate to parents the techniques that they think are effective in working with a child. In his opinion teachers cannot educate well alone and parents need to assist. Kroth notes that almost every helping profession has invited parents to share in the practice of their skills. Kroth, Whelan, and Stables (1970) support this position. In their study, they instructed parents in the use of reinforcement principles and graphing procedures. Next, they asked parents to select several skill areas to work on from a long list of skills. Those skills selected by the parents improved more than the others.

Wallace and McLoughlin (1975) and Stephens (1977) feel parent teaching helps transfer skills taught in the classroom. Since academic and social skills are frequently taught in a highly structured, reinforcing classroom, parents need to encourage these target behaviors *outside* the classroom to facilitate the child's growth. (Stephens describes in detail *Project Breakthrough,* a parent training program that was part of a statewide project in Ohio.)

Weiss and Weiss (1976) think that "overteaching" and "overlearning" benefit LD children. They offer numerous teaching and assessment activities for the parent wishing to supplement what is taught at school.

Parent Tutoring: An Individual Decision

Taking a stand on the issue is possible. Both sides to the question offer a rationale and it is proven that some parents can successfully tutor their children. A further review of the reports on parent-oriented, home-based instruction with young children enables one to assume with some confidence that parent tutoring can be effective.

Gordon, Hanes, Lamme, Schlenker, and Barnett's report (1975) on 11 early intervention programs yields encouraging results about parents as teachers. These home-based programs influenced positively the children's cognitive and affective development. In addition, Crozier's Project P.A.C.E. (Parent Action in Childhood Education) (1976) in Dubuque, Iowa, also shows the competency of parents.

Although much success accrues from these programs, remember that most feature a parent trainer who goes to the home and helps the parent via modeling, task selection, outlining management techniques, and devising recording systems and evaluation plans (Levitt & Cohen, 1975).

Each individual must decide about home tutoring. According to Kronick (1977), the basic consideration is whether or not tutoring can be accomplished without depriving any family member of the resources (time, money, activities) that should be directed toward maintaining a well-balanced life. When determining the feasibility of using parent tutoring, professionals and parents should consider these factors:

1. Grounds for deciding against tutoring include mother-father disagreement over the necessity of tutoring, health problems, financial problems, marital problems, and large families with extensive demands on parental attention (Neifert & Gayton, 1973).

Problems with homework makes many parents aware of the need for tutoring.

2. Do the parents have the resources of a professional (e.g., teacher) to assist them? The success of home tutoring may depend on cooperative efforts.
3. Can the sessions be arranged at a time when there is no interruption from siblings, callers, or other demands? These children need sustained attention in order to learn.
4. Will the child become inundated with academic instruction and resent the home sessions and/or feel overly pressured?
5. Does the parent become frustrated, tense, disappointed, and/or impatient during the tutorial sessions? These parents may better spend their time with the child in activities that are mutually enjoyable.
6. Do the tutorial sessions diminish the child's opportunities to develop social skills, interests, and/or to spend time alone?
7. Do the tutorial sessions create tensions among the family members? For instance, do the siblings view the sessions as preferential treatment?
8. Does the parent resent tutoring the child or feel guilty every time a session is shortened or missed? Are the sessions usually enjoyable and/or rewarding?

Foremost, parents should provide the child with a home environment of warmth, acceptance, and understanding. The child needs and deserves a comfortable place to retreat from the pressures, demands, and frustrations of daily living. Kronick (1977) captures the essence of this responsibility in the following passage:

> Our most primary goal must be to insure that the home is a relaxed and pleasant place, a source of strength to the child. It should not shield the child from the world but give the courage to cope with it. This means that the child must feel like an accepted, valued member of the family, sharing plans, decisions, special occasions, and concerns. I strongly feel that the home must be the child's anchor and that other considerations are secondary. Therefore, if you have to discard home remediation to create this kind of atmosphere, then discard it. (p. 327)

If the decision is made to engage in parent tutoring, attention must be directed toward doing a good job. A selected number of guidelines are presented.

1. If it is necessary to guide the child's hands during a task, stand directly behind the learner.
2. Give simple instructions and precisely convey the requirements of the task.

Parent tutoring must be conducted in a pleasant, relaxed manner.

3. Be flexible regarding the length of the session. Sometimes the child will not attend to the work for a concentrated period of time. In these instances, settle for 2 to 5 minutes of concentrated work instead of insisting on completion of the work at the risk of creating frustration and tension (Barsch, 1969; Weiss & Weiss, 1976).
4. Maintain a written record of observations (types of errors, questions asked, rate of responses) made during the tutoring. These observations may be shared with the teacher and assist in making future plans (Barsch, 1969). Keeping a record of the child's progress is often very helpful and precision-teaching techniques are excellent for charting progress.
5. Do not extend formal tutoring indefinitely. Periodically halt the tutoring. Supplement or replace it by incorporating the remedial tasks in the everyday chores and games (Kronick, 1977).
6. Make an effort to select the best time for the session. Many parents report that immediately following the evening meal is a good time (Weiss & Weiss, 1976).
7. Notice the child's learning style. Does she prefer one type of stimuli (auditory, visual, tactile, kinesthetic)? Weiss and Weiss (1976) provide parents with a checklist aimed at examining learning style.
8. Make sure the task is one the child can do. Tutoring sessions should be success-oriented (Brutten, Richardson, & Mangel, 1973).
9. Choose a place for the session which does not unduly restrict the activities of the other family members and is not too distracting.
10. Praise the learner for trying.
11. Let the child know when he is wrong, but do so in a positive or neutral manner (Gordon, Greenwood, Ware, & Olmsted, 1974).
12. Give the child time to familiarize herself with the task materials. Provide the child with an overview or introduction before beginning formal instruction (Gordon et al., 1974).
13. Encourage the child to make judgments or choices on the basis of evidence rather than by guessing or appealing to authority. Give her time to think about the problem (Gordon et al., 1974).

Several materials provide a variety of instructional activities which have been used in home teaching programs with LD children. Selected materials include

Brutten, Richardson, & Mangel (1973)
Hart & Jones (1968)
Kronick (1969)
The Exceptional Parent
Weiss & Weiss (1976)

Parents should take time to play with their children.

THE PARENT-TEACHER PARTNERSHIP

As previously mentioned, teachers should work closely with the parents in order to facilitate learning in school and at home. Parental involvement and cooperation add continuity to the child's school career and maintain the supportive foundation that the child needs in facing the changing demands of school. Kroth (1975) acknowledges the benefits of cooperative parent-teacher efforts:

> Cooperative planning between teachers and parents may prevent, alleviate, or solve many problems that arise during the educational progress of children. Teachers and parents who recognize their roles as complementary and supplementary, who approach their interactions enthusiastically and not apprehensively, and who view their relationships as a partnership will usually be rewarded with happy, achieving children and warm, personal feelings of mutual respect. (p. 10)

Mutual respect is necessary between teacher and parent.

Establishing Cooperation

Teachers and parents often harbor attitudes about each other that inhibit mutual cooperation. This attitude sometimes manifests itself through "teacher blaming" and/or "parent blaming." Such dissonance benefits no one. Sources of dissonance should be identified; and strategies promoting a cooperative and working relationship should be pursued.

Initial progress toward cooperation hinges on the development of a mutual respect. Barsch (1969) suggests that the parents prefer a teacher who approaches them as individuals, treats them with dignity, and conveys a feeling of acceptance. Parents do not want to be treated as simply a "parent of a handicapped child." He points out that "As teachers are able to convey a feeling of acceptance of the person, the parent is reciprocally more accepting of whatever counsel the teacher may offer" (p. 11).

Factors threatening cooperation include different educational levels of the parent and teacher, contrasting perceptions of the child's strengths and weaknesses, stereotyping, and terminology (Barsch, 1969). Contrasting attitudes about the child's strengths and weaknesses is a major area of concern that must be confronted. The teacher's perception of the child emerges from experience with similar and different children, her orientation toward learning disabilities, and observing the child in the school environment. The parents' perception derives from experiences with the child from infancy across a myriad of environmental situations, their orientation toward learning disabilities, experience with the child's siblings, and their stage of adjustment regarding the child's handicap.

Using a Q-sort technique, Kroth (1972) developed an instrument called Target Behavior. Teachers and parents use the instrument to compare their perceptions of the child at home or at school. If they want a comparison of school behavior, the teacher and the parent place 25 behaviors from the school list (see Table 4.2) on a formboard containing 25 squares. The squares on the formboard are arranged so that the behaviors are placed along a continuum, those *most like the child* to those *most unlike the child*. A typical formboard is presented in Figure 4.1. Each square on the board has an assigned number ranging from 1 to 9. When all the items have been placed on the board, the teacher and the parent both record the respective number assigned to each of the 25 items. A comparison of the number value for each item is made

TABLE 4.2

Items on the behavioral Q-sort (elementary level, school and home.)

School	Home
1. Gets work done on time	1. Does assigned chores
2. Pokes or hits classmates	2. Does homework on time
3. Out of seat without permission	3. Goes to bed without problems
4. Scores high in spelling	4. Comes home when should
5. Plays with objects while working	5. Argues with parents
6. Scores high in reading	6. Has friends
7. Disturbs neighbors by making noise	7. Likes school
8. Is quiet during class time	8. Cries or sulks when doesn't get own way
9. Tips chair often	9. Throws temper tantrums
10. Follows directions	10. Likes to watch TV
11. Smiles frequently	11. Likes to read
12. Often taps foot, fingers, or pencil	12. Plays alone
13. Pays attention to work	13. Eats between meals
14. Works slowly	14. Is overweight
15. Throws objects in class	15. Is destructive of property
16. Reads well orally	16. Gets ready for school on time
17. Talks to classmates often	17. Makes own decisions
18. Scores high in English	18. Chooses own clothes
19. Talks out without permission	19. Is unhealthy
20. Rocks in chair	20. Fights with brothers and sisters
21. Scores high in arithmetic	21. Has a messy room
22. Asks teacher questions	22. Responds to rewards
23. Uses free time to read or study	23. Does acceptable school work
24. Works until the job is finished	24. Is a restless sleeper
25. Walks around room during study time	25. Stretches the truth

Source: Adapted from *Communicating with Parents of Exceptional Children: Improving Parent-Teacher Relationships*, pp. 46–47, by R. L. Kroth, Denver, Colo.: Love, 1975. Copyright 1975 by Love Publishing Company. Reprinted by permission.

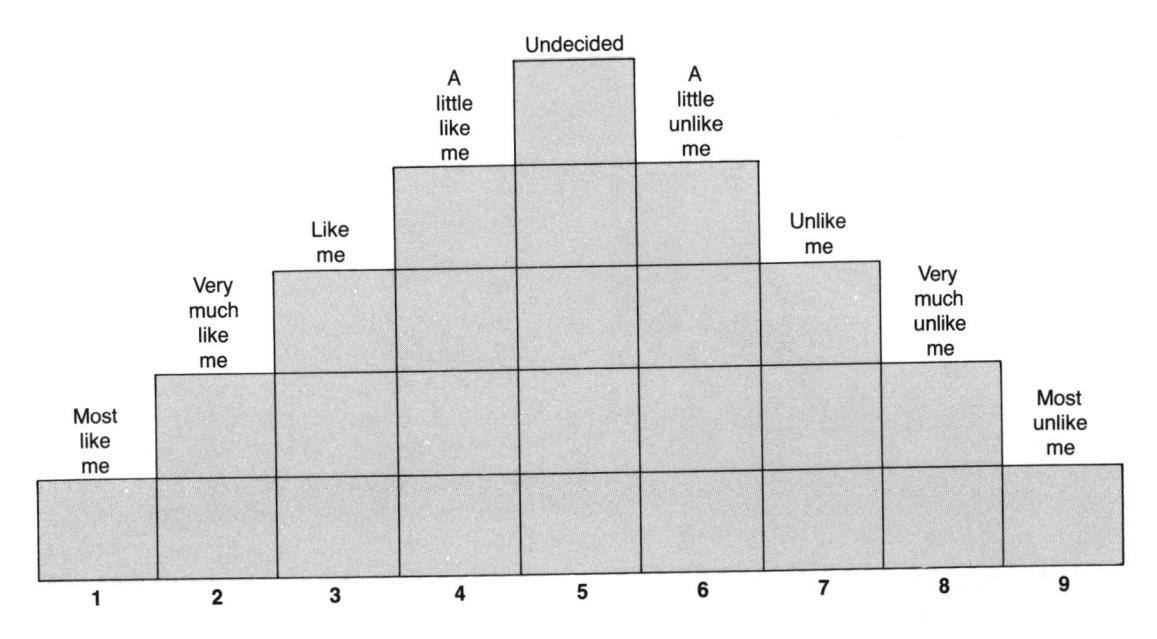

FIGURE 4.1

Behavior formboard.

Source: Adapted from *Communicating with Parents of Exceptional Children: Improving Parent-Teacher Relationships,* p. 44, by R. L. Kroth, Denver, Colo.: Love, 1975. Copyright 1975 by Love Publishing Company. Reprinted by permission.

between the parent sort and the teacher sort. The items of which the number value differs four or more points become target behaviors for parent-teacher planning and discussions. In some cases where a large discrepancy exists (e.g., follows directions), the teacher can help alleviate the parent's concerns through discussion. Or the teacher may plan a program to assist the parent in encouraging the child to behave properly at home (i.e., follow directions).

Many obstacles can inhibit cooperative parent-teacher relationships. However, the common goal of optimal growth for the child frequently enables both members to transcend the obstacles and work cooperatively.

Parent-Teacher Conferences

Parent-teacher conferences develop and maintain a cooperative partnership. Many school districts encourage the special education teacher to meet with the parents before the child begins receiving special education services. Duncan and Fitzgerald (1969) support this practice. They found that early meetings with parents served to prevent or reduce attendance problems, the number of dropouts, and discipline problems. Moreover, early meetings were associated with higher grades and good future communication.

The initial conference is extremely important. To prepare, teachers should examine the child's records and follow an initial interview guide (Kroth, 1975) Other professions (e.g., medicine, social work, counseling) consistently use guides to help conduct the session in a systematic rather than haphazard fashion. He recommends these emphases:

1. present status (chronological age, grade, class, prior teacher)
2. physical appearance and history
3. educational status

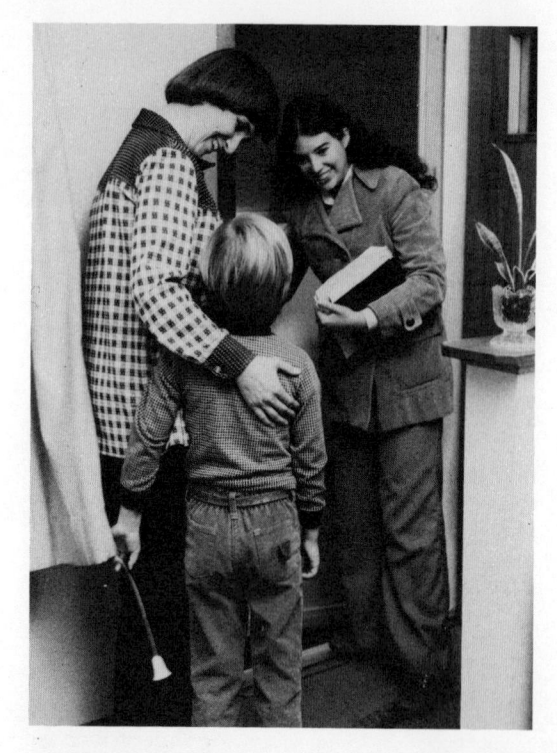

Parent-teacher conferences are essential in planning the child's educational program.

4. personal traits
5. home and family
6. work experience (usually for older children)
7. additional information

Rigid adherence to the guide is not necessary. Some flexibility may be needed regarding the topics covered, sequence of events, and length of session.

After the initial session, conferences typically consist of four parts: *(a)* establishing rapport, *(b)* obtaining pertinent information from the parents, *(c)* providing information, and *(d)* summarizing the conference (Stephens, 1977). Stephens suggests that starting with neutral topics and providing a comfortable seat help establish rapport. To obtain information, the teacher should state the purpose of the conference, ask specific questions, recognize parent feelings via reflection of their statements, and avoid irrelevances (e.g., marital problems). To provide information, the teacher should start with positive statements regarding the child's behavior and provide samples of work when possible, avoid educational jargon, and share anticipated plans. To summarize the conference, the teacher should briefly review the conference, answer questions, and thank the parents for coming.

Stephens (1977) offers several suggestions for evaluating a conference. For example, written outcomes can be compared with the actual outcomes. The areas in which planned outcomes and actual outcomes are discrepant represent areas which need improvement. Finally, he notes that three objectives are usually a maximum goal for a 45-minute conference.

Both parties must listen. A good listener (Kroth, 1975) gains much information that oftentimes can help solve problems. Schlesinger and Meadow (1976) identify listening as an important professional tool. Parents like to talk to a teacher who listens in a sympathetic, calm, and nonjudgmental manner. Several authors (Dinkmeyer & Carlson, 1973; Gordon, 1970) stress the importance of active listening (being involved in helping another define problems and clarify beliefs and values). Kroth (1975) equates such a listener to an excellent dancing partner "who seems to feel the rhythm of the conversation and moves accordingly" (p. 30). Fatigue, strong feelings, word usage, too much talking, and environmental distractions deter active listening.

Reporting Pupil Progress

In most school districts, teachers send home progress report cards six times a year covering a 6-week period. Parents receiving such reports cannot reinforce and encourage specific skill development on a daily basis. Several studies (Edlund, 1969; Kroth, Whelan, & Stables, 1970; Simonson, 1972) have explored the use of daily report card systems. It may be devised to reflect the progress in pertinent areas (see Figure 4.2).

Name: _____

Area of Progress	Excellent	Average	Needs Improvement
reading			
arithmetic			
spelling			
writing			
language			
P.E.			
art			
music			
social behavior			

Comments: _____

Date: _____

Teacher's signature: _____

FIGURE 4.2
Daily report card.

Foundations of learning disabilities

When daily report systems are used, the child's report card usually remains on her desk all day. The teacher records the progress or instructs the child to record it during the instructional activities. At the end of the day, the teacher signs each card.

Teachers who use precision teaching or who chart the child's progress can send the child's charts home each day. The charts record progress on specific skills (pinpoints). She usually measures the progress by the number of correct items and incorrect items performed in a 1-minute sample. Figure 4.3 illustrates a sample chart. For parents who want to reinforce specific skills, the chart has the advantage of listing the pinpoint. A teacher may choose to report the child's progress using any metric system (percent, rate, number correct, checklist) that the teacher-parent-child triad understands.

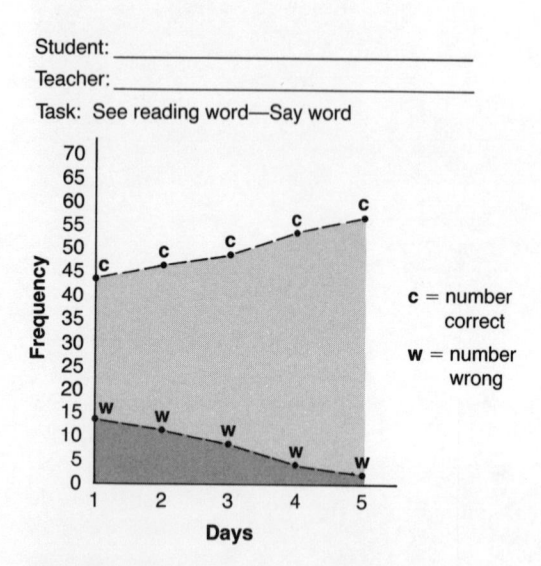

FIGURE 4.3

Sample chart recording child's progress.

Not all children can benefit from the daily reporting system. Some teachers and parents prefer weekly progress reports giving the child the opportunity to recover from a "bad day." Such reports take less of the teacher's time.

Teachers should also consider sending home notes, happy grams, or achievement certificates when the child masters a specific skill. Kroth (1975) describes numerous report systems that have been used successfully with parents of handicapped learners.

PARENTS AND PUBLIC LAW 94-142

In their efforts to obtain an accurate diagnosis or secure services, many parents encounter frustrating problems. These experiences led parents and professionals to join forces (Hallahan & Cruickshank, 1973). Although local coalitions emerged earlier, the development of the Association for Children with Learning Disabilities (ACLD) in 1964 is generally recognized as the first nationwide effort aimed at securing services for children with learning disabilities. ACLD lobbied for the passage of the Learning Disabilities Act of 1969 (Part G, Title 6). This act established LD as a category of exceptionality and provided funds to states for prototype programs, teacher training, information dissemination, and research. Since the passage of this act, some parents have turned to the courts in their quest for public services (Abeson, 1972, 1974; Kuriloff, True, Kirp, & Buss, 1974).

Litigation, coupled with parental and professional concerns, helped to pass the Education for All Handicapped Children Act of 1975 (Public Law 94-142). This law insures that all handicapped children receive a free, appropriate public education. Section 615 of PL 94-142 guarantees that such children and their parents or guardians have a right to procedural safeguards. The procedures outlined in the law are

1. The parents or guardian of a handicapped child may examine all relevant records with respect to identification, evaluation, and educational placement.
2. The parents or guardian may obtain an independent educational evaluation of the child. In addition, the state or local education agencies must provide a list of

qualified public and private agencies from whom such evaluations may be obtained.

3. Parents or guardian dissatisfied with the proposed educational program may engage in informal negotiation directly with the local education agency (LEA).
4. The parents or guardian may present complaints concerning identification, evaluation, or educational placement. The state education agency (SEA) or the LEA must provide formal procedures for parents to submit complaints.
5. Whenever a complaint has been received, the parents or guardian shall have an opportunity for an impartial due process hearing.
6. At the hearing the parents may be accompanied and advised by counsel and by individuals with special knowledge or training with respect to the problems of handicapped children. In addition they have the right to present evidence, to cross-examine, confront, and compel witnesses, to request a written or electronic verbatim record of the hearing, and to receive written findings of fact and decisions.
7. The parents or guardian may appeal the decision to the SEA. The decision of the SEA is final unless the party elects to bring civil action.
8. State and local education agencies must provide procedures to protect the rights of the child whenever the parents or guardian of the child are not known or are unavailable or the child is a ward of the state. In such cases an individual may be assigned to act as a surrogate for the parents.
9. A written, prior notice must be sent to the parents whenever the SEA or LEA proposes to initiate or change, or refuses to initiate or change, the identification, evaluation, or educational placement of the child. This notice must be written in the native language of the parents or guardian unless it is clearly not feasible to do so.
10. During the proceedings of appeals, review, and hearings regarding a complaint, the child shall remain in his or her present educational placement. If the complaint involves application for initial admission to public school, the child shall, with parent consent, be placed in the public school program until the completion of all proceedings.

Home visits promote cooperation and help the teacher to understand the child.

Yoshida, Fenton, Kaufman, and Maxwell (1978) conducted a survey of members ($N = 1,372$) on special education pupil-planning teams regarding their attitudes toward parental involvement in planning. They asked members about their attitudes to parent involvement in 24 activities. Only two activities were selected by more than 50% as appropriate for parental participation: presenting information relevant to the case (65.7%) and gathering information relevant to the case (57.4%). Other activities and corresponding percentages include: *(a)* reviewing the student's educational progress (41.1%), *(b)* reviewing the appropriateness of the student's educational program (36.7%), and *(c)* judging programming alternatives (34.0%).

These results indicate that extensive parent involvement in educational planning is likely to receive strong opposition. Many parents might end up observers only. On the other hand, Yoshida et al. (1978) point out that schools may view the parents as active participants and encourage parents to assist in making judgments about their child's program. They note that this latter approach "may increase parental support for their child's special education program and promote closer cooperation between school and home in implementing that program" (p. 533).

Weintraub and Abeson (1974) make a salient point regarding the legal revolution in special education when they state, "Thus far the revolutionaries have been the courts, the legislators, the school boards. Now it is time for us educators to make it our revolution" (p. 529). In this revolution, effective parent-teacher cooperation is basic.

PERSPECTIVE

The parent-child relationship encorporates the range of human emotions. With the trend toward more parent involvement in identification, placement, and educational programming, school personnel must prepare themselves to work more closely and effectively with parents. The teacher must be supportive, sensitive, and/or informative during crucial parental adjustment periods. Both parties must realize that the optimal growth of the child will only emerge from a pilgrimage of problem-solving ventures. Problem solving is facilitated by identification of the problem, analyzing resources, outlining alternatives, selecting an alternative, and evaluating the effectiveness of the alternative. Frustration and hard work will surely accompany the search for services; however, joy will likely accompany the solution. This process beckons the teacher and the parent to develop precise assessment techniques and gather information about resources, techniques, and materials.

School personnel's role is thus "that of consultant to the parents, not as a dominant authority in a transient relationship" (Hobbs, 1975, p. 227). Simches (1975) captures the parent involvement trend in the following passage:

By assuming new roles, parents are bringing about important changes in the educational system. Through their involvement in the classroom, parents are learning skills that enable them to help their children more effectively. Advising decision making groups, parents are helping educators find appropriate placements for children. As advocates, parents are protecting the legal rights of the handicapped, and are working to extend and expand the educational opportunities available to all children. From token involvement in the schools, parents are emerging as a potent force capable of constructively changing the entire educational system. (p. 566)

Hopefully this partnership of parents and school personnel will result in the creation of school and home environments that maximize the pleasures of parenting and teaching and minimize the sorrows and frustrations.

REFERENCES

Abeson, A. Movement and momentum: Government and the education of handicapped children—I. *Exceptional Children,* 1972, *39,* 63–66.

Abeson, A. Movement and momentum: Government and the education of handicapped children—II. *Exceptional Children,* 1974, *41,* 109–116.

Abrams, J.C., & Kaslow, F. Family systems and the learning disabled child: Intervention and treatment. *Journal of Learning Disabilities,* 1977, *10,* 86–90.

Barsch, R.H. *The parent of the handicapped child: The study of child rearing practices.* Springfield, Ill.: Charles C Thomas, 1968.

Barsch, R.H. *The parent teacher partnership.* Arlington, Va.: The Council for Exceptional Children, 1969.

Becker, W.C. *Parents are teachers: A child management program.* Champaign, Ill.: Research Press, 1971.

Bender, L. Specific reading disability as a maturational lag. *Bulletin of the Orton Society,* 1957, *7,* 9–18.

Blackham, G.J., & Silberman, A. *Modification of child behavior.* Belmont, Calif.: Wadsworth, 1971.

Bradfield, R.H. *Behavior modification: The human effort.* San Rafael, Calif.: Dimensions, 1970.

Brown, D.G. *Behavior modification in child and school mental health: An annotated bibliography on applications with parents and teachers.* (DHEW Publication No. [HSM] 71-9043). Region IV, National Institute of Mental Health, 5600 Fischers Lane, Rockville, Md. 20852, 1971. (For sale by the Superintendent of Documents, U.S. Government Printing Office, Washington, D.C. 20402, price 30 cents.)

Brutten, M., Richardson, S.O., & Mangel, C. *Something's wrong with my child: A parents' book about children with learning disabilities.* New York: Harcourt Brace Jovanovich, 1973.

Buscaglia, L. *The disabled and their parents: A counseling challenge.* Thorofare, N.J.: Charles B. Slack, 1975.

Clements, S.D. *Minimal brain dysfunction in children* (NINDS Monograph No. 3, U.S. Public Health Service Publication No. 1415). Washington, D.C.: U.S. Government Printing Office, 1966.

Cohen, S.A. Dyspedagogia as a cause of reading retardation: Definition and treatment. In B. Bateman (Ed.), *Learning disorders* (Vol. 4). Seattle: Special Child, 1971.

Cott, A. Megavitamins: The orthomolecular approach to behavioral disorders and learning disabilities. *Academic Therapy,* 1972, *7,* 245–259.

Crozier, J. Project P.A.C.E. *The Exceptional Parent,* 1976, *6*(4), 11–14.

Dardig, J., & Heward, W. *Sign here: A contracting book for children and their parents.* Kalamazoo, Mich.: Behaviordelia, 1976.

Deibert, A.A., & Harmon, A.J. *New tools for changing behavior.* Champaign, Ill.: Research Press, 1970.

Delacato, C.H. *The treatment and prevention of reading problems: The neurological approach.* Springfield, Ill.: Charles C Thomas, 1959.

Dembinski, R.J., & Mauser, A.J. What parents of the learning disabled really want from professionals. *Journal of Learning Disabilities,* 1977, *10,* 578–584.

Dinkmeyer, D., & Carlson, J. (Eds.). *Consulting: Facilitating human potential and change processes.* Columbus, Ohio: Charles E. Merrill, 1973.

Doleys, D.M., Cartelli, L.M., & Doster, J. Comparison of patterns of mother-child interaction. *Journal of Learning Disabilities,* 1976, *9,* 371–375.

Duncan, L.W., & Fitzgerald, P.W. Increasing the parent-child communication through counselor-parent conferences. *Personnel and Guidance Journal,* 1969, *47,* 514–517.

Edlund, C.V. Rewards at home to promote desirable school behavior. *Teaching Exceptional Children,* 1969, *1,* 121–127.

Exceptional Parent (Published six times per year by Psy-Ed Corporation, Room 708 Statler Office Building, 20 Providence Street, Boston, Mass. 02116.)

Feingold, B.F. *Why your child is hyperactive.* New York: Random House, 1975.

Gallagher, J. Rejecting parents? *Exceptional Children,* 1956, *22,* 273–276; 294.

Galloway, C., & Galloway, K.C. Parent classes in precise behavior management. *Teaching Exceptional Children,* 1971, *3,* 120–128.

Gordon, I.J., Greenwood, G.E., Ware, W.B., & Olmsted, P.P. *The Florida Parent Education Follow Through Program.* Gainesville, Fla.: Institute for Development of Human Resources, 1974.

Gordon, I.J., Hanes, M., Lamme, L., Schlenker, P., & Barnett, H. *Research report of parent oriented home-based early childhood education program.* Gainesville, Fla.: Institute for Development of Human Resources, 1975.

Gordon, T. *Parent effectiveness training.* New York: Peter H. Wyden, 1970.

Guerney, B.G., Jr. (Ed.). *Psychotherapeutic agents: New roles for non-professionals.* New York: Holt, Rinehart & Winston, 1969.

Hall, R.V. *Managing behavior: Parts I, II, III.* Lawrence, Kansas: H & H Enterprises, 1970.

Hallahan, D., & Cruickshank, W. *Psychoeducational foundations of learning disabilities.* Englewood Cliffs, N.J.; Prentice-Hall, 1973.

Hallgren, B. Specific dyslexia (Congenital word blindness: A clinical and genetic study). *ACTA Psychiatrica et Neurologica,* 1950, *65.* [Cited in Owen, R.W., Adams, P.A., Forrest, T., Stolz, L.M., & Fisher, S. Learning disorders in children: Sibling studies. *Monographs of the Society for Research in Child Development,* 1971, *36*(4, Serial No. 144).]

Hart, J., & Jones, B. *Where's Hannah? A handbook for parents and teachers of children with learning disorders.* New York: Hart, 1968.

Herbert, E., & Baer, D. Training parents as behavior modifiers: Self-recording of contingent attention. *Journal of Applied Behavior Analysis,* 1972, *5,* 139–149.

Hobbs, N. *The futures of children.* San Francisco: Jossey-Bass, 1975.

Karnes, M.B., & Zehrbach, R.R. Flexibility in getting parents involved in the school. *Teaching Exceptional Children,* 1972, *5,* 6–19.

Kronick, D. *They too can succeed: A practical guide for parents of learning-disabled children.* San Rafael, Calif.: Academic Therapy, 1969.

Kronick, D. A parent's thoughts for parents and teachers. In N.G. Haring & B. Bateman, *Teaching the learning disabled child.* Englewood Cliffs, N.J.: Prentice-Hall, 1977.

Kroth, R. Facilitating educational progress by improving parent conferences. *Focus on Exceptional Children,* 1972, *4*(7), 1–10.

Kroth, R.L. *Communicating with parents of exceptional children: Improving parent-teacher relationships.* Denver, Colo.: Love, 1975.

Kroth, R.L., Whelan, R.J., & Stables, J.M. Teacher application of behavioral principles in home and classroom environments. *Focus on Exceptional Children,* 1970, *3,* 1–10.

Kuriloff, P., True, R., Kirp, D., & Buss, W. Legal reform and educational change: The Pennsylvania case. *Exceptional Children,* 1974, *41,* 35–42.

Lerner, J.W. *Children with learning disabilities* (2nd ed.). Boston: Houghton Mifflin, 1976.

Levitt, E., & Cohen, S. An analysis of selected parent-intervention programs for handicapped and disadvantaged children. *The Journal of Special Education,* 1975, *9,* 345–365.

Lillie, D.L. An overview to parent programs. In D.L. Lillie & P.L. Trohanis (Eds.), *Teaching parents to teach: A guide for working with the special child.* New York: Walker & Co., 1976.

McDowell, R.L. *Managing behavior: A program for parent involvement.* Torrance, Calif.: B.L. Winch & Assoc., 1974.

McDowell, R.L. Parent counseling: The state of the art. In B.L. Watson & C. Van Etten (Eds.), Programs, materials, and techniques. *Journal of Learning Disabilities,* 1976, *9,* 614–619.

McWhirter, J.J. A parent education group in learning disabilities. *Journal of Learning Disabilities,* 1976, *9,* 16–20.

Michaels, J., & Schucman, H. Observations on the psychodynamics of parents of retarded children. *American Journal of Mental Deficiency,* 1962, *66,* 568–573.

Neifert, J.T., & Gayton, W.F. Parents and the home program approach in the remediation of learning disabilities. *Journal of Learning Disabilities,* 1973, *6,* 85–89.

Patterson, G.R. *Families.* Champaign, Ill.: Research Press, 1971.

Patterson, G.R., & Gullion, M.E. *Living with children.* Champaign, Ill.: Research Press, 1971.

Pushaw, D., Collins, N., Czuchna, G., Gill, G., O'Betts, G., & Stahl, M. *Teach your child to talk.* Cincinnati: CEBCO Stand, 1969.

Robinson, N.M., & Robinson, H.B. *The mentally retarded child: A psychological approach* (2nd ed.). New York: McGraw-Hill, 1976.

Rosen, L. Selected aspects in the development of the mother's understanding of her mentally retarded child. *American Journal of Mental Deficiency,* 1955, *59,* 522.

Schlesinger, H.S., & Meadow, K.P. Emotional support for parents. In D.L. Lillie & P.L. Trohanis (Eds.), *Teaching parents to teach: A guide for working with the special child.* New York: Walker & Co., 1976.

Schlossman, S.L. Before home start: Notes toward a history of parent education in America, 1897–1929. *Harvard Educational Review,* 1976, *46,* 436–467.

Segner, L., & Patterson, C. *Ways to help babies grow and learn: Activities for infant education.* Denver: World Press, 1970.

Silva, W. The parental merry-go-round. In D. Kronick, *They too can succeed: A practical guide for parents of learning disabled children.* San Rafael, Calif.: Academic Therapy, 1969.

Simches, R.F. The parent-professional partnership. *Exceptional Children,* 1975, *41,* 565–566.

Simonson, G. *Modification of reading com-*

prehension scores using a home contract with parental control of reinforcers. Unpublished master's thesis, University of Kansas, 1972.

Smith, R.M., & Neisworth, J.T. *The exceptional child: A functional approach.* New York: McGraw-Hill, 1975.

Smith, J., & Smith, D. *Child management: A program for parents.* Ann Arbor, Mich.: Ann Arbor, 1966.

Solnit, A., & Stark, J. Mourning and the birth of a defective child. In F.J. Menolascino (Ed.), *Psychiatric aspects of the diagnosis and treatment of mental retardation.* Seattle, Wash.: Special Child, 1971.

Stephens, T.M. *Teaching skills to children with learning and behavior disorders.* Columbus, Ohio: Charles E. Merrill, 1977.

Tomaro, M.S. Learning to live happily with Jimmy. *The Exceptional Parent,* 1972, *1*(6), 36–39.

Vallett, R.E. *Modifying children's behavior: A guide for parents and professionals.* Palo Alto, Calif.: Fearon, 1971.

Wallace, G., & McLoughlin, J.A. *Learning disabilities: Concepts and characteristics.* Columbus, Ohio: Charles E. Merrill, 1975.

Watson, B.L., & Van Etten, C. (Eds.). Programs, materials, and techniques. *Journal of Learning Disabilities,* 1976, *9,* 614–619.

Weintraub, F.J., & Abeson, A. New education policies for the handicapped: The quiet revolution. *Phi Delta Kappan,* 1974, *55,* 526–529; 569.

Weiss, H.G., & Weiss, M.S. *Home is a learning place: A parents' guide to learning disabilities.* Boston: Little, Brown, & Co., 1976.

Wilson, L. Learning disability as related to infrequent punishment and limited participation in delay of reinforcement tasks. *Journal of School Psychology,* 1975, *13,* 255–263.

Wolfensberger, W. Counseling the parents of the retarded. In A.A. Baumeister (Ed.), *Mental retardation: Appraisal, education, and rehabilitation.* Chicago: Aldine, 1967.

Wolfensberger, W., & Kurtz, R.A. Measurement of parents' perceptions of their children's development. *Genetic Psychology Monographs,* 1971, *83,* 3–92.

Wortis, J. Successful family life for the retarded child. *Stress on families of the mentally handicapped. Proceedings of the Third International Conference of the International League of Societies of the Mentally Retarded,* Brussels, Belgium, 1966.

Yoshida, R.K., Fenton, K.S., Kaufman, M.J., & Maxwell, F.P. Parental involvement in the special education pupil planning process: The school's perspective. *Exceptional Children,* 1978, *44,* 531–534.

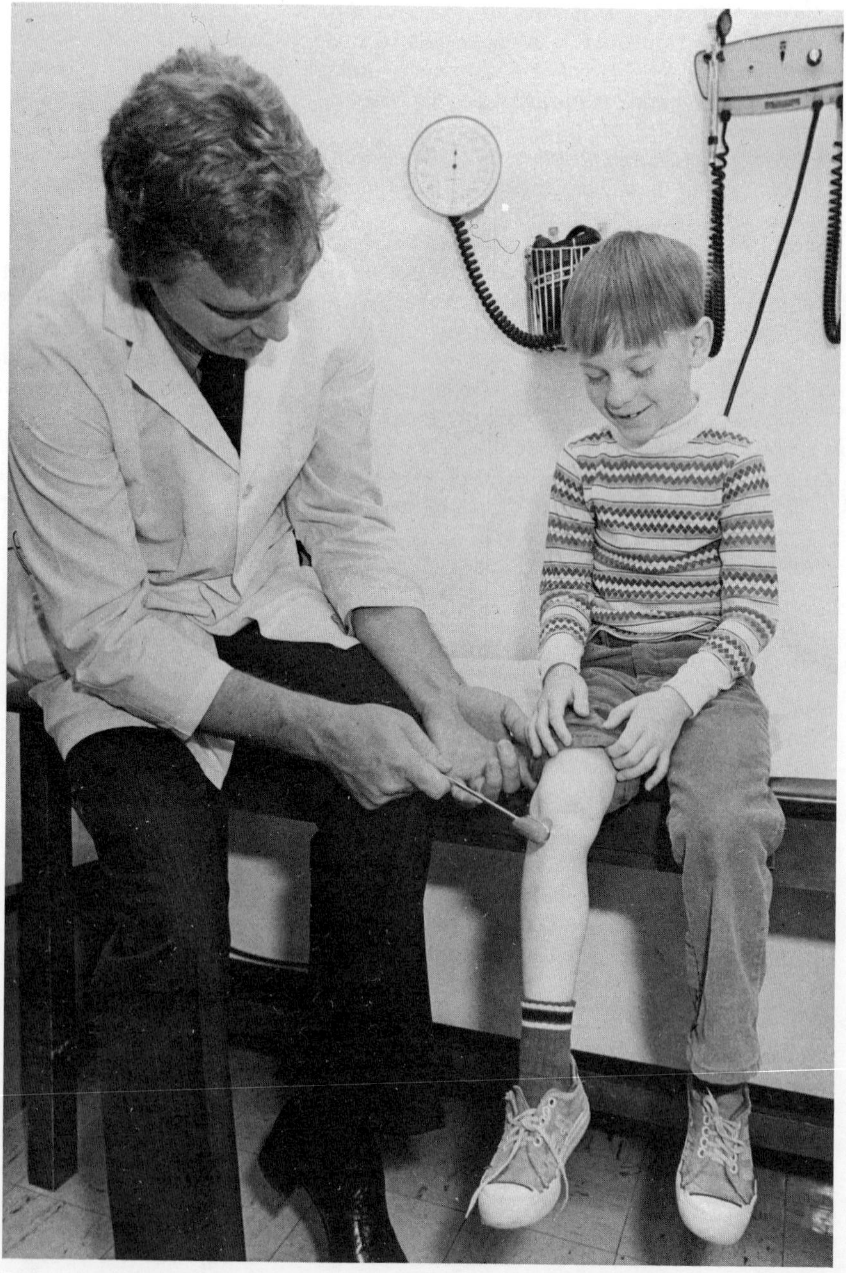

5

Medicine and learning disabilities

Kirk (1975) states that education has discarded the medical approach in an attempt to relate learning disability to the teaching and learning process. If educators have discarded this notion, why include a chapter about medicine in this text? First, Kirk says the "medical approach" was discarded—not the real and potential contributions from the field of medicine. Second, the medical profession, like education and psychology, is so intertwined with the area of learning disabilities that separation is difficult. This situation generates problems for the practitioner; the differing viewpoints of each discipline often obstruct cooperation and communication. Third, an appreciation of the medical profession and its potential for support may help the teacher answer questions, counsel parents, assess learning problems, and plan and evaluate educational programs. This chapter provides a basic foundation about medical services, specialists, and treatments.

HISTORY

Historically, medicine and learning disabilities are closely linked. As mentioned in Chapter 1, the evolution of the area is divided into three distinct periods: *(a)* genesis, *(b)* birth, and *(c)* growing pains. During the genesis period (1647–1959), medical studies of brain-damaged adults resulted in theories of brain function. Physicians contributed most during this phase. During the last three decades of the genesis period and throughout the birth period (1960–1970), psychologists and educators worked with medical specialists in an attempt to translate theory into educational strategies. The growing pains period (1970 to present) has been characterized by a phenomenal growth of public and private school programs. In spite of a de-emphasis of medical aspects in contemporary educational strategies, individuals in the field of medicine continue to establish theories and conduct research of significance for the learning disabled.

The rapid growth of politically active, well-informed parent groups in the 1950s further facilitated interaction between educators and physicians. While the organizations do not restrict membership, most of their members are parents or relatives of an LD child. The keen interest of these individuals in medical progress is evident in the program content and speakers scheduled for their local, state, and national meetings.

The medical community is maintaining an active interest in the LD child. Extensive medical research is reported each year (Adams, Kocsis, & Estes, 1974; Campbell, 1975; Lapointe, 1976); "how to do" articles are regularly published for physicians (Barlow, 1974; Camp, 1976; Goldstein, 1974; Gordon, 1975); pertinent papers are read at medical conferences and institutes; and several drugs (e.g., benzedrine, deaner, dexedrine, and ritalin) are officially marketed for use with LD children. Given the early contributions to the area, the interest of powerful parent groups, and the attention of the medical profession, it seems likely medicine will continue to be active and influential in this area.

THE MEDICAL MODEL

While there are many medical models (London, 1972), the "disease model" has allegedly had a disproportionate influence on psychology and education. Essentially, it focuses upon the individual in an attempt to identify abnormalities. This identification is a careful process of cataloging relevant variables (taking the "history" and various biological and psychological tests) and establishing causal relationships among the variables. Once an etiology or relationship is identified, a treatment plan is designed, implemented, and evaluated. Several writers (MacMillan, 1973; Stuart, 1970; Trippe, 1966; Ullman & Krasner, 1965) criticize the application to education of what they term the *medical model*. They allege that this application has led educators to three erroneous assumptions: *(a)* maladaptive behavior is a symptom of a hypothesized underlying pathology; *(b)* assessment of etiology and classifying disorders are valid components of the educational roles; and *(c)* resolution of the hypothesized pathology should occur before educational intervention. These writers call for an end of its use.

Kauffman and Hallahan (1974), however, persuasively argue that the critics misinterpret the medical model. They offer six features that make it a useful paradigm:

1. The necessity of treatment is based on empirical data.
2. Priorities are established for assessment and treatment.
3. Treatment effects are evaluated empirically.
4. Beneficial treatment may be offered even in the absence of knowledge of etiology or understanding of the therapeutic mechanism, although etiologies are sought and known etiologies may imply specific treatment.
5. The need for prosthesis, prophylaxis, and therapy is recognized.
6. Ecological variables are considered. (p. 99)

Teachers should carefully assess arguments condemning the application of the medical model education, ascertain the qualifications of the antagonist addressing the subject, and carefully evaluate each argument proposed. Be wary of broad, negative characterizations of other professions and models to account for shortcomings in special education. The medical model—specifically the disease model—has a tested history of successfully guiding the physician (Kauffman & Hallahan, 1974).

Medical professionals are responsible for initiating and reporting investigations of neurological, biochemical, and nutritional factors affecting children. The educator then monitors research (medical, psychological, and educational), interprets findings in relation to the teaching process, and develops intervention strategies.

MEDICAL SPECIALISTS

Parents want to know the teacher's opinion of a treatment; general education colleagues ask advice for making referral decisions; and the children themselves are often under medical treatment when placed. In response, every school or school system should establish a general policy for dealing with the medical aspects of teaching. This policy should address general guidelines for responding to questions about medical treatments, rules for dispensing or monitoring medications, procedures for implementation of a medically related treatment (such as a special diet), and principles for interaction with medical specialists. Teachers need to know about the medical specialists with whom they may interact: the pediatrician, neurologist, ophthalmologist, optometrist, otologist, audiologist, psychiatrist, or psychologist.

The Pediatrician

Until the middle of the 19th century (Garrison, 1965), professionals in medicine viewed children as differing from adults only by their size, inferiority of intellect, and feelings. Later physicians recognized that good medical care must include an in-depth understanding of a child's physical, mental, and social development. Consequently, pediatrics emerged, focusing specifically on the health care of children. It includes care of the sick child, prevention of disease, and maintenance of good health. Now professionals are increasingly concerned with the relationship between children and their families, their peers, the school, and the society in which they live (Garrard, 1973).

Society is beginning to recognize the right of children to have basic needs met regardless of the capacity or willingness of the parent to supply them. In response, the pediatricians attempt to provide health care to all children and comprehensive physical, social, and emotional support to hospitalized children. They also are now beginning to actively cooperate with other disciplines that share concern and responsibility for the health, education, and well-being of children. Oppé (1975) summarizes the contemporary responsibilities of the pediatrician: *(a)* genetic counseling, *(b)* diagnosis, intervention, and immunization, *(c)* nutrition, *(d)* cooperation with other professionals, *(e)* education, and *(f)* preventive health care.

Since there is no precise classification system of learning disorders, the role of pediatricians is yet to be defined in the total management plan. Now they often act independently of any specified procedure. Some pediatricians focus on "pure" medical services while others see their role as central in physical and mental health matters. Pediatricians in the latter role practice in language development, school adjustment, and academic learning. While several individuals (Boder, 1976; Denhoff, 1976; Garrard, 1973; Hogan & Ryan, 1976) have commented in general on the role of the pediatrician as a member of an interdisciplinary team, specific responsibilities have been suggested by Bateman and Frankel (1972) and Richmond and Walzer (1973). These responsibilities include:

1. Know the special education personnel and services available in the locality.
2. Adopt a primary focus of delivery of medical services. In addition, maintain a cooperative relationship with other service agencies.
3. Recognize the need for special education and support its services.
4. Diagnose and treat physical and physiological handicaps that might impair learning.
5. Interpret to others medical findings and their relevance.
6. Specify appropriate medical therapy for any identified defect or emotional problem.
7. Use all available services for preventive intervention, including programs for the disadvantaged, early childhood screening, and community resources.

In general, pediatricians are concerned with a broad spectrum of services that include care for the sick child, preventive medicine, and positive interaction with other areas of society. Even though they do not now have a specific role in the total treatment schema, it is obvious that they can be extremely helpful by providing diagnosis, treatment, counseling, and research.

The Neurologist

Neurology is the science of the structure and function of the healthy and the diseased nervous system. Since a correct diagnosis must often precede rational therapy, a neurologist is often consulted when nervous disorders are suspected. As a diagnostician, the neurologist seeks to identify or eliminate abnormalities of the nervous system as a cause for the problem being considered.

The Nervous System

Many people have speculated about the brain and its function. Scientific study over the ages has yielded much information about the human nervous system and its various structures. Detailed knowledge exists about how the complex parts function.

The *nerve cell,* the basic unit of the nervous system, consists of a body, one long structure called the *axon,* and many shorter structures called *dendrites* (see Figure 5.1). An electrical disturbance or impulse received by the dendrites passes through the cell body and down the axon where other dendrites pick it up. Dendrites connect to adjoining cell axons at points called *synapses*. This cell is uniquely specialized to receive and conduct excitatory or inhibitory electrical stimuli. Aggregates of various forms of it construct the entire nervous system.

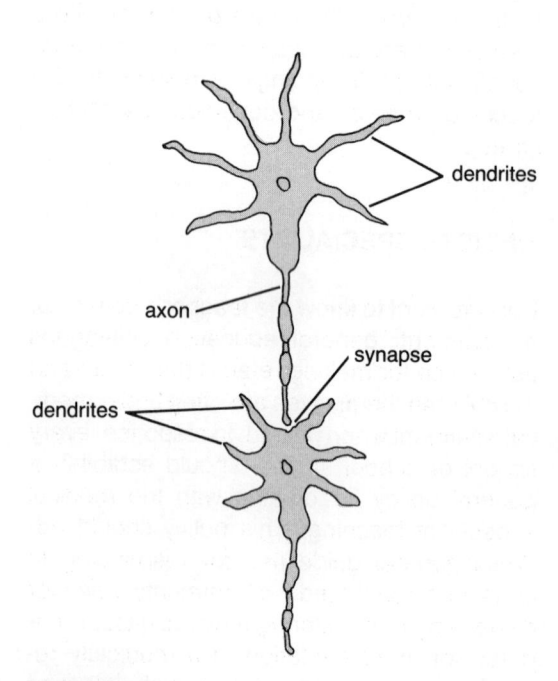

FIGURE 5.1

Nerve cell.

Two major parts comprise the nervous system: *(a)* the central nervous system (CNS), and *(b)* the peripheral nervous system (PNS). The CNS, consisting of the spinal column and the brain, is encased in the bony structures of the skull and vertebral column. The PNS lies outside these bony structures and connects the CNS to the rest of the body.

The CNS forms the integrative and thinking portions of the system. Its spinal column serves two purposes: *(a)* a connecting link between the brain and body, and *(b)* a center for motor activity integration. As illustrated in Figure 5.2, the brain consists of three major parts: *(a)* cerebrum, *(b)* cerebellum, and *(c)* the brain stem. The largest part, the cerebrum, occupies the upper portion of the skull where it controls the conscious functions of the nervous system. It is here that the highest levels of neural functioning take place, including those inherent in intellectual activity. The cerebellum lies beneath the cerebrum in conjunction with the brain stem and cerebral cortex and coordinates the voluntary muscle system to maintain balance and harmonious muscle movement. The brain stem, consisting of the diencephalon, midbrain, pons, and medulla oblongata, is phylogenetically the oldest part of the brain (Curtis, Jacobson, & Marcus, 1972), having changed very little with human evolution. It serves three major functions: *(a)* to connect the cerebral cortex, spinal cord, and cerebellum; *(b)* to control heart and respiratory rates; and *(c)* to integrate various motor reflexes and sensory input. Specifically, the diencephalon, the major relay, integrates all sensory systems except smell; the midbrain controls eye movement and the state of brain wakefulness; the pons is associated with sensory input and motor outflow to the face; and the medulla oblongata controls integrative functions for the reflex activities of respiration cardiovascular operation and is associated with control of the throat, neck, and mouth.

The Diagnosis

Because of the inseparable relationship between the CNS and the process of learning, parents often consult a neurologist when a child has unexplained difficulty with learning tasks. Walton (1971) and Vuckovich (1968) outline the basic procedures of a neurological diagnosis:

1. The collection of information consists of recording the history related to the existing

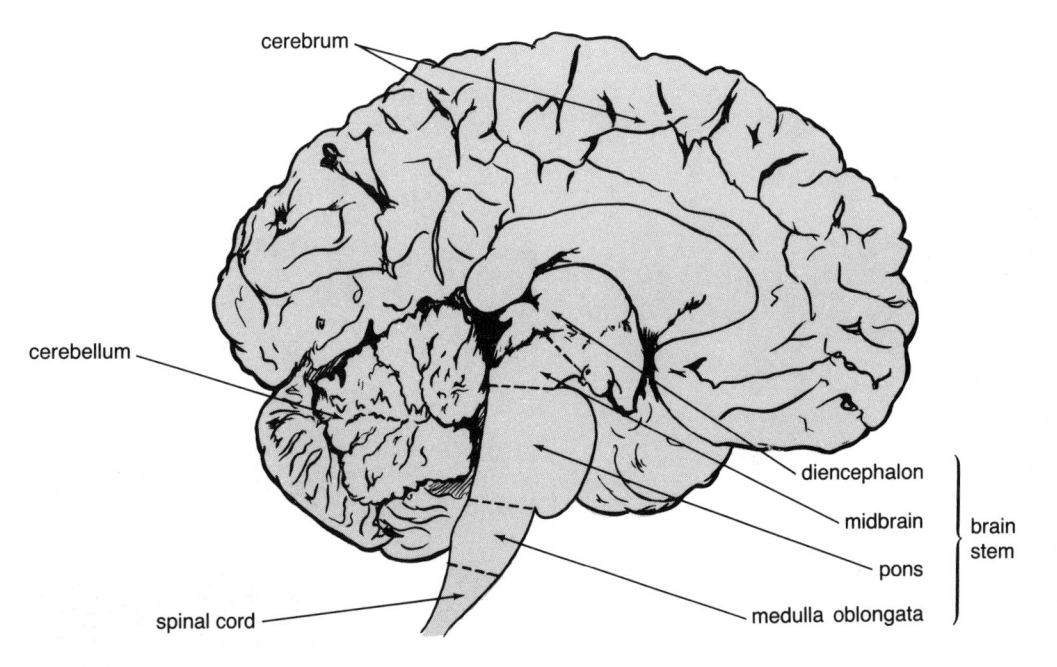

FIGURE 5.2

Regions of the undamaged, mature brain (sagittal section).

symptoms and complaints of the patient, previous health, and information about nervous problems in other members of the family (living or dead).
2. The neurological examination consists of assessing six components:
   a. The patient's mental state of awareness, normality of mood, and behavioral and social adjustment.
   b. Praxis and gnosis of the body image. *Praxis* is the ability to perform purposive skilled movements (e.g., dressing, shaving, opening a box of matches). Inability to perform these movements without obvious motor or sensory impairment may indicate a disorder called *apraxia*. *Gnosis* is the ability, based upon reception of sensory stimuli, to recognize the nature and significance of objects.
   c. The patient's ability to use speech.
   d. The skull and skeleton for size, shape, symmetry, bony protuberances, points of tenderness, cranial bruit (murmur), and deformity of movement limitations in the spine or joints.
   e. The special senses of smell, taste, vision, hearing, and the motor system.
   f. Signs of disease in other systems.

In spite of this comprehensive procedure, LD children are extremely difficult to diagnose with certainty as neurologically impaired. One reason for this is that the child's neurological system is still maturing and it is difficult to differentiate between a lag in maturity and an actual disorder. Consequently, the neurologist working with children often deals with what has been termed *soft signs,* minimal and subtle deviations from normal responses (e.g., awkward gait, clumsiness). In these cases the neurologist may form a presumptive diagnosis based on his initial findings. The presumptive diagnosis, of course, must then be confirmed or finally clarified by more "technical" means of diagnosis (Zulch, 1969), for example, the electroencephalograph (EEG), which is used to measure the electrical activity of the brain; visual-motor tests such as the *Bender Visual-Motor Gestalt Test* (Bender, 1938) and the *Draw-A-Man Test* (Harris, 1963); tests of gross-motor ability; tests of fine sensory-

A neurological exam includes an EEG.

motor skills; and an assessment of the presence of hyperkinesis.

In addition to diagnostic and therapeutic contributions, education has drawn terminology from the field of neurology. The prefix *a* means "absence of," *dys* means "disturbance of," *hyper* means "increased," and *hypo* means "decreased." If the Greek suffix *phasis* is taken to represent the conceptualization requisite for functional speech, then *aphasia* describes the loss of this ability, while the word *dysphasia* is used when the disorder is less severe. Examples of some commonly used terms using *a* meaning "absence of" (Barr, 1974) are

agnosia

gnosis = knowledge
Lack of ability to recognize the significance of sensory stimuli.

agraphia

grapho = to write
Inability to express thoughts in writing.

alexia

lexis = word
Loss of the power to grasp the meaning of written or printed words and sentences.

aphasia

phasis = speech
A defect of the power of expression by speech or of comprehending spoken or written language.

apraxia

pratto = to do
Inability to carry out purposeful movements in the absence of paralysis.

ataxia

taxis = order
A loss of power of muscle coordination, with irregularity of muscle action.

The prefix *dys* can be added to most of the same suffixes to which *a* is added (e.g., *dyslexia*), thus indicating a less severe condition.

Summary

Traditionally, a referral to a neurological specialist was to help establish or reject the presence of specific nervous system disorders and to identify the developmental level of the child. The advantage for the teacher was in having helpful guidelines for the selection of specific materials and teaching approaches to be used with the child. Denckla (1973) reports that information about minimal brain dysfunction or learning disabilities has become common knowledge and that many pediatricians are now competent to diagnose, prescribe medical interventions, and consult with the teacher. Consequently, she suggests that the role of the neurologist should shift to developing reliable, objective evaluation procedures for identification.

In spite of the fact that knowledge of neurology as it relates to learning disabilities is still fragmentary (Vuckovich, 1968), the diagnostic and therapeutic services of the neurologist will continue to be frequently used. In response, the teacher should have a working knowledge of the neurological examination and diagnostic procedures in order to facilitate communication between the medical practitioner and educator.

The Ophthalmologist and Optometrist

Classroom tasks often rely heavily on visual processes. Colors, shapes, letters, and other stimuli may be distorted for the child with faulty vision. A test of vision is an initial step in diagnosis.

The Eye

The eye, a remarkable, complicated organ, enables the gathering of the data necessary for survival and pleasure. Figure 5.3 illustrates the many parts of the eye that may be damaged or diseased.

Refractive errors make up approximately one-half of all visual defects (Kirk, 1972). In the normal eye, light rays are concentrated so that the image focuses on the tissue of the

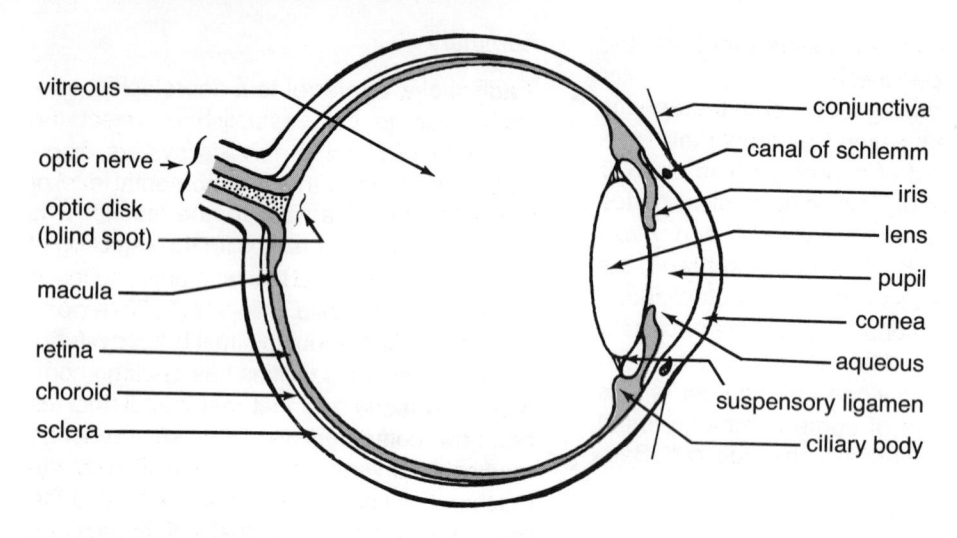

FIGURE 5.3

The eye.

retina (called the *refractive process*). The normal, mature eye, can focus on an image 20 feet away without muscular effort or refractive changes. When objects are closer or further than 20 feet, the curvature of the lens alters so the image will still focus upon the retina (called *accommodation*). Visual keenness (acuity) is expressed as a ratio based upon the basic "20 feet" figure: 20/200 indicates that an individual can distinguish at 20 feet what the normal eye can distinguish at 200 feet. Errors in refraction include

1. Farsightedness (hyperopia), in which the eye is too short from front to back. The image focuses behind the retina, resulting in a blurred or unclear image.
2. Nearsightedness (myopia), in which the eye is too long from front to back. The image focuses in front of the retina.
3. Astigmatism, which results from an irregularity in the cornea or lens of the eye. Light rays cannot focus at the same point on the retina, so some of the image may fall in front of the retina and some behind it, causing blurred vision.

Children sometimes have defective muscular control of the eyes. Strabismus (crossed eyes) is caused by a lack of muscle coordination. A defect in muscular balance of the eyes results in heterophoria. While not as noticeable as strabismus, difficulty in visual fusion results. The child cannot integrate the two images, one from each eye, into a single image.

The disorders discussed thus far have all been associated with the eye as a specific organ. A major problem arises with the attempt to define what is meant by "vision." Should functions of the central nervous system (CNS) and the peripheral nervous system (PNS) both be included in considerations for a definition, or should one consider the eye alone? In the following passage Krippner (1971) refers to the work of Flax (1967):

> a useful distinction between PNS and CNS disorders... would at least clarify the issue even if all professionals did not agree on the definitions. To Flax, PNS disorders refer to deficiencies of the end-organ system of vision (i.e., the eye); they include visual acuity, refractory error, fusion, convergence, and accommodation, all of which involve the eye mechanism and which are responsible for producing clear, single, binocular vision. CNS disorders involve deficiencies in organizing and interpreting images received by the eyes and sent to the brain. In CNS disorders, a clear, single visual image may be

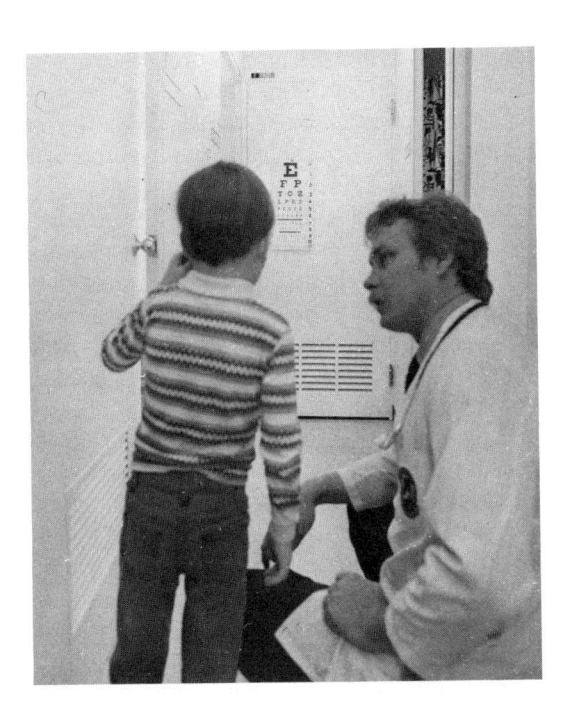

A child experiencing learning disabilities may have difficulty integrating two images, one from each eye, into a single image.

present but the child still cannot decode the presented word because of problems in organization and interpretation of what is seen. (p. 74)

Present assessments for a learning disability center on the presence of problems of visual processing, a CNS function. Problems of the eye not producing clear vision (a PNS function) are referred to the ophthalmologist or optometrist for further assessment or correction.

The Ophthalmologist

Ophthalmology relates to the care and cure of diseases and injury to the eye and related structures. This specialist is required to complete medical school, serve an internship in general medicine and surgery, and pursue additional specialized training in the structure, function, and diseases of the eye. He may prescribe eyeglasses and contact lenses and is legally permitted to diagnose and treat all eye disorders.

The Optometrist

Optometry relates to the examination of the eyes, the analysis of their function, and the use of preventive or corrective measures to insure maximum vision and comfort. The optometrist pursues a general course of study in college and then enters a graduate school of optometry from which he receives an O.D. degree. Not being a physician, he cannot treat eye diseases or prescribe medication, but he is licensed to prescribe refractive lenses (eyeglasses, contact lenses) and to treat functional aspects of vision.

The Controversy

Many optometrists practice "visual training" with children who have learning problems. Visual training is based on Skeffington's concept (Betts, 1958) of developmental vision, which proposes that proper vision for complex tasks such as reading is a learned activity involving the CNS as well as the eyes. According to Keogh (1974), the basic assumptions of such training are "that vision has motoric and sensory-motor bases; that problems in learning are due to disturbances of underlying functions in terms of visual efficiency and sensory-motor organization; that vision and visual organization can be trained; and that visual training will affect educational performance" (p. 220). The optometrist believes that ocular malfunctioning has a causal relationship to learning problems rather than being a symptom. But to the opthalmologist, the lack of smooth eye functioning is symptomatic, not etiological, of learning difficulties (Goldberg & Arnott, 1970; Keeney, 1968).

Optometrists and ophthalmologists bitterly debate this issue (Getman, 1972; Getz, 1973; Greenspan, 1971); optometrists charge that ophthalmologists lack scholarship and intellectual honesty (Flax, 1972). Countercharges by ophthalmologists claim that visual training is worthless, costly, and lacking in efficacy (Benton, 1973). Reviews of the literature

Foundations of learning disabilities

(Keogh, 1974) indicate that sampling problems, poor program procedures, and weak research methodology make existing evidence unsuitable for drawing conclusions. Benton (1973) suggests that when dealing with an LD child the optometrist or ophthalmologist should limit activity to the following:

1. He should take a careful history, including birth, development, home and family life, medical problems, emotional problems and school problems.
2. He should do a thorough eye examination including muscle functions and perception. Only refractive errors of significance should be corrected. Muscle abnormalities should be corrected as far as possible.
3. He should do a neurological survey aimed at discovering signs of minimal brain dysfunction. If positive findings are present, the child should be referred to a neurologist.
4. He should test the child's reading level or obtain test results from a teacher. This serves as a guide to the amount of extra help that may be needed for remediation.
5. He should look for signs of hyperactivity and short attention span and refer such children to their pediatrician or family doctor for evaluation and possible medication.
6. He should explain his estimate of the child's situation to parents and teachers in terms they can understand and make recommendations they can follow.
7. He should conduct follow-up examination every two or three months to see if the child is improving. (p. 336)

He concludes that "extensive programs of training in vision, visual perception, eye exercises, and ocular gymnastics beyond the above recommendations are an unnecessary waste of time and money" (p. 336).

The Otologist and Audiologist

Otology specializes in the care and prevention of damage and disease to the ear. The otologist, like the ophthalmologist, is a medical doctor who has continued training in a specialized area of medicine. He is licensed to diagnose and treat all disorders of the ear. The audiologist, on the other hand, is a nonmedical specialist permitted to assess the extent of hearing loss and to prescribe appropriate prosthetic devices.

For learning, the sense of hearing is crucial. Teachers frequently use the auditory mode to present material. In addition, hearing is essential to language development. While severe losses of hearing are relatively easy to identify, children with slight or mild hearing losses often escape detection. Several informal tests of hearing ability (conversation at 20 feet, whisper tests, and watch ticking tests) are used to obtain a rough measure; but the most accurate method is with a pure-tone audiometer. This instrument produces "pure" tones of known intensity and frequency and permits each ear to be tested separately. *Intensity* refers to the relative loudness (volume) of a sound, while *frequency* refers to the number of vibrations per second of a second wave (the more vibrations, the higher the pitch). In speech the most important frequencies are between 500 and 2000 vibrations per second (see Figure 5.4).

In a test, the individual listens to sounds of known intensity and frequency and indicates (raises a hand, nods, etc.) when he hears the sound. How "loud" a sound has to be before the child hears it is determined. The volume (loudness) of sound is measured in units called *decibels (dB)*. Consequently, if a child must have the volume of a specific sound increased 30 decibels above the level at which it is detected by the normal ear, the child has a 30 decibel hearing loss. Kirk (1972) lists the levels of hearing loss as

slight   27–40 dB loss
mild   41–55 dB loss
marked   56–70 dB loss
severe   71–90 dB loss
extreme   91 dB or more

There are two main types of hearing loss: *(a)* conductive and *(b)* sensory-neural. A conductive loss reduces the volume of a sound

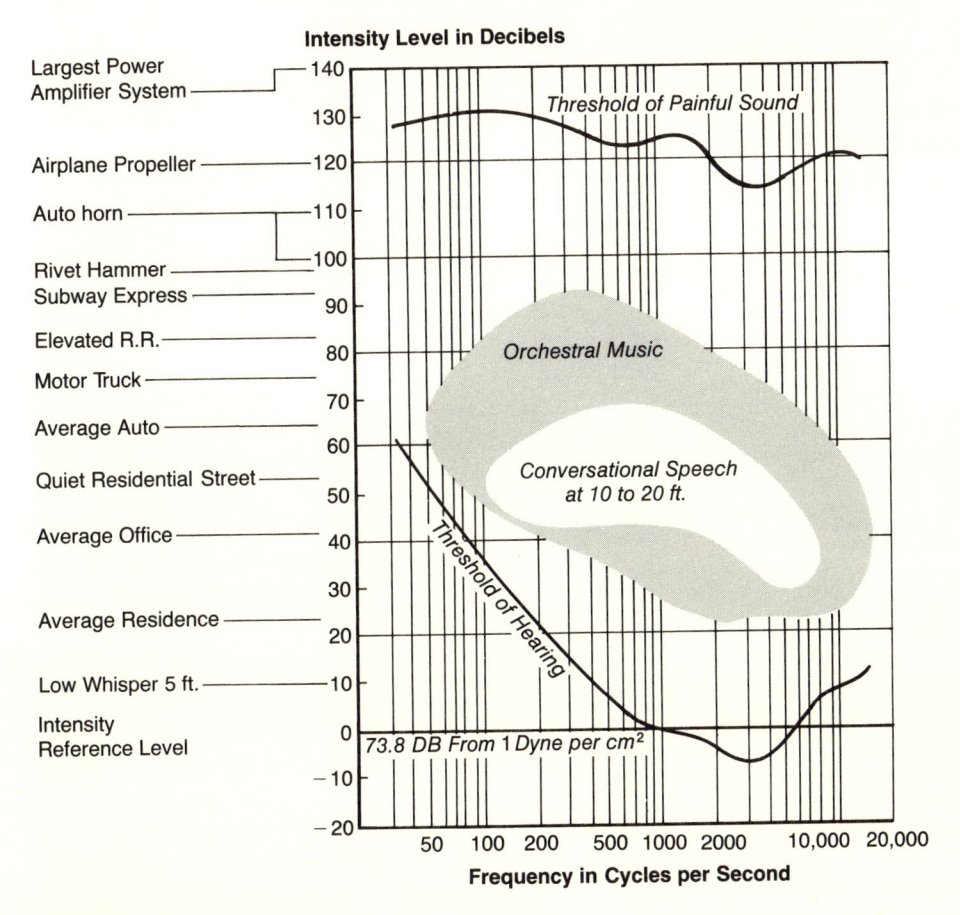

FIGURE 5.4

Range of human hearing.

Source: Adapted from *Instructor's manual to accompany Educating Exceptional Children* by S.A. Kirk, prepared by F.E. Lord. Boston: Houghton Mifflin, 1972, p. 93 (Plate No. XII). Reprinted by permission of Wayne-Green Publisher and Maico Hearing Instruments.

reaching the auditory nerve in the inner ear. A sensory-neural loss results from defect or damage to the inner ear or auditory nerve. A sensory-neural loss is usually more serious, both in terms of hearing loss and remediation. In most learning situations, the primary problem resulting from a hearing loss (conductive or sensory-neural) is what is *not* heard rather than the volume of the stimuli. Because sounds used in human speech vary in frequency (the consonants *s, sh,* and *z* are high frequency, while vowels such as *o* and *u* are low), the effect of hearing loss often is garbled speech. A child with a slight or mild loss might hear, "Three blind mice, see how they run" as " ree blin mi , ee ow they run " (Cruickshank & Johnson, 1958, p. 351).

Learning behaviors resulting from hearing losses are often similar to those of the LD child. Consequently, the otologist and audiologist play an important role in the diagnostic process. On the one hand, correction of a hearing loss and educational remediation may eliminate many of the pseudosymptoms of a learning disability, while rejection of a hearing loss as a cause of learning problems will aid

When the audiometer makes a loud sound, Ken raises his hand.

the diagnostician in identifying relevant variables of the problem.

The Psychiatrist and Psychologist

Psychiatry and *psychology* are the study of human behavior, including etiology, treatment, and pathology. Psychiatry is a branch of medical science, while psychology is a separate discipline. Both use systematic observation to determine the laws and principles of behavior.

The child psychiatrist and psychologist are extensively trained to deal with the child's emotional problems, their etiology, and the pathologies associated with them. They can often help the LD child cope with his frustrations and behavior problems. In addition, they can support and counsel the family. Children express their problems in behavior and, as parents must deal with this behavior, parents can be involved in the treatment (Mirel & Solomon, 1971). Parent attitudes, values, and family interactions undeniably influence the child and his school success. Conversely, school experiences come home to the family, with the child's academic success and failure altering basic family patterns. With serious problems, families often seek the counsel of a psychiatrist or psychologist.

These specialists offer useful information to the classroom teacher. Considering their training and access to information not generally available, they are a valuable resource of ideas for use in diagnosis and treatment.

Although many educators and physicians cooperate very nicely, some teachers complain that medical specialists in private practice do not understand the problems of the teacher, refuse to cooperate, or make unrealistic demands. As pointed out in Chapter 1, the physician was the primary professional consulted during the genesis and birth stages of the learning disability history. Many medical personnel continue to view the educator's role as carrying out the prescriptions of supposedly more expert professional disciplines. In addition, medical specialists work on a fee basis and cannot afford excessive time for directions, speculations, and rationales. They must show results for their patients (who are not the schools or teachers) and are often uninformed regarding the realities of teaching.

The teacher's responsibility related to medicine greatly changed with the current acceptance of the position that learning disabilities is primarily an educational phenomenon (Larsen, 1978). Teachers are not expected to become pseudo-medico experts or to passively accept medical recommendations and directions about educational procedures. They should, however, be thoroughly knowledgeable about the historical development of their speciality (i.e., its past and present accepted practices), highly competent in their educational role, and proficient in obtaining and effectively using ancillary and community services. In regard to medicine, the teacher should specifically (a) know, understand, and follow the general school policy related to education and medicine, (b) have a brief but serviceable understanding of the medical specialities most likely to contribute to programs for the learning disabled, and (c) have a general knowledge of current medically oriented treatments advocated for use with LD children and adolescents.

TREATMENTS

Cerebral Dominance

The cerebrum is a two-part structure; each part is called a *hemisphere.* Each hemisphere relates to opposite sides of the body. A large tract of fibers (the *corpus callosum*) connects the two and seems to transfer information. The surface of each hemisphere (called the *cortex*) receives sensory information from the body's receptor organs (skin, eyes, ears) on the opposite side of the body. The function of the two sides varies with specific activity. For example, both sides of the cerebrum control vision and hearing. Motor movements appear to be coordinated in a centrilateral fashion: the left hemisphere dominant for speech and language functions, and the right hemisphere for complex visual processes.

In the 1930s Orton studied the effects of brain damage acquired in adulthood on language and attempted to apply his results to children alleged to be brain injured (Myers & Hammill, 1976). Concerned with reading difficulty, Orton hypothesized that reversal of letters and words was the result of failure to establish the left hemisphere (location of speech functions) as dominant over the right. According to Lerner (1976),

> Orton's therapeutic reasoning was therefore as follows: language function originates in the left cerebral hemisphere, and the left cerebral hemisphere is also the center for motor movement on the right side of the body; therefore, the language center in the left hemisphere could be strengthened and made dominant by strongly establishing the right-sided motor responses of the body. Right-handed and right-sided activities should be strongly encouraged and practiced, while left-sided activities should be discouraged or eliminated. (p. 48)

Such a procedure, according to Orton, would reduce the language problems caused by the right hemisphere's interference with the signals of the left. Orton may also be interpreted as recommending that *one* side (either right or left) be made dominant.

A concept related to dominance is laterality. The laterality theory maintains that learning is adversely affected if an individual does not establish a tendency to perform most functions with one side of the body. That is, if one mixes laterality (the tendency to mix left-right preference for using hands, feet, eyes), the probability of learning problems is increased.

While most researchers and professionals in medicine, psychology, and education place little practical value on either theory (Freeman, 1967; Robbins & Glass, 1969), teachers occasionally encounter a parent, colleague, or other professional who believes their methodology.

Neural Retraining

Proponents of the neural retraining approach share the common premise that one can retrain, reprogram, or in some way improve the

Foundations of learning disabilities

functioning of the CNS through specific, selected activities. Representative examples of this approach are "patterning" and sensory-integrative therapy.

Patterning

Temple Fay, a noted Philadelphia neurosurgeon and founder of the Neuro-Physical Rehabilitation Clinic in Philadelphia, pioneered many different aspects of neurology (Hallahan & Cruickshank, 1973). During the 1940s and 1950s he described pattern movements that formed the core of treatment for various brain injuries in children and adults. Glen Doman, a physical therapist, and Carl Delacato, an educational psychologist, met Fay and adopted many of his concepts. Widespread popularity and notoriety followed the publication of the basic tenets of their theory and corresponding treatments (Delacato, 1959; Doman, Spitz, Zucman, Delacato, & Doman, 1960).

Doman and Delacato hypothesize that each individual develops through stages that correspond to the evolutionary stages of man. Consequently, as each child develops he progresses through stages in which the use of specific CNS functions must be sequentially mastered. This process begins with the phylogenetically most ancient and proceeds to the more recently developed CNS functions. Hence the process develops accordingly; the spinal cord medulla, then the pons, the midbrain, followed by the cortex, and finally the establishment of hemispheric dominance. They maintain that there are six functional attainments of the human being (motor skills, speech, writing, reading, understanding speech, and tactile ability); failure to pass through a developmental sequence will result in problems of mobility and communication. By measuring the level of development (neurological organization) it becomes possible to prescribe activities that will improve development and thus prevent or eliminate learning problems. As presented in Table 5.1, the level of neurological development is determined by evaluating behaviors (Delacato, 1963).

The unique factor of their patterning approach is their assumption that the functions of the CNS should be treated. Silver (1975) notes that in this method stimuli normally provided by the environment are poured into the afferent sensory system; however, the intensity and frequency are great enough to draw a response from the corresponding motor system.

Once a level of unsatisfactory development is identified, they impose an intense regimen of remedial motor activity. If the individual is physically unable to perform the motor exercises, another person moves the limbs through the prescribed motions. The individual must relearn and properly perform each stage of motor learning: creeping, crawling,

TABLE 5.1

Behaviors that identify the level of neurological development.

Developmental Stage	Behavior
Spinal cord medulla	Normal reflex movement
Pons	Sleeping position appropriate to laterality
Midbrain	Smooth, rhythmical, cross patterned creeping
Cortex	Cross patterned, balanced, smooth, and rhythmical walking
Hemispheric dominance	Clearly established dominance of one side of the body

and walking. In addition to these exercises, the approach includes breathing exercises, sensory stimulation, restriction of fluids, salt, and sugar, sleeping in prescribed body positions, and the training of eye and hand use. They feel that by establishing hemispheric dominance in this method, full neurological organization and the elimination of learning problems will result.

Some proof of success exists (Delacato, 1966), but other writers (Kershner, 1968; Robbins & Glass, 1969; Stone & Pielstick, 1969) analyzing these studies or attempting replication have found the theory, specific treatment procedures, and research to be lacking. An excellent review of the literature on patterning is presented by Hallahan and Cruickshank (1973). The intensity of the debate was highlighted in 1968 when several prestigious professional organizations joined together and expressed strong concern in an official statement:

1. Promotional methods appear to put parents in a position in which they cannot refuse such treatment without calling into question their adequacy and motivation as parents.
2. The regimens prescribed are so demanding and inflexible that they may lead to neglect of other family members' needs.
3. It is asserted that if the therapy is not carried out as rigidly prescribed, the child's potential will be damaged, and that anything less than 100% effort is useless.
4. Restrictions are often placed upon age-appropriate activities of which the child is capable, such as walking or listening to music, though unwarranted by any supportive data and knowledge of any long-term results published to date.
5. Claims are made for rapid and conclusive diagnosis according to a "Development Profile" of no known validity. No data on which construction of the profile has been based have ever been published, nor are there known attempts to cross-validate it against any accepted methods.
6. Undocumented claims are made for cures in a substantial number of cases extending even beyond disease states to making normal children superior, easing world tensions, and possibly "hastening" the evolutionary process.
7. Without supporting data, Doman and Delacato indicate many typical child-rearing practices as limiting a child's potential, thereby increasing the anxiety of already burdened and confused parents (Adapted from p. 94 of Hallahan & Cruickshank, 1973).

Despite the reservations of professionals in education and medicine, many parents are zealous advocates of patterning. Teachers should be able to discuss the pro and con of patterning treatments with assurance and from a factual base.

Sensory-Integrative Therapy

Ayres (1965, 1969, 1972, 1975) suggests that in order for the cerebrum to perform its function, auditory and visual sensory input must be adequately organized at the brain stem level. This organization enables the two levels of the brain to interact and satisfactorily perform the tasks demanded of them.

> Disorders consistently observed in learning disabled children that are suggestive of inadequate sensory integration in the brain stem are immature postural reactions, poor extraocular muscle control, poorly developed visual orientation to environmental space, difficulty in the processing of sounds into percepts, and the tendency toward distractibility. (Ayres, 1972, p. 342)

Treatment consists of carefully controlled sensory input through vestibular and somatosensory systems. The treatment is designed to enhance sensory integration, thereby improving the ability of the brain to function.

Ayres (1969) developed a test battery that samples behavior in motor accuracy, perceptual-motor skills, figure-ground visual perception, kinesthesia, tactile perception, and space perception. Moreover, she has reported investigations concerning her hypothesis (Ayres, 1972, 1977, 1978). Unlike several investigators using neural retraining, Ayres does not hastily jump from theoretical concepts to conclusions. For example, she suggests that some children respond well to sensory integrative therapy and some do not. Consequently, her (1978) work also focuses on establishing procedures for identifying which children will benefit and which will not. While her hypothesis appears plausible, further investigation is necessary.

Pharmacology

The press and parents continually debate the issue of using drugs to control behavior of children in school and at home (Berman, 1976; Gray, 1975; Hentoff, 1971; Ladd, 1970). Estimates of the number of school children receiving medication vary: 200,000 children (U.S. Department of Health, Education, & Welfare, 1971); 15–20% of elementary school children (Grinspoon & Singer, 1973); and 10–15% of students in some school districts (Walker, 1975). Since teachers of LD children have considerable contact with children on medication or recommended for medication and with parents seeking advice about drug therapy, an extensive review of the topic is included.

Drugs are obtained from animals, vegetables, and minerals. Some are made synthetically. In the past, people obtained most drugs naturally and used them in the raw form. They made use of dried or fresh animal organs and, in some cases, they isolated an active ingredient (e.g., alcohol) from the natural source. These practices led to some rather exotic prescriptions—at least from our contemporary viewpoint. For example, Phillip of Spain, a noted 13th century Spanish physician, suggested eating the liver from a vulture that had been drunk for nine days as a cure for epilepsy. Other examples are highlighted in phrases such as "tongue of lizard," "toe of frog," and "eye of newt." One should be careful, however, not to assume that the sorcerers, magicians, and herb healers were all fraudulent. Some drugs with accepted medical use today have been prepared throughout history (e.g., insulin from animal glands, digitalis from roots, and a variety of minerals such as copper sulfate and magnesium sulfate). Now synthetic manufacturing is common. It is a more satisfactory source of drugs because a high level of consistency and purity can be maintained.

Drugs are chemical substances which, by interacting with the chemical action of a biological system, change the internal functions and/or behaviors. The term *drug* is defined by the Federal Food, Drug, and Cosmetic Act as applying to:

1) articles recognized in the official pharmaceutical standards such as *The United States Pharmacopeia, National Formulary, British Pharmacopeia, Pharmacopeia Internationalis,* or other such official volumes;
2) articles intended for use in the diagnosis, cure, mitigation, treatment or prevention of disease in man or animals;
3) articles other than food which are intended to affect the structure or any function of the body of man or animals; and
4) articles intended for use as a component of any article specified in clauses 1, 2, or 3.
(Asperheim & Eisenhauer, 1973, p. 3)

For practical purposes, drugs are any substance (other than food) containing a chemical that alters the normal function and behavior of a biological system.

Drug Nomenclature

A problem for individuals not trained in medicine is the process used for naming a drug. Every drug approved for medical use has four names: First, the chemical name that describes the drug's structural formula for pharmacists. Second, the official name listed in one or the other of two official references for drug standards in the United States: *United States Pharmacopeia* (USP) and *National Formulary* (NF). While not officially recognized, the most popular drug reference is the *Physicians' Desk Reference (PDR)*, which contains summaries of the composition, action, uses, mode of administration, dosage, side effects, and contraindications of commercial pharmaceutical products. Third, the generic name assigned by the organization first developing the drug. Fourth, the trade name assigned by the drug manufacturer for marketing purposes. For example, one of the more common drugs prescribed for hyperactive children is ritalin. The chemical name is methyl α–phenyl–2–piperidine–acetate hydrochloride; its official name is methylphenidate hydrochloride; its generic name is methylophenidate hydrochloride; and its trade name is ritalin. Communication problems about drug names usually stem from one individual using the generic name and another using the trade name.

Drug Action

The human body is composed of elemental atoms combined in various ways to form molecules, which in turn form cells. Aggregates of cells form the various tissue and organs of the body. Cells differ because they vary in the chemical combinations (i.e., the specific manner in which certain atoms and molecules are "bonded" to each other) of their atoms and molecules. As a result of medical and chemical research, many of these basic combinations can be described in terms of chemical formulas and equations that represent the action and reaction of atoms and molecules to each other.

In the human being, altering the chemical combinations among atoms, molecules, and cells also results in changes in product or function. Drugs (chemicals) change the biologic action of selected cells. The precise method is as yet unknown. It is known, however, that different cell groups (e.g., brain versus liver) have different reactions to the same drug. Consequently, all drugs specify a main effect and side effects. An example is the pain-killing effect of morphine as a main effect and constipation and dependency as side effects (of course, if one were treating diarrhea, the binding effect would be considered the main effect and the dependency and pain depression would be side effects). In addition to main and side effects, research has also established estimates of the specific amount of drug (dose) necessary to produce a desired effect. Likewise, estimates of the degree of effectiveness per dose (potency) among various drugs are now known.

The Literature

Bradley (1937) reports marked improvement in the behavior of children receiving benzedrine. Since Bradley's work, numerous papers and conference reports have become available on the value of drug therapy with children (Eisenberg, Conners, & Sharpe, 1965; Knights & Hinton, 1969; Molitch & Sullivan, 1937; Wade, 1976). Most reviews on the research dealing with the effect of stimulant drugs on hyperactivity (Eisenberg, 1972; Kornetsky, 1970; Millichap & Fowler, 1967; Safer, Allen, & Barr, 1972) agree to some extent with Conners' (1971) conclusions:

> Stimulant drugs reduce inattentive behavior, undirected motor behavior, and the number of punishments received for disruptive behavior, and tend to increase both the child's attention to learning tasks and the amount of positive teacher contact with the pupils. (p. 478)

The successful use of stimulants with some hyperactive children appears paradoxical; highly active children become less active when given the stimulant. Perhaps the stimulant chemically reacts to increase the arousal level and effectiveness of the CNS. In a conference report sponsored by the Office of Child Development and the Office of the Assistant Secretary for Health and Scientific Affairs (1971), stimulants are said to help the child to mobilize and increase his ability to concentrate on relevant stimuli and to organize body movements more purposefully. Similarly, Conners (1971) thinks that hyperactive youths on stimulants learn better because they are more attentive to the task and/or are more aroused and motivated. Activity is proven to increase by stimulant drugs; however, the important feature concerning hyperactive behavior is that they increase the *quality* as well as the total amount of activity.

In contrast to the abundance of reports about the effect of stimulants, work with tranquilizers has been minimal (Gearheart, 1977). This situation may be due in part to the documented dependence-producing properties of tranquilizers and the consistent finding that improvement in behavior frequently occurs at the expense of deterioration in performance (Sroufe, 1975).

While much of the reported literature indicates positive results for drug therapy, some researchers report converse and inconclusive findings. Lobb (1968) and Bell and Zubek (1961) indicate that children learn less well when receiving stimulants. Others (Freeman, 1966, 1970; Liberman, 1961; McConnell & Cromwell, 1964; Millichap, Aymat, Sturgis, Larson, & Egan, 1968) question the validity of findings that drugs are beneficial.

Sulzbacher (1973), in a review of 1,359 studies of drug treatment, raises the question of research methodology. Of the 1,359 studies examined, they rejected 603 as studies of nonbehavioral effects or as having a complete report unavailable (see Table 5.2). They analyzed the remaining 756 studies for methodological procedure. Only 29 attempted to directly measure change in specified behaviors. Stated another way, 96.2% of the studies lacked sufficient control or inferred a behavior change indirectly.

Schrag and Divoky (1975) allege serious discrepancies in basic methodology and data collection procedures of studies submitted to

TABLE 5.2

Sulzbacher literature review.

Total number studies surveyed		1,359
Studies of unrelated (nonbehavioral) effects of psychoactive drugs		−560
Unavailable reports		−43
Total number studies of drug effects on the behavior of children		756
	Number	Percentage of total (n = 756)
Uncontrolled studies (no placebos or double-blind)	548	72.5
Controlled studies categorized by dependent variable:		
"Clinical impression" or professional opinion	34	4.5
Rating scale	99	13.1
Standard psychological tests	46	6.1
Direct measurement of behavior	29	3.8
	756	100.0

Source: Adapted from Psychotropic Medication with Children: An Evaluation of Procedural Biases in Results of Reported Studies by S. I. Sulzbacher, *Pediatrics,* 1973, *51,* p. 514. Copyright 1973 by American Academy of Pediatrics. Reprinted by permission.

the Federal Drug Administration in 1971 purporting to demonstrate the safety and effectiveness of cylert. They further claim that in gaining permission to manufacture and distribute cylert, the drug company pressured Federal Drug Administration officials to approve the application despite the discrepancies. Employees of the drug company later published an article in an educational journal and stated that "pemoline (cylert) is a highly useful clinical alternative to the amphetamines and methylphenidate as an adjunct in the management of hyperkinetic behavior" (Page, Janicki, Bernstein, Curran, & Michelli, 1974, p. 503).

The conflicting findings and allegations surrounding the research on drug efficacy and the adverse public response to prescribing drugs for school children (Berman, 1976; Gray, 1975; Randall, 1972) create a dilemma for the classroom teacher. The teacher wishes to encourage the use of every helpful technique available, but she often lacks the training and expertise to make sound judgments about drug therapy. Most teachers simply trust that specific drugs have been tested and judged acceptable by appropriate professionals. To some extent they agree with Denhoff, Davids, and Hawkins (1971), who state:

If these drugs can help certain children focus their attention and concentration, and thus profit more from the many hours spent in school, then they serve a useful function for these children at this particular time in their academic and psychosocial development. (p. 498)

Guidelines for the Teacher

The teacher supports the child in addition to tutoring him. He must both protect the child from adverse elements in the environment and introduce propitious ones. In regard to pharmacology, the teacher might best discharge this responsibility by providing relevant data to the family and physician (Neisworth, Kurtz, Ross, & Madle, 1976). Specifically, the teacher should translate labels such as *hyperactive* into observable behaviors, determine the severity of the behaviors by collecting baseline data, and help determine if the label is validated by the frequency and intensity of classroom behaviors.

Before considering drug treatment, professionals should consider other means of controlling hyperactive behavior. Bower and Mercer (1975) report evidence that proves the success of verbal mediation, behavior modification, modeling, and reduction of environmental distractions. Teachers can readily

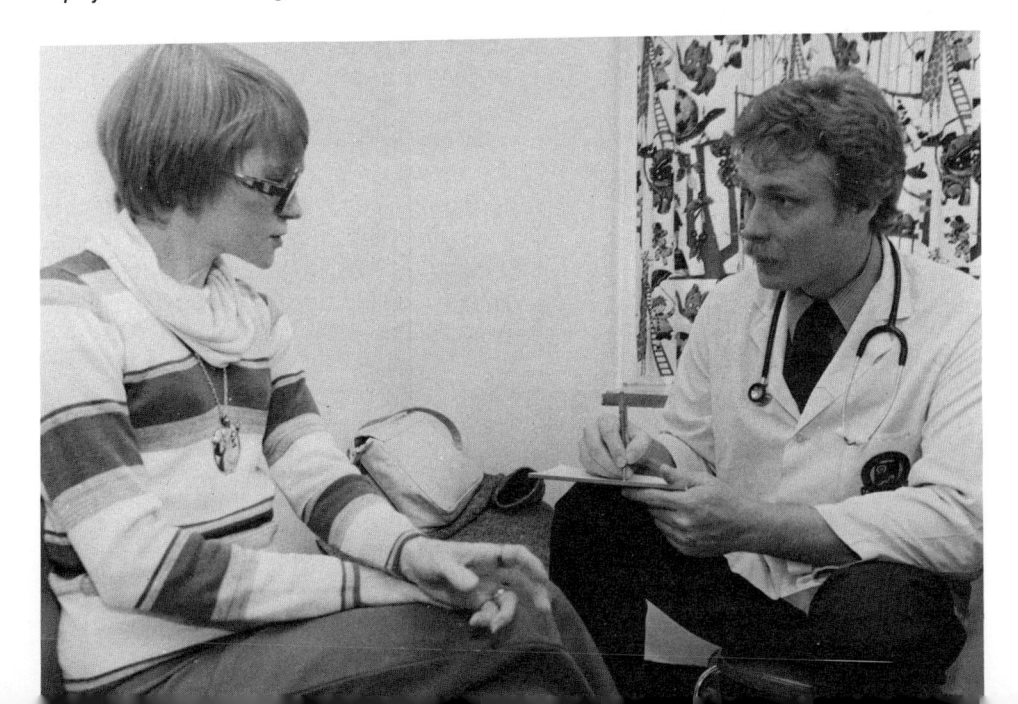

A physician discussing with a parent the use of stimulant drugs to control hyperactivity.

use these treatments. Moreover, Gearheart (1977) reports that teachers should continue to use various techniques for controlling hyperactive behavior even if the child is on medication.

If the child already is on medication, the teacher has further obligations:

1. The teacher should identify and monitor the drug's side effects. This task necessitates that he know the name of the drug and its possible side effects, personally checking the USP, NF, or PDR to note any secondary effects. Although this may mean a visit to a nearby medical school library or physician's office, there is no substitute for direct knowledge. All relevant information should be copied and placed in a folder or notebook for reference.
2. The teacher can keep a systematic accurate record of the behaviors to be altered by the drug. This information may be crucial in documenting the need for dosage adjustments. Because of her proximity, the teacher may be the most qualified person for monitoring the effects of the drug.
3. The teacher should keep in touch with the family and if requested, the physician about how the drug affects the child.
4. The teacher should carefully take drug effects into account when planning the child's daily activities. For example, if the child is drowsy, irritable, or inattentive after receiving the medication, the teacher can avoid group work or teaching new concepts during this period. No one can expect the child to perform efficiently during such periods.

Orthomolecular Medicine

Many people enthusiastically support treatments centering on hypothesized deficiencies in body function. These treatments fall into the broad category of orthomolecular medicine, which is defined by Pauling (1968) as "the treatment of mental disease by the provision of the optimum molecular environment for the mind, especially the optimum concentrations of substances normally present in the human body" (p. 265). Examples of these treatments are megavitamin therapy, food additives, hypoglycemia, trace elements, and allergic reactions.

Megavitamin Therapy

This treatment consists of prescribing massive doses of vitamins for children with learning and behavior problems. The therapist assumes that vitamin deficiencies cause hyperactivity, learning problems, and other symptoms associated with the LD child.

Megavitamin therapy originated from the work of Hoffer, Osmond, and Smythies (1954) with schizophrenics. The approach was popularized by a widely quoted article in which Cott (1971) describes a megavitamin treatment for learning disabled children. In a careful review of this article, Silver (1975) takes issue with Cott on the following points:

1. The subjects of the "learning disability study" may have been the same population Cott called *autistic* and *schizophrenic* in a 1969 report published in *Schizophrenia*.
2. Although Cott claims his results are being duplicated by physicians, clinics, and at the New York Institute for Child Development, he offers no references for these studies.
3. Cott claims megavitamin therapy is valuable for clinical treatment of learning disabilities but cites no data to support this assertion.
4. Most of the claims for megavitamin therapy are based on subjective reporting, questionable research designs, and studies relating megavitamin treatment to schizophrenia. In relation to schizophrenia and megavitamins, the American Psychiatric Association (APA Task Force, 1973) and the Canadian Mental Health Association (Ban, 1973) both take strong positions on the ineffectiveness of this therapy.

Megavitamin therapy has also been extremely popular with amateur and professional athletes to increase performance. But according to Bob Ferry, former basketball player for the Detroit Pistons, "I remember one season in Detroit, we all took a lot of vitamins. I don't think we played any better, but three of our wives got pregnant" (Reed, 1977, p. 71).

The most prudent course may be that of Silver (1975): "If one chooses to treat children with learning disabilities with megavitamins, he or she must be aware that such treatment is based on the state of the art and not the state of the science" (p. 412).

Food Additives

Feingold (1973, 1975a, 1975b, 1976) proposes that hyperactivity and learning problems may be caused by salicylates and chemicals added to foodstuffs. He thinks some children react adversely to one or more chemicals present in synthetic colors and flavors and to the salicylates occurring naturally in foods such as apples, oranges, tomatoes, peaches, and a variety of berries. He has identified 34 food colors, 1,610 synthetic flavors, and 1,120 other chemicals added to foods. Since it is impractical to determine the specific agent causing problems for a child, he prescribes the Kaiser-Permanente (K-P) Diet. This diet eliminates foods containing natural salicylates (e.g., apples, oranges, cucumbers, strawberries, tea, tomatoes), foods containing artificial colors and flavors, and various miscellaneous items, such as toothpaste, perfumes, and compounds containing aspirin.

Many people strongly believe in the usefulness of the diet. Feingold (1976) notes that "the K-P Diet, which eliminates all artificial food colors and flavors as well as foods with a natural salicylate radical, will control the behavioral disturbance in 30 to 50% (depending upon the sample) of both normal and neurologically damaged children" (p. 588). A national association of parents supporting the Feingold diet (Feingold Association of the United States, 759 National Press Building, Washington, D.C. 20045) has been organized with two stated purposes: *(a)* to persuade food processors to provide more complete and detailed labeling on their products, and *(b)* to encourage the national use of a logo or design which would identify foods that are free of artificial flavors and colors.

Some children's diets are very carefully controlled.

But some professionals express concern about the claimed success. For example, Spring and Sandoval (1976) undertook a close examination of the research, concluding that:

1. There are no reliable data proving that a recent epidemic of hyperactivity is due to use of synthetic colors and flavors added to food.
2. Meager clinical evidence has been overinterpreted.
3. The K-P Diet may result in strong placebo responses.
4. The results of two controlled studies (Conners, Goyette, Southwick, Lees, & Andrulonis, 1976; Harley, Ray, Matthews, Cleeland, Tomasi, Eichman, & Chun, 1976) are ambiguous and should be interpreted with caution.
5. Further public advocacy should be halted until efficacy of the diet is established by controlled research.

Harley (1976) reports preliminary results of a comprehensive University of Wisconsin study and states that his group's data do not offer strong support for the efficacy of the experimental diet. On the other hand, Rose (in press) used a single subject design with two children and double blind conditions to test the claims of advocates of the Feingold diet. He found a functional relationship between the ingestion of artificial food colors and an increase in the occurrence of hyperactive behavior. In addition, he reports a treatment effect that consistently lasted two days; no placebo effect; and differential sensitivity of the dependent measures to the treatment effects (i.e., activity level increased, but aggressive behavior did not increase).

Food additives may be a cause of learning difficulty, but it has yet to be unequivocally proven. Teachers should use caution when answering questions or discussing the treatment with parents and colleagues.

Hypoglycemia

Some people theorize that LD children are deficient in blood sugar level. They maintain that there is a decrease in blood sugar level about an hour after eating that effectively lowers the child's energy for learning. If the level remains low for a prolonged period of time, symptoms of cerebral dysfunction develop: mental confusion, hallucinations, convulsions, and eventually deep coma. The nervous system is deprived of the glucose needed for its normal metabolic activity. Treatment depends on the primary etiology and includes surgical intervention and dietary change aimed at avoiding extremes in blood glucose level. The diet is high in protein and fat, low in carbohydrate content, and is given in frequent small feedings during the day and before bedtime.

Although citing no references, Cott (1971) states that learning disabled children eat foods high in cereals, carbohydrates, and prepared with sugar, and that an abnormally high incidence of hypoglycemia exists for this group. Because no strong proof now exists of this relationship, there is no implication for treatment.

Trace Elements

The body needs trace elements (copper, zinc, magnesium, chromium, etc.) and common elements (calcium, potassium, sodium, iron, etc.) to function normally. One unsupported theory proposes that LD children lack one of these essential elements. Proponents of this theory prescribe the ingestion of a wide spectrum of these elements (replacement therapy). Despite the lack of evidence supporting either cause or cure, occasionally children receive this therapy.

Allergic Reactions

Some suggest that learning disabilities are the result of CNS allergies to certain foods (Havard, 1973; Philpott, Mandell, & von Hilsheimer, 1972). A lengthy and expensive test supposedly identifies the cause. The relationship between allergies and learning disabilities has yet to be established; until further study, no conclusions can be reached.

Other Treatments

Biofeedback

Smith (1975) quotes Weiner as defining feedback as "a method of controlling a system by reinserting into it the results of its past performance" (p. 95). For example, when the room temperature gets too cold, the thermostat turns on the heat. Biofeedback uses electronic devices to monitor physiological processes not normally under voluntary control. These processes translate electronically into a visual cue or sound tone allowing the individual to gain voluntary control over internal physiological systems. One controls the external signal by altering internal dynamics. No satisfactory explanation exists. However, the technique is proven useful in helping adults develop control of their own heart rate, blood pressure, electrical activity of the brain, and muscle tension (Brown, 1977; Green & Green, 1977). An excellent review of biofeedback research is reported in *Biofeedback and Self-Control,* published annually by Aldine.

Braud, Lupin, and Braud (1975) report one of the few attempts to use a biofeedback process with children. To reduce muscular activity and tension in a hyperactive boy, a tone sounded when the tensing of the child's forehead muscle group exceeded a certain point. The child was instructed to "keep the tone off" by sitting still and relaxing. Muscular tension and activity decreased both within and across training sessions. As long as he practiced the laboratory techniques, his school and home behavior improved. An improvement of 25–56 months on four subtests of the *ITPA*, school achievement test improvement, and gains in self-confidence and self-concept were also reported. Braud et al. point out, however, that performance deteriorated when parent and school cooperation lagged. In spite of these problems, they judged biofeedback as a very promising technique.

Simpson and Nelson (1974) combine biofeedback, operant conditioning, and relaxation training to help children develop self-control over motor behaviors and maintain attention. Their results warrant continued investigation. Even though biofeedback shows promise, the teacher should use caution in interpreting and discussing the efficacy of the strategy until more studies are done.

Miscellaneous Treatments

Two documented treatments are listed under the categories of *(a)* nutritional factors and *(b)* maturational lag. Hallahan and Cruickshank (1973) report extensively on nutrition and Ross (1976) presents the maturational lag position. Another treatment (but with a minimum of supportive evidence) includes Ott's (1976) suggestion that hyperactivity and learning problems may be partly due to radiation stress from fluorescent lighting. In a similar vein, experiments in which hyperactive children were taught systematic relaxation techniques have been reported as having positive results (Carter & Synolds, 1974; Word & Rozynko, 1974).

IN RETROSPECT

This chapter does not consider all the medical specialities contributing to the area of learning disabilities. Among others, researchers in endocrinology, biochemistry, and genetics have the potential for important treatment breakthroughs. It is the teacher, however, who spends the most time with the LD child. The physician in private practice is not trained and, in most cases, not interested in assuming the major responsibility. Thus, medical knowledge in the day-to-day teaching situation helps but is limited.

In practice, the major task involves "numerous disciplines bringing their skills and expertise to the educator, who in the long run must be the implementer" (Cruickshank, 1977, p. 56). Teachers must be prepared to accept the responsibility of being the "implementer." Acceptance of this role carries the obligation of having some knowledge of the medical specialists and treatments with which professional interaction occurs. More importantly, however, the teacher should be a competent practitioner of the teaching arts and only integrate knowledge from other disciplines to aid better education.

REFERENCES

Adams, R.M., Kocsis, J.J., & Estes, R.E. Soft neurological signs in learning disabled children and controls. *American Journal of Diseases of Children,* 1974, *128,* 614–618.

APA Task Force on Vitamin Therapy in Psychiatry. *Megavitamin and orthomolecular therapy in psychiatry.* Washington, D.C.: American Psychiatric Association, 1973.

Asperheim, M. & Eisenhauer, L. *The pharmacological basis of patient care* (2nd ed.). Philadelphia: W.B. Saunders, 1973.

Ayres, A.J. Patterns of perceptual-motor dysfunction in children: A factor analytic study. *Perceptual Motor Skills,* 1965, *20,* 335–368.

Ayres, A.J. Deficits in sensory integration in educationally handicapped children. *Journal of Learning Disabilities,* 1969, *2,* 160–168.

Ayres, A.J. Improving academic scores through sensory integration. *Journal of Learning Disabilities,* 1972, *5,* 338–343.

Ayres, A.J. Sensorimotor foundations of academic ability. In W.M. Cruickshank & D.P. Hallahan (Eds.), *Perception and learning disabilities in children* (Vol. 2). Syracuse, N.Y.: Syracuse University Press, 1975.

Ayres, A.J. Cluster analyses of measures of sensory integration. *American Journal of Occupational Therapy,* 1977, *31,* 362–366.

Ayres, A.J. Learning disabilities and the vestabular system. *Journal of Learning Disabilities,* 1978, *11,* 18–29.

Ban, T.A. The niacin controversy: The possibility of negative effects. *Psychiatric Opinion,* 1973, *10,* 19.

Barlow, C.F. "Soft signs" in children with learning disorders. *American Journal of Diseases of Children,* 1974, *128,* 605–606.

Barr, M.L. *The human nervous system: An anatomical viewpoint* (2nd ed.). New York: Harper & Row, 1974.

Bateman, B., & Frankel, H. Special education and the pediatrician. *Journal of Learning Disabilities,* 1972, *5,* 178–186.

Bell, A., & Zubek, J.P. Effects of deanol on the intellectual performance of mental defectives. *Canadian Journal of Psychology,* 1961, *15,* 172–175.

Bender, L. *A visual-motor gestalt test and its clinical uses* (Research Monograph No. 3). New York: American Orthopsychiatric Association, 1938.

Benton, C.D. Comment: The eye and learning disabilities. *Journal of Learning Disabilities,* 1973, *6,* 334–336.

Berman, S. How schools drug your children. *Science Digest,* 1976, *79*(4), 72–77.

Betts, E.A. Leaders in education: The one who established the importance of vision to children. *Education,* 1958, *79,* 1–3.

Biofeedback and self-control. Chicago, Ill.: Aldine, published annually.

Boder, E. School failure—Evaluation and treatment. *Pediatrics,* 1976, *58,* 394–403.

Bower, K.B., & Mercer, C.D. Hyperactivity: Etiology and intervention techniques. *The Journal of School Health,* 1975, *45,* 195–202.

Bradley, C. The behavior of children receiving benzedrine. *American Journal of Psychiatry,* 1937, *94,* 577.

Braud, L.W., Lupin, M.N., & Braud, W.G. The use of electromyographic biofeedback in the control of hyperactivity. *Journal of Learning Disabilities,* 1975, *8,* 420–425.

Brown, B.B. *Stress and the art of biofeedback.* New York: Harper & Row, 1977.

Camp, B.W. Current thoughts about learning disabilities. *Journal of the American Medical Women's Association,* 1976, *31,* 433–440.

Campbell, S.B. Mother-child interaction: A comparison of hyperactive, learning disabled, and normal boys. *American Journal of Orthopsychiatry,* 1975, *45,* 51–57.

Carter, J.L., & Synolds, D. Effects of relaxation training upon handwriting quality. *Journal of Learning Disabilities,* 1974, *7,* 236–238.

Conners, C.K. Recent drug studies with hyperkinetic children. *Journal of Learning Disabilities,* 1971, *4,* 476–483.

Conners, C.K., Goyette, C.H., Southwick, D.A., Lees, J.M., & Andrulonis, P.A. Food additives and hyperkinesis: A controlled double-blind experiment. *Pediatrics,* 1976, *58,* 154–166.

Cott, A. Orthomolecular approaches to the treatment of learning disability. *Schizophrenia,* 1971, *3,* 95.

Cruickshank, W.M. Myths and realities in learning disabilities. *Journal of Learning Disabilities,* 1977, *10,* 57–64.

Cruickshank, W.M., & Johnson, G.O. (Eds.). *Education of exceptional children and youth* (2nd ed.). Englewood Cliffs, N.J.: Prentice-Hall, 1958.

Curtis, B., Jacobson, S., & Marcus, E. *An introduction to neurosciences.* Philadelphia: W.B. Saunders, 1972.

Delacato, C.H. *The treatment and prevention of reading problems: The neurological approach.* Springfield, Ill.: Charles C Thomas, 1959.

Delacato, C.H. *The diagnosis and treatment of speech and reading problems.* Springfield, Ill.: Charles C Thomas, 1963.

Delacato, C.H. *Neurological organization and reading.* Springfield, Ill.: Charles C Thomas, 1966.

Denckla, M.B. Research needs in learning disabilities: A neurologist's point of view. *Journal of Learning Disabilities,* 1973, *6,* 441–450.

Denhoff, E. Learning disabilities: An office approach. *Pediatrics,* 1976, *58,* 409–411.

Denhoff, E., Davids, A., & Hawkins, R. Effects of dextroamphetamine on children: A controlled double-blind study. *Journal of Learning Disabilities,* 1971, *4,* 491–498.

Doman, R.J., Spitz, E.B., Zucman, E., Delacato, C.H., & Doman, G. Children with severe brain injuries: Neurological organizations in terms of mobility. *Journal of the American Medical Association,* 1960, *174,* 257–262.

Eisenberg, L. Symposium: Behavior modification by drugs. 3: The clinical use of stimulant drugs in children. *Pediatrics,* 1972, *49,* 709–715.

Eisenberg, L., Conners, C.K., & Sharpe, L. A controlled study of the differential application of out-patient psychiatric treatment of children. *Japanese Journal of Child Psychiatry,* 1965, *6,* 125–132.

Feingold, B.F. *Introduction to clinical allergy.* Springfield, Ill.: Charles C Thomas, 1973.

Feingold, B.F. Hyperkineses and learning disabilities linked to artificial food flavors and colors. *American Journal of Nursing,* 1975, *75,* 797–803. (a)

Feingold, B.F. *Why your child is hyperactive.* New York: Random House, 1975. (b)

Feingold, B.F. Hyperkineses and learning disabilities linked to the ingestion of artificial food colors and flavors. *Journal of Learning Disabilities,* 1976, *9,* 551–559.

Flax, N. *Visual function in dyslexia.* Paper presented at the annual meeting of the American Academy of Optometry, Chicago, 1967.

Flax, N. The eye and learning disabilities. *Journal of the American Optometric Association,* 1972, *43,* 612–617.

Freeman, R.D. Drug effects on learning in children: A selected review of the past thirty years. *Journal of Special Education,* 1966, *1,* 17–44.

Freeman, R.D. Controversy over "patterning" as a treatment for brain damage in children. *Journal of the American Medical Association,* 1967, *202,* 385–388.

Freeman, R.D. Review of medicine in special education: Another look at drugs and behavior. *Journal of Special Education,* 1970, *4,* 377–384.

Garrard, S. Role of a pediatrician in the management of learning disorders. *The Pediatric Clinics of North America,* 1973, *20,* 737–754.

Garrison, F.H. History of pediatrics. In I.A. Abt (Ed.), *Abt-Garrison history of pediatrics.* Philadelphia: W.B. Saunders, 1965.

Gearheart, B.R. *Learning disabilities: Educational strategies* (2nd ed.). Saint Louis: C.V. Mosby, 1977.

Getman, G.N. The mileposts to maturity. *Optometry Weekly,* 1972, *63,* 321–331.

Getz, D.J. *Vision and perception training.* Chula Vista, Calif.: College of Optometrists in Vision Development, 1973.

Goldberg, H.K., & Arnott, W. Ocular mobility in learning disabilities. *Journal of Learning Disabilities,* 1970, *3,* 160–162.

Goldstein, E.H. A multidisciplinary evaluation of children with learning disabilities. *Child Psychiatry and Human Development,* 1974, *5,* 95–107.

Gordon, N. Learning difficulties: The role of the doctor. *Developmental Medicine and Child Neurology,* 1975, *17,* 99–102.

Gray, F. Drugging for deportment. *The Nation,* 1975, *221,* 423–425.

Green, E., & Green A. *Beyond biofeedback.* New York: Delacourt Press, 1977.

Greenspan, S.B. *Research studies of visual and perceptual-motor training.* Duncan, Okla.: Optometric Extension Program, 1971.

Grinspoon, L., & Singer, S. Amphetamines in the treatment of hyperkinetic children. *Harvard Education Review,* 1973, *43,* 515–555.

Hallahan, D.P., & Cruickshank, W.M. *Psychoeducational foundations of learning disabilities.* Englewood Cliffs, N.J.: Prentice-Hall, 1973.

Harley, J.P. *Diet and behavior in hyperactive children: Testing the Feingold hypothesis.* Paper presented at the meeting of the American Psychological Association, Washington, D.C., 1976.

Harley, J.P., Ray, R., Matthews, C.G., Cleeland, C.S., Tomasi, L., Eichman, P., & Chun, R. *Food additives and hyperactivity in children.* Research report presented at the annual meeting of the Nutrition Foundation, Naples, Florida, 1976.

Harris, D. *Children's drawings as measures of intellectual maturity.* New York: Harcourt, Brace, & World, 1963.

Havard, J. School problems and allergies. *Journal of Learning Disabilities,* 1973, *6,* 492–494.

Hentoff, N. Using drugs in classrooms. *Current,* 1971, *126,* 40–45.

Hoffer, A., Osmond, H., & Smythies, J. Schizophrenia: A new approach: II. Results of a year's research. *Journal of Mental Science,* 1954, *100,* 20.

Hogan, G.R., & Ryan, N.J. Evaluation of the child with a learning disorder. *Pediatrics,* 1976, *58,* 407–409.

Kauffman, J.M., & Hallahan, D.P. The medical model and the science of special education. *Exceptional Children,* 1974, *41,* 97–102.

Keeney, A.H. Dyslexia and associated diseases as seen by the ophthalmologist and orthoptist. *American Orthoptic Journal,* 1968, *18,* 98–102.

Keogh, B.K. Optometric vision training programs for children with learning disabilities: Review of issues and research. *Journal of Learning Disabilities,* 1974, *7,* 219–231.

Kershner, J.R. Doman-Delacato's theory of neurological organization applied with retarded children. *Exceptional Children,* 1968, *34,* 411–456.

Kirk, S.A. *Educating exceptional children* (2nd ed.). Boston: Houghton Mifflin, 1972.

Kirk, S.A. Reply to Diane Divoky, *Journal of Learning Disabilities,* 1975, *8,* 318–319.

Knights, R.M., & Hinton, G.G. The effects of methylphenidate (ritalin) on the motor skills and behavior of children with learning problems. *Journal of Nervous and Mental Disease,* 1969, *148,* 643–653.

Kornetsky, C. Psychoactive drugs in the immature organism. *Psychopharmacologia,* 1970, *17,* 105–136.

Krippner, S. On research in visual training and reading disability. *Journal of Learning Disabilities,* 1971, *4,* 66–76.

Ladd, E.T. Pills for classroom peace. *Saturday Review,* 1970, *53*(47), 66–68.

Lapointe, C.M. Token test performances by learning disabled and achieving adolescents. *British Journal of Disorders of Communication,* 1976, *11,* 121–133.

Larsen, S. Learning disabilities and the professional educator. *Learning Disability Quarterly,* 1978, *1,* 5–12.

Lerner, J.W. *Children with learning disabilities* (2nd ed.). Boston: Houghton Mifflin, 1976.

Liberman, R. A criticism of drug therapy in psychiatry. *Archives of General Psychiatry,* 1961, *4,* 131–136.

Lobb, H. Trace GSR conditioning with benzedrine in mentally defective and normal adults. *American Journal of Mental Deficiency,* 1968, *73,* 239–246.

London, P. The end of ideology in behavior modification. *American Psychologist,* 1972, *27,* 913–920.

MacMillan, D. *Behavior modification in education.* New York: Macmillan, 1973.

McConnell, T.R., & Cromwell, R.L. Studies in activity level: VII. Effects of amphetamine drug administration on the activity level of retarded children. *American Journal of Mental Deficiency,* 1964, *68,* 647–651.

Millichap, J.G., Aymat, F., Sturgis, L.H., Larson, K., & Egan, R.A. Hyperkinetic behavior and learning disorders. 3: Battery of neuropsychological tests in controlled trial of methylphenidate. *American Journal of Diseases of Children.* 1968, *116,* 235–244.

Millichap, J., & Fowler, G. Treatment of "minimal brain dysfunction" syndromes. *Pediatric Clinics of North America,* 1967, *14,* 767–776.

Mirel, E., & Solomon, P. Child psychiatry, In P. Solomon & V.D. Patch (Eds.), *Handbook of psychiatry* (2nd ed.), Los Altos, Calif.: Lange Medical Publications, 1971.

Molitch, M., & Sullivan, J. The effect of benzedrine sulfate on children taking the new Stanford achievement test. *American Journal of Orthopsychiatry,* 1937, *7,* 519–522.

Myers, P., & Hammill, D. *Methods for learning disorders* (2nd ed.). New York: John Wiley, 1976.

Neisworth, J.T., Kurtz, P.D., Ross, A., & Madle, R.A. Naturalistic assessment of neurological diagnoses and pharmacological interventions. *Journal of Learning Disabilities,* 1976, *9,* 149–152.

Office of Child Development and the Office of the Assistant Secretary for Health and Scientific Affairs. *Report of the conference on the use of stimulant drugs in the treatment of behaviorally disturbed young school children.* Washington, D.C.: Department of Health, Education, and Welfare, 1971.

Oppé, T.E. Introduction to pediatrics. In V.C. Kelly (Ed.), *Practice of pediatrics* (Vol. 1). New York: Harper & Row, 1975.

Ott, J.N. Influence of fluorescent lights on hyperactivity and learning disabilities. *Journal of Learning Disabilities,* 1976, *9,* 417–422.

Page, J.G., Janicki, R.S., Bernstein, J.E., Curran, C.F., & Michelli, F.A. Pemoline (cylert) in the treatment of childhood hyperkinesis. *Journal of Learning Disabilities,* 1974, *7,* 498–503.

Pauling, L. Orthomolecular psychiatry. *Science,* 1968, *160,* 265–271.

Philpott, W.H., Mandell, M., & von Hilsheimer, G. *Allergic, toxic, and chemically defective states as causes and/or facilitating factors of emotional reactions, dyslexia, hyperkinesis, and learning problems.* Paper presented at the meeting of the Ninth International Conference of the Association for Children with Learning Disabilities, Atlantic City, New Jersey, February 1972.

Randall, R. Drugs for children—Miracle or nightmare? *The Providence Journal,* February, 1972, p. 1.

Reed, J.D. They hunger for success. *Sports Illustrated,* 1977, *46*(10), 65–74.

Richmond, J., & Walzer, S. The central task of childhood—Learning. The pediatrician's role. *Annals of the New York Academy of Sciences,* 1973, *205,* 390-394.

Robbins, M.P., & Glass, G.V. The Doman-Delacato rationale: A critical analysis. In J. Hellmuth (Ed.), *Educational therapy* (Vol. 2). Seattle: Special Child, 1969.

Rose, T.L. The functional relationship between artificial food colors and hyperactivity. *Journal of Applied Behavior Analysis,* 1978, *11,* 439-446.

Ross, A. *Psychological aspects of learning disabilities and reading disorders.* New York: McGraw-Hill, 1976.

Safer, D., Allen, R., & Barr, E. Depression of growth in hyperactive children on stimulant drugs. *New England Journal of Medicine,* 1972, *287,* 217-220.

Schrag, P., & Divoky, D. *The myth of the hyperactive child.* New York: Pantheon Books, 1975.

Silver, L.B. Acceptable and controversial approaches to treating the child with learning disabilities. *Pediatrics,* 1975, *55,* 406-415.

Simpson, D.D., & Nelson, A.E. Attention training through breathing control to modify hyperactivity. *Journal of Learning Disabilities,* 1974, *7,* 274-283.

Smith, A. *Powers of mind.* New York: Random House, 1975.

Spring, C., & Sandoval, J. Food additives and hyperkinesis: A critical evaluation of the evidence. *Journal of Learning Disabilities,* 1976, *9,* 560-569.

Sroufe, L.A. Drug treatment of children with behavior problems. In F. Horowitz (Ed.), *Review of child development research* (Vol. 4). Chicago, Ill.: University of Chicago Press, 1975.

Stone, M., & Pielstick, N.L. Effectiveness of Delacato treatment with kindergarten children. *Psychology in the Schools,* 1969, *6,* 63-68.

Stuart, R.B. *Trick or treatment: How and when psychotherapy fails.* Champaign, Ill.: Research Press, 1970.

Sulzbacher, S.I. Psychotropic medication with children: An evaluation of procedural biases in results of reported studies. *Pediatrics,* 1973, *51,* 513-517.

Trippe, M.J. Educational therapy. In J. Hellmuth (Ed.), *Educational therapy* (Vol. 1). Seattle: Special Child, 1966.

Ullman, L.P., & Krasner, L. (Eds.). *Case studies in behavior modification.* New York: Holt, Rinehart & Winston, 1965.

U.S. Department of Health, Education, and Welfare. *HEW News,* March 19, 1971.

Vuckovich, D.J. Pediatric neurology and learning disabilities. In H. Myklebust (Ed.), *Progress in learning disabilities* (Vol. 1). New York: Grune & Stratton, 1968.

Wade, M.G. Effects of methylphenidate on motor skill acquisition of hyperactive children. *Journal of Learning Disabilities,* 1976, *9,* 443-447.

Walker, S. Drugging the American child: We're too cavalier about hyperactivity. *Journal of Learning Disabilities,* 1975, *8,* 354-358.

Walton, J. *Essentials of neurology* (3rd ed.). Philadelphia: Lippincott, 1971.

Word, P., & Rozynko, V. Behavior therapy of an eleven-year-old girl with reading problems. *Journal of Learning Disabilities,* 1974, *7,* 551-554.

Zulch, K.J. The place of neurology in medicine and its future. In P.J. Vinken & G.W. Bruyn (Eds.), *Handbook of clinical neurology* (Vol. 1). New York: John Wiley & Sons, 1969.

section II

Specific learning disorders

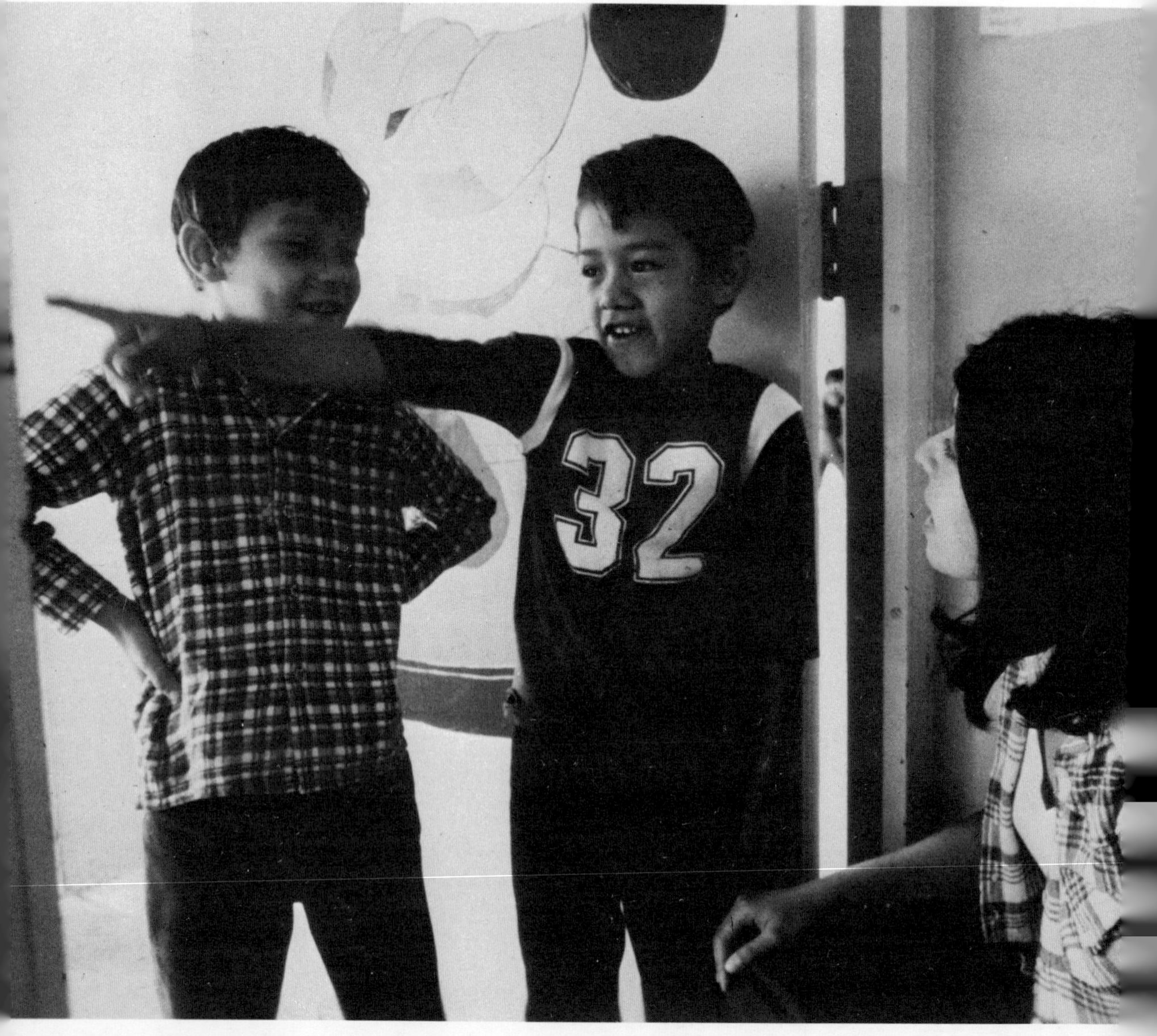
32

6

Language disabilities

Language differentiates humans from lower animals. This elaborate code communicates facts, thoughts, ideas, feelings, and desires. It enhances socialization and thinking and enables us to transmit culture from generation to generation. We can use this tool to speak of unseen events in the past and future. In essence, language allows us to control our environment.

Basic to an understanding of language is the fact that the human brain displays cerebral dominance, allowing lateralization and specification of particular brain functions. The brain's left hemisphere produces and decodes language (Eisenson, 1972). At least 96% of the population, regardless of handedness, process linguistic stimuli in the left hemisphere (Geschwind, 1973).

What is the relationship between language and learning? Vygotsky (1962) theorizes that inner speech is the equivalent of cognition. Numerous writers argue that cognition and language are intricately meshed, each influencing the other (Bruner, Olver, & Greenfield, 1966; Luria, 1961; McNeill, 1970; Piaget, 1952).

Although language is one of the greatest human achievements, little is known about it. All over the world preschool children begin to speak without formal instruction. How they acquire language remains a mystery. Hallahan and Kauffman (1976) write:

> Within the past few years ... an awareness has grown of the need to consider language problems. One of the reasons for this upsurge in interest has probably been the expanding body of knowledge within the field of psycholinguistics. Since the early 1960s many advances have been made concerning normal language development. Until recently, very little was known about language development, particularly language acquisition. (p. 180)

LANGUAGE AND LEARNING DISABILITIES

Historically researchers in learning disabilities have heavily emphasized visual-motor problems, but a concern for language problems is also readily detected. As noted in Chapter 1, the works of Orton (1937), de Hirsch (1952), Johnson and Myklebust (1967), and Kirk (1966) reflect an increasing concentration on language problems. With the shift away from concentration on visual-motor problems, and the advent of increasing work in psycholinguistics, the field of learning disabilities is rapidly becoming more involved with language problems. This emphasis is evident in the NACHC definition (USOE, 1968): "Children with special learning disabilities exhibit a disorder in one or more of the basic psychological processes involved in understanding or in using spoken or written languages" (p. 34). The majority of such individuals have language deficits (McGrady, 1968); Marge (1972) estimates 50%. Language does play a significant role in learning and for many LD students a relationship exists between learning problems and language deficits.

Numerous interrelated factors comprise language and the topic may be examined from several viewpoints. In this chapter information generated from the field of linguistics (the scientific study of the nature of language) and psycholinguistics serves as a primary base for discussing the development, pathology, assessment, and remediation of language deficits. To provide the reader with an initial framework, this chapter presents information in *(a)* theories of language acquisition, *(b)* components of language, *(c)* language disabilities, *(d)* assessment of such disabilities, *(e)* remediation, and *(f)* assessment and remediation of problems in written expression.

THEORIES OF LANGUAGE ACQUISITION

Although several theories offer explanations of language acquisition, most positions fall within three major camps: *(a)* behavioristic, *(b)* nativistic, and *(c)* interactionistic. Table 6.1 summarizes briefly these positions.

The behavioristic position, popularized in Skinner's (1957) book, *Verbal Behavior,* relies on learning principles to explain language acquisition. Other proponents of the behavioristic position include Braine (1971), Jenkins and Palermo (1964), and Staats (1971). The behaviorist believes that the infant begins with no knowledge of language but possesses the necessary underlying mechanisms. The child learns through selected reinforcement of vocal sounds and through reinforcement of imitation. The selected reinforcement of babbling (e.g., parent attention and delight) and the shaping of vocal behavior account for the initial stages of learning. Behaviorists emphasize environmental influences and the universal laws of learning (operant conditioning principles).

Chomsky (1957, 1965) reflects the nativistic position, along with Lenneberg (1964, 1967) and McNeill (1966, 1970). In contrast to the behaviorists, nativists emphasize the role of innate abilities. For example, Chomsky claims that a child possesses an innate capacity for dealing with linguistic universals. He feels the child generates a theory of grammar to help

TABLE 6.1

Language acquisition theories and proponents.

Theory	Proponents
Behavioristic Theory Language is learned through a series of stimulus response chains that are reinforced by the environment. The child is born with underlying mechanisms necessary for language development.	Skinner (1957) Braine (1971) Jenkins & Palermo (1964) Staats (1971)
Nativistic Theory The child is predetermined at birth to learn language. The environment triggers its emergence and the child formulates a theory of grammar based on linguistic universals.	Lenneberg (1964, 1967) Chomsky (1957, 1965) McNeill (1966, 1970)
Interactionistic Theory Language develops as the child passes through a series of developmental stages. The child possesses the innate capacity to learn it but must internalize linguistic structures by the environmental processes of assimilation and accommodation.	Piaget (1960)

understand and produce an infinite number of sentences. Lenneberg believes the child is biologically predisposed to learn language as her brain matures. In the nativistic position, humans are "pre-wired" for language development and the environment simply triggers its emergence.

The major proponent of the interactionistic position, Piaget (1960), theorizes that the child develops language developmentally through the complimentary interaction of her perceptual-cognitive capacities and experience. The child's environmental and neurological maturation determines learning. Language and thought thus develop simultaneously as the child passes through a series of fixed developmental stages requiring progressively more complex strategies of cognitive organization. Interactionists consider language ability to be innate; however, unlike the nativist, the interactionist believes the child must internalize linguistic structures assimilated from the environment and become aware of communication's social functions.

In the early 1960s, theoretical conflicts began (Bloom, 1975). On one hand, the biologists (Lenneberg, 1967) and the linguists (Chomsky, 1965) viewed the child as a product of her own maturation. Barring physical or mental complications, they believed the child's fate is predetermined. This view places heavy emphasis on the child (i.e., she is biologically prepared or linguistically preprogrammed to develop language). In contrast, the behaviorists stressed the influence of the environment. Again, the child's role appears to be a passive one (i.e., development depends largely on which individuals in her environment respond to her behavior). The interactionistic position emphasizes the child's active participation in terms of the *processes* or *strategies* that appear to influence interactions with the environment as she learns to talk (Bloom, 1975). To date, neither theory has unequivocal empirical or theoretical support.

Many researchers today are very actively pursuing questions involving the acquisition and nature of language. As a result, it is likely that the future will hold increased awareness on this topic.

LANGUAGE COMPONENTS

Professionals must understand the major linguistic components if they are to work with

TABLE 6.2

Phonetic feature specification of consonants.

Phonetic Features[b]	Phonetic Segments[a]																										
	p	b	m	t	d	n	k	g	ŋ	f	v	s	z	θ	ð	š	ž	č	ǰ	l	r	w	ʍ	y	h	ʔ
Voiced	−	+	+	−	+	+	−	+	+	+	−	+	−	+	−	+	−	+	+	+	−	+	+	+	−	−
Nasal	−	−	+	−	−	+	−	−	+	−	−	−	−	−	−	−	−	−	−	−	−	−	−	−	−	−
Stop	+	+	+	+	+	+	+	+	+	−	−	−	−	−	−	−	−	+	+	−	−	−	−	−	−	+
Affricate	−	−	−	−	−	−	−	−	−	−	−	−	−	−	−	−	−	+	+	−	−	−	−	−	−	−
Liquid	−	−	−	−	−	−	−	−	−	−	−	−	−	−	−	−	−	−	−	+	+	−	−	−	−	−
Glide	−	−	−	−	−	−	−	−	−	−	−	−	−	−	−	−	−	−	−	−	−	+	+	+	+	+
Sibilant	−	−	−	−	−	−	−	−	−	−	−	+	+	−	−	+	+	+	+	−	−	−	−	−	−	−
Labial	+	+	+	−	−	−	−	−	−	+	+	−	−	−	−	−	−	−	−	−	−	+	+	−	−	−
Alveolar	−	−	−	+	+	+	−	−	−	−	−	+	+	−	−	−	−	−	−	+	−	−	−	−	−	−
Interdental	−	−	−	−	−	−	−	−	−	−	−	−	−	+	+	−	−	−	−	−	−	−	−	−	−	−
Velar	−	−	−	−	−	−	+	+	+	−	−	−	−	−	−	−	−	−	−	−	−	+	+	−	−	−
Glottal	−	−	−	−	−	−	−	−	−	−	−	−	−	−	−	−	−	−	−	−	−	−	−	−	+	+
Palatal	−	−	−	−	−	−	−	−	−	−	−	−	−	−	−	−	+	+	+	−	−	−	−	+	−	−

[a]Examples:
 ŋ = walki*ng*
 θ = (voiceless) e*th*er
 ð = (voiced) ei*th*er
 š = *sh*oe
 č = *ch*ew
 ž = delu*si*on
 ʍ = *wh*istle
 ʔ = *H*ugo

[b]These 13 features explain how and where within the vocal tract each of the 26 English consonant phonemes is produced. The 7 features representing manner of articulation include
1. *Voiced.* The presence of a laryngeal tone.
2. *Nasal.* Sound is directly through the nasal cavities.
3. *Stop.* The flow of air is abruptly interrupted.
4. *Affricate.* Sound is made by forcing air through a narrow constriction.
5. *Liquid.* Some obstruction in the airstream but not enough to cause friction.
6. *Glide.* Sound is determined by movement to or from the vowel with no obstruction of the air flow.
7. *Sibilant.* Friction between two articulators producing a "hissing" noise.

The 6 features representing place of articulation include
1. *Labial.* Lip rounding or lip closure.
2. *Alveolar.* Tongue makes contact with the upper gum region.
3. *Interdental.* Between the teeth.

TABLE 6.2 cont.

4. *Velar.* Tongue makes contact with soft palate.
5. *Glottal.* Sudden release of a pulse of air.
6. *Palatal.* Tongue makes contact with hard palate.

Source: Adapted in part from *An Introduction to Language,* p. 53, by V. Fromkin & R. Rodman. New York: Holt, Rinehart & Winston, 1974. Copyright © 1974 by Holt, Rinehart & Winston, Inc. Reprinted by permission of Holt, Rinehart and Winston.

students who have language problems. These components are phonology, morphology, semantics, syntax, and pragmatics.

Phonology

Phonemes, the smallest existing units of sound, are arranged in various ways to form words. For example, the word *bat* has three phonemes: b/ae/t. Different languages are made up of different sounds, yet there appears to be one universal set of sounds from which all languages draw (Hopper & Naremore, 1973). For example, every language uses the common phonemes /p/, /t/, /k/, /s/, and /n/, while very few languages employ the phonemes /r/ and /l/. According to Jakobson and Halle (1956), common phonemes are the easiest to master because they manifest the greatest articulatory and auditory contrasts. Children all over the world master these sounds first. Phonemes requiring finer distinctions (those which distinguish one language from another) are the most difficult to master and are acquired last.

Distinctive feature analysis compares phonemes. This type of analysis classifies phonemes according to where (i.e., place of articulation) and how (i.e., manner of articulation) they are articulated. All phonemes have characteristic features that differentiate them from other phonemes. As noted in Table 6.2, the distinctive feature system is composed of 13 features that describe the consonant phonemes. A consonant phoneme is classified according to whether this feature is characteristic of that phoneme (+) or not characteristic of that phoneme (−). Fromkin and Rodman (1974) classify vowels according to where they are produced in the mouth (e.g., high, mid, or low; front, central, or back).

The first contrast the child makes is between vowels and consonants. Vowels are produced with no oral obstruction, whereas consonants involve obstructing the flow of air through the mouth. This contrast represents the broadest articulatory and auditory contrast; phonemes acquired after this involve increasingly finer and more subtle contrasts. Thus, the distinctive feature analysis is a process of differentiation and enables the child to learn the sound system feature by feature. It is thought that this process is a more efficient method of acquisition than acquiring each of the 44 sounds in the English language phoneme by phoneme.

Babbling during infancy does not appear to be related to the acquisition of the child's sound system. When the child first starts to use meaningful speech, she begins learning the sound system (Wood, 1976). Active acquisition of the phonological component normally finishes when the child is approximately 6 years old.

Not only must the child learn all the phonemes of her language, but she must also learn the rules that specify how these phonemes can be sequenced to form words. Since phonemes cannot be strung together randomly and still be meaningful, these rules determine which phonemes can end a word, begin a word, or follow another phoneme within a word. Every native "knows" these rules. For example, a native speaker of English would never begin a word with the phoneme sequence *ng,* yet this sequence is permissible at the beginning of words in Vietnamese. There are no English words that consist entirely of consonants and no English words end in the *h* sound of *hat.* Through the use of phonological rules, a child learns how to produce sounds that form meaningful utterances. These rules also allow the language user to apply the appropriate past tense or plural endings to words, to recognize foreign accents, and to know what is or is not a sound in one's own language (Fromkin & Rodman, 1974).

Reading words involves sounding out letters.

Morphology

The morphological component supplies the basic units of meaning in word structure. Morphemes, the smallest units of meaning, are composed of one or more phonemes. A morpheme differs from a syllable in that a morpheme is a meaning-based unit and a syllable is a sound-based unit. For example, the word *unnatural* can only be divided into two morphemes, *un* and *natural.* Any further subdivision of these two morphemes would not result in meaningful units. However, this same word can be divided into four syllables: *un, nat, u, ral.*

Morphemes are two types: free and bound. Free morphemes, which cannot be further subdivided into meaningful units, are considered the base words of language. The words *car, monster, black* and *an* are free morphemes as opposed to the prefixes *pre, anti,* and *un,* which must be attached to free morphemes in order to convey the meaning of a word. These latter morphemes are called *bound morphemes* and include prefixes, suffixes, tenses, and plurals.

Children first acquire free morphemes around 1 year of age. As they learn sounds and the sequences of sounds that form meaningful units, their morphological development expands.

Berko (1958) demonstrated that 1st grade children form rules that specify how morphemes can be sequenced together. Using nonsense words, she found that children could attach the appropriate inflectional endings. For example, she showed the subjects a picture of a fat bird and called it a *wug.* Then she showed them a picture of two birds and the children correctly labeled them as two *wugs.* For past tense endings, she showed a picture of a man "binging" (hitting the ceiling) and said, "Today the man is binging, so yesterday he _____." The children supplied the correct form, *binged.*

Morphemes, especially bound morphemes, require knowledge of meanings. To understand *ing,* the child must know more than the meaning of a simple unit of language; she must be aware of sentence action as an ongoing function. Similarly, she must also know that *ed* signifies that the action occurred in the past. Thus, a child who knows 300 words may actually know more than 300 morphemes and it would be inaccurate to consider the words as the sole evidence of what meanings the child understands. Morphemes are also important components of basic word structure and their appropriate use is vital to the development of the adult meaning system.

Semantics

Semantics supplies the meanings for words and sentences as they relate to ideas, situations, and events. Young children do not always attach the same meanings to words as adults do. Oftentimes the conceptions of children are narrow and generally limited by a lack of experience.

The child acquires her first words through parental reinforcement (Taylor, 1976). Thus, the meanings she attaches to these initial words are primarily determined by the circumstances in which they were uttered and reinforced. Taylor (1976) claims that children acquire only a few words through this process and later semantic acquisition develops through a series of stages. Wood (1976) outlines several stages of semantic acquisition.

Stage One

In the first stage of semantic development, a child gives meanings to words according to the functions they perform. The meanings of these "one-word" sentences are determined by the context in which the utterance occurred. An 18-month-old child may use the word *doggie* quite frequently, but the contexts in which she says it may differ ("There is a doggie," "That is my doggie," "Doggie is barking," "Doggie is chasing a kitty") and imply different meanings. The child is not just labeling her environment; she is actually expressing a sentence-like thought.

Stage Two

In about two years the child begins to produce two-word utterances with meanings related to concrete actions, such as *Doggie bark* or *My doggie*. She conveys more specific information verbally, continuing to expand vocabulary and utterance length. However, until around the age of 7, the child defines words merely in terms of visible actions. For example, to a 6 year old, a *fish* is "a thing that swims in a lake"; a plate is "a thing you eat dinner on." Also, during this stage, the child will typically respond to a prompt word, such as *pretty*, with a word that could follow it in a sentence, such as *flower*. Older children, around 8 years of age, frequently respond with a verbal opposite, such as *ugly* (Brown & Berko, 1960).

Stage Three

At 8 years of age, the child's word meanings relate directly to experiences, operations, and processes. A child whose neighbor owns a horse may include this attribute in her word comprehension of horse, in addition to the attributes of *animal, four-legged,* and *a thing that can be ridden.* When asked where horses live, the child may respond, "At the Kahn's." According to an adult definition, this answer is not correct. Her own experiences define her vocabulary, not those of adults. At 12 years of age, children begin to give "dictionary-like" definitions for words (Wood, 1976). When asked to define *bear,* she might respond, "A large warm-blooded animal that hibernates in the winter." At this time their word definitions approach the semantic level of adults.

Hopper and Naremore (1973) believe that semantic language development is an act of concept development (i.e., the child begins the language-learning task with very broad meanings for words and gradually begins to define words in a more narrow manner by assigning specific attributes to their meanings). Children must also learn which words can logically and realistically follow each other in sentences and convey intended meanings. For example, it would not be semantically correct to say, "The book ate the goldfish."

Acquisition of Specific Semantic Concepts

Children acquire spatial concepts easier and earlier than they acquire concepts related to time (Wood, 1976). Children learn *up–down, in–out,* and *on–off* easiest, in that order. Next they acquire the location terms *above–below* and *over–under* and lastly, visibility terms: *ahead–behind, in front of–in back of.*

Beginning temporal terms are *first–last, early–late,* and *before–after.* Most 5-year-old children know these terms, although some have difficulty with the *before–after* concept (Clark, 1971). For example, the kindergarten child, when told that she will get some ice cream after she finishes her work, frequently persists in asking, "Is it time for ice cream yet?" She does not realize that something has to happen "before" she gets the treat.

Syntax

Syntax specifies the way in which words can be joined together to express intended meanings. These rules account for the grammatical aspects of sentences. For example, they determine the ordering of morphemes, reveal ambiguities, determine the relationship between different parts of a sentence, and enable one sentence to be related to another (Fromkin & Rodman, 1974). In English, meaning is critically determined by the way in which words are strung together. For example, *John hit Mary* does not mean the same thing as *Mary hit John*. Due to the complexity of syntax rules, most children do not master this concept fully until they reach 10 years of age (Wood, 1976). Taylor (1976) adds that for many individuals, syntactic acquisition is a lifelong process.

Wood (1976) outlines six acquisition stages focusing on productive competence (expression) and not on receptive competence (listening comprehension). Most children usually understand more of their language than they can express. In the first stage, the child uses one word to express sentence-like meaning. These words, usually nouns (content words), are used conjointly with body movements and voice intonation to express meaning. Each one-word utterance has a variety of meanings, so adults must rely on the latter two cues and the context of the situation to determine meaning.

Stage Two, the modification stage, occurs around the age of 18 to 24 months. At this time the child begins to understand the basic grammatical relations and starts combining words to form two-word sentences. Her sentences use nouns and a mixture of words from all grammatic classes, for example, *Daddy go, pretty baby,* and *no cookie.*

Stage Three, the structure stage, typically begins when the child is 2 to 2½ years old. Her sentences will contain a subject and a predicate. For example, whereas in Stage Two she would have said *Daddy go,* in Stage Three she says *Daddy is going.*

In Stage Four the child begins to perform operations on sentences. This stage begins sometime after age 2 and continues through the preschool years. She learns to add an element to one of her basic sentences through the process of *conjunction.* For example, *where* can be added to the simple sentence, *Daddy go,* to form a more complex sentence, *Where Daddy go?* The child can also perform the *embedding* operation: the sentence, *No glass break,* becomes *The glass didn't break.* Stage Four also involves *permutation.* Thus she can transform the question, *Man here?* to *Is the man here?* In essence, in this stage the child's utterances become more grammatically correct.

In Stage Five, usually reached by age 5, the child becomes aware that not all words in the same grammatic class have the same attributes. This categorization stage lasts through the early elementary years. For example, plural and singular nouns require the use of different determiners and verbs. All words within a grammatic class can be used in the same position within a sentence, but appropriate selection of words depends upon the grammatic relation one wishes to express. For example, *this* is inappropriate for use in the sentence, *This chairs are heavy.* Appropriate grammatic categorization for expressing plurality requires that the proper determiner (singular or plural) and appropriate verb be used. This same principle applies to prepositional phrases, which can belong to three classes: time, place, or manner. To be grammatically correct, the child must select the appropriate prepositional phrase. For example, the sentence, *We cried to the movie,* is not grammatically correct because an inappropriate prepositional phrase is used. In essence, in this stage the child learns the appropriate semantic attributes of words and assigns these words to the appropriate grammatic classes.

Stage Six, the stage of complex structures, begins around the age of 5 when the child is learning to understand and produce sentences implying a command *(Give me the toy)*, a request *(Please pass the salt),* and a promise *(I promise to stop).* Implied commands are the easiest for children to acquire but are often confused with the requests. The promise verb is very difficult for children to understand (Chomsky, 1969; Kessel, 1970) and, according to Wood (1976), may not be mastered until age 10.

Because the child must form tentative rules about language, syntax is the most complex of all the language components. These rules allow production of an infinite number of sentences, including some not previously heard. She must "try out" these rules by generating sentences and then modifying or altering these rules according to her experiences (e.g., reinforcement). The child's language must be functional; if those around her do not understand her desires, she must change her language rules. However, a problem may occur when the child reaches Stage Five. At this point she usually has enough language to make herself understood, even if her sentences are not grammatically correct. The criterion for reinforcement is usually comprehension, not grammatical correctness; therefore, the child may continue to get reinforced for using incorrect grammar (Taylor, 1976). However, incorrect usage may cause problems in the assignment of appropriate attributes to grammatic classes. Furthermore, a child who does not understand the basic linguistic structures underlying word order encounters serious problems in the comprehension and expression of language.

Pragmatics

Pragmatics supplies the rules of social interaction, which are extremely important for effective communication. Due to the constraints of each communication situation, neither children nor adults speak the same way all the time. Hopper and Naremore (1973) report that the speaker changes speaking style according to five factors that exist in the situational context: *(a)* the people present, *(b)* what has been said before—message, *(c)* the topic being discussed—content, *(d)* the goal of the conversation—task, and *(e)* the time and place—surrounding physical context. Refinement of pragmatics requires many years of experience in speaking situations.

Summary of the Development of Language Components

Language acquisition is indeed complex and involves many cognitive abilities. Although each component of language is outlined in a series of ages and stages (see Table 6.3), not every child follows this exact format. Due to their different environments and genetic endowments, children respond differently to the language-learning situation. How fast a child learns is usually determined by developmental rate rather than by chronological age or mental ability (Wood, 1976). Thus, not every 2 year old will be in Stage Two and not every child will follow the acquisition sequence in the steps outlined. The critical factor is that certain language concepts must be acquired before others.

In general, children grasp language gradually, acquiring its rules, forms, and functions in a pattern. This pattern can be summarized as follows: Essential is acquired before less essential, simple and short are acquired before long and complex, few is acquired before many, concrete is acquired before abstract, gross and distinct are acquired before subtle and fine, isolated items individually are acquired before items in relation, regular is acquired before irregular, forms with more general application are acquired before forms with restricted application, and basic functions are acquired before particular details (Taylor, 1976).

TYPES OF LANGUAGE DISABILITIES

Language disabilities may be categorized in a variety of ways. Many language pathologists refer to them within the framework of an input-integration-output model (Osgood, 1964).

TABLE 6.3

Summary of language development.

Approximate Age	Phonology	Morphology	Semantics	Syntax
12–18 mos.	Contrasts vowels and consonants	First words function as declaratives, interrogatives, and imperatives		Stage I—Holophrastic stage—uses sentence-like word with nonverbal cues and gestures
18–24 mos.			Stage I—Meanings are assigned by the situation context	Stage II—Modification stage—uses patterned speech to express grammar and modifies a topic word with another word
24–30 mos.			Stage II—The child uses two-word sentences, meanings are related to concrete actions, and the length of utterances is expanded but words are still defined by visible actions	Stage III—Structure stage—uses subject-predicate structure
3 yrs.	/b/, /m/, /n/, /f/, /w/, /h/	Builds vocabulary and uses expansions and contractions to produce new words		Stage IV—Operational stage—performs operations such as permutation, conjunction, and embedding to express more complicated relationships

Age	Phonology	Morphology	Semantics/Syntax
4 yrs.	/p/, /d/, /g/, /k/, /y/, /l/, /t/	Compounding—identity, salient features, related features, etymological features	Stage V—Categorization stage—classifies words into grammatic classes
5 yrs.	/v/, /s/, /z/, /š/, /ž/, /č/, /r/	Early bound morphemes—plurals, possessives, verb tenses, present progressive, simple past, third person present, irregular past, future	Stage VI—Complex structure stage—acquires more difficult structures of language, such as *ask*, *tell*, and *promise*
6 yrs.	/j/, /θ/, /ǰ/, /ŋ/	Later bound morphemes—adjective forms, deriving diminutives and agentives	
8 yrs.			Stage III—word meanings are directly related to experiences, operations, and processes
12 yrs.			Child's word definitions have approached the adult semantic level

The speech clinician works with John one period a day.

This model deals with problems in reception or decoding (input), inner language (integration or processing), and expression or encoding (output). The distinction between receptive and expressive abilities is an important one. Some researchers feel that reception is what the child *comprehends,* whereas expression is what the child *produces.* This distinction between comprehension and production is frequently made in discussions of language development, assessment, and remediation. Researchers generally agree that comprehension develops prior to production (Eisenson, 1972; Fraser, Bellugi, & Brown, 1963). The comprehension-production and the input-integration-output areas are readily discernible in a discussion of types of language disabilities organized within the framework of phonology, morphology, semantics, syntax, and pragmatics.

Phonological Problems

LD children frequently exhibit phonological problems involving auditory symbolic units. Many of these problems are manifested in semantics, syntax, morphology, or pragmatics; only close analysis reveals that the child is experiencing difficulty with phoneme discrimination. For example, the child may hear *Go get the nail* when the command was actually *Go get the mail.* She does not respond appropriately because she cannot discriminate between the phonemes /n/ and /m/. A child making phoneme discrimination errors will appear to display deficits in many areas—but the real problem is in the area of phonology.

Consonants

LD children often show a predictable and consistent pattern of errors within the distinctive features framework. Table 6.4 contrasts each of the 26 English consonant phonemes according to Jakobson and Halle's (1956) distinctive-feature analysis. The numbers represent the number of distinctive features not shared by the two phonemes being compared. For example, /p/ and /b/ are differentiated by only one distinctive feature, while /p/ and /j/ are differentiated by five. As previously discussed, LD children exhibit a predictable pattern of errors within the distinctive features framework (i.e., they tend to misperceive phonemes requiring very fine discriminations). Phonemes separated by only one distinctive feature, such as /m/ and /n/ or /p/ and /b/, comprise the majority of the phoneme confusions. Thus, LD children may

TABLE 6.4

Predicted consonant-phoneme error patterns of learning disabled children.

	p	b	m	t	d	n	k	g	ŋ	f	v	s	z	θ	ð	š	ž	č	ǰ	l	r	w	ʍ	y	h	ʔ
p	—																									
b	1	—																								
m	2	1	—																							
t	2	3	4	—																						
d	3	2	3	1	—																					
n	4	3	2	2	1	—																				
k	2	3	4	2	3	4	—																			
g	3	2	3	3	2	3	1	—																		
ŋ	4	3	2	4	3	2	2	1	—																	
f	1	2	3	3	4	5	3	4	5	—																
v	2	1	2	4	3	4	4	3	4	1	—															
s	4	5	6	3	4	4	4	5	6	3	4	—														
z	5	4	5	3	2	3	5	4	5	4	3	1	—													
θ	3	4	5	3	4	5	3	4	5	2	3	3	4	—												
ð	4	4	4	4	3	4	4	3	4	3	2	4	3	1	—											
š	3	5	6	4	5	6	4	5	6	3	4	2	3	3	4	—										
ž	5	4	5	5	4	5	5	4	5	4	3	3	2	4	3	1	—									
č	4	5	6	4	5	6	4	5	6	5	6	4	5	5	6	2	3	—								
ǰ	5	4	5	5	4	5	5	4	5	6	5	5	4	6	5	3	2	1	—							
l	5	4	5	3	2	3	5	4	5	4	3	3	2	4	3	5	4	7	6	—						
r	4	3	4	4	3	4	4	3	4	3	2	4	3	3	2	4	3	7	5	1	—					
w	4	3	4	6	5	6	4	3	4	3	2	6	5	5	4	6	5	8	7	5	4	—				
ʍ	3	4	5	5	6	7	3	4	5	2	3	5	6	4	5	5	6	7	8	5	5	1	—			
y	5	4	5	5	4	5	5	4	5	4	3	5	4	3	5	4	4	3	3	2	5	4	4	3	3	4	—
h	4	5	6	4	5	6	4	5	6	3	4	4	5	3	4	4	5	6	7	5	4	4	3	3	—	
ʔ	3	4	5	3	4	5	3	4	5	4	5	5	6	4	5	5	6	5	6	6	5	5	4	4	1	—

be expected to confuse phonemes that differ by only one or two features as contrasted in Table 6.4. These children would rarely confuse phonemes differing by more than four or five features.

More specific observations (Wiig & Semel, 1976) show that numerous LD children confuse the voiced and unvoiced consonants, such as /p/ for /b/ or /d/ for /t/ and vice versa. The next most frequent type of error occurs between the consonants that differ only in place or manner of articulation. For example, /b/, /d/, /v/, /g/, /z/, and /th/ are often confused with one another.

The child may also have difficulty with the discrimination of initial consonant blends. Some of the most common problems involving blends include

1. /pr/, /fr/, and /kr/ confused with /pl/, /fl/, and /kl/
2. /tr/ and /dr/ confused with /tw/ and /dw/
3. /pr/, /tr/, /kr/, /dr/, /gr/, and /fr/ confused with each other
4. /sp/, /st/, /sk/, /sm/, /sn/, /sl/, and /sw/ confused with each other (Wiig & Semel, 1976)

For the most part the confusion associated with the blends can be predicted according to their place and manner of articulation. Children often mix up /sp/, /st/, and /sk/ with one another; an examination of the distinctive features reveals that /p/, /t/, and /k/ are only separated by two features.

Phoneme discrimination problems occurring with consonant blends can be classified according to error severity (Wiig & Semel,

1976). For example, if the word *train* is misperceived as *pain,* the error is more severe than if *train* is misperceived as *drain.* The confusion between /tr/ and /dr/ involves a finer discrimination than that between /tr/ and /p/. Moreover, a child who confuses words from different grammatic classes (e.g., noun, adjective, verb) within the context of a sentence presents a more serious problem than the child who substitutes words from the same grammatic class. For example, the child who interprets the sentence *The great bell rang loudly* as *The gray bell rang loudly* (adjective confusion) is making a less serious mistake than the child who interprets the sentence as *The great bell rang lunch* (noun for adverb confusion). According to Wiig and Semel (1976), confusion within a grammatic class is easier to remediate than confusion across grammatic classes. Across-class confusion may indicate that the child does not attend to the semantic cues inherent in the sentence. As the number of semantic cues in the sentence increases, the chances of the sentence being inaccurately perceived diminish. For example, *Pour the water in the pail* is not likely to be perceived as *Pour the water in the rail,* whereas the sentence *The cat is gone* could easily be misperceived as *The rat is gone* or *The bat is gone.*

Several investigators (Johnson, 1968; Johnson & Myklebust, 1967) have found that many LD children have a limited ability to conceptualize. Some of these children decode phonemes by contextual cues. Thus, if they have a limited ability to form accurate concepts in the first place, many errors can occur through this type of decoding process. Phonemic analysis should provide the correct analysis and synthesis of semantic categorization within sentences, not vice versa. Thus, LD children must be evaluated for specific phoneme discrimination errors. Such analysis directly applies to reading instruction. Heilman (1976) reports that a child cannot profit from phonics instruction if he is not able to discriminate between the different speech sounds.

Vowels

Vowel discrimination problems primarily involve the front vowels (Wiig & Semel, 1976). For example, a child may have difficulty in discriminating between the words *sit, set,* and *sat* because they all contain front vowels. Also, since vowels can be represented by different graphemes, many auditory-visual problems can arise (e.g., *leave, freeze,* and *elite* all contain the same vowel sound [/ē/] yet have different spellings). These problems are manifested in reading, writing, and spelling. Sometimes children show the reverse of the preceding problem (i.e., one or two graphemes can be used to describe several vowel sounds). For example, the graphemes /ie/ sound differently in the words *die* and *view.* In addition, many English word endings are pronounced similarly but are characterized by different graphemes. By auditory analysis, the words *doctor* and *mother* end with the same vowel-consonant pattern. Thus LD children are confused by vowel discrimination. It is apparent that problems concerning phonemes can cause the child to make many errors in academics as well as in everyday speaking situations.

Morphological Problems

Wiig, Semel, and Crouse (1973) report that many LD children cannot easily form the third person of verbs, possessives, and adjectival inflections. This problem shows a lack of knowledge and use of English morphology (Vogel, 1974; Wiig, Semel & Crouse, 1973). Also, some children cannot process time-related verb tenses. For example, *walked* and *walking* express the past and present, but some LD children can use only the present (Wiig & Semel, 1976). When auxiliary verbs are added to the sentences, such that *I am walking* becomes *I was walking* or *I will be walking,* the child is further confused.

Semantic Problems

Although many LD children develop their vocabularies within the normal range, Wiig and

Semel (1976) report that close analysis reveals a number of problems. For example, these children tend to assign a very narrow set of attributes to each word so that each word has limited meaning. This problem is exemplified when they persist in confusing dual meaning words (e.g., *watch*).

An overhead projector can be used to present vocabulary or math problems.

They also tend to misinterpret sentences that include the *to be* verb (Wiig & Semel, 1976). Phrases that carry the same meaning, such as *the green chair* and *the chair is green* are often not interpreted by LD children as being equivalent. As discussed in the semantics acquisition section, children normally pass through several stages of semantic development before they acquire adult definitions. Since LD children define their words according to the frequency with which the particular words are used, their definition of words may change as a function of their linguistic environment and not as a function of linguistic refinement or maturity. The narrow assignment of attributes to words may also limit the scope of the LD child's definitions and result in her not interpreting the meaning of words that do not conform to "her" dictionary. In general, many learning disabled children assign very gross, broad, functional meanings to their words and do not attend to the subtle and fine semantic features.

Adjectives

Wiig and Semel (1976) offer a suggested hierarchy of difficulty for adjective comprehension by LD children (See Table 6.5). This hierarchy suggests that LD children readily comprehend adjectives that are characterized by gross dimensions, such as size, shape, and color; however, adjectives with less distinctive dimensions (e.g., denoting space, time, seriation) tend to be more difficult. Moreover, numerous investigators (Semel & Wiig, 1975; Wiig & Roach, 1976; Wiig & Semel, 1973, 1974b, 1976) report that such children do not easily comprehend sentences containing a string of adjectives (e.g., *the big, furry, black, wild hunting dog*) or sentences that express comparative relationships (e.g., *Are cars bigger than bicycles?*).

Adverbs

Many LD children have difficulty processing adverbs (Wiig & Semel, 1976). For example, they cannot recall adverbs that are in the final position of a sentence. Usually, because of the recency phenomenon, words in the final position are the most easily recalled; therefore, this deficit must be attributed to a semantic decoding problem and not to memory. Furthermore, Wiig and Semel report that LD children have trouble processing adverbs that end in *ly* (e.g., *swiftly*) and with situationally bound adverbs (e.g., *here, there, somewhere, someplace, sometime*).

Prepositions

Learning disabled children usually easily process prepositions that signify a definite, static position (Wiig & Semel, 1976). They

TABLE 6.5

Suggested hierarchy of difficulty for adjective comprehension by learning disabled children.

Aspect	Adjectives
Color	red, blue, green
Size	big, small, large
Size–Color	big red, small blue, large green
Shape	round, square, oblong
Size–Color–Shape	big red round, small yellow square, large green oblong
Length	long, short
Height	tall, short
Width	wide, narrow, thin
Age	old, young, new
Taste	sweet, sour, bitter
Smell	sweet, pungent, stale
Attractiveness	pretty, ugly, beautiful
Speed	fast, slow
Temperature	hot, cold, tepid
Quality	rough, smooth, hard
Affect	happy, sad, angry
Distance	near, far, distant
Comparatives–	bigger, hotter, nearer
Superlatives	biggest, hottest, nearest

Source: Adapted from *Language Disabilities in Children and Adolescents*, p. 49, by E.H. Wiig & E.M. Semel. Columbus, Ohio: Charles E. Merrill, 1976. Copyright 1976 by Bell & Howell Co. Reprinted by permission.

tend to process one-syllable prepositions better than two-syllable prepositions. In addition, prepositions that denote a position in space or time (e.g., *above–below, in front of–behind*) present further problems.

Pronouns

To comprehend pronouns, the child must abstract and categorize their functions in relation to time and space. All pronouns can be characterized in terms of spatial-temporal features even though the various subclasses of pronouns (personal, demonstrative, interrogative, etc.) are not a homogeneous group (Wiig & Semel, 1976). Specifically, LD children have considerable difficulty with personal pronouns *(I, you, he,* etc.*)*, demonstrative pronouns *(this, these, those)*, indefinite pronouns *(somewhere, someone, something)*, and negative pronouns *(nobody, nothing, no one)*.

Syntactic Problems

LD children may demonstrate particular deficiencies in the processing of syntax (Meier, 1971, Rosenthal, 1970; Semel & Wiig, 1975; Wiig & Roach, 1975; Wiig & Semel, 1976). Obvious deficits include comprehension problems in sentences, sentence repetition, semantic mood, passive sentences, and negation.

Sentence Comprehension

Misunderstanding sentences may reflect a lack of linguistic rule learning and memory deficits (Menyuk & Looney, 1972a, 1972b; Rosenthal, 1970; Semel & Wiig, 1975; Wiig & Roach, 1975). This deficit is quite apparent in the processing of oral syntax. For example, Semel and Wiig (1975) found that on an oral sentence comprehension test LD children experienced the most difficulty in discriminating

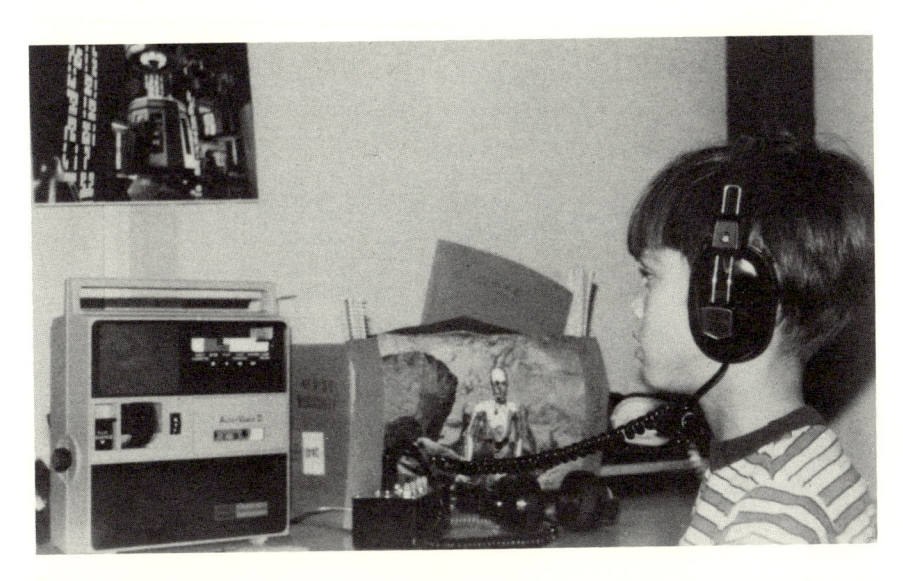

This boy practices sentence comprehension by listening to instructional tapes.

between *who* and *what,* question and statement, *this* and *that,* and direct and indirect objects in sequence. In addition, these children could not recall critical verbal elements located in the middle of a sentence.

Sentence Repetition

Using Newcombe and Marshall's (1967) experimental sentence test, Wiig and Roach (1975) found that LD adolescents made significant quantitative reductions in the immediate repetition of sentences. These reductions were predominantly characteristic of four types of sentences.

The first type included sentences that were syntactically correct but contained semantically inappropriate words. For example, when repeating the sentence, *Colorless green ideas sleep furiously,* 9 of 30 subjects omitted from one to three words. Five substituted the adverb *quietly* for the adverb *furiously* and the noun *ideas* for the noun *dreams* and changed the verb tense of *sleep* from present to past, such that their sentence became *Colorless green dreams slept quietly.* In contrast, none of the 30 control subjects produced such a sentence.

The second type of sentence comprehension error occurred with sentences containing correctly or incorrectly sequenced modifier strings. For example, when asked to repeat the sentence, *She has bought five large, brown leather cases,* 12 of the 30 subjects omitted the size adjective, 1 substituted a size adjective, and 4 changed the modifier sentence to read *five brown, large leather cases.* In comparison, 3 controls omitted the size adjective and 3 changed the sequence of the adjectives. Thus, the major area of discrepancy for the LD adolescents was the omission of one of the adjectives.

Sentences consisting of random word strings presented a third type of processing problem. For example, when asked to repeat the sentence, *Walk some by hand of clearly table very,* only 5 LD subjects did so correctly compared to 13 control subjects.

Syntactically complex sentences were the fourth type of problem sentences. For example, when asked to repeat the sentence, *The sky that the dream thought jumped cheaply,* 9 LD adolescents made substitution errors and 7 omitted one, two, or three words. In contrast, only 3 controls omitted a word and 1 made a substitution error.

In general, the results of this study indicate that the LD adolescents primarily made substitution and omission errors. The control subjects tended to "normalize" syntactically or semantically incorrect sentences. Very few LD subjects exhibited this tendency, which suggests that they were not coding the information in terms of linguistic structure.

Comprehension of Semantic Mood

Many LD children cannot comprehend syntactic mood (i.e., inferences of obligations signified by the auxiliary verbs *must, have to,* and *ought*) (Wiig & Semel, 1976). In general, they cannot discriminate the difference between sentences of this type. This problem is further complicated with the addition of tense and aspect. For example, they may respond similarly to the sentences *I will be going, I will go, I will probably go, I may go, I think I will be going, I think I may go, I think I might go,* and *I might go.*

Comprehension of Passive Sentences

Errors in the comprehension of passive sentences are characterized by a reduced ability to analyze and synthesize subject-object relationships simultaneously and delays in the growth of cognition and logic (Wiig & Semel, 1976). This type of error pattern is observed when an LD child is asked to process sentences containing two pronouns. For example, the reversible passive sentence, *She was kicked by him,* contains two pronouns, *she* and *him,* and either pronoun could have been the actor. Thus, no semantic cues are available to assist in the processing. On the other hand, the irreversible passive sentence, *The ball was kicked by Jane,* contains semantic cues that determine who kicked what (i.e., the ball could not kick Jane). When the actor is not mentioned in the sentence, the child has further difficulty. For example, the child may interpret the sentence, *Mail is delivered every day,* as *I get mail every day* (Wiig & Semel, 1976).

Comprehension of Negation

Wiig and Semel (1976) observed that LD children have a hard time processing sentences with certain features of the negated aspect. Children process the more obvious negated elements more easily than those requiring finer discriminations. The features include *(a)* saliency of the negated aspect, *(b)* proximity and sequence of the negated aspect, and *(c)* logical complexity of the negated aspect. First, a salient negated aspect is more easily understood than other types of negated aspects. *The truck is not brown* is an example of a salient negated aspect. Second, children comprehend negated elements referring to proximity and sequence easier than negations of logical complexity. *The truck is not in the garage* is an example of a negative aspect related to proximity; *The car is not bigger than the truck* is an example of a negative aspect involving the logical complexity of a comparison between two objects.

Pragmatic Problems

How LD children handle pragmatics has not been investigated. However, as previously reported, they typically have difficulty comprehending linguistic cues that require fine discriminations. Thus, many appear to function quite well with language when it is presented in concrete terms that do not require interpretations, inferences, comparisons, or attention to underlying cues. Because elements are basic to the appropriate social use of language, it is likely that many LD children manifest deficiencies with regard to pragmatics. Specifically, these children probably do not perceive the situational cues surrounding the communicative function. For example, Joni walks into a room where her mother is talking on the phone. In a loud voice, she asks her if she can go out and play. Her inappropriate loudness could indicate her failure to understand that her mom is involved in an activity incompatible with listening and responding to her.

Many LD children exhibit problems in interpreting the nonverbal aspects of social situations (Johnson & Myklebust, 1967; Wiig & Harris, 1974; Wiig & Semel, 1976). These children move inappropriately in space, stand

Assessment of Phonological Skills

Before phonological testing, evaluate the child for hearing problems. Although hearing impairments may not be apparent, some children may not accurately hear speech sounds at certain frequencies. A routine audiological examination includes an assessment of hearing ability at different frequencies and determines whether or not the child can localize speech sounds (i.e., tell the direction from which the sound is coming). Since the phonological component of language requires good listening skills, attention skills, and the ability to discriminate between phonemes, it is feasible to divide phonological assessment into the areas of auditory attention, auditory figure-ground, and auditory discrimination.

Auditory Attention

Tests included in this category determine the child's ability to attend to relevant stimuli and sustain this attention with and without the presence of distracting stimuli. Kornetsky and Eliasson (1969) adapted the *Continuous Performance Test* (Rosvold, Mirsky, Sarason, Bransome, & Beck, 1956) by using auditory stimuli to assess auditory attention. In this test the target auditory stimuli are present randomly among other stimuli and the listener is required to respond only to the target stimulus.

One can easily devise procedures for assessing auditory attention. The following guidelines are helpful:

1. Make sure the target auditory stimuli are within the child's comprehension level.
2. Present the target auditory stimuli randomly among other auditory stimuli.
3. Require an immediate and simple response each time the target auditory stimuli are presented.
4. Record the correct responses.

Following these guidelines, a sample informal procedure for assessing auditory stimuli is presented.

Tom doesn't understand how to communicate well with his classmates.

too close to people, misinterpret directional gestures, bump into objects and people, talk at the wrong times, and break into closed groups (Wiig & Semel, 1976). Naturally, such children are often annoying to peers, teachers, and other individuals; frequently they are socially rejected. Although these behaviors are generally considered to be nonverbal aspects of communication, they overlap with pragmatics.

ASSESSMENT OF LANGUAGE ABILITIES

When assessing the language abilities and disabilities, a variety of formal and informal measures must be used. No one test can provide a valid profile. Unfortunately, the testing procedure is often time consuming. Many tests also require considerable training before they can be administered, scored, and interpreted correctly. Even though there is an abundance of standardized tests available for the assessment of language disabilities (see Appendix A) teachers should choose with care and interpret results with caution.

A. Determine the child's comprehension level of the target stimuli by having her select a picture denoting the meaning of the word when she hears it.

For example:
1. Hear *apple*
   Point to picture of apple.
2. Hear *banana*
   Point to picture of banana.
3. Hear *peach*
   Point to picture of peach.
4. Hear *grape*
   Point to picture of grape.
5. Hear *pear*
   Point to picture of pear.
6. Hear *grapefruit*
   Point to picture of grapefruit.
7. Hear *orange*
   Point to picture of orange.

Criterion: 6/7 correct for use as target auditory stimuli.

B. Record these items randomly dispersed among other one-word items. Have the child raise her hand each time she hears one of the target words. A sample tape might include "city, car, *grape, banana*, bicycle, red, yellow, *peach*, happy, *apple*, baseball, vanilla, *orange*, boat, ball, building, *pear, grapefruit*, water, fish, *orange*."

Criterion: Correctly identifies 90% of the target stimuli by raising hand.

Record Performance: 6/8 correct.

Modifications: The target stimuli may vary from a nonsense sound to high-interest content. The target stimuli may include sentences that contain a certain dimension (e.g., color, a specific word, place, activity). Finally, the rate of presentation may be varied.

Auditory Figure-Ground

Tests designed to measure this ability determine how well a child can attend to the relevant language stimuli in the presence of competing environmental noise. An excellent test for this type of analysis is the *Goldman-Fristoe-Woodcock Test of Auditory Discrimination* (Goldman, Fristoe, & Woodcock, 1970). This test features an *Auditory Discrimination Noise* subtest (cafeteria noise used as background noise) and an *Auditory Discrimination Quiet* subtest.

Informal procedures for assessing auditory figure-ground may be similar to the procedures used for assessing auditory attention. The major modification involves presenting the auditory stimuli with and without background sounds. For example, background music, nonlinguistic music, and/or linguistic sounds may be used as background sound when making the tapes.

Auditory Discrimination

Several tests measure auditory discrimination but only those which have particular merit for the assessment of children with learning disabilities are discussed. Tests measuring this ability should reveal specific phoneme discrimination errors and/or phoneme sequencing deficits. The *Goldman-Fristoe-Woodcock Test of Auditory Discrimination* provides a format for analyzing phoneme error patterns

In this programmed auditory perception activity, Marcia is listening to a record that gives instructions for marking a worksheet. After each direction, she must choose the correct color crayon and make the right mark in the proper place on the sheet.

in terms of their distinctive features. This type of analysis often reveals the fine discrimination problems characteristic of many LD children.

The *Travis-Rasmus Speech Sound Discrimination Test* (Travis & Rasmus, 1931) and the *Short Test of Sound Discrimination* (Templin, 1943) also analyze phoneme error patterns in terms of the distinctive features framework. These tests differ from the *Goldman-Fristoe-Woodcock Test of Auditory Discrimination* because they feature nonsense sounds. Because nonsense words do not evoke any semantic connotations, the child has no undue aid.

The *Stanford Diagnostic Reading Test* (Karlsen, Madden, & Gardner, 1966) has five subtests that measure aspects of auditory perception: *(a) Auditory Discrimination, (b) Beginning and Ending Sounds, (c) Sound Discrimination, (d) Blending,* and *(e) Syllabication.* The *Auditory Discrimination* subtest provides an extensive analysis of phoneme error patterns in terms of location, type, consistency, and severity. This subtest assesses vowels and blends as well as consonants. The *Beginning and Ending Sounds* subtest requires the child to identify the beginning and ending sounds of words. Errors in identification should be analyzed separately although the scoring manual puts scores together to yield a grade equivalent. The grade equivalent is not as important as the analysis of the particular mistakes the child makes. For example, the child could be making only one type of feature discrimination error which causes her to achieve a very low score. The *Sound Discrimination* subtest assesses discrimination of all the vowels, diphthongs, and consonants by requiring the child to identify phonemic elements based on visual-symbolic input. The *Blending* subtest provides specific data on the errors pattern concerned with which clusters of phonemes are consistently confused and which initial or final segments are consistently omitted or confused. The *Syllabication* subtest requires the child to identify the first syllable boundary in one, two, or three-syllable words that are presented visually. This test provides useful data about the child's reauditorization ability.

If these standardized tests are not available, or if the child cannot be assessed by the assessment specialist for a number of weeks, Stephens (1977) suggests an informal measure for assessing auditory discrimination. This test assesses the extent to which the child can distinguish one sound from another.

1. Select material that is within the examinee's listening comprehension.
2. Set a criterion level below which performance is inadequate.
3. Pronounce the material one unit at a time; tell him or her to repeat exactly what you say.
4. Note inaccuracies in pronunciation. (p. 162)

If it is suspected that the child is having difficulty with the discrimination of particular phonemes, an informal measure can be used. First, a list is developed of CVC (consonant, vowel, consonant) words that begin or end with the phonemes to be tested. Then the examiner says the words one at a time and asks the child to repeat them. For example, if the teacher suspects that the child may be confusing the phonemes /p/ and /b/, the following list of words could be used for the assessment.

initial position	final position
pat	tab
den	cup
dad	cub
pen	tap
bat	rip
pit	sab
big	rib
pib	sad
bit	mop
bad	mob

These words could also be presented as word pairs, such as *pen–ben,* and the child could be asked to tell whether the words were the same or different.

Assessment of Morphological Skills

Only a few tests exist that assess morphology. These tests assess knowledge of word formation and the application of this knowledge in determining word meaning. Three commonly used tests for assessing morphology are *(a)* the *Berko Experimental Test of Morphology* (Berko, 1958), *(b)* the *Grammatic Closure* subtest of the *ITPA* (Kirk, McCarthy, & Kirk, 1968), and *(c)* the *Michigan Picture Language Inventory* (Lerea, 1958; Wolski, 1962).

The *Berko Experimental Test of Morphology* assesses the child's knowledge of noun plurals, past tenses, singular possessives, plural possessives, derivation, third-person singular of verbs, adjectival inflections, progressive tense, and compounding. Wiig, Semel, and Crouse (1973) found that this test distinguished between high-risk, learning disabled, and normal children. The test, although not commercially available, is easily developed from Berko's (1958) description of the items. There are no normative data but the test results are easy to analyze in terms of each child's particular pattern of errors.

The *Grammatic Closure* subtest of the *ITPA* is like the *Berko Test* in areas covered. In addition, it assesses the use of adjectives, adverbs, prepositions, and pronouns. Newcomer, Hare, Hammill, and McGettigan (1975) found that this test maintains a close correlation with tests of reading and writing ability.

The *Michigan Picture Language Inventory* assesses the rules for singular and plural nouns, personal pronouns, possessives, adjectives, demonstratives, articles, adverbs, prepositions, and verbs. Due to the test's detail and design it is highly informative.

Informal Test of Morphology

An informal test of specific morphological rules is easily developed by following the design of the *Berko Test*. For example, an assessment of the child's knowledge of plural nouns consists of questions patterned after the Berko format. The child should be told that she will be required to fill in the blank with the appropriate word. This test can be given verbally using nonsense or real words. The same format could be used for the assessment of singular possessives.

Examiner: Yesterday I saw one thing on the porch but today I saw five. So, today I saw five _____.

Child: Things.

Examiner: This coat belongs to John. So, the coat is _____.

Child: John's.

Examiner: This is John's coat. So, the coat belongs to _____.

Child: John.

Many different types of questions can be generated depending on what particular rule or class of words the examiner wishes to evaluate.

Assessment of Semantic Skills

An understanding of semantics is essential to those assessing the language of young children. As discussed previously, it is believed that children do not acquire adult meanings until around the age of 12. This information helps examiners to interpret children's answers in a more meaningful way. Also, it is known that many children do not give verbal opposites in response to a prompt word before age 8; therefore, this type of item for young children appears questionable unless the tester is certain the child understands the demands of the task. Moreover, examiners need to consider that many older children from age 8 to 12 explain the world in terms of their own experiences. It is impossible for anyone to know what each child has experienced and, consequently, an answer that may be wrong in terms of a test may be perfectly valid in terms of the child's experiences.

Much of the research about semantics was conducted in the 1970s. Most language assessment tests were published before 1970.

Newer tests incorporating recent findings are needed.

Semantics includes concept formation, categorization, associations, definitions, logical relationships, verbal problem solving, and cause-effect relationships (Guilford, 1967). No one test provides specific information on all of these abilities. Thus, it is usually feasible to select a few target areas for a detailed assessment. The following tests provide specific information in a variety of semantic skill areas.

The *Peabody Picture Vocabulary Test* (Dunn, 1965) assesses receptive knowledge of words and concepts pinpointing specific vocabulary problems. On each item, the child is required to select a picture that matches the word the examiner orally presents. The words are mostly nouns but some verbs and adjectives are included.

The *Boehm Test of Basic Concepts* (Boehm, 1970) deals with concepts of quantity and number, space, and time. The child must select a picture representing the stimulus word that is presented orally.

The *Botel Reading Inventory* (Botel, 1970) contains a *Word Opposites: Reading Listening* subtest, which assesses the child's knowledge of verbal opposites. This subtest features a multiple-choice format. The results permit identification of specific vocabulary problems.

The *Auditory Association* subtest of the *ITPA* (Kirk, McCarthy, & Kirk, 1968) assesses the child's ability to comprehend verbal analogies. In order to understand verbal analogies, the child must have good knowledge of verbal opposites, logical relations, and verbal associations (Wiig & Semel, 1976). This global aspect of the test requires that its results be corroborated with data from other tests in order to specify problem areas. Wiig, Lapointe, and Semel (1975) report that scores from this subtest correlated positively with receptive vocabulary scores on the *Peabody Picture Vocabulary Test* and with scores from the comprehension of syntactic structures section of the *Northwestern Syntax Screening Test* (Lee, 1971). In addition, they report findings that suggest that poor performance by LD children on verbal analogies may persist into adolescence.

The *Wiig-Semel Test of Linguistic Concepts* (Wiig & Semel, 1973, 1974a, 1974b) evaluates the child's knowledge of linguistic concepts that require logical operations. The conceptual relations assessed include comparative, passive, spatial, familial, and temporal-sequential. For example, to assess comparisons, the teacher asks, "Are jets slower than turtles?" To all questions, the child responds yes or no. According to Wiig and Semel, this test differentiates learning disabled children from their age peers.

The *Detroit Tests of Learning Aptitude* (Baker & Leland, 1959) contains the *Likenesses and Differences* subtest, which assesses the child's ability to identify and classify concepts and objects. The child must tell how things are alike and different (e.g., morning and afternoon) and each response is scored on a four-point scale.

Informal tests are useful in assessing morphological skills.

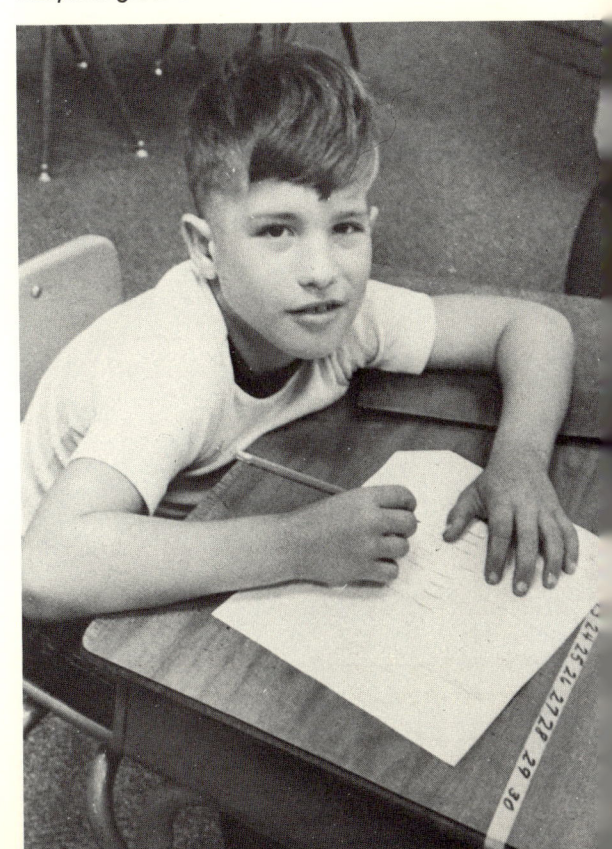

Specific learning disorders

Informal Assessment of Semantic Skills

Because of the complex nature of the tasks assessing semantics, informal testing procedures may be difficult to devise (e.g., in the areas of logical relationships, cause-effect relationships, and verbal problem solving). For areas such as verbal opposites, basic concept formation, word definitions, and categorization, informal testing is very appropriate.

For the assessment of the basic concepts, Milton Bradley Company manufactures a set of cards (Space Relationship Cards) that display a pictorial representation of 22 basic concepts. Each card illustrates two concepts (e.g., a large tree and a small tree). The examiner can ask the child to point to the large tree and the response can be recorded on a checklist (See Table 6.6). For another informal device, these cards can be cut in half so the child can pair them with their opposite.

An assessment of attribute assignment and concept formation can be performed with colored shapes. For example, ask the child to perform a series of graduated tasks. Given a box of assorted designs of various shapes, sizes, and colors, the child should (a) find a square, (b) find a red square, (c) find a large red square, and (d) find three large red squares.

Assessment of Syntactic Skills

In a study with LD adolescents, Semel and Wiig (1975) found a positive correlation between syntactic deficits and low academic achievement. Thus, the assessment of syntax usage provides a specific analysis of the child's particular types of grammatical errors and should be included in a language evaluation.

Some tests helpful in assessing syntax are the *Assessment of Children's Language Comprehension* (*ACLC*) (Foster, Giddan, & Stark, 1972), the *Northwestern Syntax Screening Test* (*NSST*) (Lee, 1971), and the

TABLE 6.6

Basic concept assessment with Milton Bradley Space Relationship Cards.

Concept	Right	Wrong	Concept	Right	Wrong
1. here–there			10. wide–narrow		
2. left–right			11. short–tall		
3. off–on			12. big–little		
4. right–left			13. down–up		
5. thin–thick			14. in–out		
6. go–come			15. near–far		
7. to–from			16. top–bottom		
8. back–front			17. around–through		
9. over–under			18. high–low		
TOTAL SCORES					

Token Test (DeRenzi & Vignolo, 1962). The *ACLC* evaluates the child's ability to process critical verbal elements and identifies the parts of speech and speech sequences that are causing the child difficulty. The *ACLC* can serve as an instructional model (Van Etten & Watson, 1977). For example, the teacher begins with vocabulary and gradually adds combinations with syntactic elements. Furthermore, Semel and Wiig (1975) have found that the *ACLC* identifies receptive language deficits.

The *NSST* evaluates knowledge of linguistic rules, simultaneous analysis and synthesis of syntactic elements, and auditory memory. In it, the child must process, interpret, and recall syntactic structures of increasing difficulty. This test differentiates LD adolescents from their peers (Semel & Wiig, 1975).

The *Token Test* measures the ability to process commands. Beginning with a simple verb-subject format, it increases in difficulty by adding modifier strings, particles, complex syntactic structures, and compound oral commands. This test identifies subtle receptive language deficits (Lapointe, 1975).

Informal Measures of Syntax

Depending on the specific skill that the examiner desires to assess, many different informal measures can be devised. A tape-recorded sample of the child's language provides initial data. To elicit the language sample, show the child some pictures of people or animals in action (e.g., a mother tying a boy's shoe). Ask the child questions about what is happening in the picture. Twenty sentences may provide sufficient data to analyze gross syntactic errors. A profile of syntax usage is presented in Table 6.7. Analyze the sample in terms of syntactic word omissions, criticial verbal elements, word substitutions, or failure to apply the appropriate linguistic rules (plurality, tense, etc.).

Assessment of Pragmatic Skills

No standardized test now exists to specifically assess pragmatics. Wiig and Semel (1976) recommend six tests for the assessment of social perception skills in children. They are (a) the *Bender-Gestalt Test for Young Children* (Bender, 1938), (b) *Wechsler Intelligence Scale for Children (WISC): Object Assembly* (Wechsler, 1949), (c) *WISC: Block Design*, (d) *WISC: Picture Arrangement*, (e) *Detroit Tests of Learning Aptitude: Memory for Designs* (Baker & Leland, 1959), and (f) the *Vineland Social Maturity Scale* (Doll, 1947). These tests discern how well the child perceives fine nonverbal cues or attends to social aspects of communication.

An informal assessment of pragmatics could provide situation-specific information. For example, a child may be shown a picture of an angry woman talking to a child next to a broken window. Then the examiner asks questions:

1. What has happened?
2. What is going to happen?
3. What is the woman saying?
4. What is the child saying?
5. Where is the conversation taking place?

Another example could be a picture of a classroom with a teacher who is talking in front of a group of children. The child is asked:

1. Who is talking?
2. Should anyone be listening?
3. Where was the picture taken?

Examples of this latter type may be useful to teachers who have students who are rude in group situations (i.e., they are constantly interrupting others or are responding inappropriately to verbal situations). These children may not be perceiving the situation accurately.

TABLE 6.7

Profile of syntax usage.

Sample elicitation procedure:	Verbs		Pro-nouns		Words							Sen-tences		
	Agreement	Tense	Possessive pronoun usage	Personal	Additions pronoun usage	Omissions	Substitutions	Modifiers	Negatives	Plurals		Incomplete	Complete	Totals

Date: _____

Students' names:

Thus, the problem may not be due to a lack of manners or respect; they may simply be unable to assimilate the environment within the proper context.

Illinois Test of Psycholinguistic Abilities

Although the *ITPA* (Kirk, McCarthy, & Kirk, 1968) is not designed according to the components of language featured in this chapter, its widespread use in LD warrants coverage of the test. This section discusses the test in terms of purpose, model, usage, research, and training programs.

Purpose

The *ITPA* was the first tool specifically designed for the assessment of a child's intraindividual differences (i.e., it focuses on comparing a child's development to herself). It also presents normative data for the comparison of interindividual differences (i.e., how the child compares with her peers). Its authors postulate that the data generated from the test allow the teacher to plot the child's strengths and weaknesses. This profile of strengths and weaknesses, in turn, suggests specific teaching strategies that match the child's learning characteristics.

The Model

Although it is primarily based on Osgood's (1957) two-dimensional model of language, it is not exactly parallel. However, both are concerned with language transmission processes and levels of mental organization. In addition to the two categories in Osgood's model, the model used for the *ITPA* includes a third category, channels of communication. (See Table 6.8.)

Using this model, the authors formulated 12 psycholinguistic constructs and developed a subtest for each of the constructs. These subtests are summarized in the following list.

Representational Level

1. *Auditory Reception.* Assesses the understanding of simple questions that are presented auditorially. For example, the examiner may ask, "Do dogs fly?" and the child must respond *yes* or *no.* (Reception process; auditory-vocal channel.)
2. *Visual Reception.* Evaluates the ability to associate concepts from a visual stimulus. For example, the child is presented with a picture of a boy running. Then she is presented with a second page displaying four pictures with one of the pictures showing a boy running. She must select the correct picture. (Reception process; visual-motor channel.)
3. *Auditory Association.* Assesses the ability to relate concepts that are presented auditorially. For example, the child may hear the sentence, "Soup is hot and ice cream is _____." She must supply the correct word, *cold.* (Association process; auditory-vocal channel.)
4. *Visual Association.* Measures the ability to relate concepts through the visual channel. For example, the child is shown a picture of a dog, which is in the middle of four other pictures displaying objects. The child must find the object that goes with the dog (e.g., a bone). (Association process; visual-motor channel.)
5. *Verbal Expression.* Assesses knowledge of the attributes of several common objects that are presented visually. After being shown an object, she must tell everything she knows about it. (Expression process; auditory-vocal channel.)
6. *Manual Expression.* Evaluates the ability to express ideas through gestures. The child must show through pantomime how an object (such as a guitar) is used. (Expression process; visual-motor channel.)

Automatic Level

1. *Visual Closure.* Measures the ability to complete a visual stimulus. The child must find partially hidden objects in an incomplete picture. For example, the examiner shows the child a picture of several dogs and then asks her to look at the rest of the

TABLE 6.8

Dimensions of the ITPA *model.*

Levels of Organization	Channels of Communication	Psychological Processes
Representational level (symbolic learning)	Auditory-vocal (auditory input—vocal output)	Reception process (input of information)
Automatic level (habituated responses)	Auditory-motor (auditory input—motor output)	Association process (organization and integration of information)
	Visual-vocal (visual input—vocal output)	Expression process (output of information)
	Visual-motor (visual input—motor output)	

This boy is examining objects on the Verbal Expression subtest of the ITPA.

picture and see how many more dogs she can find. (Association process; visual-motor channel.)

2. *Grammatic Closure.* Assesses knowledge of syntactic and morphologic rules. The examiner shows a visual stimulus and tells the child, "Here is a dog. Now here are two _____." The child should respond with *dogs.* (Association process; auditory-vocal channel.)

3. *Auditory Closure.* Evaluates the ability to complete a stimulus word that is presented auditorially. For example, if the examiner says the word *cho olate,* omitting the /k/ sound, the child must say the complete word, *chocolate.* (Association process; auditory-vocal channel.)

4. *Sound Blending.* Requires the ability to segment and resynthesize phonemic elements. The examiner presents each phonemic segment of a word at half-second intervals, such as *b–oo–k.* The child must respond with the correct word, *book.* (Association process; auditory-vocal channel.)

5. *Auditory Sequential Memory.* Evaluates the ability to repeat a sequence of digits presented auditorially. For example, the teacher presents the digit string 2–5–7 and requires the child to reproduce this sequence exactly. (Association process; auditory-vocal channel.)

6. *Visual Sequential Memory.* Assesses the ability to recall meaningful sequences of objects presented visually. For example, the examiner displays a sequence of symbols for 5 seconds and requires the child to reproduce the sequence exactly using chips provided for the task. (Association process; visual-motor channel.)

Table 6.9 displays the 12 subtests according to the three dimensions. Note that the test does not use the visual-vocal or auditory-motor channels even though these channels are in the model.

TABLE 6.9

ITPA subtests categorized according to dimensions.

Levels and Channels	Reception	Psychological Processes Association	Expression
Representational Level Auditory-Vocal Visual-Motor	Auditory Reception Visual Reception	Auditory Association Visual Association	Verbal Expression Manual Expression
Automatic Level Auditory-Vocal		Grammatic Closure Auditory Closure Sound Blending Auditory Sequential Memory	
Visual-Motor		Visual Closure Visual Sequential Memory	

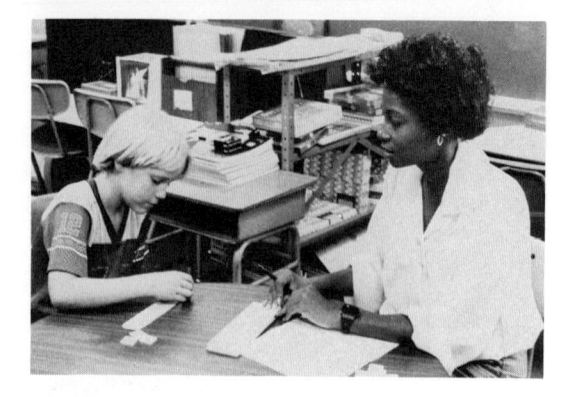

A student completes the Visual Sequential Memory subtest of the ITPA.

Usage

The *ITPA* assesses specific psycholinguistic abilities in children ranging in age from 2–10 years. The test data can be interpreted with four types of scores: *(a)* raw data, *(b)* psycholinguistic age, *(c)* scaled score, and *(d)* estimated IQ score. Its authors recommend the use of scaled scores for analyzing the strengths and weaknesses of individual learners. *ITPA* subtest scores enable the examiner to compare a child's overall psycholinguistic abilities to her abilities in specific psycholinguistic areas. A child with no particular difficulties would score equally in all 12 areas of the test and thus would present a very flat profile. Kirk and Kirk (1971) found that five disability patterns comprise the subtest profile:

1. Channel deficits in which all (or most) of the subtests in the auditory-vocal channel or the visual-motor channel are below those in the other channel.
2. Channel deficits at only one level, e.g., if auditory and vocal tests at the representational level or at the automatic level are low.
3. Level deficits in which all of the functions at either the automatic level or the representational level are deficient.
4. Process deficits in which the scores on subtests in one process are below the scores on other processes.
5. Other deficits, such as isolated deficits in one function or in two unrelated areas. (pp. 77–79)

Remediation is prescribed according to the child's ability profile. Although the *ITPA* does not focus on comparison of interindividual differences, it does provide data for doing so.

The *ITPA* differentiates problem areas characteristic of a particular handicapped population. Ferrier (1966), Hallom (1964), and Foster (1963) found that children with functional speech disorders performed poorly on tasks requiring automatic-sequential ability. Bilovsky and Share (1965) reported that mongoloid children exhibited significant weaknesses on tests requiring auditory-vocal automatic and auditory-sequencing abilities. Brown and Rice (1967) indicated that EMR children manifested particular deficiencies at the automatic sequential level. The *ITPA* also differentiates social classes (Mittler & Ward, 1970; Stephenson & Gay, 1972) and ethnic groups (McCarron, 1971; Webb, 1968).

Research

Ysseldyke and Salvia (1974) report the following test-retest reliability scores for the *ITPA* subtests:

1.	*Auditory Reception*	.36–.79
2.	*Visual Reception*	.21–.69
3.	*Auditory Association*	.62–.90
4.	*Visual Association*	.32–.75
5.	*Verbal Expression*	.45–.74
6.	*Manual Expression*	.40–.70
7.	*Grammatic Closure*	.49–.87
8.	*Visual Closure*	.57–.82
9.	*Auditory Sequential Memory*	.61–.89
10.	*Visual Sequential Memory*	.12–.71
11.	*ITPA*	.66–.91

Ysseldyke and Salvia have found that the low reliability scores raise many questions concerning the identification of strengths and weaknesses of individual learners.

More than 20 studies now shed light on the relationship between the *ITPA* and tests of academic achievement. The bulk of the research reports correlations of reading achievement scores with the *ITPA* subtest scores. From these studies, Newcomer and Hammill (1976) report that only three subtests

(*Grammatic Closure, Auditory Association,* and *Sound Blending*) and the composite score yield correlation coefficients high enough to be considered useful (*r* = .35). Moreover, they found that when these scores were controlled for the influence of intelligence, only the *Grammatic Closure* subtest reached the .35 level.

In their study, only *Grammatic Closure* significantly correlated with achievement in spelling. Twenty-two other studies reported either nonsignificant or negligible correlations for all 12 subtests. Thus, Newcomer and Hammill concluded that the *ITPA* subtests are not useful predictors of spelling achievement.

Correlations of the *ITPA* subtest scores with arithmetic achievement produced findings similar to the reading correlations. The *Grammatic Closure* subtest, the *Auditory Association* subtest, and the composite score were the only measures found to correlate with achievement at the .35 level. However, when intelligence was controlled, none of the three produced scores high enough to be useful.

As such, *Grammatic Closure* is the only useful subtest. However, it actually measures competence in English morphology and is likely to be strongly influenced by race and social class. None of the studies reviewed by Newcomer and Hammill (1976) controlled for these factors. Therefore, definitive conclusions regarding the predictive value of this subtest should not be made without further investigation. Now research findings do not support the use of the *ITPA* for the prediction of academic success or failure.

Training Programs

The *ITPA* is the basis for a variety of psycholinguistic training programs. The purpose of these programs is to stimulate psycholinguistic development in children who have a specific language deficit or an overall language lag. Four main assumptions underlie the development of these programs: *(a)* certain language skills are identifiable and measurable, *(b)* adequate development of these skills is necessary for success on school-related tasks, *(c)* these language skills can be improved through psycholinguistic training, and *(d)* remediation of these language skills will improve performance in academic areas. Newcomer and Hammill (1976) note that research findings raise serious questions concerning the validity of the first three assumptions. Furthermore, they point out that the fourth assumption has not yet been explored.

They also report on the results of studies [originally reviewed by Hammill and Larsen (1974)] in which psycholinguistic-based training programs were used. Since the studies were all performed under different conditions, the results are difficult to analyze. Ten of the major factors differentiating these studies are *(a)* types of subjects used, *(b)* age of subjects, *(c)* number of subjects, *(d)* inclusion or exclusion of a control group, *(e)* approach to training (individualized or group instruction), *(f)* type of experimental training (*ITPA*-based materials or author-designed materials), *(g)* duration of the training period (days, weeks), *(h)* number of hours per training session, *(i)* type of personnel performing the training (professional or nonprofessional), and *(j)* the year in which the study was performed. After reviewing the 39 studies, they concluded that the effects of *ITPA*-based psycholinguistic training programs have not been validated. They state four possible explanations:

1. The *ITPA* is an invalid measure of psycholinguistic functioning.
2. The intervention programs and/or techniques are inadequate.
3. Most psycholinguistic dimensions are either untrainable or highly resistant to stimulation.
4. There exists methodological inadequacies in the studies. (p. 78)

Lund, Foster, and McCall-Perez (1978) reevaluated 24 of the 38 studies originally reviewed by Hammill and Larsen (1974) and report results that conflict with the Hammill and Larsen evaluation. From their study, Lund et al. conclude that some of the training programs *did* show significant positive results as measured by the *ITPA*. They also report that there were some studies from which no information could be drawn. They conclude that the claim made by Hammill and Larsen (i.e., psycholinguistic training is nonvalidated) is false.

Hammill and Larsen (1978) refuted the claim made by Lund et al. (i.e., psycholinguistic training is effective in some cases) by reevaluating the 24 studies examined by the latter research group. Hammill and Larsen report that their original evaluation of 23 of the 24 studies was accurate.

Moreover, Smead (1977) reports that in four studies that she reviewed, instruction based on modality preferences as assessed by the *ITPA* did not produce different results from instruction not based on the *ITPA*. Now there is little empirical support for using the *ITPA* as either a diagnostic tool for identifying specific psycholinguistic strengths and weaknesses or as the basis for remediation programs. The controversy continues and data are needed from good empirical studies.

REMEDIATION OF LANGUAGE DEFICITS

Initial Language Programs

A number of LD language remediation programs were primarily developed for use with other categories of exceptional children. Three of the most widely used programs were designed by Hortense Barry (1961), Mildred McGinnis (1963), and Doris Johnson and Helmer Myklebust (1967).

Barry's program (1961) was originally used with young aphasic children. It follows a developmental format aimed at strengthening inner, receptive, and expressive language. It recommends inner language training to help the child relate to the environment; for example, symbolic toys (e.g., dolls, cars) help the child relate in a meaningful manner. Receptive language training focuses on teaching the child to recognize the names of a large number of objects. Expressive language training involves shaping children's meaningful utterances and encouraging the youngster to express herself verbally. The teacher introduces and reinforces different parts of speech at different stages of the program.

Also designed for use with aphasic children, McGinnis' program (1963) was influenced by her previous work with the deaf. She describes language-delayed children as manifesting either of two types of aphasia: *(a)* expressive or motor and *(b)* receptive or sensory. Her training program, called the *Associative Method,* systematically develops and associates all of the skills needed to comprehend and produce language. It helps prepare aphasic children to function as close to their age and grade level as possible. Thus, academics play a basic part in the program. Since McGinnis believes that an aphasic child should not be expected to comprehend any words that she cannot produce, she stresses oral language more than receptive language. Her highly structured approach follows a simple to complex sequence (e.g., simple speech acts are taught first and then combined into complex skills). This program is most often used with older children or adolescents.

Johnson and Myklebust's program (1967) also was strongly influenced by work in the areas of aphasia and deafness. They believe that semi-autonomous systems in the brain underlie and control learning. These systems may be independent of each other (intraneurosensory) or they may complement each other and function in an interrelated manner (interneurosensory). Their premise is that any one of these systems could be damaged while the others could remain intact. Thus, the child could experience a learning disability of a fairly specific nature. Johnson and Myklebust identify five different areas in which a learning disability may be apparent: *(a)* auditory language, *(b)* reading, *(c)* written language, *(d)* arithmetic, and *(e)* nonverbal language. In addition, they outline specific training procedures for each of the five areas. The overall program operates on the principle of individualized instruction at the child's level of readiness and involvement. Their approach assumes that the child can comprehend more than she can express (contradictory to the program designed by McGinnis) and, thus, it stresses receptive language training before expressive language.

Psycholinguistic Approaches

The clinical model of the *ITPA* has been the basis for several language programs. The most widely discussed programs include those developed by Bush and Giles (1977), Hartman (1966), and Minskoff, Wiseman, and Minskoff (1972).

In *Aids to Psycholinguistic Teaching,* Bush and Giles (1977) discuss remediation activities for young children according to the *ITPA* subtests. Each chapter includes a definition of the particular psycholinguistic ability, a method for assessment, and training procedures for remediation of specific deficits.

Hartman's Preschool Diagnostic Language Program (1966) was originally designed for use with culturally disadvantaged children. This program is primarily intended for use with preschool children who are language deprived. Myers and Hammill (1976) have found that children with language-learning disorders may also benefit. The first few months of the program focus on diagnosing each child's language problems and designing a remediation program. Children with common disability areas are then grouped together for remediation. The manual provides specific recommendations and guidelines concerning how the children should be grouped, how the room should be arranged, how the teacher should spend her time, and what types of daily remediation should take place.

Minskoff, Wiseman, and Minskoff (1972) created the MWM Program for Developing Language Abilities. They outline remediation procedures for all 12 areas of the *ITPA*. It is designed for use with 4–7-year-old children. Myers and Hammill (1976) reveal that the effectiveness or validity of this program has not been researched due to its recent development. However, they do report that the overall program is well sequenced and the screening procedures included are conducive to specifying target populations. Future efficacy studies might prove that the MWM Program has much clinical and educational value.

As mentioned earlier, the effectiveness of psycholinguistic training has not been demonstrated. Perhaps forthcoming research will either establish the value of psycholinguistic training or provide insights regarding future directions.

Linguistic Approaches

The language programs discussed in the previous sections have drawn upon the fields of neurology and learning theory. Two more recent programs, the Developmental Syntax Program (Coughran & Liles, 1974) and the Interactive Language Development Training Program (Lee, Koenigsknecht, & Mulhern, 1975), are based on the work of developmental linguists and language theorists. Their programs focus on the particular language skills the child should have and the best way to train the child. These programs do not deal with etiology and origin of the problems. Unfortunately, they are meant to strengthen only syntactic skills and do not include training procedures for the other language components. Within the next few years other linguistically based programs will most likely be developed.

The Developmental Syntax Program (Coughran & Liles, 1974) can easily be implemented in a public school and does not require much teacher training. Based on reinforcement theory, this approach includes programs and training procedures for articles, pronouns, possessive pronouns, adjectives, verbs (regular, irregular, present tense, progressive tense, and past tense), and plurality. Each program consists of three phases: *(a)* ear training, *(b)* production and carryover, and *(c)* generalization to a different context. These research-based programs are developmentally sequenced. The overall program includes guidelines for reinforcement modes. No research has been reported on this program.

184 Specific learning disorders

The second linguistically based language program, the Interactive Language Development Training Program (Lee et al., 1975), provides remedial guidelines for training individuals or small groups of young children. The program uses a conversational setting to teach both receptive and expressive language skills. Its training approach involves a storytelling format in which the stories reflect experiences familiar to the children. The teacher asks questions about the story plots and follows the given guidelines for evaluation. The interactive feature, unique to this approach, provides an educationally relevant means of assessing and training the child's syntactic language skills. The overall program consists of two levels. The first level provides training guidelines for basic sentence structures, coordination, and simple transformations. The second level provides guidelines for advanced development of the verb phrase, secondary verbs, conjunctions, and complex transformations. Research findings indicate that this program is well suited to its stated purpose (Wiig & Semel, 1976).

Linguistically Based Remediation

This section illustrates selected activities based on linguistic constructs. Each activity focuses on a specific skill or skill area. Learning disabled children typically do not manifest global language deficits; therefore, remediation is usually aimed at specific skills. For example, the child experiencing difficulty with time-related verb tenses may benefit only minutely from a total language-training program. Remediation of particular problems appears to be the most efficient training route for both the teacher and child.

Phonology

Phonetic Bingo focuses on improving the child's ability to discriminate between phonemes differing by one or two distinctive features. In Phonetic Bingo, each child receives one card from a set containing the appropriate phonemes (e.g., the /b/, /d/, /p/, /t/, /g/, and /v/ set).

1	2	3	4	5
p	d	g	t	p
g	v	p	v	t
b	t	d	g	v
t	g	b	p	b
d	p	t	d	g

The caller selects a card and calls out the phoneme. If the child has that particular phoneme in the appropriate column (e.g., 2 /p/), she can place a space marker over that phoneme. The winner of the game is the first player to cover five phonemes in a row.

Fishing for Blends concentrates on the child's ability to discriminate between phonetically similar blends. The teacher calls out a word, such as *skate,* and the child must find the correct blend from a group of fish-shaped cards displaying the /s/ blends (i.e., *st, sk, sw, sl*). If the player is correct, she gets to keep the fish. Whoever has the most fish wins.

Matching Vowels attempts to strengthen the child's ability to discriminate between vowel sounds. Pupils sit around a game board (e.g., a start-to-finish sequence) displaying pictures of CVC words, such as *cat, bug, pig.* Each child places a marker at the start position. The first child draws a card from the card stack. Each card shows one vowel (i.e., *a, e, i, o,* or *u*). The child moves to the first CVC word picture on the game board containing that vowel sound. Whoever reaches the end of the game board first wins.

Morphology

Making Compound Words deals with the child's ability to construct new words using base-morphemic words. Each child has a set of 20 word cards. The teacher displays a compound word picture, such as a milkman. The children must make the corresponding word using two of their word cards. The teacher gives a point to the child producing the correct answer first. Whoever earns the most points wins.

An aide shows letter cards to a small group of children.

Time Slot focuses on increasing the child's ability to use time-related verb tenses. The child is given a set of cards displaying words with time-related verb tenses, such as *walked, walking,* and *will walk.* She then places each card in an envelope labeled *yesterday, today,* or *tomorrow.* By looking at matching symbols on the back of the cards and envelopes, the child can self-check her answers.

Semantics

Sentence Sayer focuses on improving the child's ability to obtain meanings from the sentence context. The teacher gives the child a worksheet containing 10 sentences in which a key word is omitted (e.g., *The man mowed the _____ with the lawn mower*). Under each sentence is a set of alternative words. The child must select the appropriate word for the blank.

Crazy Concepts aims at strengthening the child's ability to understand concepts denoting size and quantity. The teacher hands the child a series of cards with printed questions. (For example, *Are dogs bigger than horses?*) The child circles either *yes* or *no.* The child receives immediate feedback by turning the card over to see the correct answer.

Who, Where, When stresses the child's ability to understand the concepts in the title. The teacher gives the child a set of cards displaying words telling who *(boy),* where *(store),* or when *(today).* The child then places each word in the appropriate who, where, or when envelope. To make this task self-correcting, each word card has drawn on the back either a triangle (for who cards), a circle (for where cards), or a square (for when cards). The child can match her answers with the appropriate shape printed on the front of the envelope.

Syntax

Sentence Construction focuses on increasing the child's ability to construct sentences exhibiting correct word order. The child is provided with five envelopes which each contain words from a particular class (e.g., nouns, verbs, articles, adverbs, and adjectives). The child must construct a certain number of sentences using the words from each envelope. To get the child started, initially a format could

This academic game has a start-to-finish format.

be provided. For example, she could be asked to make five sentences following the pattern of article, adjective, noun, verb, adverb (e.g., *The black dog went home*).

The Sentence Game aims at increasing the child's ability to use syntactically correct sentences. Several children sit around a game board displaying stimulus pictures and/or words that are marked off in squares along a winding path. Each child places a marker at the start position, spins a spinner or rolls a die, and moves the designated number of spaces. The square her marker lands on contains the word that she must use appropriately in a sentence. If the sentence is complete and sequentially correct, the player remains on the square. If the player cannot use the word correctly, she moves back one square at a time until she produces a correct sentence. The first player to reach the end wins.

The What Came First Game focuses on improving the child's ability to recall the correct order of critical verbal elements in a sentence. The child listens to a tape recording of 20 sentences of various lengths. Each sentence contains three critical verbal elements, such as *The boy hit the dog with the rock.* (This example includes agent, action, and object.) The child receives a worksheet displaying 20 sets of three pictures that correspond to the sentences. When the child hears a sentence (e.g., *The boy hit the dog with the rock*), she must number the corresponding pictures (i.e., boy, dog, rock) according to which came first, second, and third.

Pragmatics

The Loud or Soft Game focuses on improving the child's awareness of appropriate use of voice intensities. The child is provided with a recording describing several communication situations. She responds to each by writing *loud* or *soft* on her worksheet. For example, one situation might describe a church scene; the child is asked, "Would you use a loud or soft voice to ask your mother a question?"

Other situations might describe a football game, parade, or classroom scene. After each situation is presented, the correct answer should be provided with a short discussion on why.

Communication Comic aims at improving the child's ability to understand situational factors. The teacher gives the child comic strip segments that, when placed together in the appropriate order, depict an entire communication event. The child must place the segments in their proper sequence. These segments can be made self-correcting by placing their appropriate sequence number on the reverse side.

Tricky Voices deals with the child's ability to use the appropriate voice intonation for expression. The child listens to a tape recording of several pairs of sentences that express the same idea but are said with two different voice intonations. For example, she hears *I like you* first in an angry voice and then in a kind voice. She must select sentence number one or two as correct. After each set of sentences is presented, the correct answer should be provided with an explanation.

Games help teach various language skills.

WRITTEN EXPRESSION

Written expression, one of the highest forms of language development, involves the visual-symbolic reflection of comprehension, concept development, and abstraction. It differs from handwriting in that the latter is primarily a visual-motor task that does not require complex cognitive abilities. Handwriting includes such tasks as copying, tracing, scribbling, and writing from dictation. Written expression, on the other hand, presents a graphic record of how an individual can organize her thoughts and ideas to convey a message.

Cartwright (1967) divides written expression into four major components: fluency, vocabulary, structure, and content. This division allows very specific analysis.

Components

Fluency

Cartwright (1967) defines *fluency* as quantity of verbal output. This component is related to age and includes sentence length and complexity (McCarthy, 1954; Meckel, 1963). Cartwright (1968) found that the average sentence length of an 8-year-old child is eight words and that this length increases one word per year through age 13. He suggests that any deviation of more than two words indicates a problem.

The types of sentences a child uses also reflects fluency problems. Cartwright (1969) identifies four types of sentences (incomplete, simple, compound, and complex) that can be used to measure competency. He suggests that the number of compound and complex sentences increases with age and the use of incomplete and simple sentences decreases with age.

Vocabulary

Vocabulary is the number of different words expressed in the written task. The student's vocabulary should increase with age and experience (Cartwright, 1969). The Type Token Ratio (TTR) (Johnson, 1944) is a measure of vocabulary that compares the total number of words used to the ratio of different words used. For example, the sentence, *The two boys went fishing in Noonan's Lake early yesterday morning,* has a high TTR (1.0), as 11 total words are used and all 11 words are different. In contrast, the sentence, *The little girl saw the little boy in the little house,* has a fairly low TTR (.63), as 11 total words are used but only 7 of these words are different. A low TTR could indicate inadequate vocabulary for the written expression task. This technique can also be used for measuring long compositions; however, Carroll (1938) notes that the number of different vocabulary words decreases as the total number of words in the composition increases. Thus, when comparing several compositions produced by the same student or by different students, the same type of sample should be taken. For example, the first 50 words should be used from each composition instead of selecting the first 50 words from some compositions and the last 50 words from others.

Vocabulary can also be assessed by measuring the number of unusual words. For this assessment, a sample of the student's written expression (first 50 words of a composition) should be compared with a list of words frequently used by other children [e.g., the Dolch (1955) word list]. The number of words used by the child that do not appear on the list indicates the extent of her vocabulary.

Structure

Structure includes the mechanical aspects of writing (e.g., punctuation, capitalization, rules of grammar). A high score on a grammar test does not always indicate that the child knows the grammatical rules (Cartwright, 1966). Internalization of these rules is necessary before the child can correctly apply them. Cartwright (1966) reports that a lack of understanding of sentence structure and basic grammatical rules results in inappropriate usage of punctuation and capitalization.

One method suggested by Cartwright (1969) for the assessment of structure is the Grammatical-Correctness Ratio (GCR) (Stuckless & Marks, 1966). The GCR quickly analyzes the total number of grammatical errors produced by a child. To obtain the GCR, a sample of the student's written expression (e.g., 50 words from a composition) is scored by counting the number of grammatical errors. The error count is then subtracted from 50 and this difference is divided by 50. To obtain a percentage score, this last number is multiplied by 100. Because the final result can be displayed as a percentage, GCRs can be calculated for any number of words and still yield a score that can be compared with the student's previous scores. A GCR score can also be calculated for one specific type of error as well. Thus, this extremely flexible method accurately measures and compares samples of written expression.

Content

Content, the fourth component of written expression, can be divided into at least three factors: accuracy, ideas, and organization (Cartwright, 1969). The nature of the written assignment determines how different factors should be weighed. For example, accuracy carries more weight when the written exercise is a presentation of historical facts. Cartwright suggests that each factor be scored on a scale from zero to 10. This type of analysis identifies each student's particular problem areas. Thus, the student who consistently scores low in organization may need to perform tasks using outlines. Cartwright further suggests that teachers should add or delete categories depending upon the assignment; however, reliable criteria should always be used for analyzing written expression.

Problems and Remediation of Written Expression

Written expression is usually not acquired until an individual has had extensive experience with reading, spelling, and verbal expression. Thus, these problems are generally not diagnosed until the second grade or beyond. Many times these problems are not caught until the middle school years when a

Pictures stimulate written expression.

heavy emphasis is placed upon the refinement of writing skills. This situation may account for the dearth of information reported concerning written expression problems of LD children (i.e., these problems are not detected until the later school years and may thus be considered secondary to the child's other academic problems). The remainder of this section discusses written expression problems and remediation procedures in terms of the four components, fluency, vocabulary, structure, and content, as described by Cartwright (1969).

Fluency

Learning disabled children with limited oral language experience show little written output. They speak in simple or incomplete sentences, so their writing reflects these characteristics.

Johnson and Myklebust (1967) suggest an exercise for shaping fluency. The teacher selects an object and places it in front of the child. The child is told to write the name of the object and then write a word or words describing it. Next, the child is told to write a sentence telling how or where the object is used. When action pictures are used in this exercise, the child is told to write about who is in the picture and what they are doing. The important and necessary ingredient for the success of this exercise is the amount of instruction provided at each step.

Some LD students can speak well yet cannot write a simple sentence. These children may need to first say the sentence aloud before writing it. This technique provides visual-graphic feedback and strengthens the child's ability to integrate information from one modality to another.

Another problem exhibited by older LD children involves syntactic difficulties. They may not have learned the syntactic rules that specify the many different ways in which words can be ordered to form meaningful sentences. For example, some may have learned only the structure of the basic sentence (e.g., simple, active, declarative, interrogative) that is characterized by the word order sequence of agent–action–object. They may incorrectly encode all sentences as if they were in this sequence. Such children would benefit from instruction involving the development of syntactic skills, such as those activities found on pp. 185–186.

Vocabulary

Wallace and McLoughlin (1975) indicate that some students have poor spoken and written vocabularies because of a lack of experiences. This problem may be displayed through overuse of words common to the student's immediate environment. Their performance on written expression tasks probably results in a low TTR. Remediation could include structured field trips that involve follow-up discussions of what was seen and heard. Viewing films, listening to guest speakers, making a picture dictionary, and reading books, magazines, and newspapers also may increase a student's vocabulary. Whenever she uses a new vocabulary word appropriately, the student should be praised.

Learning disabled children need help in building up their vocabularies.

Wiig and Semel (1976) report that some LD children have adequate vocabularies for their age range but have assigned a small number of attributes to each word. In this case, each vocabulary word may have only one meaning and may only be used by the child in one particular situation. This limited situation-specific use for words could cause the child to perform very well on some written expression tasks, while not being able to perform at all on others. In addition, some children may consistently have problems with written expression—"narrow" meanings may have them always on the search for the right word. Procedures for remediation of this type of problem are discussed in the section on remediation activities for semantic problems.

Structure

Some written expression problems stem from a lack of understanding of linguistic rules, resulting in an inability to produce sentences displaying correct syntactic and grammatical order (Wallace & McLoughlin, 1975). The most frequent manifestations are word omissions, distorted word order, incorrect verb and pronoun usage, incorrect word endings, and lack of punctuation (Johnson and Myklebust, 1967).

As previously discussed, the syntactic component of language can present a multitude of problems to LD students. These difficulties may not show up in the child's oral language since competence in fluency and a large vocabulary give the impression that the student is a proficient communicator. Several samples of the student's written expression may uncover even the mildest problem in syntactic written expression. (Suggestions for the remediation of syntactic difficulties are presented in the section on remediation activities for syntactic problems, p. 185-186.)

Content

Problems in content (i.e., thoughts, ideas, and organization) may also be disguised orally by an LD child with a large vocabulary and oral fluency. She talks a lot about nothing, often repeating what others say or rephrasing the same thought repeatedly. Taking trips or viewing slides may stimulate creative and original thinking.

Wallace and McLoughlin (1975) believe that some LD youngsters cannot express themselves in writing because they cannot classify and categorize input information. Such children's writing shows gross disorganization and disconnected thoughts. Exercises in categorization and classification of objects and ideas should help.

Conclusion

Learning disabled youngsters with oral language problems may manifest these same problems in written expression, since writing problems are related to an inadequate language background. Some problems disguised by oral competence can be quickly detected when the child is required to write. Language training procedures may frequently be the most appropriate route for remediation of writing problems.

Teachers of LD children should develop and use a consistent method for evaluating written expression. Cartwright's (1969) model is a reliable and systematic approach for determining a child's strengths and weaknesses. Since LD children usually do not manifest global deficits, his model presents a unique approach for the isolation of specific problems.

SUMMARY

This chapter discusses language as it relates to learning disabilities, theories of language acquisition, and the components of language. Types of language disabilities and the assessment of language abilities are discussed according to the five components of language: phonology, morphology, semantics, syntax, and pragmatics. The *Illinois Test of Psycholinguistic Abilities (ITPA)* is presented in terms of purpose, model, usage, research, and training programs. The section on remediation of language deficits features initial language programs, linguistic approaches, and specific remediation activities for the five language components. Finally, written expression and remediation of problems in this area are discussed in terms of Cartwright's (1969) model, which includes the four components of fluency, vocabulary, structure, and content.

REFERENCES

Baker, H.J., & Leland, B. *Detroit Tests of Learning Aptitude.* Indianapolis: Bobbs-Merrill, 1959.

Barry, H. *The young aphasic child: Evaluation and training.* Washington, D.C.: Volta Bureau, 1961.

Bender, L. *A visual motor gestalt test and its clinical use* (Research Monograph No. 3). New York: American Orthopsychiatric Association, 1938.

Berko, J. The child's learning of English morphology. *Word,* 1958, *14,* 150–177.

Bilovsky, D., & Share, J. The ITPA and Down's syndrome: An exploratory study. *American Journal of Mental Deficiency,* 1965, *70,* 78–82.

Bloom, L. Language development review. In F.D. Horowitz (Ed.), *Review of child development research* (Vol. 4). Chicago: The University of Chicago Press, 1975.

Boehm, A.E. *Boehm Test of Basic Concepts.* New York: Psychological Corp., 1970.

Botel, M. *Botel Reading Inventory.* Chicago: Follett Educational Corp., 1970.

Braine, M. On two types of models of the internalization of grammars. In D. Slobin (Ed.), *The ontogenesis of grammar.* New York: Academic Press, 1971.

Brown, L.F., & Rice, J.A. Psycholinguistic differentiation of low IQ children. *Mental Retardation,* 1967, *5,* 16–20.

Brown, R., & Berko, J. Psycholinguistic research methods. In P.H. Mussen (Ed.), *Handbook of research methods in child development.* New York: Wiley, 1960.

Bruner, J.S., Olver, R.R., & Greenfield, P.M. *Studies in cognitive growth.* New York: Wiley, 1966.

Bush, W.J., & Giles, M.T. *Aids to psycholinguistic teaching* (2nd ed.). Columbus, Ohio: Charles E. Merrill, 1977.

Carroll, J.B. Diversity of vocabulary and the harmonic series law of word-frequency distribution. *Psychological Record,* 1938, *2.*

Cartwright, G.P. *Techniques of analysis of written language.* Paper presented at the annual meeting of the American Educational Research Association, February 1966.

Cartwright, G.P. *Multivariate analyses of the written language abilities of normal and educable mentally retarded children.* Paper presented at the annual meeting of the American Educational Research Association, February 1967.

Cartwright, G.P. Written language abilities of normal and educable mentally retarded children. *American Journal of Mental Deficiency,* 1968, *72,* 499–508.

Cartwright, G.P. Written expression and spelling. In R.M. Smith (Ed.), *Teacher diagnosis of educational difficulties.* Columbus, Ohio: Charles E. Merrill, 1969.

Chomsky, C. *The acquisition of syntax in children from 5 to 10.* Cambridge, Mass.: MIT Press, 1969.

Chomsky, N.A. *Syntactic structures.* The Hague: Mouton, 1957.

Chomsky, N.A. *Aspects of the theory of syntax.* Cambridge, Mass.: MIT Press, 1965.

Clark, E. On the acquisition of the meaning of *before* and *after. Journal of Verbal Learning and Verbal Behavior,* 1971, *10,* 266–275.

Coughran, L., & Liles, B. *Developmental syntax program.* Austin, Tex.: Learning Concepts, 1974.

de Hirsch, K. Specific dyslexia or strephosymbiolia. *Folia Phoniatrica,* 1952, *4,* 231–248.

DeRenzi, E., & Vignolo, L.A. The Token Test: A sensitive test to detect receptive disturbances in aphasics. *Brain,* 1962, *85,* 665–678.

Dolch, E.W. *Methods in reading.* Champaign, Ill.: Garrard, 1955.

Doll, E.A. *Vineland Social Maturity Scale.* Circle Pines, Minn.: Educational Test Bureau, 1947.

Dunn, L. *Peabody Picture Vocabulary Test.* Circle Pines, Minn.: American Guidance Service, 1965.

Eisenson, J. *Aphasia in children.* New York: Harper & Row, 1972.

Ferrier, E.E. Investigation of the ITPA performance of children with functional deficits of articulation. *Exceptional Children,* 1966, *32,* 625–629.

Foster, C.R., Giddan, J.J., & Stark, J. *ACLC: Assessment of children's language comprehension.* Palo Alto, Calif.: Consulting Psychologists Press, 1972.

Foster, S. *Language skills for children with persistent articulatory disorders.* Unpublished doctoral dissertation, Texas Women's University, 1963.

Fraser, C., Bellugi, U., & Brown, R. Control of grammar in imitation, comprehension and production. *Journal of Verbal Learning and Verbal Behavior,* 1963, *2,* 121–135.

Fromkin, V., & Rodman, R. *An introduction to language.* New York: Holt, Rinehart & Winston, 1974.

Geschwind, N. The brain and language. In G.A. Miller (Ed.), *Communication, language, and meaning: Psychological perspectives.* New York: Basic Books, 1973.

Goldman, R., Fristoe, M., & Woodcock, R.W. *Goldman-Fristoe-Woodcock Test of Auditory Discrimination.* Circle Pines, Minn.: American Guidance Service, 1970.

Guilford, J.P. *The nature of human intelligence.* New York: McGraw-Hill, 1967.

Hallahan, D.P., & Kauffman, J.M. *Introduction to learning disabilities: A psycho-behavioral approach.* Englewood Cliffs, N.J.: Prentice-Hall, 1976.

Hallom, J.J. *An exploratory study to determine the psycholinguistic abilities of a group of six-year-old children with severe articulation problems.* Unpublished master's thesis, Sacramento State College, 1964.

Hammill, D.D., & Larsen, S.C. The effectiveness of psycholinguistic training. *Exceptional Children,* 1974, *41,* 5–14.

Hammill, D.D., & Larsen, S.C. The effectiveness of psycholinguistic training: A reaffirmation of position. *Exceptional Children,* 1978, *44,* 402–414.

Hartman, A.S. *Preschool diagnostic language program.* Harrisburg, Pa.: Department of Public Instruction, 1966.

Heilman, A.W. *Phonics in proper perspective* (2nd ed.). Columbus, Ohio: Charles E. Merrill, 1976.

Hopper, R., & Naremore, R.C. *Children's speech: A practical introduction to communication development.* New York: Harper & Row, 1973.

Jakobson, R., & Halle, M. *Fundamentals of language.* The Hague: Mouton, 1956.

Jenkins, J.J., & Palermo, D.S. Mediation processes and the acquisition of linguistic structure. In U. Bellugi & R. Brown (Eds.), The acquisition of language. *Monographs of the Society for Research in Child Development,* 1964, *29*(1, Whole No. 92).

Johnson, D.J. The language continuum. *Bulletin of the Orton Society,* 1968, *28,* 1–11.

Johnson, D.J., & Myklebust, H.R. *Learning disabilities: Educational principles and practices.* New York: Grune & Stratton, 1967.

Johnson, W. Studies in language behavior. I. A program of research. *Psychological Monographs,* 1944, *56*(2).

Karlsen, B., Madden, R., & Gardner, E.F. *Stanford Diagnostic Reading Test.* New York: Harcourt Brace Jovanovich, 1966.

Kessel, F. The role of syntax in children's comprehension from age six to twelve. *Monographs of the Society for Research in Child Development,* 1970, *35*(6), 48–53.

Kirk, S.A. *The diagnosis and remediation of psycholinguistic disabilities.* Urbana: University of Illinois Press, 1966.

Kirk, S.A., & Kirk, W.D. *Psycholinguistic learning disabilities: Diagnosis and remediation.* Urbana, Ill.: University of Illinois Press, 1971.

Kirk, S.A., McCarthy, J.J., & Kirk, W.D. *Illinois Test of Psycholinguistic Abilities* (Rev. ed.). Urbana, Ill.: University of Illinois Press, 1968.

Kornetsky, C., & Eliasson, M. Reticular stimulation

and chlorpromazine: An animal model for schizophrenic over-arousal. *Science,* 1969, *165,* 1273–1274.

Lapointe, C. *Token Test performances by learning disabled and academically achieving adolescents.* Unpublished master's thesis, Boston University, 1975.

Lee, L. *Northwestern Syntax Screening Test.* Evanston, Ill.: Northwestern University Press, 1971.

Lee, L., Koenigsknecht, R.A., & Mulhern, S.T. *Interactive language development teaching.* Evanston, Ill.: Northwestern University Press, 1975.

Lenneberg, E. A biological perspective of language. In E. Lenneberg (Ed.), *New directions in the study of language.* Cambridge, Mass.: MIT Press, 1964.

Lenneberg, E.H. *Biological foundations of language.* New York: Wiley, 1967.

Lerea, L. Assessing language development. *Journal of Speech and Hearing Research,* 1958, *1,* 75–85.

Lund, K.A., Foster, G.E., & McCall-Perez, F.C. The effectiveness of psycholinguistic training: A reevaluation. *Exceptional Children,* 1978, *44,* 310–319.

Luria, A.R. *The role of speech in the regulation of normal and abnormal behavior.* New York: Liverwright, 1961.

Marge, M. The general problem of language disabilities in children. In J.V. Irwin & M. Marge (Eds.), *Principles of childhood language disabilities.* Englewood Cliffs, N.J.: Prentice-Hall, 1972.

McCarron, L.T. *Psycholinguistic profiles of Mexican-American disadvantaged children.* Paper presented at the annual meeting of the Western Psychological Association, San Francisco, April 1971.

McCarthy, D. Language development in children. In L. Carmichael (Ed.), *Manual of child psychology.* New York: John Wiley & Sons, 1954.

McGinnis, M.A. *Aphasic children.* Washington, D.C.: Volta Bureau, 1963.

McGrady, H. Language pathology and learning disabilities. In H. Myklebust (Ed.), *Progress in learning disabilities* (Vol. 1). New York: Grune & Stratton, 1968.

McNeill, D. Developmental psycholinguistics. In F. Smith & G.A. Miller (Eds.), *The genesis of language: A psycholinguistic approach.* Cambridge, Mass.: MIT Press, 1966.

McNeill, D. The development of language. In P.H. Mussen (Ed.), *Carmichael's manual of child psychology* (Vol. 1) (3rd ed.). New York: Wiley, 1970.

Meckel, H.C. Research on teaching composition and literature. In N. Gage (Ed.), *Handbook of research on teaching.* Chicago: Rand McNally, 1963.

Meier, J.H. Prevalence and characteristics of learning disabilities found in second grade children. *Journal of Learning Disabilities,* 1971, *4,* 1–16.

Menyuk, P., & Looney, P. A problem of language disorder: Length versus structure. *Journal of Speech and Hearing Research,* 1972, *15,* 264–279. (a)

Menyuk, P., & Looney, P. Relationships between components of the grammar in language disorders. *Journal of Speech and Hearing Research,* 1972, *15,* 395–406. (b)

Minskoff, E., Wiseman, D.E., & Minskoff, J.G. *The MWM program for developing language abilities.* Ridgefield, N.J.: Educational Performance Associates, 1972.

Mittler, P., & Ward, J. The use of the Illinois Test of Psycholinguistic Abilities on British four-year-old children. *British Journal of Educational Psychology,* 1970, *40,* 43–54.

Myers, P.I., & Hammill, D.D. *Methods for learning disorders* (2nd ed.). New York: John Wiley & Sons, 1976.

Newcombe, F., & Marshall, J.C. Immediate recall of sentences by subjects with unilateral cerebral lesions. *Neuropsychologia,* 1967, *5,* 329–334.

Newcomer, P., & Hammill, D.D. *Psycholinguistics in the schools.* Columbus, Ohio: Charles E. Merrill, 1976.

Newcomer, P., Hare, B., Hammill, D., & McGettigan, J. Construct validity of the Illinois Test of Psycholinguistic Abilities. *Journal of Learning Disabilities,* 1975, *8,* 32–43.

Orton, S.T. *Reading, writing and speech problems in children.* New York: Norton, 1937.

Osgood, C.E. Motivational dynamics of language behavior. In M.R. Jones (Ed.), *Nebraska symposium motivation.* Lincoln: University of Nebraska Press, 1957.

Osgood, C. *Method and theory in experimental*

psychology. New York: Oxford University Press, 1964.

Piaget, J. *The origins of intelligence in children.* New York: International University Press, 1952.

Piaget, J. *The psychology of intelligence.* Patterson, N.J.: Littlefield, Adams, 1960.

Rosenthal, J.H. A preliminary psycholinguistic study of children with learning disabilities. *Journal of Learning Disabilities,* 1970, *3,* 391–395.

Rosvold, H.E., Mirsky, A.F., Sarason, I., Bransome, E., & Beck, L. A continuous performance test of brain damage. *Journal of Consulting Psychology,* 1956, *20,* 343–350.

Semel, E.M., & Wiig, E.H. Comprehension of syntactic structures and critical verbal elements by children with learning disabilities. *Journal of Learning Disabilities,* 1975, *8,* 53–58.

Skinner, B.F. *Verbal behavior.* New York: Appleton-Century-Crofts, 1957.

Smead, V.S. Ability training and task analysis in diagnostic/prescriptive teaching. *The Journal of Special Education,* 1977, *11*(1), 113–125.

Staats, A. Linguistic-mentalistic theory versus an explanatory S-R learning theory of language development. In D.I. Slobin (Ed.), *The ontogenesis of grammar.* New York: Academic Press, 1971.

Stephens, T.M. *Teaching skills to children with learning and behavior disorders.* Columbus, Ohio: Charles E. Merrill, 1977.

Stephenson, B.L., & Gay, W.D. Psycholinguistic abilities of black and white children from four SES levels. *Exceptional Children,* 1972, *38,* 705–709.

Stuckless, E.R., & Marks, C.H. *Assessment of the written language of deaf students* (USOE Cooperative Research Project 2544). University of Pittsburgh, 1966.

Taylor, I. *Introduction to psycholinguistics.* New York: Holt, Rinehart & Winston, 1976.

Templin, M. A study of sound discrimination ability of elementary school pupils. *Journal of Speech and Hearing Disorders,* 1943, *8,* 127–132.

Travis, L.E., & Rasmus, B. The speech sound discrimination abilities of cases with functional disorders of articulation. *Quarterly Journal of Speech,* 1931, *17,* 217–226.

U.S. Office of Education. *First annual report of National Advisory Committee on Handicapped Children.* Washington, D.C.: U.S. Department of Health, Education, & Welfare, 1968.

Van Etten, C., & Watson, B. Language assessment: Programs and materials. *Journal of Learning Disabilities,* 1977, *10,* 395–402.

Vogel, S.A. Syntactic abilities in normal and dyslexic children. *Journal of Learning Disabilities,* 1974, *7,* 47–53.

Vygotsky, L.S. *Thought and language.* Cambridge, Mass.: MIT Press, 1962.

Wallace, G., & McLoughlin, J.A. *Learning disabilities: Concepts and characteristics.* Columbus, Ohio: Charles E. Merrill, 1975.

Webb, P.K. *A comparison of the psycholinguistic abilities of Anglo-American, Negro, and Latin-American lower-class preschool children.* Unpublished doctoral dissertation, North Texas State University, 1968.

Wechsler, D. *Wechsler Intelligence Scale for Children.* New York: Psychological Corp., 1949.

Wiig, E.H., & Harris, S.P. Perception and interpretation of nonverbally expressed emotions by adolescents with learning disabilities. *Perceptual and Motor Skills,* 1974, *38,* 239–245.

Wiig, E.H., Lapointe, C., & Semel, E.M. *Relationships among language processing and production abilities of learning disabled adolescents.* Paper presented at the annual meeting of the American Speech and Hearing Association, Washington, D.C., 1975.

Wiig, E.H., & Roach, M.A. Immediate recall of semantically varied "sentences" by learning disabled adolescents. *Perceptual and Motor Skills,* 1975, *40,* 119–125.

Wiig, E.H., & Semel, E.M. Comprehension of linguistic concepts requiring logical operations by learning disabled children. *Journal of Speech and Hearing Research,* 1973, *16,* 627–636.

Wiig, E.H., & Semel, E.M. Development of comprehension of logico-grammatical sentences by grade school children. *Perceptual and Motor Skills,* 1974, *38,* 171–176. (a)

Wiig, E.H., & Semel, E.M. Logico-grammatical sentence comprehension by learning disabled adolescents. *Perceptual and Motor Skills,* 1974, *38,* 1131–1134. (b)

Wiig, E.H., & Semel, E.M. *Language disabilities in children and adolescents.* Columbus, Ohio: Charles E. Merrill, 1976.

Wiig, E.H., Semel, E.M., & Crouse, M.A. The use of English morphology by high-risk and learning disabled children. *Journal of Learning Disabilities,* 1973, *6,* 457–465.

Wolski, W. *Language development of normal*

children four, five, and six years of age as measured by the Michigan Picture Language Inventory. Unpublished doctoral dissertation, University of Michigan, 1962.

Wood, B.S. *Children and communication: Verbal and nonverbal language development.* Englewood Cliffs, N.J.: Prentice-Hall, 1976.

Ysseldyke, J.E., & Salvia, J. Diagnostic-prescriptive teaching: Two models. *Exceptional Children,* 1974, *41,* 181–185.

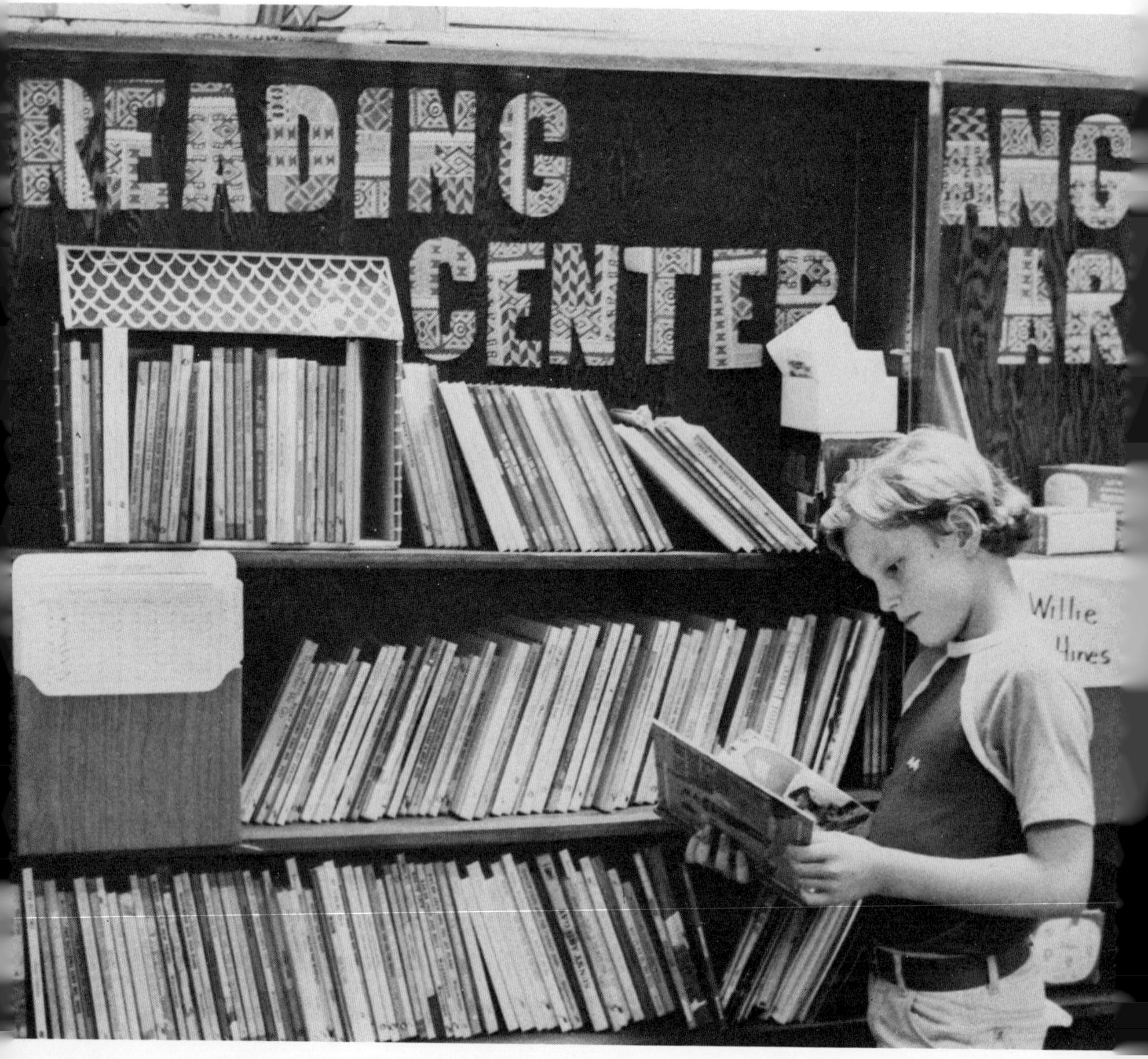
READING
CENTER
Willie

7

Reading disabilities

Reading, a visual-auditory task, involves obtaining meaning from symbols (letters and words). It is a basic tool that serves an individual for a lifetime. The ability to read permits a person to develop and maintain employable skills; participate in social, cultural, and political affairs; and fulfill emotional and religious needs. In addition, reading offers recreation and enjoyment (Kirk, Kliebhan, & Lerner, 1978). Despite its importance to daily functioning, one child out of every seven (approximately 8,000,000) will not learn to read adequately (National Advisory Committee on Dyslexia and Related Disorders, 1969). In 1970, a Harris survey revealed that approximately 18 million Americans are functionally illiterate (Haring & Bateman, 1977). Moreover, Haring and Bateman (1977) found that approximately 50% of the unemployed youth (CA = 16–21 years) and 75% of juvenile offenders have serious reading problems. According to Brabner (1969), most pupils who fail a grade do so because they cannot read well. Reading failure adds to a pupil's frustration, feelings of inadequacy, and dissatisfaction with school (Haring & Bateman, 1977).

Specific learning disorders

Learning Disabilities and Reading

Most LD youngsters cannot read well. As reported in Chapter 1, the history of the LD movement has emphasized reading disabilities (Hinshelwood, 1917; Orton, 1937). An examination of the estimated prevalence rates of reading disabilities and learning disabilities provides a framework for viewing the two groups. Approximately 15% of all school children have trouble reading (Haring & Bateman, 1977), but the estimated prevalence of LD is much lower (e.g., USOE [1976] recommends 1–3%). Thus, many children with mild reading disabilities have not been categorically identified as learning disabled. On the other hand, the majority of children who have severe reading disabilities that are not due to mental retardation, cultural disadvantage, emotional disturbance, and/or sensory impairments are readily classified as LD. Figure 7.1 displays the likely relationship between mild and severe reading problems and learning disabilities. In special education programs where the LD prevalence figure is higher than 3%, it is likely that more of the pupils with mild reading disabilities are included in the LD population.

Reading disabled children often become distressed and frustrated.

Factors Related to Reading Disabilities

Why do children have trouble with reading? Kirk, Kliebhan, and Lerner (1978) organize factors into three areas: *(a)* physical, *(b)* environmental, and *(c)* psychological. Table 7.1 lists these factors and their various compo-

→ severe reading disabilities due to mental retardation, emotional disturbance, sensory impairments, and/or cultural disadvantage

→ LD and severe reading disabilities

→ LD with primary learning problem in another area (e.g., language, math, written expression)

Key

◯ = mild reading problem

◯ = severe reading problem

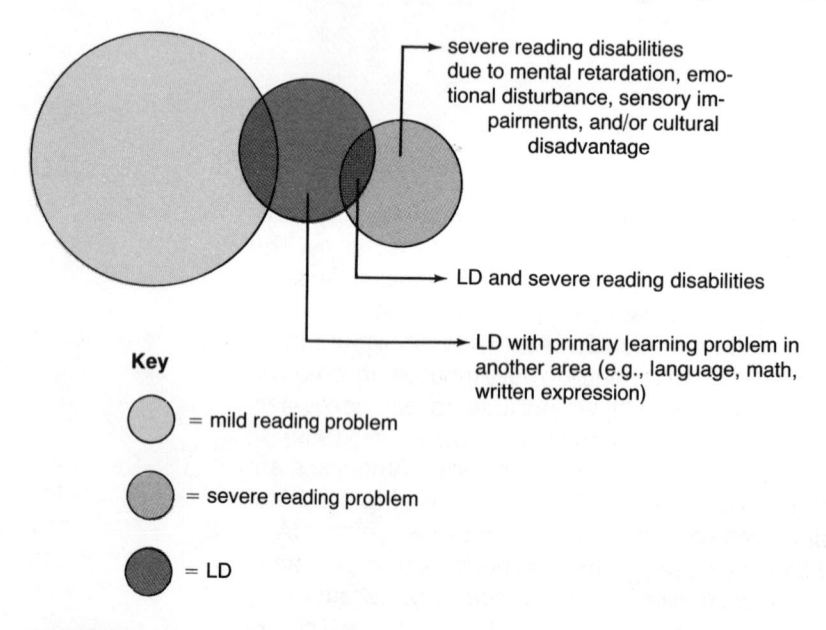

● = LD

FIGURE 7.1

Relationship between mild and severe reading disabilities and LD.

TABLE 7.1

Factors related to reading disabilities.

Physical

   *Neurological dysfunction
   *Cerebral dominance and laterality
    Visual defects
    Auditory defects
   *Heredity and genetics

Environmental

   *Inadequate teaching
    Cultural differences
    Language differences
    Emotional-social problems

Psychological

   *Auditory perception
   *Visual perception
   *Language disorders
   *Selective attention
   *Memory
    Intelligence

*These factors have received more attention in learning disabilities than the others.

nents. Remember that these factors do not *cause* reading problems.

Physical Factors

Hinshelwood (1917) examined neurological correlates of reading problems. His findings about reading and acquired brain damage appear in his book *Congenital Word Blindness*. Later, Orton (1937) claimed that the inability to read is a function of a lack of cerebral dominance. Noticing the reversal errors in reading and writing (e.g., *was* for *saw*), he labeled this condition *strephosymbolia*, meaning "twisted symbols." The work of Hinshelwood and Orton stimulated much research in the area of neurological dysfunction and reading disabilities. Now much of the literature concerning genetics and reading disabilities is reported in studies on *dyslexia* (a term that infers brain pathology as a cause of reading disability). (Dyslexia is discussed later on p. 200.)

Environmental Factors

Inadequate or poor teaching receives attention in special education. Many special educators (Cohen, 1973; Engelmann, 1969; Haring & Bateman, 1977) believe that children fail to read primarily as a result of inadequate instruction. Kirk, Kliebhan, and Lerner (1978) report proof that success in reading depends heavily on the teacher as a key ingredient. On the other hand, Haring and Bateman report on research (Abt Associates, 1976) that indicates that *method of instruction* enters into learning success. Thus, inadequate instruction may consist of poor teaching and/or the use of an inappropriate method.

Psychological Factors

As noted in Chapter 9, the relationship between auditory and visual perception (as measured by commonly used perception tests) and reading is not firmly established. Numerous researchers (Dykman, Ackerman, Clements, & Peters, 1971; Keogh & Margolis, 1976) report that many LD pupils cannot pay attention, a problem highly correlated to learning difficulty. Haring and Bateman (1977) report that some LD children have poor selective attention to graphemic features. In a review of research on attention, Samuels (1973) concludes that attention and achievement are linked.

   LD children cannot remember well what they hear and see. In a review of research concerning auditory and visual memory and its relationship to reading, Samuels (1973) reports that poor visual memory is associated with poor reading. Wallace and McLoughlin (1975) report that visual sequential memory problems affect the ordering of letters and words within a sentence (e.g., *nomkey* for *monkey*, *ballbase* for *baseball*). They also note that children with auditory sequential memory problems omit speech sounds and syllables. Finally, as noted in Chapter 9, the relationship between auditory and visual memory skills (as measured by commonly used tests) and reading is not firmly established.

Specific learning disorders

Combinations of Factors

It is likely that a combination of factors contributes to reading problems. Regardless of the cause of a reading disability, it is helpful if the teacher approaches instruction with a primary concern for factors that she can control (e.g., reading method, material, intensity of instruction, reinforcement).

Types of Reading Problems

Although reading problems originate from a variety of factors, they generally produce similar difficulties. The teacher must be alert to certain behaviors. Table 7.2 presents some of the characteristics exhibited by children with reading disabilities.

Dyslexia

The term *dyslexia* refers to difficulty in learning to read. Primarily a medical term, it is associated with neurophysiological disorder (Bryan & Bryan, 1975). Specifically, Bryan and Bryan (1975) define it as

> a syndrome in which a child has unusual and persistent difficulty in learning the components of words and sentences, in integrating segments into words and sentences and in learning other kinds of representational systems, such as telling time, directions and seasons. (p. 215)

The perspective on dyslexia is also educational. Lerner (1976) notes that the precise definitions of dyslexia vary considerably and include:

> (a) evidence of an etiology of brain damage, (b) the observation of behavioral manifestations of central nervous system dysfunction, (c) the indication of a genetic or inherited cause of the reading problem, (d) the presence of a syndrome of maturational lag, (e) use as a synonym for reading retardation, and (f) use to describe a child who has been unable to learn to read through the regular classroom methods. (p. 250)

Much of the literature from the medical perspective originated in Europe and focuses on genetics, brain damage, and CNS dysfunction as causes. This orientation is reflected in the writings of Hinshelwood (1971), Orton (1937), Hallgren (1950), Hermann (1959), Critchley (1966), Money (1966), and Johnson and Myklebust (1967). In comparison, the educational orientation primarily comes from American educators and psychologists who believe that dyslexia simply is a reading disability of individuals who have average or above average intelligence.

Although over 20,000 books, articles, and papers concern this problem, evidence of an etiology based on brain damage or CNS dysfunction is still not firmly established. For the most part, educators prefer the term *severe reading disability* instead of *dyslexia*. In 1968 HEW established the National Advisory Committee on Dyslexia and Related Reading Disorders to examine the issues. In 1969, the

Pointing to words sometimes helps.

TABLE 7.2

Selected reading habits of reading disabled children.

Characteristics	Comments
Reading Habits	
Tension movements	Frowning, fidgeting, using a high-pitched voice, and lip biting.
Insecurity	Refusing to read, crying, and attempting to distract the teacher.
Loses place	Losing place frequently (is often associated with repetitions).
Lateral head movements	Jerking head.
Holds material close	Deviating extremely (from 15–18 inches).
Word Recognition Errors	
Omissions	Omitting a word (e.g., *Tom saw(a)cat*).
Insertions	Inserting words (e.g., *The dog ran* [fast] *after the cat*).
Substitutions	Substituting one word for another (e.g.)., *The house ~~horse~~ was big*).
Reversals	Reversing letters in a word (e.g., *no* for *on*, *was* for *saw*).
Mispronunciations	Mispronouncing words (e.g., *mister* for *miser*).
Transpositions	Reading words in the wrong order (e.g., *She away ran* for *She ran away*).
Unknown words	Hesitating for 5 seconds at a word she cannot pronounce.
Slow choppy reading	Not recognizing words quickly enough (e.g., 20–30 words per minute).
Comprehension Errors	
Cannot recall basic facts	Unable to answer specific questions about a passage (e.g., *What was the dog's name?*).
Cannot recall sequence	Unable to tell sequence of story read.
Cannot recall main theme	Unable to recall the main topic of the story.
Miscellaneous Symptoms	
Word-by-word reading	Reading in a choppy, halting, and laborious manner (e.g., no attempts are made to group words into thought units).
Strained, high-pitched voice	Reading in a pitch higher than conversational tone.
Inadequate phrasing	Inappropriately grouping words (e.g., *The dog ran into* [pause] *the woods*).

committee offered the following statement: "In view of these divergencies of opinion, the Committee believes that the use of the term *dyslexia* serves no useful purpose" (p. 38).

It is apparent that perspectives from education and medicine have contributed a substantial body of knowledge on dyslexia. More importantly, both disciplines continue to investigate. Working together could no doubt produce worthwhile gains (Lerner, 1976).

Development of Reading

Teachers of pupils with reading disabilities need a perspective concerning the development of reading skills. Harris (1970) divides reading development into five stages: *(a)* development of reading readiness, *(b)* the initial stage in learning how to read, *(c)* rapid development of reading skills, *(d)* wide reading stage, and *(e)* refinement of reading skills.

Development of Reading Readiness

Readiness refers to the level of development needed for efficient learning. Kirk, Kliebhan, and Lerner (1978) report that observation and research suggest that many factors contribute to reading readiness. Specifically, they list *(a)* mental maturity, *(b)* visual abilities, *(c)* auditory abilities, *(d)* speech and language development, *(e)* thinking and attention skills, *(f)* motor development, *(g)* social and emotional maturity, and *(h)* interest and motivation. They believe that these factors comprise a network of interrelated, interacting components. The readiness period spans a period from birth until reading instruction begins. For many children, the period continues throughout the kindergarten year.

Mental age as it relates to readiness has received extensive attention. Many educators hold that a minimum mental age between 6-0 and 6-6 is essential. This position, primarily based on studies conducted in large classrooms in the 1930s (Gates, 1937), today is being viewed critically. For example, educators now realize that difficulty of material, pace of instruction, the method used, amount of individualized help, and the child's specific abilities modify the minimum mental age required for efficient learning. Kirk, Kliebhan, and Lerner (1978) note that research results have not determined the optimum mental age for beginning reading instruction. They point out that waiting until age 6 has been questioned frequently (p. 229).

Initial Stage

The initial learning usually begins in first grade but with some children it may begin in kindergarten or earlier, or the second grade or later. Most research concerns this highly controversial stage. The unrest centers around the "code-emphasis approach" versus the "meaning-emphasis approach." Whereas the code approach stresses the early introduction of the sound-symbol system and the teaching of phonics, the meaning approach stresses the initial learning of whole words and sentences by sight. Phonic instruction comes later in this approach.

Chall's (1967) now classic book titled *Learning to Read: The Great Debate* reports on an extensive investigation of several approaches to beginning reading. In this book, Chall concludes that code-emphasis methods produce better results. In another comprehensive study of beginning reading instruction, Bond and Dykstra (1967) arrive at different conclusions. For example, they report that no one method is so outstanding that other methods should not be considered. Now a variety of methods (basal, basal plus supplement, phonics, linguistics, language experience, programmed reading) are used.

Kirk, Kliebhan, and Lerner (1978) present a three-phase model that clarifies learning to read. Their phases consist of *(a)* reading wholes, *(b)* learning details, and *(c)* reading without awareness of details. As presented in Figure 7.2, points *(a)* and *(b)* apply to this initial stage. *Reading wholes* refers to providing the child with some initial words and sentences to learn by sight. To learn these words children rely heavily on memory and configuration clues. *Learning details* involves discriminating between words and acquiring the sound-symbol associations. In essence the child learns the code and develops word-attack skills during this phase of learning details.

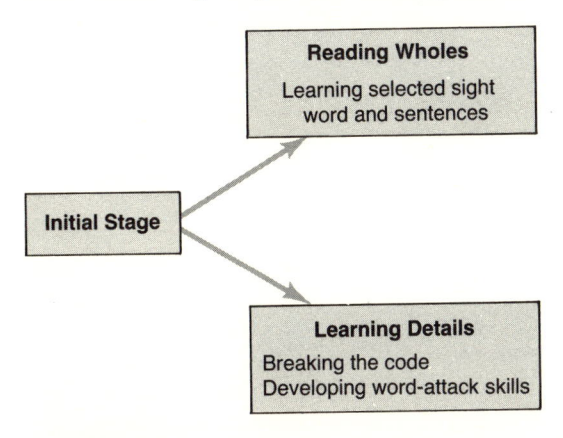

FIGURE 7.2

Common components of the initial stage of learning to read.

Using a task analysis approach, Venezky (1975) outlines subskills for sight-word recognition, for decoding, and for general instructional design. Table 7.3 presents these subskills. Many skills that are commonly included in readiness or beginning reading programs are omitted from his list. Specifically, Venezky refers to the omission of such skills as letter name knowledge, fine motor performance, visual discrimination of objects and shapes, and ocular-motor control. He omits them because he wishes to emphasize teaching skills (involving letters, sounds, and words) that relate directly to reading.

Stage of Rapid Development of Reading Skills

Normally in the second and third grades, the child refines reading skills acquired earlier. The third phase (reading without awareness of details) of Kirk, Kliebhan, and Lerner's (1978) three-phase model applies to this stage. Children reading at this stage do so visually until they encounter an unknown word. Having mastered at this point most of the sound-symbol relationships, the child tries

TABLE 7.3

Venezky's delineation of beginning reading subskills.

Sight-Word Recognition Subskills

Visual discrimination of letter strings, including attention to order of letters and attention to the entire word
Association and retention of labels for the letter strings
Retrieval and articulation of labels when shown the strings

Decoding Subskills

Letter differentiation
Association of sound and letter
Blending sounds
Identification of a sound within a word
Sound matching within words

General Instructional Design Skills

Attending to letter order
Attending to letter orientation
Attending to word detail
Sound matching
Sound blending

a variety of word-attack approaches. In their continued reading development, they mainly increase vocabulary and improve comprehension skills. Once children reach this stage, instruction mainly focuses on vocabulary development, improving skills, and maintaining interest. But few children with severe reading disabilities (in word recognition) ever reach this stage of development during their elementary years.

Stage of Wide Reading

Normally during the intermediate grades the child realizes the pleasure of reading. It becomes a very *meaning*-oriented task. Children voluntarily read books (e.g., *Hardy Boys, Nancy Drew*) and magazines. These enthusiastic readers recognize and comprehend words easily. Children with severe reading disabilities seldom reach this level.

204 Specific learning disorders

Refinement of Reading Stage

Normally in the junior high school years comprehension, critical reading, studying, and reading rate improve. Continuing into adulthood, this stage principally demands practice in reading skills.

Decoding/Word-Attack Objectives for Grades K–3

In addition to understanding the general stages of reading development, the teacher should be aware of a hierarchical ordering of instructional objectives in reading. Table 7.4 offers some selected decoding/word-attack objectives for Grades K–3.

DIAGNOSIS OF READING PROBLEMS

Diagnosis can provide the teacher with relevant information. In addition to indicating the child's current reading ability, assessment measures may indicate particular errors and aid the teacher in planning instructional objectives. Although there are now many useful commercial tests, do not overlook informal measures. This section explores three categories of tests: *(a)* norm referenced, *(b)* criterion referenced, and *(c)* informal. Appendix A lists additional tests.

Reading for pleasure strengthens abilities.

Norm-Referenced Tests

Norm-referenced tests are standardized on large groups of children. One child's performance can thus be compared with the popula-

TABLE 7.4

Decoding/word-attack objectives for reading (grades K–3).

Suggested Grade Level	Objective (examples in parentheses)
K	Auditorially discriminates between the regular consonant sounds in initial position.
1	Produces the regular consonant sounds.
1	Auditorially discriminates between the regular consonant sounds in final position.
1	Auditorially discriminates between the regular short vowel sounds: $\breve{o}$ as in *ostrich*, $\breve{e}$ as in *Ed*, $\breve{u}$ as in *umbrella*, $\breve{i}$ as in *Indian*, $\breve{a}$ as in *apple*.
1	Produces the regular short vowel sounds.
1	Produces the long vowel sounds.
1	Recognizes the long vowel sign: $\bar{a}, \bar{e}, \bar{i}, \bar{o}, \bar{u}$.
1	Auditorially discriminates between the regular short vowel sounds and long vowel sounds.
1	Decodes two- and three-letter words that have short vowel sounds.
1	Substitutes initial consonant to form new words.

TABLE 7.4 cont.

Suggested Grade Level	Objective (examples in parentheses)
1	Substitutes final consonant to form new words.
1	Substitutes medial vowel to form new words.
1	Decodes words with same phonogram/phonemic pattern (at, cat, bat).
1	Reads the preprimer level Dolch sight words.
1	Reads the primer level Dolch sight words.
1–2	Reads the grade one level Dolch sight words.
2	Produces the consonant blends in isolation: bl, br, cl, cr, dr, dw, fr, fl, gl, gr, mp, nd, pl, pr, qu, sc, sl, st, str, sw, scr, sm, sn, sp, spl, squ, sk, spr, tr, tw, -st, -nt, -nk, -thr.
2	Decodes words with consonant blends.
2	Substitutes initial consonant blends to form other words.
2	Identifies forms and sounds of consonant digraphs in initial position: sh, ch, ph, th, wh.
2	Identifies forms and sounds of consonant digraphs in final position: sh, ch, gh, ng, ph, th, sh.
2	Decodes four- and five-letter words that have regular short vowel sounds.
2	Decodes words in which the vowels are long.
2	Decodes words with final consonant blends.
2	Decodes words ending in v-c plus silent e, (make, smoke, bone).
2	Decodes consonant variants (s—has, see; g—garden, large; c—music, ice).
2	Decodes long e and i sound of y.
2	Decodes vowel diphthongs: oi, oy, ou, ow, ew.
2	Decodes words in which vowel is controlled by r (far, fur, bar, more).
2	Forms compound word with two known words (e.g., baseball).
2	Identifies root/base words in inflected forms of known words (helpful, help; darkness, dark; unhappy, happy; recall, call).
2	Decodes words in which final silent e is dropped before adding ending (smoke, smoking).
2	Identifies sounds and forms of consonant digraphs in medial position (wishing).
2	Decodes vowel digraphs/vowel teams: oa, ai, ay, ee, ea, ie, ei.
2	Identifies sounds of a followed by l, w, or u.
2	Decodes suffixes (less, ful, ness, er, est, ly).
2	Decodes prefixes (un, re, dis, pre, pro, ex, en).
2	Identifies multiple sounds of long a (ei, weigh; ai, straight; ay, day; ey, they).
2	Decodes words with vowel digraph/vowel team irregularities (bread, heart).
2	Reads the grade two level Dolch sight words.
3	Decodes silent k in kn (know).
3	Decodes silent gh (though).
3	Decodes words ending in ed (ed, crooked; t, looked).
3	Decodes dg (edge).
3	Reads the grade three level Dolch sight words.

tion upon which the test was standardized. Scores are reported in a number of ways. The total number of corrent items comprises a *raw score.* It can be converted to a *reading grade level score,* which indicates the grade level at which the child is performing. For example, a grade level score of 2.6 indicates that the child's raw score is the same as the median score of children in the sixth month of the second grade who took the test. Likewise, a *reading age score* is based on the age of the children rather than grade level. A reading age score of 8–9 indicates that the child's reading level is the same as the median score of children in the normal population aged 8 years and 9 months. *Percentiles* state how a child ranks or compares with other children according to his own grade or age. If Rico's percentile is 72, it indicates that his performance was better than 72% of the norm population and poorer than 28%. Some reading tests also provide *stanine scores,* which are normalized standard scores that rank a child of a given grade or age from a low of 1 to a high of 9.

There are many general survey tests of reading, which tell at which level a child is reading. Three of the most widely used norm-referenced survey tests in reading are

1. *Gates-MacGinitie Reading Tests* (Teachers College Press). This test of silent reading is designed to be administered by the classroom teacher to a group in about 45–55 minutes. Tests for grades 1, 2, and 3 contain subtests of vocabulary and comprehension; an additional test for grades 2 and 3 measures speed and accuracy. There also are tests for grades 4–12 that contain subtests of vocabulary, comprehension, speed, and accuracy.

2. *Metropolitan Achievement Tests: Reading* (Harcourt Brace Jovanovich). The form for grades K.7 to 1.4 takes approximately one hour to administer; it tests listening for sounds, word knowledge, and comprehension. Tests for grades 1.5 to 3.4 also take approximately 1 hour to administer and measure word knowledge, word analysis, and comprehension. Word knowledge and comprehension are tested in the elementary, intermediate, and advanced forms for grades 3.5 to 9.5; administration time is approximately 45 minutes.

3. *SRA Achievement Series: Reading* (Science Research Associates). This group test for grades one through nine includes vocabulary and comprehension subtests. It can be administered in approximately 1 hour.

In contrast to the general reading survey tests, diagnostic reading tests provide a more precise, comprehensive analysis of specific reading abilities and disabilities (i.e., the teacher finds out *how* the child attempts to read). Most diagnostic reading tests are standardized, but some do not include norm-referenced data. Many reading subskills are measured in diagnostic reading test batteries. Four well-known diagnostic test batteries are discussed.

1. *Durrell Analysis of Reading Difficulty* (Harcourt Brace Jovanovich). This test, designed for individual administration by a trained professional, may be used with nonreaders to children in the 6th grade. Subtests deal with oral and silent reading, listening, and word recognition in addition to supplementary tests on visual memory of word forms, phonics, auditory analysis, spelling, and handwriting.

2. *Gates-McKillop Reading Diagnostic Tests* (Teachers College Press). This individually-administered battery for nonreaders is available in two forms. The subtest areas include oral reading (with error analysis), flash presentation and untimed presentation of words, flash presentation of phrases, knowledge of word parts, recognition of visual forms representing sounds, and auditory blending. Additional tests assess spelling, oral vocabulary, syllabication, and auditory discrimination.

3. *Spache Diagnostic Reading Scales* (California Test Bureau). In this battery of tests designed for children in grades 1 and up, three word lists and 22 graded reading passages are used to assess word recognition, word analysis, and comprehension. There also are

supplementary phonics tests. Independent, instructional, and frustration reading levels are determined.

4. *Woodcock Reading Mastery Tests* (American Guidance Service). This test takes approximately 20–30 minutes to administer and yields scores in each of the five subtest areas (letter identification, word identification, word attack, word comprehension, and passage comprehension) in addition to a total reading score. It contains two forms and may be used as either a norm-referenced test or a criterion-referenced test.

In addition to diagnostic test batteries, some diagnostic reading tests exist that measure a child's ability in a specific skill area.

1. *Botel Reading Inventory* (Follett). This group-administered test for children in grades 1–10 contains subtests that determine instructional levels in a variety of reading skills: phonics, word recognition, and word opposites in reading and listening.

2. *Doren Diagnostic Reading Test of Word Recognition* (American Guidance Service). This group- or individually-administered test assesses children in grades 2–8. Phonic skills in the following subtest areas are measured: letter recognition, beginning sounds, whole-word recognition, words within words, speech consonants, ending sounds, blending, rhyming, vowels, discriminate guessing, spelling, and sight words.

3. *Gray Oral Reading Test* (Bobbs-Merrill). This oral reading test is designed for individual administration to children in grades 1–12. Thirteen graded oral reading passages are included; reading accuracy and rate of read-

This teacher is administering the Woodcock Reading Mastery Tests.

208 Specific learning disorders

ing are combined to obtain a grade level score. Comprehension questions are included but they are not scored.

Criterion-Referenced Tests

Whereas norm-referenced tests *compare* a child's performance to the scores of others, criterion-referenced tests *describe* performance (in terms of fixed criteria). In the latter method, the teacher finds out what skills the child has learned, what he is learning now, and what skills still must be taught. Teachers use criterion-referenced reading tests to determine if the child has mastered specific reading instructional objectives (e.g., recognition of *ed* endings, use of the *ch* consonant digraph). Test items are presented in an ordered hierarchy so that the child is assessed in terms of the sequence of reading skills. If his performance on each skill does not reach the pre-established criterion of success (e.g., 95% level of proficiency), the teacher provides instruction specifically for that skill. When the child's performance demonstrates mastery of a specific skill according to the determined criterion, he progresses to the next skill in the sequence. The child's progress is determined by comparing his current performance with his previous performance.

The *RRC Diagnostic Reading Inventory* (Regional Resource Center, University of Oregon) is a criterion-referenced reading test featuring the use of *rate of correct and incorrect responses* from 1-minute behavior samples. Each subtest consists of a probe sheet, which is used for the 1-minute timings. Each probe assesses a specific reading skill. The skills assessed in the *Diagnostic Reading Inventory* include:

1. *Consonant Sounds.* Student orally sounds consonants while pointing to the letter.
2. *Vowel Sounds.* Student orally sounds long and short vowels while pointing to the letter.
3. *Blending I.* Student reads three-letter phonically regular nonsense words.
4. *Consonant Teams.* Student reads consonant teams in nonsense words.
5. *Irregular Words.* Student reads irregular words.
6. *Blending II.* Student reads nonsense words containing blends such as digraphs and diphthongs.
7. *"Van's Cave."* Student orally reads a story from a primer.
8. *Classroom Reader.* Student orally reads from classroom reader.

The manual recommends that the teacher administer each subtest approximately five times over a period of several days. Several samples provide more reliable results than a single sample. Figure 7.3 displays a subtest probe sheet (Irregular Words) and Table 7.5 contains a sample record sheet for the *Diagnostic Reading Inventory*. The record sheet readily displays the student's strengths and weaknesses in the subtest areas. For example, Greg needs immediate instruction in the areas of simple blending and sight words. Also, the rate of saying vowel and consonant sounds needs to be increased. However, its authors stress that their guideline rates may need altering for individual children. The use of rate data has not been extensively incorporated in standardized reading tests; its use probably will increase in forthcoming tests.

Dana reads while his teacher times him and makes notes.

away	three	little	said	my	help
find	come	blue	where	yellow	for
you	jump	down	is	the	here
go	look	make	all	good	have
are	want	ride	please	our	news
out	was	like	must	came	saw
who	did	eat	with	say	that
so	they	be	there	now	soon
went	after	will	from	could	put
them	when	every	know	just	how
again	give	over	any	some	live
then	as	take	where	fly	because
use	sleep	many	gave	does	been
its	very	write	your	made	read
off	best	which	work	their	us
these	pull	about	much	eight	bring
only	never	laugh	kind	try	done
keep	ten	six	light	far	cut

Time: One minute

Comments:

Number Correct: _____

Number Incorrect: _____

FIGURE 7.3

Subtest probe sheet for irregular words.

Source: Adapted in part from *Regional Resource Center Diagnostic Inventories,* Eugene, Oregon: University of Oregon. The material is in public domain.

TABLE 7.5

Diagnostic Reading Inventory record sheet.

Name: Greg   Teacher: Jones
Grade: 4   School: Piney Circle

SUBTEST NAME	TIME	DAY 1 Date ___ standard X non-stand ___ admin. by: ___		DAY 2 (weekend) Date ___ standard X non-stand ___ admin. by: ___		DAY 3 Date ___ standard X non-stand ___ admin. by: ___		DAY 4 Date ___ standard X non-stand ___ admin. by: ___		Suggested Rates for Determining Proficiency[a]	
		correct	error	correct	error	correct	error	correct	error	correct	error
Consonant Sounds	1 min.	18	0	25	0	18	0	35	0	60–80	2 or less
Vowel Sounds	30 sec.	14	0	12	4	11	1	15	3	30–40	2 or less
Blending I	1 min.	6	6	5	2	4	10	9	8	90–100	2 or less
Con. Teams	30 sec.	6	4	7	4	7	4	8	3	45–50	1 or less
Irreg. Words	1 min.	8	3	15	3	21	3	17	9	80–100	0
Blending II	1 min.	2	4	2	2	b				80–100	2 or less
Oral Reading "Van's Cave"	1 min.	9	7	18	4	26	6	28	11	100–120	2 or less
School Book:	1 min.	21	1	18	6	24	7	28	5	100–120	2 or less

Title: "Tony's Adventure"   Page: 48   Grade Level: 2.1
Publisher: Science Research Associates   Basal / (Regular) (circle one)

[a] Based on Haughton's (1972) report of research by Starlin.
[b] Blank boxes show that rate is so low, further testing is not warranted.

Source: Adapted in part from *Regional Resource Center Diagnostic Inventories,* Eugene, Oregon: University of Oregon. The material is in the public domain.

The *Individual Pupil Monitoring System—Reading* (Houghton Mifflin) includes five levels, each of which is divided into the three reading skill areas of word attack, vocabulary and comprehension, and discrimination/study skills. The teacher keeps a record of the progress of his students on the Teacher's Management Record; in addition, each student records his own performance on a Pupil Progress Record. Other criterion-referenced programs for assessing and teaching reading include *Brigance Diagnostic Inventory of Basic Skills* (Curriculum Associates, Inc.), *Read-On* (Random House), and *Skills Monitoring System—Reading* (Harcourt Brace Jovanovich).

Informal Measures

A teacher can easily devise useful informal criterion procedures to assess any measurable skill in reading. For example, the teacher can assess letter recognition, sound-symbol knowledge, recognition of sight words, or reading rate in basal reader by presenting the student with a task and recording responses. (Table 7.2, p. 201, provides an error-analysis framework for observing and recording student responses. Chapters 3 and 14 provide numerous suggestions for using and developing informal assessment procedures.) This section presents three informal measures: *(a) Informal Reading Inventory, (b)* graded word lists, and *(c)* daily observations.

Informal Reading Inventory

The *Informal Reading Inventory* gives information about the child's general reading level. It uses reading passages from various graded levels. The child reads aloud and the teacher records his errors. He continues reading until he makes no more than two errors per 100 words. The teacher asks questions about each passage to check comprehension skills. According to Johnson and Kress (1965), through this method the teacher can informally estimate the child's reading ability at three reading levels: independent, instructional, and frustration.

At the *independent reading level,* the child can read the graded passage with high accuracy (i.e., he recognizes 98–100% of the words and answers the comprehension questions with 90–100% accuracy). At this level, the teacher can hand out supplementary materials for independent reading.

The level at which the child needs some help is the *instructional reading level.* The child can recognize 95% of the words and comprehends approximately 75% of the material. The teacher should provide directed reading instruction.

At the *frustration reading level,* the child cannot read without considerable difficulty. His word recognition is 90% or less with a comprehension score of 50% or less. Reading material at this level cannot be used for instruction.

In addition to recording the child's word recognition and comprehension, the teacher can also note various types of reading errors. On his copy of the reading material, the teacher should record such errors as omitting words or parts or words, inserting or substituting words, reversing a word or its letters, and repeating words.

Graded Word Lists

The child's word recognition grade level can also be informally determined through the use of *graded word lists* (Kirk, Kliebhan, & Lerner, 1978). A word list with words ranging from preprimer to 3rd grade level can be devised by randomly selecting words from the glossaries of graded basal readers. The words for each grade level should be typed on separate cards for the child to read and the teacher should have all the words listed on one sheet of paper. As the child reads the words aloud, the teacher marks the errors on his sheet of paper and makes note of the child's method of attacking difficult words. When the child recognizes at least 99% of the words on the list, he is at the independent level. When the child incorrectly responds to 2-10% of the words, he is functioning at the instructional level. When he misses more than 10% of the words, he is at the frustration level.

Daily Observations

Experienced teachers can carefully make day-to-day observations to obtain diagnostic information. Strang (1969) notes that teachers can obtain insights about behavior and immediately respond to the child's strengths and weaknesses. The teacher can watch the child in various situations, such as during instructional lessons, testing sessions, and recreational reading.

READING APPROACHES AND MATERIALS

Haring and Bateman (1977) recommend three steps in teaching learning disabled children to read: *(a)* teach them to attend to relevant phoneme features, *(b)* provide many repetitions of sound-symbol associations, and *(c)* systematically apply reinforcement for reading behavior. In this section the following approaches to reading instruction are discussed: *(a)* basal, *(b)* phonic, *(c)* linguistic, *(d)* alphabetic, *(e)* language experience, *(f)* individualized, *(g)* programmed, and *(h)* specialized. Although each method may be useful, the teacher must weigh the attributes and limitations of each approach or material. As Gearheart (1976) states, "we know that all of these approaches are effective with some children some of the time and that no one approach is effective with all children all of the time" (pp. 78-79).

Basal Reading Approach

Many teachers use a basal reading series as the core of their reading program. Most series include a sequential set of reading texts and supplementary materials such as workbooks, flash cards, placement and achievement tests, and filmstrips. In addition, a teacher's manual explains the purpose of the program and provides precise instructional plans and suggestions for skill activities. The readers in a series usually begin with preprimers and gradually increase in difficulty continuing through the sixth-eighth grade. The series systematically presents reading skills in word recognition, comprehension, and word attack and controls the vocabulary from level to level. Some materials designed for multiracial and disadvantaged groups incorporate story settings and content to appeal to a variety of backgrounds and ethnic groups. Also, now many readers introduce the earlier use of phonics. The basal reading series is carefully designed to be a comprehensive foundation on which the resourceful teacher can build and create other reading experiences.

Phonic Approach

The phonic approach teaches word recognition through a sounding-blending process. After learning the sounds of vowels, consonants, and phonic blends, the child learns to sound out words by combining sounds and blending them into words. Thus, the child learns to produce unfamiliar words by associating speech sounds with letters or groups of letters. Teachers may use either the synthetic method or the analytic method (Matthes, 1972). In the synthetic method, children learn that letters represent certain sounds (e.g., *b, buh*) and then find out how to blend or synthesize the sounds to form words. This method emphasizes isolated letter sounds before the child progresses to words. The analytic method teaches letter sounds as integral parts of words (e.g., *b* as in *baby*). The child must generalize from familiar words to new words on the basis of similar phonic elements. Various phonic methods and materials differ on details, but the main objective is to teach the child to attack new words independently.

After conducting an extensive review of research on reading instructional methods, Chall (1967) indicates the importance of phonic instruction and states:

> The research from 1912 to 1965 indicates that a code-emphasis method—i.e., one that views

Reading disabilities

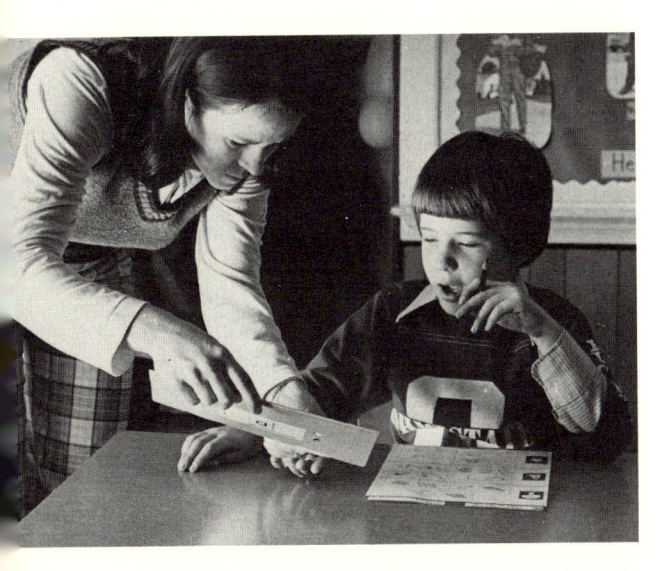

The auditory wheel shows a short a *and the child makes up a word using that vowel.*

beginning reading as essentially different from mature reading and emphasizes learning of the printed code for the spoken language—produces better results, at least up to the point where sufficient evidence seems to be available, the end of the third grade. (p. 307)

Five programs or methods based on the phonic approach are *(a) Open Court Basic Readers* (Trace, 1964), *(b) Basic Reading* (McCracken & Walcutt, 1963), *(c) Phonovisual Method* (Schoolfield & Timberlake, 1960), *(d) Hegge-Kirk-Kirk Remedial Reading Drills* (Hegge, Kirk, & Kirk, 1936), and *(e) The Writing Road to Reading* (Spalding & Spalding, 1962).

Open Court Basic Readers

Consisting of six textbooks and one workbook, this series uses a letter-by-letter and sound-by-sound approach to teach children to pronounce words. In the first book the child learns a sound at the beginning of each lesson, then the child makes associations with spellings of that sound. The remaining books include a variety of stories.

Basic Reading

In the lessons in this series, both long and short sounds of a letter are presented and on the page following each lesson the child is given a chance to use the sound. In the pre-primer and primer there are 135 lessons on sounds and the two additional books for the 1st grade include 182 more lessons and stories.

Phonovisual Method

In this phonetic system the sounds of consonants and vowels are orally introduced through the use of wall charts. Through the pictures on the wall charts (e.g., a monkey for /m/), the child is taught to associate each letter sound with a visual image.

Hegge-Kirk-Kirk Remedial Reading Drills

These reading drills are systematically developed and are divided into four parts. Part I introduces the most frequent sounds including sounds of short vowels and consonants; Part II consists of certain combinations of the previously learned sounds. Part III presents less frequently used sounds in whole words; and supplementary exercises are provided in Part IV.

The Writing Road to Reading

In this method, 70 phonograms, representing 45 basic sounds, are presented. Only phonetic sounds are used and the letters are not referred to by name. The child says the sound for each phonogram and then writes the letter symbol. After phonograms have been mastered, words are taught and are presented in groups that correspond to phonetic rules. Irregular forms of words that do not follow phonetic rules are taught as sight words.

Linguistic Approach

Although linguistic scholars have not actually attempted to develop a total reading approach, there are many linguistic approaches to reading that have been generated from the ideas of various linguists. Linguists, mainly concerned with oral communication, have provided important information concerning the nature and structural properties of language. Bloomfield and Barnhart (1961) and

Fries (1963) provide a linguistic framework for the teaching of reading that emphasizes "decoding" or changing the printed words into verbal communication. In many linguistic reading materials, a whole-word approach is used. In beginning reading, words are introduced that contain a short vowel and consist of a consonant-vowel-consonant pattern. Thus the words are selected on the basis of similar spelling patterns (e.g., *cab, lab, tab*) and the child must discover and generalize the relationship between speech sounds and letters (i.e., between phonemes and graphemes). This approach does not use exercises in sounding and blending; words are taught in word families and only as wholes. Words that have phonemically irregular spellings are introduced as the child progresses; he learns them as sight words. After learning words in the spelling patterns, he must put them together to form sentences. Kirk, Kliebhan, and Lerner (1978) found that LD children cannot easily generalize the relationship between sounds and letters, so direct instruction during each step of the learning process may be required. Materials using the linguistic approach are *Let's Read; Merrill Linguistic Readers; Miami Linguistic Readers; SRA Basic Reading Skills; The Linguistic Readers;* and *The Structural Reading Series.* (Addresses of the publishers may be found in the references for this chapter.)

Alphabetic Approach

The alphabetic approach in beginning reading instruction is often used with LD students. The following four modified alphabetic approaches are discussed: *(a)* initial teaching alphabet, *(b)* Words in Color, *(c)* UNIFON, and *(d)* diacritical marking system.

Initial Teaching Alphabet

The initial teaching alphabet (i.t.a.) uses a modified alphabet to insure a consistent correspondence between sound and symbol. Originally used in the British schools, the i.t.a. was introduced in the United States by Downing (1965). Each letter in the traditional 26-letter alphabet does not always have just one sound. However, because the i.t.a. presents one symbol for each sound, a consistent relationship exists between each of the 44-letter characters and its respective sound. This pattern helps eliminate confusing irregularities in spelling. The 44 characters include all the letters of the traditional alphabet (with the exceptions of *x* and *q*) and 20 other letters that either look like traditional letters joined together or new symbols. These additional letters represent special phonemes, such as the *th* sound. In addition, to reduce confusion, a larger version of the letter indicates uppercase letters instead of capital letters (Tanyzer & Mazurkiewicz, 1967). Some examples of words in the i.t.a. include *larj (large), thout (thought), laf (laugh), askt (asked),* and *wun (one).* The initial teaching alphabet is used only in the beginning stages of reading; then, as soon as he is fluent in the i.t.a., the child transfers his skills to the traditional alphabet. Spache and Spache (1973) report that although research findings on the i.t.a. are often contradictory and inconclusive, it shows promise and warrants longitudinal research efforts.

Words in Color

This program (Gattegno, 1962) in alphabet-phonics uses color to indicate sounds contained in words; 47 speech sounds (phonemes) are represented by 47 different colors or shades of colors. Thus, regardless of its spelling, each sound is represented by the same color. For example, white represents the sound of short *a* whether the spelling is *a (pat)* or *au (laugh);* likewise, another color represents all variations of the sound of long *a,* such as *ay,* or *eigh.* Wall charts help the student learn the sounds and colors. On the first 21 of these charts, 20 vowel sounds and 27 consonant sounds are each presented in a different color. Vowels, then consonants are introduced. The remaining 8 charts present various spellings for each sound. The series also includes three introductory books, a book of stories, and worksheets. Children learn the sounds of letters through color names; letter names are not taught. They copy words and sentences from the blackboard and visual dictation is used to point out successions of sounds from written sequences. As the child learns to use words in black and white, the use of color is discontinued.

UNIFON

The UNIFON (Malone, 1965) alphabet consists of 40 synthetic capital letters. Regular symbols represent the short vowels but new symbols are given for long vowel sounds, vowel diphthongs, and some consonant digraphs (e.g., *ng, sh, ch, th*). UNIFON does not deal with double and silent letters.

Diacritical Marking System

In the diacritical marking system (Fry, 1964), phonetic marks are added to the letters in the traditional alphabet. For example, long vowels have a bar over them, silent letters have a slash mark through them, and digraphs have a bar under both letters (e.g., *fiv̸e, with*). Short vowels and regular consonants are not changed. As the child's reading skill progresses, use of the marks diminishes.

Language Experience Approach

The language experience approach (LEA) integrates the development of reading skills with the development of listening, speaking, and writing skills. What the child is thinking and talking about make up the materials. According to Lee and Allen (1963), LEA deals with the following thinking process: *(a)* what a child thinks about, he can talk about, *(b)* what a child says, he can write (or someone can write for him), and *(c)* what a child writes (or others write for him), he can read.

Highly individualized, LEA stresses each child's unique interests. The experiential background of the child plays a major role in determining his reading material. The child dictates stories to the teacher, which initially may be taken from the child's own drawings and art work. The teacher writes down the stories and they become the basis of the child's initial reading experiences. Thus, the

The language experience approach enables Greg to pursue his interest in model airplanes.

child learns to read his own written thoughts. Teachers encourage each pupil to proceed at his own rate; the teacher tries to broaden and enrich the experiences of the child so he will have a broader base from which he can think, speak, and read. Eventually, with help, the child can write his own stories. Story notebooks may be traded among children. The LEA helps maintain motivation and interest, since initially the child creates the content.

Individualized Reading Approach

In an individualized reading program each child independently selects his own reading material according to his interests and ability and progresses at his own rate. Thus it is essential to have available a large collection of books at varied reading levels with many subjects represented at each level of difficulty. After each child chooses his reading material, he paces himself and keeps records of his progress. Teachers instruct word recognition and comprehension skills as each child needs them. The child and teacher confer once or twice a week during which time the teacher may ask the child to read aloud and discuss his reading material. From these conferences he keeps a record of the child's capabilities and progress in order to plan activities to develop specific skills. His role is to diagnose and prescribe; success depends on his resourcefulness and competency. Because this approach involves self-learning and lacks a systematic check of the mastery of basic steps in the reading process, Kirk, Kliebhan, and Lerner (1978) feel that the value of this method is questionable with LD children.

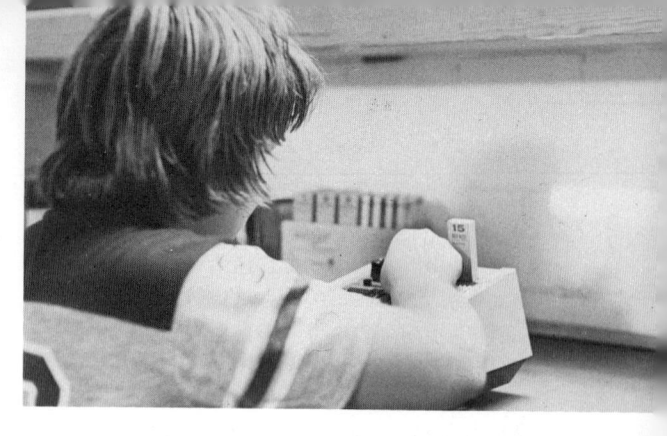

A tachistoscope briefly exposes words and phrases to strengthen visual memory. Brent learns how to combine parts of sentences and carry his reading down to the next line.

In an individualized reading program, the student chooses his own reading materials.

Programmed Reading Approach

Programmed reading materials can be presented either in a workbook format or a teaching machine. The materials are designed to be self-teaching and self-corrective. Subject matter is presented in small steps or frames that are in a systematic and logical sequence. The child must make a response to the question in each frame and then he checks his own responses by sliding down a marker. Responses may be in the form of answering *yes, no, true,* or *false;* completing a sentence; writing a word; or completing a word by filling in letters. When working with a machine, the child responds by pulling a lever or knob, pushing a button, or turning a crank. With all programmed materials he receives immediate feedback. He thus progresses at his own pace and receives correction or positive reinforcement at each step. *Programmed Reading* (Buchanan, 1966), an example of this method, emphasizes a sequenced linguistic-phonic approach.

Specialized Techniques

This section includes specialized methods of teaching reading that are not included in the previously discussed approaches. The five methods presented are *(a)* Fernald, *(b)* Gillingham, *(c)* Distar, *(d)* rebus, and *(e)* neurological impress.

Fernald Method

Fernald (1943) offers a multisensory approach to reading that simultaneously involves four sensory modalities: visual, auditory, kinesthetic, and tactile (VAKT). The vocabulary is selected from stories the child has dictated, and each word is taught as a whole. The method consists of four stages.

In Stage 1, the teacher writes the word to be learned on paper with a crayon. The child then traces the word with his fingers making contact with the paper (tactile-kinesthetic). As he traces it, he says the word aloud (auditory). In addition, the child sees the word (visual) while he is tracing it and hears the word as he says it (auditory). This process is repeated until the child can write the word correctly without looking at the sample. If the word is correct, it is placed in a file box. The child writes a story using these words and the story is typed so he can read the words. In Stage 2, the child is no longer required to trace each word but learns each new word by looking at the teacher's written copy of the word, saying it to himself, and writing it. The child learns new words in Stage 3 by looking at a printed word and saying it to himself before writing it. At this point the child may begin reading from books. In Stage 4, the child is able to recognize new words from their similarity to printed words or parts of words previously learned. Thus he can generalize his reading skills. According to Kirk, Kliebhan, and Lerner (1978), "If the four stages are followed in sequence and mastery assured at each stage before moving on, the slow learner and the learning-disabled pupil should learn to read and become eager to use reading materials" (p. 138).

Gillingham Method

The Gillingham method (Gillingham & Stillman, 1968) is a highly structured, phonetically oriented approach based on the theoretical work of Orton (1937). Following an alphabetic system, the method requires that each letter sound be taught using a multisensory approach. Consonants and vowels having only one sound are presented on drill cards (consonants on white cards and vowels on salmon-colored cards) and letters are introduced by a key word (e.g., *fun* for *f*). Associative processes are used beginning with the child associating or forming linkages between the name and sound of the letter with its printed symbol. The child repeats the name of the letter and the sound of the letter (i.e., oral spelling). Then without showing the drill card, the teacher makes a sound and asks the child to name the letter having that sound. In the final association process, the teacher writes the letter and explains its form. The child then traces the letter over the teacher's lines, copies it, writes it from memory, and writes it

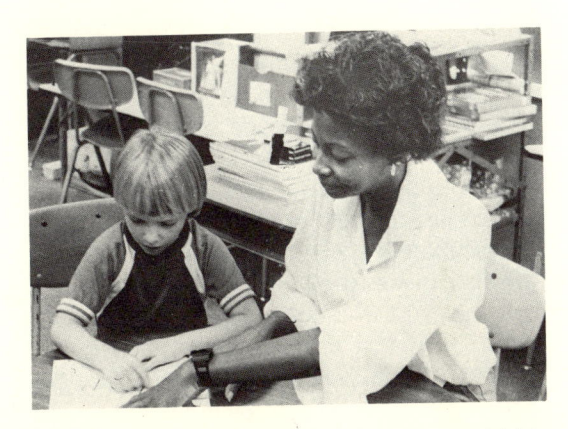

The teacher asks the child to trace a word with his finger.

The Gillingham method requires tracing of letters.

with his eyes looking away. When the child has learned the first group of 10 letters, he is taught to blend and read words.

Spelling is introduced after blending in a four-point program. When the teacher says a word, the student repeats the word, names the letters, writes the letters as he says them (simultaneous oral spelling), and reads the word he has written. Sentence and story writing is introduced after the child is able to write any three-letter phonetically pure word. Nonphonetic words are taught through drill. Thus the Gillingham method emphasizes repetition and drill; no other reading and/or spelling materials are to be used. Two adaptations of the Gillingham method include *Recipe for Reading* (Traub & Bloom, 1970) and *Multi-Sensory Approach to Language Arts for Specific Language Disability Children* (Slingerland, 1974). Dechant (1970) and Gates (1947) criticize this method because the teaching procedures are rigid; it lacks meaningful, interesting activities and children tend to develop a labored reading style. However, Otto, McMenemy, and Smith (1973) found the approach works with modifications.

Distar Reading Program

The Distar reading program (Engelmann & Bruner, 1969) is an intensive and highly structured programmed instructional system designed to remediate below-average reading skills of any age child. The children are grouped (no more than five in a group) according to their current abilities. Each day, one 30-minute lesson is presented. As the child masters skills according to his performance on tests, he changes groups. A detailed guide precisely specifies everything the teacher is to say and do. The method uses a behavioral approach by giving the children positive reinforcement for correct responses. The Distar program includes: *(a)* symbol-action games to teach sequencing skills and left-to-right orientation, *(b)* blending tasks to teach children to spell words by sounds ("say it slow") and to blend quickly ("say it fast"), and *(c)* rhyming tasks to teach the relationships between sounds and words. Take-home sheets are used to practice skills. Becker and Engelmann (1977) and Stallings (1974) report that results from Project Follow Through indicate that Distar effectively helped children in Head Start programs to learn reading skills.

Rebus Approach

The rebus approach to reading instruction involves the use of picture words (rebuses) rather than spelled words. Reading material uses pictures instead of printed words. Since each picture has only one obvious meaning, reading is quite easy (e.g., *dog* is simply a picture of a dog). The *Peabody Rebus Reading Program* (Woodcock, 1967) includes three programmed workbooks and two readers. Each workbook contains 384 frames that present a simple question or reading task. The child selects an answer and applies a small amount of water on the response area. If the response is correct, the area changes color to green. If the response is incorrect, the area becomes red and the child does not move to the next frame until he has made a correct response. Thus, the student proceeds at his own pace. *Introducing Reading—Book One* introduces a rebus vocabulary of 35 words and several basic reading skills, such as the use of context clues. Thirty-three additional rebuses are added in *Introducing Reading—Book Two* and structural analysis skills are presented. The third programmed workbook, *Introducing Reading—Book Three,* introduces some phonic skills and is used with two rebus readers, *Red and Blue Are On Me* and *Can You See a Little Flea.* Upon completion, the child will have a reading vocabulary of 122 spelled words. Through substitution of spelled words for the rebuses, the child makes the transition to the traditional reading situation. Haring and Bateman (1977) claim that the use of pictures adds an additional step to the reading task; they discourage the use of pictures in teaching reading to LD children.

Neurological Impress Method

The relatively new neurological impress method (Heckelman, 1969; Langford, Slade, & Barnett, 1974) was originally developed to teach reading to children with severe reading disabilities. The method consists of oral unison reading at a rapid pace by the student and the teacher. The student is seated slightly in front of the teacher and the teacher's voice is directed into the student's ear at a close range. The student or teacher slides his finger to the location of the words as they are being spoken. The method is based on the theory that a new learning process is established from the auditory feedback from the reader's voice and the voice of someone else reading the same material. There have been few research studies reported using this approach with LD children.

Sources of Reading Activities and Methods

Chapter 14 includes numerous teaching activities and techniques for teaching reading skills. However, specific teaching activities are available from a variety of commercial sources: Bailey (1975), Hall (1969), Hammill & Bartel (1978), Kirk, Kliebhan, & Lerner (1978), Russell & Karp (1938), Spache (1972), Stephens (1977), Wallace & Kauffman (1978), Wiederholt, Hammill, & Brown (1978).

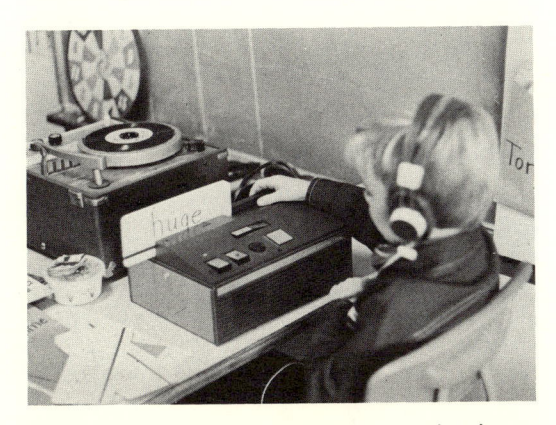

The Language Master provides practice in vocabulary skills.

SPELLING

Spelling refers to forming words through the traditional arrangement of letters. Spelling in the written form (orthography) is considered to be a more important skill than oral spelling. Spelling is usually instructed at the beginning of the second grade or at the end of the first grade.

As noted in Chapter 6, the English language presents inconsistent relationships between phonemes (i.e., speech sounds) and graphemes (i.e., written symbols). There are 26 letters in the traditional alphabet; however, many more phonemes are used in English speech. Thus, differences may exist between the spelling of various words and the way the words are pronounced. Many LD children have trouble spelling. Lerner (1976) reports that children who have trouble recognizing words in reading (decoding system) usually exhibit poor spelling skills (encoding system) as well.

Development of Spelling Skills

Some educators propose a linguistic approach (use of rules that emphasize a sound-letter method). They maintain that there is an underlying regularity between phoneme-grapheme correspondence and spelling words should be selected on the basis of unpredictable linguistic patterns. Hodges and Rudorf (1966) used a computer program designed to *predict* the spelling of 17,000 words according to rules that emphasized relationship between sound and symbol, effect of the phoneme position in a syllable, effect of speech emphasis, and effect of sounds that immediately precede or follow a given sound. In the results, (a) the computer correctly spelled 49% of the words, (b) 37.2% of the words were spelled with only one error, (c) 11.4% had two errors, and (d) 1.3% had three or more errors. These findings support the linguistic approach, proving that predictable spelling patterns do exist with some regularity. In addition, Hammill, Larsen, and McNutt (1977) conducted a survey of 100 third-through eighth-grade teachers concerning their instructional methods. The majority of the teachers listed one of the following three basal spelling series, all based on linguistic theory: *(a) Spell Correctly* (Benthul, Anderson, Utech, Biggy, & Bailey, 1974), *(b) Word Book* (Rogers, Ort, & Serra, 1970), and *(c) Basic Goals in Spelling* (Kottmeyer & Claus, 1968, 1972).

Traditional spelling programs consist of word lists that have been selected according to frequency of use rather than linguistic patterns. Teachers then introduce word lists based on necessity and utility in writing and emphasize spelling rules when warranted.

Fernald's (1943) multisensory approach features a more structured method. As discussed previously in this chapter, the VAKT technique includes a tracing task (tactile-kinesthetic) that reinforces the child's visual image of the word. Thus, spelling skill is increased through strengthening the child's visual sequential memory.

According to Westerman (1971), spelling involves various skills in the visual, auditory, and motor sensory modalities. The child must be able to exhibit visual and auditory recognition and discrimination of the letters of the alphabet and must have motor control to write the word. In addition, he must know the language's linguistic structure. When skills in the visual, auditory, and motor sensory modalities are cross-integrated, spelling becomes automatic. However, a deficit in any one of these areas can manifest itself in spelling difficulties. Thus, when problem factors are diagnosed (e.g., poor auditory or visual memory and sequencing skills, poor auditory analysis, lack of fine motor control), activities should be designed to strengthen and reinforce the deficient area and thereby lead to efficient spelling ability.

Diagnosis of Spelling Problems

Many commercial spelling tests now available yield a grade level score. These tests are generally part of an achievement battery of tests [e.g., *Wide Range Achievement Test* (Jastak & Jastak, 1965)]. On the other hand, diagnostic tests provide information concerning a child's performance in various specific areas. For example, the *Gates-Russell Spelling Diagnostic Test* (1937) contains nine subtests that measure some of the factors underlying spelling ability (e.g., method of word attack, word pronunciation, and auditory discrimination).

Larsen and Hammill (1976) developed a norm-referenced diagnostic test, *The Test of Written Spelling,* which yields a standard score, a grade level score, and an age-equivalent score of the child's ability to spell both predictable and unpredictable words. The test contains 60 words and can be administered to individuals or to groups in approximately 20–30 minutes.

Kottmeyer's (1970) *Diagnostic Spelling Test,* a criterion-referenced test, measures specific spelling elements (e.g., doubled final consonants, nonphonetic spellings, long and short *oo*). The test uses a dictation format; the examiner says the word and an illustrative sentence and the child is required to write the word. One test is provided for children in the second and third grades, and a second test is designed for children in the fourth grade and above.

More diagnostic information can be obtained through informal procedures that concentrate on an analysis of specific errors. Cartwright (1969) notes:

Scotty's problems in visual memory show up in this spelling test.

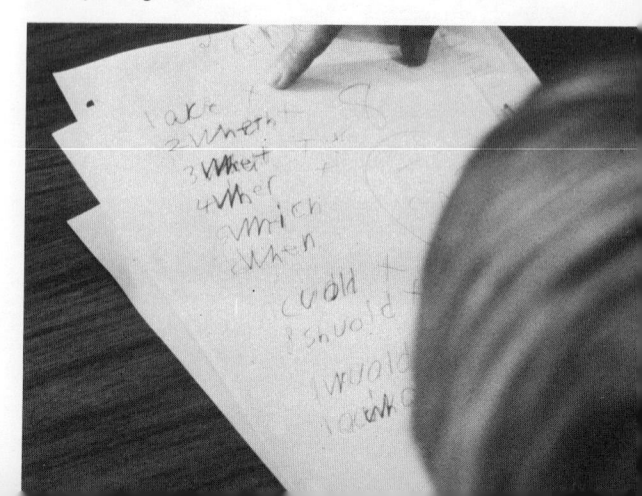

The primary purpose of appraisal of spelling ability is to discover consistent patterns of strengths and weaknesses. Knowing that a student consistently makes certain types of errors, the teacher can initiate a remedial program enabling him to generalize to new spelling situations with minimum difficulty. (p. 110)

Through direct observation of a child's spelling behavior, the teacher can identify specific and consistent spelling errors. Once the teacher knows the specific problems, he can plan individualized programs which will lead to spelling proficiency.

Cartwright (1969) suggests the use of a spelling error analysis chart to provide a profile of spelling strengths and weaknesses. For example, each time the child makes a specific error (e.g., errors pertaining to plurals, silent letters, contractions, and double letters), it is recorded on the chart. Edgington (1967) suggests some specific types of errors that should be noted (e.g., addition of unneeded letters; omissions of needed letters; reversals of whole words, consonant order, and/or syllables; errors due to a child's misinterpretation or dialect; phonetic spelling of nonphonetic words).

The child's proficiency in spelling frequently used words and frequently misspelled words may also be determined. After studying 10,000 words, Horn (1926) reveals that 10 words accounted for 25% of all words used. In order of frequency, these words include: *I, the, and, to, a, you, of, in, we, for.* He also notes that 100 words accounted for 65% of the words written by adults. In addition, Kuska, Webster, and Elford (1964) present a list of 100 commonly misspelled words that are linguistically irregular and do not follow spelling rules. These words, referred to as "demons," include: *ache, because, clothes, double, enemy, fault, guessed, hungry, kitchen, lettuce, meant, ninety, piano, rotten, success, whose,* and *writing.*

In addition to the dictated spelling test most commonly used, the Cloze procedure provides a visual means of testing spelling. The child may be required to complete a sentence by writing the correct response in the blank (e.g., "The opposite of down is _____" [*up*]). In addition, the child may complete a word or supply missing letters (e.g., "The clouds are in the s   " [*sky*] or "Please give me a glass of w t r" [*water*]).

SUMMARY

This chapter discusses the relationship between reading disabilities and learning disabilities. It is possible that few children with mild reading disabilities are considered learning disabled. Factors related to reading disabilities are discussed in terms of physical correlates, environmental correlates, and psychological correlates. It is noted that most reading disabilities result from a combination of factors. Types of reading behaviors and specific reading errors are presented within the framework of reading habits, word recognition errors, comprehension errors, and miscellaneous symptoms. Dyslexia is discussed from a medical and educational perspective. The development of reading is organized according to five stages: *(a)* development of reading readiness, *(b)* initial stage of learning to read, *(c)* stage of rapid development, *(d)* stage of wide reading, and *(e)* stage of refinement of reading. In addition, instructional objectives for word attack skills are featured in Table 7.4. The diagnosis of reading problems is presented in terms of norm-referenced tests, criterion-referenced tests, and informal measures. The *Diagnostic Reading Inventory* is stressed as a useful criterion-referenced instrument and informal reading inventories are highlighted as useful informal measures. Reading methods and approaches are presented and discussed in the following order: *(a)* basal reading, *(b)* phonic, *(c)* linguistic, *(d)* alphabetic, *(e)* language experience, *(f)* individualized reading, *(g)* programmed reading, and *(h)* specialized. The position is stressed that the teacher must constantly evaluate the attributes and weaknesses of the reading approaches for each child and select the most feasible approach based on assessment and clinical judgment. Also, selected sources of reading activities and methods are presented. Finally, spelling is presented in terms of skill development and diagnosis.

REFERENCES

Abt Associates. *Education as experimentation: A planned variation model* (Vol. 3). Boston: Abt Associates, 1976.

Bailey, E.J. *Academic activities for adolescents with learning disabilities.* Evergreen, Colo.: Learning Pathways, 1975.

Becker, W.C., & Engelmann, S. *The Oregon direct instruction model: Comparative results in Project Follow Through: A summary of nine years of work.* Eugene, Oreg.: University of Oregon Follow Through Project, 1977.

Benthul, H.F., Anderson, E.A., Utech, A.M., Biggy, M.V., & Bailey, B.L. *Spell correctly.* Morristown, N.J.: Silver Burdett, 1974.

Bloomfield, L., & Barnhart, C.L. *Let's read—A linguistic approach.* Detroit: Wayne State University Press, 1961.

Bond, G.L., & Dykstra, R. The cooperative research program in first-grade reading instruction. *Reading Research Quarterly,* 1967, 2, 5–142.

Botel Reading Inventory. (Available from Follett Educational Corp., 1010 W. Washington Blvd., Chicago, Ill. 60607).

Brabner, G., Jr. Reading skills. In R.M. Smith (Ed.), *Teacher diagnosis of educational difficulties.* Columbus, Ohio: Charles E. Merrill, 1969.

Brigance Diagnostic Inventory of Basic Skills. (Available from Curriculum Associates, 8 Henshaw St., Woburn, Mass. 01801).

Bryan, T.H., & Bryan, J.H. *Understanding learning disabilities.* Port Washington, N.Y.: Alfred, 1975.

Buchanan, C. *Programmed reading.* New York: McGraw-Hill, Sullivan Associates, 1966.

Cartwright, G.P. Written expression and spelling. In R.M. Smith (Ed.), *Teacher diagnosis of educational difficulties.* Columbus, Ohio: Charles E. Merrill, 1969.

Chall, J. *Learning to read: The great debate.* New York: McGraw-Hill, 1967.

Cohen, S.A. Minimal brain dysfunction and practical matters such as teaching kids to read. In F. de la Cruz, B. Fox, & R. Roberts (Eds.), *Minimal brain dysfunction.* New York: Annals of the New York Academy of Sciences, 1973.

Critchley, M. *Developmental dyslexia.* Springfield, Ill.: Charles C Thomas, 1964.

Dechant, E.V. *Improving the teaching of reading* (2nd ed.). Englewood Cliffs, N.J.: Prentice-Hall, 1970.

Doren Diagnostic Reading Test of Word Recognition. (Available from American Guidance Service, Publishers' Building, Circle Pines, Minn. 55014).

Downing, J. *The initial teaching alphabet reading experiment.* Chicago: Scott, Foresman, & Co., 1965.

Durrell Analysis of Reading Difficulty. (Available from Harcourt Brace Jovanovich, 757 Third Ave., New York, N.Y. 10017).

Dykman, R.A., Ackerman, P.T., Clements, S.D., & Peters, J. Specific learning disabilities: An attentional deficit syndrome. In H. Myklebust (Ed.), *Progress in learning disabilities* (Vol. 2). New York: Grune & Stratton, 1971.

Edgington, R. But he spelled them right this morning. *Academic Therapy Quarterly,* 1967, 3, 58–59.

Engelmann, S.E. *Preventing failure in the primary grades.* Chicago: Science Research Associates, 1969.

Engelmann, S., & Bruner, E.S. *Distar reading I and II: An instructional system.* Chicago: Science Research Associates, 1969.

Fernald, G. *Remedial techniques in basic school subjects.* New York: McGraw-Hill, 1943.

Fries, C.C. *Linguistics and reading.* New York: Holt, Rinehart & Winston, 1963.

Fry, E. A diacritical marking system to aid beginning reading instruction. *Elementary English,* 1964, 41, 526–529.

Gates, A.I. The necessary mental age for beginning reading. *Elementary School Journal,* 1937, 37, 497–508.

Gates, A.I. *The improvement of reading* (3rd ed.). New York: Macmillan, 1947.

Gates-MacGinitie Reading Tests. (Available from Teachers College Press, Teachers College, Columbia University, 1234 Amsterdam Ave., New York, N.Y. 10027).

Gates-McKillop Reading Diagnostic Tests. (Available from Teachers College Press, Teachers College, Columbia University, 1234 Amsterdam Ave., New York, N.Y. 10027).

Gates-Russell Spelling Diagnostic Test. New York: Teachers College, Columbia University, 1937.

Gattegno, C. *Words in color.* Chicago: Learning Materials, 1962.

Gearheart, B.R. *Teaching the learning disabled: A combined task-process approach.* Saint Louis: C.V. Mosby, 1976.

Gillingham, A., & Stillman, B. *Remedial teaching for children with specific disability in reading, spelling, and penmanship.* Cambridge, Mass.: Educator's Publishing Service, 1968.

Gray Oral Reading Test. (Available from Bobbs-Merrill, 4300 W. 62nd St., Indianapolis, Ind., 46206).

Hall, N.A. *Rescue: A handbook of remedial reading techniques for the classroom teacher.* Stevensville, Mich.: Educational Service, 1969.

Hallgren, B. Specific dyslexia: A clinical and genetic study. *Acta Psychiatrica Neurologica,* 1950, *65,* 1–287.

Hammill, D.D., & Bartel, N.R. *Teaching children with learning and behavior problems* (2nd ed.). Boston: Allyn & Bacon, 1978.

Hammill, D.D., Larsen, S., & McNutt, G. The effects of spelling instruction: A preliminary study. *The Elementary School Journal,* 1977, *78,* 67–72.

Haring, N.G., & Bateman, B. *Teaching the learning disabled child.* Englewood Cliffs, N.J.: Prentice-Hall, 1977.

Harris, A. *How to increase reading ability* (5th ed.). New York: David McKay, 1970.

Haughton, E. Aims—Growing and sharing. In J.B. Jordon & L.S. Robbins (Eds.), *Let's try doing something else kind of thing.* Arlington, Va.: The Council for Exceptional Children, 1972.

Heckelman, R.G. The neurological impress method of remedial reading instruction. *Academic Therapy,* 1969, *4,* 277–282.

Hegge, T., Kirk, S.A., & Kirk, W. *Remedial reading drills.* Ann Arbor, Mich.: George Wahr, 1936.

Hermann, K. *Reading disability: A medical study of word-blindness and related handicaps.* Springfield, Ill.: Charles C Thomas, 1959.

Hinshelwood, J. *Congenital word blindness.* London: H.K. Lewis, 1917.

Hodges, R.E., & Rudorf, E.H. Searching linguistics for cues for the teaching of spelling. In T.D. Horn (Ed.), *Research on handwriting and spelling.* Champaign, Ill.: National Council of Teachers of English, 1966.

Horn, E.A. *A basic writing vocabulary* (University of Iowa Monographs in Education, First Series No. 4). Iowa City: University of Iowa, 1926.

Individual Pupil Monitoring System—Reading. (Available from Houghton Mifflin, One Beacon St., Boston, Mass. 02107).

Jastak, J.F., & Jastak, S.R. *Wide Range Achievement Test.* Wilmington, Del.: Guidance Associates, 1965.

Johnson, D., & Myklebust, H. *Learning disabilities: Educational principles and practices.* New York: Grune & Stratton, 1967.

Johnson, M.S., & Kress, R.A. *Informal reading inventories.* Newark, Del.: International Reading Association, 1965.

Keogh, B.K., & Margolis, J. Learn to labor and wait: Attentional problems of children with learning disorders. *Journal of Learning Disabilities,* 1976, *9,* 276–286.

Kirk, S.A., Kliebhan, J.M., & Lerner, J.W. *Teaching reading to slow and disabled learners.* Boston: Houghton Mifflin, 1978.

Kottmeyer, W. *Teacher's guide for remedial reading.* New York: McGraw-Hill, 1970.

Kottmeyer, W., & Claus, A. *Basic goals in spelling* (3rd ed.). New York: McGraw-Hill, 1968.

Kottmeyer, W., & Claus, A. *Basic goals in spelling* (4th ed.). New York: McGraw-Hill, 1972.

Kuska, A., Webster, E.J.D., & Elford, G. *Spelling in language arts 6.* Ontario, Canada: Thomas Nelson & Sons, 1964.

Langford, K., Slade, K., & Barnett, A. An explanation of impress techniques in remedial reading. *Academic Therapy,* 1974, *9,* 309–319.

Larsen, S., & Hammill, D.D. *The Test of Written Spelling.* Austin, Tex.: Pro-Ed, 1976.

Lee, D.M., & Allen, R.V. *Learning to read through experience* (2nd ed.). New York: Appleton-Century-Crofts, 1963.

Lerner, J.W. *Children with learning disabilities* (2nd ed.). Boston: Houghton Mifflin, 1976.

Let's read. (Available from C.L. Barnhart, P.O. Box 359, Bronxville, N.Y. 10708).

Linguistic readers, The. (Available from Harper & Row, 10 East 53rd Street, New York, N.Y. 10022).

Malone, J.R. The unifon system. *Wilson Library Bulletin,* 1965, *40,* 63–65.

Matthes, C. *How children are taught to read.* Lincoln, Neb.: Professional Educators Publications, 1972.

McCracken, G., & Walcutt, C.C. *Basic reading.* Philadelphia: J.B. Lippincott, 1963.

Merrill linguistic readers. (Available from Charles

E. Merrill, 1300 Alum Creek Drive, Columbus, OH 43216).

Metropolitan Achievement Tests: Reading. (Available from Hartcourt Brace Jovanovich, 757 Third Ave., New York, N.Y. 10017).

Miami linguistic readers. (Available from D.C. Heath, 125 Spring Street, Lexington, MASS 02173).

Money, J. (Ed). *The disabled reader: Education of the dyslexic child.* Baltimore: Johns Hopkins Press, 1966.

National Advisory Committee on Dyslexia and Related Reading Disorders. *Reading disorders in the United States.* Washington, D.C.: U.S. Department of Health, Education, and Welfare, 1969.

Orton, S.T. *Reading, writing, and speech problems in children.* New York: W.W. Norton, 1937.

Otto, W., McMenemy, R., & Smith, R. *Corrective and remedial teaching* (2nd ed.). Boston, Mass.: Houghton Mifflin, 1973.

Read-On. (Available from Random House, 201 E. 50 St., New York, N.Y. 10022).

Regional Resource Center Diagnostic Reading Inventory. (Available from Regional Resource Center, Clinical Services Building, University of Oregon, Eugene, Oregon 97403).

Rogers, D.C., Ort, L.L., & Serra, M.C. *Word book.* Chicago: Lyons & Carnahan, 1970.

Russell, D.H., & Karp, E.E. *Reading aids through the grades.* New York: Teachers College Press, 1938.

Samuels, S.J. Success and failure in learning to read: A critique of the research. *Reading Research Quarterly,* 1973, *8,* 200–239.

Schoolfield, L., & Timberlake, J. *The phonovisual method.* Washington, D.C.: Phonovisual Products, 1960.

Skills Monitoring System—Reading. (Available from Harcourt Brace Jovanovich, 757 Third Ave., New York, N.Y. 10017).

Slingerland, B.H. *A multi-sensory approach to language arts for specific language disability children.* Cambridge, Mass.: Educator's Publishing Service, 1974.

Spache, E.B. *Reading activities for child involvement.* Boston: Allyn & Bacon, 1972.

Spache, G.D., & Spache, E.B. *Reading in the elementary school* (3rd ed.). Boston: Allyn & Bacon, 1973.

Spache Diagnostic Reading Scales. (Available from California Test Bureau, A Division of McGraw-Hill, Del Monte Research Park, Monterey, Calif. 93940).

Spalding, R.B., & Spalding, W.T. *The writing road to reading.* New York: William Morrow, 1962.

SRA Achievement Series: Reading. (Available from Science Research Associates, 259 E. Erie St., Chicago, Ill. 60611).

SRA basic reading skills. (Available from Science Research Associates, 259 E. Erie Street, Chicago, ILL 60611).

Stallings, J.A. *Follow Through classroom observation evaluation 1972–1973* (Executive Summary SRI Project URU-7370). Menlo Park, Calif.: Stanford Research Institute, 1974.

Stephens, T.M. *Teaching skills to children with learning and behavior disorders.* Columbus, Ohio: Charles E. Merrill, 1977.

Strang, R. *Diagnostic teaching of learning.* New York: McGraw-Hill, 1969.

Structural reading series, The. (Available from L.W. Singer, Random House, 201 East 50th Street, New York, N.Y. 10022).

Tanyzer, H.J., & Mazurkiewicz, A.J. *Early-to-read i/t/a program: Book 2.* New York: Initial Teaching Alphabet Publications, 1967.

Trace, A.S., Jr. (Ed.). *The Open Court basic readers.* LaSalle, Ill.: Open Court, 1964.

Traub, N., & Bloom, F. *Recipe for reading.* Cambridge, Mass.: Educator's Publishing Service, 1970.

U.S. Office of Education. Education of handicapped children: Assistance to states: Proposed rulemaking. *Federal Register,* 1976, *41,* 52404–52407.

Venezky, R.L. *Prereading skills: Theoretical foundations and practical applications* (Theoretical Paper No. 54). Madison, Wisc.: Wisconsin Research and Development Center for Cognitive Learning, 1975.

Wallace, G., & Kauffman, J.M. *Teaching children with learning problems* (2nd ed.). Columbus, Ohio: Charles E. Merrill, 1978.

Wallace, G., & McLoughlin, J.A. *Learning disabilities: Concepts and characteristics.* Columbus, Ohio: Charles E. Merrill, 1975.

Westerman, G.S. *Spelling & writing.* San Rafael, Calif.: Dimensions, 1971.

Wiederholt, J.L., Hammill, D.D., & Brown, V. *The resource teacher: A guide to effective practices.* Boston: Allyn & Bacon, 1978.

Woodcock, R. *Peabody rebus reading program.* Circle Pines, Minn.: American Guidance Service, 1967.

Woodcock Reading Mastery Tests. (Available from American Guidance Service, Publishers' Building, Circle Pines, Minn. 55014).

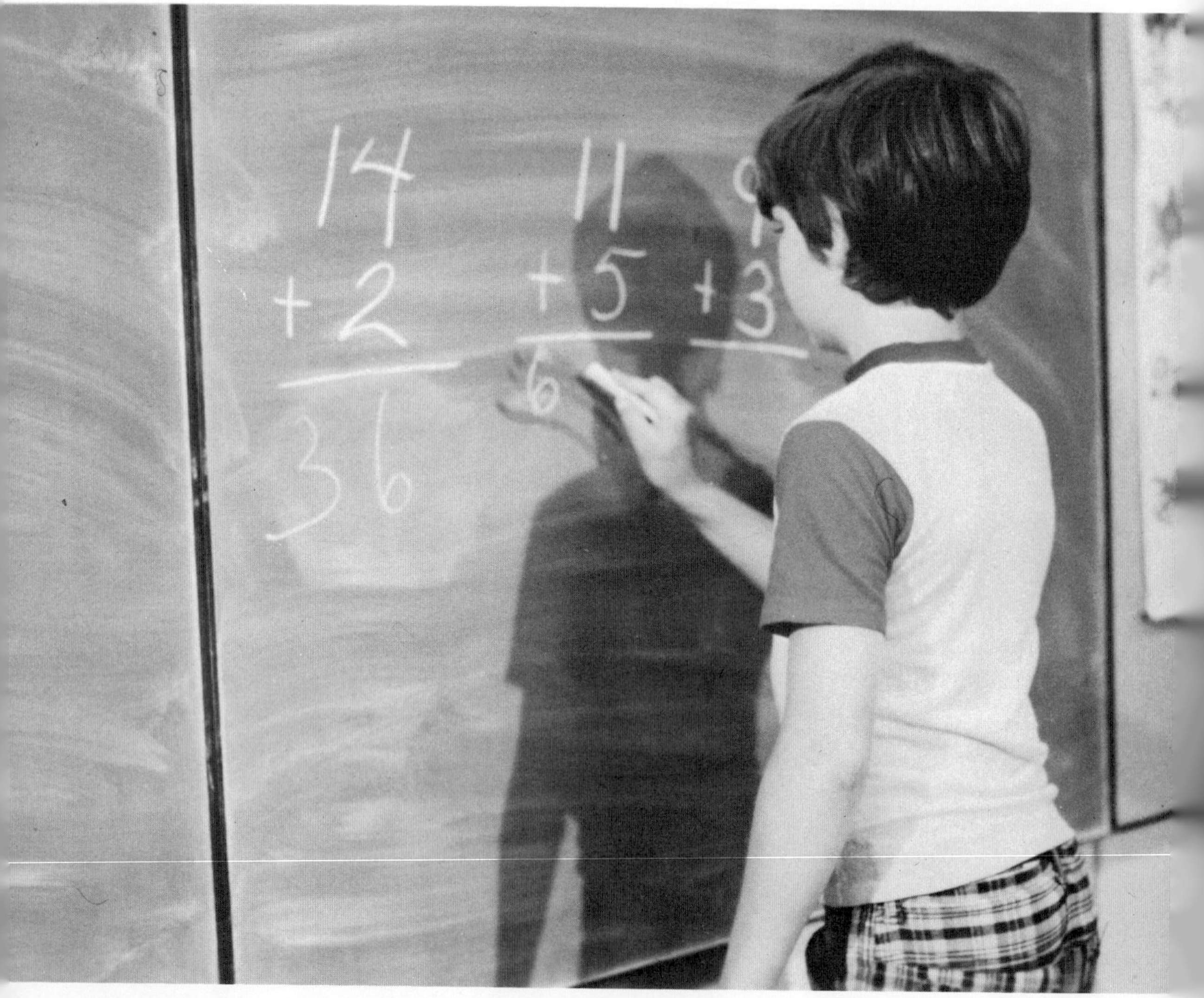
14
+2
36
11
+5
6
+3

8

Arithmetic disabilities

Traditionally arithmetic includes both verbal and written symbols. These symbols communicate such concepts as quantity, size, order, relationships, space, form, distance, and time. Some authorities refer to arithmetic as a universal language that enables people to think, record, and communicate concerning the elements and relationships involving quantity (Lerner, 1976). Moreover, it requires logical and nonverbal thinking (Stephens, 1977).

Although reading difficulties represent the most common specific academic disability, the primary academic disability of numerous LD students is math.

The work of Jack Cawley and his associates (Cawley, Fitzmaurice, Goodstein, Lepore, Sedlak, & Althaus, 1976) represents one of the few efforts aimed at examining the teaching of math to handicapped learners. To date, Cawley's work primarily focuses on mildly retarded youngsters, but it is likely that his work and other programmatic research efforts will continue to yield information applicable to the teaching of arithmetic to LD students.

DEVELOPMENT OF ARITHMETIC SKILLS

Levels of Arithmetic Tasks

Generally, math tasks are presented to youngsters at concrete, representational, and/or abstract levels. As Table 8.1 illustrates, the concrete level involves the manipulation of objects. For example, in teaching addition problems involving sums of 7, a concrete level activity could consist of having the student group seven blocks into all possible combinations of 7 (e.g., 6 + 1, 5 + 2). In teaching one-to-one correspondence at a concrete level, the learner might be required to pass out one pencil to each child in the room. Also, the abacus is a popular device for providing youngsters with concrete experiences in math. Some students demonstrate their need for or reliance on concrete level activities by counting on their fingers when requested to complete a simple addition problem. Some commercial math programs (Stern's Structural Arithmetic, Cuisenaire Rods, Unifix Cubes) feature concrete activities.

The representational level involves working with illustrations of items in performing math tasks. Items may include dots, lines, pictures of real objects, or nonsense items. For example, a worksheet that requires the student to match sets that have the same number of items is on the representational level. Most commercial math programs include such worksheets. Some LD pupils need much practice of this type in order to master a concept or fact. Oftentimes students demonstrate their reliance on this level by supplying their own graphic representations. For example, the problems 5 + 4 = ___ and 3 × 2 = ___ may be approached in the following manner:

pupil's writing } ///// ////
5 + 4 = 9

× ×
× × } pupil's writing
× ×
3 × 2 = 6

The abstract level involves working only with numerals to solve math problems. Students who have difficulty with math usually need extensive experience before they can perform and understand math at this level.

An abacus illustrates math concepts.

TABLE 8.1

Task levels in math.

Level	Primary Descriptor	Example
Concrete	Manipulation of real objects (three-dimensional).	Student manipulates blocks or abacus when solving simple math problems.
Representational	Graphic representations of objects or items (primarily two-dimensional).	Student completes worksheets that feature dots, lines, or pictures to form math tasks: ○○ + ○○ = ____ ; 🐱🐱 + 🐱 = ____ 🐱s.
Abstract	Only numerals are used in performing math tasks.	Student is given only numerals (e.g., 3 + 4 = ____).

Levels of Arithmetic Learning

Many authors relate mathematics to cognitive developmental stages. The developmental stages of Piaget as described by Pinard and Laurendeau (1969) are often incorporated into math programs. It is apparent that a specified degree of quantitative thinking is needed at each level. For example, the pupil who can solve the problem 3 + 2 = ____ but cannot solve the problem 2 + 3 = ____ lacks quantitative thinking. She should master concepts of one math skill before the next math skill is introduced. A teacher can determine her readiness for a math task by assessing her ability to compute selected math facts or by trial teaching. In trial teaching, the teacher evaluates how well instruction in certain skills "takes." Also, the learning level hierarchies discussed in Chapter 14 provide guidelines for determining whether an individual has mastered a specific skill.

Table 8.2 offers a list of skills commonly stressed at each grade level. In addition to helping the teacher select objectives for individual students, these skills also apply to many adolescent learning disabled students, since their problems in math usually involve skills taught in the upper elementary grades. Basically, the table indicates this sequence: numeration, kindergarten; addition and subtraction, first and second grades; multiplication, third grade; division, fourth grade; fractions, fifth grade; and decimals and percent, sixth grade.

In order to teach and/or learn math facts, one should master the language used in describing and computing math facts. Table 8.3, p. 233, presents some principal terms.

ARITHMETIC DISABILITIES

Factors Related to Arithmetic Disabilities

Understanding math problems of LD students is enhanced by examining several factors of arithmetic functioning. For example, one primary factor is the quality and degree of instruction. Most often ineffective or inadequate instruction causes math difficulties. These students have environmental problems, not personal deficits.

However, Kaliski (1967) notes that many of the characteristics attributed to LD students are related to arithmetic difficulties. For example, problems of perception, directionality, abstract thinking, memory, and reading are frequently attributed to LD students; each of

TABLE 8.2

Selected math skills by grade level.

Concept Area	Skill	K	1st	2nd	3rd	4th	5th	6th	Skill
Sets	1. Description	X							1
	2. Equivalent	X	X						2
	3. 1 more or less member	X							3
	4. Numbers: 1–4	X							4
	5. Zero	X							5
	6. Numbers: 0–10	X	X						6
	7. Number comparison	X		X					7
	8. Ordering	X							8
	9. Union of sets	X							9
	10. Partitioning of sets	X							10
Whole Numbers	1. Counting	X							1
	2. Ordering: 0–10	X							2
	3. Writing numbers		X						3
	4. 0–100, ordering, skip counting		X	X					4
	5. Odd or even, skip counting		X	X					5
Addition and Subtraction	1. Add: sums through 5		X						1
	2. Sub.: comb. through 5		X						2
	3. Add, sub.: comb. through 9		X						3
	4. Add, sub.: comb. through 10		X	X					4
	5. Add, sub.: comb. through 18		X	X	X				5
	6. 3 addends		X	X					6
	7. Add, without regrouping			X	X	X			7
	8. Sub., without regrouping			X	X	X			8
	9. Add, regrouping			X	X	X	X		9
	10. Sub., regrouping			X	X	X	X		10
Place Value	1. Ones and tens		X	X					1
	2. Ones through hundreds			X					2
	3. Ones through thousands			X					3
	4. Ones through hundred thousands				X	X			4
	5. Ones through hundred millions					X	X		5
	6. Large magnitude, exponents						X	X	6

Measurement

		1	2	3	4	5	6	7	8	9
1.	Time: hour, half hour	x								
2.	Time: 5 minutes		x							
3.	Length: inches		x							
4.	Length: inches, centimeters			x						
5.	Volume: cups, pints, quarts		x							
6.	Volume: gallons			x						
7.	Length: perimeter, area, volume					x	x			
8.	Money: pennies, nickels, dimes	x								
9.	Metric system								x	

Fractions

		1	2	3	4	5	6
1.	Fractions: emphasis on ½, ⅓, ¼	x					
2.	Fractions: halves through fifths		x				
3.	Fractions: halves through eighths			x			
4.	Fractions: parts of whole				x		
5.	Fractions: comparison				x	x	
6.	Fractions: improper, mixed numbers				x		x

Geometry

		1	2	3	4	5	6	7	8	9
1.	Shapes	x	x							
2.	Plane figures			x						
3.	Plane figures, congruency, parallel lines							x		x
4.	Circles			x	x					
5.	Geometric solids			x	x		x	x		
6.	Angles							x	x	x
7.	Geometry: area, volume, surface area						x	x		x
8.	Triangles							x	x	
9.	Circles: circumference, area									x

Multiplication and Division

		1	2	3	4	5	6	7	8	9	10
1.	Mult.: facts through 5		x								
2.	Mult.: facts through 9			x	x	x	x				
3.	Division: single digits			x	x	x	x				
4.	Mult.: single-digit multipliers			x	x	x	x				
5.	Division: 1-digit divisor			x	x	x	x				
6.	Mult.; regrouping					x	x	x	x		
7.	Division; multi-digit divisor					x	x	x	x		
8.	Averages						x	x			
9.	Factors, primes, multiples									x	
10.	Rounding numbers					x					x

TABLE 8.2 cont.

Concept Area	Skill	K	1st	2nd	3rd	4th	5th	6th	Skill
Graphs and Functions	1. Graphs, points and coordinates				X	X			1
	2. Graphing: 4 quadrants						X		2
	3. Graphing: 4 quadrants, functions							X	3
Fractions—Addition and Subtraction	1. Fractions: add, sub., like denominators					X	X		1
	2. Fractions: add, sub., unlike denominators						X	X	2
	3. Fractions: add, sub., mixed numbers						X	X	3
Fractions—Multiplication and Division	1. Fractions: multiplication						X	X	1
	2. Fractions: division						X	X	2
Decimals	1. Decimals						X	X	1
	2. Rounding decimals						X	X	2
Decimals—Add/Sub.	1. Decimals: add and sub.						X	X	1
Decimals—Mult./Division	1. Decimals: multiplication							X	1
	2. Decimals: division							X	2
Ratio and Proportion	1. Ratio and proportion							X	1
	2. Ratio, probability							X	2
Percent	1. Percent							X	1

TABLE 8.3

Math terms in basic computations.

Operation	Terms
Addition	8 ← addend +4 ← addend ――― 12 ← sum
Subtraction (take away)	9 ← minuend −4 ← subtrahend ――― 5 ← difference
Subtraction (add on)	9 ← sum −4 ← known addend ――― 5 ← missing addend
Multiplication	8 ← multiplicand ×5 ← multiplier ――― 40 ← product
Division	8 ← quotient 6)48 ← dividend ↑ divisor

A walk-on number line provides practice in perceptual-motor skills as well as math.

these problem areas has been related to arithmetic disabilities.

Perceptual Problems

Kaliski (1967) has found that problems with spatial relationships may result in confusion concerning concepts that are basic to quantitative thinking. For example, a child who does not fully understand the concepts of *first–last* or *beginning–end* is not ready for rational counting. Usually these and other spatial relationships are mastered during the preschool years: *top–bottom, up–down, over–under, beginning–end, near–far, first–last, front–back,* and *across.* Spatial factors are essential to quantitative thinking (Bryant & Kass, 1972), especially in differentiating between various numbers (e.g., *6* and *9* or *17* and *71*).

Problems in visual perception and visual-motor association complicate math. Such students have trouble with set identification (e.g., must count each object), recognition and production of shapes, and recognition and production of number symbols.

Directionality Problems

Directionality problems interrelate with spatial relationships. They manifest themselves in the six directions: *up–down, front–back,* and *left–right.* For example, students with directionality problems may encounter quantitative thinking difficulty using a number line, understanding positive and negative numbers, solving equations, and computing problems involving two or more columns of digits. Chalfant and Scheffelin (1969) point out that reading proceeds from left to right, whereas addition, subtraction, and multiplication are calculated right to left. For the youngster who exhibits directionality problems, division (worked from left to right) adds more confusion.

Abstract Thinking Problems

Abstract or symbolic thinking difficulties interfere with the youngster's ability to conceptualize the relationship between numerals and the objects represented by them. Also, these children lack understanding of place value and relationships between units of measurement. As noted previously, many youngsters need extensive experience at the concrete and representational levels before they can handle arithmetic problems involving only abstract symbols (numerals).

Memory Problems

Many arithmetic tasks require good memory skills. Teachers may encounter youngsters who cannot recall the name or shape of specific numbers, or number facts (e.g., multiplication). These children arrive at the correct answer in a slow and inefficient manner. For example, the teacher asked Francie to compute 8×4. Francie wrote this to figure the answers:

$$
\begin{array}{cccccc}
2 & 2 & 2 & 2 & 8 \\
\times 4 & \times 4 & \times 4 & \times 4 & 8 \\
\hline
8 & 8 & 8 & 8 & 8 \\
& & & & +8 \\
\hline
& & & & 32
\end{array}
$$

Reading Problems

Although many students who have arithmetic disabilities are excellent readers, reading is a contributing factor to some children with math problems. For example, the child may not be able to read word problems. Also, she may misunderstand the directions on a math worksheet.

Other Problems

Written language problems may contribute to arithmetic disabilities. For example, the youngster who has difficulty spacing numbers correctly might align problems incorrectly:

$$\begin{array}{r}42\\+18\\\hline\end{array} \text{ might be written as } \begin{array}{r}42\\+\ 18\\\hline\end{array}$$

Some children cannot copy arithmetic problems from the blackboard:

$$\begin{array}{r}42\\+16\\\hline\end{array} \text{ might be copied as } \begin{array}{r}24\\+19\\\hline\end{array}$$

Concrete activities help children visualize math concepts.

Some students need illustrated worksheets to understand story problems.

McLeod and Crump (1978) studied the relationship of math achievement of LD students to numerous ability areas. Their results indicate that verbal ability and visuospatial skills positively relate to match achievement. Spoken language problems may also result in math disabilities; youngsters may have difficulty learning the "language" of arithmetic. *Borrowing, carrying, times,* and *equals* have specific meanings in calculations.

Types of Arithmetic Errors

Arithmetic disabilities exist at all age levels. During the preschool and primary years, children with this problem cannot sort objects by size, match objects, understand the language of arithmetic, or grasp the concept of rational counting. During the elementary years, they have trouble with computational skills (Otto, McMenemy, & Smith, 1973). However, Bryant and Kass (1972) note that during the elementary years it is also important to examine such areas as measurement, decimals, fractions, and percentages in dealing with arithmetic disabilities. Also, the math deficits of many secondary students are similar to the deficits exhibited by younger children (e.g., place value problems and difficulty with basic math facts).

Although the specific error patterns of each student must be considered individually, it is helpful to examine some of the research regarding types of errors that students across grades exhibit. In a study of the computational errors of third graders, Roberts (1968) identified four primary error categories. These include:

1. *Wrong operation.* For example, the student subtracts when he should add.
2. *Obvious computational error.* The pupil applies the correct operation but makes an error in recalling a basic number fact.
3. *Defective algorithm.* An algorithm includes the specific steps used to compute a math problem. Stated another way, it is the problem-solving pattern used to arrive at an answer. An algorithm is defective if it does not deliver the correct answer. For example, the child who adds 24 + 16 by adding each number without regard for place value (i.e., 2 + 4 + 1 + 6 = 13) is using a defective algorithm because the correct answer is 40. In cases in which a defective algorithm is the only error, the pupil is applying the correct operation and recalling the basic facts.
4. *Random response.* In a random response no discernable relationship is apparent between the problem-solving process and the problem. For example, random responding may consist of guesses that do not even involve estimates.

Roberts (1968) reports that careless numerical errors and poor recall of addition and multiplication facts were equally distributed across ability levels. Random responses and the wrong operation occurred frequently with students of low ability (lowest quartile). Random responses accounted for the most errors in low-ability students and defective algorithm techniques accounted for the most errors of

Andy uses a multiplication chart to help him remember multiplication facts.

Specific learning disorders

pupils in the other three ability quartiles. Furthermore, in a thorough study of errors in computation by seventh graders, Lankford (1972) revealed that many errors were due to the use of erroneous algorithms. From her research, Cox (1975) reports that without intervention youngsters persist in making systematic errors for long periods of time.

Specific Error Patterns

A list of several common error patterns in addition and subtraction illustrates some of the computational problems of LD pupils.

1. *Response:*
$\quad\begin{array}{r}83\\+67\\\hline(1410)\end{array}\quad\begin{array}{r}66\\+29\\\hline(815)\end{array}$

Error pattern: The sums of the ones and tens are each recorded without regard for place value.

2. *Response:*
$\quad\begin{array}{r}67\\+31\\\hline(17)\end{array}\quad\begin{array}{r}58\\+12\\\hline(16)\end{array}$

Error pattern: All digits are added together (defective algorithm and no regard for place value).

(e.g., $\begin{array}{r}67\\+31\end{array}$ is performed as $6 + 7 + 3 + 1 = 17$.)

3. *Response:*
$\quad\begin{array}{r}{\scriptstyle 2\,1}\\476\\+851\\\hline(148)\end{array}\quad\begin{array}{r}{\scriptstyle 3\,7}\\753\\+693\\\hline(1113)\end{array}$

Error pattern: Digits are added from left to right. When the sum is greater than 10, the unit is carried to the next column on the right. This pattern reflects no regard for place value.

4. *Response:*
$\quad\begin{array}{r}{\scriptstyle 1}\\68\\+8\\\hline(156)\end{array}\quad\begin{array}{r}{\scriptstyle 1}\\73\\+9\\\hline(172)\end{array}$

Error pattern: In adding the tens column, the single digit number is added to the numeral in the tens column (i.e., the lower addend is added twice).

5. *Response:*
$\quad\begin{array}{r}627\\-486\\\hline(261)\end{array}\quad\begin{array}{r}761\\-489\\\hline(328)\end{array}$

Error pattern: The smaller number is subtracted from the larger number without regard for placement of the number. The upper number (minuend) may be subtracted from the lower number (subtrahend) or vice versa.

6. *Response:*
$\quad\begin{array}{r}{\scriptstyle 6\,1}\\1\not{7}5\\-54\\\hline(1111)\end{array}\quad\begin{array}{r}{\scriptstyle 7\,1}\\1\not{8}5\\-22\\\hline(1513)\end{array}$

Error pattern: Regrouping is used when it is not required.

7. *Response:*
$\quad\begin{array}{r}{\scriptstyle 5\,1\,1}\\\not{6}\not{3}2\\-147\\\hline(495)\end{array}\quad\begin{array}{r}{\scriptstyle 4\,1\,1}\\\not{5}\not{2}3\\-366\\\hline(167)\end{array}\quad\begin{array}{r}{\scriptstyle 4\,1}\\\not{5}63\\-382\\\hline(181)\end{array}$

Error pattern: When regrouping is required more than once, the appropriate amount is not subtracted from the column borrowed from in the second regrouping.

Place Value Problems

An examination of the arithmetic problems of LD youngsters indicates that many computational errors originate from an inadequate understanding of place value. Although place value is introduced in the primary grades, pupils of all ages continue to make mistakes because they cannot comprehend the principle that the same digit expresses different orders of magnitude depending on its location in a number. For example, all of the error patterns presented earlier reflect an inadequate understanding of place value. It seems that many factors contribute to the place value problem. In addition to the problems mentioned earlier, which contribute to arithmetic disabilities, some specific problems related to place value include:

1. Place value must be introduced before two-digit numbers are understood or computed. Since numbers greater than 10 are encountered in the primary grades, the highly abstract factor of place value is stressed at a very young age. For the most part children learn algorithms that enable them to work with two-digit numbers without comprehending the place value factors. This lack of understanding may not surface until higher level computational problems are presented in later grades.

2. In computing arithmetic facts, many parents, teachers, and peers do not "think" place value. For example, in computing the problem

$$\begin{array}{r} 48 \\ +16 \end{array}$$

most individuals say, "8 + 6 is 14, carry 1, 1 + 4 + 1 is 6, bring down the 6, and the answer is 64." This procedure is a poor model for pupils learning place value. A correct model is: "8 + 6 is 14, carry 10, 1 ten + 4 tens + 1 ten is 6 tens, bring down the 6 tens, and the answer is 6 tens and 4 ones, or 64." The lack of thinking place value exists in all arithmetic operations.

3. Most youngsters initially work only in base 10; this situation may present several problems. First, counting in base 10 does not consider place value. For example, when a youngster counts two-digit numbers by saying "11, 12, . . . 22, etc.," no consideration is given to place value. In place value terms, 11 should be thought of as 1 ten and 1 one, and 22 should be thought of as 2 tens and 1 one. Secondly, most individuals around the youngster habitually function in base 10 without overtly considering place value. For example, if you ask most individuals to read the number 45 in base 6, they will read it incorrectly. Many will read it as *forty-five* and not be able to explain that it means 4 sixes and 5 ones and is simply called "4–5." In giving directions the teacher should say, "Write the number 4 sixes and 5 ones in base 6." Third, if the youngster continues to make mistakes in base 10, errors may be learned in that base. If other bases are used, the youngster does not practice errors in the base that she primarily functions in later.

It is obvious that an inadequate understanding of place value contributes to the computational problems of LD youngsters. (In the section of this chapter containing teaching strategies, p. 248, much emphasis is placed on activities that help youngsters adequately learn place value.)

ASSESSMENT OF ARITHMETIC PROBLEMS

Diagnostic Guidelines

In assessing arithmetic skills, one must examine how a youngster computes. In most cases, a pupil goes through some steps in "figuring out" the answer. It is essential to know these steps in order to diagnose accurately. This information can be gained by observation. However, if a student does not display a faulty problem-solving pattern but responds incorrectly, ask the pupil to tell how the answer was computed. The addition and subtraction error patterns presented earlier in this chapter, p. 236, are difficulties that are readily determined by examining the pupil's problem-solving procedures. Table 8.4 illustrates some other specific types of faulty computational procedures. (Continued on pp. 238–239.)

TABLE 8.4

Types of arithmetic habits observed in elementary school pupils.

ADDITION

Errors in combinations	Errors in reading numbers
Counting	Dropped back one or more tens
Added carried number last	Derived unknown combination from familiar one

TABLE 8.4 cont.

ADDITION

Forgot to add carried number
Repeated work after partly done
Added carried number irregularly
Wrote number to be carried
Irregular procedure in column
Carried wrong number
Grouped two or more numbers
Splits numbers into parts
Used wrong fundamental operation
Lost place to column
Depended on visualization
Disregarding column position

Disregarded one column
Error in writing answer
Skipped one or more decades
Carrying when there was nothing to carry
Used scratch paper
Added in pairs, giving last sum as answer
Added same digit in two columns
Wrote carried number in answer
Added same number twice
Omitted one or more digits

SUBTRACTION

Errors in combinations
Did not allow for having borrowed
Counting
Errors due to zero in minuend
Said example backwards
Subtracted minuend from subtrahend
Failed to borrow; gave zero as answer
Added instead of subtracted
Error in reading
Used same digit in two columns
Derived unknown from known combination
Omitted a column
Used trial-and-error addition
Split numbers

Deducted from minuend when borrowing was not necessary
Ignored a digit
Deducted two from minuend after borrowing
Error due to minuend and subtrahend digits being same
Used minuend or subtrahend as remainder
Reversed digits in remainder
Confused process with division or multiplication
Skipped one or more decades
Increased minuend digit after borrowing
Based subtraction on multiplication combination

MULTIPLICATION

Errors in combinations
Error in adding the carried number
Wrote rows of zeros
Carried a wrong number
Errors in addition
Forgot to carry
Used multiplicand as multiplier
Error in single zero combinations, zero as multiplier
Errors due to zero in multiplier
Used wrong process—added
Error in single zero combinations, zero as multiplicand
Confused products when multiplier had two or more digits
Repeated part of table
Multiplied by adding
Did not multiply a digit in multiplicand

Based unknown combination on another
Errors in reading
Omitted digit in product
Errors in writing product
Errors in carrying into zero
Counted to carry
Omitted digit in multiplier
Errors due to zero in multiplicand
Error in position of partial products
Counted to get multiplication combinations
Illegible figures
Forgot to add partial products
Split multiplier
Wrote wrong digit of product
Multiplied by same digit twice
Reversed digits in product
Wrote tables

TABLE 8.4 cont.

DIVISION

Errors in division combinations	Used remainder without new dividend figure
Errors in subtraction	Derived unknown combination from known one
Errors in multiplication	Had right answer, used wrong one
Used remainder larger than divisor	Grouped too many digits in dividend
Found quotient by trial multiplication	Error in reading
Neglected to use remainder within problem	Used dividend or divisor as quotient
Omitted zero resulting from another digit	Found quotient by adding
Counted to get quotient	Reversed dividend and divisor
Repeated part of multiplication table	Used digits of divisor separately
Used short division form for long division	Wrote all remainders at end of problem
Wrote remainders within problem	Misinterpreted table
Omitted zero resulting from zero in dividend	Used digit in dividend twice
Omitted final remainder	Used second digit of divisor to find quotient
Used long division form for short division	Began dividing at units digit of dividend
Said example backwards	Split dividend
	Counted in subtracting
	Used too large a product
	Used endings to find quotient

Source: Adapted from *Diagnostic Studies in Arithmetic* by G. T. Buswell & L. John. Chicago: University of Chicago Press, 1926. Reprinted by permission.

Informal Assessment

Informal assessment means examining the pupil's daily work samples and/or administering teacher-constructed tests. The examination of daily work samples mainly serves to identify error patterns and to evaluate whether or not the seatwork is at an appropriate level. Teacher-constructed tests can effectively assess specific arithmetic skills.

Some formats of teacher-devised tests follow.

1. *Skill:* Identifies before or after for numbers to 10.

Sample items:

a. Fill in the spaces: 1 ___ 3 ___ 5 ___ 7 ___

b. What numbers are missing: 2 4 6 8

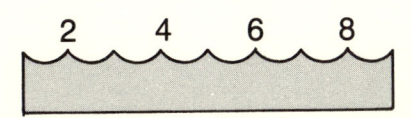

c. Fill in the spaces: BEFORE   AFTER

    ___   10   ___
    ___   8   ___
    ___   3   ___

240 Specific learning disorders

2. *Skill:* Identifies the greater or smaller for numbers 0 to 100 and uses > or <.

Sample items:

a. Put in order:

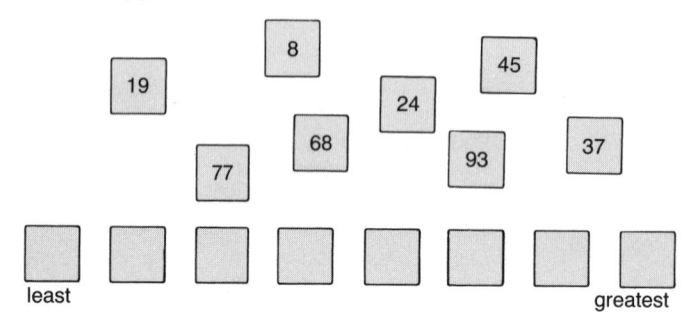

8
19
45
24
68
93
37
77

☐ ☐ ☐ ☐ ☐ ☐ ☐ ☐
least   greatest

b. Circle the greater number:

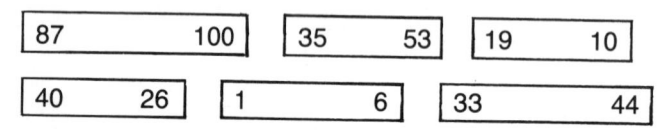

| 87 | 100 | 35 | 53 | 19 | 10 |
| 40 | 26 | 1 | 6 | 33 | 44 |

c. Put > or < in the ◯:

23 ◯ 32   8 ◯ 19   94 ◯ 76
13 ◯ 43   43 ◯ 29   65 ◯ 59

3. *Skill:* Demonstrates mastery of addition facts: sums 0 to 9.

Sample items:

a. Match:

7 + 2   4 + 5
4 + 3   5 + 2
3 + 2   1 + 1
3 + 5   3 + 3
2 + 1   0 + 1

b. Complete:

$$\begin{array}{cccccccc} 3 & 4 & 2 & 0 & 1 & 4 & 5 & 0 & 2 \\ +1 & +2 & +3 & +6 & +4 & +0 & +3 & +7 & +5 \\ \hline \end{array}$$

c. Add: 5 + 4 =   6 + 2 =
        4 + 4 =   2 + 7 =
        1 + 6 =   3 + 2 =
        3 + 0 =   8 + 1 =
        4 + 2 =   4 + 5 =

4. **Skill:** Demonstrates mastery of subtraction facts: sums 0 to 9.

Sample items:

a. Fly a kite:

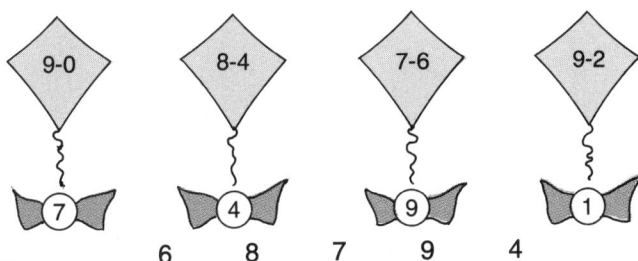

  9-0 → 7   8-4 → 4   7-6 → 9   9-2 → 1

b. Complete:

$$\begin{array}{ccccc} 6 & 8 & 7 & 9 & 4 \\ -3 & -0 & -4 & -5 & -1 \\ \hline \end{array}$$

c. Subtract: 8 − 3 =
             5 − 2 =
             7 − 1 =
             9 − 7 =

5. **Skill:** States that it is ____ o'clock when presented a clock face with two hands.

Sample items:

a. Show child a clock face with two hands. Have her tell you when it is:
   1:00
   5:00
   7:00
   9:00
   11:00

242   Specific learning disorders

b. Fill in each ▢ :

▢ o'clock

c. Match:

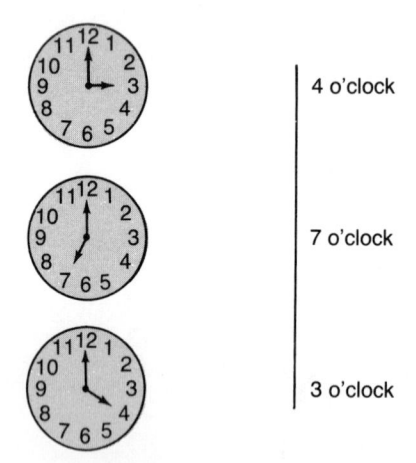

4 o'clock

7 o'clock

3 o'clock

6. *Skill:* Demonstrates mastery of addition facts: sums 0 to 18.

Sample items:

a. Add: 5 + 7 =
8 + 6 =
3 + 9 =
12 + 4 =

b. Add:
$$\begin{array}{ccccc} 8 & 9 & 12 & 3 & 14 \\ +6 & +5 & +3 & +9 & +2 \\ \hline \end{array}$$

7. *Skill:* Subtracts a one-digit number from a two-digit number without regrouping.

Sample items:

a. Subtract: 15 − 3 =
17 − 4 =
13 − 2 =
19 − 7 =

b. Subtract:
$$\begin{array}{ccccc} 18 & 49 & 25 & 37 & 19 \\ -6 & -8 & -3 & -5 & -2 \\ \hline \end{array}$$

8. *Skill:* Adds a one-digit number and a two-digit number with regrouping.

Sample items:

a. Add: 29 + 4 =
37 + 6 =
19 + 3 =
54 + 9 =

b. Add:
$$\begin{array}{ccccc} 78 & 23 & 89 & 19 & 66 \\ +3 & +8 & +5 & +2 & +7 \\ \hline \end{array}$$

9. *Skill:* Subtracts a one-digit number from a two-digit number with regrouping.

Sample items:

a. Subtract: 70 − 3 =
62 − 9 =
45 − 7 =
24 − 5 =

b. Subtract:
$$\begin{array}{ccccc} 42 & 21 & 33 & 70 & 33 \\ -6 & -8 & -4 & -9 & -5 \\ \hline \end{array}$$

10. *Skill:* Adds two-digit numbers with regrouping.

Sample items:

a. Add:
$$\begin{array}{ccccc} 47 & 56 & 39 & 25 & 17 \\ +25 & +16 & +84 & +19 & +43 \\ \hline \end{array}$$

11. *Skill:* Subtracts two-digit numbers with regrouping.

Sample items:

a. Subtract:
$$\begin{array}{ccccc} 74 & 38 & 50 & 32 & 87 \\ -27 & -19 & -24 & -17 & -69 \\ \hline \end{array}$$

12. *Skill:* Writes fractions in word and numeral forms for ½, ⅓, and ¼.

Specific learning disorders

Sample items:

a. Write the fractional numerals for each of the shaded areas in words and numeral form.

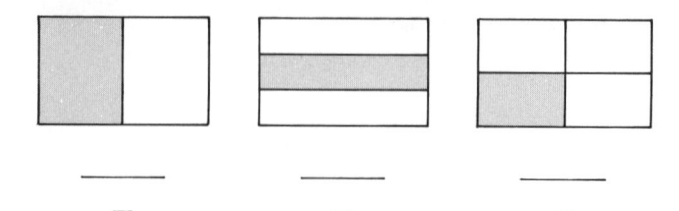

Diagnostic probes provide another type of teacher-constructed device. A simple math probe usually consists of a sheet of one type of 40–50 math facts (e.g., sums to 18), whereas a mixed probe consists of several math facts and/or presentation formats

(e.g., $\begin{array}{r}4\\ \times 2\\ \hline\end{array}$ $\begin{array}{r}6\\ -1\\ \hline\end{array}$ $8 + 2 =$ $\begin{array}{r}5\\ \times 4\\ \hline\end{array}$).

The teacher instructs the child to compute the problems for 1 minute. He records the number of correct and incorrect responses and analyzes the responses to determine error patterns and level of learning (e.g., acquisition, fluency). Additional guidelines for constructing informal arithmetic tests are presented by Ashlock (1976), Smith (1969), Stephens (1977), and Wiederholt, Hammill, and Brown (1978).

Standardized Tests

Wiederholt et al. (1978) show that the teacher can interpret test results in three analytical ways: *(a)* norm-referenced, *(b)* discrepancy, and *(c)* item. A norm-referenced analysis compares the scores of an individual with established test norms. Test norms, usually provided according to chronological ages, frequently express scores in terms of grade level, percentages, or stanines. A low score that results in a discrepancy in a youngster's performance from some norm often serves to document the need for instruction. Also, poor performance may alert the teacher to specific skill areas that need further assessment. In most cases, however, norm-referenced analysis does not directly assist the daily teaching process.

Discrepancy analysis examines test results that reflect inconsistencies. For example, a test may indicate that the pupil is achieving satisfactorily in arithmetic; however, a teacher may report that the pupil's performance in the classroom is inadequate. In other cases, the pupil's classroom performance may be good but her test results may be poor. When discrepancies exist concerning results of standardized tests, consider the nature of the standardized test, collect more data in the discrepant area, and consider motivational aspects in the classroom and testing setting.

Test-item analysis examines the specific items missed on the test; these items are often categorized by skill area. For example, items 1, 2, and 3 may involve addition without carrying and items 4 and 7 may involve addition with carrying. One drawback of test-item analysis is the limited number of items available for any one skill. Length of test, carelessness, misunderstanding directions, and numerous other factors may result in incorrect responses. Since errors occur for numerous reasons, much caution needs to be exercised in evaluating test items. The primary function of item analysis should be to alert the teacher to skill areas that need additional assessment.

Examiners must not overgeneralize about a pupil's performance in arithmetic solely on the basis of scores on a standardized test. Although these tests are useful, it is important to make additional observations (e.g., classroom setting, informal tests) of a pupil before characterizing his typical performance in any area.

Numerous math tests are presented in Appendix A. Because of their unique features, the *Key Math Diagnostic Arithmetic Test* and the *Regional Resource Center Diagnostic Math Inventories* are presented here.

Key Math Diagnostic Arithmetic Test

The *Key Math Diagnostic Arithmetic Test* (Connolly, Nachtman, & Pritchett, 1971) is appropriate for children in preschool through grade six and consists of 14 subtests divided into content, operations, and applications. *Content* includes the subtests of numeration, fractions, and geometry and symbols; *operations* includes addition, subtraction, multiplication, division, mental computation, and numeral reasoning; and *applications* includes word problems, missing elements, money, measurement, and time. The test yields a grade equivalent score for each subtest and for the total test. A diagnostic profile sheet enables the examiner to evaluate the child's performance in the three content areas and on each of the 14 subtests. The manual provides an instructional objective for each item on the test and these objectives aid in instructional planning.

This student is working on the Key Math Diagnostic Arithmetic Test.

Regional Resource Center Diagnostic Math Inventories

The *RRC Diagnostic Math Inventories* (Regional Resource Center, University of Oregon) feature the use of *rate of correct and incorrect responses* from 1-minute samples of behavior. Each subtest consists of a probe sheet that is used for the 1-minute timings. Each probe sheet assesses a specific arithmetic skill; those skills assessed in the Math Inventories I, II, and III include

Math I and II

Oral counting
Oral set recognition
Reading numerals (0–99)
Order I and II
Addition
Subtraction
Equations (addition)
Equations (subtraction)
Addition (without carrying)
Subtraction (without borrowing)

Math III

Reading numerals (0–10,000)
Order III
Addition
Subtraction
Equations (addition)
Equations (subtraction)
Addition (without carrying)
Subtraction (without borrowing)
Addition (with carrying)
Subtraction (with borrowing)
Multiplication
Division

The manual suggests that each subtest be administered approximately five times over a period of several days. Several samples (usually five) provide more reliable results than one sample. Figure 8.1 displays a subtest probe sheet (equations—addition) and Table 8.5 contains a sample record sheet for Math Inventory III. The record sheet readily displays the student's strengths and weaknesses in the subtest areas. For example, it appears that Kathy needs immediate instruction in the areas of addition equations, subtraction equations, and addition with carrying. Proficiency rates may be changed for individual children. Standardized arithmetic tests do not now use rate data. Perhaps new tests will incorporate it.

Equations (Addition)

☐ + 5 = 6   1 + ☐ = 5   ☐ + 1 = 8   ☐ + 8 = 10

6 + ☐ = 7   ☐ + 9 = 10   3 + ☐ = 4   2 + ☐ = 5

☐ + 0 = 2   4 + ☐ = 9   ☐ + 1 = 9   ☐ + 0 = 4

2 + ☐ = 3   2 + ☐ = 6   6 + ☐ = 6   ☐ + 0 = 8

☐ + 5 = 10   5 + ☐ = 8   ☐ + 4 = 6   7 + ☐ = 9

☐ + 8 = 8   2 + ☐ = 8   ☐ + 1 = 6   2 + ☐ = 4

☐ + 4 = 5   ☐ + 0 = 3   ☐ + 7 = 10   4 + ☐ = 8

☐ + 3 = 6   4 + ☐ = 7   ☐ + 10 = 10   2 + ☐ = 5

☐ + 1 = 10   7 + ☐ = 8   ☐ + 5 = 7   6 + ☐ = 10

1 + ☐ = 3   ☐ + 9 = 10   1 + ☐ = 2   ☐ + 6 = 9

Correct _____   Error (total) _____
Extra digits _____   Incorrect digits _____
Illegible digits _____   Mirror digits _____

FIGURE 8.1

Subtest probe sheet on equations (addition).

Source: Adapted in part from *Regional Resource Center Diagnostic Inventories*, Eugene, Oregon: University of Oregon. The material is in the public domain. Based on Haughton's (1972) report of research by Starlin.

TABLE 8.5

RRC Math Inventory III record sheet and proficiency rates.

Name: **Kathy** Teacher: **Jones**
Grade: **3** School: **Piney Circle**

SUB-TEST NAME	TIME	DAY 1 Date ___ standard X nonstand ___ admin. by: ___		DAY 2 Date ___ standard X nonstand ___ admin. by: ___		DAY 3 Date ___ standard X nonstand ___ admin. by: ___		DAY 4 Date ___ standard X nonstand ___ admin. by: ___		Suggested Rates for Determining Proficiency[a]	
		correct	error	correct	error	correct	error	correct	error	correct	error
Read. Num. 0–10,000	1 min.	97	3	106	1	63	1	84	0	60	0
Write Num total	1 min.	56	0	60	1	39	2	51	0	60	0
sequen.		31	1	34	1	20	4	33	0	60	0
unique		Not Administered									
Order III	1 min.	Not Administered									
Add. Facts	1 min.	29	0	24	1	30	0	32	1	50	0
Sub. Facts	1 min.	18	3	22	1	16	1	19	0	50	0
Equation (Add.)	1 min.	6	1	11	4	7	6	12	5	50	0
Equation (Sub.)	1 min.	10	7	17	6	11	5	8	4	50	0
Add. w/o carry	1 min.	29	1	28	3	20	3	24	1	50	0
Sub. w/o borrow	1 min.	26	2	25	1	16	0	18	0	50	0
Add. w/ carry	1 min.	5	13	5	16	--	--	--	--	50	0
Sub. w/ borrow	1 min.	2	27	1	30	--	--	--	--	50	0
Mult.	1 min.	11	0	13	3	7	3	11	3	50	0
Division	1 min.	3	5	1	4	--	--	--	--	50	0

[a] Based on Haughton's (1972) report of research by Starlin.

Source: Adapted in part from *Regional Resource Center Diagnostic Inventories*, Eugene, Oregon: University of Oregon. The material is in the public domain.

TEACHING STRATEGIES AND ACTIVITIES

This section provides some basics concerning how to teach math to LD youngsters. It includes selected research on teaching arithmetic, teacher-constructed activities, and commercial materials.

Selected Research

Using a single-subtest research format, Lovitt and his associates conducted several studies manipulating both antecedent and consequent events on the learning of arithmetic skills.

Antecedent Events

Smith and Lovitt (1975) used modeling to help the performance of one student improve from 0 to 100% correct following the first day of treatment. Prior to requiring the student to solve arithmetic problems, the teacher conducted the modeling session. In the modeling procedure, he solved one problem for the student and verbalized all the steps in the process. Lovitt (1978) reports that this instructional procedure was effective in 13 projects.

Lovitt and Curtiss (1968) used verbal mediation to help a boy improve performance on simple computational problems

$$(e.g., \underline{\hspace{1cm}} - 4 = 2).$$

During the treatment phase, the boy said each problem and its answer aloud before he wrote the answer. His rate improved markedly.

When Smith and Lovitt (1974) informed pupils to work faster, they improved performances. During baseline no instructions, reinforcement, or feedback were provided. In the treatment phase, the following instruction was printed on the top of each page: "Please do this page faster." No other instructions were given. The average percent increase between the baseline and treatment phases was 24%.

Blankenship and Lovitt (1976) conducted a study to examine approaches for teaching students to perform story problems. They formulated 12 classes of story problems by modifying several characteristics: number and type of nouns, verb tense, presence of an introductory sentence, extraneous information, verbal cues, form of the question, and whether the numerals were written as words or numbers. Next, they determined that the students could read all the words contained in the story problems and perform all the computations involved in the problems. To help the children reach criterion as they moved from one class of problems (12 classes) to another, three teaching techniques were used:

Technique 1:

If criterion on a set of problems was not reached (3 consecutive 100% scores) within 6 days, Technique 1 was used:

1. Teacher corrects the child's paper.
2. Student orally reads each incorrectly answered problem and says the correct answer.

Technique 2:

If the student did not reach criterion within 6 days using Technique 1:

1. Teacher corrects the child's paper.
2. Student writes out each incorrectly answered problem and provides the correct answer.
3. Teacher checks the problems and the process is repeated if an answer is incorrect.

Technique 3:

If criterion was not reached within 6 days using Technique 2:

1. Teacher corrects the child's paper.
2. Student orally reads each incorrectly answered problem.
3. Student explains how he arrived at the solution of each problem and is asked to provide another (correct) answer.

All of the students completed the entire program during the 80-day period of the project. Findings from the study include:

1. When the tense *was given* was used, student performances were not affected; however, when the verbs *purchased* or

bought were used, correct rates and correct percentages were lower.
2. When an introductory statement was included, the correct rates were lower.
3. When either the question, verbal cue, or mode of the numeral (word or number) was changed, performances were not affected.
4. When extraneous information was used, pupils' correct rates and correct percentages were lower.
5. When the techniques were used, the pupils were readily able to solve the problems. Technique 1 was used 30 times, and in 63% of the instances, the pupil reached criterion. Technique 2 was used 11 times and was effective in 73% of the instances. It was necessary to use Technique 3 only three times and it was effective twice.
6. After the instructional phase of the project was completed, the pupils were asked to perform a mixed probe containing problems from each of the 12 classes. The average correct percentage on these probes was 96%.

Blankenship and Lovitt (1976) recommend:
1. Teachers should identify types of story problems according to the numerous characteristics (e.g., extraneous information) and systematically teach them.
2. Several problems of each type should be constructed in order to give the student practice on each type of problem.
3. A group of instructional techniques should be specifically outlined and systematically used. It may be necessary to vary the techniques according to the needs of each student; however, a systematic plan appears to be an essential beginning.

Consequent Events

Consequent events influence learning (e.g., reinforcement, correct-incorrect feedback, response cost). Lovitt and Smith (1974) investigated the effects of taking points away for incorrect responses. Their subject performed erratically on simple arithmetic problems. Using a multiple-baseline design and response-cost treatment, the strategy improved her performance across three classes of arithmetic problems. Moreover, Lovitt (1978) reports success in improving pupils' performances on arithmetic problems through the use of positive reinforcement contingent on correct responses.

Teacher-Constructed Activities

Due to the many arithmetic problems that begin with simple addition, procedures using the concrete, representational, and abstract levels for teaching sums to 9 facts are described. Next, since difficulty with place value is widespread and persists across grade levels, techniques and activities for teaching place value are discussed. Finally, selected activities for teaching various arithmetic skills are presented. The skill areas and activities presented are not extensive; however, many of the activities and ideas are readily adaptable to teaching numerous arithmetic skills. Hopefully, they will serve as a springboard for developing or pursuing additional information.

Sums to Nine

Many LD children have difficulty mastering sums to 9 facts. Some children persist in using

This child understands better counting on his fingers.

250 Specific learning disorders

their fingers to compute these facts. For many children this crutch is essential for them to compute correctly. The following procedure for teaching sums to 9 greatly reduces or eliminates the need for crutches, tends to increase speed of correct computation, and often enables the youngsters to proceed to higher math facts with less difficulty.

To begin sums to 9 instruction, the following patterns[1] may be used:

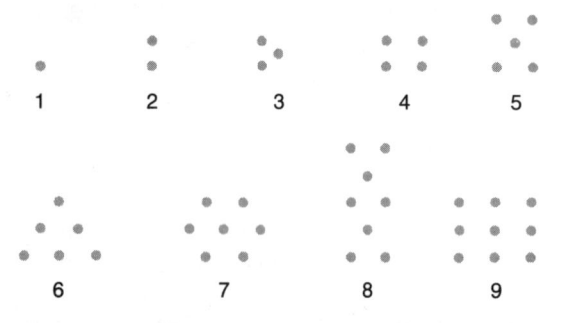

```
  •           •        • •       • •      • • •
              •        •         • •      • •
  1     2     3     4     5

  •         • •       • •      • • •
  • •       •         • •      •
  • •       • •       •        • • •
  6          7         8         9
```

The initial instructional goal involves teaching the child to recognize (name) each pattern without counting the dots. To accomplish this goal the teacher begins with a *concrete level* task using blocks or other suitable three-dimensional objects. Some activities with blocks include:

7 pattern
using blocks

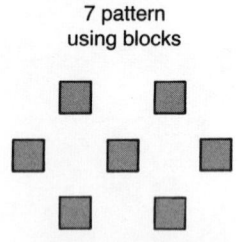

The teacher places the blocks in the 7 pattern and the child copies the pattern. Next, the teacher requests the child to produce the 7 pattern without a model.

Next, the teacher asks the child to divide a number pattern into two groups. For example:

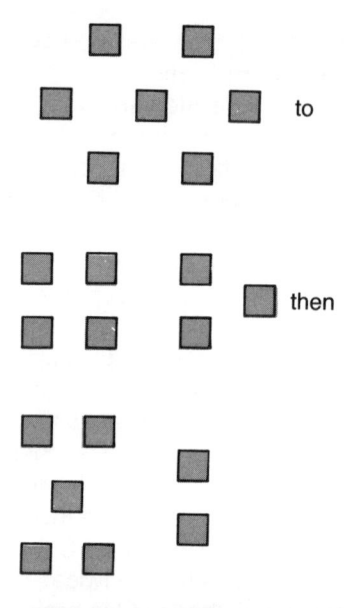

---

[1]These patterns were developed by Dr. Uprichard, professor at the University of South Florida.

to

then

At this point the teacher stresses that each pattern has a family of two-combination patterns. For example, the 5 pattern has six combinations:

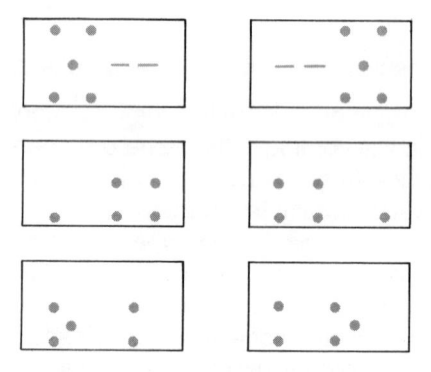

The teacher stresses that each combination is really another name for the number (sum). Thus *equals* (=) is taught as *another name for* and the word *equals* is not used (e.g., 4 + 3 is another name for 7). The child continues to manipulate the blocks into the two-combination patterns until she can do it easily.

Representational level tasks follow the concrete level activities and consist of using dots or other graphic symbols. At this level, dots form the patterns. Students work at exercises on worksheets or the blackboard; the

Arithmetic disabilities 251

tasks are similar to the activities used at the concrete level. For example, a worksheet may feature the following exercise:

Instructions: Complete two-pattern combinations (missing addends).

	6
___	6
1	___
3	___
6	___
___	5
1	___
2	___
4	___

	7
4	___
3	___
0	___
___	7
___	6
1	___
___	5
5	___

In making the patterns, the pupils must draw 3 + 4 and 4 + 3 to comprehend reversibility in addition. Also, the teacher should discourage counting in all of these activities. Pupils should practice with the dots until all two-pattern combinations (including those with zero) for each number are readily produced or identified.

After completing activities at the representational level, pupils move to the *abstract level.* At this level, they use actual numerals. A sample activity would be that on the top of the next column, for which the teacher asks the students to complete the combinations. Pupils must learn all the two-addend combinations for each number. In many cases, they must drill extensively. The game of Math War enables many youngsters to compute or recognize sums to 9 facts very quickly. (See pages 252 and 253.)

Instructions to Math War are as follows:

Instructional Objective.

See math problem sums to 9 and say answer.

Feedback Device.

Answer key and peer correction are used to provide feedback.

Materials.

Index cards or blank playing cards.

Construction.

Write all the number facts that sum to 9 on the cards. Use a total of 54 cards.

Math War Game: Sums to 9
Deck of Cards

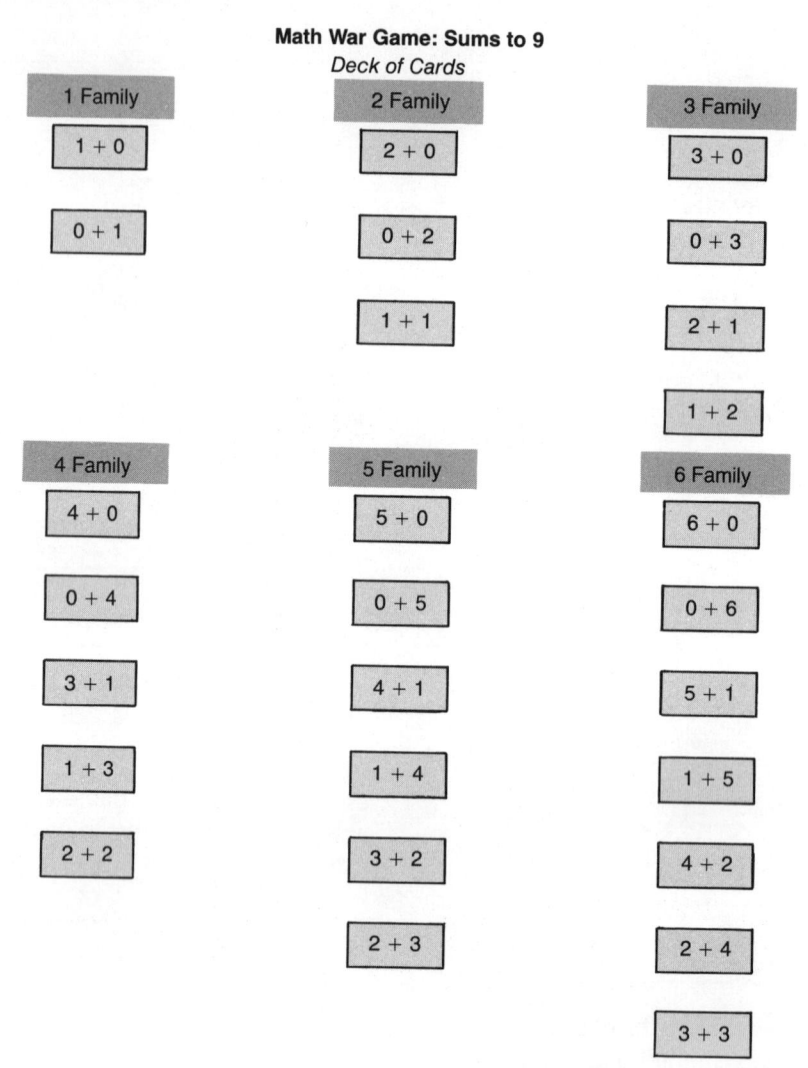

1 Family
- 1 + 0
- 0 + 1

2 Family
- 2 + 0
- 0 + 2
- 1 + 1

3 Family
- 3 + 0
- 0 + 3
- 2 + 1
- 1 + 2

4 Family
- 4 + 0
- 0 + 4
- 3 + 1
- 1 + 3
- 2 + 2

5 Family
- 5 + 0
- 0 + 5
- 4 + 1
- 1 + 4
- 3 + 2
- 2 + 3

6 Family
- 6 + 0
- 0 + 6
- 5 + 1
- 1 + 5
- 4 + 2
- 2 + 4
- 3 + 3

Directions.

Each player shuffles her 54-card deck. With cards facedown, one card at a time is turned over. The player who turns the card with the number fact with the largest sum wins all the cards that are turned. The players each turn their next card. If cards of equal sums are simultaneously turned up, players with the equivalent cards declare war. They place three cards facedown and turn the fourth card faceup. The player whose fourth card has the highest sum wins the three cards facedown and the faceup card of the opposing players. Whoever has the most cards after 54 cards are played, wins. Another way of winning consists of playing until opposing players are down to 5 or 10 remaining cards.

Modifications.

Place any set of math facts on the cards (e.g., multiplication facts, sums to 18). For homework, have each player complete the missing cards in her deck and remove the extra cards (i.e., each player always comes to school with one complete deck with no extra or missing cards).

7 Family

- 7 + 0
- 0 + 7
- 6 + 1
- 1 + 6
- 5 + 2
- 2 + 5
- 4 + 3
- 3 + 4

8 Family

- 8 + 0
- 0 + 8
- 7 + 1
- 1 + 7
- 6 + 2
- 2 + 6
- 5 + 3
- 3 + 5
- 4 + 4

9 Family

- 9 + 0
- 0 + 9
- 8 + 1
- 1 + 8
- 7 + 2
- 2 + 7
- 6 + 3
- 3 + 6
- 5 + 4
- 4 + 5

Back View

Answer Key

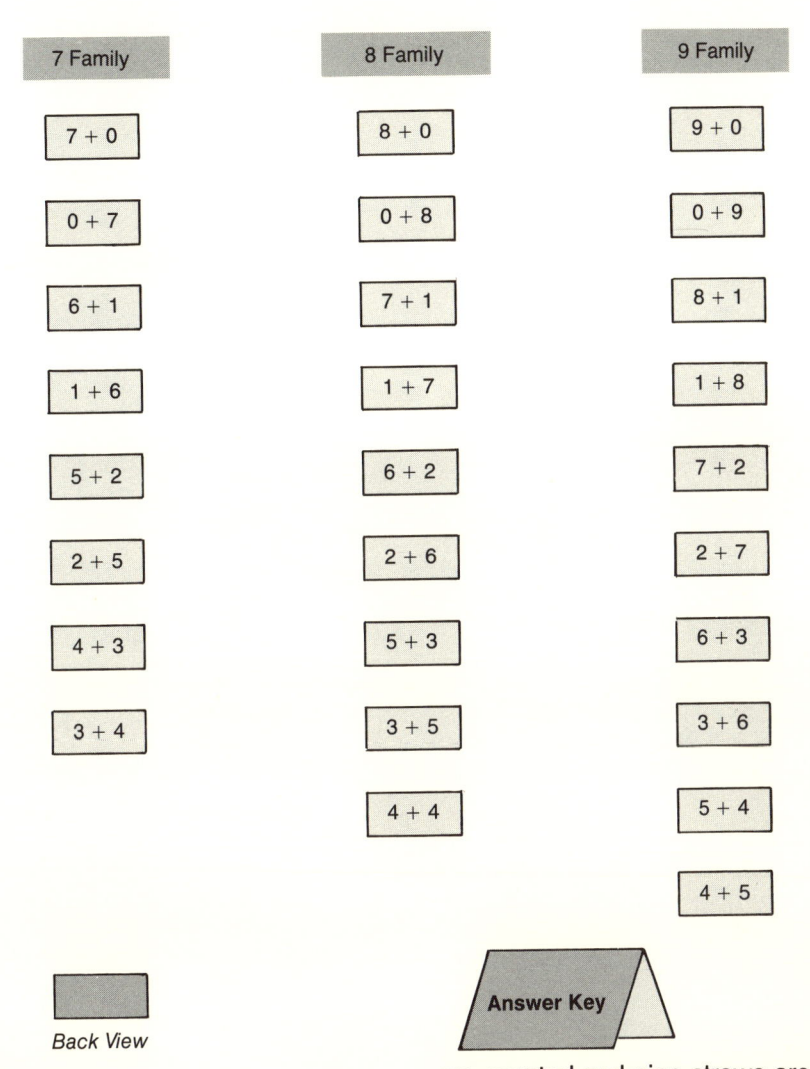

Place value.

A procedure for teaching place value with activities at the concrete, representational, and abstract levels is presented first. This procedure is followed by a list of specific instructional activities for teaching place value.

To begin place value instruction at the *concrete level,* gather two paper cups, a bundle of straws, and a set of blocks. Mount the two cups on poster board; label the right one *units* and the left one *tens.* Tell the pupil to count the blocks. For each block she counts, place a straw in the units cup. Stop when nine blocks are counted and nine straws are in the units cup. Prior to picking up the 10th straw, explain that one straw in the tens cup represents 10 objects. The pupil then takes the nine straws out of the units cup and places one straw in the tens cup. Next, the pupil continues to count the blocks and place the straws. Counting proceeds in the following manner: 1 ten and 1, 1 ten and 2, . . . 3 tens and 4, 3 tens and 5, etc. Each time a 10 is reached, empty the units cup and place a straw in the tens cup. Although the pupil is told that 1 ten and 1 is another name for 11 and 3 tens and 5 is another name for 35, during place value instruction encourage her

254 Specific learning disorders

to count using the 3 tens and 5 system. She continues with the blocks and straws until she can do the task readily.

At the *representational level,* substitute graphic symbols for the blocks, straws, and cups. A sample task might include the following:

Task: Count the items and place the correct number in each cup.

/ / / / / / / / / / / / / / / / / /
/ / / / / / / / / / / / / / /

[tens cup] [units cup]

The completed task would look like this:

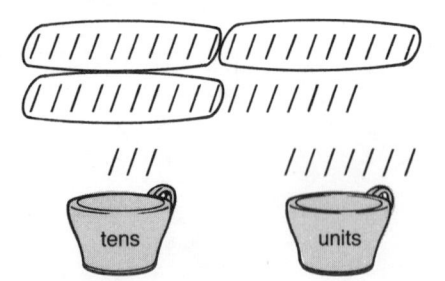

(/ / / / / / / /) (/ / / / / / / /)
(/ / / / / / / /) / / / / / /
/ / /   / / / / / /
[tens cup] [units cup]

Gradually fade the pictures of the cups and replace them with

___   ___ ;
tens   units

the items may change to pictures of real objects.

At the *abstract level,* add numbers gradually in place of items. A sequence of sample tasks might include:

Count the items and identify the number of tens and units.

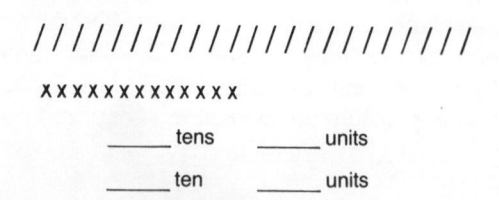

/ /
x x x x x x x x x x x x

___ tens   ___ units
___ ten   ___ units

Place value may be taught using manipulative materials.

Then: Identify the number of tens and units in each number.

24 ___ tens ___ units
36 ___ tens ___ units
87 ___ tens ___ units

These activities represent only one way of providing place value instruction at the concrete, representational, and abstract levels. Hopefully, they provide an impetus for expanding or using numerous activities across the three levels. Moreover, these procedures may be used with different bases. For example, in base 5, counting begins as follows: 3 fives and 2 ones. This strategy reinforces and/or drills the concept of place value. A collection of selected place value activities is presented next:

1. Bereiter (1968) notes that experience in different bases helps pupils understand place value. However, rather than having the pupil spend time working in a base that he will seldom encounter, Bereiter recommends using liquid measure as a place-value activity. Liquid measure does not use base 10 and provides

the pupil with an experience in a different but useful base. Specifically, Bereiter recommends using the binary system of cup, pint, quart, half-gallon, and gallon, in which each succeeding unit is equal to two of the one before. With this system, the numeral 11010 is read as *one gallon, one half-gallon, zero quarts, one pint,* and *zero cups.* The pupils may experiment and add in the system. For example:

```
   1000
 + 101
 ─────
   1101
```

states that one half-gallon plus one quart and one cup equals *(is another name for)* one half-gallon, one quart, and one cup. Carrying is managed in the following problem:

```
   1011
 +1001
 ─────
  10100
```

Since two is not allowed in the system, two cups become one pint, two pints become one quart, etc. In this problem, two half-gallons, one pint, and two cups are equal to one gallon, zero half-gallons, one quart, zero pints, and zero cups. Another advantage of this approach is that zero is very important in the system (i.e., it is important as a place holder). Finally, have the pupils engage in pouring and measuring as concrete level experiences.

2. Ashlock (1976) suggests using *chip-trading games* to teach place value. These games stress the idea of exchanging many for one. The values of chips are defined in terms of a numeration place-value pattern. For example, white chips represent units, blue chips represent tens, and red chips represent hundreds. The pupil rolls a die and receives the number of units indicated on the die. She makes exchanges for higher valued chips according to the rules of the game (four for one if base 4, 10 for one if base 10). The first player to get a chip of a certain high value wins.

3. Ashlock (1976) suggests the use of a game board and a bank to help pupils understand place value. For example:

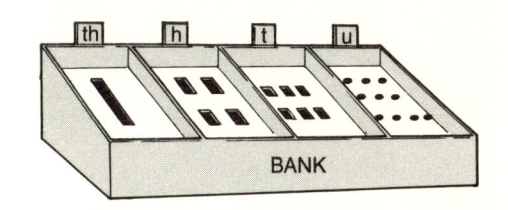

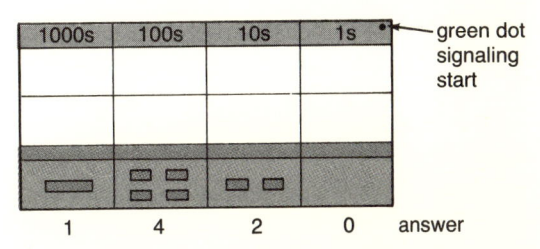

In computing the problem $\begin{array}{r}527\\+893\end{array}$ the pupil places five hundreds, two tens, and seven unit blocks in the upper row. Then she places the appropriate blocks for 893 in the second row. Starting with the units (at green dot), the pupil collects 10 units if possible and moves all remaining units below the wide line. Each 10 units collected she trades into the bank for the correct number of tens. The tens collected from the bank are placed at the top of the tens column. In this problem (see example), 10 units are traded in to the bank for one 10, and zero blocks are placed below the wide line in the units column. Next, 10 tens are traded in for a hundreds block, and two tens blocks are placed below the wide line in the tens column. She trades in ten hundreds for a thousands block, and she then places four hundreds blocks below the wide line in the hundreds column. Finally, she moves the thousands block below the wide line in the thousands column. She counts the blocks in each column and writes the answer, 1420.

4. Ashlock (1976) reports that drawing a line to separate tens and units often helps the pupil understand the need to add units to units and tens to tens. For example:

```
   t | u
   ──┼──
   2 | 8
 + 1 | 4
```

5. Bannatyne (1973) reports that inserting the initial letters for units, tens, hundreds, etc. over their respective columns helps. For example:

	t.th	th	h	t	u
		4	5	4	7
		1	7	5	6
+		3	3	1	1

Vertical lines may be in colors for additional cueing.

6. Wertlieb (1976) suggests using a pegboard to facilitate the learning of borrowing and carrying. For example:

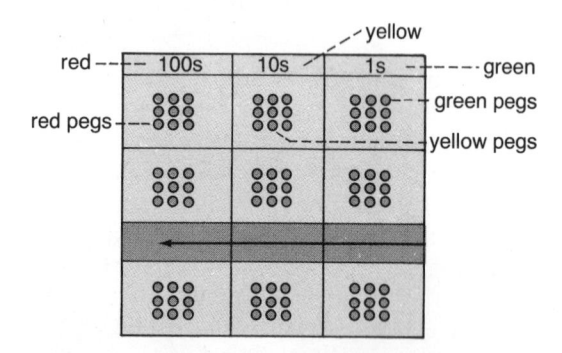

Use masking tape to divide the pegboard into three rows and three columns, each subdivision having nine holes. An arrow is drawn from right to left on a piece of tape that separates the bottom third. This line serves as an equals sign and answers to problems are always represented by inserting pegs below this line. In addition to helping the student recall the different values for each column, color coding reminds the student to start with green (go). The top two rows hold the pegs representing the first two numbers in an addition or subtraction problem. To solve

```
   5
  +6
  ---
```

she begins to transfer all the pegs in the units column to the unit section below the arrow. She discovers that not all 11 pegs will fit in the bottom row of the units column. Consequently, she must exchange 10 green pegs for one yellow peg (10 units for one ten) and carry this yellow peg into the tens column. Moreover, borrowing consists of trading one yellow for 10 green pegs and putting the green pegs in the top row of the units column.

7. Groves (1976) presents a dice game. Three different colored dice are used; the colors correspond to color-coded lines drawn on paper to represent hundreds, tens, and units places. After the pupil rolls the dice, she writes her numbers in the appropriate columns and reads it. The student with the highest number wins.

8. Wallace and Kauffman (1973) suggest making cards with numbers on one side and the number of hundreds, tens, units, etc. in that number on the other side. For example:

100s	10s	1s
4	3	1

back

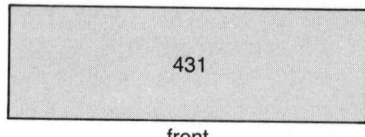

431

front

Activities for Various Arithmetic Skills

A selection of activities across several arithmetic skill areas are featured.

1. Pig Game is usually played by two students with one pair of dice. The object is to be the first player to score 100 points by adding the totals on the dice after each roll. The players take turns rolling the dice, but a player may roll as many times as she wishes as long as she does not roll a one on either or both dice. If a one is rolled on one die, the player gives up the turn and loses all points earned during that turn. If a one is rolled on both dice, the player gives up the turn and loses all her count and starts again at zero.

2. Smith (1968) suggests the use of fraction charts to help illustrate the relationship of fractions to 1 and to each other. For example:

Front

1								
1/2				1/2			
1/4		1/4		1/4		1/4	
1/8	1/8	1/8	1/8	1/8	1/8	1/8	1/8

Back

1											
1/3				1/3				1/3			
1/6		1/6		1/6		1/6		1/6		1/6	
1/12	1/12	1/12	1/12	1/12	1/12	1/12	1/12	1/12	1/12	1/12	1/12

3. Number lines are excellent for helping with simple computations. For example, 2 + 4 is taught by instructing the pupil to start at 2 and count four lines to the right and note the answer is 6.

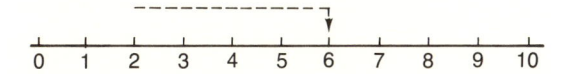

```
      ┌------------┐
      │            ▼
──┼───┼───┼───┼───┼───┼───┼───┼───┼───┼──
  0   1   2   3   4   5   6   7   8   9   10
```

4. Money cards can help pupils to determine correct change. For example, the following $10.00 change card can be used to compute correct change when a $10.00 bill is received.

$10.00 Money Card

$	$	$	$	$	$	$	$	$
(10)	(10)	(10)	(10)	(10)	(10)	(10)	(10)	(10)
(1)	(1)	(1)	(1)	(1)	(1)	(1)	(1)	(1)	(1)

To solve the problem of how much change to give when a $10.00 bill is received and the purchase is for $6.77, the student simply marks out the amount of the purchase on the card. The remaining money is the correct change.

5. Hand calculators can be used to check answers.

6. Teachers need to know numerous algorithms in order to help problem learners.

A fraction chart can help students grasp fraction concepts.

Ashlock (1976) is an excellent reference for addition, subtraction, multiplication, and division algorithms.

Additional sources for arithmetic activities include Gearheart (1976), Hammill and Bartel (1978), Platts (1964), Sharp (1971), Stephens (1977), Wallace and Kauffman (1978), and Wiederholt, Hammill, and Brown (1978).

This student uses a desk number line to compute problems.

Specific learning disorders

Commercial Materials

In using commercial materials it is important for the teacher to adapt and supplement. Some selected programs useful with LD pupils are presented next.

Structural Arithmetic

Houghton Mifflin
110 Tremont St.
Boston, Mass. 02107

Designed for K–third grade, it uses manipulative materials (cubes, number track, number guide) to give pupils concrete experiences. The program is carefully sequenced and structured to help them discover and understand abstract concepts. It emphasizes problem solving.

Cuisenaire Rods

Cuisenaire Co. of America
12 Church St.
New Rochelle, NY 10805

Primarily designed for use with pupils in grades K–2, they are often used with even sixth-grade children. The rods, usually used in supplementary activities, are color-coded (there are five color families) and proportional (the rod representing 5 is five times as long as the rod representing 1). The rods especially help children who need visual, tactile, and concrete activities.

Pacemaker Games Program

Fearon
6 Davis Drive
Belmont, CA 94002

This program features five general categories of games: *(a)* table search, *(b)* card, *(c)* guessing, *(d)* board, and *(e)* active racing. The games are best suited for pupils in grades K–2. In addition to providing pupils with the opportunity to increase number knowledge, the games help them learn how to play games correctly.

DISTAR Arithmetic I, II, and III

Science Research Associates
259 East Erie St.
Chicago, ILL 60611

DISTAR, a highly sequenced and structured program, focuses on ordinal counting, signs, addition, subtraction, multiplication, money concepts, fractions, factoring, word problems, and algebraic addition. Used with small groups, it requires that the teacher thoroughly involve the students in the activities. Children who require drill and structured activities can be aided with DISTAR. The program is primarily designed for pupils in grades K–3.

Programmed Math 2/e

Special Education Services
McGraw-Hill
1221 Avenue of the Americas
New York, NY 10020

Primarily designed for intermediate and older students, it contains individualized lesson units in 11 books. Its skill range covers addition, subtraction, multiplication, division, fractions, decimals, measurements, and consumer and personal math.

Sullivan Programmed Math

Behavioral Research Laboratories
Box 577
Palo Alto, CA 94302

Focusing on computational skills, it provides immediate feedback. Since it does not stress preacademic and arithmetic readiness skills, the youngster must already have a conceptual foundation in mathematics. The format of the books requires minimal reading until word problems are introduced.

Greater Cleveland Mathematics Program (G.C.M.P.)

Science Research Associates
(See DISTAR address.)

A highly organized, sequential math program, the G.C.M.P. is designed for pupils in grades

K–8. Models or pictures are used to develop algorithms for each operation and computational skills are used in applied situations. The program offers a variety of practice activities. The basis of the program is that mathematical understanding precedes computation exercises.

Real-Life Math

Hubbard
Box 104
Northbrook, ILL 60062

This program features a variety of role-playing activities in which individual students establish their own businesses. Students complete files, handle billing forms, and participate in financial transactions with a bank. The program attempts to teach fundamental math skills to mildly retarded and LD students in the 13–18 year age range.

Project MATH

EPC Educational Progress
Educational Development Corporation
P.O. Box 45663
Tulsa, OK 74145

A developmental mathematics program, it provides students with experiences in six areas of math: *(a)* patterns, *(b)* sets, *(c)*

In shop class, students can deal directly with math.

geometry, *(d)* measurement, *(e)* fractions, and *(f)* numbers. It is designed for use with children who have learning handicaps and is appropriate for use in preschool through high school. Project MATH was developed by Cawley and his associates (Cawley, Fitzmaurice, Goodstein, Lepore, Sedlak, & Althaus, 1976) and is one of the few math programs that has been field tested with LD children.

SUMMARY

This chapter begins with a discussion of the development of arithmetic skills. Factors that are related to arithmetic disabilities are noted and include problems in these areas: *(a)* perception, *(b)* directionality, *(c)* abstract thinking, *(d)* memory, *(e)* reading, and *(f)* other. Also, specific arithmetic error patterns and place-value problems are featured. A discussion of diagnostic guidelines, informal assessment procedures, and standardized tests is presented. Selected research is presented that focuses on teaching arithmetic to children with learning problems. Teaching strategies and activities are discussed and teacher-constructed activities for teaching sums to 9 facts, place value, and various other arithmetic skills are presented. Finally, this chapter describes several selected commercial programs.

REFERENCES

Ashlock, R.B. *Error patterns in computation: A semi-programmed approach* (2nd ed.). Columbus, Ohio: Charles E. Merrill, 1976.

Bannatyne, A. Programs, materials and techniques, *Journal of Learning Disabilities,* 1973, *6,* 204–212.

Bereiter, C. *Arithmetic & mathematics.* San Rafael, Calif.: Dimensions, 1968.

Blankenship, C.S., & Lovitt, T.C. Story problems: Merely confusing or down right befuddling. *Journal for Research in Mathematics Education,* 1976, 7, 290–298.

Bryant, N.D., & Kass, C.E. *Leadership training institute in learning disabilities* (Vol. 1). Washington, D.C.: Office of Education, Bureau of Education for the Handicapped, 1972.

Cawley, J.F., Fitzmaurice, A.M., Goodstein, H.A., Lepore, A.V., Sedlak, R., & Althaus, V. *Project MATH.* Tulsa, Okla.: Education Development Corporation, 1976.

Chalfant, J.C., & Scheffelin, M.A. *Central processing dysfunction in children: A review of research* (NINDS Monograph No. 9). Bethesda, Md.: U.S. Department of Health, Education, & Welfare, 1969.

Connolly, A.J., Nachtman, W., & Pritchett, E.M. *Key Math Diagnostic Arithmetic Test.* Circle Pines, Minn.: American Guidance Service, 1971.

Cox, L.S. Diagnosing and remediating systematic errors in addition and subtraction computations. *The Arithmetic Teacher,* 1975, *22,* 151–157.

Gearheart, B.R. *Teaching the learning disabled: A combined task-process approach.* Saint Louis: C.V. Mosby, 1976.

Groves, K. Teacher idea exchange: Using dice and the blockhead game for academic skill development. *Teaching Exceptional Children,* 1976, *8,* 103–104.

Hammill, D.D., & Bartel, N.R. *Teaching children with learning and behavior problems* (2nd ed.). Boston: Allyn & Bacon, 1978.

Haughton, E. Aims—Growing and sharing. In J.B. Jordon & L.S. Robbins (Eds.), *Let's try doing something else kind of thing.* Arlington, Va.: The Council for Exceptional Children, 1972.

Kaliski, L. Arithmetic and the brain-injured child. In E. Frierson & W. Barbe (Eds.), *Educating children with learning disabilities: Selected readings.* New York: Appleton-Century-Crofts, 1967.

Lankford, F.G., Jr. *Some computational strategies of seventh grade pupils* (Project No. 2-C-013, Grant No. OEG-3-72-0035). U.S. Department of Health, Education, & Welfare, Office of Education, National Center for Educational Research and Development (Regional Research Program) and The Center for Advanced Study, University of Virginia, 1972.

Lerner, J.W. *Children with learning disabilities* (2nd ed.). Boston: Houghton Mifflin, 1976.

Lovitt, T.C. Arithmetic. In N.G. Haring, T.C. Lovitt, M.D. Eaton, & C.L. Hansen, *The fourth R: Research in the classroom.* Columbus, Ohio: Charles E. Merrill, 1978.

Lovitt, T.C., & Curtiss, K.A. Effects of manipulating an antecedent event on mathematics response rate. *Journal of Applied Behavior Analysis,* 1968, *1,* 329–333.

Lovitt, T.C., & Smith, D.D. Using withdrawal of positive reinforcement to alter subtraction performance. *Exceptional Children,* 1974, *40,* 357–358.

McLeod, T.M., & Crump, W.D. The relationship of visuospatial skills and verbal ability to learning disabilities in mathematics. *Journal of Learning Disabilities,* 1978, *11,* 237–241.

Otto, W., McMenemy, R.A., & Smith, R.J. *Corrective and remedial teaching.* Boston: Houghton Mifflin, 1973.

Platts, M.E. *PLUS: A handbook for teachers of elementary mathematics.* Stevensville, Mich.: Educational Service, 1964.

Pinard, A., & Laurendeau, M. "Stage" in Piaget's cognitive developmental theory: Exegesis of a concept. In D. Elkind & J.H. Flavell (Eds.), *Studies in cognitive development: Essays in honor of Jean Piaget.* New York: Oxford University Press, 1969.

Regional Resource Center Diagnostic Math Inventories (Project No. 472917, Contract No. OEC-0-9-472917-4591 [608]). Eugene, Oreg.: University of Oregon.

Roberts, G.H. The failure strategies of third grade arithmetic pupils. *The Arithmetic Teacher,* 1968, *15,* 442–446.

Sharp, F.A. *These kids don't count.* San Rafael, Calif.: Academic Therapy Publications, 1971.

Smith, D.D., & Lovitt, T.C. *The influence of instructions and reinforcement contingencies on children's abilities to compute arithmetic problems.* Paper presented at the Fifth Annual Conference on Behavior Analysis in Education, University of Kansas, October 1974.

Smith, D.D., & Lovitt, T.C. The use of modeling techniques to influence the acquisition of computational arithmetic skills in learning-disabled children. In E. Ramp & G. Semb (Eds.), *Behavior analysis: Areas of research and application.* Englewood Cliffs, N.J.: Prentice-Hall, 1975.

Smith, R.M. *Clinical teaching: Methods of instruction for the retarded.* New York: McGraw-Hill, 1968.

Smith, R.M. (Ed.). *Teacher diagnosis of educational difficulties.* Columbus, Ohio: Charles E. Merrill, 1969.

Stephens, T.M. *Teaching skills to children with learning and behavior disorders.* Columbus, Ohio: Charles E. Merrill, 1977.

Wallace, G., & Kauffman, J.M. *Teaching children with learning problems.* Columbus, Ohio: Charles E. Merrill, 1973.

Wertlieb, E. The tool chest: Games little people play. *Teaching Exceptional Children,* 1976, *9,* 24–25.

Wiederholt, J.L., Hammill, D.D., & Brown, V. *The resource teacher: A guide to effective practices.* Boston: Allyn & Bacon, 1978.

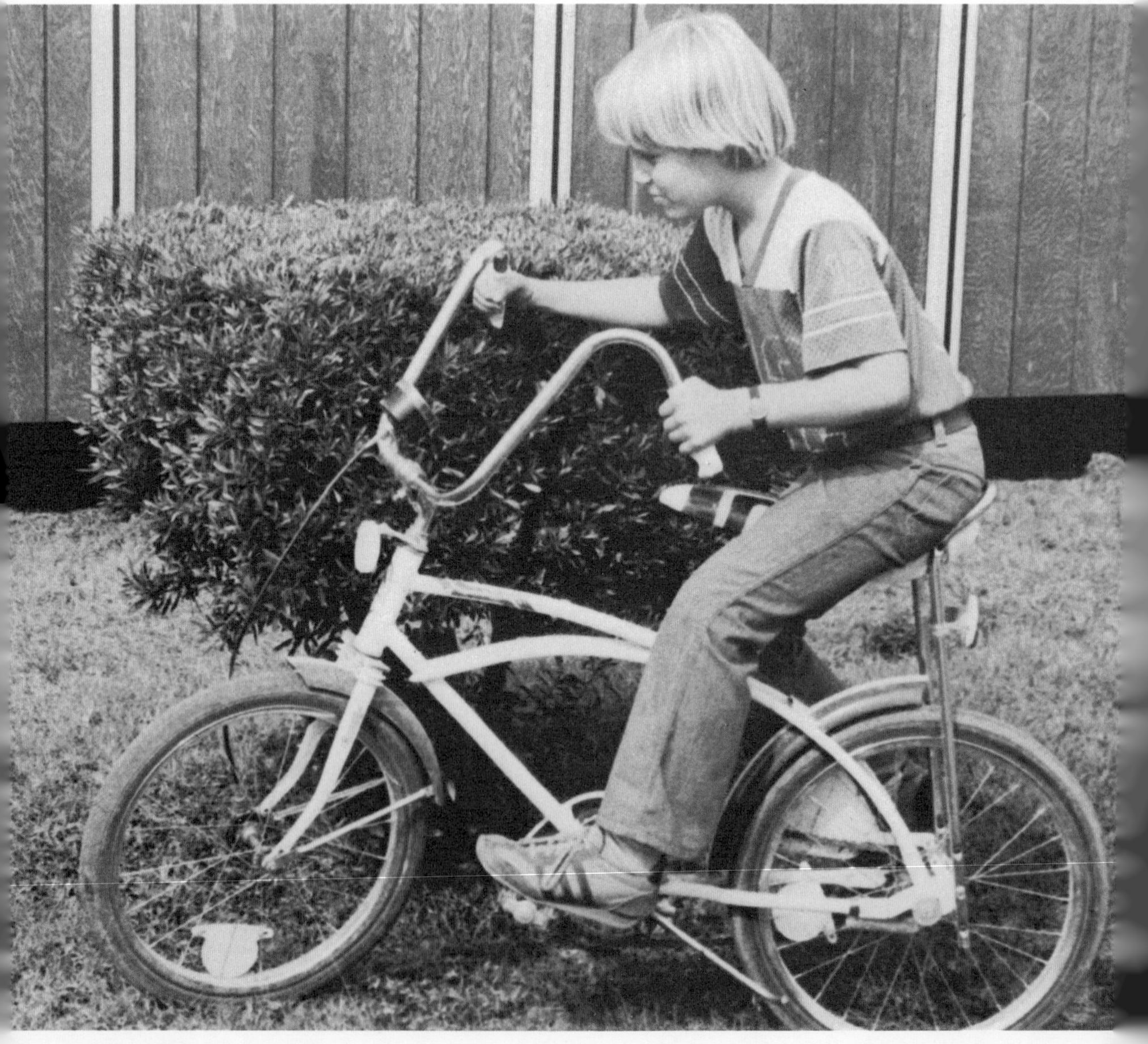

9

Perception and perceptual-motor disabilities

PERCEPTION

Perception refers to the cognitive process of making sensation meaningful. It occurs in the brain and is considered a learned skill. It serves as a basis for much behavior and involves integrating sensory stimuli (auditory, visual, tactile, kinesthetic, and olfactory) from the environment. Lerner (1976) reports that perceptual skills are very important in the early stages of academic learning.

Perceptual disabilities have received extensive attention in the area of learning disabilities. The early works of Strauss and Werner (1942) and Strauss and Lehtinen (1947) strongly emphasize perceptual disabilities. Cruickshank (1976) recently underscored the perceptual emphasis when he stated that he believed perceptual factors to be the primary problem of

Visual stimuli help some children learn better.

learning disabled individuals. In fact, he refers to LD children as *perceptual handicapped children with learning disabilities.*

Although it is a fact that perceptual skills are basic to academic learning, people disagree about how to assess the skills and training. In the *Federal Register* (USOE, 1977), perceptual disabilities remain in the definition of specific learning disabilities (disorder in basic psychological processes) but are excluded from identification criteria (i.e., no assessment is required in the perception area to identify LD). The controversy is far from ended. This section discusses types of perceptual disabilities, visual perception, auditory perception, and haptic perception. In addition, related research and selected instructional activities are touched on.

Perceptual Disabilities

Perceptual Modality

Students with perceptual difficulties exhibit a variety of problems. Some do not attend to the relevant dimensions of visual stimuli (i.e., they focus on inappropriate details and ignore very important details). Others may not be able to differentiate between selected speech sounds. Moreover, some children cannot distinguish between hard and soft objects by touch. The term *perceptual modality* frequently describes these varying deficits. This concept is based on the premise that the learning strengths and weaknesses of selected pupils are related to the preferred and nonpreferred modalities. For example, some youngsters may learn best via visual input, whereas others may learn via auditory or tactile input. In addition, a specific perceptual modality may represent a weak or inefficient pathway for learning. (In Chapter 3 numerous classroom clues are listed for detecting visual or auditory learners and recent research concerning modality-based instruction is presented.)

Many feel that for optimum learning to occur, one must consider a youngster's strong and weak modalities before planning instructional alternatives. Wepman (1964, 1968) suggests three alternatives:

1. *Teach through the youngster's best modality.*
2. *Concentrate on the weak modality.* Strengthen the weak modality so that it becomes a productive path.
3. *Consider both modalities in the instructional process.* Emphasize the strong modality to help the youngster acquire basic skills; however, specific lessons are still used to strengthen the weak modality.

Overloading the Perceptual System

The LD youngster may have difficulty simultaneously receiving and integrating information from several input modalities. For example, if input is received from the tactile, auditory, and visual modalities at the same time, the youngster's perceptual system "overloads" and the information is not meaningfully processed. Johnson and Myklebust (1967) report that symptoms of overloading include attention problems, resistance to instruction, poor recall, temper tantrums, and, in some cases, seizures. For this pupil, the teacher should avoid multisensory instructional approaches and concentrate on tasks that *primarily* stress one modality.

Whole-Part Perception

Some individuals have perceptual styles regarding the perception of the parts and whole of a stimulus (Goins, 1958). *Whole perceivers* note the object in its entirety (e.g., recognize the gestalt), whereas *part perceivers* focus on details of the object and miss the gestalt. The saying, "He can't see the forest for the trees," exemplifies the perceptual style of the part perceiver. The ability to perceive parts and wholes is essential in academic learning. For example, in reading the pupil may need to shift back and forth from part to whole perception, depending on the words being read. If a youngster encounters a word that he does not know, he must examine parts of it in order to say it correctly. If a known word is encountered, the whole word is immediately recognized and attention to detail is minimized. Moreover, whole perceivers may tend to ignore detail in such words as *money* and *merry* or *horse* and *house* and not discriminate between the words correctly. Lerner (1976) has found that in coloring pictures part perceivers may color one arm red and the other arm blue. Finally, disability in this area is likely related to figure-ground confusion.

Cross-Modal Perception

Some perceptual problems result from the inability to integrate intersensory processes (e.g., transfer an auditory input into a visual input—write a word presented auditorially). Ayres (1975) focuses on intersensory integration, and a discussion of her work is included in Chapter 5.

Visual Perception

Description

Visual perception refers to the ability to make visual sensory stimuli meaningful. Its processes involve operations in which elements of visual stimuli are interpreted and organized. Thus, it figures immensely in the educational process. Children may encounter difficulty in performing tasks involving some form of visual perception. Chalfant and Scheffelin (1969) identify five major components of visual perception: *(a)* spatial relationships, (b) visual discrimination, *(c)* figure-ground discrimination, *(d)* visual closure, and *(e)* visual memory or object recognition.

The ability to perceive the position of objects in space in relation to oneself and other objects is *spatial relations.* Children with spatial difficulties have trouble reproducing a pattern on a peg board. Also, such children experience difficulty in recognizing the sequence of letters in a word or the sequence of words in a sentence.

Visual discrimination refers to the ability to perceive dominant features in different ob-

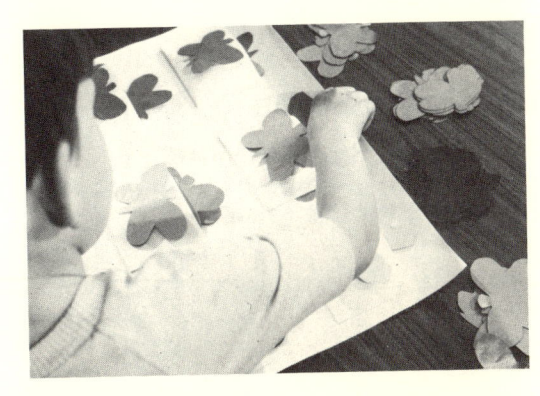

Rob works on a visual discrimination task involving matching colors.

jects and, thus, discriminate one object from another. A visual discrimination task would involve matching various shapes, designs, or objects. In learning to read, the child must visually discriminate the differences between letters and words (e.g., the different between the letters *w* and *v,* or the words *pit* and *pat*).

Figure-ground discrimination involves the ability to distinguish an object from its background. Irrelevant stimuli often distract a child with a deficit in this area. For example, a child may not be able to select and outline a specific figure that is intersected by several other figures. The child also may have difficulty focusing and concentrating on one word or line.

Visual closure refers to the ability to identify figures that are presented in fragments (i.e., the stimuli are presented with parts missing). For example, when a child identifies correctly a picture of a horse without a tail, his perceptual judgment is made based on only partial information. Likewise, in reading, when parts of words are partially covered, the reader may provide visual closure in order to recognize the words.

Visual memory is the ability to recollect the dominant features of a stimulus item or to recall the sequence of a number of items presented visually. Accurate *object recognition* includes the ability to recognize geometric shapes, objects, letters, numbers, and words. Children with deficits in this area cannot easily differentiate the letter *R* from *P*, or the shape of a block from a ball. In reading, the discrimination of letters is a crucial skill.

Diagnosis of Visual Perception Deficits

There are a number of commonly used visual perception tests. One such test in use since the late 1930s is the *Bender Visual-Motor Gestalt Test* (Bender, 1938; Koppitz, 1964). This test is to be individually administered by a trained psychologist and is composed of nine geometric designs or figures that the child is required to copy. The subject reproduces some figures from memory and others with the stimuli present. Koppitz (1964) offers scoring guidelines.

A second test of visual functioning is the *Frostig Developmental Test of Visual Perception (DTVP)* (Frostig, Lefever, & Whittlesey, 1964). This test takes less than an hour to give and may be administered individually or in small groups by the teacher. It can be used to screen children in preschool, kindergarten, and first grade and to diagnose older children. The test measures the child's ability in five separate areas: *(a)* eye-motor coordination, *(b)* figure-ground perception, *(c)* constancy of shape, *(d)* position in space, and *(e)* spatial relationships. For each of the five skill areas, the test yields *(a)* a perceptual quotient, which provides a comparison of the child's performance with that of other children of the same age, and *(b)* a perceptual age, which is an estimate of the child's developmental age level.

The *Developmental Test of Visual-Motor Integration* (Beery & Buktenica, 1967) also measures visual functioning. The test may be administered by the teacher and measures the subject's abilities in copying designs. Consisting of a series of 24 geometric forms, the test moves through five graduated levels of visual-motor skills.

The *Motor-Free Test of Visual Perception* (Colarusso & Hammill, 1972) measures visual perception without involving motor ability. Used with children aged 4 to 8, the test requires only a pointing response. In approximately 10 minutes the child sees 36 items; he must point to the correct one of four alternatives for each item.

Other tests of visual perception include the *Southern California Figure-Ground Visual Perception Test* (Ayres, 1969) and selected subtests of the *Detroit Tests of Learning Aptitude* (Baker & Leland, 1935). In addition, the *ITPA* (Kirk, McCarthy, & Kirk, 1968) assesses four aspects of visual perception: *visual reception, visual association, visual closure,* and *visual sequential memory.* Chapter 6 discusses these subtests.

Research in Visual Perception

Many practitioners provide children with visual perception training in an effort to improve aca-

Geometric shapes are sometimes used in assessing visual-perceptual skills.

demic skills that appear to be related to visual perception. For example, many teachers assume that such training significantly aids reading development. Of course visual perception is essential (a child must differentiate between letters and words in order to read); however, do these tests and training programs facilitate reading? As discussed in Chapters 3 and 14, numerous problems exist in the measurement of abilities. (Also refer to the discussion of the *ITPA* in Chapter 6 about the assessment and remediation of visual abilities.)

Visual perception studies have been reviewed by numerous investigators (Bortner, 1974; Cohen, 1969; Hammill, Goodman, & Wiederholt, 1974; Hammill & Wiederholt, 1973). The *Frostig Program for the Development of Visual Perception* (Frostig & Horne, 1964) and the *Frostig Developmental Test of Visual Perception (DTVP)* (Frostig, Lefever, & Whittlesey, 1964) have generated the most research. *The consensus of these numerous reviewers is that visual perception training alone does not have a significant effect on reading achievement.* In an examination of correlations of *DTVP* total and subtest scores with arithmetic achievement, Larsen and Hammill (1975) report that all but the eye-hand coordination subtest appear to be useful in predicting arithmetic achievement. These high positive correlations are interesting findings; further research in this area is definitely warranted. Frostig and Maslow (1969) indicate that the preponderance of negative findings (regarding reading) highlight the need for continued research on how visual perception relates to learning at various stages of development and performance. According to Hallahan and Kauffman (1976), the common-sense viewpoint regarding visual perception holds that "not all children with learning problems have visual deficits, some children with learning problems have visual deficits, and the remediation of visual perceptual disabilities may *help* in the remediation of the child's learning problems" (p. 76).

Obviously visual training should only be considered when improvement in visual perception is the primary goal (Wallace & McLoughlin, 1975). In addition, Hammill (1972) points out that its use should be viewed as highly experimental.

Until research provides a better understanding of such training, teachers can include academic content into visual perception exercises. In this approach, a child with visual perception difficulties performs tasks involving discrimination among letters, numerals, and words; the use of nonacademic content is minimized. Cohen (1969) achieved excellent results with this type of approach. In addition, Stephens (1977) provides numerous assessment procedures and activities within the visual perception framework that stress the use of academic content.

Selected Visual Perception Activities

The following selected activities may be used to help develop skills in visual perception:

1. Have the child assemble puzzles of people, animals, forms, numbers, letters, words, and/or sentences.
2. Have the child copy geometric configurations (including letters and words) with rubber bands on rows of nails on a board.

268 Specific learning disorders

3. With sets of cards, make domino-type games that require the matching of forms, letters, words, and/or numbers.
4. Play card games in which the child matches pairs of words, numbers, and/or pictures.
5. Make bingo cards using numbers, letters, and/or words.
6. Have the child match a stimulus word with a word from a list of visually similar words.
7. Use egg cartons to display how groups consist of individual "members."
8. Use a number line to provide a visual reference for helping a child solve simple addition and subtraction problems.

Some commonly used teaching materials relate to visual skills as illustrated in Table 9.1.

Auditory Perception

Description

Auditory perception refers to the ability to recognize and interpret stimuli that are heard. Although this skill is important, fewer tests and teaching materials are available for it than for visual perception. Specific components of auditory perception include discrimination, association, sequential memory, and blending.

Auditory discrimination refers to the ability to recognize differences between sounds and to identify similarities and differences between words. This skill area may also include the ability to differentiate and identify environmental sounds, such as a train whistle.

Pupils skilled in *auditory association* can relate ideas that they hear. They easily find

TABLE 9.1

Relationship between teaching materials and visual perception skills.

Skills	Parquetry	Block design	Peg board	Sorting	Matching	Sequence patterns	Stencils	Cutting	Pasting	Coloring	Geometric form copying	Puzzles
Seeing design or pattern as a whole	X	X	X				X				X	X
Color discrimination	X	X	X		X	X	X			X	X	X
Form discrimination	X	X	X		X		X	X		X	X	X
Relation of figure to background	X	X	X		X		X		X	X		X
Increased attention span	X	X	X	X	X	X	X	X		X	X	X
Temporal-spatial relationship	X	X	X									X
Size discrimination				X	X		X	X				X
Classification and grouping				X	X	X						

relationships and simple associations and categorize ideas. In addition to using reasoning to correct absurdities, they can give verbal solutions to problems that are presented orally.

Auditory memory is the ability to recognize and/or recall previously presented auditory stimuli. The recall may feature a sequential order (e.g., phone number or letters in a word) or simply remembering information presented through the auditory channel (e.g., name of a city). A child with a deficit in this area may have trouble learning the days of the week or executing a series of auditory commands. Also, the child may find difficulty in memorizing the words to a poem or a song, even if it is repeatedly heard. His problems may include trouble in recognizing or recalling sequences of unrelated words, numbers, or letters that are presented auditorially.

Auditory blending refers to the ability to make a complete word by blending phonic elements. For example, a child with a deficit in auditory blending may be unable to blend the phonemes /c/, /a/, and /r/ to complete the word *car*, even though he can differentiate the individual letter sounds in isolation.

Diagnosis of Auditory Perception Deficits

Preschool and school-aged children often take tests of auditory perception. Their teachers hope to predict their reading successes or to pinpoint those who are having difficulties. The *Auditory Discrimination Test* by Wepman (1958) is an individually administered test measuring auditory discrimination of phoneme sounds. It consists of word pairs read individually to the child while he is facing away from the examiner. The words in 30 word pairs are different in a single phoneme and have minimal sound differences (e.g., *coast–toast; big–pig*) and the words in 10 word pairs do not differ. The child must indicate whether the words in each pair are the same or different.

Another test of auditory discrimination is the *Goldman-Fristoe-Woodcock Test of Auditory Discrimination* (Goldman, Fristoe, & Wood-

Listening to records may help strengthen auditory skills.

cock, 1970). Appropriate for subjects aged 4 and up, the test measures auditory discrimination of phonemes under both quiet conditions and conditions in which there is background noise. Speech sounds are presented on a standardized tape and a response is made by pointing.

The Screening Test of Auditory Perception (STAP) (Kimmell & Wahl, 1969) is a group or individual test that measures various auditory perception skills. In one section the subject must discriminate between long and short vowel sounds; in another section he must perceive the difference between initial consonant sounds and consonant blends. The test assesses auditory sequential memory according to the subject's ability to remember and identify rhymes and to remember a rhythmic pattern. The child also is required to discriminate between same or different word pairs.

The skill of auditory blending is measured in the *Roswell-Chall Auditory Blending Test* (Roswell & Chall, 1963). Individually administered, it measures the child's ability to blend phonic sounds into complete words.

As discussed in Chapter 6, the *ITPA* (Kirk, McCarthy, & Kirk, 1968) measures auditory blending and auditory sequential memory.

In addition to standardized tests, auditory perception skills can be sampled through in-

Specific learning disorders

formal testing procedures and clinical observations in the classroom setting.

Research in Auditory Perception

In a review of the development, assessment, and teaching programs of auditory perception, Sabatino (1973) notes that, compared to visual perception, there is a paucity of information concerning the diagnosis and remediation of auditory problems. In addition, there is a lack of understanding and agreement among experts concerning the construct of auditory perception.

Hammill and Larsen (1974) reviewed studies that investigated the relationship between selected measures of auditory perceptual ability and future reading achievement. They report that the results are contradictory; however, they conclude that the auditory skills examined in their review were not sufficiently related to reading to be useful for consideration in classroom settings. In contrast, Dykstra (1966) suggests a relationship exists between reading achievement (i.e., between "good" and "poor" readers) and ability in auditory perception skills. Several studies (Christine & Christine, 1964; Golden & Steiner, 1969) indicate that poor readers exhibit difficulties in auditory perception; however, other studies (Poling, 1953; Wheeler & Wheeler, 1954) suggest that good readers may manifest deficits in auditory skills and, likewise, poor readers may demonstrate adequate auditory skills. Hammill and Larsen report that many of the studies that compared the auditory skills of "good" and "poor" readers (including Dykstra's) did not control for intelligence (e.g., the "good" readers may have higher intellectual ability than "poor" readers). Thus, they note that "good" readers may perform better on reading measures because of the influence of higher intellectual abilities. Hammill and Larsen caution the reader not to generalize the lack of relationship between auditory skills and reading to such auditory skills as acuity, listening comprehension, and/or phonic skills. These latter skills relate strongly to reading but are not the focus of auditory skills commonly associated with many auditory training approaches.

Lyon (1977) discusses some issues and related research in this area. He reports a lack of empirical evidence concerning the reliability and validity of assessment measures. Lyon's conclusions concur with the measurement problems encountered in the assessment of abilities (as discussed in Chapters 3 and 14). (Also, see the discussion of the *ITPA* in Chapter 6.) In addition, Lyon doubts the value of auditory-perceptual training programs.

Many of the auditory skills (e.g., auditory discrimination, memory, blending) assessed via standardized tests and used as a basis for planning instruction do not directly relate to reading achievement. As with visual training, until further research, the inclusion of academic content into auditory perception activities appears feasible. Thus, a child with auditory perception difficulties should perform tasks involving discrimination among the sounds of letters, words, and verbal instructions; the use of nonsense sounds and nonacademic content is minimized. Stephens (1977) provides numerous assessment procedures and instructional activities that illustrate the use of academic content in auditory perception activities.

Selected Auditory Perception Activities

The following selected activities may be used to develop auditory perception skills:

1. Say the words *money, bat,* and *puzzle.* Instruct the child to tell which word begins like the word *bottle*.
2. Play bingo with the child by calling out words and having him recognize the sound and cover the appropriate square.
3. Have the child match pictures of objects that rhyme.
4. Tell the child to listen for a specific sound in a word. Say the word and ask, "Is the sound at the beginning or end of the word?"

5. Instruct the child to classify pictures according to initial sounds, final sounds, and/or rhyming sounds.
6. Tell a story and then provide the child with pictures of the story. Have him arrange them in the correct sequence.

Haptic Perception

Description

Haptic perception refers to the process of acquiring information through the tactile and kinesthetic systems. *Tactile perception* refers to the sensation of touch; information is gained through the fingers or surfaces of the skin. Thus, a person with good tactile perception can identify a number drawn on his back or recognize an object by simply touching and feeling it. Likewise, a person deficient in this area finds that manipulative activities do not provide him with meaningful information.

Kinesthetic perception refers to sensations of the body that are received through movements of the body and muscle feeling. For example, depending on which way we move, we feel different sensations. Some children do not have full awareness of their bodily parts and muscular feelings (tension or relaxation). These children show problems with body image and coordination.

Classroom tasks require both tactile and kinesthetic skills. As such disabilities do not appear to be widespread, the available information is sparse. However, Ayres (1975) believes a relationship exists between the development of tactile and kinesthetic perception and the development of other areas of the cortex that are directly related to academic tasks. Writing and spelling may be influenced by problems in these areas. For example, the child may receive tactile sensations from holding the pencil in his hand and kinesthetic sensations from the movement of his hand while he writes. In spelling, a child may make associations with the correct spelling of a word and the movement of his hand while writing the letters (Wedell, 1973).

Diagnosis of Haptic Perception Deficits

Although a child must use his tactile and kinesthetic senses on visual and/or motor tests, few tests specifically assess these abilities. However, Ayres (1972) devised the *Southern California Sensory Integration Tests,* which include five subtests:

1. *Kinesthesia.* The examiner shields the child's eyes. The child must move his hand on a chart in a pattern similar to a previous pattern that was formed by the examiner guiding the child's hand.
2. *Manual Form Perception.* The child holds a solid geometric form without seeing it. He must select a picture that is identical to the form he is holding.
3. *Finger Identification.* The child's eyes are occluded. He must identify which of his fingers was touched by the examiner.
4. *Graphesthesia.* The examiner shields the child's eyes. The examiner then "draws" designs on the back of the child's hand with a pencil eraser. The child must reproduce the design.
5. *Localization of Tactile Stimuli.* The child's hand or forearm is shielded from view. The tester touches the hand or forearm with a ball-point pen. The child then uses his index finger to touch the place he was touched.

Stephens (1977) describes an informal test for assessing haptic learning through the sense of touch. He suggests the use of instructional material within the child's achievement level. After the student is blindfolded, he is given objects one at a time to feel. The responses of the student are recorded as he tries to identify each object.

Activities Involving Kinesthetic and Tactile Stimuli

The following selected activities focus on kinesthetic and tactile perception:

1. Fill a tray or cookie sheet with sand. Instruct the child to draw forms, letters,

A teacher administering the Bruininks-Oseretsky Test of Motor Proficiency.

words, numbers, and shapes with his finger.
2. Place notebook paper on the top side of a piece of sandpaper. Use a crayon to draw shapes, words, math equations, and letters. By pressing hard with the crayon, the lines become raised and are excellent for tracing activities. If sandpaper is not available, use a screen from a window.
3. Select a medium-sized cardboard box and cut two holes in the side. Put familiar objects and shapes (letters, numbers, geometric shapes) in the box and instruct the child to put one or both hands in the box; then ask him to pick up an object, feel it, describe it, and name it.

PERCEPTUAL-MOTOR DISABILITIES

The emphasis on perceptual-motor skills is rooted in the pioneering work of numerous investigators. Piaget (1952) stresses that early sensory-motor experiences are basic to later, more complex mental development. Sherrington (1948) claims that the motor system is the first neurological system to develop and that it provides the foundation for later perceptual growth. Hebb (1949) purports that early motor learning helps develop cortical cell assemblies. Certainly concern for perceptual-motor development is widespread in the educational and experimental literature; it is a recurring theme in the history of special education (Lerner, 1976).

Strauss and Werner (1942) and Strauss and Lehtinen (1947) provide the basic premise of the perceptual-motor orientation: motor learning is a prerequisite to higher-order learning. Although Figure 9.1 over-simplifies the perceptual-motor viewpoint, it does display the central theme.

Smith's (1969) diagram (see Figure 9.2) provides a framework for examination of the perceptual-motor processes; it may also be used to discuss auditory, visual, haptic, and olfactory perceptual processes. It is possible to stress any of these perceptual processes with this model; however, this section highlights the importance of motor learning. In this model, stimuli (from both external and internal senses) are received through the senses. It must be received accurately. The process of organizing and/or associating the sensory information occurs at the integration level. The interpretation or meaning of the sensory information is referred to as *perception*. Thus perception involves a refinement of sensory information and *perceptual-motor* refers to the interaction of this perception with motor activity. The motor activity primarily occurs at the expressive or response level. According to Smith, this output reenters the receptive component and serves as feedback to determine if the response is congruent with the stimuli previously received.

Smith (1969) describes the need for interaction among the perceptual-motor components by examining the behavior of an intoxicated person attemping to drink from a cup.

In this situation information is misperceived; data about the spatial relationship that exists between the cup, hand, and mouth are erroneously or inadequately processed; communication between the various perceptual-motor components is impaired; and the execution of proper motor movements is impeded, resulting in both over- and under-compensation. The en-

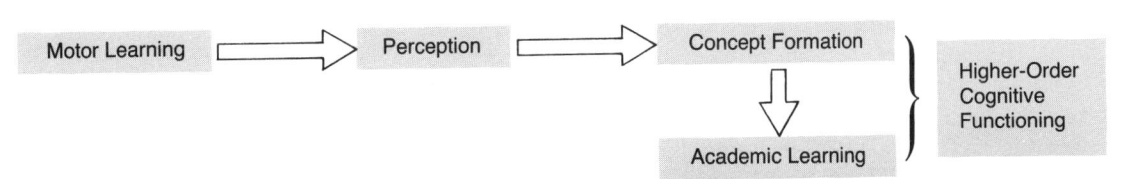

FIGURE 9.1

The relationship of motor learning to higher-order learning.

Specific learning disorders

```
Environment → [extraction of stimuli and receptive component] → [integration of incoming information with existing repertoire] → [gestural and/or vocal response] →
                                                    ↓
                                         [monitor and feedback system]
```

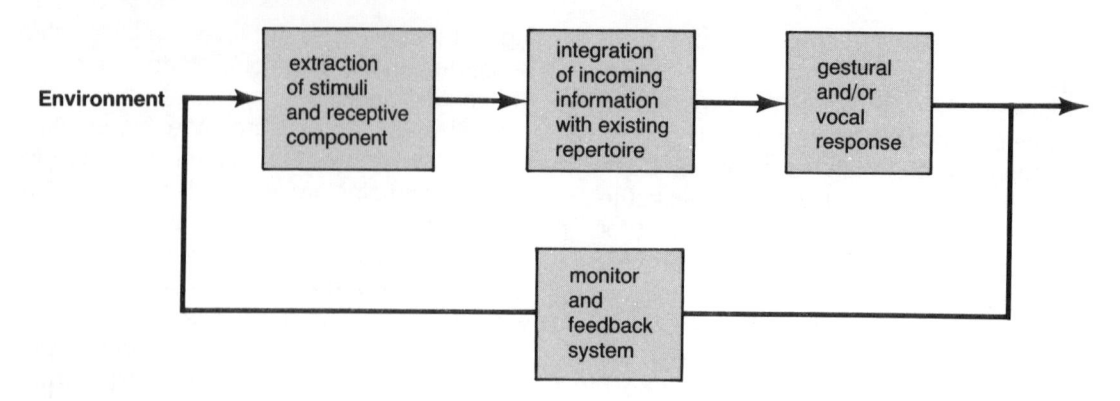

FIGURE 9.2

Perceptual-motor system.

Source. Adapted from "Perceptual-Motor Skills" by R. M. Smith. In R. M. Smith (Ed.), *Teacher Diagnosis of Educational Difficulties.* Columbus, Ohio: Charles E. Merrill, 1969, p. 50. Copyright 1969 by Charles E. Merrill Publishing Company. Reprinted by permission.

tire system is affected by disability in any or all of these components. (p. 55)

Although each writer provides his own orientation, the basic premise of the perceptual-motor position exists in the works of Barsch (1965), Kephart (1969), Frostig and Maslow (1973), Ayres (1965), Delacato (1966), Cratty (1969), and Getman (1965). Essentially, Barsch, Frostig, and Getman stress the visual-motor processes, and Kephart, Delacato, and Cratty focus on the basic motor learning. Chapter 5 examines the theories of Ayres and Delacato. This chapter presents the theories of Kephart, Barsch, and Cratty.

Kephart: Perceptual-Motor Theory

Having been influenced by Werner and Strauss at the Wayne County Training School, Kephart placed emphasis on the perceptual-motor development of the child. Kephart (1964, 1971) postulated that basically all behavior is motor, and that motor development precedes and is essential for perceptual development. He believed perception and motoric response cannot be separated. In his theory, the child develops by going through a series of graduated stages. Normally the perceptual-motor abilities of a child are developed by the age of 6; however, in the learning disabled child these skills develop abnormally, showing as learning problems in the elementary grades.

An individual interacts with the world through motor behavior. Kephart differentiated between a motor pattern and a motor skill. A *motor pattern* is a combination of movements that have a broad purpose. A *motor skill* exhibits a high degree of precision to accomplish a specific act. For example, kicking a football is a motor skill; using this skill as part of a game is a motor pattern.

When a child acquires a skill that is not part of the child's orderly sequential development, it is called a *splinter skill.* Kephart (1963) illustrated this skill by describing a child who could write his name after having memorized a series of fine finger movements which had no relation to movements of the wrist or other parts of the arm.

Motor Generalization

When motor patterns are combined and incorporated into broader motor tasks, it leads to *motor generalizations,* basic to school success. Four such generalizations through which children gain information include balance and maintenance of posture, contact, locomotion, and receipt and propulsion.

Through *balance and maintenance of posture,* the child maintains a relationship to the force of gravity. As gravity is the origin for all learning, the child must be aware of the pull of gravity and able to manipulate his body accordingly.

Reaching for, grasping, and releasing objects are *contact* skills. Knowledge about the characteristics of objects eventually helps the child to develop skills in figure-ground relationships and form perception.

Locomotion skills refer to body movement through space and include walking, jumping, and running. Thus, the child explores surrounding space and the relationship between objects in the environment.

Through *receipt and propulsion* skills incorporated in catching, throwing, pushing, and pulling, the child finds out how objects move in space. When learning *receipt* skills, the child observes objects coming toward him; *propulsion* skills refer to activities in which the child observes objects pushed away from him. By combining these movements the child learns about movement lateral to himself—which, in turn, leads to the ability to distinguish left and right sides of the body.

Perceptual-Motor Match

Another major theoretical concept discussed by Kephart (1960) is the *perceptual-motor match.* This refers to the child's ability to correlate motor information with perceptual information. Since Kephart maintains that motor development precedes visual development, he felt that a child gains information from a visual activity only if the perceptual information is matched with previously acquired motor information. For example, when an infant looks across the room and sees a ball, he may see a two-dimensional circle. However, when the ball is handed to him, he holds it, squeezes it, and feels it. Then when the ball is taken away and he sees it again, he perceives a three-dimensional object. Thus, the child has made a perceptual-motor match.

Implications

Kephart's (1960, 1971) now classic book, *The Slow Learner in the Classroom,* presents his perceptual-motor approach and includes suggestions for remediation. He believed remediation should correspond with the order of development (i.e., training the motoric development before training visual skills). In addition, he notes activities should proceed from simple to complex and generalizations should be taught prior to specific tasks.

The *Purdue Perceptual-Motor Survey* (Roach & Kephart, 1966) is based on the perceptual-motor framework. The scale, designed for children from 6 to 9 years old, includes the following skills and activities: *(a)* walking forward, backward, and sideways on a board or balance beam, *(b)* jumping and hopping on both feet and each foot alone, *(c)* identifying parts of the body, *(d)* imitating movements, *(e)* moving through an obstacle course, *(f)* moving arms and legs in various positions while lying on the back (Angels-in-the-Snow), *(g)* drawing on a chalkboard, and *(h)* performing visual achievement tasks, such as copying geometric shapes.

Barsch: Movigenic Theory

Barsch (1965, 1967, 1968) developed the movigenic theory, which is based on the belief that the development of spatial movement patterns leads to learning efficiency. Thus, learning problems are related to the individual's inefficient interaction with space. His main principles are

1. Humans are designed to move, and our activities involve movement.
2. The objective of movement is to survive, and movement efficiency increases survival chances.
3. Movement takes place in an energy surround (e.g., gravity force), and through this movement information pertaining to survival is obtained.

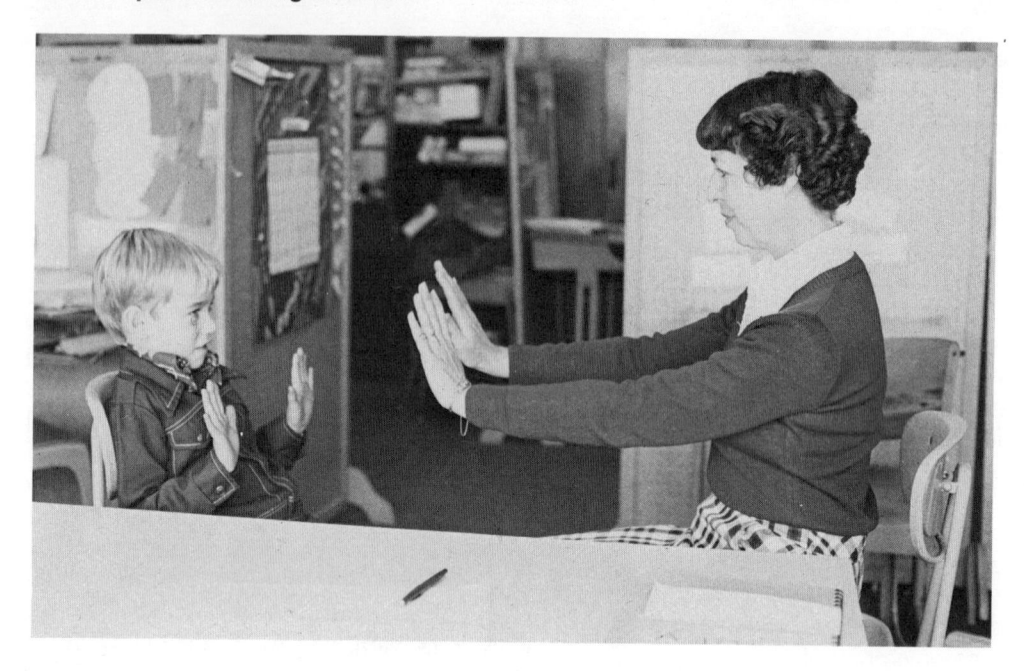

The Purdue Survey uses imitation of movement to assess skills.

4. Information is acquired through our percepto-cognitive system.
5. Since the terrain of movement is space, individuals must learn to move efficiently in space.
6. Developmental momentum moves the individual toward maturity.
7. Movement occurs in a climate of stress, and a certain amount of stress is necessary for learning.
8. Feedback is essential in the development of movement efficiency.
9. Development takes place in segments of sequential expansion, proceeding from the simple to the more complex.
10. The visual spatial phenomenon called *language* symbolically communicates movement efficiency.

Movigenic Curriculum

Based upon this theory, Barsch developed a movigenic curriculum designed to improve motor efficiency. The basic components of the curriculum include muscular strength; dynamic balance; spatial and body awareness; visual, auditory, and tactual dynamics; kinesthesia; bilaterality; rhythm; flexibility; and motor planning. Thus, the curriculum emphasizes the development of motor movement and spatial awareness. In addition, Barsch feels it is necessary for the teacher to be aware of developmental growth and to maintain a strong belief in the importance of movement to learning.

Cratty: Motor Learning

Cratty (1969, 1971, 1973) believes that movement games help both LD and normal kids learn better. He thinks that the quality and quantity of a child's motor output affect his ability and/or inclination to perform various classroom tasks. Moreover, in order for a movement activity to increase a child's cognitive abilities, there must be an association between the activity and the higher thought processes that are to be changed. However, Cratty is cautious concerning the academic benefits from motor activities and he does not claim that movement is the basis of the development of the child's mental, social abilities and emotional well-being.

Cratty (1971) developed games and exercises designed to enhance motor skills and academic learning. He notes that if a child is able to play games well, the child's self-concept and social acceptance by peers may be raised and this may enhance his academic performance. Cratty gives several examples of how movement education can be related to classroom learning. For example, in learning the shape of letters, a child may be involved in a game in which large letters are placed on the playground and the child runs or walks over the shapes of the letters. Also, Cratty feels that moderate exercise and performance of motor tasks may help produce the optimum level of alertness and arousal essential for the performance of efficient mental work.

Research and Perceptual-Motor Training

The perceptual-motor instructional programs have generated much research. These studies examine the effect of perceptual motor training on sensory-motor skills, visual-motor skills, readiness skills, and academic and/or language skills. In a review of 42 studies, Hallahan and Cruickshank (1973) report that only seven (17%) of the studies were conducted well enough to interpret the findings. Of these seven studies, they note that little can be concluded about the effectiveness of perceptual-motor training.

Myers and Hammill (1976) did not critically evaluate the methodological problems of each study but chose for examination purposes to accept the results of each study at face value. In accepting the results the authors acknowledge that their examination is biased in favor of the experimental programs (perceptual-motor training). Thirty-one of the studies examined the effectiveness of the Frostig-Horne program. In 68%, the program did not produce significant results. Thirty-one other studies researched the effectiveness of the Kephart-Getman-Cratty-Barsch approaches. Results showed that perceptual-motor approaches failed 80% of the time. Of the 14 studies on

It takes precision to throw the ball gently enough and on target so your partner can catch it.

Specific learning disorders

Delacato's techniques, only 33% showed them to be valid strategies.

On the basis of their review, Myers and Hammill conclude that perceptual-motor programs are still highly experimental and non-data-based. They point out we need more research that considers *(a)* the characteristics of children for whom such training is helpful, *(b)* the time required for achieving effectiveness, and *(c)* whether or not perceptual-motor processes can be improved via training.

In a review of studies concerning the relationship between reading difficulties and perceptual-motor deficits, Vellutino, Steger, Moyer, Harding, and Niles (1977) report that it is unlikely that perceptual disorders cause many reading problems. Instead they provide research results that support a relationship between poor reading and linguistic deficits.

Many of the perceptual-motor training programs commonly used, then, do not directly improve academic achievement or perceptual-motor development. Until further research, the inclusion of academic content in motor activities is desirable. Cratty (1971) stresses this approach in which the child can perform motor tasks involving letters, concepts (up, down), words, and telling time (e.g., let the child use his arms as clock hands to display various times). Finally, today physical education teachers find many perceptual-motor activities useful for their classes.

Selected Perceptual-Motor Activities

Gross Motor Activities

Gross motor activities involve the total musculature of the body to develop more effective body movements and a sense of spatial orientation and body awareness. The following activities stress academic content:

1. Place squares containing geometric shapes on the floor. When you call out a geometric shape, the child stands on it. The game can be modified by putting different stimuli (letters, words, numbers) on the squares and by varying the rate of calling.
2. Use masking tape to place lined configurations on the floor. Call out or write a number; the child walks through the configuration within the patterns lined on the floor.
3. Position on the floor a set of number squares containing two of each of the numbers from 1 to 15. One player at a time from two relay teams runs to the set of number squares and selects each successive number. The first team to complete the 1 to 15 number sequence wins. This game can be modified by using letter squares and requiring the teams to spell words.
4. Ask children to write on a chalkboard; this task involves the use of large muscles and is helpful in practicing the formation of various shapes, letters, and numbers.

Fine Motor Activities

1. Construct a gadget manipulation board by attaching a zipper, a button-hole strip from a shirt, nuts and bolts, a belt buckle, a shoelace, and various other devices to a thin piece of plywood. The child can prac-

Students like dot-to-dot games—while improving their fine motor skills.

tice these functional fine motor skills by manipulating the items on the board.
2. Provide activities that involve cutting with scissors.
3. Have the child dial a toy telephone in computing simple math problems (e.g., sums to 9).
4. Provide the child with a rubber stamp set to use while spelling words.
5. Use templates and stencils to enable the child to practice drawing or tracing shapes, letters, and numbers.
6. Use dot-to-dot activities involving numbers, letters, and words.

Body Image and Awareness Activities
1. Place a large piece of paper on the floor and have the child lie down on the paper, faceup. Draw lines around the child's body and cut along these lines. The resulting configuration of the child's body can be taped on the wall with the child's name over it. A photograph of the child's face may be placed on the head. Pockets can be added to the configuration and used to hold schoolwork, reinforcers, or messages. The configuration serves to help some children develop body image and awareness perceptions.
2. Place a full-length mirror in the classroom. Ask the child to face the mirror and touch various body parts. He can also use the mirror to help him understand how he looks (e.g., tuck in his shirt, comb his hair).
3. Use pencil and paper activities asking the child to color body parts or supply missing body parts.

Directionality and Space Activities
1. Ask the child to respond to the following commands:

   Show me how small (tall, wide, thin, etc.) you can be.
   Point to the farthest (nearest) wall.
   Show me how slow you can walk.
   Stand with the ball *in front of* you.
   Move *between* the two chairs.
   Move so you are *under* the table.

2. Prepare an obstacle course consisting of tires, hoops, chairs, and balance beams. Instruct the child to move through the course at various rates. When doing the course the child should pretend he is moving around breakable objects.
3. Provide the child with a place setting (plate and utensils) and instruct him to arrange it correctly (left to right).
4. Prepare a worksheet of simple pictures with various instructions, such as:

   Put a line *under* the car.
   Circle the *middle* car.
   Draw a line *between* the dog and cat.

5. Construct a road system on paper and instruct the child to guide a toy car while verbalizing turns and directions.
6. In written exercises, use arrows or red and green markers to emphasize up-down, start-stop, or left-to-right progressions.

These activities stress the mixing of academic content with motor activities. However, remember that the primary purpose of many motor activities is to have fun or directly develop selected skills. Numerous commercial programs and books provide a wealth of useful motor activities: AAHPER, 1969; Barsch, 1967, 1968; Cratty, 1971; Dubnoff, Chambers, and Schaeffer, 1969; Fairbanks and Robinson, 1969; Getman, 1969; Getman, Kane, and McKee, 1968; Hackett and Jenson, 1967; Kephart, 1971; O'Donnell, 1969; Robinson and Schmitt, 1970; Van Witsen, 1967.

Finally, Table 9.2 displays the relationship between some commonly used teaching materials and motor skills.

Handwriting

In the past handwriting was an art, executed slowly, painstakingly, and very beautifully. But today the quality of handwriting in the schools is inferior to that of a generation ago. The following situations exemplify some problems caused by poor handwriting. A million letters each year end up as "dead letters" in the U.S. Post Offices because of poorly written names

Gross-motor activities at this school involve learning coordination and cooperation.

"Get as close as you can to an object without touching it."

"Choose a partner."

"Lynn and Eric, trade places."

"Scoot as fast as you can."

"Everyone get as close as you can."

"Stand inside an object."

"Make small waves."

TABLE 9.2

Relationship between teaching materials and motor skills.

Skills	Parquetry	Block design	Peg board	Sorting	Matching	Sequence patterns	Stencils	Cutting	Pasting	Coloring	Geometric form copying	Puzzles
Eye-hand coordination	X	X	X	X	X	X	X	X	X	X	X	X
Fine muscle development		X	X	X		X	X	X	X	X	X	
Concept of spatial relationships	X	X	X			X	X	X	X	X	X	X
Left-to-right progression		X	X		X	X					X	
Laterality							X	X				
Directionality				X	X	X		X			X	X

or numerals. In addition, the majority of the 400,000 federal income tax refunds delayed in 1958 were held up because of poor handwriting. Furthermore, business people lose money every day as a result of illegible handwriting.

Many learning disabled children experience difficulty with handwriting (dysgraphia). Hildreth (1947) lists numerous contributing factors: motor problems, emotional problems, faulty visual perception of letters and words, and poor visual memory. Additional factors include poor instruction and left-handedness.

Children show a variety of handwriting problems: slowness, incorrect directionality of letters and numbers, spacing difficulty, messiness, inability to stay on a horizontal line, illegible letters, too much pencil pressure, and mirror writing. Newland (1932) examined the cursive handwriting of 2,381 people and reported their errors. Approximately 50% of the illegibilities involved the letters *a, e, r,* and *t.* Most commonly, people *(a)* failed to close letters (accounted for 24% of the errors), *(b)* closed top loops in letters like *e* (13%), *(c)* looped strokes which should be nonlooped (e.g., *i* like *e* [12%]), *(d)* used straight up strokes rather than rounded strokes (e.g., *n* for *u* [11%]), and *(e)* exhibited problem with end strokes (11%). Table 9.3 illustrates other common illegibilities.

Cursive and Manuscript Handwriting

In most schools teachers begin writing instruction with manuscript writing and introduce cursive writing around the end of second grade. However, some controversy exists concerning whether to begin writing with manuscript or cursive. Those who support manuscript writing (Johnson & Myklebust, 1967) claim that it requires less complex movements and that reading problems are reduced because most

TABLE 9.3

Common illegibilities in handwriting.

a like u		m like n	
a like o		n like u	
a like ce		o like a	
b like li		o like v	
be like bl		p like js	
b like k		r like n	
c like e		r like v	
c like a		r like i	
d like cl		t like i	
e like i		t like l	
g like y		u like ee	
g like q		u like ei	
i like e		w like n	
h like li		w like ue	
h like k		w like eu	
k like ls		x like v	
m like w		y like ij	

printed pages are in manuscript. The advocates of cursive writing (Orton, 1937; Strauss & Lehtinen, 1947) believe that cursive writing results in fewer spacing difficulties because the letters are written as units. In addition, they claim that cursive writing results in fewer reversals because of its rhythmic flow. Also, transference problems are omitted if writing begins with cursive. Although both camps present good arguments, the teacher should assess each individual situation. Many young children want to learn cursive writing because older peers and adults use it. Wallace and McLoughlin (1975) encourage teachers to teach each child the form of writing that is used by peers in the classroom.

Left-handedness

Oftentimes left-handed children tend to write from right to left. Moreover, in order to see what they have written and to avoid smudging their writing, they begin "hooking" their hand while writing.

Today we know that left-handedness is natural. In fact, Lerner (1976) reports that left-handed children learn to write as fast as right-handers. Paper should be placed in front of the left-handed child without a slant for manuscript writing. For cursive writing the top of the paper is slanted north-northeast; hooking should be avoided.

Handwriting Programs

Several commercial programs teach handwriting. Those varying from the "look-trace-copy" format include

Handwriting with Write and See (Skinner & Krakower, 1968)
The Johnson Handwriting Program (Johnson, 1971)
A Writing Manual for Teaching the Left-Handed (Plunkett, 1954)
Dubnoff School Program 1—Level 2 (Dubnoff, Chambers, & Schaeffer, 1969)

Assessing Handwriting

Many commercial programs provide error analysis charts or checklists to help analyze handwriting difficulties:

"The 15 Handwriting Demons" (Noble, 1966)
"Error Analysis Chart" (Cartwright, 1969)
"Manual for Teachers Grades One Through Four" (Freeman, 1965)

284 Specific learning disorders

In addition, Table 9.4 displays a diagnostic chart for manuscript and cursive writing that highlights some common relationships between errors, likely causes, and remediation procedures.

Teaching Handwriting

Many teachers and commercial programs break the writing process into small steps (task analysis) and provide instruction at each step. A brief checklist of writing behaviors and a 35-step skill sequence is presented in Table 9.5. Also, the teacher may find the instructional objectives by suggested grade level in Table 9.6 helpful in assessing and teaching handwriting skills.

Some teaching activities and suggestions for handwriting include

1. Chalkboard activities may be used for exercises in copying, dot-to-dot, and completing incomplete figures.
2. During writing the child needs to be in a comfortable chair with feet flat on the floor. The desk or table should be at a height which allows the child to place his forearms on the writing surface without discomfort. The nonwriting hand is used to hold the writing paper at the top.
3. Stencils and templates of shapes, numbers, and letters can be made from plastic, styrofoam, or cardboard. Once the stencil is fastened to the child's paper with paper clips, he can write or trace the forms. When the stencil or template is removed, the child can view the figure he has made.

Stenciling helps familiarize letter forms.

TABLE 9.4

Diagnostic chart for manuscript and cursive writing.

Factor	Problem	Possible Cause	Remediation
		Manuscript Writing	
Shape	Letters slanted	Paper slanted	Place paper straight and pull straight line strokes toward center of body.
		Improper mental image of letter	Have pupil write problem letters on chalkboard.
Size	Too large	Poor understanding of writing lines	Reteach size concept by pointing out purpose of each line on writing paper.
		Exaggerated arm movement	Reduce arm movement, especially on circle and part-circle letters.
		Improper mental image of letter	Have pupil write problem letters on chalkboard.
	Too small	Poor understanding of writing lines	Reteach size concept by pointing out purpose of each line of writing paper.
		Overemphasis on finger movement	Stress arm movement; check hand-pencil and arm-desk positions to be sure arm movement is possible.
		Improper mental image of letter	Have pupil write problem letters on chalkboard.
	Not uniform	Adjusting writing hand after each letter	Stress arm movement; move paper with nonwriting hand so writing hand can remain in proper writing position.

TABLE 9.4 cont.

Factor	Problem	Possible Cause	Remediation
		Manuscript Writing	
		Overemphasis on finger movement	Stress arm movement; check arm-desk and pencil-hand positions.
Space	Crowded letters in words	Poor understanding of space concepts	Reteach uniform spacing between letters (finger or pencil width).
	Too much space between letters	Improper lowercase letter size and shape	Review concepts of size and shape; provide appropriate corrections under size and shape.
Alignment	Letters not sitting on base line	Improper letter formation	Evaluate work for letter shape; stress bringing straight line strokes all the way down to base line.
		Poor understanding of base line concept	Review purpose of base line on writing paper.
		Improper hand-pencil and paper-desk positions	Check positions to make sure pupil is able to reach base line with ease.
	Letters not of consistent height	Poor understanding of size concept	Review concept of letter size in relationship to lines provided on writing paper.

		Cursive Writing	
Line quality	Too heavy or too light	Improper writing pressure	Review hand-pencil position; place wadded paper tissue in palm of writing hand to relax writing grip; demonstrate desired line quality.
Shape	Letters too oval in size	Overemphasis of arm movement and poor image of letter size and shape	Check arm-desk position; review letter size and shape
	Letters too narrow in shape	Finger writing	Check positions to allow for arm movement
		Overemphasis of straight line stroke	Make sure straight line stroke does not come all the way down to base line in letters like l, b, and t.
		Poor mental image of letter shape	Use transparent overseer for pupil's personal evaluation of shape
			In all problems of letter shape review letters in terms of the basic strokes
Size	Letters too large	Exaggerated arm movement	Check arm-desk position for over-movement of forearm
		Poor mental image of letter size	Review base and top line concepts in relation to ¼ space, ½ space, and ¾ space; use transparent overseer for pupil's personal evaluation of letter size
	Letters too small or letters not uniform	Finger movement	Check arm-desk and pencil-hand positions; stress arm movement

TABLE 9.4 cont.

Factor	Problem	Possible Cause	Remediation
		Cursive Writing	
	Letters too small or letters not uniform.	Poor mental image of letter size	Review concept of letter size (¼ space, ½ space, and ¾ space) in relation to base and top lines; use transparent overseer for pupil's personal evaluation of letter size
Space	Letters in words crowded or spacing between letters uneven	Finger movement	Check arm-desk, pencil-hand positions; stress arm movement.
		Poor understanding of joining strokes	Review how letters are joined; show ending stroke of one letter to be beginning stroke of following letter; practice writing letters in groups of five.
	Too much space provided between letters in words	Exaggerated arm movement	Check arm-desk position for over-movement of forearm.
		Poor understanding of joining strokes	Review joining strokes; practice writing groups of letters by rhythmic count.
	Uneven space between words	Poor understanding of between word spacing	Review concept of spacing between words; show beginning stroke in second word starting under ending stroke of preceding word.
Alignment	Poor letter alignment along base line	Incorrect writing position; finger movement; exaggerated arm movement	Check all writing positions; stress even, rhythmic writing movement.
		Poor understanding of base line concept	Use repetitive exercise with emphasis on relationship of base line to written word.

		Uneven alignment of letters in words relative to size	Review joining strokes.
		Incorrect use of joining strokes	Show size relationships between lower- and uppercase, and ¼ space, ½ space, and ¾ space lowercase letters; use repetitive exercise with emphasis on uniform height of smaller letters.
		Poor understanding of size concept	
Speed and Ease		Writing becomes illegible under stress and speed (grades 4, 5, and 6)	Improve writing positions; develop more arm movement and less finger movement.
		Degree of handwriting skill is insufficient to meet speed requirements	
		Writing becomes illegible when writing activity is too long	Improve all writing positions, especially hand-pencil position; stress arm movement.
		Handwriting positions have not been perfected to allow handwriting ease	
Slant	Back slant	Left-handedness	Correct hand-pencil and paper-desk positions
	Vertical	Poor positioning	Correct hand-pencil and paper-desk positions
	Too far right	Overemphasis of finger movement	Make sure pupils pull slant strokes toward center of body if right-handed and to left elbow if left-handed.
			Use slant line instruction sheets as aid to teaching slant.
			Use transparent overseer for pupil's personal evaluation.
			Review all lowercase letters that derive their shape from the slant line.
			Write lowercase alphabet on chalkboard; retrace all slant strokes in colored chalk.

TABLE 9.5

A problem checklist and writing skill sequence.

Problem Checklist

____ Forms letters from right to left rather than from left to right
____ Dissociates letters into separate parts
____ Reverses letters in words *(saw = was)*
____ Mirrors letters/numbers *(b* for *d, p* for *q)*
____ Perseverates letters
____ Writes cramped, uneven, large letters
____ Holds pencil with fist rather than fingers
____ Copies from blackboard incorrectly
____ Writes slowly
____ Writes using varied slant, pencil pressure, or spacing between letters

Skill Sequence

1.0 Makes marks with pencil or crayon held in fist
2.0 Scribbles with pencil or crayon held in fist
3.0 Draws a vertical line, imitating adult
4.0 Draws a horizontal line, imitating adult
5.0 Performs push-pull strokes imitating adult
6.0 Draws circle, imitating adult
7.0 Draws line between two parallel lines
8.0 Draws recognizable face with eyes, nose, mouth
9.0 Holds pencil or crayon in fingers
10.0 Draws horizontal/vertical line, copying model
11.0 Draws oblique lines, copying models
12.0 Draws vertical cross, imitating adult
13.0 Draws square, imitating adult
14.0 Draws oblique cross, imitating adult
15.0 Draws triangle, imitating adult
16.0 Draws diamond, imitating adult
17.0 Colors within heavy outlines, within faint outlines
18.0 Draws three-part man, six-part man
19.0 Draws letter/number shapes, copying models
20.0 Prints/writes letters, numbers, imitating adult
21.0 Draws circle, crosses, square, triangle, diamond, copying model
22.0 Prints/writes numbers and letters, copying model
23.0 Draws circle, crosses, square, triangle, diamond without model
24.0 Prints/writes selected numbers and letters without models
25.0 Forms numbers and letters from left to right
26.0 Prints/writes all letters in the alphabet, all numbers 0–9, correctly without models
27.0 Prints/writes own first name, copying model
28.0 Prints/writes own first name without model
29.0 Prints/writes own first name using a capital first letter
30.0 Prints/writes simple words, copying models
31.0 Prints/writes simple words, without models
32.0 Prints/writes own last name, copying model
33.0 Prints/writes simple sentences, copying model
34.0 Prints/writes own first and last name without model
35.0 Prints/writes simple sentences without model

TABLE 9.6

Handwriting objectives by suggested grade level.

Objective	Suggested Grade Level
1. Begin to establish a preference for either left- or right-handedness.	k, 1
2. Develop small muscle control through the use of such materials as finger painting, clay weaving, and puzzles.	k, 1
3. Understand and apply writing readiness vocabulary given orally, such as *left/right, top/bottom, beginning/end, large/small, circle, space, around, across, curve, top line, dotted line,* and *bottom line.*	k, 1
4. Begin to establish correct writing position of body, arms, hand, paper, and pencil.	k, 1
5. Draw familiar objects using the basic strokes of manuscript writing.	k, 1
6. Recognize and write own name in manuscript letters using capital and lowercase letters appropriately.	k
7. Begin manuscript writing using both lowercase and capital letters introduced to correlate with the child's reading program.	1
8. Establish preference for left/right-handedness.	2
9. Use correct writing position of body, arm, hand, paper, and pencil.	1, 2, 3, 4, 5, 6
10. Use writing paper that is standard for manuscript writing.	k, 1, 2, 3
11. Evaluate writing using a plastic overlay; identify strengths and weaknesses.	k, 1, 2, 3, 4, 5, 6
12. Write with firm strokes and demonstrate good spacing between letters, words, and sentences.	1, 2, 3, 4, 5, 6
13. Master manuscript writing (i.e., write letters independently and with good firm strokes).	1, 2
14. Write clear, legible manuscript letters at a rate commensurate with ability.	1, 2
15. Arrange work neatly and pleasingly on a page (i.e., use margins, paragraph indentations, and make clean erasures).	1, 2, 3, 4, 5, 6
16. Demonstrate ability to decode cursive writing by reading paragraphs of cursive writing both from the chalkboard and from paper.	3
17. Identify cursive lowercase and capital letters by matching cursive letters to manuscript letters.	3
18. Begin cursive writing with lowercase letters and progress to capital letters as needed.	3
19. Use writing paper that is standard for cursive writing.	3, 4
20. Use cursive writing for day-to-day use.	4, 5, 6
21. Begin to write with a pen *if* pencil writing is smooth, fluent, and neat.	4, 5, 6
22. Maintain and use manuscript writing for special needs, such as preparing charts, maps, and labels.	4, 5, 6
23. Reduce size of writing to "adult" proportions of letters (i.e., one-quarter space for minimum letters, one-half space for intermediate letters, and three-quarters space for tall lowercase and capital letters).	5, 6
24. Write clear, legible cursive letters at a rate commensurate with ability.	4, 5, 6

292 Specific learning disorders

4. The child can trace forms by placing a sheet of onion skin paper over dark-line shapes, numbers, and letters.
5. The child can draw forms, letters, and numbers by drawing between the lines. For example,

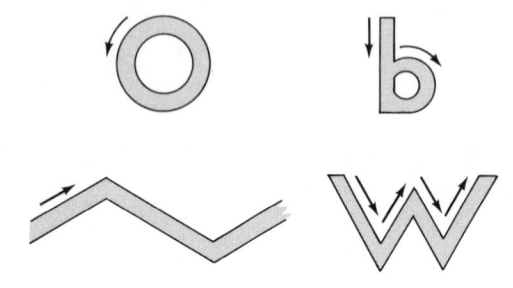

6. Slash-to-slash and dot-to-dot activities can be used to form shapes, letters, and numbers. For example,

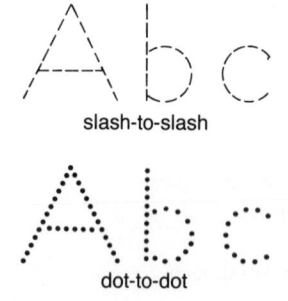

slash-to-slash

dot-to-dot

7. Paper with squares is helpful to some children who are beginning to write.

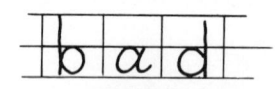

8. The child can be provided with a copy of the alphabet and numbers 0–9 to use at his desk. The child can refer to the model during writing exercises.
9. The pencil should be held lightly in the triangle formed by the thumb and the first two fingers, and the hand should rest lightly on its outer edge. Also, the child can use commercially made pencil grips.
10. The Practice Pad provides a handwriting center. Children can practice any of the handwriting skills provided by the model. When adapted to chalkboard writing, the Pad increases motivation and provides exercise for children who need large muscle movement. (See below.)

Other sources of handwriting activities and techniques are Burns, 1974; Gillingham and Stillman, 1966; Hammill and Bartel, 1978; Herrick, 1963; Otto, McMenemy, and Smith, 1973; Reger, Schroeder, and Uschold, 1968; Skinner and Krakower, 1968; Wallace and Kauffman, 1978; Wiederholt, Hammill, and Brown, 1978.

SUMMARY

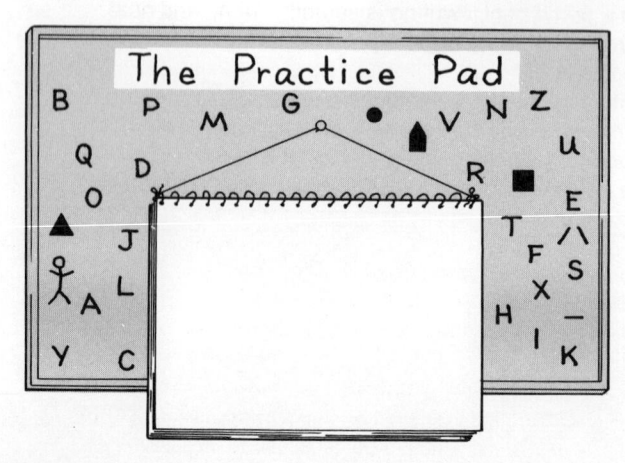

This chapter is divided into two major sections: perception and perceptual-motor disabilities. The perception section begins with a discussion of perceptual disabilities, including the topics of visual, auditory, and haptic perception; related research; and selected teaching activities. In the perceptual-motor disabilities section, the theories of Kephart, Barsch, and Cratty are discussed. In addition, information is presented on research pertaining to perceptual-motor training and selected perceptual-motor teaching activities. A discussion of handwriting includes a description of handwriting problems, a task-analysis of handwriting skills, and instructional objectives by suggested grade level. The chapter ends by exploring handwriting programs and selected teaching activities.

REFERENCES

AAHPER. *Promising practices in elementary physical education.* Washington, D.C.: American Association for Health, Physical Education, and Recreation, 1969.

Ayres, A.J. Patterns of perceptual-motor dysfunction in children: A factor analytic study. *Perceptual Motor Skills,* 1965, 20, 335–368.

Ayres, A.J. *Southern California Figure-Ground Visual Perception Test.* Los Angeles: Western Psychological Services, 1969.

Ayres, A.J. Sensorimotor foundations of academic ability. In W.M. Cruickshank & D.P. Hallahan (Eds.), *Perceptual and learning disabilities in children* (Vol. 2) *Research and theory.* Syracuse, N.Y.: Syracuse University Press, 1975.

Baker, H.J., & Leland, B. *Detroit Tests of Learning Aptitude.* Indianapolis: Bobbs-Merrill, 1935.

Barsch, R.H. *A movigenic curriculum* (Bulletin No. 25). Madison, Wisc.: Department of Public Instruction, Bureau for the Handicapped, 1965.

Barsch, R.H. *Achieving perceptual-motor efficiency* (Vol. 1). Seattle: Special Child Publications, 1967.

Barsch, R.H. *Enriching perception and cognition* (Vol. 2). Seattle: Special Child Publications, 1968.

Beery, K.F., & Buktenica, N. *Developmental Test of Visual-Motor Integration.* Chicago: Follett, 1967.

Bender, L. *Visual-Motor Gestalt Test and its clinical use* (Research Monograph No. 3). New York: American Orthopsychiatric Association, 1938.

Bortner, M. Perceptual skills and early reading disability. In L. Mann & D. Sabatino (Eds.), *Second annual review of special education.* Philadelphia: Journal of Special Education Press, 1974.

Burns, P.C. *Diagnostic teaching of the language arts.* Itasca, Ill.: Peacock, 1974.

Cartwright, G.P. Written expression and spelling. In R.M. Smith (Ed.), *Teacher diagnosis of educational difficulties.* Columbus, Ohio: Charles E. Merrill, 1969.

Chalfant, J.C., & Scheffelin, M.A. *Central processing dysfunction in children: A review of research* (NINDS Monograph No. 9). Bethesda, Md.: U.S. Department of Health, Education, & Welfare, 1969.

Christine, D., & Christine, S. The relationship of auditory discrimination to articulatory defects and reading retardation. *Elementary School Journal,* 1964, 6, 97–100.

Cohen, S.A. Studies in visual perception and reading in disadvantaged children. *Journal of Learning Disabilities,* 1969, 2, 498–507.

Colarusso, R., & Hammill, D. *The Motor Free Test of Visual Perception.* San Rafael, Calif.: Academic Therapy Publications, 1972.

Cratty, B. *Perceptual-motor behavior and educational processes.* Springfield, Ill.: Charles C Thomas, 1969.

Cratty, B. *Active learning: Games to enhance academic abilities.* Englewood Cliffs, N.J.: Prentice-Hall, 1971.

Cratty, B. *Intelligence in action.* Englewood Cliffs, N.J.: Prentice-Hall, 1973.

Cruickshank, W.M. William M. Cruickshank. In J.M. Kauffman & D.P. Hallahan (Eds.), *Teaching children with learning disabilities: Personal perspectives.* Columbus, Ohio: Charles E. Merrill, 1976.

Delacato, C.H. *Neurological organization and reading.* Springfield, Ill.: Charles C Thomas, 1966.

Dubnoff, B., Chambers, I., & Schaeffer, F. *Dubnoff school program 1—Level 2.* Boston: Teaching Resources, 1969.

Dykstra, R. Auditory discrimination abilities and beginning reading achievement. *Reading Research Quarterly,* 1966, 1, 5–33.

Fairbanks, J.S., & Robinson, J. *Fairbanks, Robinson program.* Boston: Teaching Resources, 1969.

Freeman, F.W. *Reference manual for teachers: Grades one through four.* Columbus, Ohio: Zaner-Bloser, 1965.

Frostig, M., & Horne, D. *The Frostig program for*

the development of visual perception. Chicago: Follett, 1964.

Frostig, M., Lefever, D.W., & Whittlesey, J.R.B. *The Marianne Frostig Developmental Test of Visual Perception.* Palo Alto: Consulting Psychology Press, 1964.

Frostig, M., & Maslow, P. Reading, developmental abilities, and the problem of match. *Journal of Learning Disabilities,* 1969, *2,* 571–578.

Frostig, M., & Maslow, P. *Learning problems in the classroom.* New York: Grune & Stratton, 1973.

Getman, G. The visuomotor complex in the acquisition of learning skills. In J. Hellmuth (Ed.), *Learning disorders* (Vol. 1). Seattle: Special Child Publications, 1965.

Getman, G. *Pathway school program.* Boston: Teaching Resources, 1969.

Getman, G.N., Kane, E.R., & McKee, G.W. *Developing learning readiness program.* Manchester, Mo.: Webster Division, McGraw-Hill, 1968.

Gillingham, A., & Stillman, B. *Remedial training for children with specific disability in reading, spelling, and penmanship.* Cambridge, Mass.: Educators Publishing Service, 1966.

Golden, N.E., & Steiner, S. Auditory and visual functions in good and poor readers. *Journal of Learning Disabilities,* 1969, *2,* 476–481.

Goldman, R., Fristoe, M., & Woodcock, R.W. *Goldman-Fristoe-Woodcock Test of Auditory Discrimination.* Circle Pines, Minn.: American Guidance Service, 1970.

Goins, J.T. *Visual perceptual abilities and early reading programs* (Supplementary Educational Monographs No. 87). Chicago: University of Chicago Press, 1958.

Hackett, L.C., & Jenson, R.C. *A guide to movement exploration.* Palo Alto, Calif.: Peek Publications, 1967.

Hallahan, D.P., & Cruickshank, W.M. *Psychoeducational foundations of learning disabilities.* Englewood Cliffs, N.J.: Prentice-Hall, 1973.

Hallahan, D.P., & Kauffman, J.M. *Introduction to learning disabilities: A psycho-behavioral approach.* Englewood Cliffs, N.J.: Prentice-Hall, 1976.

Hammill, D. Training visual perceptual processes. *Journal of Learning Disabilities,* 1972, *5,* 552–559.

Hammill, D., & Bartel, N. *Teaching children with learning and behavior problems* (2nd ed.). Boston: Allyn & Bacon, 1978.

Hammill, D.D., Goodman, L., & Wiederholt, J.L. Visual-motor processes: Can we train them? *Reading Teacher,* 1974, *27,* 469–478.

Hammill, D.D., & Larsen, S.C. The relationship of selected auditory perceptual skills and reading ability. *Journal of Learning Disabilities,* 1974, *7,* 429–435.

Hammill, D.D., & Wiederholt, J.L. Review of the *Frostig Visual Perception Test* and the related training program. In L. Mann & D. Sabatino (Eds.), *The first review of special education* (Vol. 1). Philadelphia: Journal of Special Education Press, 1973.

Hebb, D.O. *The organization of behavior.* New York: Wiley, 1949.

Herrick, V.E. (Ed.). *New horizons for research in handwriting.* Madison, Wisc.: University of Wisconsin Press, 1963.

Hildreth, G. *Learning the three R's.* Minneapolis: Educational Test Bureau, 1947.

Johnson, D., & Myklebust, H. *Learning disabilities: Educational principles and practices.* New York: Grune & Stratton, 1967.

Johnson, W. *The Johnson handwriting program.* Cambridge, Mass.: Educators Publishing Service, 1971.

Kephart, N.C. *The slow learner in the classroom.* Columbus, Ohio: Charles E. Merrill, 1960.

Kephart, N.C. *The brain-injured child in the classroom.* Chicago: National Society for Crippled Children and Adults, 1963.

Kephart, N.C. Perceptual-motor aspects of learning disabilities. *Exceptional Children,* 1964, *31,* 201–206.

Kephart, N.C. *The slow learner in the classroom* (2nd ed.). Columbus, Ohio: Charles E. Merrill, 1971.

Kimmell, G.M., & Wahl, J. *The STAP (Screening Test for Auditory Perception).* San Rafael, Calif.: Academic Therapy Publications, 1969.

Kirk, S., McCarthy, J., & Kirk, W. *Illinois Test of Psycholinguistic Abilities* (Rev. ed.). Urbana, Ill.: University of Illinois Press, 1968.

Koppitz, E. *Bender-Gestalt Test for young children.* New York: Grune & Stratton, 1964.

Larsen, S., & Hammill, D.D. The relationship of selected visual perceptual skills to academic abilities. *Journal of Special Education,* 1975, *9,* 281–291.

Lerner, J.W. *Children with learning disabilities* (2nd ed.). Boston: Houghton Mifflin, 1976.

Lyon, R. Auditory-perceptual training: The state of

the art. *Journal of Learning Disabilities,* 1977, *10,* 564–572.

Myers, P.I., & Hammill, D.D. *Methods for learning disorders* (2nd ed.). New York: John Wiley & Sons, 1976.

Newland, T.E. An analytical study of the development of illegibilities in handwriting from the lower grades to adulthood. *Journal of Educational Research,* 1932, *26,* 249–258.

Noble, J.K. *Better handwriting for you.* New York: Noble & Noble, 1966.

O'Donnell, P. *Motor and haptic learning.* San Rafael, Calif.: Dimension Publishing, 1969.

Orton, S. *Reading, writing and speech problems in children.* New York: Norton, 1937.

Otto, W., McMenemy, R.A., & Smith, R.J. *Corrective and remedial teaching.* Boston: Houghton Mifflin, 1973.

Piaget, J. *The origins of intelligence in children.* New York: International Universities Press, 1952.

Plunkett, M. *A writing manual for teaching the left-handed.* Cambridge, Mass.: Educators Publishing Service, 1954.

Poling, D. Auditory deficiencies of poor readers. *Clinical studies in Reading II, Supplementary Educational Monographs,* 1953, *77,* 107–111.

Reger, R., Schroeder, W., & Uschold, K. *Special education: Children with learning problems.* New York: Oxford University Press, 1968.

Roach, C., & Kephart, N. *The Purdue Perceptual-Motor Survey Test.* Columbus, Ohio: Charles E. Merrill, 1966.

Robinson, J., & Schmitt, B. *Vanguard school program.* Boston: Teaching Resources, 1970.

Roswell, F., & Chall, J. *Roswell-Chall Auditory Blending Test.* New York: Essay Press, 1963.

Sabatino, D.A. Auditory perception: Development, assessment, and intervention. In L. Mann & D. Sabatino (Eds.), *The first review of special education* (Vol. 1). New York: Grune & Stratton, 1973.

Sherrington, C.S. *The integrative action of the nervous system.* New Haven: Yale University Press, 1948.

Skinner, B.F., & Krakower, S.A. *Handwriting with write and see.* Chicago: Lyons & Carnahan, 1968.

Smith, R.M. Perceptual-motor skills. In R.M. Smith (Ed.), *Teacher diagnosis of educational difficulties.* Columbus, Ohio: Charles E. Merrill, 1969.

Stephens, T.M. *Teaching skills to children with learning and behavior disorders.* Columbus, Ohio: Charles E. Merrill, 1977.

Strauss, A., & Lehtinen, L. *Psychopathology and education of the brain-injured child.* New York: Grune & Stratton, 1947.

Strauss, A., & Werner, H. Disorders of conceptual thinking in the brain-injured child. *Journal of Nervous and Mental Disease,* 1942, *96,* 153–172.

U.S. Office of Education. Assistance to states for education of handicapped children: Procedures for evaluating specific learning disabilities. *Federal Register,* 1977, *42,* 65082–65085.

Van Witsen, B. *Perceptual training activities handbook.* New York: Teachers College, Columbia University Press, 1967.

Vellutino, F.R., Steger, B.M., Moyer, S.C., Harding, C.J., & Niles, J.A. Has the perceptual deficit hypothesis led us astray? *Journal of Learning Disabilities,* 1977, *10,* 375–385.

Wallace, G., & Kauffman, J.M. *Teaching children with learning problems* (2nd ed.). Columbus, Ohio: Charles E. Merrill, 1978.

Wallace, G., & McLoughlin, J.A. *Learning disabilities: Concepts and characteristics.* Columbus, Ohio: Charles E. Merrill, 1975.

Wedell, K. *Learning and perceptuo-motor disabilities in children.* New York: Wiley, 1973.

Wepman, J.M. *Auditory Discrimination Test.* Chicago: Language Research Associates, 1958.

Wepman, J. The perceptual basis for learning. In A. Robinson (Ed.), *Meeting individual differences in reading.* Chicago: University of Chicago Press, 1964.

Wepman, J. The modality concept. In H.K. Smith (Ed.), *Perception and reading.* Newark, Del.: International Reading Association, 1968.

Wheeler, L.R., & Wheeler, V.D. A study of the relationship of auditory discrimination to silent reading abilities. *Journal of Educational Research,* 1954, *48,* 103–113.

Wiederholt, J.L., Hammill, D.D., & Brown, V. *The resource teacher: A guide to effective practices.* Boston: Allyn & Bacon, 1978.

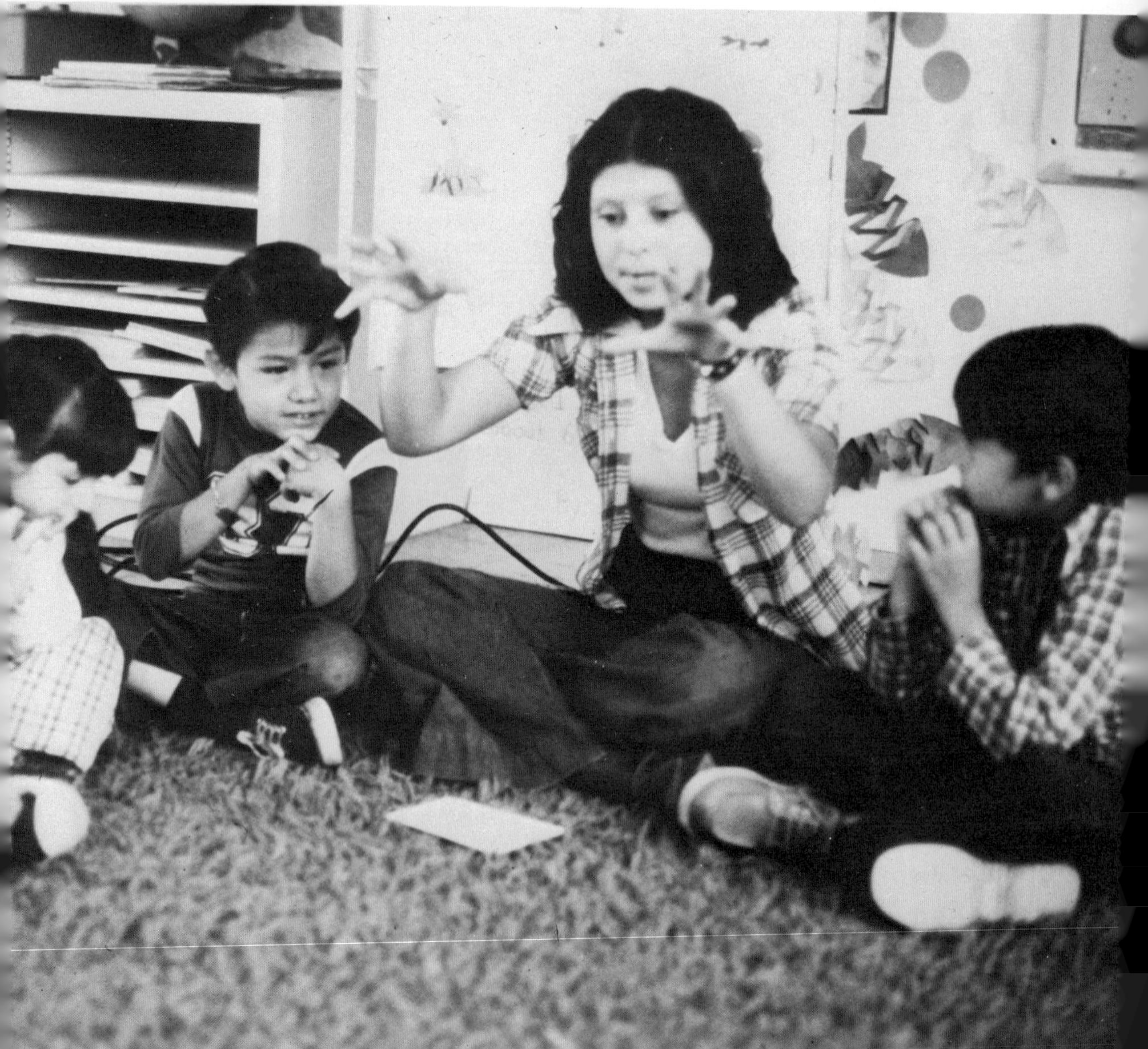

10

Social-emotional problems

Learning-disabled children often have social and emotional problems. Socially, these children find it difficult to interact with others and be friendly. They may not cooperate and participate in group discussions. Emotionally, they do not deal well with stress or frustration. Since emotional behaviors do not always involve interactions with others, they are sometimes considered separately from social behaviors. This chapter focuses on social-emotional problems that are related to learning disabilities with no distinction between emotional and social development.

Specific learning disorders

A variety of investigations (Cartledge & Milburn, 1978; Cobb, 1972; Purkey, 1970) show that social-emotional problems relate to academic achievement. Cobb and Hops (1973) conducted a study in which low-achieving first graders were taught "survival skills" (e.g., attending, following directions) in an attempt to improve reading achievement. They report that when social skills increased, so did achievement level. Similar results have been obtained (Hops & Cobb, 1973, 1974; Walker & Hops, 1976). As Cartledge and Milburn (1978) put it, "social behaviors are essential to academic success" (p. 142).

While a learning disability may cause behavior problems, alleviation of the academic difficulty does not always result in the reduction of poor behavior. This occurs because children learn these behaviors independently and continue to find them functional, adaptive mechanisms. Problems arise when society attributes values to the manner in which the environment is individually managed. When treating behavior problems, one must remember how society defines a problem behavior. Remember that these behaviors do not appear or disappear magically. They should be thought of as responses within particular environmental, personal boundaries. If the responses are viewed by society as problems, treatment must emphasize changing these behaviors. Since we cannot assume that these problems will dissolve when the child improves academically, it appears that direct instruction is the best means of reducing problems related to social-emotional development.

SOCIAL-EMOTIONAL PROBLEMS AND LEARNING DISABILITIES

Perspectives on Social-Emotional Problems and LD

A variety of behavioral characteristics are associated with social-emotional problems of LD students. Initially, their emotions develop differently from those of normal children (Rappaport, 1966, 1975). Rather than learning and developing attitudes about tasks they "can do," LD youngsters often learn what they "can't do." This lack of positive self-regard results in poor self-concept, ego development, and self-esteem. Moreover, Rappaport (1966) attributes social-emotional problems to neurologically based learning disabilities. Likewise, Johnson and Myklebust (1967) suggest that deficiencies in "social perception" are often associated with neurological learning disorders. They refer to social perception as one's "perception of the total social field, perception of oneself in relation to the behavior of others as well as to events and circumstances that involve others" (p. 295).

Valiett (1967) feels the school should help LD children learn how to relate to peers, anticipate probable outcomes of social situations, recognize and respond to moral issues, and assume personal and social responsibility. This idea is good, but the nonspecific nature of his problem behaviors restricts the utility of his approach. For example, how does one teach a child to recognize and respond to

This elementary school teacher helps Scotty feel like he's O.K.

moral issues? What moral issues are of concern?

Myers and Hammill (1976) discuss the emotional development problems of LD children. Clements and Peters (1962) give the following excerpts from the comments of parents and teachers as indications of emotional lability associated with brain malfunction:

1. He seems bright; he is quiet and obedient, but daydreams and can't read.
2. He is high-strung and nervous; his attention is hard to hold.
3. He has frequent temper outbursts, sometimes for no apparent reason.
4. He won't concentrate for more than a few minutes at a time; he jumps from one thing to another, and minds everyone's business but his own.
5. He lacks self-control; he cannot work with other children; he picks on them constantly; he is disturbing in the classroom and worse on the playground. (p. 186)

While these descriptions do illustrate kinds of emotional problems, they obviously do not lend themselves to positive remedial efforts.

Wallace and McLoughlin (1975) list the numerous prevalent problems:

1. excessive dependence on parents, teachers, and other adults
2. poor self-concept
3. distractibility
4. perseveration or difficulty switching activities
5. physically disruptive behaviors
6. withdrawal
7. hyperactivity or excessive activity and mobility

While they briefly discuss several other social-emotional problems of LD children (i.e., irritability, antisocial behaviors, low frustration tolerance), they do not offer explanations for including these particular behaviors nor do they offer any specific intervention strategies to alleviate or treat the problems. They do suggest that, while professionals such as psychiatrists, psychologists, psychotherapists, and other persons with similar training were once thought to be the exclusive therapeutic agents for such children, now teachers are involved in the treatment. In addition, they note that *"behavior modification* and *interpersonal education* have been considered the most popular and effective methods" (p. 234) of teaching new social-emotional skills.

Selected Studies Concerning Social-Emotional Problems and LD

Results of numerous studies show that behavior problems are commonly shown by LD children. In several studies, parents, teachers, and/or peers gave their perceptions of LD and non-LD children. As noted in Table 10.1, social-emotional characteristics can help differentiate LD from non-LD children. Results suggest that LD children have less favorable social interactions than their nondisabled peers. In addition, Bryan and Bryan (1978) found that classmates often view an LD child as someone they do not want as a friend.

Bryan and Wheeler (1972) and Bryan (1974a) reveal that LD children spend more time off-task (e.g., flipping pages, roaming about the room) and less time in task-oriented behaviors than a comparable group of *achiev-*

Some LD youngsters need help interacting socially.

TABLE 10.1

How the LD child is perceived by parent, teacher, and peer.

Studies	Academic Area	Social-Emotional Area
Parent (Owen, Adams, Forrest, Stolz, & Fisher, 1971; Wender, 1971; Strag, 1972)	Less verbal ability (spoken language, auditory comprehension)	Attempts to dominate peers Unable to receive affection Clings more than normal Poor impulse control Anxiety Poor perseverance Poor judgment
Teacher (Myklebust, Boshes, Olson, & Cole, 1969; Keogh, Tchir, & Windeguth-Behn, 1974)	Less able to complete assignments Orientation difficulty Behavior and motor problems	Less cooperative (negativistic, resists discipline) Less able to organize Poor consideration for others (less tactful) Less able to cope with new situations Less accepting of responsibility Less socially acceptable to others Angry and hostile Hyperactive Problems with parents
Peer (Bryan, 1974b)		Less popular/more rejected Worried and frightened Does not have a good time Is not neat and clean Is not very good-looking Nobody pays much attention to him

ing students. In addition, Bryan (1974a) reports that LD children and their teachers react qualitatively but not quantitatively different (i.e., while the amount of teacher-pupil interactions was similar, the nature of them was different).

Bryan (1977) suggests that the social-emotional problems of some LD youngsters are due to social imperceptions. Specifically, she reports that many LD children lack adequate skills in detecting subtle affective cues. Although this position is speculative, it is similar to that expressed by Johnson and Myklebust (1967) and Lerner (1976). Nonetheless, it represents an additional dimension which must be considered in remedial efforts. Bryan and Bryan (1978) report that few remedial efforts exist for working with pupils who exhibit social problems that spring from academic failure. The next section describes several etiological perspectives that provide a basis for a variety of remedial strategies.

ETIOLOGY AND TREATMENT OF SOCIAL-EMOTIONAL PROBLEMS

The origin of social-emotional problems may be attributed to a variety of theoretical perspectives ranging from the biophysical and behavioral to ecological. Table 10.2 summarizes the primary considerations and some treatment alternatives within each of these theoretical perspectives.

Biophysical Theory

Enzymes and other biochemicals monitor much bodily activity. Alteration of the characteristic amounts or functions of these substances results in abnormal behaviors. Within the biophysical context, then, social-emotional problems may result from variations in the normal amounts of body chemicals (Coppen, 1967; Ritvo, 1975; Safer & Allen, 1976).

Just as hyperactivity may be due to inadequate levels of certain monoamines (Wender, 1971), low frustration tolerance or slowness in work may result from inappropriate levels of other neurotransmitters. Pauling (1968) suggests that thiamine, nicotinic acid, pyridoxine, ascorbic acid, and other similar chemicals may trigger some forms of mental illness. He observed a remission of some psychotic symptoms after administering niacin in fairly small amounts. In addition, Cott (1972) noted improvements in children who had been given large doses of vitamins. The increasingly popular use of psychoactive

TABLE 10.2

Theoretical foundations for the existence and treatment of social-emotional problems.

Theory	Primary Consideration	Treatment Alternatives
Biophysical	Biomedical abnormalities Genetic malfunctioning Nutritional irregularities Neurological dysfunctions	Drug therapy Genetic counseling Dietary monitoring Environmental structure
Behavioral	Prior conditioning Environmental contingencies Modeling	Counter-conditioning Contingency management Modeling
Ecological	Developmental stages Individual's behaviors and reactions to them Teacher-pupil interactions	Tolerance and acceptance Behavior change within the perceiver and the perceived Improved interaction patterns

medications in the treatment of behavior problems can be attributed to suspected biophysical causes (Algozzine & Algozzine, in press; Kornetsky, 1976; Safer & Allen, 1976).

In a general sense, the relationship between nutrient intake and bodily needs (i.e., nutrition) has also been implicated in the existence of behavior problems (Gussow, 1974; Hallahan & Cruickshank, 1973). Specifically, malnutrition relates to physical growth and development (Scrimshaw, 1969) and a variety of behavioral characteristics (Birch & Gussow, 1970; Gussow, 1974; Hallahan & Cruickshank, 1973). Feingold (1975) suggests that food additives may cause hyperactivity and related learning problems, and Rose (in press) shows a functional relationship between the dietary presence of artificial food coloring and altered behavioral activity.

The characteristic levels of biochemicals are thought to be related to the behavioral characteristics exhibited by individuals. Coursin (1968) suggests that genetic factors may cause abnormal biochemical functioning, and treatment procedures exist for disorders thought to have a genetic origin (Lynch, 1970). However, the more general biophysical treatment programs include drug therapies, dietary regulation, megavitamin therapy, and environmental restructuring. While these treatments are not often administered by teachers, school personnel may serve as monitors for them (Algozzine & Algozzine, in press; Weithorn & Ross, 1975). (See Chapter 5 for a detailed discussion of biophysical treatment programs.)

Behavioral Theory

While maladaptive behavior may originate chemically within an individual, it generally takes meaning from the environment in which it occurs within the behavioral perspective. Social-emotional problems are thought to be due to inappropriate reactions to stimuli and/or to inappropriate levels of reinforcement or punishment (Rhodes & Paul, 1978; Rhodes & Tracy, 1972; Ullman & Krasner, 1965). Within this context, both classical and operant conditioning may result in behavior problems.

The classical conditioning paradigm focuses on the relationships between stimuli and the responses that they elicit. In studying the activity of the salivary glands of dogs, Pavlov (1927) observed that his animals would demonstrate similar responses to extraneous stimuli as they had to the palpable substances. His studies resulted in the following steps of classical conditioning:

1. An unconditioning stimulus elicits an unconditioned response;
2. An extraneous stimulus is paired with the unconditioned stimulus as it is eliciting the unconditioned response and becomes a conditioned stimulus;
3. When the conditioned stimulus elicits the previously unconditioned response, a conditioned response is said to have occurred.

The early work in Pavlov's laboratory focused on the establishment of conditioned responses; however, the concept of "experimental neurosis" was also being investigated (Pavlov, 1941). This was accomplished by establishing a conditioned response and then introducing a conflicting stimulus or one producing conflict by forcing an animal to respond to two stimuli that were undistinguishable. A variety of "behavioral disorders" were produced by these procedures (e.g., refusal to perform, reluctance to enter the lab, hyperactivity, tics). Watson and Rayner (1920) paired the presentation of a rat with loud noise and produced a conditioned response of fear in a young child. Gantt (1944), in a review of the literature up to 1944, reports on the techniques and procedures that were used in establishing conditioned responses in children and adults.

While Pavlov's conditioning techniques focused on the relationship between stimuli and responses in the environment, Skinner's techniques (1938) stressed the importance of responses and their consequences. Within the operant conditioning paradigm, spontaneously occurring behaviors (operants) produce an effect on the environment and a consequence to the responding organism. By manipulating the consequences of behavior, it is possible to bring the behavior under predictable control (Rhodes & Paul, 1978) (i.e., reinforcement results in increased behavior, and punishment results in decreased behavior).

From an operant point of view, behavior problems are the result of reinforcement of inappropriate actions and/or punishment or extinction (lack of reinforcement) of appropriate ones. Ferster (1961) suggests that autistic children develop their psychopathology in this way. It is easy to see how any social-emotional behavior can be altered as a result of reinforcement or punishment. For example, if task-avoiding behaviors are reinforced, they are likely to increase. Similarly, if attempts at positive peer interaction are punished, the child will stop trying and may withdraw socially.

Treatment procedures based upon behavioral theory have been developed from the classical and operant paradigms (Rhodes & Tracy, 1972). Methods such as reciprocal inhibition, systematic desensitization, and counter-conditioning use Pavlov's theory, while contingency contracting, the "engineered classroom," precision teaching, and the systematic use of rewards and punishers show Skinner's influence.

Ecological Theory

When evaluating the cause for any problem behavior, consider that the particular behavior may be developmentally appropriate and/or that the behavior may be seen as a problem because it is bothersome to someone. For example, children are not as proficient on new skills as on previously learned skills. While this beginner stage is reasonable, it may irk teachers and parents. Within the ecological perspective, behaviors *as well as* reactions to those behaviors are the cause for the existence of problems (Algozzine, 1977; Rhodes, 1967, 1970; Rhodes & Paul, 1978).

The behaviors thought to be characteristic of emotionally disturbed children have been shown to be differentially bothersome to regular classroom teachers, school psychologists, and special education teachers (Algozzine, 1976, 1977). Mooney and Algozzine (in press) demonstrated that the characteristic behaviors of LD children (i.e., perceptual problems, immature behaviors) were seen as less disturbing to teachers than were the characteristic behaviors of disturbed children. This notion of differential "disturbingness" is central to ecological theory. It suggests that the perceiver *as well as* the perceived is included in the creation of ecological problems, and that behaviors that are seen as problems in one context may not be viewed as such in another.

Treatment perspectives related to ecological theory emphasize changing behaviors as well as reactions to those behaviors. Tolerance and/or leeway for individual differences are stressed as effective treatment strategies, as are procedures that include other members of the child's ecosystem (besides the teacher). Change in behavior depends on the cooperative efforts of the child and those who interact with her.

While each etiological theory has received some support, it is likely that social-emotional problems of LD children result from a variety of specific causes and that searching for a particular cause for a specific problem within each individual child would be frustrating and nonrewarding. Typically, behaviors respond to a multitude of treatment strategies, regardless of their cause. For this reason, the selected interventions presented in the following section are general; some have their foundations in biophysical theory, while others are based on behavioral or ecological perspectives. Use them as suggestive guidelines for developing specific strategies for LD children.

Jenny excels at creative writing. Her teacher gives her encouragement to express her feelings.

SPECIFIC SOCIAL-EMOTIONAL PROBLEMS AND SELECTED INTERVENTIONS

While the more recent attempts to delimit the social-emotional behavior problems of LD youngsters have been somewhat more specific than those endeavors of earlier theorists, the increase in specificity has not been to any advantage with regard to treatment practices. Characteristics such as being high-strung, nervous, or distractible have little practical value for teachers. Even if characteristics are precisely defined, the task of developing meaningful educational activities to help the child deal with her disabling characteristic is monumental. At best, efforts have been directed toward the arrangement of contingencies in an attempt to reduce inappropriate characteristics or increase more appropriate ones (e.g., sitting quietly) (Gardner, 1974; Wallace & Kauffman, 1973; Wallace & McLoughlin, 1975). To be effective, specific behaviors that often coexist with academic task failure must be delineated. Then a variety of treatment activities can be applied to foster the social and emotional development of the child.

The following behaviors are not only characteristics of LD children but may be exhibited by any individual: poor self-concept, low frustration tolerance, anxiety, social withdrawal/ rejection, task avoidance, task interference, poor self-management skills, and slowness in work. These problems result from frustration and stress (emotional aspects), generated by limited academic performances and success. These behaviors may then create problems because they interfere with productive relationships. Although children exhibit such difficulties along with limited academic skills, these difficulties do not disappear when the skill deficiency has been improved. Thus, these behaviors require specific treatment strategies and programming.

The following format facilitates an educational program for such youngsters:

1. Describe each behavior in general, illustrative terms and in terms of a behavioral

objective. Use the objective to determine the extent to which a particular child exhibits the behavior.
2. Delineate a set of teaching activities for each behavior in terms of generalized learning principles that have been proven effective.

This format is not restrictive or all-inclusive. Primarily, it illustrates a direction for developing treatment strategies. The particular descriptions and activities that teachers, parents, or other professionals apply to the behaviors are a matter of choice. It is hoped that those presented will generate other productive means of defining and dealing with interfering social-emotional behaviors.

Poor Self-Concept

The impression one has of one's abilities in a variety of activities and settings may be referred to as *self-concept*. Since a poor self-concept cannot be directly observed, it is often inferred if a person's statements and actions reflect reduced or limited interaction potentials and/or abilities. These feelings cause problems if they interfere with productive relationships (i.e., if one's actions in response to environmental challenges are hindered or restricted by thinking, participation will result in failure).

Self-concept relates to achievement; low self-concept and low academic achievement have coexisted in a variety of populations (Kessler, 1966; Purkey, 1970; Rosenthal, 1973; Shaw, 1968). Since the LD youngster experiences achievement problems (Kirk & Elkins, 1975), he is likely to experience self-concept problems.

In identifying this student, the following operationalization may be useful: *Given an activity in which personal performance is expected, the pupil responds with statements and/or actions that reflect anticipated difficulty or result in actual failure due to perceived personal inadequacies.* The student may say "I can't do that" or "That's too hard. What do you think I am—a genius or something?" Sometimes the pupil refuses to even try.

Activities for Self-Concept Problems

1. To encourage a reluctant youngster to participate in daily programming, structure her participation around activities that are self-selected favorites. Ask pupils to list their most preferred things to do in school. Set up individual schedules to incorporate the preferred activities with less preferred ones. One pupil's schedule might include 80% favorite things and 20% less preferred. The percentages can easily be varied as confidence and interest become more developed.

2. Role play situations in which a pupil is asked to demonstrate a positive event that occurred during the day. Ask students to share their own "good things" for the day. If a youngster is reluctant to enter such a discussion, the teacher can ask others to identify the reluctant pupil's "good things" or the teacher can suggest something that happened during the day that was special for that pupil.

3. Spend several minutes (time dependent upon teacher and pupil preferences) each day discussing things that you like about a pupil who has demonstrated a low self-concept. Include statements about abilities that the youngster has as well as other personal attributes.

4. When conducting daily lessons or group activities, refer to youngsters by their names and mention a positive characteristic. For example, in calling a child to the blackboard, you might say, "Mike, who has those beautiful eyes, would you please come to the board," or "Kathy, who started doing two-digit multiplication today, would you please work the first addition problem on the board." It is helpful to stress personal attributes and developing abilities.

5. In working with a pupil who is reluctant to do drill or seatwork in basic skill areas, make

Chris opens up to her teacher about her favorite class activities.

the work look more difficult to complete than it really is. For example, "super math problems" can be constructed from basic facts. If a child needs to complete the following items:

$$\begin{array}{ccccc} 2 & 8 & 5 & 6 & 4 \\ +2 & +1 & +1 & +3 & +4 \end{array}$$

a "super fact" can be constructed that requires the same basic skills but appears much more difficult:

$$\begin{array}{r} 28,564 \\ +21,134 \end{array}$$

Completion of a page of items such as this one will likely enhance self-concept more than a similar page of single-digit facts.

Low Frustration Tolerance

A common response to having one's desires or wishes thwarted is frustration. The extent to which an individual can continue to progress toward a goal, in spite of obstacles, is known as *frustration tolerance*. When obstacles to goal attainment readily result in reduced efforts or decreased performance, low frustration tolerance exists. LD children often stop short of academically or socially challenging tasks, thereby inhibiting additional learning. They become frustrated easily by tasks that require increased effort for completion.

In identifying such a child, the following operationalization may be useful: *Given an activity or task that generates frustration but is clearly within the child's response capabilities, the child responds with behaviors that result in reduced efforts or decreased performance.* This problem may be characterized by initial attempts at task completion (i.e., different from self-concept problems) that are followed by statements or actions indicative of interference. The child might suggest that the task is "too hard," discontinue his efforts, and/or react with nongoal-directed behaviors (e.g., placing the same answer by each question regardless of appropriateness).

Activities for Low Frustration Tolerance Problems

1. When spontaneous factors interfere with an ongoing program or situation, change plans to help prevent frustration from being

generated. Explain your actions to the pupil and attempt to elicit alternative solutions from her.

2. If a situation is likely to generate unusual amounts of stress, have a variety of modifications ready that can keep the youngster involved. For example, ranges on total task performance can be substituted for total points (e.g., 17–20 correct = 100; 13–16 = 90), or the total task can be broken into two or more units (e.g., one 1-minute test can be equivalent to two 30-second ones with a break between them).

3. Reproduce a set of dot-to-dot pictures from ditto masters. Vary their complexity. Have the pupil complete the easiest one, record the time to completion, and then have the youngster complete the task in reverse, starting with the last number and proceeding toward the first. Again keep track of *progress toward the goal,* not just task completion.

4. Prepare a series of mazes at three or four levels of difficulty. Allow the youngster to complete the task at her own pace and then gradually introduce specific time constraints. As the task stress increases, reward the pupil's *progress toward the goal* rather than completed performance. Hold the time limit constant for several trials and keep track of progress. Graph the progress if the pupil is willing. Once the first level of maze difficulty has been mastered at various time intervals, repeat the procedure with a more complicated maze.

5. When presenting tasks, carefully arrange the items so difficulty levels are controlled. Present easier items initially and increase the level of difficulty within the task gradually.

Anxiety

A common reaction to an unknown or unpleasant situation is apprehension or concern. *Anxiety* may be defined as a condition of strong concern or apprehension with unspecified justification. It may result from perceived inabilities within certain performance domains. The relationship between anxiety and achievement has been studied (Hart, 1964; Sarason, Davidson, Lighthall, Waite, & Ruebush, 1960; Silverstein, 1966; Tymchuk, 1975). Anxiety can have facilitating or debilitating effects, depending on the nature and level of tasks and individual capabilities; for example, a task of intermediate difficulty may result in more interfering anxiety than an easier or harder one (Atkinson, 1957; Manzo, 1977).

In attempting to identify the anxious child the following operationalization may be useful: *Given a situation in which performance is requested and/or expected, the child engages in activities and responses that suggest an unusual amount of apprehension or concern about performance.* When asked to perform certain tasks, the anxious child may talk excessively, feel irrational fears, or display physical symptoms (e.g., nervous tics, stomach aches). These behaviors may follow requests to perform physical activities (e.g., "Kick the ball") as well as academic ones (e.g., "Answer this math problem").

Activities for Anxiety Problems

1. Arrange for the anxious youngster to observe another pupil engaged in positive responses to an anxiety-producing situation.

2. Engage the anxious youngster's curiosity in unusual aspects of an anxiety-producing situation. For example, rather than pointing out how easy it is to walk the balance beam, ask the child to imagine how difficult it would be to walk it backwards or with her eyes closed. Suggest that a person doing that would surely need help and then offer to help her try it any way that she is interested in doing.

3. Require the anxious pupil to deal with the source of anxiety for brief periods of time only. If schoolwork produces anxiety, require small units of easily completed work and gradually extend the level of knowledge and amount of work required for completion.

4. Point out the positive aspects of an anxiety-producing activity. Emphasize these aspects in teaching the youngster to handle the situation and graphically represent any progress she makes in dealing with the problem.

5. Encourage an anxious pupil to set her own goals. This strategy might mean allowing her to perform at a very low level of accuracy or participation during initial attempts at self-management.

Social Withdrawal/Rejection

A common response to incompetence or lack of ability within a social situation is rejection by more competent individuals and/or withdrawal by the incompetent ones. This withdrawal/rejection results in reduced interactional potentials and interferes with productive relationships.

When Scotty has trouble reading, he withdraws and rejects help.

Such pupils demonstrate selective types of academic incompetence (Kirk & Elkins, 1975). Moreover, they experience peer rejection (Bryan, 1974b, 1976, 1977). Bryan, Wheeler, Felcan, and Henek (1976) reveal that LD pupils receive and emit more negative statements than their peers. These findings suggest that the LD youngster is in a difficult position with regard to interpersonal relationships. She probably does not demonstrate those behaviors that foster socialization (i.e., positive comments and/or cooperative suggestions) nor does she experience them from others. She may make negative comments to reduce the likelihood of further interaction (i.e., withdrawal from the situation).

The following operationalization may be useful in identification: *Given a situation or activity that involves interaction with other individuals, the child responds with statements or actions (or receives statements or actions) that reduce the likelihood of participation.* She may be told or tell others "You did that wrong, stupid" or "Can't you ever do anything right?"

Activities for Social Withdrawal/Rejection Problems

1. Pair the withdrawn youngster with a competent, accepting peer. Arrange for the pair to participate in an activity that requires a cooperative effort. One alternative may be a spelling test in which each member of the pair must spell one-half of the total words on the test. Prior to writing or reciting an answer, the team should have a chance to discuss who should answer and what she should say. The pair will share success and failure in this activity.

2. When the youngster is engaged in a pleasant activity, have an accepting classmate express an interest in participating with the isolated pupil. Initially have the classmate participate for a short period of time and gradually increase the type and amount of participation.

3. Keep track of any occurrences of group participation and systematically reinforce them. A graphic representation of these events can help the withdrawn youngster to "see" her progress.

4. Teach a variety of social interaction skills through modeled presentations. Arrange for a high-status classmate to be reinforced for target social behaviors in the presence of the withdrawn pupil.

It's nice to have help from a friend.

5. Observe occurrences of positive social interaction; make attempts to reward those behaviors. At first these events may seem very insignificant (when compared to normal interaction) or trivial; however, it is important to recognize and use them to help foster future positive behavior.

Task Avoidance

Usually people avoid difficult or unpleasant tasks. In avoiding a complex task rather than approaching it with increased efforts, an individual is likely to reduce the probability of being successful at that task, thereby increasing the likelihood of future problems.

Learning disabled children have been shown to exhibit behaviors that look like productive efforts (e.g., they appear to be thinking about the task when they in fact are not). They may not get into trouble, but they do not complete the task, either. These children spend time flipping pages of a textbook (rather than reading it) or staring at the book for long periods of time (Bryan, 1974a). In addition, Bryan (1974a) reports that the extent to which these behaviors occur is not a function of experimentally defined levels of the tasks (i.e., easy art or hard reading). This suggests that many LD youngsters experience a generalized sense of incompetence (i.e., underachievement), which is translated into task-avoiding behaviors. Torgesen (1977) suggests that LD pupils demonstrate poor performance due to a failure to engage actively in tasks with efficient cognitive strategies.

To facilitate identification, the following operationalization is suggested: *Given an opportunity to complete an activity or task, the pupil responds with statements or actions directed toward productive efforts involving task-related activities that do not result in task completion.* Due to a perceived or actual incompetence with academic materials, such a youngster may ask to sharpen her pencil several times during work, or she may spend considerable time locating the necessary prerequisites (e.g., page of assignment, writing utensil) prior to engaging in the task.

Activities for Task-Avoidance Problems

1. When presenting independent seatwork to the task-avoiding pupil, provide "starter incentives." For example, a worksheet with the first five problems completed can serve as a pleasant surprise to the youngster who is generally not actively involved in the task initially.

2. When asking the class to take part in an activity, provide a reward for those who have started the task and completed several of the first activities within the task. By rewarding those pupils who have opened their books to

the correct page and started working, it is sometimes possible to encourage the task-avoiding pupil to become more involved. The same procedure can be useful in encouraging performance at various other times during the task sequence (i.e., starting, continuing, completing).

3. Allow the pupil to select from a variety of assignments within a skill area.

4. Keep track of the amount of time a youngster spends engaged in task-avoiding behaviors; reward slight improvements over time. Graphic representations can be useful in showing such changes. Small improvements can be made to appear much greater by controlling the scale on which the graph is based.

5. Have the task-avoiding pupil become a "teaching assistant" with the responsibility of giving directions for a class assignment. In this way, the pupil will be responsible for understanding and attending to the directions and will be interested in performing the task.

Task Interference

In response to difficult or unpleasant activities, individuals often engage in behaviors that compete with task completion efforts. In so doing, these behaviors reduce the likelihood of productive task orientations and thereby inhibit learning.

In shop class, students learn how to see a project through to completion.

Selected LD children exhibit counterproductive behaviors during academic lessons (Bryan, 1974a, Bryan & Wheeler, 1972). Bryan (1974a) defines *nontask-oriented behavior* as "non-productive behavior and/or activities not assigned by the teacher at the time of the observation" (p. 28). In this category she includes staring out of windows, roaming around the room, and generally "fooling around." Her analysis of observational results indicates that LD youngsters spent more time in these behaviors than did a selectively matched comparison group of "average achievers with no known academic or social problems" (p. 28). It should be noted that in her study Bryan includes both task-interference behaviors and task-avoidance behaviors, which are differentiated in this discussion.

In identifying the child who may be experiencing task-interference problems, the following operationalization may be useful: *Given an opportunity to complete an activity or task, the child responds with statements or actions of a nonspecific nature that are unrelated to task completion.* Actual achievement weaknesses or perceived incompetence may result in the LD child becoming engaged in a variety of task-interfering behaviors when given an activity to complete. The youngster may become involved in wandering about the room or in playing with classroom materials.

Activities for Task-Interference Problems

1. Have the pupil engage in an irrelevant or task-interfering behavior for an extended period of time. By asking a pupil to wander around the room for an extended period of time (not when she chooses to do so), the pupil tires of the behavior.

2. Build opportunities for a youngster to engage in task-interfering behaviors. For example, after the child has completed several math problems, arrange for her to whistle a favorite tune into a tape recorder for listening to later.

3. Provide opportunities to engage in irrelevant activities at a self-selected rate (a certain number of "free" trials agreed upon by the pupil and teacher). Come to an agreement with the pupil regarding the number of times she needs to engage in a particular behavior (e.g., go to bathroom, sharpen pencil). Give her that number of "free" passes to do the behavior and gradually suggest that less passes may be appropriate.

4. When a task-interfering behavior occurs, mark it down on an index card. Do not tell the pupil that you are doing so but do not try to prevent her from seeing you record it. If questioned, simply say that you are keeping track of something for your own information. It is likely that the target behavior will decrease without further treatment. It may also be helpful to point out improvements in rate of occurrence of a particular behavior if necessary; however, for most youngsters this dimension is not required.

5. In an attempt to bring irrelevant activities under predictable control, move physically closer to a pupil when he is engaged in a task-interfering behavior or place the pupil in a group with productive workers.

Poor Self-Management Skills

Children need a variety of generalized interaction skills to manage and cope with the environment, such as self-control, self-help, independent work behaviors, and social communication skills. Children experiencing achievement problems and learning disabilities are likely to experience low levels of self-management skills, a situation which inhibits productive interpersonal relationships.

Johnson and Myklebust (1967) and Bryan (1974a, 1977) feel that LD youngsters experience abnormal social perceptions; their parents and teachers may feel they are tactless or unresponsive to nonverbal cues. Lerner (1976) adds that this characteristic is likely to result in poor performance in independent activities.

The following operationalization may be useful in identification: *Given an opportunity to participate in an activity or task, the youngster responds with actions that reflect limited awareness of expected social behaviors or self-control.* This pupil may have tantrums in response to a request to participate in a group activity or make inappropriate comments during conversations. She may not be able to work independently and may be very dependent upon the teacher for direction.

Activities for Self-Management Problems

1. Prepare a list of situations in which a variety of responses is available. Divide the room into teams and give each team one of the situations to study. Have the youngsters invent as many responses as they can. Reward correct responses.

2. Arrange a role-playing situation in which a youngster becomes engaged in an activity in which self-control is exhibited and rewarded by high-status peers and the teacher. Be sure the target pupil observes the entire incident.

3. When a particular low-management behavior is observed (e.g., making inappropriate comments when someone in the room is talking), bring it to the attention of the child. It may be helpful in such a situation to explain to the child how often the particular behavior is occurring and that a record will be kept to illustrate this to her. Keep a frequency tally on an index card so that each time the target behavior occurs, a mark is made on the card for that day. Periodically, review the rate card with the pupil but do not attach any other negative consequences to it.

4. Play the Extreme Game with the target pupil and some friends. Describe a social incident that occurred in your life recently and have the pupil guess the "worse" thing that you could have done in response to that incident. Also include a discussion of the "best" alternatives.

5. Play Twenty Questions using a socially appropriate response as the criterion item. Tell the pupil you are thinking of a way to act when you meet a person for the first time. In response to her answer, suggest that you are thinking of one that is "better than" or "worse than" that one. Through this process, direct the child to the exact behavior you had in mind.

Slowness in Work

Youngsters perform work at various rates. The pupil who consistently does not finish assigned independent activities that are *within her capabilities* during a specified time limit may be exhibiting slowness in work. Torgesen (1977) suggests that the LD pupil's poor performance in different tasks may be due to inefficient strategies for task completion. Slowness in work may be evidence of such a problem; it may be an attempt to put off the anticipated failure of a particular task. It also may be due to excessive concern for correctness in responses.

In identifying such a child, the following operationalization may be useful: *Given an activity that can be completed independently, the child's performance is characterized by incomplete attempts due to slow, deliberate responses or "insufficient" time.* This child will seldom complete assignments. Often she will be inappropriately and overly concerned with neatness or accuracy or will complain that the assignment requires more time to be sufficiently performed.

Activities for Slowness in Work Problems

1. Set up a "less work for fast work" contingency. Tell the youngster that if she can finish a selected number of problems or items in a specified time, she will not be responsible for the complete assignment. The number of items expected and the time limits can be varied to accommodate individual differences.

2. To help a student who is slow because she perceives the assignment to be too difficult,

Timers help increase rate of work on this 5-minute "football game" worksheet.

have the youngster circle the "hardest" item in each line (or several of the most difficult items in a complete task) and then provide help with those items. The help can come after completion of the other items in the line or before beginning the "easy" ones. Point out that this task approach (i.e., easy first, hard later) can be useful in independent work.

3. Have the youngster select the number of items that she thinks can be done in a specified time period. Keep track of the percentage completed (number completed/number selected) and reward increases in rate (i.e., percentage completed) and number selected.

4. Have the target child attempt a timed worksheet at her ability level. Present the sheet several times during the day and keep track of increased performance. Have the child identify factors that she feels might be helpful in improving performance on a timed task.

5. Allow the child to work backwards (i.e., start with the last problem first) on an assignment. This strategy will sometimes take her mind off how many items must be done and thereby facilitate a faster approach.

SUMMARY

The LD youngster experiences a variety of social and emotional problems as a result of limited academic competence and abilities (Bryan, 1977; Bryan & Bryan, 1978; Bryan & Wheeler, 1972; Johnson & Myklebust, 1967; Lerner, 1976; Wallace & McLoughlin, 1975). These behaviors require remedial efforts. The activities presented in this chapter suggest how to begin to deal with social-emotional problems. Other applicable activities can be easily generated from this basis.

REFERENCES

Algozzine, B. The disturbing child: What you see is what you get? *The Alberta Journal of Educational Research,* 1976, *22,* 330–333.

Algozzine, B. The emotionally disturbed child: Disturbed or disturbing? *Journal of Abnormal Child Psychology,* 1977, *5,* 205–211.

Algozzine, B., & Algozzine, K. Hyperactivity and drugs: Some practical considerations. *Journal of School Health,* in press.

Atkinson, J.W. Motivational determinants of risk taking behavior. *Psychological Review,* 1957, *64,* 359–372.

Birch, H.G., & Gussow, J.D. *Disadvantaged children: Health, nutrition and school failure.* New York: Harcourt, Brace, & World, 1970.

Bryan, T. An observational analysis of classroom behaviors of children with learning disabilities. *Journal of Learning Disabilities,* 1974, *7,* 26–34. (a)

Bryan, T. Peer popularity of learning disabled children. *Journal of Learning Disabilities,* 1974, *7,* 621–625. (b)

Bryan, T. Peer popularity of learning disabled children: A replication. *Journal of Learning Disabilities,* 1976, *9,* 307–311.

Bryan, T. Learning disabled children's comprehension of nonverbal communication. *Journal of Learning Disabilities,* 1977, *10,* 501–506.

Bryan, T., & Bryan, J. *Understanding learning disabilities* (2nd ed.). Port Washington, N.Y.: Alfred, 1978.

Bryan, T., & Wheeler, R. Perception of learning disabled children: The eye of the observer. *Journal of Learning Disabilities,* 1972, *5,* 484–488.

Bryan, T., Wheeler, R., Felcan, J., & Henek, T. "Come on, Dummy": An observational study of children's communication. *Journal of Learning Disabilities,* 1976, *9,* 661–669.

Cartledge, G., & Milburn, J.F. The case for teaching social skills in the classroom: A review. *Review of Educational Research,* 1978, *48,* 133–156.

Clements, S.D., & Peters, J.E. Minimal brain dysfunctions in the school-aged child. *Archives of General Psychiatry,* 1962, *6,* 185–197.

Cobb, J.A. Relationship of discrete classroom behaviors to fourth-grade achievement. *Journal of Educational Psychology,* 1972, *63,* 74–80.

Cobb, J.A., & Hops, H. Effects of academic survival skill training on low achieving first graders. *The Journal of Educational Research,* 1973, *67,* 108–113.

Coppen, A. The biochemistry of affective disorders. *British Journal of Psychiatry,* 1967, *113,* 1237–1264.

Cott, A. Megavitamins: The orthomolecular approach to behavior disorders and learning disabilities. *Academic Therapy,* 1972, *7,* 245–259.

Coursin, D.B. Vitamin deficiencies and developing mental capacity. In N.S. Scrimshaw & J.E. Gordon (Eds.), *Malnutrition, learning and behavior.* Cambridge, Mass.: MIT Press, 1968.

Feingold, B.F. *Why your child is hyperactive.* New York: Random House, 1975.

Ferster, C.B. Positive reinforcement and behavioral deficits of autistic children. *Child Development,* 1961, *32,* 437–456.

Gantt, W. *Experimental basis for human behavior.* New York: Paul B. Huber, 1944.

Gardner, W. *Children with learning and behavior problems: A behavior management approach.* Boston: Allyn & Bacon, 1974.

Gussow, J.D. *Nutrition and mental development.* ERIC/IRCD Urban Disadvantaged Series, Number 36, 1974. (Available from ERIC Informational Retrieval Center on the Disadvantaged, Columbia University).

Hallahan, D.P., & Cruickshank, W.M. *Psychoeducational foundations of learning disabilities.* Englewood Cliffs, N.J.: Prentice-Hall, 1973.

Hart, N.W.N. Academic progress in relation to intelligence and motivation in the opportunity school. *Slow Learning Child,* 1964, *11,* 40–46.

Hops, H., & Cobb, J.A. Survival behaviors in the educational setting: Their implications for research and intervention. In L.A. Hammerlynk, L.C. Handy, & E.J. Mash (Eds.), *Behavior change.* Champaign, Ill.: Research Press, 1973.

Hops, H., & Cobb, J.A. Initial investigations into academic survival skill training, direct instruction, and first-grade achievement. *Journal of Educational Psychology,* 1974, *66,* 548–553.

Johnson, D., & Myklebust, H. *Learning disabilities: Educational principles and practices.* New York: Grune & Stratton, 1967.

Keogh, B.K., Tchir, C., & Windeguth-Behn, A. Teachers' perceptions of educationally high risk children. *Journal of Learning Disabilities,* 1974, *7,* 367–374.

Kessler, J.W. *Psychopathology of childhood.* Englewood Cliffs, N.J.: Prentice-Hall, 1966.

Kirk, S., & Elkins, J. Learning disabilities: Characteristics of child enrolled in the Child Service Demonstration Center. *Journal of Learning Disabilities,* 1975, *8,* 630–647.

Kornetsky, C. *Pharmacology.* New York: John Wiley & Sons, 1976.

Lerner, J.W. *Children with learning disabilities* (2nd ed.). Boston: Houghton Mifflin, 1976.

Lynch, H.T. *Dynamic genetic counseling for clinicians.* Springfield, Ill.: Charles C Thomas, 1970.

Manzo, A.V. Motivation and reading: Personal reflections and lessons. *Behavioral Disorders,* 1977, *3,* 13–19.

Mooney, C., & Algozzine, B. A comparison of the disturbingness of ED and LD behaviors. *Journal of Abnormal Child Psychology,* in press.

Myers, P.I., & Hammill, D.D. *Methods for learning disorders* (2nd ed.). New York: John Wiley & Sons, 1976.

Myklebust, H.R., Boshes, B., Olson, D., & Cole, C. *Minimal brain damage in children* (Final Report, U.S.P.H.S. Contract 108-65-142). Evanston, Ill.: Northwestern University Publications, 1969.

Owen, R.W., Adams, P.A., Forrest, T., Stolz, L.M., & Fisher, S. Learning disorders in children: Sibling studies. *Monographs of the Society for Research in Child Development,* 1971, *36* (No. 144).

Pauling, L.C. Orthomolecular psychiatry. *Science,* 1968, *160,* 265–271.

Pavlov, I.P. *Conditioned reflexes.* New York: Dover, 1927.

Pavlov, I. *Lectures on conditioned reflexes* (Vols. 1 & 2). New York: International Universities Press, 1941.

Purkey, W. *Self-concept and school achievement.* Englewood Cliffs, N.J.: Prentice-Hall, 1970.

Rappaport, S. Personality factors teachers need for relationship structure. In W.M. Cruickshank (Ed.), *The teacher of brain injured children: A discussion of the bases of competency.* Syracuse, N.Y.: Syracuse University Press, 1966.

Rappaport, S. Ego development in learning disabled children. In W.M. Cruickshank & D.P. Hallahan (Eds.), *Perceptual and learning disabilities in children* (Vol. 1) *Psychoeducational practices.* Syracuse, N.Y.: Syracuse University Press, 1975.

Rhodes, W.C. The disturbing child: A problem of ecological management. *Exceptional Children,* 1967, *33,* 449–455.

Rhodes, W.C. A community participation analysis of emotional disturbance. *Exceptional Children,* 1970, *36,* 309–314.

Rhodes, W.C., & Paul, J.L. *Emotionally disturbed and deviant children: New views and approaches.* Englewood Cliffs, N.J.: Prentice-Hall, 1978.

Rhodes, W.C., & Tracy, M.L. *A study of child variance* (Vol. 2). Ann Arbor, Mich.: Institute for the Study of Mental Retardation and Related Disabilities, 1972.

Ritvo, E.R. Biochemical research with hyperactive children. In D.P. Cantwell (Ed.), *The hyperactive child.* New York: Spectrum Publications, 1975.

Rose, T.L. The functional relationship between artificial food colors and hyperactivity. *Journal of Applied Behavior Analysis,* 1978, *11,* 439–446.

Rosenthal, J.H. Self-esteem in dyslexic children. *Academic Therapy,* 1973, *9,* 27–38.

Safer, D.J., & Allen, R.P. *The hyperactive child.* Baltimore, Md.: University Park Press, 1976.

Sarason, S.B., Davidson, K.S., Lighthall, F.F., Waite, R.R., & Ruebush, B.K. *Anxiety in elementary school children.* New York: John Wiley, 1960.

Scrimshaw, N.S. Early malnutrition and central nervous system function. *Merrill Palmer Quarterly,* 1969, *15,* 375–388.

Shaw, M.C. Underachievement: Useful construct or misleading illusion? *Psychology in the Schools,* 1968, *5,* 41–46.

Skinner, B.F. *The behavior of organisms: An experimental analysis.* New York: Appleton, 1938.

Silverstein, A.B. Anxiety and the quality of human-figure drawings. *American Journal of Mental Deficiency,* 1966, *70,* 607–608.

Strag, G.A. Comparative behavioral rating of parents with severe mentally retarded, special learning disability, and normal children. *Journal of Learning Disabilities,* 1972, *5,* 631–635.

Torgesen, J.K. The role of nonspecific factors in the task performance of learning disabled children: A theoretical assessment. *Journal of Learning Disabilities,* 1977, *10,* 27–34.

Tymchuk, A.J. Personality and sociocultural retardation. In R.L. Jones & D.L. MacMillan (Eds.), *Special education in transition.* Boston: Allyn & Bacon, 1975.

Ullman, L.P., & Krasner, L. (Eds.). *Case studies in behavior modification.* New York: Holt, Rinehart & Winston, 1965.

Vallett, R. *The remediation of learning disabilities.* Palo Alto, Calif.: Fearon, 1967.

Walker, H.M., & Hops, H. Increasing academic achievement by reinforcing direct academic performance and/or facilitative nonacademic responses. *Journal of Educational Psychology,* 1976, *68,* 218–225.

Wallace, G., & Kauffman, J.M. *Teaching children with learning problems.* Columbus, Ohio: Charles E. Merrill, 1973.

Wallace, G., & McLoughlin, J.A. *Learning disabilities: Concepts and characteristics.* Columbus, Ohio: Charles E. Merrill, 1975.

Watson, J.B., & Rayner, R. Conditioned emotional responses. *Journal of Experimental Psychology,* 1920, *3,* 1–14.

Weithorn, C.J., & Ross, R. Who monitors medication? *Journal of Learning Disabilities,* 1975, *8,* 458–461.

Wender, P. *Minimal brain dysfunction in children.* New York: Wiley-Interscience, 1971.

section III

Educational services for the learning disabled

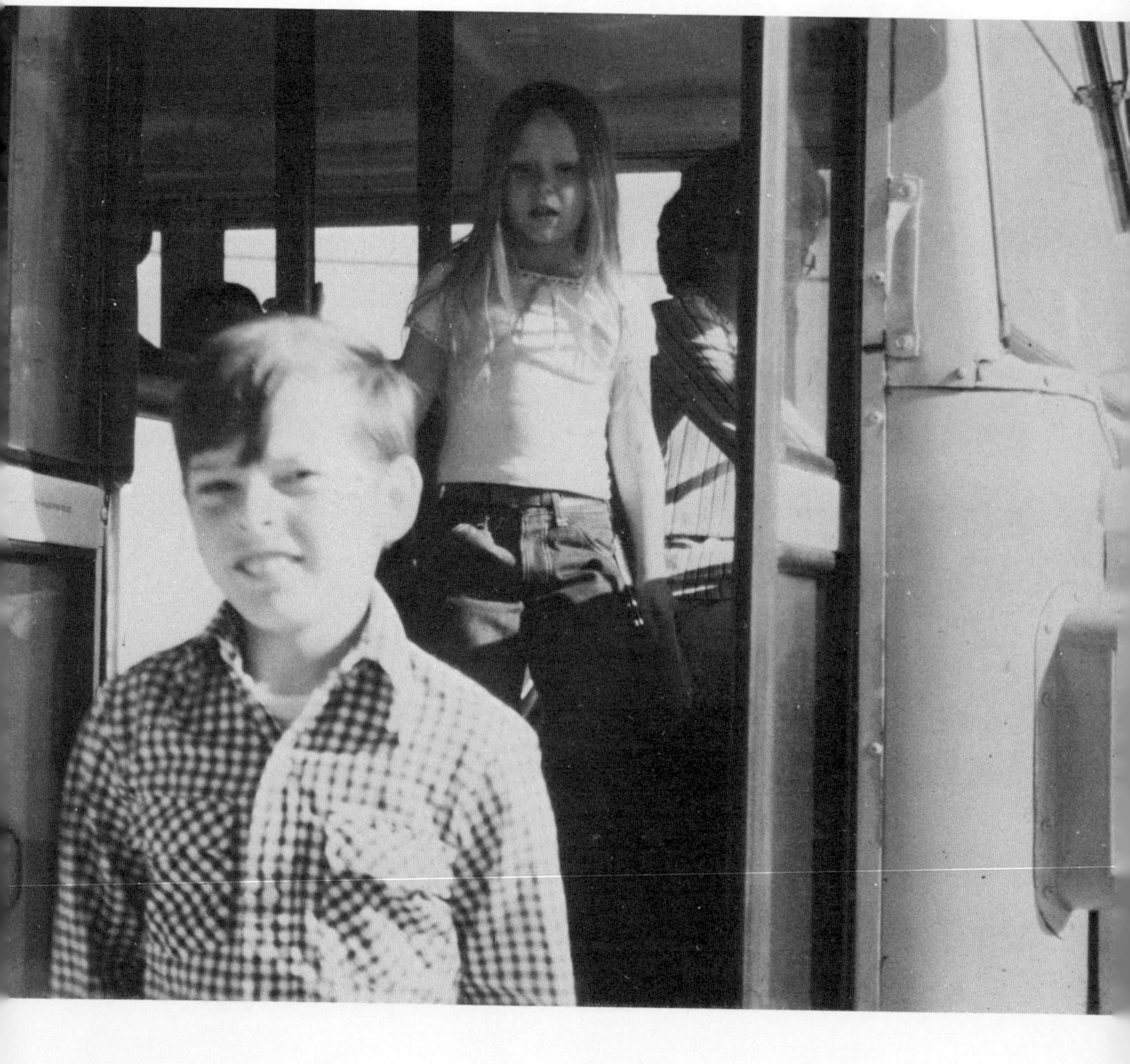

11

Providing educational services

Public Law 94–142 requires that each handicapped student receive a free, appropriate education. To insure this right, the law mandates that an Individualized Educational Program (IEP) be developed for each child and approved by the parent (see Chapter 14 for a detailed description of an IEP). In developing the IEP, the special education team is faced with the task of placing the student in an educational setting tailored to the student's learning and social-emotional needs. Many types of services may be provided within a school district and it is apparent that the setting itself has a strong influence on the student, the teacher, and the family. This chapter discusses *(a)* the selection of special education services and *(b)* the various educational service provisions and related practices that are used with LD students.

SELECTION OF SPECIAL EDUCATION SERVICES

The needs of each student determine the selection of services. The needs are assessed by a special education team who gather and interpret diagnostic information. Unfortunately, in many cases, this team cannot *primarily* rely on the student's needs in proposing special education services. Additional factors include the existing and possible resources available. Moreover, placement decisions are strongly influenced by legislation. For example, one of the provisions included in PL 94-142 is that students must be educated in environments that are the least restrictive.

Least Restrictive Environment and Mainstreaming

The term *least restrictive environment* requires that no pupil is removed from regular class participation any more than is appropriate. The IEP must document to what extent the pupil can participate in the regular program. In addition, Hayes and Higgins (1978) note that handicapped pupils need to be able to participate in the variety of educational programs and services available to nonhandicapped pupils (e.g., art, music, industrial arts, consumer education, and homemaking). Historically, handicapped pupils were pulled out of regular classrooms and placed in self-contained classes. The least restrictive principle stops this "all-or-nothing" approach to placement and stresses the need for using a continuum of services sensitive to diverse needs.

A perspective on this idea is enhanced by examining Deno's (1970) "cascade" system that describes services in terms of seven levels. As a student moves from Level 1 to Level 7, the degree of segregation from regular class peers increases.

1—regular class assignment with or without supportive services
2—regular class assignment plus supplementary instructional services

Small-group instruction is essential in mainstreaming.

3—part-time special class
4—full-time special class
5—special school assignment within public school system
6—homebound instruction
7—placement in facilities operated by health or welfare agencies

Rationale for Mainstreaming

PL 94-142 does not mention the term *mainstreaming;* however, its use is widespread. According to Hayes and Higgins (1978), many educators feel confused about it and have overreacted. They note that *mainstreaming* and *least restrictive environment* are not interchangeable; the two terms are parallel in many areas but do differ. In mainstreaming, handicapped pupils, including the learning disabled, receive instruction with their nonhandicapped peers to the maximum extent possible. While least restrictive environment promotes the integration, it primarily stresses that placement be based on the individual needs of the student. In essence, least restrictive environment is a broader concept than mainstreaming.

Numerous factors and reasons provide a rationale for mainstreaming. First, the research has failed to demonstrate that handicapped youngsters progress more quickly when segregated (Birch, 1974; Kaufman, Gottlieb, Agard, & Kukic, 1975). Second, it is believed that the stigma associated with special class placement is removed when the handicapped child remains in the regular class (Kaufman et al., 1975). Third, interaction with nonhandicapped peers is often beneficial to handicapped students (Kaufman et al., 1975). Fourth, mainstreaming lessens the need for labeling; thus, the potential negative effects of labels are reduced. Fifth, many parents do not want segregation. Finally, court decisions now specify that regular class placement is preferable (Kaufman et al., 1975).

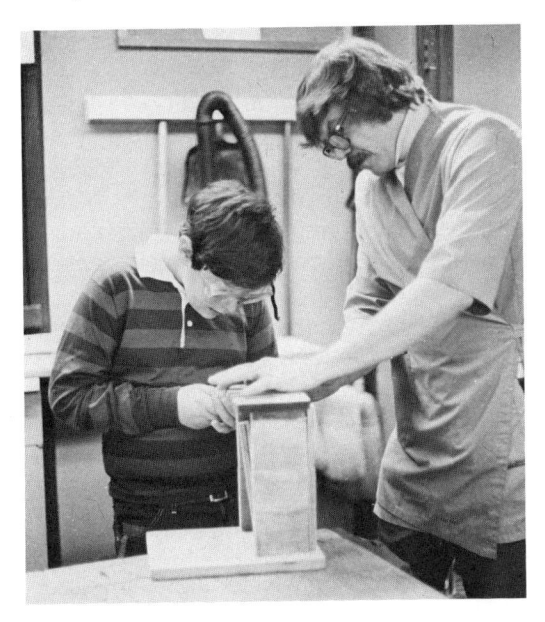

Many LD youngsters function well in regular shop classes.

Criticism of Mainstreaming

Although the mainstreaming movement is rapidly spreading, it is faced with many problems and skepticism by some prominent educators. For example, Cruickshank (1977) expresses several concerns and reports that no definitive research exists that demonstrates that one type of educational placement is less restrictive than others. In addition, he claims that the majority of regular classroom teachers lack the preparation that is required to serve the needs of LD students. Furthermore, he feels that many administrators do not understand the nature of the problem and, as a result, they do not provide adequate support to teachers.

Similarly, Lovitt (1978) points out that mainstreaming has been primarily promoted by legislators who have not consulted with school personnel who are charged with implementing it. Clearly, if regular class teachers are to teach handicapped children, they must learn how to do it well. Before teaching, they must be able to

1. understand how handicaps affect learning
2. recognize handicaps and develop prescriptive learning experiences
3. individualize instruction
4. understand the emotions of handicapped students
5. use the services of supportive personnel
6. effectively communicate with parents of handicapped youngsters

It is apparent that the ideas of least restrictive placement (National Advisory Council on Education Professions Development, 1976) and mainstreaming influence where learning disabled youngsters receive instruction. However, regardless of trends, the placement of each youngster rests primarily on his needs and the available resources. With the numerous options available, it is often difficult to select the optimal placement for each student. Payne, Polloway, Smith, and Payne (1977) suggest that the following criteria be considered in selecting a placement.

1. *Severity of the problem*—Specific academic and social difficulties must be weighed initially. Behavioral characteristics and work/study skills should also be considered.
2. *Regular class situation*—Skills and attitudes of the teacher and the number of students enrolled will be crucial determinants.
3. *Availability of school supportive personnel*—Placement decisions will be greatly affected by the resource people that can be tapped to support the regular teacher if mainstreaming is the option to be chosen.

4. *Outside resources*—Tutoring help by volunteers from the community can be of significant assistance. (p. 141)

Learning disabled children have a wide range of needs, and schools vary concerning the types of resources available. Thus, needs and resources must be examined *student by student* and not be guided by trends or philosophies insensitive to uniqueness. Within this framework educators must provide LD youngsters with as many alternatives as possible.

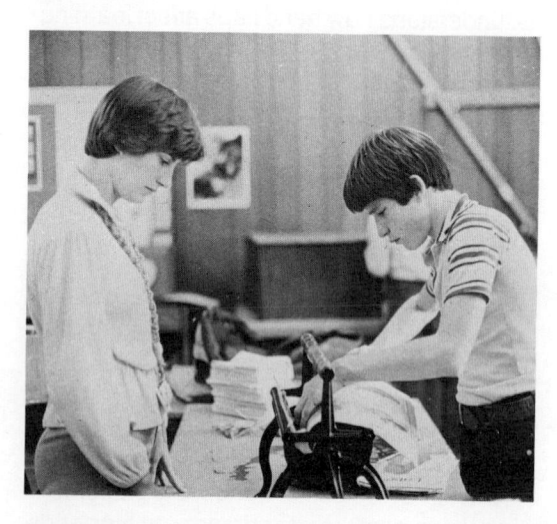

Nonacademic activities, such as rolling paper logs, help foster motivation in LD youngsters.

Placement Selection

It is important to view placement within this step-by-step framework:

1. Define SLD.
2. Outline eligibility criteria.
3. Screen.
4. Make referral.
5. Determine eligibility.
6. Develop individualized educational program (IEP) and select placement.
7. Establish dismissal criteria.

On this continuum, placement is the sixth step and occurs in conjunction with the development of an IEP.

Definition of SLD and Eligibility Criteria

PL 94–142 includes procedures for each step. The definition of *SLD* and selected eligibility criteria presented in Chapter 2 include PL 94–142 requirements.

Screening

Screening refers to a process of rapid assessment of a population in order to obtain potential SLD pupils. PL 94–142 requires that all children, regardless of handicap, be identified; screening is a necessary step in this identification process and can include teacher rating, single tests, and batteries of tests (presented in Chapter 12). Table 11.1 illustrates a sample checklist for screening (used in Hillsborough County, Florida). Typically screening for SLD pupils includes both standardized and informal measures in academic skill areas. Other important areas for screening include hearing and vision, speech and language, classroom behavior, health status, and parental information.

Referral

Referral is the process whereby a parent or guardian, school personnel, or appropriate public agencies may request assessment of a student's abilities. Screening information usually serves as a basis for making a referral. In developing a referral system it is helpful to use a standard form. In order to reduce inappropriate referrals it is helpful to require specific information (e.g., specific academic problems, behavioral observations, attempted instructional strategies) on the referral form and systematically review all referrals at the school level. This review may be conducted by the referring teacher, the SLD teacher, the guidance counselor, or other personnel as necessary (e.g., school principal). Oftentimes the review meeting results in meeting the student's needs without proceeding with the referral. Finally, if the referral appears needed, parental permission to conduct evaluation is required.

TABLE 11.1

Teacher observation checklist for screening referral.

Name _____ Grade _____ Date of birth _____

The following identification guidelines help analyze symptom complexes and facilitate appropriate management and educational procedures for the learning disabled child. Rate each characteristic on a 0–5 scale in terms of increasingly observed behavior, *1* indicating behavior exhibited to a slight degree, *5* indicating behavior exhibited to a very large degree. Remember that appropriate behavior varies with chronological age. If only part of the statement is applicable, underline the specific characteristic that applies to the child.

- ____ Significant discrepancy between ability and achievement
- ____ Difficulty with activities involving rhythm.
- ____ Difficulty judging size, shape, or distance.
- ____ General awkwardness. Poor balance.
- ____ Difficulty with tasks requiring fine coordination.
- ____ Confuses left and right body parts.
- ____ Reverses letters or words when reading.
- ____ Reverses letters, words, or numbers when writing.
- ____ Confuses letters, words, or numbers that look alike.
- ____ Confuses letters, words, or numbers that sound alike.
- ____ Omits letters or words when reading or writing.
- ____ Difficulty recognizing familiar words in unfamiliar context.
- ____ Drawings are immature, lacking organization and detail.
- ____ Difficulty remembering ideas, facts, or rules.
- ____ Difficulty learning facts, such as address or phone number.
- ____ Difficulty learning a series, such as the alphabet.
- ____ Forgets almost immediately what has been seen or heard.
- ____ Confused by oral directions. Difficulty following directions.
- ____ Difficulty with concepts involving time.
- ____ Achieves high in some areas and low in others.
- ____ Poor printing or writing. Difficulty copying from the board.
- ____ Arithmetic more than one grade level below grade placement.
- ____ Reading more than one grade level below grade placement.
- ____ Difficulty learning sight words. Lacks word attack skills.
- ____ Does not comprehend the significance of what is read.
- ____ Spelling more than one grade level below grade placement.
- ____ Thinks slowly. Has delayed response to questions or commands.
- ____ Poor abstract reasoning ability.
- ____ Performs inconsistently from day to day or hour to hour.
- ____ Short attention span. Difficulty concentrating.
- ____ Impulsive. Responds without considering consequences.
- ____ Distracted by minor sights or sounds. Notices everything.
- ____ Difficulty focusing on center of attention.
- ____ Repeats a task or movement when it is no longer appropriate.
- ____ Hyperactive. Excessive motor activity.
- ____ Low tolerance for frustration. Gives up easily.
- ____ Poor judgment in social and interpersonal relations.
- ____ Poor adjustment to change of routine.
- ____ Sudden unexplainable shifts from one emotion to another.
- ____ One eye occasionally turns in or out.
- ____ Speech irregularities. Distorts or omits sounds.
- ____ Easily fatigued by mental exertion.

Signature of Teacher _____ *Date* _____

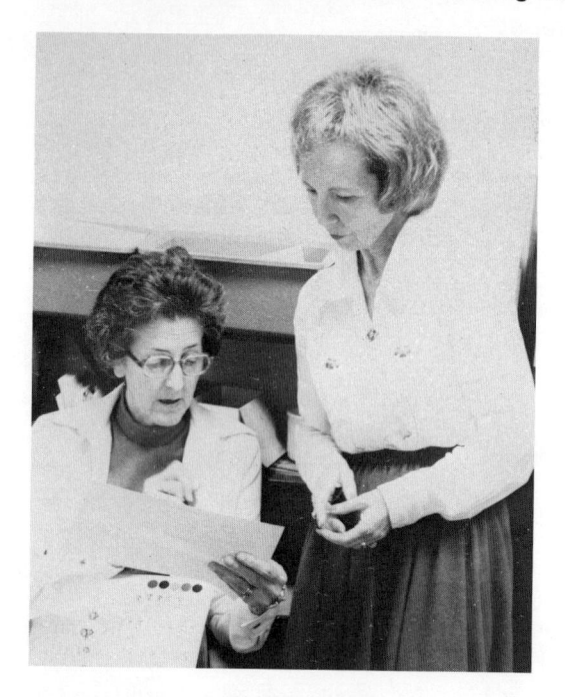

A principal and SLD teacher discuss a referral.

Determine Eligibility

An evaluation team must document the existence of a learning disability according to the procedures outlined in the 1977 *Federal Register* (USOE, 1977). These evaluation procedures are discussed in Chapter 2.

Develop IEP

Once the eligibility of the student for SLD programming is determined, the IEP is developed. A detailed discussion of the IEP is presented in Chapter 14.

Select Placement and Establish Dismissal Criteria

A variety of placements have been used for SLD students. The next section of this chapter presents these placement alternatives. In addition, later portions will discuss dismissal criteria.

EDUCATIONAL SERVICE PROVISIONS AND RELATED PRACTICES

The service or placement options presented in Figure 11.1 represent a core of alternatives that are necessary to serve a heterogeneous population of LD students. The program alternatives may be divided into three major categories: regular class-based, special class-based, and special school-based. Inspection of the 10 types of programs indicates that as the program alternatives move from the regular class to the special school, segregation, labeling, and severity of need of the recipients usually increase. In establishing objectives for an LD youngster, it is important to adopt a tentative commitment to a program level and not consider placement in any program as permanent or terminal. Educators must provide LD youngsters with programs that will *continuously* respond to their unique needs. Opportunities for moving LD pupils from the more segregated programs to the more integrated programs need to be regularly considered and effected whenever feasible. In addition, placement *within* a particular program alternative needs to be considered when it appears that such a change would be beneficial. For example, a change from one regular classroom to another may be enacted because a specific teacher has certain qualities or an instructional program specifically suited to an individual pupil.

Regular Class-Based Programs

The regular classroom placement represents the most integrated level of placement. In these programs the child spends the majority of the day in the regular classroom with youngsters of the same age. Smith and Neisworth (1975) note that the key to success for the exceptional child placed in the regular classroom rests with the regular classroom teacher. They list a series of factors that deserve consideration:

1. The teacher's judgment of the child's capacity for progress, the teacher's attitude toward having exceptional children in the classroom with other students, and the way in which he or she acts and reacts toward the child.
2. The procedures the teacher uses in forecasting and dealing with the inevitable problems

Providing educational services 325

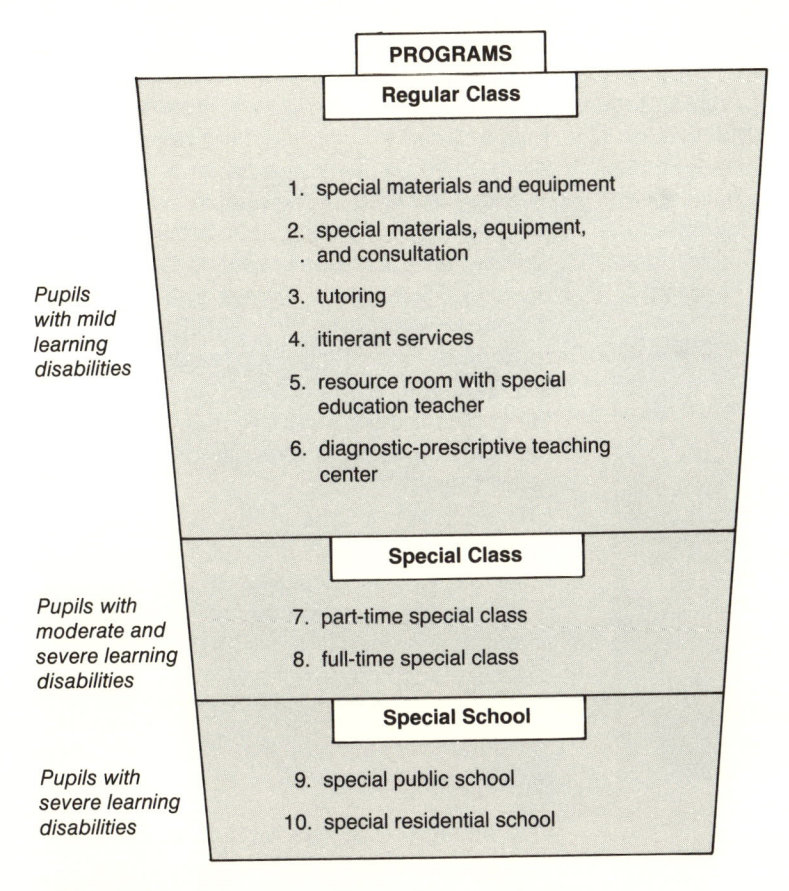

```
                         ┌─────────────┐
                         │  PROGRAMS   │
                    ┌────┴─────────────┴────┐
                    │    Regular Class      │
                    └───────────────────────┘
                    
                    1. special materials and equipment
                    2. special materials, equipment,
  Pupils               and consultation
  with mild         3. tutoring
  learning          4. itinerant services
  disabilities      5. resource room with special
                       education teacher
                    6. diagnostic-prescriptive teaching
                       center
                    
                    ┌───────────────────────┐
                    │    Special Class      │
                    └───────────────────────┘
  Pupils with       7. part-time special class
  moderate and      8. full-time special class
  severe learning
  disabilities
                    ┌───────────────────────┐
                    │    Special School     │
                    └───────────────────────┘
  Pupils with       9. special public school
  severe learning  10. special residential school
  disabilities
```

FIGURE 11.1

Ten program alternatives for evaluating learning disabled students according to level of program segregation and degree of need.

Source. Adapted from "Programs and Services" by C. D. Mercer & J. S. Payne. In J. M. Kauffman & J. S. Payne (Eds.), *Mental Retardation: Introduction and Personal Perspectives.* Columbus, Ohio: Charles E. Merrill, 1975, p. 128. Copyright 1975 by Bell & Howell Company. Reprinted by permission.

of peer acceptance that will occur between the exceptional child and other youngsters.
3. The efforts of the teacher to maintain as reasonable and normal an environment for the exceptional student while providing the necessary circumstances to facilitate increased levels of functioning on the child's part.
4. The skill with which the teacher is able to deal with the emotional behavior and problems of the exceptional child as a result of his not being able to compete with other youngsters in certain areas he considers to be important. In like manner, the teacher will need to be aware of and skillful in handling the jealousy of other students when the teacher must give special attention to the exceptional youngster. (pp. 273–274)

It is apparent that this teacher has an enormous responsibility. It is very important these cooperative and capable people receive the proper preparation and support. Moreover, LD children should not be placed in regular classrooms with teachers who do not believe that the LD student will profit from the experience.

Special Materials and Equipment

Occasionally a teacher can work with his LD youngsters in the classroom with the help of additional materials and equipment. The materials may consist of a high-interest–low-vocabulary reading series, a programmed reader, a Language Master, manipulative materials for math, a pencil holder, or any material or hardware that enables individualized instruction. To use this plan it is very important for the teacher to have a reasonable pupil-teacher ratio (e.g., mid-20s to 1, or lower).

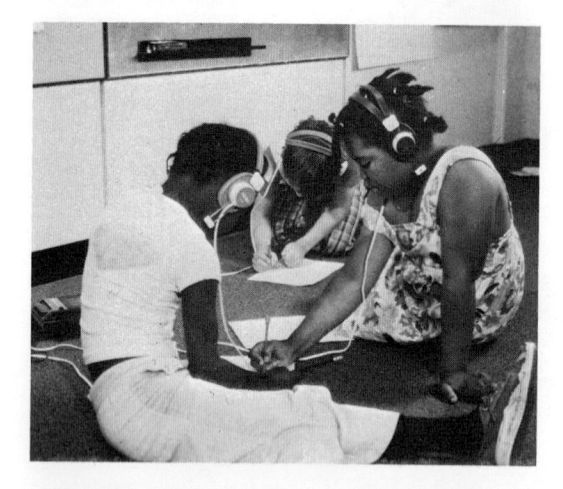

Math tapes provide these students with individualized instruction.

Special Materials, Equipment, and Consultation

The teacher may be provided with special materials and limited consultation. The consultation is usually offered by an LD teacher and may consist of demonstrating the use of selected materials or equipment, performing an educational assessment, developing specific learning strategies, or providing an inservice program. As with the previous program, a reasonable pupil-teacher ratio is mandatory.

Tutoring

Tutoring usually refers to one-to-one instruction for part of the school day. Some states help fund the costs of tutoring handicapped youngsters. The practice of tutoring is widespread for several reasons. Sometimes it is used in lieu of special class placement. In addition, it is used to assist youngsters who are being reintegrated into the regular classroom or to aid youngsters who need additional help in order to function in the regular classroom. In some situations, tutoring is provided outside the school. For example, parents may employ tutors to help their children learn specific skills. Outside tutors should work with the respective teacher of the tutee to insure continuity in the youngster's instructional program. Tutors may be trained teachers, university students, aides, and/or volunteers. For tutors who are not trained to teach LD youngsters, the guidance of a qualified teacher may prove helpful.

Despite its widespread use, tutoring has not been heavily researched (Stephens, 1977). It receives its justification from its extensive use and from research results that indicate that specific academic skills can be taught through directive teaching. Stephens (1977) provides much helpful information regarding the responsibilities and training of tutors.

Peer Tutoring

Peer tutoring is commonly practiced in regular education (Cloward, 1967). Allen (1976) reports that the results of research on peer tutoring indicate a positive effect for the tutor (i.e., it helps the tutor with academics or behavior difficulties or both). Allen notes that the effects on the tutee are generally positive, but the results are not conclusive. He reports that the critical factor in establishing a mutually beneficial tutor-tutee arrangement is the competence of the tutor regarding content. As a result of his review of the research in peer teaching, Allen offers the following comments:

1. Young children prefer a tutor of the same sex, but the sex of the tutor has not produced differential effects on the tutee. However, youngsters of the same sex tend to have more mutual interests.
2. Tutoring sessions that last too long may produce negative effects. Recommended are twenty- to thirty-minute sessions held two to three times a week.

In a student-tutoring system, both children benefit.

3. Tutoring should occur in a location with minimal disturbance. Hallways and playgrounds are generally too distracting.
4. It should be explained to parents that tutoring supplements teacher instruction but does not replace it.
5. All types of students (low achieving, high achieving, etc.) may be used as tutors. However, make sure the tutor has mastered the instructional content before tutoring occurs.
6. The goals and the activities of the tutoring sessions should be specified.

Peer tutoring has been successfully used to (a) improve academic skills, (b) foster self-esteem, (c) help the shy youngster, (d) help students who have difficulty with authority figures, (e) improve race relations, and (f) promote positive relationships and cooperation among peers. Although little research exists regarding its effects, it seems to hold much promise. For example, (a) peer tutoring usually benefits the tutor and tutee, (b) once it is initiated It does not require much of the teacher's time, and (c) regular classroom teachers can use it for assisting the mainstreamed LD youngster.

Itinerant Services

An itinerant program involves providing regular class teachers with consultative and in-

The LD teacher may demonstrate to the classroom teacher how to use manipulative math materials.

structional services for those pupils whose learning problems are not severe enough to warrant resource room instruction or special class placement. An itinerant teacher usually operates from a central office and visits the schools periodically. The itinerant teacher frequently spends much of his time evaluating and teaching pupils who have special needs. Since these services are limited to weekly or biweekly visits, the basic responsibility for instruction of LD pupils remains with the regular teacher. Furthermore, the itinerant teacher must be careful in scheduling (i.e., the regular teacher needs to be consulted regarding the best time for a pupil to work with the itinerant teacher). Occasionally, the itinerant services are bolstered through the use of volunteers and/or teacher aides.

The Resource Room

The resource room is now the most prevalent service arrangement used for learning disabled pupils. In this plan the LD pupil spends the majority of the day in a regular class and goes to the resource room for a specified period of time (e.g., 45 to 60 minutes) each day. The resource room teacher, located in the school, works closely with numerous teachers to coordinate the instructional programs of the pupils. The various service alternatives of the resource room presented in Figure 11.2 indicate how the plan can be used to accommodate the different needs of both students and teachers.

The resource room is widely used apparently because of its flexible service delivery format. Wiederholt, Hammill, and Brown (1978) specify numerous advantages:

1. Students can benefit from specific resource support while remaining integrated with their friends and age-mates in the school.
2. The resource teacher has an opportunity to help more children than does a full-time special class teacher. This is especially true when the resource teacher provides indirect services to children with mild or moderate problems by consulting extensively with their teachers.
3. Resource programs are less expensive to operate than special self-contained classes.

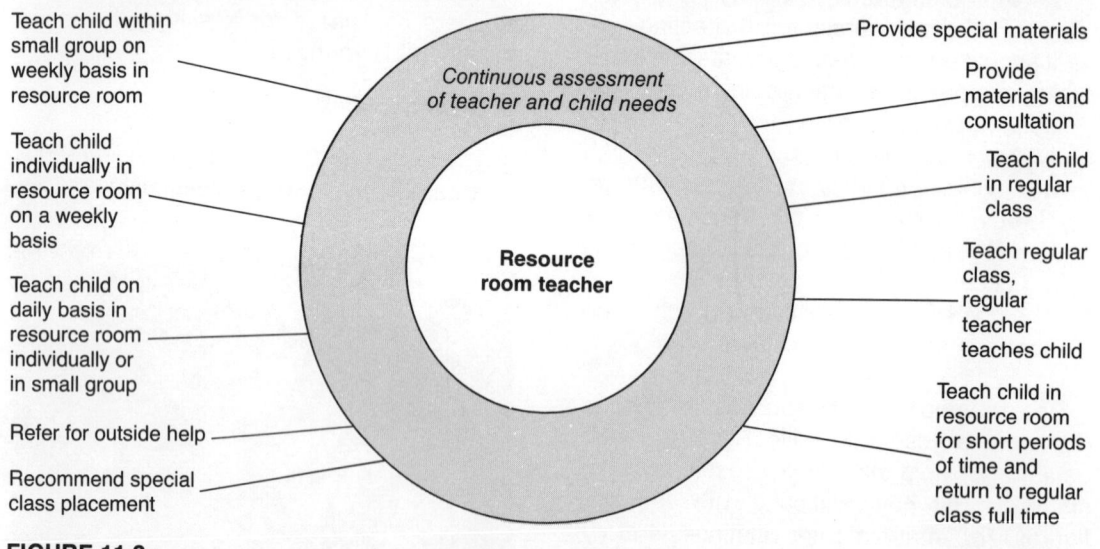

FIGURE 11.2

Service alternatives for the resource room teacher.

Source. Adapted from "Programs and Services" by C. D. Mercer & J. S. Payne. In J. M. Kauffman & J. S. Payne (Eds.), *Mental Retardation: Introduction and Personal Perspectives.* Columbus, Ohio: Charles E. Merrill, 1975, p. 131. Copyright 1975 by Bell & Howell Company. Reprinted by permission.

4. Because young children with mild, though developing, problems can be accommodated, later severe disorders may be prevented.
5. Flexible scheduling means that remediation can be applied entirely in the classrooms by the regular teacher with some resource support or in another room by the resource program personnel when necessary; also, the schedule can be quickly altered to meet the children's changing situations and needs.
6. Since the resource program will absorb most of the handicapped children in the schools, the self-contained special education classes will increasingly become instructional settings for truly and relatively severely handicapped students, the children for whom the classes were originally developed.
7. Because of the resource teacher's broad experience with many children exhibiting different educational and behavioral problems, he/she may in time become an in-house consultant to the school. (pp. 10–11)

Since the resource room teacher provides daily services to approximately 20 LD youngsters and their respective teachers, obviously his role demands a highly competent, personable individual. Specifically, Wiederholt (1974) feels the following qualities are essential: *(a)* the ability to work effectively and harmoniously with teachers and ancillary staff, *(b)* the ability to assess the educational needs of pupils, and *(c)* the ability to design and implement prescriptive educational programs.

Wiederholt, Hammill, and Brown (1978) describe several types of resource room models. However, it is likely that most LD youngsters are served in one of three types: categorical, cross-categorical, or noncategorical. Categorical programs serve *only* LD youngsters. Cross-categorical serve exceptional children from among several categorical areas (i.e., educable mentally retarded, emotionally handicapped, and learning disabled). Noncategorical meet the educational needs of youngsters with mild learning problems who may or may not be classified *handicapped*. Wiederholt et al. list four specific advantages of the noncategorical approach:

1. The noncategorical approach minimizes the stigma that might result from labeling and segregation.
2. Most students are able to receive help in their neighborhood school since many elementary schools are large enough to have one or more noncategorical resource teachers. Therefore, this situation eliminates or reduces the necessity of busing handicapped children to a school that has an appropriately labeled class or resource program.
3. The time lapse between the teacher's referral and the initiation of special services for the child is minimized since placement in the resource program is an individual school matter that involves only the principal, the teachers, and the parents.
4. In the noncategorical alternative, since medical and psychological work-ups are provided only at the schools' specific request, the school psychologist is freed from the role of psychometrist.

Although the resource room is gaining popularity as an instructional plan for serving LD youngsters, its efficacy has not been extensively examined. Weiner (1969), Sabatino (1971), and Ferinden, Van Handel, and Kovalinsky (1971) studied the effectiveness of the resource room. Using a pre-posttest for-

Tom and Alicia are scheduled to attend the resource room one period a day.

mat, Weiner found that LD children (*N* = 72) significantly improved academically after attending a resource room for 1 hour a day throughout the school year. No LD students gained markedly in self-concept (as measured by the *Draw-A-Person Test*). Sabatino found that daily contact (40-minute sessions) of LD youngsters with the resource room teacher produced better results than semiweekly contact (30-minute sessions). Ferinden et al. concentrated on correcting perceptual disturbances of 11 children who remained in regular classes and received supplemental instruction from a special teacher in a resource room. Using a pre-posttest design, they reported that after 8 months of treatment, the children improved in their perception (as measured by the *Bender Gestalt Test*) and in their math skills (18 months). Although not significant, the average gain in reading achievement was 8 months.

In summary, it appears that the resource room program is worthwhile. Although the research to date is beset with definition and methodological problems, it appears that until further research suggests otherwise, the resource room will continue to be used as a model to serve mainstreamed LD students.

Diagnostic-Prescriptive Teaching Center

Youngsters can be taken for short periods of time to centers staffed by a team of special educators and diagnosticians. The center's staff members assess a youngster's performance and design an educational program tailored to his needs. As part of their evaluation, the staff members observe the pupil in the classroom and work closely with the regular teacher to develop appropriate teaching strategies. When the pupil returns to his class, his instruction is based on the program recommended by the center's staff.

Special Class-Based Programs

Part- and Full-time Special Classes

Initially, public schools used special classes for LD youngsters. Cruickshank, Bentzen, Ratzeburg, and Tannhauser (1961) provide one of the first descriptions of a special class designed for brain-injured and hyperactive children. Their plan features a highly structured program and a reduction of distracting stimuli. In general, these classes consist of 8 to 12 pupils, a special education teacher, an aide, and the services of supportive personnel (e.g., speech clinician, physical education teacher, music teacher, visiting teacher). The pupils may either receive their entire academic instruction within the self-contained class or attend regular classes for portions of their academic instruction.

Since special classes do not provide much integration with other segments of the school, much consideration should be given to assigning a pupil to such a class. Many educators question the efficacy of using special classes for mildly handicapped youngsters (Dunn, 1968). For example, Dunn (1973) notes:

> The self-contained special-class plan has been most severely criticized when used with slow-learning and disruptive children. Too often the plan has been used to put out of sight pupils the regular teachers do not want. It is to be hoped, however, that this practice will not disguise the appropriateness of the plan, especially for children with severe learning disabilities and for younger children. Certain of these children may need an intensive, specialized curriculum to learn specific skills so as to take a greater part in the regular school program later in their school careers. (p. 28)

McCarthy and McCarthy (1969) estimate that less than 1% of LD youngsters are placed in special classes; most of these pupils seem to be best educated in a less segregated placement. Special class placement should only be considered for the child with the serious learning disability (e.g., Strauss syndrome, severe dyslexia, aphasia).

When the special class is deemed appropriate, certain criteria are essential:

1. The special class teacher should be trained to teach the types of students in the class.

2. The students should be selected on the basis of learning or social-emotional problems, *not* on the basis of socio-economic status or race.
3. Each child should receive intensive and systematic instruction tailored to his unique needs.
4. A wide variety of teaching materials and resources should be available to the teacher.
5. The class size should be considerably smaller than a regular class.
6. A variety of teaching styles is needed to accommodate the different needs of the pupils.
7. Each pupil's progress should be constantly monitored. Reintegration into the mainstream should be considered when it appears feasible.
8. The class should have administrative support.

Finally, Smith and Arkans (1974) caution educators not to be swept into the mainstreaming efforts to the extent that self-contained classes are abolished. A regular classroom teacher who is responsible for the educational needs of 20 to 35 students simultaneously cannot realistically meet the educational demands of youngsters with severe learning problems. It appears that the self-contained program remains a viable alternative to educate those students who require it.

Special School-Based Programs

Special Public School

Students with severe learning and/or emotional problems who have difficulty functioning in the regular school may attend a special day school on either a part-time or full-time basis. In school systems combining regular and special schools, LD pupils are transported to a central school for part of the day. The pupils receive educational services that are not provided in their home schools. In school divisions where services for LD youngsters are not available in the regular school, the pupils may receive their entire educational program within a special day school.

Special Residential School

In some instances, LD children attend a residential school. These schools, normally private, offer low teacher-pupil ratios, intensive instruction, and counseling. If the residential school primarily serves exceptional children, it may be viewed as segregated and generally isolated from the mainstream. If the school serves all types of youngsters, including the LD pupil, it may represent an integrated placement and be consistent with the mainstream movement. Some primary considerations involved in a special school placement include (a) severity of the problems, (b) costs to the family, (c) transportation, (d) degree of segregation, (e) home conditions, and (f) parental requests.

Reintegration of Students

Students in special programs should be returned to their regular programs as soon as they are able to function successfully there. Stephens (1977) reports that little research exists regarding practices for reintegrating students. Using experience as a guide, Stephens offers several basic rules for reintegrating students:

1. Placement changes should be based on the performance of the youngster.
2. Students and parents should be provided assistance to help them adjust to modifications or a reduction of special education services.
3. Trial placements should be initiated only when essential.
4. The respective teachers should share their observations of the youngster and be involved in placement decisions.
5. Fading techniques are helpful when changing placements.
6. Due process procedures should be used whenever a change in service provisions is recommended.

Practical skills are experienced in this special school.

Reintegration or dismissal from an LD program originates from a reevaluation of the student's needs and progress. The IEP format offers the teacher an excellent opportunity to examine the feasibility of program dismissal or reassignment. If his observations or evaluation data indicate that a change is warranted, he can initiate a meeting to reevaluate the existing IEP.

Who Should Teach Learning Disabled Students?

Learning disabilities represent the only exceptionality in which there is considerable controversy over who should teach the students. Through the International Reading Association (IRA), reading specialists have challenged LD specialists concerning the privilege of teaching LD youngsters. Similarly, through the American Speech and Hearing Association (ASHA), speech and language specialists have voiced their intention to manage the instructional programs of LD children. Lovitt (1978) attributes the emergence of these territorial rights issues to ambiguous and varied definitions, professional training, and state regulations:

Sometimes diagnosticians observe within the classroom to determine a program to meet each child's needs.

1. Each respective discipline has its own definition of LD or interprets the definition of LD from a viewpoint consistent with its specific intentions. For example, reading specialists note that reading disabilities are the most prevalent academic problem of LD students. In like manner, language specialists point out that the initial sentence of the NACHC definition ties LD to a language disability.

2. Little communication exists concerning professional training in the disciplines. In many instances, students or professionals in one discipline know very little about the training of persons in the other disciplines.

3. State regulations for certification of LD or remedial reading teachers lack consistency across states. The speech and language specialists readily point out that their standards are more consistent and generally more rigorous than those used in LD or remedial reading.

These problem areas, coupled with the reduction of funding for reading and speech programs and the increased funding for LD programs, have intensified the territorial rights issue.

A special issue of the *Journal of Learning Disabilities (JLD)* is devoted to the territorial rights problem. In this issue, Sartain (1976) expresses the viewpoint of the reading specialist. He recommends that LD specialists work with children with severe reading problems and that remedial reading teachers manage the children with moderate and mild reading problems.

Stick (1976) represents the speech pathologists' viewpoint and contends that speech pathologists should be involved in the instruction of LD children. With LD youngsters he recommends that speech pathologists focus on usage of grammatical forms, auditory perceptual skills, linguistic abilities, and the ability to process information and express oneself.

In the same *JLD* issue, Larsen (1976) and Wallace (1976) represent the LD specialist. Larsen contends that LD specialists should be the primary managers of LD youngsters but notes that speech personnel and reading specialists should be assigned important teaching responsibilities. Wallace encourages cooperative training and research efforts across the disciplines.

From the perspective of the parents and the children, it is relatively unimportant who does the teaching. They simply want competent, useful instruction. In some circumstances such instruction may be from only one of the aforementioned professionals; in other situations it may involve all three. Obviously improved communication and coordination are needed among professionals. Remember that caution must be exercised *student by student* to insure that individual students receive the instruction they need.

Procedural Safeguards

Certain procedures for involving the parent in placement decisions are outlined in PL 94-142. Chapter 4 thoroughly examines these procedures. Basically they explain due process and focus on the principle of *informed consent* regarding testing and placement de-

After a day of fun and learning, it's time to go home.

cisions. Also included in the due process procedures are guidelines for maintaining the confidentiality of records. Again, informed consent is the key factor. Stephens (1977) provides several guidelines concerning record keeping:

1. Collect only information about which parents and students are informed.
2. Make sure the parents consent to the collection of the information.
3. Develop procedures for verifying the accuracy of information and destroy inaccurate information or information that is no longer useful.
4. Make sure that parents have full access to the information and recognize their right to challenge its accuracy.
5. Give only the parents and school personnel who deal directly with the child access to the records. All others need written parental permission.

SUMMARY

Placement must be done in full consideration of the rights of the student and parent. In addition, it should represent the youngster's least restrictive environment. From a "best practice" viewpoint, the needs of each individual student should guide the placement decision. Numerous alternatives are needed to provide for the diverse needs of LD students. Ten alternatives that appear appropriate for LD students are presented: *(a)* special materials and equipment, *(b)* special materials, equipment, and consultation, *(c)* tutoring, *(d)* itinerant services, *(e)* resource room with special education teacher, *(f)* diagnostic-prescriptive teaching center, *(g)* part-time special class, *(h)* full-time special class, *(i)* special public school, and *(j)* special residential school. Of these, the resource room is the primary plan used with LD students. Since reintegration is a feasible goal for most LD youngsters, several procedures are listed to facilitate reintegration. The territorial rights issue is highlighted with a discussion of the respective claims of speech and language specialists, remedial reading teachers, and LD specialists concerning the management of the LD youngster's instructional program. Finally, record-keeping practices and confidentiality of records are examined.

REFERENCES

Allen, V.L. (Ed.). *Children as teachers: Theory and research on tutoring.* New York: Academic Press, 1976.

Birch, J. *Mainstreaming: Educable mentally retarded children in regular classes.* Leadership Training Institute/Special Education, University of Minnesota, 1974.

Cloward, R. Studies in tutoring. *Journal of Experimental Education,* 1967, *36,* 14–25.

Cruickshank, W.M. Least-restrictive placement: Administrative wishful thinking. *Journal of Learning Disabilities,* 1977, *10,* 193–194.

Cruickshank W., Bentzen, F.A., Ratzeburg, R.H., & Tannhauser, M. *A teaching method for brain-injured and hyperactive children.* New York: Syracuse University Press, 1961.

Deno, E. Special education as developmental capital. *Exceptional Children,* 1970, *37,* 229–237.

Dunn, L.M. Special education for the mildly retarded—Is much of it justifiable? *Exceptional Children,* 1968, *35,* 5–22.

Dunn, L.M. (Ed.). *Exceptional children in the schools: Special education in transition* (2nd ed.). New York: Holt, Rinehart & Winston, 1973.

Ferinden, W., Van Handel, D., & Kovalinsky, T. A supplemental instructional program for children with learning disabilities. *Journal of Learning Disabilities,* 1971, *4,* 84–93.

Hayes, J., & Higgins, S.T. Issues regarding the IEP: Teachers on the front line. *Exceptional Children,* 1978, *44,* 267–273.

Kaufman, M.J., Gottlieb, J., Agard, J.A., & Kukic, M.B. Mainstreaming: Toward an explication of the construct. *Focus on Exceptional Children,* 1975, *7*(3), 6–17.

Larsen, S.C. The learning disabilities specialist: Role and responsibilities. *Journal of Learning Disabilities,* 1976, *9,* 498–508.

Lovitt, T. Learning disabilities. In N. Haring (Ed.), *Behavior of exceptional children: An introduc-*

tion to special education (2nd ed.). Columbus, Ohio: Charles E. Merrill, 1978.

McCarthy, J., & McCarthy, J. *Learning disabilities.* Boston: Allyn & Bacon, 1969.

National Advisory Council on Education Professions Development. *Mainstreaming: Helping teachers meet the challenge.* Washington, D.C.: Author, 1976.

Payne, J.S., Polloway, E.A., Smith, J.E., Jr., & Payne, R.A. *Strategies for teaching the mentally retarded.* Columbus, Ohio: Charles E. Merrill, 1977.

Sabatino, D.A. An evaluation of resource rooms for children with learning disabilities. *Journal of Learning Disabilities,* 1971, *4,* 84–93.

Sartain, H.W. Instruction of disabled learners: A reading perspective. *Journal of Learning Disabilities,* 1976, *9,* 489–497.

Smith, J.O., & Arkans, J.R. Now more than ever: A case for the special class. *Exceptional Children,* 1974, *40,* 497–502.

Smith, R.M., & Neisworth, J.T. *The exceptional child: A functional approach.* New York: McGraw-Hill, 1975.

Stephens, T.M. *Teaching skills to children with learning and behavior disorders.* Columbus, Ohio: Charles E. Merrill, 1977.

Stick, S. The speech pathologist and handicapped learners. *Journal of Learning Disabilities,* 1976, *9,* 509–519.

U.S. Office of Education. Assistance to states for education of handicapped children: Procedures for evaluating specific learning disabilities. *Federal Register,* 1977, *42,* 65082–65085.

Wallace, G. Interdisciplinary efforts in learning disabilities: Issues and recommendations. *Journal of Learning Disabilities,* 1976, *9,* 520–526.

Weiner, L.H. An investigation of the effectiveness of resource rooms for children with specific learning disabilities. *Journal of Learning Disabilities,* 1969, *2,* 223–229.

Wiederholt, J.L. Planning resource rooms for the mildly handicapped. *Focus on Exceptional Children,* 1974, *5,* 1–10.

Wiederholt, J.L., Hammill, D.D., & Brown, V. *The resource teacher: A guide to effective practices.* Boston: Allyn & Bacon, 1978.

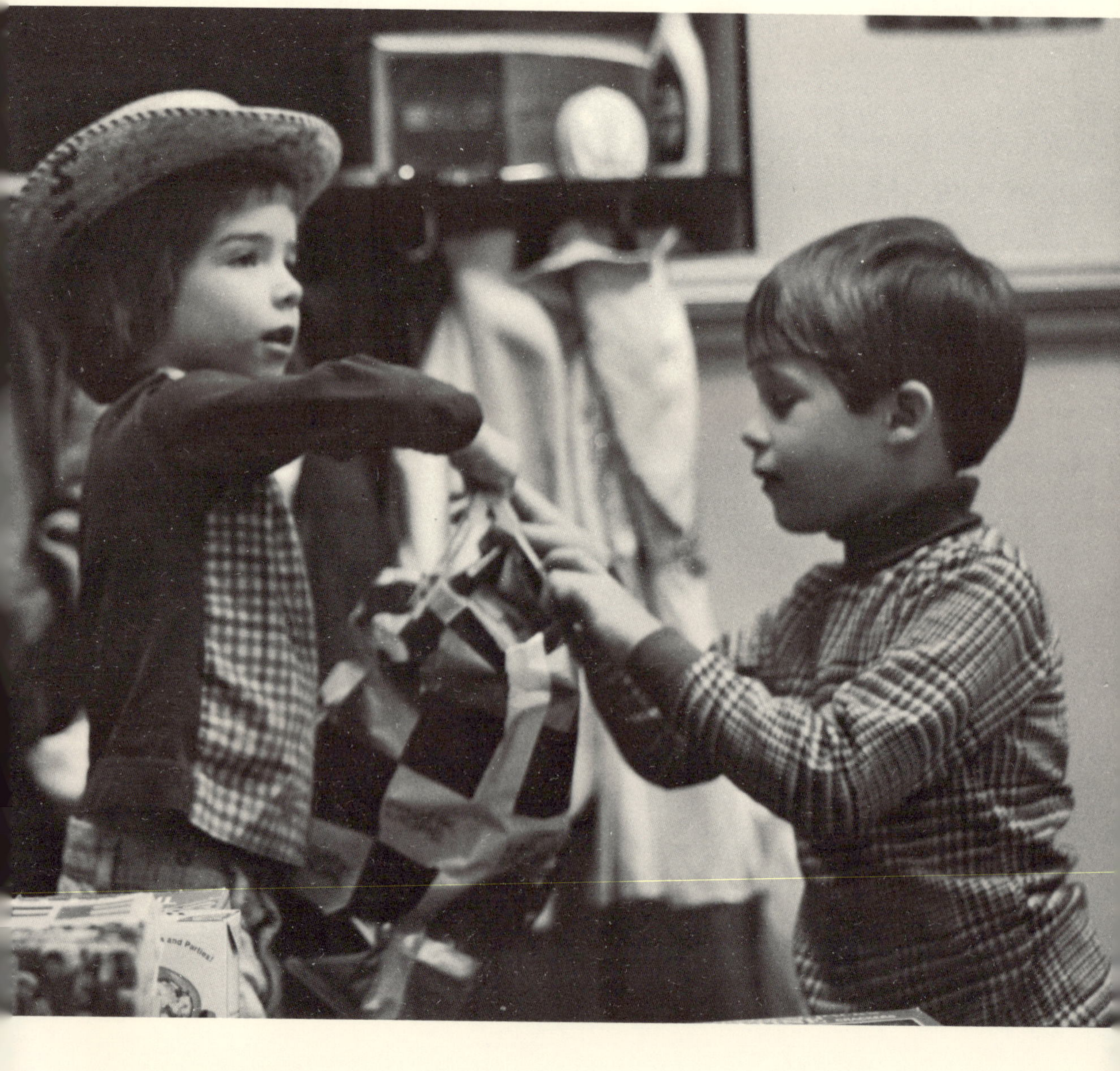
and Parties!

12

Early identification and intervention

Infants and preschool children (below the age of 6) who are likely to experience learning problems beginning in the primary grades are referred to as *at risk* or *high-risk children.* During the last decade the early identification of these children has received substantial support from parents and professionals in medicine, psychology, and education. They feel that many learning, social-emotional, and educational problems can be prevented or remediated if identification and intervention are provided before the child enters school.

Rationale for Early Identification and Intervention

PL 94–142 emphasizes early identification and intervention. It mandates that all handicapped children aged 3 to 21 must have available to them a free, appropriate, public education, tailored to their unique needs. In addition, it includes early childhood incentive grants of up to $300 per child to eligible states for providing such services to children aged 3–5.

Concern for early identification springs from an impressive yet inconclusive body of knowledge on the short-term and long-term progress of high-risk children who receive early intervention. Undoubtedly the now classic studies of Skeels (1966) and Kirk (1958) did much to initiate an interest in early intervention and a commitment to it. Likewise, the numerous projects with high-risk children (Garber & Heber, 1973; Gray & Klaus, 1965; Hayden & Haring, 1976; Shearer & Shearer, 1976) that have ensued in the last decade have done much to foster early identification and intervention. Existing projects, both descriptive and evaluative, combine with the mounting research regarding the effects of early experience on cognitive and social development (Thompson & Grusec, 1970; Tjossem, 1976) to provide a sound rationale for the emphasis on early identification and intervention.

Advantages of Early Identification and Intervention

The advantages encompass the following viewpoints:

1. *Prevention* activities may foster the learning of skills that are prerequisite for later learning (Hayden, 1974).
2. *Remediation* of a handicapping condition may result (Hayden, 1974).
3. Oftentimes parents are overly concerned about a child whom they suspect has a problem. When precise diagnosis is possible, it may help the parents adjust and accept the child and focus on helping in the specified problem area. In essence, they can stop worrying and concentrate their efforts on a specific behavior (Hayden, 1974).
4. A young child is more susceptible to behavioral change than an older child because she is in a period of rapid cognitive and social growth. During this period she acquires both inappropriate and appropriate behaviors (Stimbert, 1971).
5. The young child's motivation system is relatively simple, and events and activities are easily implemented. Also, many of the modern preschool toys can be motivational and may be used in instruction (Stimbert, 1971).
6. Many personality theorists stress the importance of the early years on *personality* development. Such behaviors as gender identity, peer relations, morals, impulse control, dependence-independence, and frustration tolerance become well established during the preschool years (Stimbert, 1971). Early identification and intervention may lead to instruction that has a positive effect on personality development.

Early intervention helps prevent learning problems for many high-risk children.

Problems of Early Identification

Although much support exists for early identification and intervention, numerous concerns and problems parallel this support.

Reluctant Physician

Of the numerous professionals concerned about early identification, the physician is often in the most advantageous position for making the initial identification. Many of these children do not have a physical handicap and a firm diagnosis cannot be established. Their problems are in the social, educational, and behavioral areas. Due to the unsure diagnostic status and nonmedical characteristics of high-risk children, many physicians are reluctant to identify them (Tjossem, 1976). Moreover, early intervention services for these children are usually nonmedical; physicians may be unaware of them. Her failure to identify or refer a high-risk child can delay the delivery of services.

Tenuous Diagnosis

Procedures of identification often lack sophistication, especially where the young mildly handicapped are concerned. Severely handicapped children display symptoms and behaviors that enable a diagnostician to confidently identify a very young child at risk. Aldrich and Holliday (1971) investigated the identification of severe versus mild problems. They revealed that whereas the first suspicion of retardation for profoundly retarded individuals occurred at 7.8 months of age, it occurred at 34.5 months for the mildly retarded. Moreover, the elapsed time between suspicion and confirmation for the profoundly retarded was 6.2 months and for the mildly retarded it was 12 months. This study demonstrates that mild cognition problems are more difficult to recognize and confirm than severe cognition problems.

The problem of accurate early detection becomes even more evident in the field of learning disabilities. The early warning signals of specific learning disabilities may be very subtle, vary in degree, and occur within a wide range of behaviors. For example, a Strauss syndrome child may be readily identified during the preschool years, whereas a child with reading problems may not be accurately identified until the first grade when reading is first introduced.

Developmental Differences

The possibility of maturational lag (Bender, 1957) or developmental imbalances (Gallagher, 1966) poses another problem in early identification. During the early years of rapid growth, individual children may exhibit unique developmental patterns. For some, the central nervous system (CNS) develops slowly. These children may exhibit perceptual-motor and attention problems. The CNS also may develop in a differential manner, causing the child to demonstrate high ability in one area (e.g., language) but very limited skills in another area (e.g., fine motor). However, as the CNS matures, these problems may diminish. These unique patterns make it difficult to determine if the child is high-risk or simply needs more time to mature. The pediatrician may be right when she says, "Dorothy will outgrow

Young children develop at different rates.

this." However, a serious problem emerges if she is wrong and the child does not receive needed assistance.

Since it is extremely difficult to evaluate the development of the CNS, the best practice may be to give assistance to the child whom the diagnostician suspects as being high-risk. If the diagnosis is correct, the child receives the needed educational intervention; if the diagnosis is incorrect, the child usually benefits from the extra instruction.

Labeling

Labeling has become a major issue. Because the accurate detection of high-risk children is very difficult, many children are mislabeled. Rosenthal and Jacobson (1966) feel that labels affect teacher expectancies (i.e., if she knows that a child is labeled *learning disabled,* she will expect certain behaviors). Such expectancies have been proven to have a negative influence on the child's educational progress. It is purported that the teacher expects less and accepts less from the labeled child in the areas of academic performance and social behavior (Algozzine, Mercer, & Countermine, 1977; Foster, Schmidt, & Sabatino, 1976; Foster & Ysseldyke, 1976). In addition, labels give the child a stigma to peers. They may view her negatively and openly say so.

Obviously labels harm both the misdiagnosed (labeled *high-risk* when she is not) and the correctly diagnosed child. If teachers and staff could avoid developing negative expectancies, the problem of labeling would be greatly reduced. As mentioned, early intervention by a trained teacher will likely benefit any child who receives it. However, without safeguards, early identification has a built-in expectancy phenomenon that may be harmful.

Prediction Study Problems

How reliable and valid prediction instruments are remains uncertain (Keogh & Becker, 1973). Numerous studies exist regarding prediction, but several problems have surfaced in this area. Since the prediction instrument forecasts whether a child will have later learning problems, it is important that the value of the instrument be considered in terms of the educational program in which the child is placed. For example, in validating a prediction instrument the accuracy of the prediction depends on the type of instructional program in which the child is placed (i.e., if intervention is initiated, the child will perform well and the prediction power of the instrument appears low). Fortunately, numerous prediction studies have been reported with kindergartners who did not receive special intervention. Thus, the validity of these instruments regarding children entering regular education programs has been established. From the review of these studies presented later in this chapter, it appears that high-risk kindergarten children can be identified somewhat accurately. Given this current level of accuracy in prediction with 5 and 6 year olds, it would be difficult to justify future studies which did not supply intervention to 5-year-old children identified or suspected as being high-risk.

Miscellaneous Problems

Two other significant problems exist regarding early identification:

1. The diagnostic information used to identify a high-risk child often lacks relevance for

Toys may help elicit the cooperation of young children during assessment.

teachers. For example, a poor performance on a *Bender-Gestalt Test* does not readily translate into relevant teaching goals.
2. The historical data on preschoolers are frequently inaccurate or unavailable. Parents often cannot recall information (developmental milestones, infant diseases) essential to clinical evaluation.

Early identification and intervention have enough support to warrant substantial emphasis. However, the problems involved behoove professionals to delinate the "best practices" from existing information. In recognition of the need to delineate best practices, the remainder of this chapter reviews prediction studies and early intervention programs.

EARLY IDENTIFICATION

At times it seems that human activities would cease if individuals did not engage in predicting future events. If we did not anticipate or expect certain events to happen, farmers would not plant crops, car manufacturers would not produce cars, insurance companies would not sell policies, and perhaps an aspiring young person would not send gifts to the apple of his/her eye. The accuracy of one's predictions directly influences one's degree of confidence.

The process of early identification lacks the preciseness that is needed to engage in it with extreme confidence. At this point it is the responsibility of diagnosticians to improve the accuracy of early identification procedures. The prediction of which young children will experience school failure must be approached cautiously and thoroughly.

Prediction Models

In order to improve in accuracy, the diagnostician should use an evaluation model to determine the usefulness of any instrument. Table 12.1 displays the 2 x 2 matrix, revealing four possible relationships between the performance on the diagnostic instrument and performance on the criterion measure (measure being predicted to, e.g., reading achievement). Based on a poor score or performance, the diagnostic instrument predicts that the child is high-risk (condition present); a good score or performance yields a prediction of no risk (condition absent). Although any handicapping condition exists on a continuum, decisions on whether or not to place a child in a special program is a dichotomous one: the child is or is not placed. Thus, Table 12.1 is realistic for decision-making purposes. Once the child is diagnosed, she can either

TABLE 12.1

The evaluation of diagnostic instruments in early identification.

Performance on Criterion Measure

		Poor	Good
Performance on Diagnostic Instrument	Poor (LD present)	Predicted poor and achieving poorly PP	Predicted poor and achieving "good" PG
	Good (LD absent)	Predicted good and achieving poorly GP	Predicted good and achieving "good" GG

exhibit LD (high risk) or not. In the area of learning disabilities the accuracy of the original prediction is usually determined by administering achievement tests (criterion measures) at a later date.

Quadrant PP represents individuals who performed poorly both on the diagnostic instrument and the criterion measure (i.e., predicted LD and became LD). The decision to place these children in a special program would be accurate. Quadrant PG represents children who performed poorly on the diagnostic instrument but performed well on the criterion measure. Placement of children in this quadrant represents false positives (i.e., prediction that a child is LD when the child is not LD). The placement of these children in a special program is not warranted.

Quadrant GP represents children who performed "good" on the diagnostic instrument but did poorly on the criterion measure. Placement of children in this quadrant results in false negatives (i.e., children who are LD but are not identified [condition not present] by the diagnostic instrument). Quadrant GG includes the children who did well on both the diagnostic instrument and the criterion measure. These children are correctly identified; therefore, educational placement decisions regarding them are accurate. It is apparent that the children in quadrants PP and GG are correctly identified, whereas the children in quadrants PG and GP are incorrectly identified. Thus, a predictive instrument may be evaluated by examining the number of children located in each quadrant.

Horizontal Evaluation of the Matrix

One way of examining the placement of children in each quadrant is by determining the percentages for each quadrant by going from left to right or horizontally. This approach involves examining the matrix as based on prediction scores. For the sake of illustration, Table 12.2 has a number of children in each quadrant. Inspection of the table reveals that 100 children (quadrants PP and PG) performed poorly on the diagnostic test. Quadrant PP indicates that 80 of these children were correctly identified; quadrant PG shows that 20 were incorrectly identified (false positives). Thus, the percentages for quadrants PP and PG are 80% and 20%, respectively. These percentages mean that of the children identified by the test as LD, 80% actually ended up as LD and 20% did not become LD. The numbers in quadrants GP and GG indicate that 300 children performed well on the

TABLE 12.2

Evaluating the matrix horizontally.

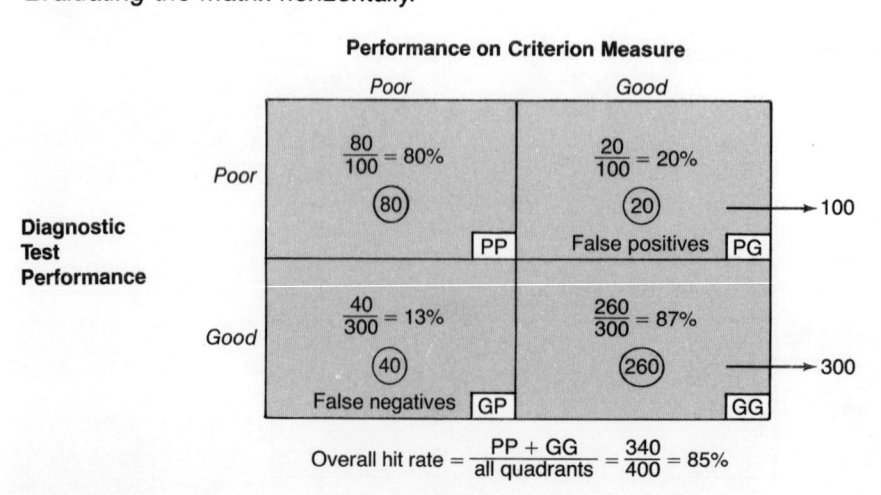

Performance on Criterion Measure

	Poor	Good	
Diagnostic Test Performance Poor	$\frac{80}{100} = 80\%$ (80) PP	$\frac{20}{100} = 20\%$ (20) False positives PG	→ 100
Good	$\frac{40}{300} = 13\%$ (40) False negatives GP	$\frac{260}{300} = 87\%$ (260) GG	→ 300

Overall hit rate = $\frac{PP + GG}{\text{all quadrants}} = \frac{340}{400} = 85\%$

diagnostic instrument. Of these 300, 40 children (13%) were misdiagnosed (false negatives) because they actually became LD, and 260 children (87%) were correctly diagnosed because they did not become LD. Finally, the overall hit rate (number of children correctly identified) for the diagnostic instrument is determined by dividing the total number of children in quadrants *PP* and *GG* (340) by the total number of children in all quadrants (400).

Organizing a matrix allows the user to examine different ratios and determine appropriate cutoff points. For example, Table 12.2 reveals an impressive overall hit rate of 85%, but general accuracy is not always a major concern. A study by Whiting, Clarke, and Morris (1969) vividly illustrates the problem of only examining the overall hit rate. They tested the validity of the *Stott Test of Motor Impairment* by administering it to 106 children. They used a pediatric exam as a validating criterion for motor impairment. Table 12.3 displays the results. Gallagher and Bradley (1972) comment,

> The authors [Whiting, et al.] report a statistically significant relationship between test and pediatrician. However, such a description misses the point. One can either report that there was correspondence between pediatrician and test on 102 of 106 cases, giving an impressive 96 percent agreement; or point out that three-sevenths of those truly impaired were missed by the test, a not so impressive 42 percent error. (p. 94)

Inaccurate interpretations may result if the matrix is only examined from a horizontal viewpoint. For example, in Table 12.2 the overall hit rate is an impressive 85% and the false negative rate (GP) looks good at 13%. However, out of 120 children (quadrants *PP* and *GP*) who actually performed poorly on the criterion measure, the diagnostic instrument missed 33% (40 out of 120) of them. Since this mistake may result in 33% of the children who need special intervention not receiving it, it is a very important observation. This observation is obtained from deriving the percentages in a vertical fashion.

Vertical Evaluation of the Matrix

By using ratios that are obtained vertically, one can compute percentages based on performance on the criterion measure. For example, in Table 12.4 an inspection of quadrants *PP* and *GP* reveals that 120 children scored poorly on the criterion test (i.e., these children are LD). Of these 120 children, the diagnostic

TABLE 12.3

Evaluation matrix for Whiting, Clarke, and Morris's (1969) study.

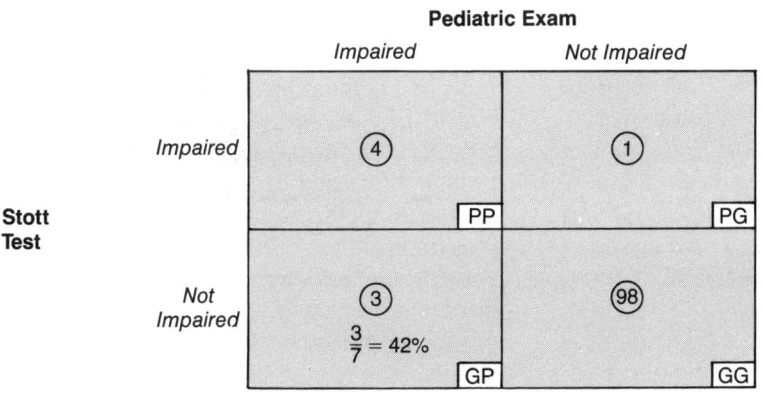

		Pediatric Exam	
		Impaired	Not Impaired
Stott Test	Impaired	4 (PP)	1 (PG)
	Not Impaired	3 $\frac{3}{7}$ = 42% (GP)	98 (GG)

Overall hit rate = $\frac{102}{106}$ = 96%

TABLE 12.4

Evaluating the matrix vertically.

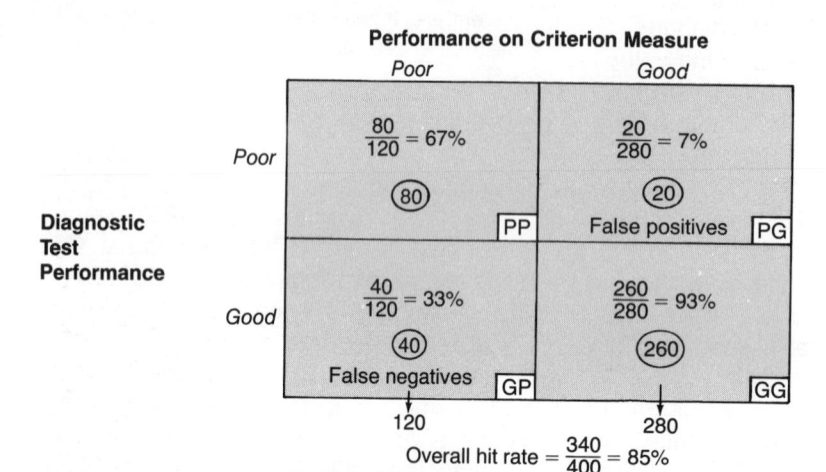

		Performance on Criterion Measure	
		Poor	Good
Diagnostic Test Performance	Poor	$\frac{80}{120} = 67\%$ ⓼⓪ PP	$\frac{20}{280} = 7\%$ ②⓪ False positives PG
	Good	$\frac{40}{120} = 33\%$ ④⓪ False negatives GP	$\frac{260}{280} = 93\%$ ②⑥⓪ GG
		↑ 120	↑ 280

Overall hit rate $= \frac{340}{400} = 85\%$

instrument correctly identified 80 and misdiagnosed 40. Thus, 67% of the poorly performing children were accurately diagnosed, and 33% (false negatives) were not identified. An inspection of quadrants *PG* and *GG* shows that 280 children performed well on the criterion measure; these children represent the group who are not LD. Of the 280 children, 260 (93%) were correctly identified, and 20 (7%—false positives) were incorrectly identified.

Comprehensive Evaluation of the Matrix

A quick inspection of Tables 12.2 and 12.4 shows that the horizontal and vertical methods yield different percentages with the same data. In a review of early identification studies, Mercer (1975) reports that most prediction studies only provide a horizontal evaluation. Satz and Fletcher ("Early Screening," in press) point out, that grossly inaccurate conclusions may be made if the vertical method is not used. Using the work of Meehl and Rosen (1955), they provide a strong argument for using the vertical method; however, they do not discuss the useful information that is derived from the horizontal method. Gallagher and Bradley (1972) combine portions of the vertical and horizontal methods to evaluate the matrix. They use the horizontal approach to compute false positives (quadrant *PG*) and the vertical approach to compute false negatives (quadrant *GP*). In essence, Gallagher and Bradley use the two error scores, the overall hit rate, and visual inspection to evaluate the matrix.

It is apparent that the horizontal and vertical methods yield different but useful information. However, the usefulness of the information depends on accurately interpreting the data from each procedure. The matrix primarily serves to improve the accuracy of decision-making regarding placement. In this respect, an examination of false positives and false negatives is critical in determining cutoff points. Gallagher and Bradley (1972) report that these error ratios are linked together; therefore, a change in the cutoff point changes both ratios simultaneously. For example, on the prediction instrument, a cutoff point of 20 may be selected for identifying LD children. Figure 12.1, p. 346, displays the realtionship between the false positives and false negatives with a cutoff of 20.

An attempt to reduce the false positive error (misidentification of normals) by lowering the cutoff score will increase the false negative error (the number of real LD children who are missed by the lower cutoff). A thorough study of these errors must include a horizontal and a vertical evaluation. The wisest approach in evaluating the matrix would be to examine the percentages from both ways. These eight

These correctly identified children are benefiting from special instruction.

scores and an overall hit rate provide maximum information (see Table 12.5) from which the user may make decisions concerning the usefulness of individual prediction instruments or procedures.

The correct interpretation of each percentage is basic to determining the usefulness of prediction procedures. In order to facilitate accurate interpretations of the percentages as shown in Table 12.5, p. 346, the following brief meanings of each percentage are provided.

VALID POSITIVES (*positive* means the condition [LD] is present)

1. Poor/Poor Horizontal. PP_h (80%) represents the percentage of children who were identified as LD by the prediction instrument and who become classified as LD.
2. Poor/Poor Vertical. PP_v (67%) represents the percentage of children who were classified as LD by the criterion measure and who were identified as LD by the prediction instrument.

FALSE POSITIVES

3. Poor/Good Horizontal. PG_h (20%) represents the percentage of children who were identified as LD by the prediction instrument but who did not become classified as LD.
4. Poor/Good Vertical. PG_v (7%) represents the percentage of children who were not classified as LD on the criterion measure but who were identified as LD by the prediction instrument. False positives result in placing a child in a special program when it is not warranted. Mercer, Algozzine, and Trifiletti (in press) note that false positives are tolerable when the program minimizes the negative effects of labeling.

FALSE NEGATIVES (*negative* means the condition [LD] is absent)

5. Good/Poor Horizontal. GP_h (13%) represents the percentage of children who were not identified by the prediction instrument as LD and who became classified as LD.

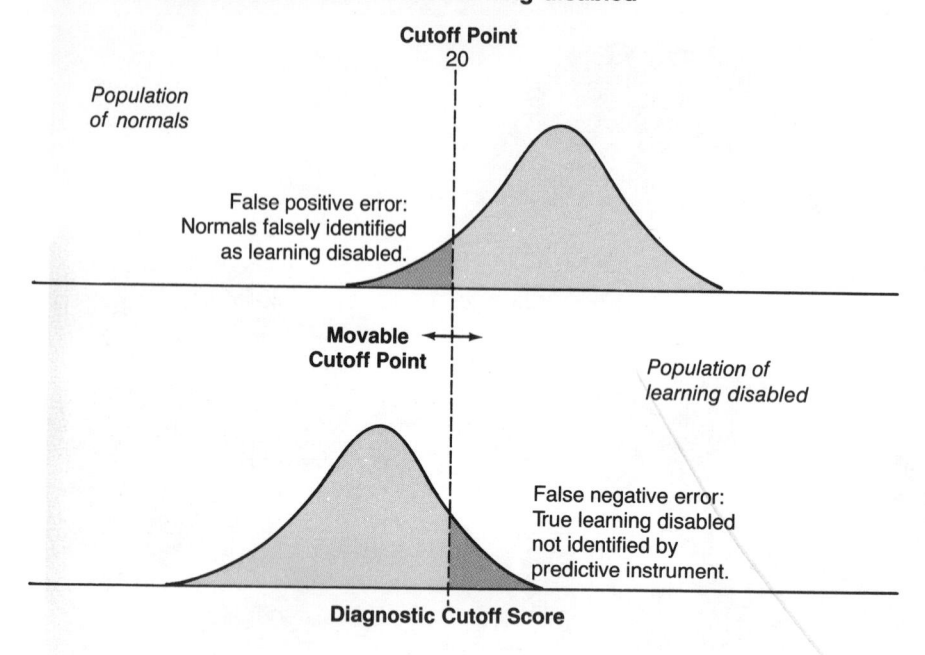

FIGURE 12.1

Errors in relation to cutoff point.

Source. Adapted in part from "Early Identification of Developmental Difficulties" by J. J. Gallagher & R. H. Bradley. In I. J. Gordon (Ed.), *Early Childhood Education: The Seventy-First Yearbook of the National Society for the Study of Education* (Part II). Chicago, Ill.: Distributed by The University of Chicago Press, 1972, p. 93. Reprinted by permission of the National Society for the Study of Education.

TABLE 12.5

Evaluating the matrix horizontally and vertically.

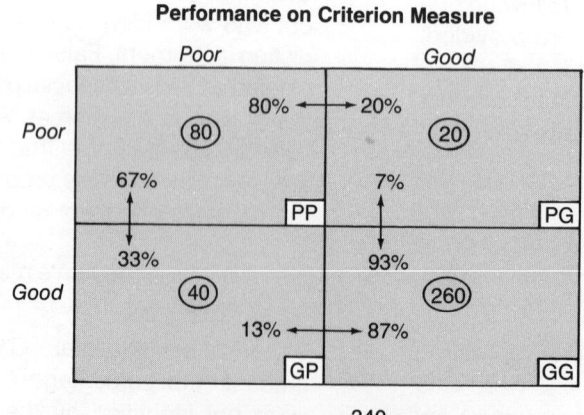

Overall hit rate = $\frac{340}{400}$ = 85%

of delays in age-experienced skills (e.g., language and formal operations) of older children. As pointed out by Satz et al., the theory postulates that developmental reading disorders "are explained as delays in those crucial *early* sensori-perceptual and *later* conceptual-linguistic skills that are intrinsic to the acquisition of reading" (p. 12).

The standardization Satz battery consists of 22 variables. To arrive at an optimal predictor score from the variables, Satz et al. (in press) perform a discriminant function analysis. The analysis yields a composite predictor score that places a child in a high- or low-risk category and gives a "best fit" between predictors and criterion measures each year. Thus, Satz's cutoff score is not fixed at the time of kindergarten testing and varies in each follow-up year. The criterion variable consists of a classroom reading level as determined by a questionnaire given to individual teachers. Based on these levels the children are divided into four reading groups: severely disabled, mildly disabled, average, and superior. From a special educator's viewpoint it is feasible in designing the evaluation matrix for Satz's studies to consider only the severely disabled as high-risk. This group consisted of 10–20% of his population and many of these learners would not even qualify for special education. For example, the recommended incidence figure for learning disabilities (of which reading problems are the primary reason for referral) is 2%, thus reflecting a more severe problem than defined by Satz's severely disabled reader. At the end of second grade the severely disabled reader is defined as being at primer level or below and at the end of the fifth grade the severely disabled reader is defined as being at third reader (approximately third grade) or below. In evaluating his data Satz usually includes the mildly disabled reader in the high-risk group, but on several occasions (Satz & Friel, 1974; Satz et al., in press) the severe individuals were the only ones included in the high-risk group. In the analysis of test batteries presented in Table 12.6, only severes are considered as high-risk.

Satz's Studies

Table 12.6 shows that the first four studies involve a longitudinal investigation with 473 kindergarten white males.

1. Of the 22 predictor variables, several emerged as superior after 3 years. In rank order they are *(a)* finger localization test, *(b)* alphabet recitation test, *(c)* recognition-discrimination test, and *(d)* day of testing. The remaining 18 tests contributed less than 1% to the total hit rate.
2. At the end of 6 years, the rank order of the predictor variables was *(a)* finger localization test, *(b) Peabody Picture Vocabulary Test (PPVT), (c) Beery Developmental Test of Visual Motor Integration,* and *(d)* alphabet recitation test.
3. The criterion variable of classroom reading level was validated with standardized achievement testing.
4. In addition to a reading disability, the severes exhibited an overall achievement disability.
5. Two abbreviated test batteries consisting of the best predictor variables were developed. The *Satz Abbreviated Screening Battery* ($N = 5$) takes about 30–50 minutes to administer and includes the following: *(a)* finger localization test, *(b)* reception-discrimination test, *(c) PPVT, (d) Beery Developmental Test of Visual Motor Integration,* and *(e)* socioeconomic status. The second abbreviated battery ($N = 8$) adds three more tests to the preceding five: *(a)* dichotic listening, *(b) Wepman Test of Auditory Discrimination,* and *(c) Embedded Figures.*
6. During the period from second to fifth grade, more children shifted into the severe group.

An examination of the longitudinal study (first four studies in Table 12.6) conducted by Satz and his colleagues yields several noteworthy observations. For example, the major strengths of the Satz battery are the overall hit

TABLE 12.6

An analysis of test batteries as predictors using horizontal and vertical percentages.[a]

Study	Sample	Prediction Instrument	Length of Prediction	Criterion Test	Valid Positives PP$_h$	Valid Positives PP$_v$	False Positives PG$_h$	False Positives PG$_v$	False Negatives GP$_h$	False Negatives GP$_v$	Valid Negatives GG$_h$	Valid Negatives GG$_v$	Overall Hit[b]
Satz & Friel (1974)	473 kindergartners (white males)	Satz Battery	End of 1st grade; 2 yrs.	Teacher rating of reading using a scale	16	100	84	21	0	0	100	79	79
Reported in Satz et al. (in press)	458/473 kindergartners (white males)	Satz Battery	End of 2nd grade; 3 yrs.	Classroom reading level	28	89	72	31	2	11	98	69	71
Reported in Satz et al. (in press)	419/473 kindergartners (white males)	Satz Battery	End of 2nd grade; 3 yrs.	Classroom reading level & *IOTA* word recognition	34	91	66	34	3	9	97	66	70
Reported in Satz et al. (in press)	442/473 kindergartners (white males)	Satz Battery	End of 5th grade; 6 yrs.	Classroom reading level	63	58	37	9	11	42	89	91	84
Satz, Friel, & Rudegeair (1976)	new children; 175 kindergartners (white males)	Abbreviated Satz Battery	End of 2nd grade; 3 yrs.	Classroom reading level	29	89	71	25	2	11	98	75	76

Study	Sample	Predictor	Criterion	Interval							
Satz & Friel (1978)	105/132 kindergartners (male, female, black, white)	*Abbreviated Satz Battery*	Classroom reading level; *IOTA* word recognition	End of 2nd grade; 2 yrs.	44	89	56	26	3	11	97	74	77
Satz et al. (in press)	114 kindergartners (male, female, black, white); Follow-up	*Abbreviated Satz Battery*	Classroom reading level	End of 1st grade; 2 yrs.	60	71	40	11	7	29	93	89	86
Satz et al. (in press)	Same as above	*Language Battery*	Classroom reading level	End of 1st grade; 2 yrs.	55	71	45	13	7	29	93	87	84
de Hirsch, Jansky, & Langford (1966)	53 kindergartners	de Hirsch index of 37 variables	Gray Oral; Gates Reading	2 yrs.	71	91	29	10	3	9	97	90	91
Feshback, Adelman, & Fuller (1974)	572 kindergartners	*de Hirsch Predictive Index*	Gates-MacGinitie Reading Test	15 mo.	61	26	39	74	25	7	75	93	73
Eaves, Kendall, & Crichton (1972)	50 kindergartners	*Predictive Index, Draw a Person, & name printing*	Medical diagnosis of MBD	Concurrent; immediate	88	96	12	4	4	11	96	89	92
Eaves et al. (1974)	42 kindergartners; Follow-up	*MPI*; neuropediatric exam; psychological exam	Recommended grade placement	End of 2nd grade; 2 yrs.	65	81	35	27	14	19	86	73	76

TABLE 12.6 cont.

Study	Sample	Prediction Instrument	Length of Prediction	Criterion Test	Valid Positives PP$_h$	PP$_v$	False Positives PG$_h$	PG$_v$	False Negatives GP$_h$	GP$_v$	Valid Negatives GG$_h$	GG$_v$	Overall Hit[b]
Eaves et al. (1974)	163 kindergartners	MPI	2 yrs.	Recommended grade placement	59	63	41	10	8	37	92	90	85
Book (1974)	425 kindergartners	MRT, Bender, Slosson	9 mos.	Level achieved on Scott Foresman Reading Series	93	48	7	3	31	52	69	97	75
Book (1974)	425 kindergartners	MRT, Bender, Slosson	2 yrs.	Level achieved on Scott Foresman Reading Series	55	94	45	13	1	6	99	87	88

Note.
[a] Only studies that provide enough data to complete the matrix are listed.
[b] The median overall hit is 79.

rate for the 6 years and the accuracy in identifying valid negatives (i.e., a high percentage of the children identified as low risk do not become disabled readers). The battery appears to have more difficulty in accurately identifying the high-risk children. These problems are apparent in the overall low percentages in the PP_h and PP_v (6 years only) columns and in the high percentages in the PG_h, PG_v (exclude 6 years), and the GP_v columns (6 years only).

At the conclusion of the investigation, Satz et al. (in press) provided information that allows an inspection of the prediction accuracy using four classificiations. Using the abbreviated battery scores, 442 children were assigned to four levels (severe + +, mild +, average −, superior − −) and probabilities were examined regarding treatment/no-treatment decisions. If + + were the only group to receive treatment, the following percentages would result:

PP_h	PP_v	PG_h	PG_v
64%	53%	36%	8%
GP_h	GP_v	GG_h	GG_v
11%	47%	89%	92%

Overall Hit
84%

These percentages are similar to the 6-year findings. In terms of treatment decisions, it appears that 42/90 (GP_v) of the severes would not receive treatment. This error (false negatives) reduces prevention efforts. Moreover, 27/75 (PG_h) of the children identified as severe would receive unwarranted treatment. This error (false positives) increases the likelihood that the child will face the undesirable effects of labeling. Regarding valid negatives, 100% of the children identified as superior (− −) were correctly placed in the no-treatment condition. Again, the Satz battery—although strong in identifying low-risk children—has difficulty identifying those at high risk.

The Satz, Friel, and Rudegeair (1976) study is a cross-validation study of the battery. The results of this study (see Table 12.6) are similar to the original 3-year prediction study (horizontal row 2).

Satz and Friel (1978) report on the findings of an investigation with 105 kindergartners who were followed for 2 years. Unlike the 6-year study, their sample includes males, females, blacks, and whites. They used the *Satz Abbreviated Battery* ($N = 8$); the results present the same pattern found in the 6-year results. When only the severe group is used as high risk for special education, the problem area is in identifying high-risk children—the strengths are in the overall hit rate and the identification of valid negatives.

In the final Satz et al. (in press) study, a language battery was administered to 114 kindergartners for the purpose of comparing it with the Satz abbreviated battery. The language battery consisted of the verbal fluency test, *ITPA* Grammatical Closure Test, *Syntax Test* (Scholes, Tanis, & Turner, 1975), the *Berry-Talbot* (morphology), and the *PPVT*. In this battery, socioeconomic status ranked highest, followed by grammatical closure, *PPVT,* word fluency, *Berry-Talbot,* and *Syntax*. As noted in Table 12.6, the language battery and Satz's abbreviated battery produced very similar results.

Due to the unique definition of *severe,* the high number of false negatives, and the changing of cutoff scores each year to obtain a "best fit" between predictor and criterion measures, the Satz battery should be used with full consideration of its strengths and weaknesses. Also, one must consider the time, materials, and personnel that are needed for administration.

de Hirsch's Studies

De Hirsch, Jansky, and Langford (1966) conducted a well-known prediction study with a small sample of 53 lower-middle-class kindergartners. Their original battery consisted of 37 variables and the criterion measures were standard reading tests *(Gray Oral* and *Gates).* At the end of a 2-year follow-up, they found:

1. No background information was a significant predictor.
2. IQ was correlated to reading but not to spelling and writing.
3. Prediction for the girls was more accurate.
4. CA was a significant predictor.
5. Blacks equaled whites except for the spelling.

From the 37 predictor variables they recommend the following *Modified Predictive Index:* (a) pencil use, (b) Bender Visual-Motor Gestalt Test, (c) Wepman Auditory Discrimination Test, (d) Number of words used in a story, (e) categories, (f) Horst Reversals Test, (g) Gates Word-Matching Subtests, (h) Word Recognition I, (i) Word Recognition II, and (j) Word Reproduction. The full de Hirsch index (see Table 12.6) yielded an impressive 91% hit rate. Overall the percentages are good, with the exception of false positives. This error results in misplacing children into intervention. Gallagher and Bradley (1972) indicate that these results are seriously marred because the authors applied the index to the same population on whom it was developed. They note that the de Hirsch index needs cross validation. In a later work, Jansky and de Hirsch (1972) developed a *Final Screening Index* based on 355 children. The five subtests of this index correlate .66 with second grade level. The most powerful predictors on the index are letter naming and picture naming.

Feshback, Adelman, and Fuller (1974) administered the *de Hirsch Predictive Index* to 572 kindergartners. The criterion test was the *Gates-MacGinitie Reading Test,* administered in the second grade. The percentages in Table 12.6 indicate that the overall hit rate is a low 73% and the false positives are usually high. Overall these results provide little support for using the *de Hirsch Predictive Index.*

Eaves, Kendall, and Crichton (1972) administered the *de Hirsch Predictive Index* and two other measures to 50 kindergartners. The criterion measure consisted of medical and psychological exams to diagnose minimal brain dysfunction (MBD) and immaturity. The criterion measure was administered immediately and compared with the predictors. The results in Table 12.6 are formidable but this study is a concurrent validity study and these results are not based on the performance of the children followed over a period of time.

However, Eaves, Kendall, and Crichton (1974) conducted a 2-year follow-up study of these children. They used the *de Hirsch Modified Predictive Index (MPI),* a neuropediatric exam, and a psychological exam as the prediction battery, and teacher-recommended grade placement as the criterion measure. The overall hit rate for this extensive battery is 76%. The battery produced a high percentage of false positives.

In another prediction study with 163 kindergartners, Eaves, Kendall, & Crichton (1974) used the *MPI* as a prediction instrument and teacher-recommended grade placement as the criterion measure. The overall hit rate was a high 85%, but many false negatives (37% GP_v) occurred. This battery was especially strong in identifying valid negatives.

Book (1974) conducted a 2-year prediction study using a battery consisting of the *Metropolitan Readiness Test,* the *Bender Gestalt,* and the *Slosson Intelligence Test.* The prediction instrument classified the children into six categories. Book followed them for 2 years. The criterion measure consisted of level of reading in the Scott Foresman Reading Series. Overall, the percentages in Table 12.6 are impressive for the 2-year follow-up. The overall hit rate, the valid negatives, and the false negatives are good. The weak area is in the high number of false positives.

Summary

Satz et al. (in press) report that several conditions need to be adhered to in prediction research:

1. A sufficient amount of time should exist between the initial testing and the criterion measure (e.g., 4–6 years).
2. The population should be large and homogeneous (e.g., all middle class, all boys) to eliminate the confounding variables of sex, race, and socioeconomic level.
3. The prediction instrument should be cross-validated with a separate group of children.
4. The prediction instrument should originate from a theoretical base.

To date, only the work of Satz and his colleagues meets these conditions. However, it does not appear that the results of their research justify the expense and time incurred from administering the battery of tests. Further work with all the batteries appears warranted. To date, the Book (1974) and de Hirsch batteries identify a high percentage of false positives. Likewise, the Satz battery identifies a large percentage of false positives. Any of the three may eventually yield the delicate combination of variables that is needed for the highly accurate identification of high-risk children during or before they reach kindergarten. Badian (1976) reports that special predictive batteries have yet to yield high enough predictive validity to compensate for their disadvantages in cost, effort, and time.

Single Instruments as Predictors

The majority of prediction studies use single instruments as predictors. These instruments are readily categorized into readiness, intelligence, language, and perceptual-motor tests. In addition, several investigators have examined physical factors. Of the 70 studies reviewed, only a few report the data that are needed to generate a matrix. Table 12.7 examines these few.

Readiness Tests

An inspection of Table 12.7 indicates that the *Metropolitan Reading Readiness Test (MRRT)* yields some impressive percentages for a single instrument (Ferinden & Jacobson, 1970; Lessler & Bridges, 1973). The *MRRT* does a good job of identifying valid positives over both a short and long range. In the large sample it has the most difficulty with false negatives, yet it yields a good overall hit rate. Lessler and Bridges (1973) compared the *MRRT* with the *Lee Clark Reading Readiness Test (LC)* and the *California Test of Mental Maturity (CTMM)* and conclude that the *MRRT* is the best predictor of the three.

Moreover, the *Metropolitan Readiness Test (MRT)* is a frequently used test of academic readiness (Maitland, Nadeau, & Nadeau, 1974). Badian (1976) presents a summary of correlations between the *MRT* and later reading achievement (see Table 12.8). The median correlation for 37 studies is .58. Table 12.8, p. 358, shows correlations for the *Lee Clark* and the *Clymer Barrett Prereading Battery*. Badian concludes that on the average, group-administered readiness tests yield better prediction results than both group intelligence tests and most individually administered intelligence tests. Moreover, letter naming is simple to administer and has a high correlation with later achievement. Dykstra (1967) notes that this test is one of the best predictors of later reading achievement.

Intelligence Tests

Only one study using an intelligence test as a predictor was located that provided enough information to generate a matrix. Lessler and Bridges (1973) used the *California Test of Mental Maturity (CTMM)* as a predictor and the *California Achievement Test (CAT)* and teacher rating as criterion measures. The percentages in Table 12.7 reveal a respectable overall hit rate of 80%, with a higher percentage of false negatives being the problem area. The correlations (reported in Table 12.8) of intelligence tests with achievement range from .39 to .53. These correlations are generally lower than those of readiness tests.

Language Tests

Many theorists and researchers purport that adequate language development is a precur-

TABLE 12.7

An analysis of single tests as predictors using horizontal and vertical percentages.

Study	Sample	Prediction Instrument	Length of Prediction	Criterion Test	Valid Positives PP_h	PP_v	False Positives PG_h	PG_v	False Negatives GP_h	GP_v	Valid Negatives GG_h	GG_v	Overall Hit[a]
Readiness Tests													
Ferinden & Jacobson (1970)	67 kindergartners	Evanston Early Identification Scale	8 mos.	WRAT Reading	56	50	44	17	20	50	80	83	73
Ferinden & Jacobson (1970)	64 kindergartners	WRAT Reading	8 mos.	WRAT Reading	63	100	37	27	0	0	100	73	81
Ferinden & Jacobson (1970)	67 kindergartners	MRRT	8 mos.	WRAT Reading	57	85	43	28	8	15	92	72	76
Lessler & Bridges (1973)	293 1st graders	MRRT	9 mos.	CAT & teacher rating	86	87	14	14	13	13	87	86	86
Lessler & Bridges (1973)	196 1st graders; Follow-up	MRRT	End of 2nd grade; 21 mos.	CAT & teacher rating	91	62	9	10	39	38	61	90	73
Lessler & Bridges (1973)	293 1st graders	Lee Clark Reading Readiness Test	9 mos.	CAT & teacher rating	82	77	18	17	22	23	78	83	80
Intelligence Tests													
Lessler & Bridges (1973)	293 1st graders	Calif. Test of Mental Maturity	9 mos.	CAT & teacher rating	82	78	18	18	22	22	78	82	80

Language Tests

Lyons & Bangs (1972)	35 1st graders	LLAT	1½ yrs. with special intervention	SRA Arithmetic	67	35	33	33	65	65	35	67	46
Lyons & Bangs (1972)	23 1st graders	LLAT	1½ yrs. without special intervention	SRA Arithmetic	91	71	9	11	33	29	67	89	78
Lyons & Bangs (1972)	35 1st graders	LLAT	1½ yrs. with special intervention	SRA Reading	30	70	70	64	25	30	75	36	46
Lyons & Bangs (1972)	23 1st graders	LLAT	1½ yrs. without special intervention	SRA Reading	82	75	18	18	25	25	75	82	78

Perceptual-Motor Tests

Keogh & Smith (1970)	26 kindergartners	Bender	6 yrs.	CAT Reading	47	88	53	44	9	13	91	56	65
Keogh & Smith (1970)	26 kindergartners	Bender	6 yrs.	CAT Arithmetic	40	100	60	45	0	0	100	55	65

Physical Factors

Galante, Flye, & Stephens (1972)	71 kindergartners	Unusual birth history	7 yrs.	Stanford Achievement & Horn Expectancy	56	41	44	14	24	59	76	86	72
Galante, Flye, & Stephens (1972)	71 kindergartners	Birth order	7 yrs.	Stanford Achievement & Horn Expectancy	25	27	75	37	34	73	66	63	52

Note.
[a] The median overall hit is 73.

TABLE 12.8

Correlations of prediction instruments with achievement.

Predictive Test	No. of Correlations	Range	Median
Readiness Tests			
MRT	37	.22–.78	.58
Lee-Clark	11	.43–.74	.57
Clymer-Barrett	5	.40–.69	.61
MSST	4	.53–.82	.64
Letter naming	19	.39–.79	.55
Intelligence Tests			
Group IQ tests	22	.10–.73	.45
WISC and WPPSI	11	.20–.57	.39
Stanford-Binet	5	.31–.62	.53
Language Tests			
PPVT	4	.16–.62	.345
ITPA	7	.13–.43	.32
Perceptual-Motor			
Bender	25	.17–.68	.39
Figure drawings	6	.23–.46	.28
Frostig DTVP	8	.06–.62	.425

Note.
MRT = Metropolitan Readiness Test
PPVT = Peabody Picture Vocabulary Test
ITPA = Illinois Test of Psycholinguistic Abilities
MSST = Meeting Street School Screening Test
DTVP = Developmental Test of Visual Perception

Source. Adapted in part from "Early Prediction of Academic Underachievement" by N. A. Badian. Paper presented at the meeting of the 54th Annual International Convention of the Council for Exceptional Children, Chicago, April 1976, p. 44. Reprinted by permission of N. A. Badian.

sor to academic achievement. Language skills develop at a rapid rate during the preschool years; a test sensitive to a delay in this development might predict later academic failure. Table 12.7 charts the prediction results of the *Language and Learning Assessment for Training Test (LLAT)*. Lyons and Bangs (1972) used it to predict reading and arithmetic over 2 academic years. In these studies of 35 children, intensive intervention was provided to the high-risk group. Intervention powerfully influenced the very low percentages (overall hit rate = 46%). This study indicates that the later achievement of kindergartners depends to a large extent on the child's educational program. In the studies in which the high-risk children did not receive special intervention, the *LLAT* yielded high percentages, with an overall hit rate of 78%. The language tests in Table 12.8 have low correlations with achievement.

Perceptual-Motor Tests

The *Bender Visual-Motor Gestalt Test* is frequently used to identify high-risk children. Badian (1976) presents 25 *Bender* academic achievement correlations from 12 studies. As noted in Table 12.8, the median correlation in this group of studies is a low .39. In the Keogh and Smith (1970) study, the *Bender* yielded a low overall hit rate of 65% but produced some interesting individual percentages. For example, it has good false negative percentages but does this at the expense of producing a large number of false positives. Ferinden and Jacobson (1970) and Keogh and Smith (1961) note that a good score on the *Bender* usually means the child will achieve satisfactorily, but that a low *Bender* is not predictive. Koppitz (1964) and Norfleet (1973) report that the test predicts effectively for lower socioeconomic children but poorly with higher SES children. Views of its value as a predictor vary, but data justifying its use over other single instruments appear lacking.

Physical Factors

The overwhelming majority of prediction studies with the mildly handicapped have been initiated at kindergarten. Information regarding the early identification of the high-risk child prior to the age of 5 is sparse. Several investigators are examining physical factors as predictors of learning disabilities (Galante, Flye, & Stephens, 1972); this area may help facilitate the accurate identification of the infant and preschool high-risk child.

The studies of physical factors as predictors may be grouped into prospective and retrospective studies. They focus on perinatal and developmental history (Denhoff, Hainsworth, & Hainsworth, 1972; Hoffman, 1971; Pasamanick, Rogers, & Lilienfeld, 1956; Wilborn & Smith, 1974), physical anomalies (Waldrop & Goering, 1971; Waldrop, Pedersen, & Bell, 1968), and dental enamel defects (Cohen & Diner, 1970). In the prospective studies, children are followed from prenatal checkups onward. In the retrospective studies, the records and histories of children with learning problems are examined. In the retrospective procedure it is important to remember that there is much room for error (e.g., parents may not relate an accurate history).

Mercer and Trifiletti (1977) summarize studies concerning perinatal and developmental history as prediction factors (see next page). An examination of Table 12.9 shows that in the histories of LD children, prolonged labor, difficult delivery, creeping late, walking late, and developing speech late are prevalent.

The percentages of minor physical anomalies and dental enamel defects found in children with learning problems are presented by Mercer and Trifiletti (1977) (Table 12.10, p. 361). The high percentages of LD children with a small head circumference and dental enamel defects highlight an observation of this list.

In the conclusion of her review of the physical factors, Badian (1976) notes,

> Although many of the findings in the infancy studies are contradictory, there appears to be a consensus that a later-born male, who has a history of pre- or peri-natal difficulties and who is not of superior intelligence, is a child at high risk for school learning difficulties. If he is also a boy with several minor physical anomalies, the risk of hyperactive and difficult behavior, and school failure, is very high. (p. 11)

Remember that no single anomaly or historical event can be considered as indicative of learning problems. Constellations of abnormalities, however, are often successful in predicting high-risk children. The Waldrop, Pedersen, and Bell (1968) list uses minor structural anomalies to predict learning problems. The Hoffman (1971) *Learning Problem Indication Index* (LPII) and *Revised LPII* by Wilborn and Smith (1974) combine perinatal history and developmental abnormalities to

TABLE 12.9

Percentage of perinatal history and developmental history prediction factors for learning disabled children.

Prediction Factors	Hoffman (1971) Exp. Group (N = 100)	Hoffman (1971) Control Group (N = 200)	Silver (1971) Exp. Group (N = 372)	Quinn & Rapoport (1974) Exp. Group (N = 81)	Wilborn & Smith (1974) Exp. Group (N = 432)
Perinatal History Factors					
Problems during pregnancy	25%			12.3%	19.2%
Prolonged labor	25%	.5%			11.8%
Difficult delivery	5%	1.5%			24.8%
Prematurity	8%	1%		2.7%	9.1%
Blood incompatability		1%			2.7%
Low birth weight	11%	.5%			9.1%
Cyanosis	10%	.5%			4.5%
Adoption			6.5%[a]		
Developmental History Factors					
Creeping late or abnormal (9 mos.)	50%	7%			9.4%
Walking late (16 mos.)	26%	1%			5.8%
Speech late or abnormal (18 mos.)	70%	4.5%			23.8%
Ambidexterity after 7 yrs.	33%	3%			
Tiptoe walking prolonged beyond 1 mo.	14%	5%			

Note.
[a]This percentage may be compared to the 3.8 national average for adoption in 1971.

Source. Adapted from "The Development of Screening Procedures for the Early Detection of Children with Learning Problems" by C. D. Mercer & J. J. Trifiletti. *The Journal of School Health,* 1977, 47, 527. Copyright 1977 by American School Health Association. Reprinted by permission.

TABLE 12.10

Percentages of minor physical anomalies found in learning disabled children.

Minor Physical Anomalies	Quinn & Rapoport (1974) Exp. Group (N = 81)	Cohen & Diner (1970) Exp. Group (N = 215)	Cohen & Diner (1970) Control Group (N = 130)
Head			
Head Circumference > 1.5 s.d.[a]	53%		
Electric hair[b]	17%		
Eyes			
Epicanthus	24%		
Hypetelorism	32%		
Ears			
Adherent lobes	18%		
Asymmetrical	9%		
Low seated	4%		
Malformed	1%		
Mouth			
High palate	37%		
Furrowed tongue	2%		
Hands			
Fifth finger curved	23%		
Single transverse palmar crease	0%		
Feet			
Gap between first and second toe ≥ ¼ in.	6%		
Partial syndactylia of two middle toes	6%		
Third toe length greater than or equal to second toe	4%		
Dental enamel defects		48%	9.3%

Note.
[a]Standard deviation.
[b]Fine, thin hair.
Source. Adapted from "The Development of Screening Procedures for the Early Detection of Children with Learning Problems" by C. D. Mercer & J. J. Trifiletti. *The Journal of School Health*, 1977, 47, 529. Copyright 1977 by American School Health Association. Reprinted by permission.

predict learning problems. Since it appears that certain constellations of physical factors represent viable predictors of learning problems, it seems plausible to combine them with predictor items from existing instruments in all areas (language, etc.) to produce more powerful procedures for identifying high-risk children. Besides, this information can usually be gathered in a few minutes by a school nurse or teacher.

Teacher Perception as a Predictor

A simple procedure for identifying high-risk children is to ask the teacher. Most studies have used a scale or checklist. Kottmeyer (1947) surveyed the predictive accuracy of

142 teachers' observations for 3,156 children. He reports that their mean accuracy rate was 71.4% and that years of teaching experience was positively correlated with accuracy (e.g., 5 years = 65.9%; 10 years = 75.7%). However, in a more recent study, Kapelis (1975) found no difference in the accuracy of beginning and experienced teachers' judgment. Furthermore, Kottmeyer notes that the teachers were able to predict reading problems about 5% better than the *Metropolitan Readiness Test.*

The school psychologist should receive a report from the child's teacher.

In a study involving the screening of 1,200 kindergartners, Haring and Ridgway (1967) found that teacher observations are a key factor in the early identification of LD. In fact, "the individual behavior analysis done by teachers may prove to be a more effective procedure than group testing in identification" (p. 393). Ferinden and Jacobson (1970) report that 80% of the children identified by teachers actually became problem learners. The teachers made these predictions without the help of a checklist. Ferinden and Jacobson claim that teacher perception coupled with the use of other instruments could yield accuracy of almost 90% or more in screening for potential learning problems. Benger (1968) reports that teachers used a 5-point rating scale to surpass all the tests in a large battery *(Binet,*

Frostig, PPVT, Wepman) in predicting first grade reading. Cowgill, Friedland, and Shapiro (1973) note that the end-of-year reports by kindergarten teachers were successful in predicting learning disabilities. Glazzard (1977) compared the predictive effectiveness of *(a) The Gates-MacGinitie Reading Tests:* Readiness Skills, *(b) The Gates-MacGinitie Reading Test,* Primary A, Form 1, and *(c)* the Kirk teacher rating scale by administering them to 87 kindergartners. She found that all three instruments were effective in predicting first grade reading; however, she concludes that the Kirk teacher rating scale is the most *efficient.*

Table 12.11 reveals some very impressive percentages for teacher perception. In the Keogh and Smith (1970) studies, the teachers were extremely accurate in identifying valid negatives and in identifying the children who actually end up with learning problems *(PP$_v$).* Feshback, Adelman, and Fuller (1974) report that teachers' ratings predicted learning problems at least as efficiently as the de Hirsch battery. It appears Kottmeyer (1947) was right when he concluded that a school system with budget concerns could rely on the judgments of experienced teachers to get fairly accurate predictive results.

Early Identification Perspectives and Guidelines

Selecting Areas of Assessment

The practitioner has much to consider in selecting a procedure or instrument. Figure 12.2, p. 364, presents the major factors that deserve consideration. Initially, one needs to choose which area(s) of assessment will provide relevant information and do an adequate job of predicting to the criterion measure.

Keogh and Becker (1973) recommend the use of screening measures that are close to the criterion measures in both *content* and *time.* Specifically, identification should focus on whether the preschool child has the skills and abilities to succeed in kindergarten or

TABLE 12.11

An analysis of teacher perception as a predictor using horizontal and vertical percentages.

Study	Sample	Prediction Instrument	Length of Prediction	Criterion Test	Valid Positives PP_h	PP_v	False Positives PG_h	PG_v	False Negatives GP_h	GP_v	Valid Negatives GG_h	GG_v	Overall Hit[a]
Keogh & Smith (1970)	20 kindergartners	Teacher rating scale	5 yrs.	CAT Arithmetic	43	100	57	24	0	0	100	76	80
Keogh & Smith (1970)	20 kindergartners	Teacher rating scale	5 yrs.	CAT Reading	71	100	29	13	0	0	100	87	90
Feshbach, Adelman, & Fuller (1974)	585 kindergartners	Student rating scale	15 mos.	Gates-MacGinitie Reading Test	83	30	17	3	24	70	76	97	77

Note.
[a]The median overall hit is 80.

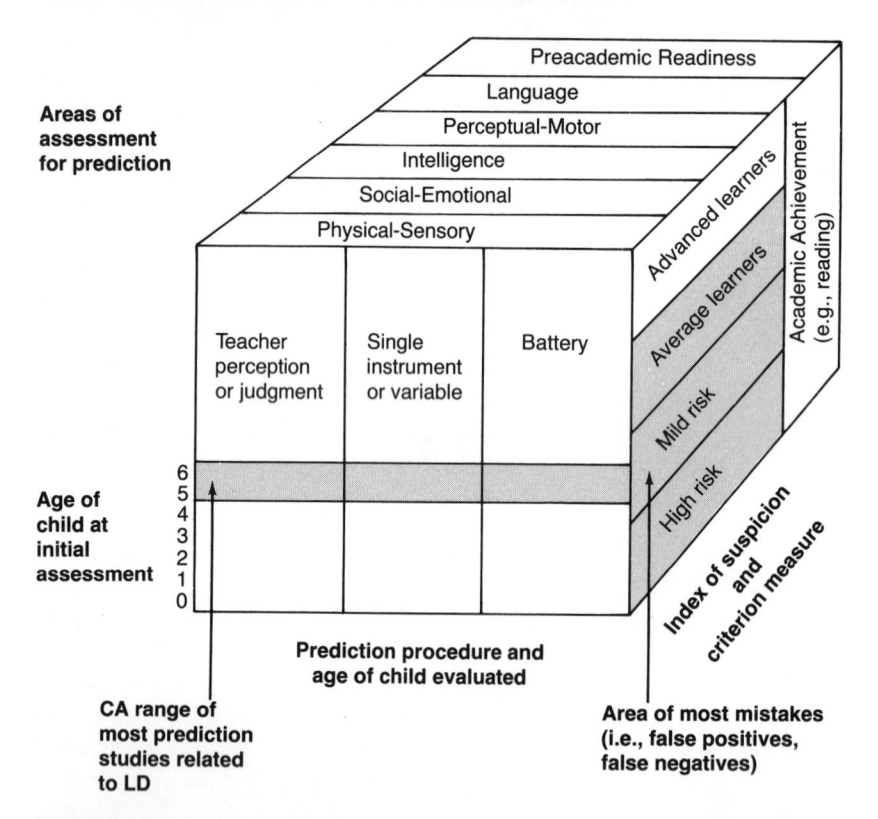

FIGURE 12.2.

Components of early identification.

whether the kindergartner has the skills to succeed in first grade. Preacademic skills in reading, math, and language are usually stressed when screening, and criterion measures are close in content and time. Magliocca, Rinaldi, Crew, and Kunzelmann (1977) identified high-risk preschoolers by means of a frequency sampling technique. The children worked on 1-minute samples (less than 10 minutes of testing) of *academic behavior* (e.g., see letters—say letters; matching colors). They were considered high risk if their frequency of correct responses was in the lower 25% of frequency scores generated by the total kindergarten group. A comparison of the list of high-risk learners identified by the frequency sampling with teacher identification yielded a correlation above .9. This approach concentrates on the immediate needs of the child and deemphasizes long-range predictions.

Keogh and Becker (1973) stress the need for identifying the competence of high-risk children. The recognition of specific skills and abilities provides information that often aids the development of an instructional or preventive program. In addition, the assessment of skills similar to tasks performed in kindergarten or first grade helps determine the child's specific instructional objectives.

Although frequently omitted, the social-emotional area deserves consideration. High-risk individuals can be detected by the assessment of ability to share, work independently, organize play, wait (patience), attend to tasks, and interact with peers and adults (Keogh & Becker, 1973).

All behaviors deserve more study, but existing information provides tentative support for the use of preacademic and academic tasks. Other areas may be added if time and resources are available.

Determining Prediction Procedures

The major procedures for selection are teacher perception, single instrument, or battery. All three may be used to assess in one or more areas. In addition, a unique battery may be formed using a combination of single measures alone or combined with teacher perception. Existing data strongly support teacher perception. Some references that may help in the development of teacher scales include

1. Denhoff, Hainsworth, and Hainsworth (1971), *The Meeting Street School Screening Tests*
2. Novack, Bonaventura, and Merenda (1973), *Rhode Island Pupil Identification Scale*
3. Schleichkorn (1972), checklist
4. Mardell and Goldenberg (1975), Project DIAL

When to Begin Early Identification

Most LD prediction studies test kindergartners. Some evidence indicates that these instruments may be more accurate if administered in the spring of the kindergarten year (Novack, Bonadventura, & Merenda, 1973).

The emphasis of PL 94–142 on providing a free, appropriate public education to the young handicapped child (CA = 3 years) stresses the need for better identification at younger ages. It is apparent that this area needs more study regarding physical indices, developmental history, and socioeconomic status in the early identification of the high-risk infant and preschool child.

Choosing a Criterion Measure

The criterion measure, in essence, represents reality; thus it is important that it be a relevant and valid measure. LD prediction studies have primarily used reading achievement measures for criterion. Other measures include placement level of a child in a reading group, measures in other academic areas, special education placement, teacher judgment, or a combination of measures.

Establishing an Index of Suspicion

The determination of the index of suspicion (degree of handicapping condition) is very often critical. This factor controls whether or not a child receives special intervention. A major consideration at this step is to establish a cutoff score that provides the desired balance between the errors (i.e., false positives and false negatives). False positives may be tolerable when the program is designed to minimize the potential debilitating effects of labeling and allows children the opportunity to work themselves back into the mainstream. False negatives may be tolerable if the no-risk status is not a static decision and children who actually need special intervention are recognized by sensitive teachers and/or measures within a short period of time. In most instances the exclusion of a child who needs special intervention is a more serious error than the inclusion of a child who does not need it. However, for special education purposes the high-risk child is one who is likely to experience serious learning or adjustment problems. Cutoff scores that classify 10–20% of a population as high risk are identifying a much broader population than those eligible for special education.

Conclusions

Based on her review of prediction studies and her own early identification research, Badian (1976) concludes:

> It may be difficult to identify children with potential learning problems because, as some authors have pointed out, among kindergarten children there are very few consistent and identifiable patterns of characteristics associated with future learning problems. Certainly, from the point of view of administrative expediency, as well as from that of predictive accuracy, kindergarten teacher judgments, perhaps based on a behavioral checklist, together with a simple test of ability to name letters and shapes, would seem to contribute as much or even more toward the identification of children likely to underachieve, as the test batteries specially designed for such identification. (p. 29)

Prediction data are being gathered in several major early identification projects. Mardell and Goldenberg (1975) report that initial data from Project DIAL (Developmental Indicators for the Assessment of Learning)[1] are encouraging. It features a battery that concentrates on gross and fine motor skills, concepts, and communication skills.

Project SCREEN (Senf-Comrey Ratings of Extra Educational Need)[2] is another effort in Illinois to develop adequate screening and intervention programs for children with learning disabilities (Senf & Comrey, 1975). SCREEN assesses kindergarten and first grade pupils. Its four tests concentrate on self-concept, visual-auditory skills, figure copying, and basic knowledge. Its teacher rating scale consists of 40 items and focuses on cognitive-perceptual skills, behavioral adjustment, social adjustment, and immaturity. In a series of four articles on SCREEN in the *Journal of Learning Disabilities* during 1975, no data are provided regarding its predictive power.

Projects such as DIAL and SCREEN often provide the practitioner with information, techniques, or forms that may be adapted. Their accuracy must await follow-up data. Finally, it is important to note that early identification without follow-up intervention is useless. Early intervention is the necessary sequel to early identification.

EARLY INTERVENTION

Rationale for Early Intervention

Animal Studies

Animal deprivation and enrichment studies provided impetus for examining the effects of early experiences on human development. Animal research is highlighted by the research of Hebb (1949) with rats, Thompson and Heron (1954) with dogs, Harlow (1965) with monkeys, and numerous others (see Thompson & Grusec, 1970). Payne, Mercer, and Epstein (1974) report that two major points emerged from the animal research: *(a)* an enriching or restrictive environment greatly influences the social and cognitive development of the organism, and *(b)* early experiences affect later learning attributes. Regarding the animal research, Caldwell (1970) notes, "The animal literature suggests that the critical time for manipulation of experiences is during the early infancy of the animals under study" (p. 719).

Human Studies: Lack of Mothering

Much of the early experience literature with humans concentrates on the effects of unusual child-rearing practices on cognitive and social behavior. Thus the initial investigations focus on culturally deprived children. In two of the earliest studies, Spitz (1945) and Ribble (1944) examined the development of infants who received differential degrees of "mothering" activities. They both conclude that lack of mothering resulted in physical deterioration (marasmus) and general retardation. They did not consider the physical setting or degree of environmental stimulation as factors; consequently, their work was severely criticized by Pinneau (1950, 1955).

Human Studies: Sensory Deprivation (Institutions)

In a series of investigations, Rheingold (1956, 1961) compared children reared at home with children reared in institutions and found no significant differences. This finding challenged the lack-of-mothering hypothesis. In addition, Dennis and Najarian (1957) studied infants raised in three institutions and found differential results. They conclude that institutionalization per se is not directly related to retardation, but the degree of physical and social deprivation is the key factor. Thus the lack-of-mothering hypothesis gave way to the position that deficits appear in institutionalized

---
[1] More information is available from DIAL, Inc., Box 911, Highlands Park, Illinois 60035.

[2] For more information write to Project SCREEN, State of Illinois, Office of the Superintendent of Public Instruction, 188 West Randolph Street, Chicago, Illinois 60601.

children because of restricting environments and lack of learning opportunities.

Human Studies: Restricting Environment (Lower-Class Homes)

In an effort to investigate environments that appeared to lack adequate stimulation, numerous researchers began studying children reared in lower-class homes. Coleman and Provence (1957) and Coleman (1966) report that these children were restricted in opportunities to learn and this restriction hindered later school performance. Hess and Shipman (1965) claim that the interaction patterns in lower-class homes are very restricting and hinder cognitive and social growth.

Classic Early Intervention Studies

Concern for the debilitating effects of an impoverished environment on young children opened the way for initial interest in early intervention. If restricting environments impeded the social and cognitive growth of children, it was then reasoned that early enrichment efforts would help prevent or ameliorate disabilities.

As a result of previous work (Skeels & Dye, 1939) with two infants, Skodak and Skeels (Skeels, 1966) embarked on a study to determine the effects of early intervention. They selected an experimental group of 13 children under 3 years of age. The average IQ of the group was 64; 11 of the children were classified as *retarded*. A contrast group of 12 children under 3 years of age was selected. The average IQ of this group was 86; 10 were classified as *intellectually normal.*

The contrast group remained in an orphanage and received adequate health and nutritional services. Overall the environment was not very stimulating. In contrast, the experimental group were transferred to a state school where they received care on a one-to-one basis from adolescent retarded patients. The adolescent "parent" was given instructions on how to care for the child.

At the end of just 2 years, the 13-member experimental group showed a mean gain in IQ of 28 points. After approximately 5 years, 11 of them were adopted and placed in good homes. In 1965, 25½ years after the study began, a follow-up revealed highly significant differences in the two groups. For example, 11 members of the experimental group married and had a total of nine children, all of normal intelligence. In the contrast group 2 married and had five children, with one diagnosed as *retarded.* The experimental group completed a median of 12 grades, whereas the control group completed a median of less than 3 grades. All experimental subjects were either self-supporting or functioning as homemakers; one of them received a BA degree. In the contrast group, 4 were institutionalized and unemployed. In general, the occupational level for the experimental group was much higher than that of the contrast group. Skeels (1966) concludes,

> It seems obvious that under present-day conditions there are still countless infants with sound biological constitutions and potentialities for development well within the normal range who will become mentally retarded and noncontributing members of society unless appropriate intervention occurs. It is suggested by the findings of this study and others published in the past 20 years that sufficient knowledge is available to design programs of intervention to counteract the devastating effects of poverty, sociocultural, and maternal deprivation. . . . The unanswered questions of this study could form the basis for many life long research projects. If the tragic fate of the 12 contrast group children provokes even a single crucial study that will help prevent such a fate for others, their lives will not have been in vain. (pp. 54–55)

Kirk (1958) was interested in measuring the effects of an enrichment program on the social and mental growth of 81 retarded preschoolers. He divided the children into four groups. Experimental children (28 living at home and 15 living in an institution) attended nursery schools, but the control children (26 living at home and 12 in an institution) did not. In a short time, the experimental children achieved IQ gains ranging from 10 to 30 points, whereas the IQs of the control children declined. Over a period of years the differences between the groups were maintained.

The deprivation studies and the impressive results of the Skeels (1966) and Kirk (1958) studies helped provide the impetus for the era of massive early intervention programs. This expansion of programs paralleled the rapid growth of the area of learning disabilities. Thus, although the early intervention programs have not directly focused on LD children, they do provide an important source for developing the best LD practices. Early intervention rapidly developed for lower-class children (begun by Head Start in 1965) and to a lesser extent for handicapped children.

Head Start

Project Head Start, enthusiastically initiated in 1965, attempted to disrupt the cycle of poverty. Brazziel (1967) called it "the country's biggest peace-time mobilization of human resources and effort" (p. 244).

From 1965 to 1974, Head Start received over 3.1 billion dollars and served over 5.3 million children *(Report to the Congress, 1975)*. It has emerged through three rather distinct periods (Caldwell, 1974; Payne & Mercer, 1976).

Many preschool youngsters have been involved in Project Head Start.

Period of Optimism

In the initial period (1965-1967), generous funding and extreme optimism characterized Head Start. Moreover, program development was exploratory and somewhat haphazard; evaluations consisted mainly of case studies.

Critical Period

In the second period, people began to question the lasting effects of Head Start. This period is highlighted by the Westinghouse Report (Cicirelli, Evans, & Schiller, 1970). Payne, Mercer, Payne, and Davison (1973) summarize the main points of the study:

> 1. Summer Head Start programs did not produce early cognitive and affective gains that continued in the first grade and beyond.
> 2. Full-year programs produced marginal cognitive gains which continued through the first three grades, but no affective gains were made.
> 3. Programs worked best in Negro centers, in some urban areas, and in the Southeast region of the nation.
> 4. Project children were below national norms on the Illinois Test of Psycholinguistic Abilities (I.T.P.A.) and the Stanford Achievement Tests, although Metropolitan Readiness Test scores approached national norms.
> 5. Parents liked the program and took active part in it. (pp. 93-94)

Although the Westinghouse Study had numerous limitations and its results were severely questioned, its presentation via the media generated skepticism and widespread disappointment.

Consolidation and Refinement

Since 1969, Head Start seems to be in a consolidation and refinement period, characterized by the development and evaluation of numerous intervention programs. Fortunately, in the early years of Head Start numerous sponsors developed intervention models, and during this refinement period many of these models have been systematically investigated. These investigations are discussed in the next section.

Head Start Models and Evaluation

Head Start models represent a wide spectrum of educational theories and practices, centering on these four models: *(a)* positive reinforcement/directive-teaching, *(b)* cognitive development, *(c)* open classroom, and *(d)* combination.

Primarily through Planned Variation and Follow Through (two longitudinal research projects initiated at the national level), data are being gathered concerning the effectiveness of the various intervention models. Follow Through was initiated because early research indicated that the gains that many Head Start children achieve "wash out" by the third grade. Many educators reported that the wash out of initial gains resulted from factors not related to Head Start (i.e., environment of home and community, and local school programs) *(Report to the Congress,* 1975). It was reasoned that intervention must continue to maintain gains. Follow Through provided sponsors with the opportunity to continue intervention into the primary grades. McDaniels (1975) notes that more data will become available from Follow Through. This data should yield some definitive conclusions. Meanwhile, he reports on some interim data from Follow Through but cautions against hasty generalizations and misinterpretations. The interim data reveal that after 3 years of Follow Through, the structured models (University of Oregon Engelmann-Becker Model and University of Kansas Behavior Analysis Model) produced the greatest gains in academic achievement. The results also show that the majority of the models produced scores higher than comparison control group scores. McDaniels reports that it is encouraging that interim results match expectations of the respective sponsors.

In another report, Stallings (1974) investigated 20 first grade and 20 third grade classrooms of seven different sponsors:

1. University of Kansas—structured—positive reinforcement
2. University of Oregon—structured—directive teaching
3. High/Scope Foundation (Michigan)—cognitive development (e.g., Piaget)
4. Education Development Center (Massachusetts)—open classroom (e.g., English Infant School Theory)
5. Far West Laboratory—combinations of Piaget, Dewey, and English Infant School
6. University of Arizona—combinations of Piaget, Dewey, and English Infant School
7. Bank Street College—combinations of Piaget, Dewey, and English Infant School

Stallings's (1974) results include:

1. Each model is distinctly different from each other and consistently implemented across different sites.
2. In a comparison of children in the seven models and with matching non-Follow Through classes, the structured models (1 and 2) produced the greatest academic gains in reading and math.
3. High scores on *Raven's Coloured Progressive Matrices* (nonverbal reasoning) were earned by children in the more flexible classrooms (2 to 7). In these classrooms a wide variety of materials are used, numerous activities occur, and children select their own groups and seating part of the time. In addition, in these flexible classrooms adults interact with the children more on a one-to-one basis and ask more open-ended questions.
4. On the *Intellectual Achievement Responsibility Scale,* children in the more "open" and flexible classrooms achieved higher scores. For example, children in the flexible classrooms take responsibility for success but not for failure. Children in the highly structured classrooms take responsibility for failure but attribute success to their teacher's competence or other external forces. Only the Education Development Center produces results in which the children take responsibility for both success and failure.

5. A brief summary of other findings indicates that the best model for the following behaviors include:
   a. *Independent behavior*—Education Development Center, Far West Laboratory
   b. *Task persistence*—University of Arizona, University of Kansas
   c. *Cooperation*—Bank Street College, High/Scope Foundation, Education Development Center
   d. *Questions asking*—Far West Laboratory, Bank Street College, University of Kansas, High/Scope Foundation, Education Development Center

Stallings (1974) concludes that "the seven Follow Through models . . . are bringing different strengths to their pupils, and each is bringing advantages not usually found in traditional classrooms" (p. 9). Finally, remember that some sponsors do not value all the measures used to assess the programs. For example, the behavioral sponsors do not support indirect or inferential testing (e.g., focus of control, *Raven*).

Parent Involvement

In a different vein, Tjossem (1976) reports that preschool instruction per se is not the agent for producing long-term cognitive gains. He stresses the importance of delivering intervention to the child via the parent and claims that this method represents the most viable approach. Overall, the support for parent and family involvement in early intervention is impressive. In reviews of early intervention by Bronfenbrenner (1974), Horowitz and Paden (1973), and Levitt and Cohen (1975), the role of the parent as the teacher of the child is strongly supported. Moreover, the Florida Parent Model developed by Gordon, Greenwood, Ware, and Olmsted (1974) represents one of the prominent parent-oriented models and provides an established Follow Through parent intervention model.

Early Intervention with the Handicapped

Most early intervention studies and models have been generated with disadvantaged children. The research from this area, plus a handfull of specific studies on the handicapped, provide a wealth of information. In addition, Head Start is beginning to serve such children.

Milwaukee Project

Heber and Garber (1975) are conducting a longitudinal study designed to prevent

Successful early intervention programs involve the parents.

Early intervention programs often include group activities.

cultural-familial retardation. Using the results of an inner-city community survey, they concluded that mothers' intelligence, socioeconomic status, and community significantly contribute to cultural-familial retardation. Forty mothers with IQs of 75 or less and their infants were selected for the study. The intervention for the experimental group included maternal "rehabilitation" and infant stimulation. The program stressed the preparation of the mothers for vocational positions and trained them in child-rearing and homemaking skills. The infants participated in a sequence of activities that began with one-to-one activities at home and gradually proceeded to participation in a daily 7-hour, 5-days-per-week preschool program. The curriculum had a cognitive-language orientation implemented via a structured environment and prescriptive teaching.

The children in the experimental group ($N = 17$) have made substantially more progress than the control children ($N = 18$) at each evaluation interval. After approximately 5 years, the results reflect the gains of the experimental group. The *ITPA* was administered to all children at CA = 54 months. The mean score of the experimental children was the 63-month level, whereas the mean score of the control group was the 45-month level. In general, the language of the experimental group was described as volubly expressive, linguistically sophisticated, and verbally fluent. The mean IQ of the experimental group at CA = 66 months was 122 compared to the control group's mean of 91. At the various evaluation intervals the difference in mean IQ has ranged from 25 to 31 points in favor of the experimental children. Also Heber and Garber (1975) report that the mother-child interactions of the experimental children are more sophisticated and satisfying. Although Heber and Garber note that the ultimate evaluation will come from the performance of the children in the educational system, they suggest on the basis of existing data that cultural-familial retardation can be mitigated if help is given to the mothers during pregnancy and to the infants during early development.

Portage Project

The Portage Project (Shearer & Shearer, 1976) is a home-based intervention program for handicapped infants and preschoolers. A home teacher, (trained professional or paraprofessional) visits 15 families for 1½ hours, 1 day per week. An individualized curriculum is developed weekly on the basis of the child's skills in language, self-help, cognition, motor ability, and socialization. Precision teaching (Lindsley, 1964) is used to record the progress.

The Alpern-Boll Developmental Profile (Alpern & Boll, 1972) is primarily used to screen the children, and individual planning is facilitated by the *Portage Guide to Early Education* (Bluma, Shearer, Frohman, & Hilliard, 1976). This guide consists of a developmental checklist in the five curriculum areas, a set of 580 curriculum cards that match the checklist items, and instructional suggestions for each of the 580 behaviors. Initial results (IQ gains, behavioral gains, parent teaching skills) from the project are very favorable (Peniston, 1972; Shearer & Shearer, 1976).

Many children learn to recognize and form letters in early intervention programs.

Down's Syndrome Project

At the University of Washington, Hayden and Haring (1976) conduct programs for Down's syndrome children. The programs and the respective ages served are

1. Infant Learning Class—2–5 weeks to 18 months
2. Early Preschool—18 months to 3 years
3. Advanced Preschool—3 years to 5 years
4. Kindergarten—4.5 years to 6 years

The major objective of the programs is to promote a child's skill areas (gross and fine motor, social, communication, cognitive, and self-help) within an approximate normal developmental rate.

In the infant class, the parents and children come to the Experimental Child Unit once a week for a 30-minute training session in motor and cognitive development. Parents and staff work together by practicing exercises designed to promote the cognitive and motor development of the child. In the early preschool, the children attend 1½-hour sessions for 4 days a week. Specific performance objectives are established in each curriculum area and the children are assessed daily or weekly on the *Down's Syndrome Preschool Performance Inventory*. In the advanced preschool, the children attend 2-hour sessions 4 times a week. The activities are similar to those in the early preschool but more emphasis is placed on language behavior and on preacademic skills requisite for reading and arithmetic. Hayden and Haring (1976) report that children enrolled in the advanced preschool continue to make gratifying progress. Children who enter the program at an early age (e.g., 3 months) reach their respective developmental criteria sooner than children who enter the program at a later age (e.g., 2 years). In 1974, the mean IQ for the children who had been in the program since they were 6–9 months old was from 84.8 to 88, whereas the mean IQ gain for the children entering later was from 61 to 74.7.

In the kindergarten class, children attend 2-hour sessions 4 times a week. Much emphasis is placed on cognitive development. During the winter of 1974, five of these children were continuing in a sight reading program and four were in the "Systems 80 Phonic Program." The children in the phonics program completed a mean of five primers (range 2 to 12) and the sight vocabulary of the other children ranged from 36 to 50 words (mean 41). Hayden and Haring (1976) maintain that a crucial question remains: Can these early gains in response to educational programming be maintained as the children get older? To date, the results are impressive and parents and professionals await with optimistic anticipation and exuberance the long-range findings of this exciting study.

It is apparent that early intervention programs are emerging and yielding some impressive results for children up to 6 years old. Two other projects that serve handicapped preschoolers include Project Memphis[3] and Project PEECH.[4]

Guidelines for Early Intervention

Several programs have generated impressive findings with retarded and disadvantaged children who exhibit many of the characteristics commonly found in the LD population (e.g., academic failure, poor motor skills, language deficits, and poor social skills). Selected findings from these programs are now presented to foster improved programming for high-risk or LD children:

1. Family involvement in early intervention appears crucial if long-terms gains of the children are to be maintained (Bronfenbrenner, 1974).
2. Academically oriented structured programs yield the greatest short-term gains in reading and math (McDaniels, 1975; Stallings, 1974).
3. Intervention initiated with infants has been very impressive (Hayden & Haring, 1976; Heber & Garber, 1975). Hayden and Haring (1976) report that the earlier the intervention, the better the results.
4. Parents can be effective teachers of their handicapped and high-risk children (Levitt & Cohen, 1975).
5. Paraprofessionals can be trained as home teachers to work with parents (Gordon, 1975; Levitt & Cohen, 1975). One to two hours of work with the parents each week has yielded positive results.
6. In summarizing the results of her Follow Through study, Stallings (1974) states:

A study of the instructional procedures used in classrooms and the achievement of children indicates that time spent in reading and math activities and a high rate of drill, practice, and praise contribute to higher reading and math scores. Children taught by these methods tend to accept responsibility for their failures but not for their successes. Lower absence rates, higher scores on a nonverbal problem-solving test of reasoning can be attributed in part to more open and flexible instructional approaches in which children are provided a wide variety of activities and materials and where children engage independently in activities and select their own groups part of the time. (p. 9)

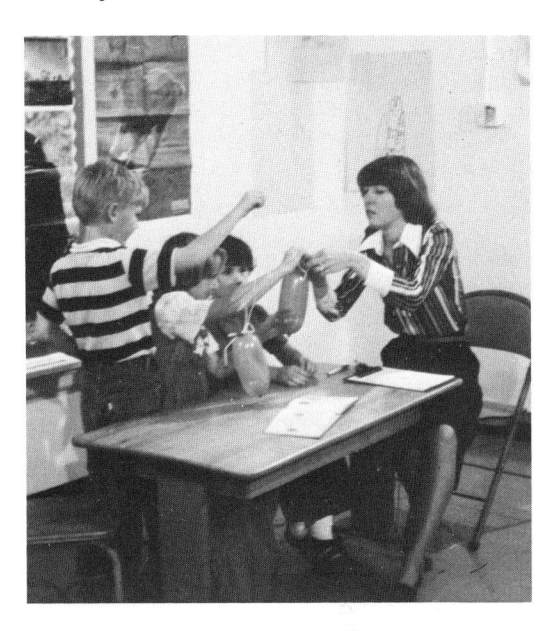

Children look forward to early intervention activities.

---

[3] Project Memphis: Dr. Alton Quick, Director, Department of Special Education and Rehabilitation, Memphis State University, Memphis, Tennessee 38152. For materials: Fearon Publishers, 6 Davis Drive, Belmont, California 94002.
[4] Project PEECH: Mrs. Lois A. Cadman, Region IX Education Service Center, 3014 Old Seymour Road, Wichita Falls, Texas 76309.

7. Curriculum has included the use of hierarchies with the charting of progress, open-ended experiences originating from classroom stimuli, and spontaneous group interaction.
8. Follow-up data indicate that both IQ gains and achievement gains can be sustained through grades 2 and 3 (Horowitz & Paden, 1973). For initial gains to be maintained it appears that intervention must continue. Some reason that improvement in the parent-child interaction and relationship is the key to maintaining the child's gains (Bronfenbrenner, 1974; Tjossem, 1976). Also, it appears that better public school programs would help children maintain an adequate rate of development.

Perspective

Since the early results tend to match the expectations of the specific model, it appears that a well-founded program would include a combination of approaches. The combination program enables the practitioner to incorporate the respective outcomes or objectives of each model. Children may enjoy the best of several approaches if they participate in a program that features some structure, direct academic intervention, daily charting of progress, free-choice activities, developmental task activities, and spontaneous learning experiences.

Conclusion

In a nation of plentiful resources, rich in energetic and committed people, the negative consequences of an unstimulating environment must be diminished by providing the most promising intervention strategies. By fostering the cognitive, academic, social, and emotional growth of children, individuals can be assisted in their pursuit of self-fulfillment. It is hoped that the information on early identification and intervention in this chapter brings us a step closer to developing "best practices" for those children who need early intervention.

REFERENCES

Aldrich, R.A., & Holliday, A. *The mental retardation service delivery system project* (Research Report No. 3). Seattle: Health Resources Study Center, University of Washington, 1971.

Algozzine, B., Mercer, C.D., & Countermine, T. The effects of labels and behavior on teacher expectations. *Exceptional Children,* 1977, *44,* 131–132.

Alpern, G., & Boll, T. *Developmental profile.* Indianapolis, Ind.: Psychological Development Publications, 1972.

Badian, N.A. *Early prediction of academic underachievement.* Paper presented at the meeting of the 54th Annual International Convention of the Council for Exceptional Children, Chicago, April 1976. (ERIC Document Reproduction Service No. ED 122 500)

Bender, L. Specific reading disability as a maturational lag. *Bulletin of the Orton Society,* 1957, *7,* 9–18.

Benger, K. The relationships of perception, personality, intelligence, and grade one reading achievement. In H.K. Smith (Ed.), *Perception and Reading.* Newark, Del.: International Reading Association, 1968.

Bluma, S., Shearer, M., Frohman, A., & Hilliard, J. *Portage guide to early education* (Rev. ed.). Portage, Wis.: Cooperative Educational Service Agency No. 12, 1976.

Book, R.M. Predicting reading failure: A screening battery for kindergarten children. *Journal of Learning Disabilities,* 1974, *7,* 43–56.

Brazziel, W. Two years of Head Start. *Phi Delta Kappan,* 1967, *48,* 344–348.

Bronfenbrenner, U. *Is early intervention effective?* (A Report on Longitudinal Evaluations of Preschool Programs, Vol. 2, Department of Health, Education and Welfare Publication Number OHD 76–30025). Washington, D.C.: U.S. Government Printing Office, 1974.

Caldwell, B. The rationale for early intervention. *Exceptional Children,* 1970, *36,* 717–727.

Caldwell, B.M. A decade of early intervention programs: What we have learned. *American Journal of Orthopsychiatry,* 1974, *44,* 491–496.

Cicirelli, V.G., Evans, J.W., & Schiller, J.S. The impact of Head Start: A reply. *Harvard Educational Review,* 1970, *40*(1), 105–129.

Cohen, H.J., & Diner, H. The significance of developmental dental enamel defects in neurological diagnosis. *Pediatrics,* 1970, *46,* 737–747.

Coleman, J.S. *Equality of educational opportunity.* Washington, D.C.: United States Government Printing Office, 1966.

Coleman, R.W., & Provence, S. Environmental retardation (hospitalism) in infants living in families. *Pediatrics,* 1957, *19,* 285–292.

Cowgill, M.L., Friedland, S., & Shapiro, R. Predicting learning disabilities from kindergarten reports. *Journal of Learning Disabilities,* 1973, *6,* 577–582.

de Hirsch, K., Jansky, J., & Langford, W.S. *Predicting reading failure.* New York: Harper & Row, 1966.

Denhoff, E., Hainsworth, P.K. & Hainsworth, M.L. Learning disabilities and early childhood education: An information-processing approach. In H. Myklebust (Ed.), *Progress in learning disabilities* (Vol. 2). New York: Grune & Stratton, 1971.

Denhoff, E., Hainsworth, P.K., & Hainsworth, M.L. The child at risk for learning disorder. *Clinical Pediatrics,* 1972, *11,* 164–170.

Dennis, W., & Najarian, P. Infant development under environmental handicap. *Psychological Monographs,* 1957, *71*(7).

Dykstra, R. The use of reading readiness tests for diagnosis and prediction: A critique. In T.C. Barrett (Ed.), *The evaluation of children's reading achievement.* Newark, Del.: International Reading Association, 1967.

Eaves, L.C., Kendall, D.C., & Crichton, J.U. The early detection of minimal brain dysfunction. *Journal of Learning Disabilities,* 1972, *5,* 454–562.

Eaves, L.C., Kendall, D.C., & Crichton, J.U. The early identification of learning disabilities: A follow-up report. *Journal of Learning Disabilities,* 1974, *7,* 632–638.

Ferinden, W.E., Jr., & Jacobson, S. Early identification of learning disabilities. *Journal of Learning Disabilities,* 1970, *3,* 589–593.

Feshback, S., Adelman, H., & Fuller, W.W. Early identification of children with high risk of reading failure. *Journal of Learning Disabilities,* 1974, *7,* 639–644.

Foster, G., Schmidt, C., & Sabatino, D. Teacher expectancies and the label "learning disabilities." *Journal of Learning Disabilities,* 1976, *9,* 58–61.

Foster, G., & Ysseldyke, J. Expectancy and halo effects as a result of artificially induced teacher bias. *Contemporary Educational Psychology,* 1976, *1,* 37–45.

Galante, M.B., Flye, M.E., & Stephens, L.S. Cumulative minor defects: A longitudinal study of the relation of physical factors to school achievement. *Journal of Learning Disabilities,* 1972, *5,* 75–80.

Gallagher, J. Children with developmental imbalances: A psychoeducational definition. In W.M. Cruickshank (Ed.), *The teacher of brain-injured children: A discussion of the bases for competency.* Syracuse: Syracuse University Press, 1966.

Gallagher, J.J., & Bradley, R.H. Early identification of developmental difficulties. In I.J. Gordon (Ed.), *Early childhood education: The seventy-first yearbook of the National Society for the Study of Education* (Part II). Chicago, Ill.: Distributed by the University of Chicago Press, 1972.

Garber, H., & Heber, R. *The Milwaukee Project: Early intervention as a technique to prevent mental retardation.* Stoors, Conn: The University of Connecticut Technical Paper, 1973.

Glazzard, M. The effectiveness of three kindergarten predictors for first-grade achievement. *Journal of Learning Disabilities,* 1977, *10,* 95–99.

Gordon, I.J. *The Florida parent education early intervention projects: A longitudinal look.* Urbana, Ill.: ERIC Clearinghouse on Early Childhood Education, 1975.

Gordon, I.J., Greenwood, G.E., Ware, W.B., & Olmsted, P.P. *The Florida parent education Follow Through program.* Gainesville, Fla.: Institute for Development of Human Resources, 1974.

Gray, S.W., & Klaus, R.A. An experimental preschool program for culturally deprived children. *Child Development,* 1965, *36,* 887–898.

Haring, N.G., & Ridgway, R.W. Early identification of children with learning disabilities. *Exceptional Children,* 1967, *33,* 387–395.

Harlow, H. Total social isolation: Effects on Macaque monkey behavior. *Science,* 1965, *148,* 666.

Hayden, A.H. Perspectives of early childhood education in special education. In N.G. Haring (Ed.), *Behavior of exceptional children: An in-*

troduction to special education. Columbus, Ohio: Charles E. Merrill, 1974.

Hayden, A.H., & Haring, N.G. Early intervention for high risk infants and young children: Programs for Down's syndrome children. In T.D. Tjossem (Ed.), *Intervention strategies for high risk infants and young children*. Baltimore: University Park Press, 1976.

Hebb, D.O. *The organization of behavior.* New York: Wiley, 1949.

Heber, R., & Garber, H. The Milwaukee Project: A study of the use of family intervention to prevent cultural-familial mental retardation. In B.Z. Friedlander, G. Kirk, & G. Sterritt (Eds.), *The exceptional infant* (Vol. 3). New York: Brunner/Mazel, 1975.

Hess, R.D., & Shipman, V.C. Early experience and the socialization of cognitive modes in children. *Child Development*, 1965, *36*, 869–886.

Hoffman, M.S. Early indications of learning problems. *Academic Therapy*, 1971, *7*, 23–35.

Horowitz, F.D., & Paden, L.Y. The effectiveness of environmental intervention programs. In B.M. Caldwell & H.N. Ricciuti (Eds.), *Review of child development research* (Vol. 3). Chicago: The University of Chicago Press, 1973.

Jansky, J., & de Hirsch, K. *Preventing reading failure: Prediction, diagnosis, and intervention.* New York: Harper & Row, 1972.

Kapelis, L. Early identification of reading failure: A comparison of two screening tests and teacher forecasts. *Journal of Learning Disabilities*, 1975, *8*, 638–641.

Keogh, B.K., & Becker, L.D. Early detection of learning problems: Questions, cautions, and guidelines. *Exceptional Children*, 1973, *40*, 5–12.

Keogh, B.K., & Smith, C.E. Group techniques and proposed scoring system for the *Bender Gestalt Test* with children. *Journal of Clinical Psychology*, 1961, *17*, 172–175.

Keogh, B.K., & Smith, C.E. Early identification of educationally high potential and high risk children. *Journal of School Psychology*, 1970, *8*, 285–290.

Kirk, S.A. *Early education of the mentally retarded: An experimental study.* Urbana, Ill.: University of Illinois Press, 1958.

Koppitz, E.M. *The Bender Gestalt Test for young children.* New York: Grune & Stratton, 1964.

Kottmeyer, W. Readiness for reading. *Elementary English*, 1947, *24*, 355–366.

Lessler, K., & Bridges, J.S. The prediction of learning problems in a rural setting: Can we improve on readiness tests? *Journal of Learning Disabilities*, 1973, *6*, 90–94.

Levitt, E., & Cohen, S. An analysis of selected parent-intervention programs for handicapped and disadvantaged children. *The Journal of Special Education*, 1975, *9*, 345–365.

Lindsley, O.R. Direct measurement and prosthesis of retarded children. *Journal of Education*, 1964, *147*, 62–81.

Lyons, J.S., & Bangs, T. Effects of preschool language training on later academic achievement of children with language and learning disabilities: A descriptive analysis. *Journal of Learning Disabilities*, 1972, *5*, 585–592.

Magliocca, L.A., Rinaldi, R.T., Crew, J.L., & Kunzelmann, H.P. Early identification of handicapped children through a frequency sampling technique. *Exceptional Children*, 1977, *43*, 414–420.

Maitland, S., Nadeau, J.B.E., & Nadeau, G. Early school screening practices. *Journal of Learning Disabilities*, 1974, *7*, 645–649.

Mardell, C., & Goldenberg, D. For prekindergarten screening information: DIAL. *Journal of Learning Disabilities*, 1975, *8*, 140–147.

McDaniels, G.L. The evaluation of Follow Through. *Educational Researcher*, 1975, *4*(11), 7–11.

Meehl, P.E., & Rosen, A. Antecedent probability and the efficiency of psychometric signs, patterns or cutting scores. *Psychological Bulletin*, 1955, *52*, 194–216.

Mercer, C.D. *Preliminary review of early identification indices for learning disabled children.* Paper presented at the meeting of the Conference of the State of Florida Association for Children with Learning Disabilities, Tampa, October 1975.

Mercer, C.D., Algozzine, B., & Trifiletti, J.J. Early identification: Issues and considerations. *Exceptional Children*, in press.

Mercer, C.D., & Trifiletti, J.J. The development of screening procedures for the early detection of children with learning problems. *The Journal of School Health*, 1977, *47*, 526–532.

Myklebust, H.R. Learning disability: Definition and overview. In H.R. Myklebust (Ed.), *Progress in learning disabilities* (Vol.1). New York: Grune & Stratton, 1968.

Norfleet, M.A. The *Bender Gestalt* as a group

screening instrument for first grade reading potential. *Journal of Learning Disabilities,* 1973, *6,* 383–388.

Novack, H.S., Bonaventura, E., & Merenda, P.F. A scale for early detection of children with learning problems. *Exceptional Children,* 1973, *40,* 98–105.

Pasamanick, B., Rogers, M.E., & Lilienfeld, A.M. Pregnancy experience and the development of behavior disorder in children. *American Journal of Psychiatry,* 1956, *112,* 613–618.

Payne, J.S., & Mercer, C.D. Head Start. In S.E. Goodman (Ed.), *Handbook on contemporary education.* New York: R.R. Bowker, 1976.

Payne, J.S., Mercer, C.D., & Epstein, M.H. *Education and rehabilitation techniques.* New York: Behavioral Publications, 1974.

Payne, J.S., Mercer, C.D., Payne, R.A., & Davison, R. G. *Head Start: A tragicomedy with epilogue.* New York: Behavorial Publications, 1973.

Peniston, E. *An evaluation of the Portage Project.* Unpublished manuscript, 1972. (Available from the Portage Project, Cooperative Educational Service Agency No. 12, Portage, Wis.)

Pinneau, S.A. A critique on the articles by Margaret Ribble. *Child Development,* 1950, *21,* 203–228.

Pinneau, S.A. The infantile disorders of hospitalism and anaclitic depression. *Psychological Bulletin,* 1955, *52,* 429–452.

Quinn, P.O., & Rapoport, J.L. Minor physical anomalies and neurologic status in hyperactive boys. *Pediatrics,* 1974, *53,* 742–747.

Report to the Congress. Project Head Start: Achievements and problems. Washington, D.C.: Office of Human Development, Department of Health, Education, and Welfare, 1975.

Rheingold, H.L. The modification of social responsiveness in institutional babies. *Monograph of the Society for Research in Child Development,* 1956, *21*(2).

Rheingold, H.L. The effect of environmental stimulation upon social and exploratory behavior in the human infant. In B.M. Foss (Ed.), *Determinants of infant behavior.* New York: Wiley, 1961.

Ribble, M.A. Infantile experience in relation to personality development. In J. McV. Hunt (Ed.), *Personality and the behavior disorders.* New York: Ronald Press, 1944.

Rosenthal, R., & Jacobson, L. Teachers' expectancies: Determinants of pupils' IQ gains. *Psychological Reports,* 1966, *19*(1), 115–118.

Satz, P. & Fletcher, J. Early screening tests: Some uses and abuses. *Journal of Learning Disabilities,* in press.

Satz, P., & Friel, J. Some predictive antecedents of specific reading disability: A preliminary two-year follow-up. *Journal of Learning Disabilities,* 1974, *7,* 437–444.

Satz, P., & Friel, J. Predictive validity of an abbreviated screening battery. *Journal of Learning Disabilities,* 1978, *11,* 347–351.

Satz, P., Friel, J., & Rudegeair, F. Some predictive antecedents of specific reading disability: A two-, three- and four-year follow-up. In J.T. Guthrie (Ed.), *Aspects of reading acquisition.* Baltimore: Johns Hopkins Press, 1976.

Satz, P., Taylor, H.G., Friel, J., & Fletcher, J. Some predictive and developmental precursors of reading disability: A six-year follow-up. In D. Pearl & A. Benton (Eds.), *Dyslexia: A critical appraisal of current theory.* Oxford: Oxford University Press, in press.

Schleichkorn, J. The teacher and recognition of problems in children. *Journal of Learning Disabilities,* 1972, *5,* 501–502.

Scholes, R.S., Tanis, D., & Turner, A. Syntactic and strategic aspects of the comprehension of indirect and direct object constituents in children. *Communication Science Laboratory Quarterly Report,* 1975.

Senf, G., & Comrey, A. State initiative in learning disabilities: Illinois' Project SCREEN, Report I: The SCREEN, early identification procedure. *Journal of Learning Disabilities,* 1975, *8,* 451–457.

Shearer, D.E., & Shearer, M.S. The Portage Project: A model for early childhood intervention. In T.D. Tjossem (Ed.), *Intervention strategies for high risk infants and young children.* Baltimore: University Park Press, 1976.

Silver, L.B. Familial patterns in children with neurologically-based learning disabilities. *Journal of Learning Disabilities,* 1971, *4,* 348–358.

Skeels, H.M. Adult status of children with contrasting early life experiences. *Monographs of the Society for Research in Child Development,* 1966, *31*(3).

Skeels, H.M., & Dye, H.B. A study of the effects of differential stimulation on mentally retarded children. *Convention Proceedings of American*

Association of Mental Deficiency, 1939, *44,* 144–136.

Spitz, R.A. Hospitalism: An inquiry into the genesis of psychiatric conditions in early childhood. *Psychoanalytic Study of the Child,* 1945, *1,* 53–74.

Stallings, J.A. *Follow Through classroom observation evaluation 1972–1973* (Executive Summary SRI Project URU-7370). Menlo Park, Calif.: Stanford Research Institute, 1974.

Stimbert, V.E. A technology of preschool education. *Educational Technology,* 1971, *11*(2), 9–13.

Thompson, W.R., & Grusec, J.E. Studies of early experience. In P.H. Mussen (Ed.), *Carmichael's manual of child psychology* (Vol. 1, 3rd ed.). New York: John Wiley & Sons, 1970.

Thompson, W.R., & Heron, W. The effects of restricting early experience on the problem-solving capacity of dogs. *Canadian Journal of Psychology,* 1954, *8,* 17–31.

Tjossem, T.D. Early intervention: Issues and approaches. In T.D. Tjossem (Ed.), *Intervention strategies for high risk infants and young children.* Baltimore: University Park Press, 1976.

Waldrop, M.F., & Goering, J.D. Hyperactivity and minor physical anomalies in elementary school children. *American Journal of Orthopsychiatry,* 1971, *41,* 602–607.

Waldrop, M.F., Pedersen, F.A., & Bell, R.A. Minor physical anomalies and behavior in preschool children. *Child Development,* 1968, *39,* 391–400.

Whiting, H.T., Clarke, T.A., & Morris, P.R. A clinical validation of the *Stott Test of Motor Impairment. British Journal of Social Clinical Psychology,* 1969, *8,* 270–274.

Wilborn, B.L., & Smith, D.A. Early identification of children with learning problems. *Academic Therapy,* 1974, *9,* 363–371.

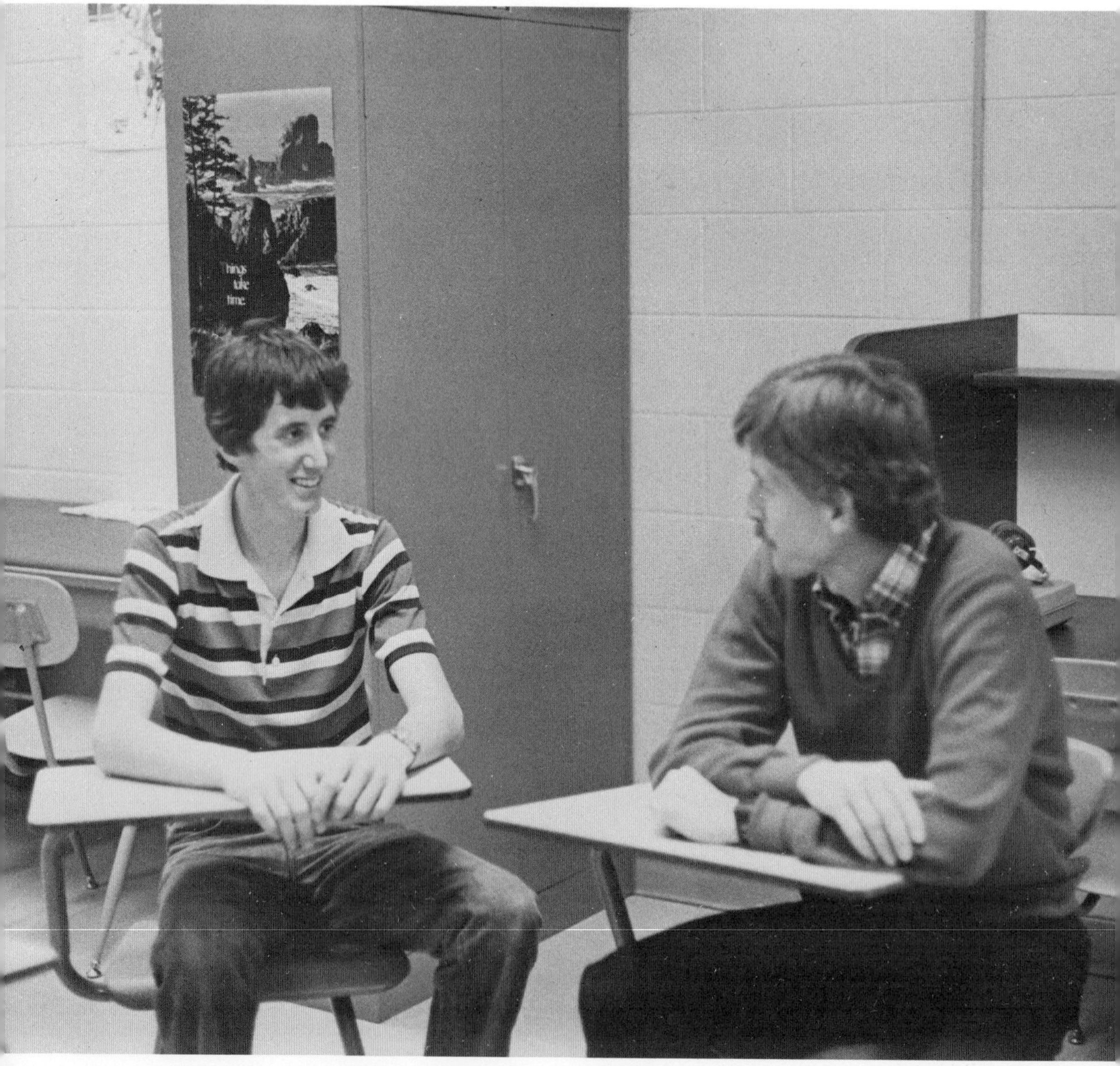

13

The learning disabled adolescent

Theories and practices about learning disabilities focus primarily on children 6 to 12 years of age. This orientation resulted from several factors. First, pressure for educational programs originated with parents and organizations concerned with young children who could not master the basic skills of reading, writing, arithmetic, and spelling. Second, as this pressure for service produced tangible programs, the educational procedures and materials were oriented toward the elementary school. Even today, most assessment, developmental, and remedial materials are directed toward the initial stages of the academic curriculum. Third, teacher training programs in colleges and universities tended to prepare individuals to work with young children. In addition, most research focuses on young children. Fourth, with few exceptions, the high school establishment overtly and covertly resisted providing services for the LD student.

This disproportionate attention to the elementary-aged child is also partially rooted in the assumption that early remediation prevents later learning problems. A common strategy has been one of "catching and correcting" learning problems early (see Chapter 12). Several years of experience, however, have demonstrated that this early approach has not eliminated or significantly decreased the number of LD adolescents. Many children enter adolescence and continue to have learning problems; thus, the interest in teen-agers with learning disabilities is increasing. This interest, along with the mandates of Public Law 94–142 and Section 504 of Public Law 93–112, provides a strong impetus for preparing services for the adolescent.

Differences between elementary school and high school goals, organization, and structure obviously necessitate different educational programs. Unfortunately, few procedures for educating this population have been systematically examined and/or empirically validated. The professional literature contains little about adolescents and existing references are often redundant. Theories about young children continue to be applied to adolescents, facts from experimental research are few, and expert opinion is conflicting. As a result, individuals responsible for providing services have little to guide them other than instinct, best guess, and trial and error.

Because the LD adolescent seems more like his nonhandicapped peers than different, the following section will briefly discuss "adolescence" and the American high school.

FACTORS RELATED TO THE LD ADOLESCENT

Adolescence

The term *adolescence* is derived from the present participle of the Latin verb *adolescere*, meaning to "to grow up." During this period of continuous physical growth, the child tests social and cultural values and gains social skills. It has been variously defined as a period of physical development (Konopka, 1973; Lorenz, 1974), a chronological age span (Berger & Hackett, 1974; Cottle, 1973), a developmental stage (Keniston, 1975; Rapoport & Rapoport, 1975), and a sociocultural phenomenon (Goethals, 1975). Even though maturational age is often more significant than chronological age (Miller, 1974), for the purposes of this chapter *adolescence* is defined as a chronological age span (i.e., the period from 12 to 15 years is early adolescence, 15 to 18 years is middle adolescence, and 18 to 22 years is late adolescence).

The adolescent must accomplish certain developmental tasks. To Havighurst (1952), the developmental task "arises at or about a certain period in the life of the individual, successful achievement of which leads to his happiness and to success with later tasks, while failure leads to unhappiness in the individual, disapproval by the society, and difficulty with later tasks" (p. 2). The primary developmental tasks associated with early and middle adolescence include *(a)* developing new and more mature relations with both male and female peers, *(b)* developing a masculine or feminine social role, *(c)* accepting one's physique and effectively using the body, *(d)* developing emotional independence from parents and other adults, *(e)* achieving assurance of economic independence, *(f)* selecting and preparing for an occupation, *(g)* preparing for marriage and family life, *(h)* developing intellectual skills necessary for civic competence, *(i)* desiring and achieving socially responsible behavior, and *(j)* guiding behavior according to a set of values and an ethical system.

In every generation, adolescents evoke negative reactions from adults. According to Rogers (1977), Socrates viewed adolescents as disrespectful to their elders, tyrants, ill-mannered, and luxury-loving. Haan (1972) depicts the adolescent as inconsistent, involved in superficial socializing, given to considerable fantasizing, lacking insight, and having little philosophical interest in life. While some adults view adolescents positively, youth generally accept the pessimistic opinion of the majority and tend to view themselves somewhat negatively (Rogers, 1977).

Probably none of the common characterizations is completely true. Concepts of adolescence are generally derived from adults (Salzman, 1972), who stereotype all youth as students (Coleman, 1974). In addition, some groups of adolescents disproportionally influence adult opinion. The facts are that some teen-agers are model citizens, some are profligate, and that the everyday adolescent is between the two extremes.

Contrary to the belief of many parents, adolescence does not transform a person from what he was as a child. The patterns established and solidified during childhood continue during adolescence. Marked changes do occur but continuity of development is the rule. While there has been much dispute about adolescent tumult (Offer, 1969), Conger (1977) stated that it does not "for the great majority lead to the high degree of emotional turmoil, violent mood swings, and threatened loss of control suggested by some clinical theorists" (pp. 30–31).

Several common characteristics, however, do distinguish adolescence from childhood and adulthood. (While these characteristics interact and occur together, they have been separated for the purposes of discussion.)

1. The adolescent's physical growth results in adult stature and appearance. He grows rapidly during the first year of life and then gradually slows down until adolescence, when the rate again quickens. Common physiological changes are:
    a. rapid increases in height and weight with accompanying clumsiness and incoordination
    b. facial bone and feature changes from child to adult appearance
    c. increases in body strength and redistribution of body fat
    d. growth of pubic and auxiliary body hair

The necessity to cope with rapid body changes, coupled with psychological and sexual development, poses adjustment problems for him and the surrounding adults. Maturity of appearance also influences adult expectations and judgments of the individual, regardless of ability to meet the expectations.

2. The adolescent is mobile and functionally independent. While the child's movement patterns center about the home and school, the adolescent moves freely throughout the community and beyond. His movement is usually unsupervised; societal control is weakened. In addition, he becomes more functionally independent, able to survive without adult support. This realization also weakens societal controls.

3. He continually tries to establish an identity. His major problem is to arrange knowledge of himself into a meaningful whole—a rough process for both adolescent and parents. He spends more time at the "hangout" than at home, shifting from solitary to group pursuits. A strong consciousness of self (generally absent in childhood) contributes to a preoccupation with clothes, how he looks, and adherence to the peer group norms.

4. Adolescents are influenced more by peer group than are children or adults. It is the single most important influence, helping adolescents develop independence from family, broadening perspectives, and providing support for rebellion (Rogers, 1977). Conger (1977) suggests that adolescent peer relationships fall into three categories: the crowd, the clique, and individual friendships. Membership in a clique is requisite for membership in the crowd. Cliques, small in size, provide for closer relationships than the crowd. Close individual friendships are usually limited to one or two "best" friends and are not necessary for membership in a clique. Crowds provide the center for social activity, while the clique helps the in-

Peer relationships are very important to the adolescent.

dividual prepare for functioning in the crowd.

5. The adolescent matures sexually. The advent of sexual development brings problems and tasks that are different for boys and girls. Generalizations about children without regard to sex are acceptable, but in adolescence the individual is a boy or a girl first and then an adolescent. Elkind (1974) states, "It is only at adolescence that sexual status supercedes age status" (p. 150). As with the establishment of an identity, learning appropriate sex roles is a gradual "bumpy" process for both adolescents and parents.

6. He develops formal and/or abstract thinking abilities. While his IQ will remain fairly stable as he ages, his mental ability will change. He is now able to propose a variety of causes and solutions for the same events. He uses deductive reasoning in manipulating hypothetical propositions; he uses abstract rules and generalizations to attack problems. These abilities permit scientific and philosophical thinking, an understanding of history, and the ability to plan for the future. For example, he realistically envisions a vocation. Unlike his childhood attraction to the excitement and glamour of a job, he now considers how and where he wants to earn a living. What and how information is to be taught in high school must take into account this maturation in thinking ability.

7. The adolescent is not passive. He has mental, emotional, and physical aspects. He actively interacts with the environment and the demands made upon him. In contrast, most children tend to accept (with relatively little question) what is told them.

8. The adolescent seeks to establish independence and an identity, tending to be critical of the world and authority. In spite of this desire, he needs security. These two conflicting forces make the adolescent unpredictable and ambivalent about how to react to the world.

9. The adolescent wants to conform to his peers, especially in behavior and dress. In his effort to conform to the peer norms and yet establish independence and identity, the adolescent sometimes experiments with undesirable behaviors.

10. The adolescent usually has a long attention span but low tolerance for boredom. This trait, combined with the needs of independence and conformity, may result in unacceptable school behavior.

11. He is extremely self-motivating. It is not a matter of stimulating the adolescent to do something; the problem is to get him to

direct his attention and activity into desirable directions.

The LD teen-ager is an adolescent first and then an exceptional individual. Many of the general characteristics of the adolescent period displayed by an individual interact with the disability. For example, the student with a reading disability who has developed formal thinking abilities may construct compensatory strategies that mask the basic reading problem. His desire for independence, coupled with an aversion for appearing different from the peer group, may stimulate the development of sophisticated defense mechanisms to protect him from detection or being "shown up." These interactions produce multifaceted problems of motivation, behavior management, and curriculum content for the high school LD specialist.

The High School

Types of High Schools

Secondary schools provide formal schooling after the elementary experience and precede higher education. Alexander, Saylor, and Williams (1971) classify them into four general types: *(a)* comprehensive, *(b)* general, *(c)* specialized, and *(d)* vocational.

The *comprehensive high school* offers a broad program of academic, practical, prevocational, and vocational education, corresponding to the educational needs of the community. Conant (1959) notes that such schools provide a general education for all future citizens, a program for students planning to enter the world of work, and a program for students planning to enter a college or university.

The *general high school* offers a restricted program of study and does not meet the standards of the comprehensive school, which is usually larger. Its student body is not as representative of society, and its program of study is primarily academic preparation.

The *specialized high school*, usually located in a large urban area or school district, offers a program of study adapted to the needs of a special group of students. Admission is restricted to members of this group. The program offerings vary from specialized academics and fine arts to specific vocational training.

Jim learns about carbon dioxide in science class.

Linda folds clothes from the dryer in a room devoted to learning home skills.

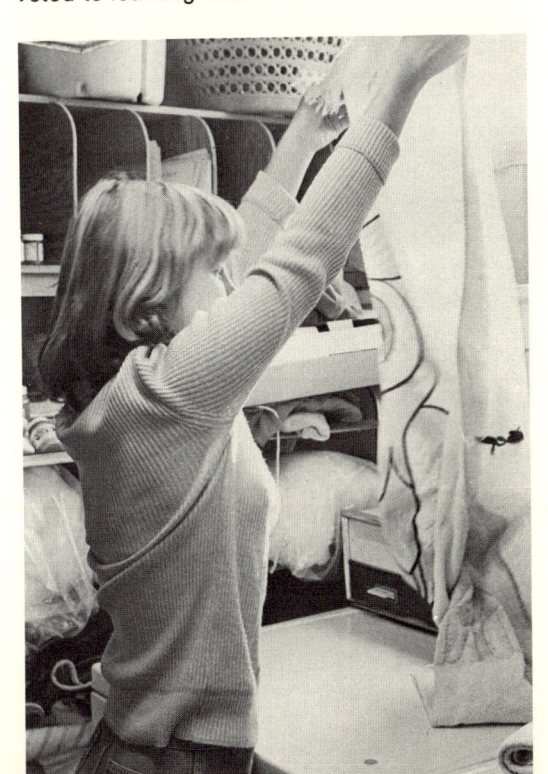

The *vocational high school* is usually open to all adolescents in the school district although it may be required that the student be 16 to 18 years of age for admission. Coursework in academics is offered; but the standards are not as high as in the comprehensive or specialized schools, and the vocational training may not be as advanced as in the specialized schools.

Many junior high schools and middle schools are similar to general high schools. They focus on academics (with limited offerings in practical fields) and introduce subjects such as music, art, and physical education.

Goals of the High School

Traditionally, high schools have had several functions and goals in society. They provide a universal education opportunity, develop individual potential, transmit cultural heritage, develop a system of values, stimulate personal development, and prepare the adolescent for adulthood. The best-known statement of objectives for the high school is the *Cardinal Principles of Secondary Education,* prepared by the Commission on the Reorganization of Secondary Education (1918). These principles include *(a)* health, *(b)* command of fundamental processes, *(c)* worthy home membership, *(d)* vocation, *(e)* civic education, *(f)* worthy use of leisure, and *(g)* ethical character.

The Educational Policies Commission (1938) attempted to give more specific direction to curriculum planners in a statement titled *The Purposes of Education in American Democracy.* Its broad purposes and specific objectives include

1. *self-realization*—an inquiring mind; communications and quantitative skills; character; health, recreation, intellectual, aesthetic interests
2. *human relationship*—respect for humanity, friendships, cooperation, courtesy, appreciation of the home and homemaking
3. *economic efficiency*—work; occupational information, choice, efficiency, adjustment, and appreciation; personal economics; consumer competence
4. *civic responsibility*—social understanding and justice, critical judgment, tolerance, conservation, social applications of science, world citizenship, law observance, political citizenship, devotion to democracy

Concern with accountability and a renewed interest in behavior theory (discussed in Chapter 1) have stimulated statements of goals and objectives for the high school. A declaration from a 1968 curriculum workshop (Anderson & Van Dyke, 1972) includes seven to nine specific objectives for the goals of *(a)* personal development and self-realization, *(b)* social commitment and human relationships, *(c)* civic competence and responsibility, and *(d)* economic competence. The Bicentennial Conference Report on America's Secondary Schools (Chaffee & Clark, 1976) states six goals:

1. personal self-confidence (self-image); flexibility; ability to cope
2. basic language and computation skills; human "survival" skills, including consumer skills, family and parenthood training, career exploration; skills to understand and to use political, economic, and social systems
3. civic education, including the concept of social cohesion
4. moral development
5. occupational competency; employability
6. aesthetic development; skills for lifelong learning and leisure time. (p. 16)

Aims, goals, and principles guide the development of curriculum content, instructional practices, and in some measure determine the expectations set for the students. A comparison of the goals for elementary education and secondary education reveals basic differences that have resulted in the development of separate educational programs. For example, at the elementary level the instructional orientation is on mastery of basic skills, while the secondary schools focus on developing facility in *applying* the basic skills.

TABLE 13.1

Expectations of elementary and secondary students.

Elementary	Secondary
The student has gaps in his basic knowledge and skills.	The student has mastered the basic knowledge and skills.
The student is dependent on adults for guidance and support.	The student, to a large degree, is independent of adults for guidance and support.
The student is a passive learner who usually accepts the curriculum content.	The student is an active learner who questions the world and seeks knowledge.
The student has incomplete mastery of personal and social skills.	The student has acceptable personal and social skills.

High school students need to know practical skills, such as using the photocopier.

In addition, the elementary school program is aimed at the introduction and mastery of personal and social skills, while the secondary school program assumes that mastery has occurred. As a result, expectations of the students are quite different (see Table 13.1).

In the primary grades (K–3) of elementary school, each teacher has a single group of children. He is personally responsible for the education of each child in the group. If a child has difficulty, he gives individual attention, develops special interventions, and allots extra time for mastery. If a child has a deficit in social and personal skills, he views it as his responsibility to help. The only exception to this pattern is evidence of some departmentalization in the upper elementary grades (4–7).

In the high school, as is commonly known, an individual teacher will meet four or five different groups of students daily. While the elementary school teacher has instructional responsibility for a daily total of 25 to 75 children, the high school teacher instructs 125 to 175 or more students. For him, individualization may be impossible. A second difference is the "content orientation" of the high school teacher. He is a specialist in some discipline or skill with responsibility for transmitting a certain amount of information in only that one area. This leads to several practices that have an impact on the adolescent:

1. Specialty areas develop reputations for catering to a particular group of students. For example, advanced mathematics students are stereotyped as having specific traits. If an individual student does not have the requisite skills, belong to the right crowd, or "fit in," he will be made to feel unwelcome or ignored by the staff and other students.

2. Very little tolerance of deviance in social and personal behavior is accepted. If the student cannot or will not conform, he is quickly removed and placed in "special" classes and programs. Once an individual is identified as a certain type (e.g., "the grind," "the jock," "the clown," "the troublemaker"), it is very difficult to change the nickname. Some elements of the self-

fulfilling prophecy (Rosenthal & Jacobson, 1968) and peer pressure undoubtedly contribute to maintaining the label and behaviors.
3. An assumption is made that each student in the class has mastered the necessary basic skills to understand and learn the course content.

For the student who has ability but lacks prerequisite skills, the high school classroom curriculum stands inflexible. Unless the teacher takes a special interest, it is the student's responsibility to gain the necessary skills and master the course content. Because the teacher feels responsible for the course content rather than for the individual student, the pupil must manage his own learning and behavior.

Of course not all teachers ignore student needs and problems. Unfortunately, however, the teacher's training contributes to the problem by fostering *(a)* the content orientation, *(b)* concern for maintaining order rather than identifying the cause and remediating unruliness, and *(c)* a need for completing a prescribed amount of curriculum content. Course loads, expectations, and societal attitudes about what an adolescent "should be" do not permit the individualization and tolerance of deviance, which is possible in the elementary school.

All these factors complicate education—the interactions between the characteristics of adolescence, the unique goals, expectations, and structure of the high school, and a learning disability. Provision of adequate schooling as mandated by law will require careful planning, alteration of some present practices, provision of adequate support systems and financing, and modification of attitudes—in both the teaching staff and the adolescent.

Definition of Learning Disabilities

The difficulties in developing an acceptable definition of *learning disabilities* and some of the commonly used definitions are discussed in Chapter 2. Selecting the best definition and using it successfully is difficult because professionals disagree sharply about what is appropriate for the adolescent. Hammill (1975) and Strother (1971), for example, advocate using the definition of the National Advisory Committee on Handicapped Children (USOE, 1968). Goodman and Mann (1976) find this definition unsatisfactory because it is based on work with children rather than adolescents, is vague concerning psychological processes, and includes other handicaps (brain injury, dyslexia, perceptual handicaps).

In spite of the number of definitions available and persuasive arguments by professionals, in most cases the agency funding the LD program decides on a definition. Schools use one selected by their state department of education or the U.S. Office of Education. Commonly selected is this one used in PL 94–142 (USOE, 1977):

> "Specific learning disability" means a disorder in one or more of the basic psychological processes involved in understanding or in using language, spoken or written, which may manifest itself in an imperfect ability to listen, think, speak, read, write, spell, or to do mathematical calculations. The term includes such conditions as perceptual handicaps, brain injury, minimal brain disfunction, dyslexia, and developmental aphasia. The term does not include children who have learning problems which are primarily the result of visual, hearing, or motor handicaps, of mental retardation, of emotional disturbance, or of environmental, cultural, or economic disadvantage. (p. 65083)

The criteria published with the law for determining the existence of a specific learning disability do not include procedures for determining "process problems." Goodman and Mann (1976) and Marsh, Gearhart, and Gearheart (1978) note that most experts agree that the process component has little relevance at the secondary level. The definition continues to lack preciseness, but until further investigations yield a more precise definition, the 1977 USOE definition must be viewed as serviceable.

Prevalence of Adolescent Learning Disabilities

Several investigators have studied the incidence of learning disabilities among school children. Bryant and McLoughlin (1972), for example, reviewed and discussed 21 such studies. There is yet, however, to be a research-based prevalence figure accepted by members of the profession. Myers and Hammill (1976) attribute this to the lack of a "definitive, operational definition of the 'conditions' being identified" (p. 12). Unfortunately, knowledge of prevalence is critical to the development of school programs because it aids educators in providing estimates of the population to be served, in making budget projections, in informing other professionals and parents of the number needing services, and in projecting personnel needs.

In lieu of a prevalence figure based on research, use of a pragmatic estimate may be appropriate. Some professionals and organizations (Lerner, 1976; National Advisory Committee on Dyslexia and Related Reading Disorders, 1969) prefer a liberal estimate of 15% or more while other estimates are less (see Chapter 2, Table 2.5). Wissink (1972) surveyed 100 leaders in the area of learning disabilities regarding their estimates of incidence in the school population. Half of the respondents (39 responded) suggested an estimate of 5% or less. PL 94-142 contained an eligibility estimate of 2% (USOE, 1976) but was later amended in 1977 to eliminate the estimate (USOE, 1977). Estimates of LD adolescents can be calculated using the data in Table 13.2 and a choice of prevalence level.

Take care in interpreting prevalence figures based on estimates, especially those on LD adolescents. Actual numbers may vary due to dropout rates, maturation and compensation, and the "masking" effect of the secondary program. Such variations influence funding patterns, program development, and personnel projections. In addition, differences between localities make application of prevalence estimates difficult. A school district should select a prevalence rate that seems to best fit the local norm rather than fit the school district to a national estimate.

Characteristics of Learning Disabilities

It is likely that there are identifiable characteristics of learning disabilities in adolescence that are different from those of childhood; however most of the published lists of LD characteristics (see Chapter 2) are descriptive of only children. By the time an individual becomes an adolescent he may have learned to control, modify, mask, or compensate for many of these behaviors. Maturation of the musculoskeletal and central nervous systems may also interact with his learning experiences to eliminate some of the commonly linked characteristics. Consequently, many of these lists of identifying characteristics are of limited use for the professional.

TABLE 13.2

Prevalence estimates for adolescent learning disabilities.[a]

Students Enrolled	1974–1975	1% LD	2% LD	3% LD	5% LD	7% LD	15% LD
Public 9th grade	4,006,000	40,060	80,120	120,180	200,000	280,420	600,900
Public 10th grade	3,843,000	38,430	76,860	115,290	192,150	269,010	576,450
Public 11th grade	3,455,000	34,550	69,100	103,650	172,750	241,850	518,250
Public 12th grade	3,088,000	30,880	61,760	92,640	154,400	216,160	463,200
Nonpublic high schools	1,240,000	12,400	24,800	37,200	62,000	86,800	186,000
Total population 14–17 years of age (includes school dropouts)	16,876,000	168,760	337,520	506,280	843,800	1181,320	2531,400

Note.
[a] Based on data from Grant and Lind (1976).

A small body of literature specifically addresses LD adolescents (Brutten, Richardson, & Mangel, 1973; Deshler, 1975; Hagin, 1971; Maietta, 1970; Mauser, 1974; Russell, 1974; Siegel, 1974; Strother, 1971). Characteristics summarized from these reports include:

1. alienation from family
2. awkwardness
3. daydreaming
4. delinquency
5. difficulty in anticipating the behavior of others
6. difficulty in changing behavior patterns
7. difficulty in generalizing from experience
8. difficulty in interpreting and using symbols
9. difficulty in selecting from alternatives
10. distractibility
11. emotional problems
12. feelings of inadequacy
13. few established principles or ideals
14. frustration
15. hyperactivity
16. immaturity
17. inflexibility
18. inner rage
19. major cognitive deficits
20. passive or active aggression
21. perceptual confusions
22. persistent confusion
23. poor logical reasoning
24. quickly yields to pressure
25. severe underachievement
26. short attention span
27. tendency toward impulsive decisions and judgments
28. truancy

These characteristics must be viewed with caution and applied with prudence. Most are the result of clinical judgment or classroom observation rather than controlled empirical study. Variations probably exist between the populations examined and many of the characteristics listed can be expected of normal teen-agers.

Deshler (1975) reviewed the literature related to characteristics of LD adolescents. He suggests LD adolescents show four distinctive features: *(a)* both strengths and weaknesses in social, emotional, and learning areas, *(b)* deficits in the basic academic skills of reading and arithmetic, *(c)* poor self-concept and motivation, and *(d)* the common characteristics also found in children, more subtly manifested.

It seems clear that carefully designed research is needed. The initial steps, however, are to devise an acceptable definition, to establish precise criteria for identification, and to systematically identify and investigate characteristics of LD adolescents. Until this is done there will be debate, discrepancies between labeled groups, and wide variations in LD populations and subsequent secondary programs.

Juvenile Delinquency and Learning Disabilities

In spite of the viewpoint of authors such as Jacobson (1974), who contends that "incipient delinquent behavior grows from schoolroom frustrations experienced by the child who generally appears normal, but who is handicapped by a learning problem" (p. 189), it appears more accurate to say that there *may* be some relationship between delinquency and learning disabilities. For example, according to Poremba (1975),

> The typical delinquent of 1974 is 13½ years old and functions at an intellectual level of 95 IQ, which is in the average range of intelligence. Academically, he is 3 to 5 years behind his grade placement. His most serious lag is in reading, with spelling next, then writing and arithmetic, followed by other subjects. Males outnumber females by about four to one. (p. 124)

Common characteristics do not, however, constitute "cause and effect" relationships. Despite reports and opinions (Berman, 1974; Geiger, 1961; Henley, 1969; Keldgord, 1968) that brain damage and delinquency are related and that poor school achievement is highly correlated with delinquency (Duling, Eddy, & Risko, 1970; Holte, 1972), there is yet to be reported acceptable empirical evidence that a learning disability causes juvenile delinquency.

EDUCATIONAL PROGRAMS FOR THE LD ADOLESCENT

Thus far, LD adolescents have been described in abstractions, statistical numbers, and generalities. A profile of a real learning disabled teen-ager is reflected in the description of Stuart:

Stuart is an enigma to his teachers at Artesia High School. His attention is good, he understands explanations well, and his oral answers are usually precise. Stuart's class standing, however, is low in almost every subject. His written reports and assignments are incomprehensible and his handwriting is undecipherable. He reads in a slow, halting, embarrassed manner and his spelling is atrocious. When asked about the nature of his problem, Stuart shrugs or says, "I'm just trying to survive."

Stuart is 16 years of age and during his two years at Artesia he has accumulated only 12½ credits, which classifies him as a freshman. There is no doubt concerning his intelligence, as his records consistently indicate intelligence test scores in the high normal range. In the last few years his parents have become frustrated and developed a pattern of acceptance-rejection. They have been told throughout Stuart's schooling that he is a bright boy and they cannot understand his lack of performance in school. They tend to think Stuart is lazy although he does well in his after school job and on his home chores.

Stuart must make a choice soon. He will be 18 in 24 months and the state in which he resides has given 18 year olds full citizenship with all the rights and responsibilities that accompany it. Frankly, Stuart is intimidated at the thought of being on his own in a world that demands so much competence. His father, in frustration, has occasionally vowed that if Stuart is not succeeding in school when he reaches 18 he can quit, get a job, and support himself. Stuart is considering the Army as his only solution and over the years has gradually downgraded his career choice from physician to infantryman. Stuart is well aware of the need for a diploma in the world he will face. A decade ago Stuart could have dropped out of school, entered the world of work, and readily achieved a meaningful life. Today, an incomplete education may prevent him from even demonstrating what he can do.

With minor variations, Stuart is like many other youngsters. For them there are no definitive answers to these practical questions: What is an appropriate educational program? What service delivery models are most effective? How can a secondary program be best implemented?

Philosophical Questions

In addition to practical questions, there are philosophical ones. The first philosophical tenet that must be considered in designing programs for the secondary student is that of placement in the least restrictive environment. The second tenet, which also is contained in PL 94–142, is that individualization should occur; for every student formally identified as learning disabled, a written education plan must be developed and approved (see Chapter 14). In addition, each plan must be reviewed at least once a year.

Normalization

Both the tenets have roots in the principle of *normalization* (Wolfensberger, 1972). It proposes that educational programs should at-

```
Maximum possible
deviancy from normal                              Normal behavior
behavior and appearance                           and appearance

All specialized education                         Normal education
and support systems                               policy and procedure
possible
```

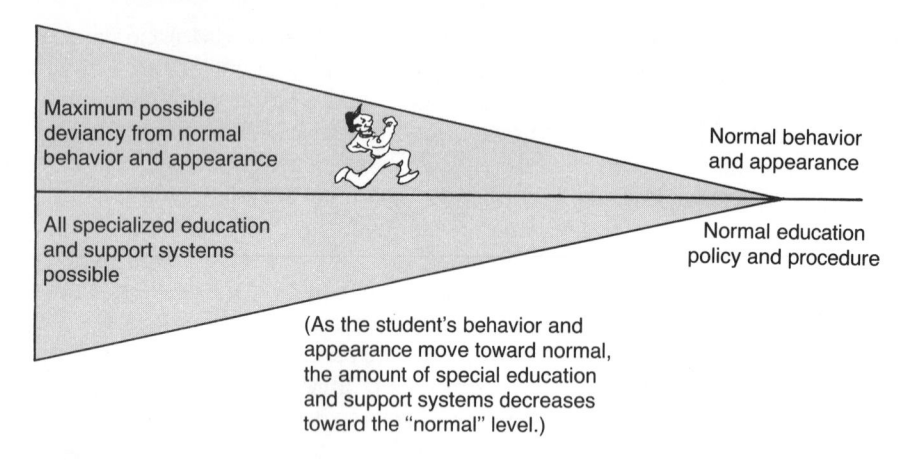

(As the student's behavior and appearance move toward normal, the amount of special education and support systems decreases toward the "normal" level.)

FIGURE 13.1.

The normalization continuum.

tempt to aid the child, regardless of severity of handicap, to progress toward the state of "being normal," both in behavior and appearance. Figure 13.1 illustrates a model that organizes educational services along a continuum from a maximum level of support to the normal level of support (see Chapter 11 for a discussion of services). Regardless of the entry point on the continuum, effort is directed toward modifying behavior and increasing skills in the direction of normalcy.

While few educators would disagree with the model, it is often ignored in practice. As the individual student acquires new skills, his special education program continues to offer highly specialized and individualized support systems. As the student begins to approximate the norm, he is placed in a regular setting; but all too often, he then quickly fails to demonstrate acceptable skills and/or behaviors. What occurs is that the student maintains near normal performance when receiving high levels of specialized support but cannot function adequately in the general classroom setting. Consequently, before a student can be expected to function satisfactorily in the normal setting, the demands and support systems of the special class should approximate the normal classroom.

Special and General Education

Two views of the special education concept are possible: *(a)* Special education is designed for a specialized population and is a separate system from general education, or *(b)* Special education is a specialized part of the general education system designed to meet the needs of a special population in cooperation with the general educator. While lip service has been given to the latter, actual practice indicates that special education is a separate educational system with its own funding, teaching staff, and curriculum. In addition, little cooperative effort of any significance has been established between general and special education. These practices have resulted in the creation of empires and special interests that do not mesh well with the philosophical tenets of least restrictive environment and normalization. For maximum success in meeting the legislated mandates, special education must become an integral part of the educational mainstream in both theory and practice.

Responsibility for Learning

Close examination of PL 94–142, the professional literature (Hopkins & Conard, 1976;

The LD specialist must work with secondary teachers in planning programs for LD students.

Schiefelbusch & Haring, 1976; Willenberg, 1977), and public statements (Frierson, 1978; Page, 1978) reveals a strong implication that responsibility for learning lies with the educator. It appears that if educators properly structure the learning environment with attention to antecedents and consequents, learning invariably will occur. As an ideal this may be true; however, in practice educators simply do not control all the necessary antecedents and consequents. Any special educator working with adolescents who expects to independently "arrange" the environment and have learning naturally follow is going to encounter difficulty. At the high school level the educator can provide the best possible environment and have the best materials available, but if the teen-ager finds street life more exciting than learning and does not attend school (or prefers to goof off when he does attend), very little is going to be accomplished. In high school, the student and teacher must intensively interact. Both have responsibilities.

Standards

Another philosophical question is, What standards should be used to measure success or failure when the student is placed in the general classroom? This serious issue quickly stirs community controversy. Over two-thirds of all junior high and senior high schools now use the letter grade system (National Education Association, 1974). If established grading systems are used, at what level is success achieved? If the curriculum content, teaching strategies, and/or grading policies are modified beyond what is ordinarily done for students not labeled exceptional, does a separate standard for success exist? In practice, LD pupils will probably be expected to meet the established standards for some classes (depending on the skills of the individual student) and modified standards in others. In school systems that require satisfactory performance on a basic skills test, LD adolescents must meet the basic standards to receive a high school diploma. With the emphasis placed on *grades* in high school, the LD specialist must be sensitive to the needs and will of the student, school, and community.

Factors Influencing Program Development

In developing an educational program, several factors must be considered (see Figure 13.2). Since the focus is on teen-agers, characteristics of adolescence, organization and goals of the high school, and the type of high school influence program organization and content. The definition selected for use also dictates program elements. For example, if a definition is selected that contains a strong "process" statement, provision for process should be included in the program structure. Mandates of state and federal legislation also influence program development.

Not only must these influencing factors and the philosophical considerations be scrutinized individually, but potential interactions must be considered. Reconciling the requirements of PL 94–142 with these factors illustrates some of the programming questions generated. Some of the required provisions of the law and the resulting questions and problems might include:

Educational services for the learning disabled

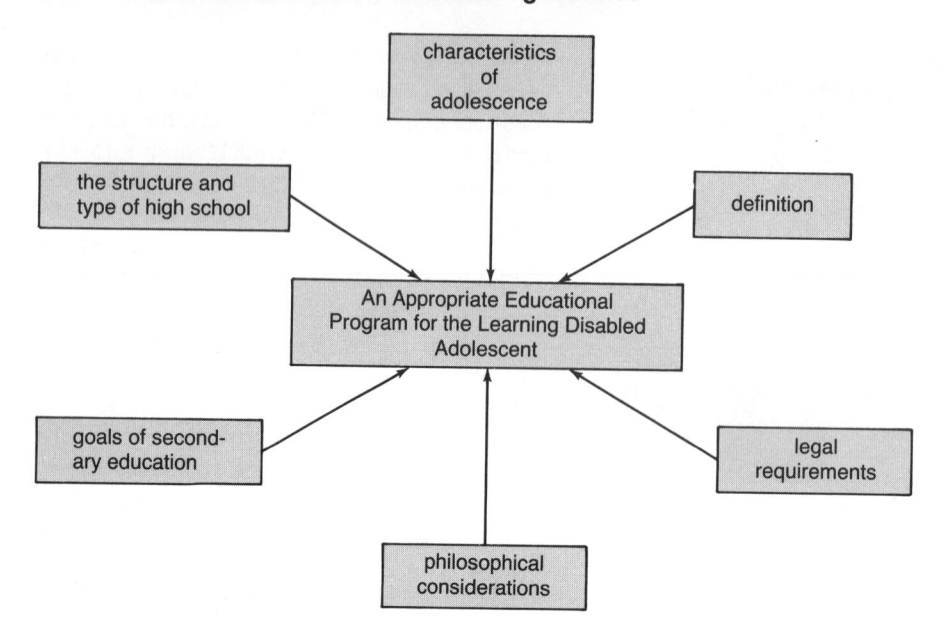

FIGURE 13.2.

Major factors influencing program development.

Factors shown: characteristics of adolescence; the structure and type of high school; definition; goals of secondary education; legal requirements; philosophical considerations — all influencing *An Appropriate Educational Program for the Learning Disabled Adolescent*.

1. A free, appropriate public education and related services must be provided for every handicapped child. With the variety of courses in the comprehensive, general, specialized, and vocational high schools, *who* will determine what is an appropriate program? Many of the related services (special teachers, speech programs, individualized enrichment programs) taken for granted in the elementary school are not available in the high school. This situation is particularly true of the general high school. Will specialized high schools be required to provide special support services for the handicapped student who otherwise meets the admission requirements?

2. Each child will be provided with nondiscriminatory individualized evaluation and full rights of due process in all placement decisions. With most evaluation instruments for learning disability programs designed for elementary school-aged children, is a nondiscriminatory evaluation possible?

3. Each student is to be educated in conformity with an individualized education plan. This plan is a written statement and must be developed and/or approved by: *(a)* an agency representative other than the teacher, *(b)* the teacher, *(c)* one or both parents, *(d)* the child (when appropriate), and *(e)* evaluation personnel. High school teachers, however, know little about individual planning. Other problems include determining which teachers are to participate, when the adolescent is to be included, and what input the teen-ager is to have. These latter problems are particularly troublesome considering that adolescents are reluctant to be different.

4. The content of the individualized plan must include *(a)* a statement of annual goals, including short-term instructional objectives, *(b)* a statement of present level of performance, *(c)* a statement of specific special education and related services, *(d)* projected dates for initiation and duration of service, and *(e)* appropriate objective criteria and evaluation procedures for

determining progress. With most high schools organized into departments, unanswered questions include: Does the present level of educational performance statement include statements for every course in which the adolescent is enrolled or only for basic skills? Are the objectives to be specific to each course or are they to be the general objectives of secondary education? Should the high school develop a special evaluation system that cuts across all the specialized content, develop a system for each course, or make each individual teacher responsible for the evaluation system?

A Service Delivery Model

A model for service delivery at the high school level should provide a range of services from a self-contained program to placement in the general education classroom or community. The model illustrated in Figure 13.3 has four main components.

1. Procedures for identifying eligible adolescents must be developed and implemented. The process includes at least three major components. First, an annual screening should be scheduled for all freshmen and transfer students. This screening might take the form of asking teachers to refer students who appear to exhibit some or all of a list of behaviors indicative of an adolescent with learning disorders. Second, students should be encouraged by their teachers to refer themselves. Zigmond (1978) reports encouraging results with self-referrals when the LD specialists explained their program to homeroom groups and encouraged students to "drop by." Third, students who were placed in LD programs in elementary schools should be identified and reevaluated when entering the secondary school. These "legacy" students may or may not meet the criteria for inclusion in the high school program. Since the identification process has one goal—to identify students who may have a disability severe enough to warrant placement in the program—the process should not be limited only to incoming students. Some provision should be made for periodically screening the entire high school population.

2. Students identified in Step 1 should receive a formal assessment and diagnosis of their skills. This procedure should follow the legal guidelines and result in identifying individuals who meet the criteria for program placement. Students who do not meet the criteria for the learning disabilities program should be referred for other appropriate services and/or remain in their general education placement.

3. The students who meet the criteria for placement in the learning disability program should have an IEP written and approved. The content of this plan should be consistent with the law (see Chapter 14).

4. Based on the IEP and placement criteria, placement should be made within a continuum of services including the self-contained setting, the resource room, and the adapted general education placement.

Severe LD adolescents usually cannot function in most general high school classes. Some investigators (Kaufman, Gottlieb, Agard, & Kukic, 1975; Koegh & Levitt, 1976; MacMillan & Becker, 1977) believe that placement for these youngsters without meaningful instructional integration would not be productive. The term *self-contained setting* implies that for them, no movement into the general mainstream is appropriate. Because many of these students have the language, social skills, and talent for success in fine arts, athletics, or other nonacademic areas, the term *modified self-contained setting* is used. In this type of placement, the pupils receive an orientation toward academics and career/vocational development: integration into the general mainstream will occur where possible. Placement in the resource room may be

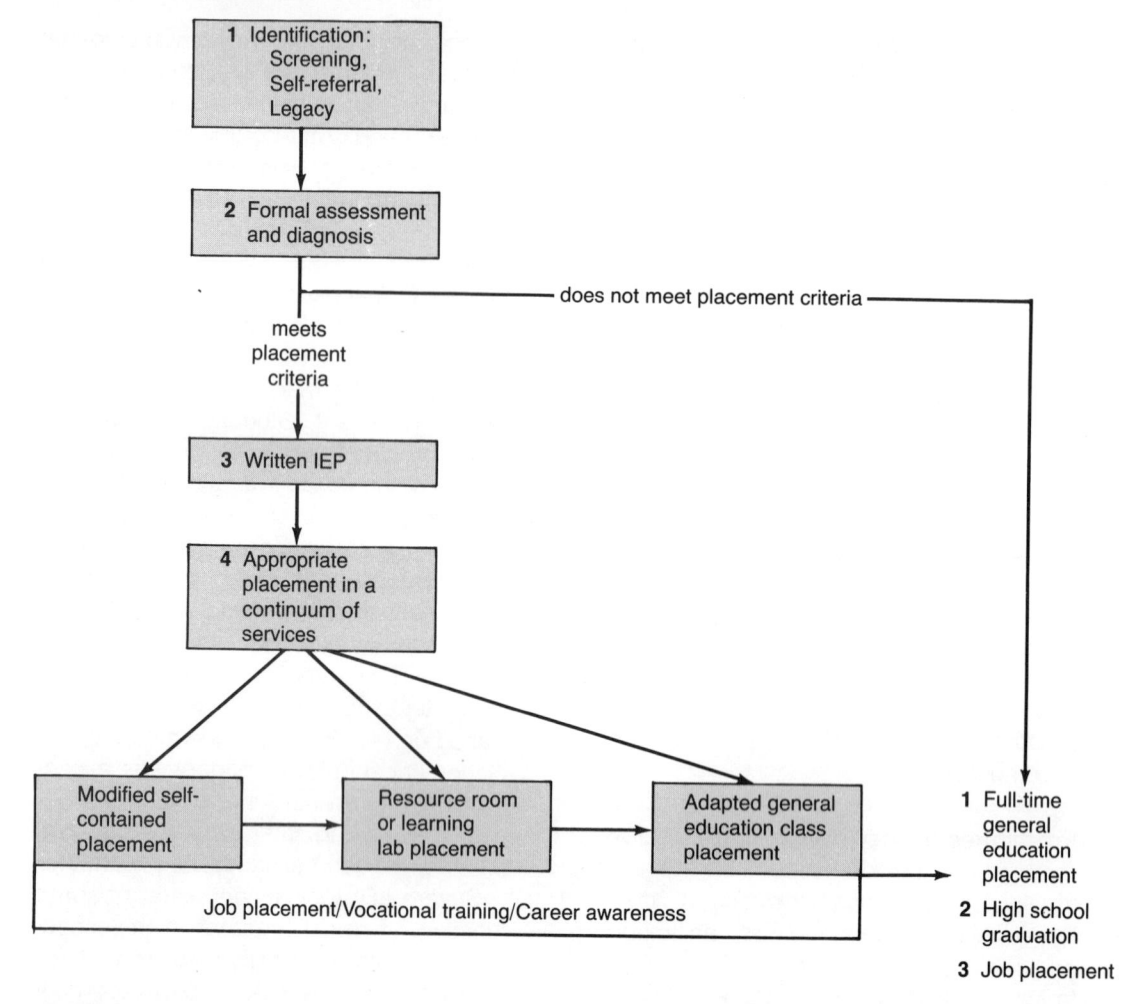

FIGURE 13.3.

A service delivery model for the high school.

possible if these students develop the requisite skills.

Mild and moderate learning disabled teen-agers require a strong remedial component to strengthen their deficient skills. They learn best in a resource room or learning laboratory. Depending on the goals set for each individual student, activities in the resource room will vary from instruction in specific skills to career exploration. In practice, the students will spend part of their day in the resource room for remedial-tutorial activities and part of their day in general education classes (academic and nonacademic). Wiederholt, Hammill, and Brown (1978) provide a detailed description for designing and operating a resource room.

An extension of the resource room is placement in an adapted general education classroom. Some students cannot function in a full-time classroom but can profit from modified general education "adapted" classes. Content specialists from regular education teach these classes with modifications. In a sense, these teachers are part special educators and part general educators. They prepare students for eventual full-time placement in regular classes and provide the same content available to nonhandicapped students. Some adolescents may continue indefinitely in this setting.

Finally, each student should have the opportunity for job training and/or career-awareness instruction. Vocational instruction with on-the-job training will be emphasized more for the self-contained program, while career exploration will become the focus as the student moves toward full-time general education placement.

Depending on the skill level of the students, there are three ultimate goals of any secondary learning disability program. First, regardless of initial placement the program should move the student toward full-time general education. Care must be taken, however, to insure that the student has the requisite skills for each advancement through the model. Second, in every case possible, an attempt should be made to insure that the adolescent has an opportunity to earn the necessary credits toward high school graduation. Third, the severely learning disabled student with a poor prognosis for graduation should be scheduled for vocational training, functional skill development, and eventual job placement.

This model makes provision for normalization and recognizes the fact that some students need immediate vocational preparation rather than academic skill remediation or development. It is apparent that application of the model will vary across programs and settings; this situation is to be expected due to the unique needs and resources of each locality. In practice, large, comprehensive schools will have the resources to offer the complete model. Smaller and more specialized schools may not be able to offer each separate placement. Some evidence (Goodman & Mann, 1976) exists, however, to suggest that the modified self-contained and resource room placements can be combined into one setting with the students spending varying amounts of time in the combined setting.

Although the model appears feasible, there are many problem areas that may prevent smooth operation, such as scheduling problems, time demands, personality conflicts, funding, and a lack of established procedures and precedents. In essence, high school personnel must examine existing resources and secure the best services possible.

Facilitating Accommodation

Even in the modified self-contained placement, the LD adolescent should participate in the general curriculum whenever possible. In many cases some alteration of the learning environment will be necessary for success; along these lines, Marsh, Gearheart, and Gearheart (1978) suggest several procedures:

1. *Communication with feeder schools.* A high school draws students from several junior high or middle schools. Communication between personnel of the schools is necessary to insure that *(a)* continuity of curriculum exists, *(b)* the necessary student records arrive at the high school, *(c)* program planning permits effective student transition to the new school, and *(d)* an adequate orientation to the high school is provided for the student and his family.
2. *Enrollment and scheduling assistance.* The classes for which a student enrolls can be a major cause of poor adjustment and failure. The LD specialist should assist whenever possible in developing a course schedule that will contribute to initial adjustment and success. He should help the student develop *course equilibrium* (i.e., registering for a course load that has a balance between demanding and easy courses). In some cases he may advise *course substitution.* This means that if the school provides courses that are less demanding but still satisfy required credits,

the student can avoid the high-risk courses. An approach similar to course substitution is *course supplantation,* in which the special education staff teaches some content areas in the alternative setting. This instruction is counted as course credit and listed on the transcript under the regular course name.

3. *Special textbooks.* Some companies have developed history, science, and other texts that cover the same material as standard textbooks but are less difficult to read. Alternative and modified curricula are also available. Examples include *Project MATH* (Educational Development Corporation, Tulsa, Okla.) and *Me Now* and *Me and My Environment* (Hubbard Publishing, Northbrook, Ill.) In addition, the teacher may modify the standard curriculum content or materials for better accommodation by the learning disabled. Weiss and Weiss (1974) describe several useful examples of this technique.

4. *The Omega list.* The LD specialist should know which teachers are the last choice (Omega list) for placement of an LD student. Likewise, the specialist should have an Alpha list of the teachers for first choice. Marsh, Gearheart, and Gearheart (1978) point out that the list should not be written because it could cause a serious breach in professional relationships.

5. *Course objectives.* Obtaining course objectives and requirements from the general educator may be very useful to the LD specialist in planning study schedules and selecting materials for use in the placement. Coordination between the activity of the special setting and the general classroom should aid the student to prepare for the important events of the regular class.

6. *Course salvaging.* The LD specialist must develop a system for monitoring the student's progress. With advance knowledge, it may be possible to intercede before a student fails. Every course failed increases the length of time necessary to accumulate graduation credit.

The guidance counselor assists the LD student in scheduling classes.

7. *Technical vocabulary.* The specific language of the content areas requires selective reading. Students might benefit from a handbook that includes the technical vocabulary and communication skills for each course. Another method would be to develop a list of technical words and integrate them into the activities of the special education placements.

Accommodation is probably the cumulative effect of many small efforts. Consequently, it is the responsibility of the LD specialist to seek every alternative in modifying the learning environment to increase effective learning and success.

The Learning Disabilities Specialist

The high school LD specialist will offer direct and indirect services. In providing these services he must fulfill the roles of *teacher* and *case manager.* To be effective as a teacher, the individual must be proficient in the following competencies: curriculum analysis, analytic teaching, organizing and managing the learning environment, mobilizing resources, and systems analysis (Wiederholt, Hammill, & Brown, 1978).

Due to the high school's organizational structure and focus on content specialties,

This teacher is helping a student with specific vocabulary words.

The LD specialist must develop materials that are not available commercially.

the LD specialist also becomes an advocate. In practice, he is a case manager who not only teaches but interacts with general educators, administrators, and parents. He may get involved in jurisdictional disputes—for example, if he and a regular teacher disagree on a scheduling or programming decision and cannot reach a compromise, he has no alliances. The general educator, though, can expect support from other department members. An administrator may rule in favor of the regular teacher so as not to alienate an entire department.

According to Zigmond, Silverman, and Laurie (1978), to be successful in both roles, the specialist must be able to satisfactorily perform the following direct services.

1. Interpret a psychological report and identify the educational relevance of findings in the report.
2. Assess the secondary-level learning-disabled student with appropriate informal, criterion-referenced, or competency-based tests as well as formal, standardized, norm-referenced assessments.
3. Conduct and interpret interviews with students and observations of them in and out of class, to learn about their particular interests and motivations.
4. Develop individualized instructional programs, utilizing the assessment information. This includes adjusting the difficulty level of a particular task and incorporating information regarding the child's attitude, interests, and values into the instructional plans.
5. Teach in the basic skill areas of reading, written language, and math.
6. Select commercially available instructional programs appropriate for the educational objectives as well as for the age and interests of adolescents with learning disabilities.
7. Create age-appropriate, high-interest instructional materials that may not be available commercially.
8. Use classroom management techniques with individuals and groups of students that motivate optimal efforts for achievement, reduce interfering maladaptive behaviors, encourage internal monitoring of behaviors, and enhance the students' self-concepts and peer interactions.
9. Engage groups of adolescents in discussion or activities that explore school sur-

vival skills, values clarification, attitudes, self-concept, and the like.
10. Provide learning-disabled students with an occupational exploration/preparation program which includes "hands on" experiences in one or more occupational fields. (pp. 287–288)

Zigmond, Silverman, and Laurie (1978) also suggest that the LD specialist should provide numerous indirect services. Many of these should focus on working with regular teachers. Specifically, they would include modeling management techniques, assisting in adapting curriculum, making suggestions for accommodating individual learner styles, analyzing the system for service delineation, and operating as an advocate for the LD students. Other services center on working with parents to provide (a) management techniques, (b) tutorial strategies, (c) referral sources, and (d) sessions to plan realistic academic and vocational goals.

Suggestions for Developing a Secondary Program

A problem in developing practical programs is that the "state of the art" is still relatively unknown. Few reports refer to secondary programming; most results conflict. In addition, studies are "trial and error" with little empirical verification. Another problem in developing guidelines is the variation in groups identified as *learning disabled* and the variation in size and type of high school. The following suggestions include (a) premises for program development, (b) guidelines for definitions and placement criteria, (c) program goals, and (d) curriculum considerations.

Premises

Based on the philosophical considerations and influence factors, the following premises are presented as a base for program development.

1. The provision for placement in a secondary program should include the severe, moderate, and mildly learning disabled. As discussed in Chapter 11, the placement options include 10 alternatives. A large comprehensive high school may offer all of the regular and special class alternatives within the same campus, while general and specialized high schools with smaller enrollments may offer fewer alternatives. For example, a rural general high school may have the resources to offer only placement in a general education classroom, a resource room, and an adapted special class.
2. The curriculum content of the secondary program must include provisions for career education. Some adolescents with learning disabilities develop career interests and others are in the process of examining career options. Some choices may demand a college education, some will require a high school diploma, and others may not need a formal degree. Some LD adolescents set unobtainable goals and others choose realistic careers. Parents have their own ideas about what the teenager should do and they, too, may be either realistic or unrealistic. Regardless of the circumstances, each individual should select and train for a possible career. Many LD adolescents have average or above average intellectual ability; the range of vocational options must be commensurate with their talent levels.
3. The LD program should remain close to the general program in distance and schedule. Their classes should not all be in one central location. Scheduling large groups of LD students into the same class sections and arranging special transportation usually violates the normalization principle.
4. The school program orientation must be based on the student's needs and abilities. For example, if the student is reading at the second grade level after 10 years of schooling, it is not always realistic to expect to bring the reading level to grade placement in the 9 or 18 months remaining of school. Likewise, a student working

The learning disabled adolescent 401

LD students need a variety of experiences before they select a career. Cher helps prepare a hot lunch for her classmates.

part-time as a carpenter's helper has a greater immediate need to learn measurement skills than to know algebra.

5. The secondary program does not include process training. Most research on process involves children. Considering the maturation of the musculoskeletal and central nervous systems during adolescence (Marsh, Gearheart, & Gearheart, 1978), this research may have little relevance to the teen-ager. In addition, there is limited evidence to support the use of process training at all (Hallahan & Cruickshank, 1973; Hallahan & Kauffman, 1978; Hammill & Larsen, 1974; Haring & Bateman, 1977; Newcomer & Hammill, 1976; Salvia & Ysseldyke, 1977; Ysseldyke, 1978). While it may be appropriate in the clinic or research setting, high school teachers should focus on academic, career, and behavioral objectives.
6. Use of Levels one, two, and/or three of the service delivery model in Chapter 11 implies that the student will meet or have the potential to meet the minimum require-

ments of the general education class in which he is placed. While the LD specialist can offer aid to the student in the form of helping to read the assignments and arranging for extra help, he cannot effectively tutor all the content specialties. Consequently, the student and regular teachers must also assume responsibility for the program.

Definition and Placement

In view of the influence which PL 94–142 will have, the definition used in the law should be accepted as a general *baseline* definition. While some agencies may use other definitions, the funding patterns written into the law will stimulate most programs to meet at least the minimum requirements as defined in the law.

Assessment should disclose the degree of deviancy from the norm rather than the nature of the disability. The placement criteria cited in the law (USOE, 1977) should be used as the baseline for placement (see Chapter 2). The major feature of these criteria involves a *severe discrepancy* between ability and achievement not attributed to another disability. However, experts disagree concerning what constitutes a severe discrepancy. Thompson (1970) maintains that any developmental lag in reading less than 3 years is not an indication of learning disability. Bryan and Bryan (1975), on the other hand, suggest that a 1½-year discrepancy in achievement and expected achievement warrants special attention. Goodman and Mann (1976) establish the placement criteria to be a 2-year difference except when the achievement exceeds the beginning seventh grade level.

Table 13.3 suggests specific placement criteria for a secondary LD program. These criteria were adapted from those of Goodman and Mann (1976). Steps 1–3 can be evaluated using a variety of accepted achievement, intellectual, and psychological instruments. A detailed discussion of specific instruments is provided by Goodman and Mann. Achievement above a sixth grade level is considered

TABLE 13.3

Suggested placement criteria for a secondary learning disability program.

Evaluation Sequence	Criteria	LD Placement Indicated	LD Placement Not Indicated
Step 1	No sensory, motor, intellectual, environmental impairments resulting in achievement discrepancies.	Student exhibits a discrepancy (underachievement) and this recurring problem is not attributed to the conditions listed.	Any of the conditions listed in the criteria exist.
Step 2	Intelligence falls into the normal range as measured by an accepted individual intelligence test.	Measured intelligence falls into normal range.	Measured intelligence is less than that required for normal range.
Step 3	Severe discrepancy exists between achievement and intellectual ability in oral expression, listening comprehension, mathematics calculation, or mathematics reasoning.	Measured achievement is below the sixth grade level in one or more of the criteria areas.	Measured achievement is above the sixth grade level in the criteria areas.
Step 4	Adolescents meeting criteria 1–3 are ranked on a continuum from most in need of service to least in need.	Assignment of individual to secondary LD program at most appropriate point in cascade of service.	Ranking indicates individual best assigned to Level one of service model (Chapter 11).

functional (i.e., a student with skill achievement in Step 3 at the seventh grade level or better is considered to have the potential for successful completion of high school work in the general classroom). The final step in the suggested placement criteria is to rank the students identified in Steps 1–3 on a continuum from most in need of service to least in need. The purpose of the ranking is to identify the adolescents most in need of immediate services and to aid in locating the entry point into the cascade of services.

Goals

It is impossible to list a simple set of universal goals applicable to all high school LD programs. The general aim is to establish specific goals for each individual. As illustrated in Figure 13.4, such goals include *(a)* the established goals of the high school, *(b)* individual compensatory goals, and *(c)* career-awareness goals. Adolescents ranked as least in need can probably achieve many of the general high school goals. The students ranked as most in need will probably work on developing basic skills or establishing procedures for compensation so that they can survive the everyday world. While awareness of appropriate career alternatives is especially important for those most in need, career awareness goals should be selected for every student.

Curriculum

Curriculum is the vehicle for accomplishing program goals. Five general suggestions are offered:

1. Each student needs a developmental or remedial curriculum approach. A de-

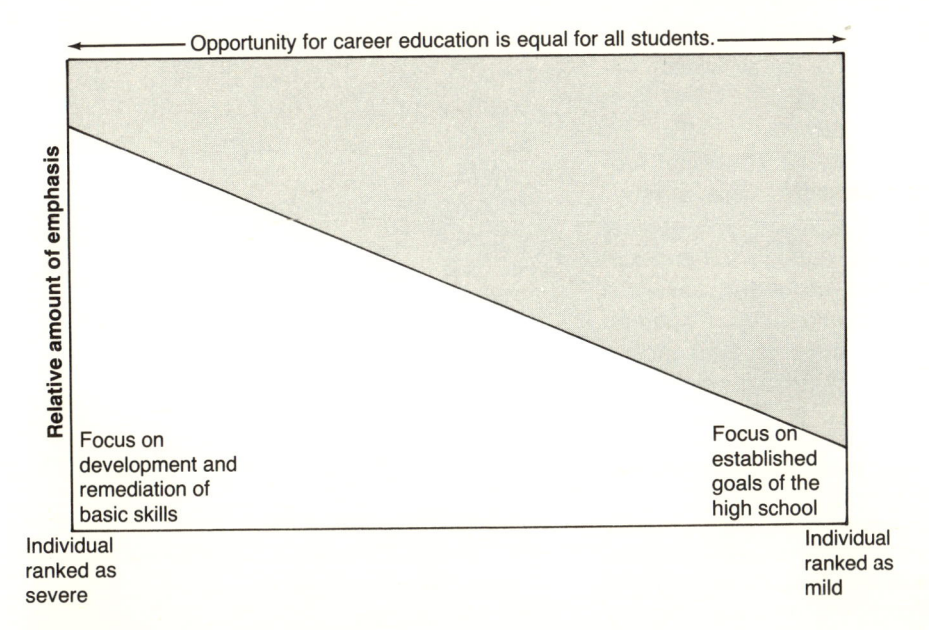

FIGURE 13.4.
Curriculum content of a program of LD adolescents.

Graph axes and labels:
- Y-axis: Relative amount of emphasis
- Top: Opportunity for career education is equal for all students.
- Lower left: Focus on development and remediation of basic skills
- Lower right: Focus on established goals of the high school
- Bottom left: Individual ranked as severe
- Bottom right: Individual ranked as mild

velopmental program may be appropriate for the students most in need (severely learning disabled). It also implies that the student will spend large portions of his day within the LD program. Essentially, the developmental approach is a carefully sequenced, comprehensive program for teaching a basic skill in its entirety. For students who have developed skills at higher levels, a remedial approach may be more appropriate. These students will spend more of their day in the general education classroom than the developmental learner because they have only specific skill deficits that need remediation. The importance of making developmental versus remedial decisions is in the implications for selection of materials, use of teaching strategies, and scheduling practices.

2. Increasingly, the student should learn acceptable social and emotional behaviors. The teacher must be very sensitive and perceptive to the adolescent emotional needs of the LD student. Aiding the shy, withdrawn freshman to become more assertive, or helping the socially inept sophomore to acquire the social graces prized by the right crowd may be as important in the student's progress as increasing ability in math or reading skills. This is not to imply that the teacher should function as a psychologist, therapist, or social worker but that a balance between cognitive and affective curriculum components must be achieved for a successful program.

3. The curriculum must be a unified whole. It should be clear to both the teacher and student how each component leads to accomplishing the goals and how activities in the LD program and in the regular class relate.

4. The curriculum should include an adequate feedback system. Many of the available commercial curriculum programs include a combination of objectives and evaluation tests to provide information for making instructional decisions. If a commercial program or teacher-made materials do not include a feedback system, the LD specialist should devise one. A feedback system is essential for *(a)* adjusting the teaching pace and techniques to fit the individual student, *(b)* identifying specific

areas of difficulty that will require additional instruction, and *(c)* providing accountability data.

5. The curriculum materials should be adapted from the regular education program whenever possible. This strategy keeps the student in touch with general education materials, appeals to his desire for conformity, and saves the specialist considerable preparation time. Goodman and Mann (1976) suggest five general criteria for assessing curricular systems:

   a. The curriculum will include a comprehensive, structured, developmental sequence of the subject matter content.
   b. The appearance and format of the program should be appealing to the older student.
   c. The scope and sequence of the program should be clearly delineated and preferably presented in a behaviorally objective format.
   d. The program should have an accompanying curricular management-evaluation system.
   e. The program should focus on mastery of basic skills. (p. 134)

Some materials[1] with potential for use in secondary learning disabilities programs include:

Math

Heath Mathematics Program (D. C. Heath, Lexington, Mass.)
Arithmetic: Step by Step, Kit A, Kit B (Continental Press, Elizabethtown, Pa.)
Basic Modern Math (Addison-Wesley, Menlo Park, Calif.)
Spectrum (Laidlaw, River Forest, Ill.)
Basic Essentials of Mathematics (Steck-Vaughn, Austin, Texas)
Pacemaker Practical Arithmetic Series (Fearon, Belmont, Calif.)
Mathematics for Individual Achievement (Houghton Mifflin, Boston, Mass.)
Target Series—Occupation Employment Phase (Mafex Associates, Johnstown, Pa.)

---
[1] See Hammill & Bartel (1978) for addresses of publishers.

Reading

Phoenix Reading Series (Prentice-Hall, Englewood Cliffs, N.J.)
Specific Skill Series (Barnell-Loft, Baldwin, N.Y.)
Reading for Concepts (McGraw-Hill, New York, N.Y.)
Reading Attainment System (Grolier Educational Corp., New York, N.Y.)
PAL Publications (Xerox Publications, Columbus, Ohio)
Corrective Reading Series (SRA, Chicago, Ill.)
Real Life Reading Skills (Scholastic Book Service, New York, N.Y.)
Getting It Together (SRA)
The Mature Student's Guide to Reading and Comprehension (SRA)
Point 31 (Reader's Digest, Pleasantville, N.Y.)

Spelling

Continuous Progress in Spelling (The Economy Co., Oklahoma City, Okla.)
Learn to Spell (The Economy Co.)

English

Keys to Good Language (The Economy Co.)
Language Exercises (Steck-Vaughn)
English for Everyday Living (Ideal School Supply Co., Oak Lawn, Ill.)
Action Series (SRA)
SCOPE (Scholastic Book Service)
Mott Basic Language Skills Program (Allied Education Council, Middletown, Conn.)

Contemporary and Future Problems

Lack of available information causes educators attempting to develop programs enormous difficulties. The practitioner must use a trial-and-error approach. Problems previously discussed include definition, prevalence rates, philosophical considerations, the structure of the high school, and untested models. Five other specific problems include establishing a referral system, scheduling, the Carnegie unit and graduation credit, grading standards, and financing secondary programs.

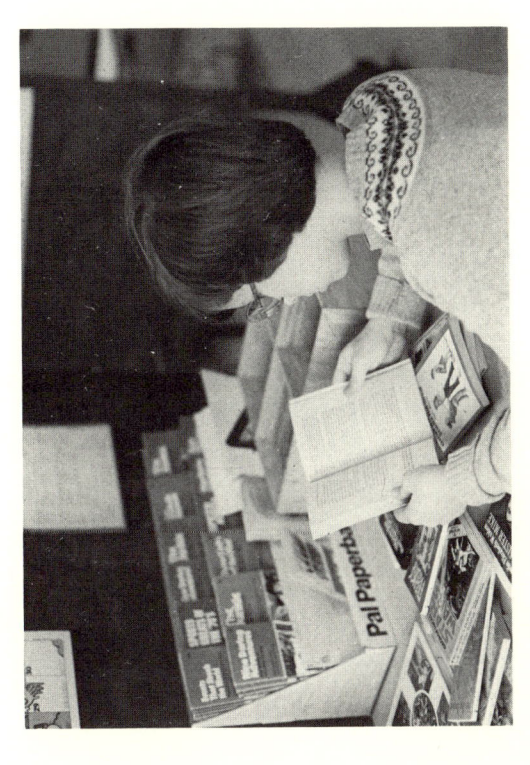

Special materials maintain interest and encourage reading.

Establishing a Referral System

Most LD adolescents are discovered before junior or senior high school. Regardless, three facts remain: *(a)* teachers are reluctant to refer older students to special education, *(b)* it is unrealistic to expect secondary teachers to identify LD students without some preparation for the task, and *(c)* thorough screening for learning disabilities is rare at the elementary level (Senf & Comrey, 1975) and nonexistent at the secondary level. Consequently, identification and referral procedures appropriate for the secondary school must be developed, teachers must be instructed in the use of the procedures, and the entire process should be validated.

Scheduling

Due to the wide variety of scheduling practices in high schools it is impossible to develop *the* solution to scheduling that fits every situation. Nevertheless, LD classes must be fit in. Ideally, the LD program should have priority. In practice, the system's political structure often makes this impossible. Usually a student failing in the general class because of low or nonfunctioning basic skills can be rescheduled into learning disability classes with little resistance, especially if the student is a behavior problem. The student who compensates for skill deficits, manipulates teachers, or resists placement is more difficult to remove from the regular program. The part-time placement component of the model suggested for service delivery may alleviate some of the problems, but inflexible schedules remain as one of the single most difficult day-to-day problems facing the specialist.

The Carnegie Unit and Graduation Credit

To graduate from high school a student must accumulate a sufficient number of required Carnegie units. A unit represents a year's study in any major subject, constituting approximately a quarter of a full year's work (i.e., four major subjects taken in one year generate four Carnegie units). It is designed to afford a standard measurement for the work done in secondary schools. In many schools work in special classes goes uncredited. This situation contributes to high school teachers' reluctance to refer students or agree to schedule changes. Until a satisfactory compromise is reached on this matter, no one will want to opt for special placement that jeopardizes earning credit for graduation.

Grading Standards

Most teachers torn between conflicting issues in grading are genuinely interested in the progress of their students and want them to graduate from high school. However, they are under pressure to have the grade mean something (i.e., to discriminate good work from poor work). Grades and grading standards are sensitive areas. For the specialist the problem requires tact, diplomacy, and negotiating skills. As the student's advocate, he must bargain for just rewards when the student works hard and demonstrates progress in achieving his goals both in the general and special classroom. Unfortunately, the progress may be below or just at the minimum accepted for credit. While a number of solutions have been tried, none has proven totally acceptable (Frierson, 1975).

Financing Secondary Programs

Most school systems are on tight budgets, and the costs of an adequate secondary LD program are prohibitive. Lack of money to purchase adequate materials, buy support services, and develop service delivery models may be second only to scheduling as the worst day-to-day problem.

CONCLUSION

Little is known about the secondary LD student and how to best provide for him. As yet unestablished are an acceptable definition, empirically established characteristics, well-defined program models, and effective curricula and teaching strategies. Consequently, the reader must cautiously interpret and apply current recommendations and suggestions. Perhaps valid practices will be soon forthcoming as teacher trainers, administrators, teachers, parents, and adolescents confront today's problems.

REFERENCES

Alexander, W.M., Saylor, J.G., & Williams, E.L. *The high school: Today and tomorrow.* New York: Holt, Rinehart & Winston, 1971.

Anderson, L.W., & Van Dyke, L.A. *Secondary school administration* (2nd ed.). Boston: Houghton Mifflin, 1972.

Berger, B.M., & Hackett, B.M. On the decline of age grading in rural hippie communes. *Journal of Social Issues,* 1974, *30,* 163–183.

Berman, A. Learning disabilities and juvenile delinquency: Results of a psychoneurological approach. In B. Kratoville (Ed.), *Youth in trouble: The learning disabled adolescent.* San Rafael, Calif.: Academic Therapy Publication, 1974.

Brutten, M., Richardson, S.O., & Mangel, C. *Something's wrong with my child.* New York: Harcourt, Brace, Jovanovich, 1973.

Bryan, T.H., & Bryan, J.H. *Understanding learning disabilities.* Port Washington, N.Y.: Alfred, 1975.

Bryant, N.D., & McLoughlin, J.A. Subject variables: Definition, incidence, characteristics, and correlates. In N.D. Bryant & C.E. Kass, *Final report: Leadership training institute in learning disabilities* (Vol. 1) (USOE Grant No. OEO-0-71-4425-604, Project No. 127145). Tucson, Ariz.: University of Arizona, 1972.

Chaffee, J., Jr., & Clark, J.P. (Eds.). *New dimensions for educating youth.* Denver: U.S. Department of Health, Education, and Welfare, 1976.

Coleman, J.S. Comments on responses to youth: Transition to adulthood. *School Review,* 1974, *83,* 139–144.

Commission of the Reorganization of Secondary Education. *Cardinal principles of secondary education* (U.S. Office of Education, Bulletin 1918, No. 35). Washington, D.C.: U.S. Government Printing Office, 1918.

Conant, J.B. *The American high school today.* New York: McGraw-Hill, 1959.

Conger, J.J. *Adolescence and youth: Psychological development in a changing world* (2nd ed.). New York: Harper & Row, 1977.

Cottle, T.J. Memories of half a life age. *Journal of Youth and Adolescence,* 1973, *2,* 201–212.

Deshler, D.D. Psycho-social characteristics of learning disabled adolescents. In *Learning disabilities in the secondary school: Title III: Curricular development for secondary learning disability.* Norristown, Pa.: Montgomery County Intermediate Unit, 1975.

Duling, F., Eddy, S., & Risko, V. *Learning disabilities of juvenile delinquents.* Morgantown, W. Va.: Department of Educational Services, Robert F. Kennedy Youth Center, 1970.

Educational Policies Commission. *The purposes of education in American democracy.* Washington, D.C.: National Education Association, 1938.

Elkind, D. *A sympathetic understanding of the child—Birth to sixteen.* Boston: Allyn & Bacon, 1974.

Frierson, E.C. *A classroom guide to grading without judgment.* Nashville, Tenn.: EDCOA Publications, 1975.

Frierson, E.C. Presentation at *All I've got is me,* a workshop for classroom teachers, Orlando, Florida, February 1978.

Geiger, S. Early recognizable personality deviations. *Federal Probation,* 1961, *25,* 4–10.

Goethals, G.W. Adolescence: Variations on a theme. In R.J. Havighurst & P.H. Dreyer (Eds.), *Youth.* Chicago: University of Chicago Press, 1975.

Goodman, L., & Mann, L. *Learning disabilities in the secondary school: Issues and practices.* New York: Grune & Stratton, 1976.

Grant, W.V., & Lind, C.G. *Digest of educational statistics, 1975 edition.* Washington, D.C.: U.S. Government Printing Office, 1976.

Haan, N. Personality development from adolescence to adulthood in the Oakland growth and guidance studies. *Seminars in Psychiatry,* 1972, *4,* 399–414.

Hagin, R.A. How do we find him? In E. Schloss (Ed.), *The educator's enigma: The adolescent with learning disabilities.* San Rafael, Calif.: Academic Therapy, 1971.

Hallahan, D.P., & Cruickshank, W.M. *Psychoeducational foundations of learning disabilities.* Englewood Cliffs, N.J.: Prentice-Hall, 1973.

Hallahan, D.P., & Kauffman, J.M. *Exceptional children: Introduction to special education.* Englewood Cliffs, N.J.: Prentice-Hall, 1978.

Hammill, D.D. Adolescents with learning disability: Definition, identification, and incidence. In *Learning disabilities in the secondary school: Title III: Curricular development for secondary learning disability.* Norristown, Pa.: Montgomery County Intermediate Unit, 1975.

Hammill, D.D., & Bartel, N.R. *Teaching children with learning and behavior problems* (2nd ed.). Boston: Allyn & Bacon, 1978.

Hammill, D.D., & Larsen, S. The effectiveness of psycholinguistic training. *Exceptional Children,* 1974, *41,* 5–15.

Haring, N.G., & Bateman, B.D. *Teaching the learning disabled child.* Englewood Cliffs, N.J.: Prentice-Hall, 1977.

Havighurst, R.J. *Developmental tasks and education* (2nd ed.). New York: David McKay, 1952.

Henley, A. Delinquents are his patients. *Today's Health,* 1969, *47,* 48–49.

Holte, A. *Confessions of a juvenile judge.* Paper presented at the Ninth International Conference of the Association for Children with Learning Disabilities, Atlantic City, New Jersey, 1972.

Hopkins, R.L., & Conard, R.J. Putting it all together: Super school. In N.G. Haring & R.L. Schiefelbusch (Eds.), *Teaching special children.* New York: McGraw-Hill, 1976.

Jacobson, F.N. Learning disabilities and juvenile delinquency: A demonstrated relationship. In R.E. Weber (Ed.), *Handbook on learning disabilities: A prognosis for the child, the adolescent, the adult.* Englewood Cliffs, N.J.: Prentice-Hall, 1974.

Kaufman, M.J., Gottlieb, J., Agard, J.A., & Kukic, M.B. Mainstreaming: Toward an explication of the construct. *Focus on Exceptional Children,* 1975, *7,* 1–12.

Keldgord, R.E. Brain damage and delinquency; A question and a challenge. *Academic Therapy Quarterly,* 1968, *4,* 93–99.

Keniston, K. Prologue: Youth as a stage of life. In R.J. Havighurst & P.H. Dreyer (Eds.), *Youth.* Chicago: University of Chicago Press, 1975.

Keogh, B.K., & Levitt, M.L. Special education in the mainstream: A confrontation of limitations? *Focus on Exceptional Children,* 1976, *8,* 1–11.

Konopka, G. Requirements for healthy development of adolescent youth. *Adolescence,* 1973, *8,* 291–316.

Lerner, J.W. *Children with learning disabilities* (2nd ed.). Boston: Houghton Mifflin, 1976.

Lorenz, K. Genetic decay. *Intellectual Digest,* 1974, *4*(8), 23–30.

MacMillan, D.L., & Becker, L.D. Mainstreaming the mildly handicapped learner. In R.D. Kneedler & S.G. Tarver (Eds.), *Changing perspectives in special education.* Columbus, Ohio: Charles E. Merrill, 1977.

Maietta, D.F. The role of cognitive regulators in learning-disabled teen-agers. *Academic Therapy,* 1970, *5,* 177–186.

Marsh, G.E., Gearheart, C.K., & Gearheart, B.R. *The learning disabled adolescent: Program alternatives in the secondary school.* Saint Louis: C.V. Mosby, 1978.

Mauser, A.J. Learning disabilities and delinquent youth. *Academic Therapy,* 1974, *4,* 390–402.

Miller, D. *Adolescence: Psychology, psychopathology, and psychotherapy.* New York: Jason Aronson, 1974.

Myers, P.I., & Hammill, D.D. *Methods for learning disorders* (2nd ed.). New York: John Wiley, 1976.

National Advisory Committee on Dyslexia and Related Reading Disorders. *Reading disorders in the United States.* Washington, D.C.: U.S. Department of Health, Education, and Welfare, 1969.

National Education Association. *What research says to the teacher: Evaluation and reporting of student achievement.* Washington, D.C.: National Education Association, 1974.

Newcomer, P.L., & Hammill, D.D. *Psycholinguistics in the schools.* Columbus, Ohio: Charles E. Merrill, 1976.

Offer, D. *The psychological world of the teenager.* New York: Basic Books, 1969.

Page, B. Presentation at *All I've got is me,* a workshop for classroom teachers, Orlando, Florida, February 1978.

Poremba, C.D. Learning disabilities, youth and delinquency: Programs for intervention. In H.R. Myklebust (Ed.), *Progress in learning disabilities* (Vol. 3). New York: Grune & Stratton, 1975.

Rapoport, R., & Rapoport, R. *Leisure and the family life cycle.* London: Rutlege & Kegan Paul, 1975.

Rogers, D. *The psychology of adolescence* (3rd ed.). Englewood Cliffs, N.J.: Prentice-Hall, 1977.

Rosenthal, R., & Jacobson, L. *Pygmalion in the classroom: Teacher expectations and pupils' intellectual development.* New York: Holt, Rinehart & Winston, 1968.

Russell, R.W. The dilemma of the handicapped adolescent. In R.E. Weber (Ed.), *Handbook on learning disabilities.* Englewood Cliffs, N.J.: Prentice-Hall, 1974.

Salvia, J., & Ysseldyke, J.E. *Assessment in special education.* Boston: Houghton Mifflin, 1977.

Salzman, L. Adolescence: Epoch or disease? *American Journal of Orthopsychiatry,* 1972, *42,* 342–343.

Schiefelbusch, R.L., & Haring, N.G. Perspectives on teaching special children. In N.G. Haring & R.L. Schiefelbusch (Eds.), *Teaching special children.* New York: McGraw-Hill, 1976.

Senf, G., & Comrey, A. State incentive in learning disabilities: Illinois project SCREEN, Report 1: The SCREEN early identification procedure. *Journal of Learning Disabilities,* 1975, *8,* 451–457.

Siegel, E. *The exceptional child grows up.* New York: E.P. Dutton, 1974.

Strother, C.R. Who is he? In E. Schloss (Ed.), *The educator's enigma: The adolescent with learning disabilities.* San Rafael, Calif.: Academic Therapy, 1971.

Thompson, A. Moving toward adulthood. In L. Anderson (Ed.), *Helping the adolescent with the hidden handicap.* Los Angeles, Calif.: California Association for Neurologically Handicapped Children, 1970.

U.S. Office of Education. *First annual report of National Advisory Committee on Handicapped Children.* Washington, D.C.: U.S. Department of Health, Education, & Welfare, 1968.

U.S. Office of Education. Education of handicapped children: Assistance to states: Proposed rulemaking. *Federal Register,* 1976, *41,* 52404–52407.

U.S. Office of Education. Assistance to states: Procedures for evaluating specific learning disabilities. *Federal Register,* 1977, *42,* 65082–65085.

Weiss, H., & Weiss, M. *A survival manual.* Great Barrington, Mass.; Treehouse Associates, 1974.

Wiederholt, J.L., Hammill, D.D., & Brown, V. *The resource teacher: A guide to effective practices.* Boston: Allyn & Bacon, 1978.

Willenberg, E.P. Foreword. In B.R. Gearheart, *Learning disabilities: Educational strategies.* Saint Louis, Mo.: C.V. Mosby, 1977.

Wissink, J.F. *A procedure for the identification of children with learning disabilities.* Unpublished doctoral dissertation, The University of Arizona, Tucson, 1972.

Wolfsensberger, W. *The principle of normalization in human services.* Toronto: National Institute on Mental Retardation, 1972.

Ysseldyke, J.E. Remediation of ability deficits: Some major questions. In L. Mann, L. Goodman, & J.L. Wiederholt (Eds.), *Teaching the learning-disabled adolescent.* Boston: Houghton Mifflin, 1978.

Zigmond, N. *A program of comprehensive service for secondary students with learning disabilities.* Paper presented at the meeting of the 56th Annual International Council for Exceptional Children Convention, Kansas City, Missouri, May 1978.

Zigmond, N., Silverman, R., & Laurie, T. Competencies for teachers. In L. Mann, L. Goodman, & J.L. Wiederholt (Eds.), *Teaching the learning-disabled adolescent.* Boston: Houghton Mifflin, 1978.

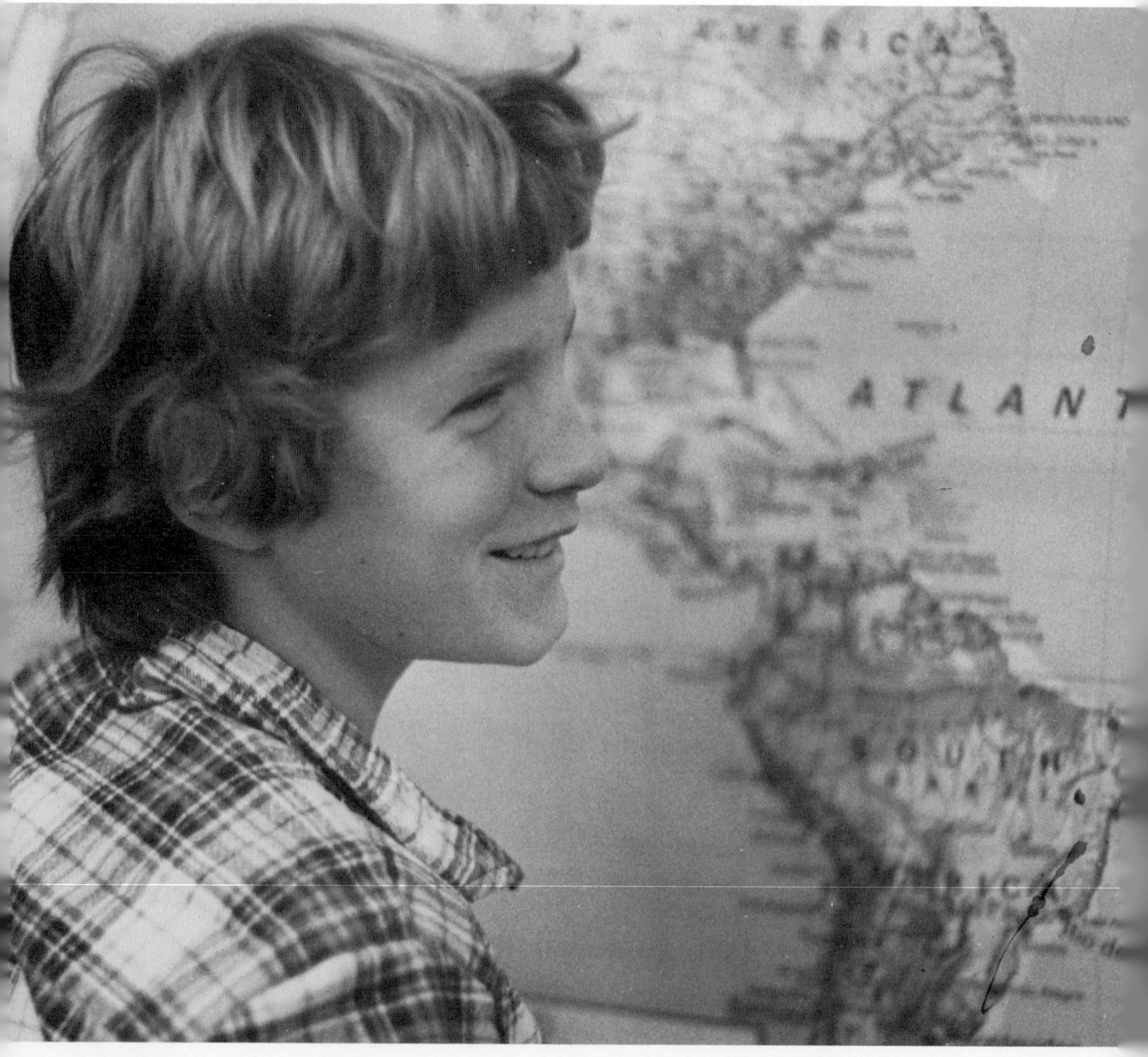
AMERICA
ATLANT

14

Teaching children and adolescents

For many special education teachers the school year begins with someone handing them a stack of folders and saying, "These are your new students." The thick folders may include psychological reports, results of medical examinations, academic achievement test scores, comments from previous teachers, and work samples. Many teachers scrutinize each folder in an effort to find information that may help develop an individualized instructional plan. Other teachers may briefly glance at the folders for pertinent health-related information (e.g., seizures) and then file them.

Due to different theoretical orientations, teachers vary greatly on how they plan and implement an instructional program. Some teachers rely heavily on standardized achievement tests and/or psychological process tests such as the *ITPA* or the *Developmental Test of Visual Perception*. Others depend on their own informal measures. Regardless of a teacher's orientation it is apparent that numerous alternatives are available in planning and implementing programs.

Because LD children do not learn sufficiently through traditional teaching, special educators are faced with the responsibility of designing and delivering instructional programs that enable these children to progress at an acceptable rate. Although such a rate is arbitrary, oftentimes a program is considered successful if it enables the children to return to the regular class and make satisfactory progress.

DIAGNOSTIC-PRESCRIPTIVE TEACHING ON A DAILY BASIS

Diagnostic-prescriptive teaching describes the instructional process used with LD children. Its procedures vary across numerous parameters, in both qualitative and quantitative ways. However, a common goal is to match the learner, the task, and instructional interventions in a manner that facilitates maximum cognitive and emotional growth. The establishment and *continuation* of this match are usually accomplished through the four steps outlined in Figure 14.1.

The first step, identifying a target skill, is directly tied to an educational assessment or diagnosis. Depending on the teacher's orientation, the *initial* target skill may be derived from an informal teacher-made test or from standardized tests. Subsequent skills must be derived from day-to-day evaluation procedures, which are usually informal. During instruction the teacher decides if the difficulty level of the task is appropriate. The child should acquire the skill without prolonged failure and/or frustration. Earned success is a key concept in monitoring task difficulty; the student must view the task as demanding enough to realize some sense of accomplishment when criterion is reached. An optimum success-error ratio probably varies from child to child. Informal reading inventories traditionally suggest a 95% success to 5% failure ratio for instructional tasks. Lovitt and Hansen (1976) suggest a correct reading rate of 45–65 words per minute with eight or less errors and 50%–75% comprehension as guidelines for placement in a basal. However, because this area needs research, teachers must rely on observation to establish a good ratio for each learner. The identified skill may span academic and/or social areas. For example, it may focus on spelling consonant-vowel-consonant-silent *e* (cvce) words or learning to take turns in a game.

Step II consists of providing instruction. The teacher selects a stimulus or material (commercial or teacher-made) that presents the task to the student. Furthermore, she determines how she wants the child to respond (e.g., written, spoken). Also, she must decide how she will respond to the student. Some common responses include simple correct-incorrect feedback, reinforcement, additional task-related information, a question, and/or modeling of the correct response. In Step II she must also plan assignments to be completed without her help (e.g., homework and practice activities). Stephens (1977) suggests that teachers not use homework to introduce new skills. Chapter 3, p. 80, provides some guidelines to assist teachers with Step II.

Evaluation, the third step, is an essential feature. In order to monitor a pupil's progress and/or determine the effectiveness of a specific instructional technique, evaluation must occur frequently (e.g., daily). Several procedures available to the teacher include

1. *Amount of work completed and performance on standardized tests.* This type of evaluation is based on the amount of work a student completes during a specified period of time. It may include pages read, the number of math problems computed, or the number of workbook pages completed. The work is usually checked by the teacher. Unfortunately, this type of evaluation does not include criterion that insures mastery by the student. It is often coupled

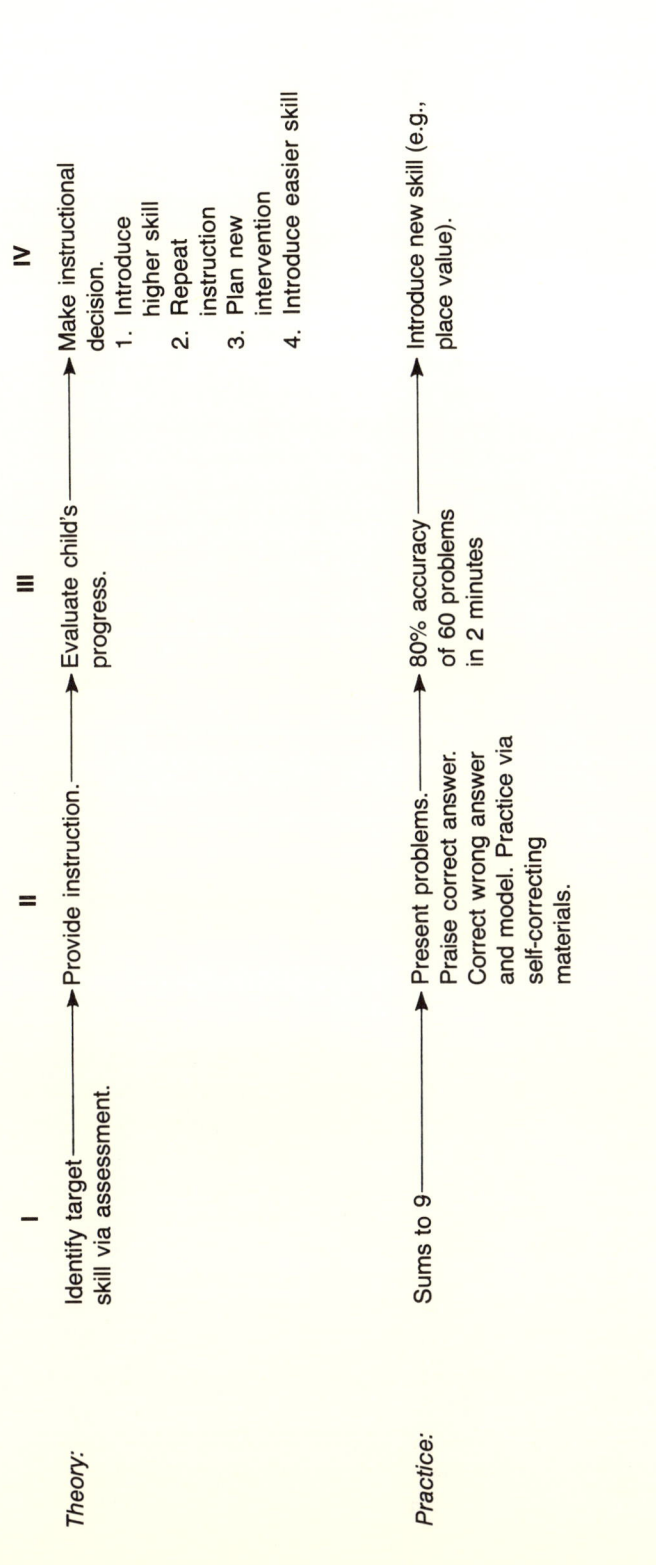

	I	II	III	IV
Theory:	Identify target skill via assessment. →	Provide instruction. →	Evaluate child's progress. →	Make instructional decision. 1. Introduce higher skill 2. Repeat instruction 3. Plan new intervention 4. Introduce easier skill
Practice:	Sums to 9 →	Present problems. Praise correct answer. Correct wrong answer and model. Practice via self-correcting materials. →	80% accuracy of 60 problems in 2 minutes →	Introduce new skill (e.g., place value).

FIGURE 14.1
Four steps of diagnostic-prescriptive teaching.

with the administration of standardized achievement tests at infrequent intervals. These achievement tests seldom influence daily instruction and are for the most part post hoc. Although standardized tests are used in evaluation, they seldom influence the day-to-day instruction. They are not sensitive to pupil progress on a daily basis and do not evaluate the effectiveness of various instructional techniques while they are being used.

2. *Progress on a skill hierarchy.* A student can be carefully monitored within a specified skill hierarchy. Oftentimes, criterion for the mastery of each skill is established (e.g., 90% correct). When one skill is mastered, the next skill on the hierarchy is introduced. Progress is readily determined by noting the number of skills mastered.
3. *Charting of progress.* Charting is the main feature of precision teaching (Lindsley, 1964). The teacher selects an instructional pinpoint and charts the student's progress on that pinpoint. The number of correct and incorrect responses on the instructional pinpoint (e.g., see word— say word) for a specified time period (frequently 1 minute) provides the data for the chart. The student usually achieves criterion by attaining a certain rate of correct responses (e.g., 60–80 words read correct per minute with two or less errors). Charting is frequently used with a specified skill hierarchy; however, it is a procedure that is independent of the skill (pinpoint) selected.

The evaluation results provide the information for initiating Step IV. If the student masters a task, the teacher initiates a new task and repeats the teaching cycle. If a student does not master the task, three options are available for the teacher: repeating the same instructions, introducing a new teaching strategy, or changing to an easier task. When she selects one of the options, the teaching cycle is repeated. In essence, diagnostic-prescriptive teaching is a test-teach-test-teach cycle.

INDIVIDUALIZED EDUCATIONAL PROGRAMS

PL 94–142 directly affects teaching practices by stating that an Individualized Educational Plan (IEP) must be developed and implemented for pupils receiving special education. Table 14.1 illustrates an IEP format that incorporates the essentials of a plan. According to the law the IEP must state *(a)* the child's present performance levels, *(b)* annual and short-term instructional objectives, *(c)* the specific educational services to be provided and the extent to which the child will be able to participate in regular education, *(d)* the projected date for initiation and anticipated duration of such services, and *(e)* appropriate objective criteria and evaluation procedures and schedules for determining, on at least an annual basis, whether objectives are being achieved.

A distinction must be made regarding IEP procedures and the identification process. Although the identification and IEP processes are related, they require different team members (e.g., parent involvement) and different diagnostic-assessment information, and they function under different time requirements. Whereas identification focuses on determining the student's eligibility for placement in a specific learning disabilities (SLD) program, the IEP is aimed at planning an instructional program specifically tailored to the student's needs. It is often a good practice for the SLD teacher to work with the student for several sessions prior to the IEP conference. During this time she can determine realistic objectives and specific teaching techniques. According to Turnbull, Strickland, and Hammer (1978a),

The IEP has the potential of being the catalyst for a more individualized and specified approach to education, increased accountability of educators, and shared decision-making between teachers and parents. It can be viewed as a burden of more paperwork or as an opportunity to improve the quality of education for

TABLE 14.1

Individualized Education Program.

FORM A

Name _____ D.O.B. _____ C.A. _____ E.A. _____ School _____ Grade _____

SLD Resource Teacher _____ Staffing Date _____ Placement Date _____

Eligibility Data: Student meets current eligibility criteria for SLD. See eligibility/staffing summary (in Chapter 3). Duration of service contingent upon annual staffing recommendations and educational planning conferences.

IEP Participants:
Teacher(s) _____
LEA representative _____
Parent/Guardian _____
Evaluation-eligibility team member _____
Other(s) _____

Educational Programs and Services: Regular classroom placement with curriculum modification; SLD program _____ hours per day, _____ days per week; _____

Level of Functioning:

Academic Levels: *Behavioral Levels:*   *Physical Levels:*
(Preacademic, academic, vocational)

SKILL   SOURCE   SKILL   SOURCE   SKILL   SOURCE

_____ _____   _____ _____   _____ _____

_____ _____   _____ _____   _____ _____

TABLE 14.1 cont.

Annual Goals and Short-term Objectives: See IEP Form B.

Special Considerations: (Resources used within and outside school)

Regular program participation: _____

	Beginning	Ending

Special strengths: _____

Intervention Strategies: _____

Educational Planning Conferences: For formulation and review of Individualized Education Plan.

Classroom teacher _____ Date _____ Parent _____ Date _____

FORM B

Long-range Goals: (include academic, behavioral, and physical where appropriate)

A. Goal: to _____ as measured by _____ achieved _____
B. Goal: to _____ as measured by _____ achieved _____
C. Goal: to _____ as measured by _____ achieved _____

Goal Development: (include this section for each long-range goal)

Long-range goal: _____

_____

_____

Beginning
Date

Projected
Ending
Date

Short-range Objectives Leading to Long-range Goals

1 _____
2 _____
3 _____
4 _____
5 _____
6 _____

| Methods and Materials | Objectives |||||| Methods/Materials Changed |
	1	2	3	4	5	6	
Objectives changed							
Objectives mastered							

Date	Comments

handicapped students and the diagnostic-prescriptive skills of teachers. (p. 46)

Participants in IEP Meetings

The law specifies who participates in IEP meetings: *(a)* a representative of the schools, other than the child's teacher, who is qualified to provide or supervise special education, *(b)* the student's teacher (i.e., the special education teacher if the student is receiving special education; otherwise, the regular teacher), *(c)* one or both parents, *(d)* the student, when appropriate, and *(e)* others at the discretion of the parent or school personnel.

Schools must follow certain procedures regarding parent participation, especially those insuring their presence at the meeting. Specific steps include

1. Notify them early enough. The purpose, time, and location of the meeting, and who will be in attendance should be included in the notice.
2. Schedule the meeting at a mutually agreed upon time and place.
3. If neither parent can attend, the school should use other methods to insure parent participation, such as telephone calls or home visits.
4. If a meeting is held without a parent in attendance, the school must document attempts to involve the parent. These attempts include telephone calls, copies of correspondence, and records of home visits.

Components of an IEP

Levels of Performance

The student's present level of performance may be obtained from placement information (e.g., evaluations of academic, language, and cognitive skills); however, additional assessment is usually necessary to formulate specific objectives in various subject areas. On the IEP, level-of-performance data must be precise enough to direct the teacher in formulating initial objectives. Norm- or criterion-referenced evaluation instruments are designed to provide such data. Criterion-referenced instruments appear more suitable than tests that primarily yield comparative scores. These instruments typically include systematic skill sequences and provide information that directly leads to objectives (e.g., instruct child in sums to 9 facts). Finally, levels of performance may be assessed in the following areas: social adaptation, emotional maturity, prevocational-vocational skills, psychomotor skills, and academic achievement.

Annual Goals

In order to plan annual goals, evaluation data must be carefully examined. These goals must be tailored to individual needs—academic and otherwise—and encompass the entire spectrum of short-term objectives in each specified area. They must describe what the child should be able to do at the end of the school year. Although these goals can only be an educated approximation, progress toward them can be systematic. Turnbull, Strickland, and Hammer (1978b) note:

> Although teachers are not legally responsible for achieving the annual goals, they are responsible for setting realistic expectations and for providing relevant, systematic instruction toward these goals. If learning disabled students do not achieve as predicted on the IEP, goals and objectives should be revised. (p. 71)

Short-term Objectives

Short-term objectives must be listed for each student and described in specific, objective, measurable terms. These objectives help extend present levels of performance toward annual goals. As noted earlier, if criterion-referenced evaluation measures are used this task is much simpler, because the mastery of specific skills is readily pinpointed on a continuum of listed competencies. By using well-designed curriculum guides that specify objectives, the process usually becomes orderly, systematic, and less time consuming.

Description of Services

A statement of the specific services and materials provided for the child includes *(a)* who teaches the child, *(b)* what content is included in the instructional program, (e.g., master short vowels in cvc words, master simple addition sums to 9) and *(c)* what materials are used *(Distar* Reading, Dr. Spello, Cuisenaire Rods). Also, the extent of the child's participation in the regular program must be established. For example, the plan may state that the child functions in the regular classroom all but 1 hour a day. The role of the regular teacher concerning the child is determined (e.g., the child will sit in the front of the regular classroom, use individualized spelling tapes developed jointly by the regular teacher and the SLD teacher).

Dates of Service

The plan outlines the projected dates for initiation and anticipated duration of services.

Evaluation

The use of objective criteria and frequent assessment are encouraged. However, the law only requires an annual evaluation to determine if the annual goals are being achieved. Evaluation procedures are presented in Chapter 3 and in the latter portion of this chapter.

Requirements of an IEP insure a certain amount of commonality in planning instruction for SLD students; however, its specific components leave the teacher with much flexibility in selecting assessment, instructional, and evaluation procedures. It is hoped that both the requirements and flexibility combine to generate individualized, resourceful instructional programs.

Although many teachers share common orientations, no two teachers teach exactly alike. They select from the numerous theories, strategies, and techniques to create individual styles. The remainder of this chapter provides information relevant to instruction and the creation of teaching styles. It is presented in four sections: *(a)* Instructional Approaches, *(b)* Planning Instruction, *(c)* Developing and Maintaining Effective Interaction Skills, and *(d)* Summary.

INSTRUCTIONAL APPROACHES

Task Analysis Versus Ability Training

Quay (1973) feels there are three principal types of teaching strategies. First, he believes that the exceptional learner suffers from impairments or dysfunctions in processes that are essential to learning. In Type 1 instruction, the teacher focuses on improving the impaired process (e.g., lack of motor coordination). Today's teaching activities are expected to facilitate learning at some time in the future. For example, a child may receive gross-motor training with the purpose of improving reading at a later time. In learning disabilities, Type 1 has primarily been promoted by the perceptual-motor theorists (e.g., Barsch, 1967; Cratty, 1971; Kephart, 1971).

Type 2, like Type 1, focuses on correcting (for future benefit) a faulty process within the child that interferes with learning. It differs in that its activities empirically or logically relate to the desired terminal behavior. For example, a child may receive form discrimination training in order to improve the terminal behavior of reading. It is apparent that reading involves many skills of which form discrimination is one. Type 2 instruction has been highlighted in the perceptual discrimination programs of Frostig and Horne (1964) and in the psycholinguistic programs of Bush and Giles (1977), Kirk and Kirk (1971), and Minskoff, Wiseman, and Minskoff (1972).

Type 3 is based on the principle that the child's learning processes are intact and that her difficulty is a result of a limited behavioral repertoire. This approach stresses the idea that the focus of the handicap is primarily outside the child (i.e., an experience deficit). Type 3 teaching techniques involve direct instruction in either the terminal behavior or its immediate antecedents. In essence, the instructional activity is an actual part of the terminal behavior. For example, a child learns to read by reviewing words or practicing word attack skills. Quay (1973) notes that Type 1 and Type 2 strategies lack empirical support and the link between the specific activities and the desired educational goal has not been established. Quay recommends that Type 3 approaches deserve first consideration and should only be discarded when they are found ineffective. He reports that substantial evidence exists that supports their effectiveness.

Ysseldyke and Salvia (1974) classify diagnostic-prescriptive teaching approaches into two different models: *(a)* the ability training model and *(b)* the task analysis model. Their ability training model incorporates Quay's (1973) Type 1 and Type 2 approaches. The task analysis model is similar to Quay's Type 3 approach.

Ysseldyke and Salvia (1974) report that the ability model lacks relevance for instruction because there is no empirical support for the position that motor, psycholinguistic, and/or perceptual training is an essential prerequisite to the acquisition of academic skills. In addition, they note that few tests on ability are reliable enough for making decisions regarding programming. They indicate that the task-analysis approach more effectively meets the critical assumptions of prescriptive teaching; and, like Quay (1973), they strongly recommend its use. Furthermore, they report that extensive research and experimentation are needed to establish the relationship between reliable, valid aptitude measures and effective instructional techniques.

In a similar vein, Stephens (1977) delineates two primary teaching models: *(a)* the ability-training approach and *(b)* the skill-training approach. Basically, this dichotomous arrangement parallels the position of Ysseldyke and Salvia (1974). Moreover, Stephens states that the major assumptions of the ability approach include the following:

1. Reliable and valid aptitude measures exist.
2. Aptitude deficits can be corrected.
3. Aptitude weaknesses are causally related to performance deficits.

Additionally, Stephens lists the major assumptions of the skill approach:

1. Direct skill instruction corrects inadequate responses.
2. Behavior change is a function of its consequences.
3. Pupils can learn to generalize specific responses across conditions.

He reports that the ability approach is based upon more unproven assumptions than the skill approach. He agrees with Quay (1973) and Ysseldyke and Salvia (1974) in recommending the skill-oriented approach.

A Combination Approach

Like previous writers, Smead (1977) severely criticizes the present form of the ability training approach; however, she extends her review by raising several questions concerning the task-analysis approach. She claims that the short history of task analysis precludes the existence of extensive data. However, she uses theoretical positions and some data to raise several questions concerning the model:

1. Do natural hierarchical sequences of learning skills exist?
2. Does the most efficient learning occur in small, carefully guided steps, or in massive general experience?
3. Is the overwhelming concern with task manipulation justified, or should child variables receive more attention?
4. Can teachers become good task analysts, or will each individual's view of learning uniquely influence the task analysis process?

Smead (1977) notes that neither the ability model nor the task-analysis model alone covers the entire teaching continuum. For example, she reports that both the ability approach and the task-analysis approach do not include such factors as values and motivation.

Furthermore, she claims that the staunch task-analysis model excludes a means of assessing teacher and setting characteristics[1] as they relate to learning.

Obviously the assumptions implicit in her questions are debatable. For example, not all of Stephen's (1977) assumptions of the skill training approach directly relate to her questions. She appears to interpret the model in a very narrow sense. This narrow interpretation is evident in several of her statements. For example, she notes that the short history of task analysis precludes the existence of much research. But if she viewed the task analysis model within the larger framework of a skills approach [as suggested by Quay (1973), Stephens (1977), and Ysseldyke and Salvia (1974)], she could have cited an impressive amount of data (cited in Chapter 3) to support a skill-oriented model. Also, she views the task-analysis model as being overwhelmingly concerned with task manipulation and not sensitive enough to child variables. Again, a broader interpretation of the approach appears warranted. In many skill-oriented instructional settings, child variables (e.g., stimulus preferences, reinforcement preferences, rate of learning) guide the teaching activities. It is likely that such a radical, narrow perspective on task analysis is not prominent in applied settings. However, even if one disagrees with her criticisms of the approach, she has raised some issues and offered recommendations that deserve attention.

For example, Smead (1977) claims that neither model is fully adequate and a combination of the two approaches is needed to cover the full spectrum of diagnostic-prescriptive teaching. She cautions against rejecting either model and supports further study in both. She offers numerous suggestions for combining and examining various factors in each model:

1. The flaws in present ability instruments should be remediated and their efficacy reassessed. Emphasis should be placed on establishing adequate reliability and construct validity. Moreover, efficacy studies should measure improvement against actual school achievement-related dependent measures.
2. Rather than concentrating on single modalities, investigators need to examine the relationship between modalities. According to Silverston and Deichman (1975), perceptual shifting, intersensory transfer, and modality preference appear to be fruitful areas for investigation.
3. New aptitudes that have ecological validity within a specific setting need to be identified. She notes that Glaser (1972) promotes this identification of new aptitudes that capture the ongoing interaction between the learner and aspects of the educational setting. For example, preference for input organization may be an aptitude that interacts with academic stimulus material to improve rate of learning.
4. The task analysis and ability training models should be coordinated so each can provide essential information. In this arrangement the ability model provides the concern for individual differences and "because" statements, whereas task analysis offers a skill network and specific instructional objectives.
5. Attempts should be made to base ability on observable behavior in the classroom.
6. Abilities that account for skill acquisition problems on task-analytic, criterion-referenced tests need to be pinpointed and remediation strategies need to be developed.
7. Provisions need to be made for examining the influence of teacher and setting variables on the achievement of objectives. Charting is suggested.
8. Consideration should be given to learner motivation, values, and attitudes in the combined approach.

The ability versus task-analysis dichotomy is a general classification system that differentiates most of the LD instructional approaches. However, other parameters per-

---

[1] Classroom environment—number of students, arrangement of seats, temperature of room, etc.

meate the approaches and serve to facilitate classification and understanding. For example, some approaches tend to stress teaching methods, whereas others focus on specific content. Table 14.2 presents the primary instructional approaches used in LD and their respective classification parameters. The primary instructional approaches are classified differently by numerous writers. Myers and Hammill (1976) identify seven approaches: perceptual motor, language, multisensory, test related, structured, phonic, and neurological organization. Tarver and Hallahan (1976) report five approaches: perceptual motor, linguistic, structured, behavior modification, and clinical teaching. More recently, Lovitt (1978) identifies perceptual, multisensory, precision teaching, and remedial as primary instructional approaches in LD.

In this text, seven approaches are presented: perceptual motor, psycholinguistic, academic materials, multisensory, learner developmental, content developmental, and applied behavior analysis. It is important for the teacher to examine these and determine their usefulness for teaching. Moreover, this examination must include available research findings that show the strengths and weaknesses of each approach.

Perceptual-Motor Approach

Many educators maintain that the learning problems of LD children originate from inadequate perceptual-motor (P-M) skills. Correcting the poor P-M skills might, then, improve academic skills. For example, a child may work on figure-ground activities with an expected result of improving reading.

Since the approach focuses on improving P-M skills, it is readily identified within the ability training model. In addition, it emphasizes curriculum *content* more than instructional method. For example, P-M training may include activities in gross motor, fine motor, body image, and eye-hand coordination but does not usually outline specific or rigid methods for guiding instruction. Its classification, then, is as an ability training approach with a primary emphasis in curriculum content.

The P-M approach is highlighted by Barsch (1967), Cratty (1971), Frostig and Horne (1964), and Kephart (1971). In many of the programs, P-M skills are assessed via selected instruments, and instruction is designed to correct inadequate P-M areas. As indicated in literature reviews (Hallahan & Cruickshank, 1973; Hammill, Goodman, &

TABLE 14.2

Classification parameters of instructional approaches commonly used in learning disabilities.

Instructional Approaches	Process or Ability	Skill	Method [a]	Content
Perceptual motor	✓			✓
Psycholinguistic	✓		✓	✓
Academic materials		✓	✓	✓
Multisensory	✓	✓	✓	
Learner developmental	✓			✓
Content developmental		✓		✓
Applied behavior analysis		✓	✓	

Note.
[a] Dotted checks infer method but do not directly dictate it; they are less method oriented than the solid checks.

Weiderholt, 1974), the research on the effects of P-M training on academic growth is unimpressive. Chapter 9 includes a detailed presentation of perceptual-motor theories, teaching activities, and research results.

Psycholinguistic Approach

In the area of LD, psycholinguistic teaching has mainly focused on the input-association-output model developed by Osgood (1957). Proponents of this approach assume that inadequate psycholinguistic skills (reception, association, and expression) result in academic learning problems. Remediation commonly includes activities that emphasize the development of reception, association, and memory skills in the auditory and visual channels. It is expected that training these skills improves academic achievement. This approach is highlighted by the use of the *ITPA* for assessment; instructional programs include numerous commercial programs and books [*The Peabody Language Development Kits* (Dunn & Smith, 1966), *The MWM Program for Developing Language Abilities* (Minskoff, Wiseman, & Minskoff, 1972), and *Aides to Psycholinguistic Teaching* (Bush & Giles, 1977)]. Due to the use of the *ITPA* and the commercial programs based on it, many educators (Lerner, 1976; Myers & Hammill, 1976) classify this approach as a test-related instructional program.

This approach, with its emphasis on correcting the psycholinguistic deficits with an expected carry-over to academics, is readily viewed within the framework of the ability training model. This approach does have implications for instructional methods, but focuses mainly on content (i.e., visual memory exercises, auditory reception activities). The implications for methods originate from the practice of teaching to the preferred or strong modality (e.g., provide a visual learner with instructions that primarily feature visual stimuli). In an extensive review, Newcomer and Hammill (1976) report that the effectiveness of psycholinguistic training has yet to be substantiated. A comprehensive presentation of psycholinguistic theory, practices, and research is included in Chapter 6.

Academic Materials Approach

Commercial materials in special education have mushroomed during the last decade. Hundreds of publishers' display booths are featured at major special education conventions. Teachers can select from a large array of reading, spelling, writing, and math programs. Most of these programs make many instructional decisions for the teacher. For example, they feature a skills sequence, provide practice activities, suggest step-by-step teacher behavior, and give questions to be used. As acknowledged by Durkin (1974), when this approach dictates what is to be taught and how, it can reduce teaching to a clerical role. On the other hand, materials used wisely can be a tremendous resource. Most are attractive, follow commonly used instructional procedures, and save the teacher from having to make her own. The emphasis on academic skills places this approach in the skill training model. Although the materials approach includes some methods (e.g., *Distar*), it is primarily characterized by a heavy emphasis on content.

Unfortunately, research regarding the effectiveness of various materials is minimal. The task of appropriately matching materials to

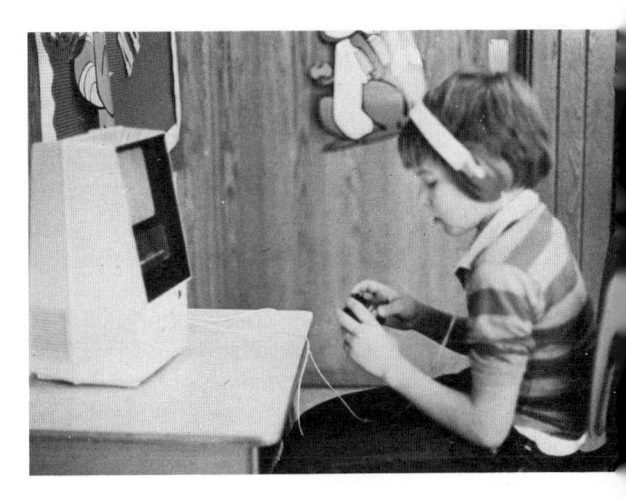

Numerous programmed materials are used with LD youngsters.

children is the responsibility of the teacher. This process requires continuous assessment and monitoring of the child's progress as well as a familiarity with a wide variety of materials.

Multisensory Approach

The multisensory approach is based on the premise that for some children, learning is facilitated if content is presented via several modalities. Frequently, kinesthetic and tactile stimulation are used along with the visual and auditory modalities. The multisensory programs that feature tracing, hearing, writing, and seeing are often referred to as VAKT (visual-auditory-kinesthetic-tactile). To increase tactile and kinesthetic stimulation, sandpaper letters, finger paint, sand trays, raised letters, and sunken letters are used.

The Fernald (1943) method and the Gillingham and Stillman (1966) method are reading approaches that highlight VAKT instruction. The Fernald method stresses whole word learning. The Gillingham-Stillman method originated from the work of Orton (1937) and features sound blending. Slingerland (1971) adapted the Orton-Gillingham approach to develop a multisensory language arts program for LD children. Lovitt (1978) reports on two studies in which the Slingerland techniques were compared to other reading programs. He notes that the data indicate that students in all programs improved and no one program emerged as better than the others.

The neurological impress method is another multisensory approach used with individuals who have severe reading problems. In this approach the pupil and teacher together read aloud rapidly. The child follows by moving his finger along the words. It is reasoned that the auditory process provides stimulation and feedback. These multisensory approaches to reading are discussed in Chapter 7.

Some teachers successfully teach arithmetic by using VAKT techniques such as the following:

1. Teacher writes the arithmetic fact while saying it (e.g., $4 \times 4 = 16$).
2. Child traces the arithmetic fact while saying it.
3. Child copies the arithmetic fact and says it.
4. Child writes the arithmetic fact from memory.
5. Child reads the arithmetic problem, says the answer, and writes the answer.

Although the multisensory approach has gained recognition for its use in teaching skills, it is not limited to the skill-training model. Actually, its roots are in the ability model, where specific modality learning is stressed. However, the multisensory approach features distinct instructional procedures and may be viewed as independent of specific content. Multisensory techniques are often used with individuals who have severe learning problems. The approach deserves serious consideration by LD teachers.

Learner-Developmental Approach

The learner-developmental approach stresses the position that cognitive growth occurs in stages. The learner progresses from one stage to another and a readiness for different tasks parallels this growth. Specific tasks correspond to each developmental stage and tasks associated with a higher stage are not presented to the individual until she reaches it.

To begin instruction the learner is usually assessed in terms of the specific hierarchy of normal developmental stages. Getman's visuomotor model (Getman, 1965), Piaget's developmental stages (Flavell, 1963), Doman and Delacato's Neurological Organization Theory (Delacato, 1966), and Johnson and Myklebust's (1967) language program represent some of these developmental orientations. Once the individual is assessed, instruction is aimed at the lowest undeveloped stage and proceeds to the next higher stage as the child progresses. This approach assumes that behavior development is sequential and more complex behaviors develop out of less complex behaviors. According to Johnson and Morasky (1977), if one accepts the basic premises of the developmental approach, several advantages are recognized:

1. It provides a normative standard for different age levels, one that is often useful in assessing an individual's relative status of functioning.
2. When an accurate discernment of a child's critical learning stage is assessed, it can be very useful in planning remediation.
3. Instruction is aided by the structure of a skill sequence. Deciding the next step in treating a problem is a difficult decision and a sequential model simplifies the process.

Some of the criticisms leveled against the approach include

1. Many problem behaviors are remediated and/or improve with intervention without regard to a specific developmental hierarchy. In these situations it appears that a return to lower level skills is redundant and, perhaps, a waste of time.
2. The interaction of development (maturation) and experience is not clearly explained.
3. Developmental approaches that rely on singular systems of etiological and problem explanations have difficulty accounting for various phenomena of human growth (e.g., spontaneous remission of problem behavior).

A comparison of the behavioral and developmental positions provides some insights into both approaches. The developmentalist plans treatment programs by providing the child with tasks appropriate for her developmental level. The treatment and preventive programs of the behaviorist and the developmentalist do not markedly differ; both endorse beginning tasks at a level commensurate with the individual's ability. However, the difference in orientation to treatment may lie in specific task selection and timing. A developmentalist is oftentimes guided by a mental age or a specific developmental profile in determining what tasks are appropriate. New tasks may not be introduced because the child's level suggests she is not ready. On the other hand, a behaviorist would introduce new tasks on the basis of the child's measured progress and would not generally consider cognitive

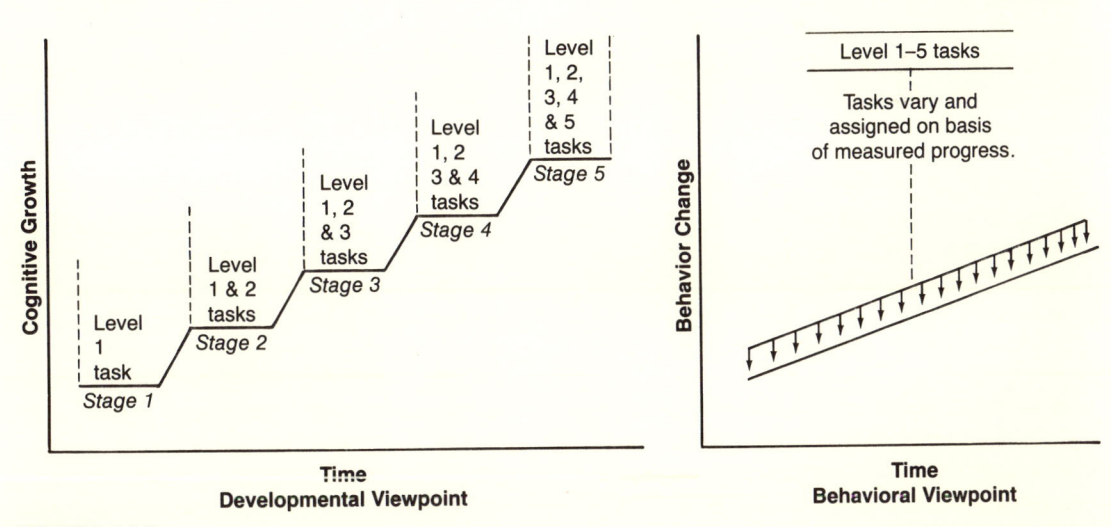

FIGURE 14.2

The developmental and behavioral viewpoints of learning progress.

Source. Adapted in part from *Learning Theory Research in Mental Retardation: Implications for Teaching* by C. D. Mercer & M. E. Snell. Columbus, Ohio: Charles E. Merrill, 1977, p. 318. Copyright 1977 by Bell & Howell Company. Reprinted by permission.

426 Educational services for the learning disabled

level. Figure 14.2 illustrates the differing viewpoints. The learner-developmental approach is best classified within the ability-training model and it stresses content (i.e., tasks are controlled by the developmental level of a child on a specific developmental hierarchy).

Content-Developmental Approach

In the content-developmental approach, a hierarchy of skills in a subject area (reading, mathematics, writing) is formulated. The pupil is assessed in terms of each subject skill hierarchy and instruction begins at the lowest skill not mastered. Thus, the skill hierarchies provide a framework for educational assessment, instructional objectives, and curriculum development. In addition to using skill hierarchies, this approach features task analysis and criterion-referenced tests and tasks.

The criterion approach typically involves three steps:

1. The pupil takes a pretest on a criterion skill.
2. The pupil is placed on a specific instructional activity based on the pretest.
3. The teacher periodically administers the criterion test until mastery is demonstrated. When mastery is achieved she introduces a new skill and the cycle is repeated.

A variety of materials may be used to teach selected skills; here, current events are explored.

Stephens (1977) provides a detailed description of criterion-based teaching in which assessment is usually based on percent correct, not on rate. He suggests the following guidelines for determining level of learning:

1. *mastery* (100% correct responses)
2. *learned*—(90–99% correct responses)
3. *instructional*—(70–90% correct responses)

4. *frustration*—(69% or less correct responses)

Critics of this approach claim it lacks empirically based skill hierarchies in each subject area. Also, they point out that the ordering of skills for the most efficient learning may vary across learners.

The content-developmental approach fits best within the skill-training model. Moreover, it tends to stress content more than method (i.e., the subject skill area hierarchy controls the content).

Applied Behavior Analysis

Applied behavior analysis (ABA) represents one of the newer approaches used in the field of special education. Specifically its application in learning disabilities is receiving extensive attention in the writings of Hallahan and Kauffman (1976), Haring and Schiefelbusch (1976), Lovitt (1975a, 1975b, 1975c, 1976, 1977), and Stephens (1977). It is apparent that ABA is gaining recognition; many educators note that it holds much promise regarding both current and future instructional practices. Since ABA is a viable instructional approach and is not discussed in detail in any other chapter, its major features are included in this section under the topics of *(a)* measurement system, *(b)* precision teaching, *(c)* learning principles, and *(d)* evaluation of teaching procedures.

Measurement System

As Hallahan and Kauffman (1976) note, one of the most important features of ABA is its emphasis on direct, continuous, and precise measurement of behavior. *Direct* measurement entails focusing on behaviors that can be directly observed and counted. It stresses the need to deal with specific academic (see words—say words, sums to 9 facts) and social behaviors (taking turns in a game). *Continuous* measurement requires that a behavior be counted and recorded over a period of time, usually daily. Such continuous data helps the teacher make daily instructional decisions. *Precise* measurement requires that observation and recording systems be reliable. The reliability is often determined by comparing the findings of two or more independent observers on the same behavior during the exact same time period. The greater their agreement, the more reliable the data.

Precision Teaching

Lindsley (1964) initially developed precision teaching. It incorporates the direct, continuous, and precise measurement system of ABA by tutors and classroom teachers. The teacher should

1. Select a target behavior.
2. Develop a task sheet or probe for evaluation of pupil progress in daily timings.
3. Graph the data daily, set instruction aims, and teach.
4. Analyze data and make instructional decisions.

Target behaviors are usually determined by administering probe sheets. These sheets include academic tasks and are used to sample the child's behavior. Typically the child works on the probe sheet for 1 minute and the teacher records the rate of correct and incorrect responses and notes any error patterns. Figure 14.3 displays a probe sheet of a task aimed at assessing addition facts with sums to nine. The target behavior is selected on the basis of rate of correct and incorrect responses and/or consistent error patterns and is often referred to as an instructional *pinpoint*. A pinpoint is not usually established until the student performs the task on the probe sheet several times. This baseline procedure provides the teacher with a more reliable index of how well the student can do than is achieved by simply recording the student's performance once.

The task sheet may be the original assessment probe or it may be uniquely designed to stress specific facts (e.g., addition involving 0). Daily timings usually consist of having the

428 Educational services for the learning disabled

Name _____ Correct _____ Error _____
Date _____ Comments _____

| 6 | 5 | 4 | 9 | 8 | 2 | 5 |
|+2 |+3 |+4 |+0 |+1 |+7 |+0 |

| 8 | 4 | 1 | 3 | 5 | 3 | 5 |
|+0 |+3 |+1 |+2 |+2 |+6 |+4 |

| 7 | 4 | 3 | 8 | 7 | 2 | 4 |
|+1 |+2 |+3 |+1 |+0 |+5 |+0 |

| 1 | 3 | 2 | 6 | 5 | 1 | 0 |
|+0 |+1 |+2 |+1 |+4 |+6 |+0 |

| 3 | 2 | 2 | 3 | 3 | 4 | 5 |
|+4 |+4 |+1 |+1 |+0 |+5 |+1 |

| 6 | 7 | 1 | 1 | 1 | 1 | 1 |
|+3 |+2 |+2 |+3 |+4 |+5 |+8 |

FIGURE 14.3
Probe sheet used to present addition facts—sums to 9.

pupil work on the task sheet for 1 minute and recording the correct and incorrect responses.

Precision teachers record the daily performances and graph the results (charting). The Standard Behavior Chart[1] receives widespread use. As noted in Figure 14.4, it features a logarithmic scale and allows the recording of rates ranging from 0.000695 per minute to 1000 per minute. White and Haring (1976) offer a complete description of the Standard Behavior Chart.

Some teachers, preferring a simpler graph, use an equal interval chart. These can be made from "square-ruled" graph paper.

Teachers record the frequency of the behavior along the vertical axis and the number of sessions or timings on the horizontal axis. Figure 14.5 presents an equal interval chart.

An instructional aim provides the student and teacher with an instructional goal. In precision teaching the aim is usually defined in terms of the rate of correct and incorrect responses per minute. Ideally, the aim should represent a mastery level of the skill. To date, there is some disagreement concerning the rates that reflect proficiency across academic tasks. Rates collected by various investigators are presented in Table 14.3. These rates are either suggested as proficiency levels or indicate the performance levels of peers who are achieving adequately. Inspec-

[1] A commercial version of the chart is available from Behavior Research Co., Box 2251, Kansas City, Kansas 66103.

FIGURE 14.4

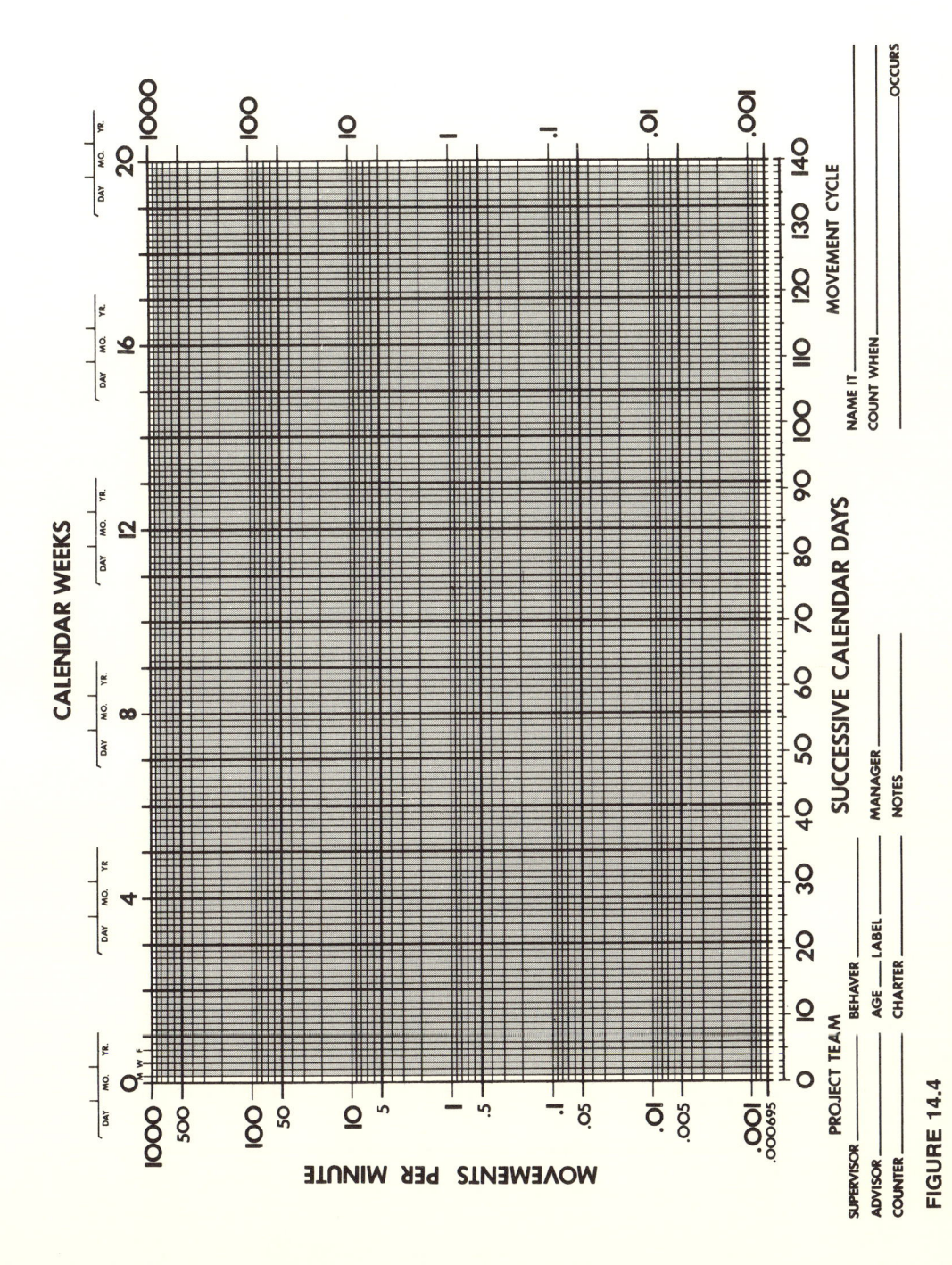

Standard Behavior Chart.

Name _____
Setting _____

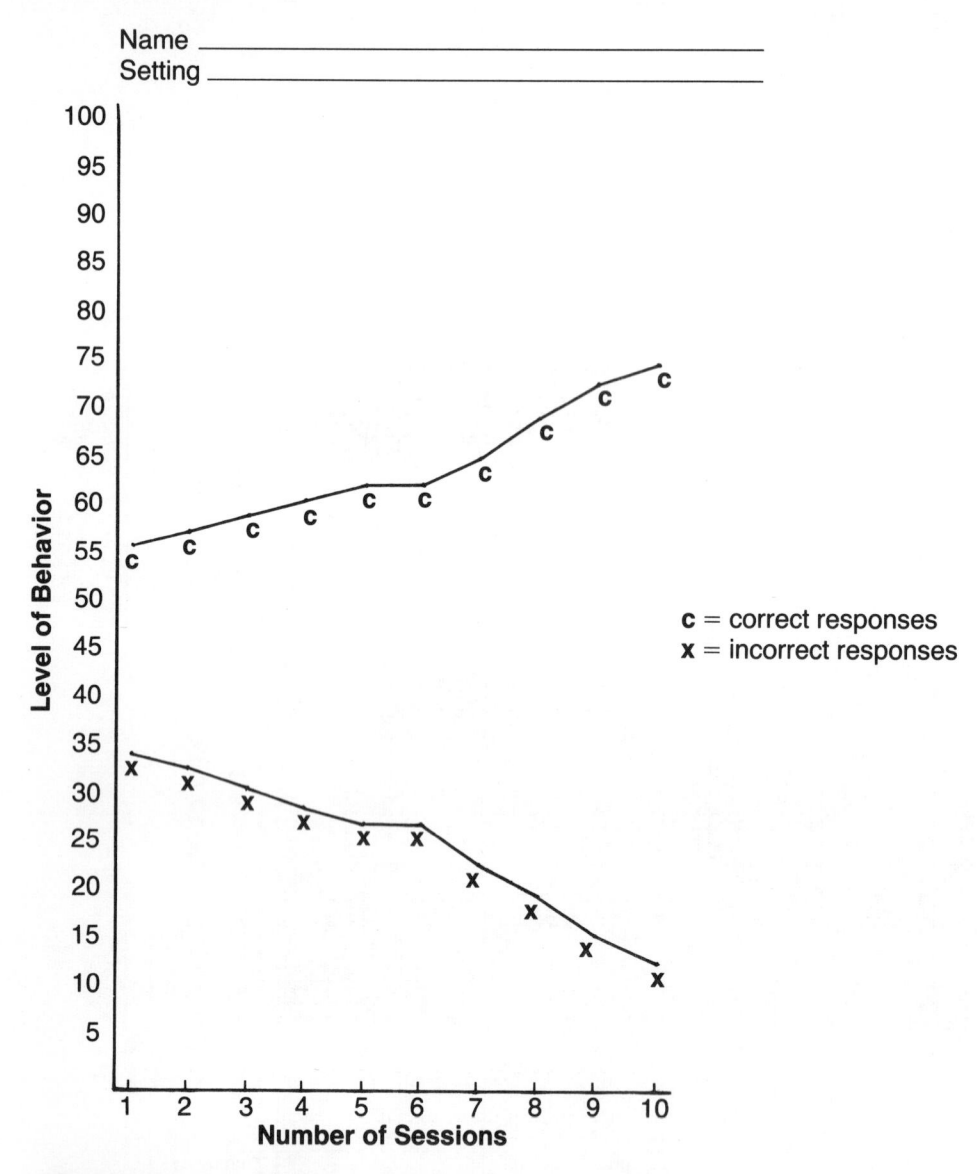

FIGURE 14.5

Equal interval chart.

tion of the rates reveals some wide discrepancies in the rate of letter sounds said, but there is reasonable consistency in other areas. For example, 100+ correctly read words per minute is consistent across the studies. In math, 30–40 correct computations per minute appears to be feasible.

Certain learner characteristics, such as age, grade level, and achievement level are likely to influence the establishment of appropriate aims. Table 14.4 lists rate data of adults and high and low achieving children in grades 1–6. Wolking (1973) sampled the performance (1-minute timings) of 740 individuals on

TABLE 14.3

Data-based performance rates.

Author	Reading - Letter sounds said Corr.	Error	Reading - Words read orally Corr.	Error	Reading - Say words Corr.	Error	Reading - Alphabet names Corr.	Error	Math - Addition facts Corr.	Error	Math - Subtraction facts Corr.	Error	Writing - Small letters Corr.	Error	Writing - Random numbers Corr.	Error
Kunzelmann (1969)													50	0		
Haughton (1971)	100	n.a.[b]							30–40	0[a]						
Henderson, Clise, & Silverton (1971)			100–200	2[c]												
Starlin (1971)	40	2[c]			50+	2[c]										
Haughton (1972)	30	n.a.	100	n.a.												
Ellis & Prelander (1973)																
Wolking (1973) Grade 3 High Achievers	44	0	120–132	0	104	0	104	0	34	0	21	0	30	0		
Alper, Nowlin, Lemoine, Perine, & Bettencourt (1974)	80	2[c]	100–120	2[c]	60–80	2[c]	80	2[c]								
Haring & Gentry (1976)	61	4			58	7			29	0	25	.4	36	1	38	1

Note.
[a]basic computation
[b]not available
[c]or less

TABLE 14.4

Performance rates across age levels.

Academic Skills	One Corr.	One Error	Two Corr.	Two Error	Three Corr.	Three Error	Grades Four Corr.	Four Error	Five Corr.	Five Error	Six Corr.	Six Error	Adult Corr.	Adult Error	
Wolking's (1973) Data															
Reading Skills															
Hear instructions— say words	120 / 108	0 / 0	132 / 108	0 / 0	132 / 132	0 / 0	156 / 144	0 / 0	174 / 156	0 / 0	180 / 156	0 / 12	252	0	High[a] / Low
See small letters— say letter names	68 / 24	4 / 22	84 / 48	0 / 6	104 / 64	0 / 4	124 / 76	0 / 0	122 / 88	0 / 3	142 / 104	0 / 0	196	0	High / Low
See small letters— say letter sounds	36 / 1	4 / 8	52 / 16	0 / 4	44 / 24	0 / 4	50 / 36	0 / 3	52 / 30	0 / 3	64 / 34	0 / 6	108	4	High / Low
See regular words— say words	50 / ½	8 / 38	100 / 6	0 / 11	108 / 28	0 / 8	126 / 54	0 / 8	138 / 74	0 / 4	148 / 104	0 / 2	198	0	High / Low
See irregular words— say words	50 / 0	8 / 0	90 / 6	0 / 17	104 / 16	2 / 6	128 / 48	0 / 12	134 / 74	0 / 8	150 / 90	0 / 6	198	0	High / Low
Writing Skills															
See numbers, random— write numbers	25 / 11	0 / 0	30 / 29	0 / 0	44 / 39	0 / 0	66 / 52	0 / 0	79 / 61	0 / 0	100 / 80	0 / 0	145	0	High / Low
See letters, random— write letters	25 / 11	0 / 0	27 / 30	0 / 0	40 / 41	0 / 0	61 / 48	0 / 0	74 / 61	0 / 0	88 / 72	0 / 0	127	0	High / Low
Spelling Skills															
Hear regular words— say letters	4 / 0	0 / 0	14 / 1	2 / 6	24 / 4	0 / 6	32 / 10	0 / 6	32 / 20	0 / 4	36 / 22	0 / 4	48	0	High / Low
Hear irregular words— say letters	2 / 0	6 / 0	12 / 2	4 / 5	18 / 5	2 / 6	28 / 8	0 / 6	32 / 14	0 / 4	32 / 16	0 / 5	48	0	High / Low

Number Skills													
Hear instructions—write numbers, sequential	22	2	38	0	62	0	81	0	88	0	116	0	156	0	High
	6	3	26	3	36	0	63	2	87	0	94	0			Low
See addition problems—write numbers	12	1	23	0	34	0	48	0	58	0	86	0	132	0	High
	1	4	9	2	14	3	34	0	33	1	54	0			Low
See subtraction problems—write numbers	5	4	10	1	21	0	28	0	31	0	46	0	72	0	High
	0	0	2	4	9	4	16	2	18	2	20	1			Low

Academic Skills	Kindergarten-Two		Three-Adult	
	Corr.	Error	Corr.	Error
Starlin & Starlin's (1973a, 1973b, 1973c), Data				
Reading Skills				
Words read per minute				
Independent	50–70	2 or less	100–200	2 or less
Instructional	30–49	3–6	50–99	3–6
Spelling Skills				
Letters spelled per minute				
Independent	30–50	2 or less	50–70	2 or less
Instructional	15–29	3–7	25–49	3–7
Arithmetic Skills				
Numerals written in answer per minute				
Independent	20–30	2 or less	40–60	2 or less
Instructional	10–19	3–8	20–39	3–8

Note.
[a]Obtained high or low level of academic achievement.

numerous academic tasks. He noted that by sixth grade the median child attained approximately 95% of adult accuracy and 65% of adult speed on the academic tasks. As noted in Table 14.4, Starlin and Starlin (1973a, 1973b, 1973c) provide academic performance data for K–2 individuals and grade 3–adult. Their reading data are based on words read per minute, whereas spelling data reflect number of letters spelled per minute, and arithmetic data are based on numerals in the answer written per minute.

Since research has not conclusively determined specific aims for academic tasks, the teacher must use considerable discretion in setting aims with individual pupils. As noted by Haring and Gentry (1976), the teacher should select aims that can be justified via empirical support or considerable experience. One way of facilitating aim selection is to collect rate data from children who are achieving satisfactorily and use their performances as aims. Another way involves the teacher performing the task and using a proportion of her performance as an aim.

Once the graphing procedures are established and the aims are set, teaching begins. Teaching in the ABA model is usually direct, simple, and with no constraints. Commercial materials, drill sheets, flash cards, games, media modeling, and systematic consequation using positive reinforcement all may be used. As for procedures, Lovitt (1977) supports the use of a single-element process. For example, in teaching reading he suggests:

1. tell the pupil to read faster
2. have the pupil read silently before he reads orally
3. schedule practice on newly introduced words
4. schedule practice on missed words
5. provide points or chips for correctly read words
6. schedule practice on simple phrases
7. schedule practice on various phonic elements, for example, initial consonants; medial, short vowels (pp. 15–16)

For math he recommends:

1. show the pupil how to perform a certain type of problem
2. tell the pupil which problems were correctly or incorrectly solved
3. give points for correctly computed problems
4. tell the pupil to work faster or to compute more accurately
5. provide the pupil with various aids as he works the problem, for example, abacus, number line, Cuisenaire Rods, flash cards. (p. 16)

White and Haring (1976), Haring and Gentry (1976), and Haring and Eaton (1978) are developing an instructional hierarchy that has implications for teaching. Using the premise that learning occurs in developmental stages, they are formulating an instructional hierarchy with related teaching activities for each stage. They propose several stages of learning, displayed in Figure 14.6. For a detailed discussion of the instructional hierarchy, read White and Haring (1976).

Regarding practice, Stephens (1977) recommends *simple* practice if the child has not mastered the skill and *mixed* practice if she shows skill mastery. Mixed practice consists of tasks that vary from the original form (single column subtraction) (e.g., include both single-digit addition and subtraction on a drill sheet in horizontal and parallel forms). Using the instructional hierarchy, simple practice would occur at Stage 2 and mixed practice would occur at Stages 3–5. Until the instructional hierarchy has supportive data it must be approached in an experimental fashion. Currently the relationship of rate data to the proposed stages is being investigated.

Charted data enable the teacher to determine if the pupil is making acceptable progress. Significant learning patterns often develop and an understanding of them enables her to ascertain possible reasons for success or failure and make data-based decisions. The basic underlying orientation in examining patterns is simple: *An increase in the rate of appropriate or correct responses and a de-*

Learning Stage   *Teaching Procedure*

1. Response ⟶ Model and demonstration
2. Acquisition ⟶ Drill, demonstration, prompts and cues
3. Proficiency ⟶ Drill and reinforcement
4. Maintenance ⟶ Practice and reinforcement
5. Generalization ⟶ Discrimination training, differentiation training, application problems

FIGURE 14.6

Instructional hierarchy.

crease in the rate of inappropriate or incorrect responses is the most desirable pattern. In a detailed discussion of patterns, Koorland and Rose (1978) present numerous patterns that commonly occur. To illustrate the process of analyzing the charts and making program changes, Table 14.5 explains several common patterns mentioned by Koorland and Rose.

Learning Principles Commonly Used in Applied Behavior Analysis

Learning principles used in ABA are primarily those discussed within the framework of behavior modification or operant conditioning. They manipulate antecedent and subsequent events in a way that modifies behavior. Basically the principles focus on reinforcement, punishment, and extinction. A detailed discussion of these principles is not within the scope of this book; however, the reader may wish to consult any of the following sources for study: Hallahan and Kauffman (1976), Haring and Schiefelbusch (1976), Neisworth and Smith (1973), White and Haring (1976), and Worell and Nelson (1974). The ABA approach is based on the skills-training model and it stresses method more than specific content.

The Evaluation of Teaching Procedures

Stephens (1977) reports that three designs are commonly used to evaluate the effectiveness of classroom instruction: *(a)* pre- and post-design, *(b)* reversal design, and *(c)* multiple-baseline design. Although these de-

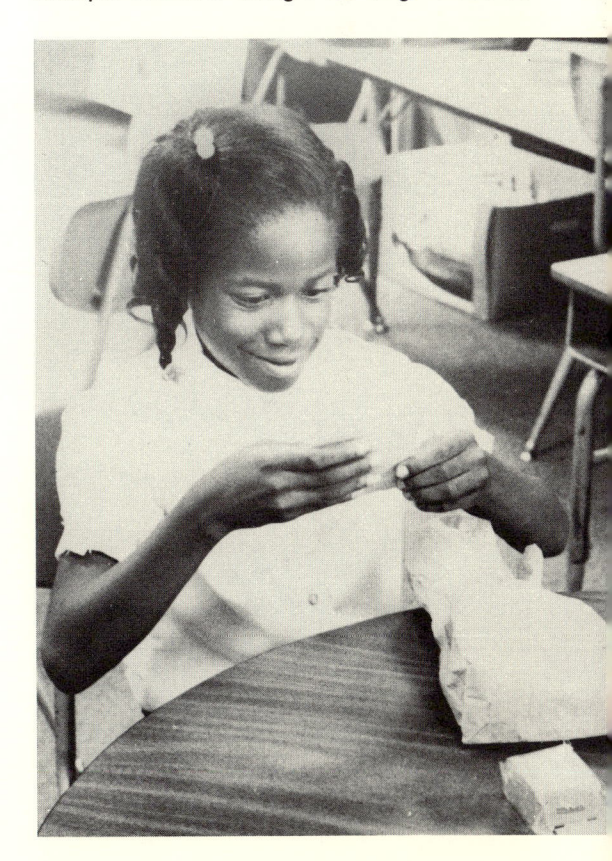

This student receives a reinforcer for a job well done.

TABLE 14.5

Common learning patterns.

Patterns	Analysis
Single Data Patterns	
Pattern 1	This pattern indicates a change is needed. The behavior was improving but is now leveling off. An instructional change is needed in order to continue the acceleration.
Pattern 2	In this pattern the vertical line indicates an instructional change in the program. This pattern shows a desirable change in behavior after the instructional change.
Pattern 3	This is a common pattern in academic learning. The behavior will frequently drop to a lower frequency than before the instructional change; but if it begins to accelerate, the program is working.
Correct and Incorrect Data Patterns **c** = correct responses **x** = incorrect responses	
Pattern 4	This pattern is very desirable. The correct responses are accelerating and the incorrect responses are decelerating.
Pattern 5	Correct responses are accelerating but so are incorrect responses. A change is needed.
Pattern 6	This is the worst possible situation; correct responses are decreasing and incorrrect responses are increasing. A program change is needed immediately.

Teaching children and adolescents 437

Patterns	Analysis
Pattern 7 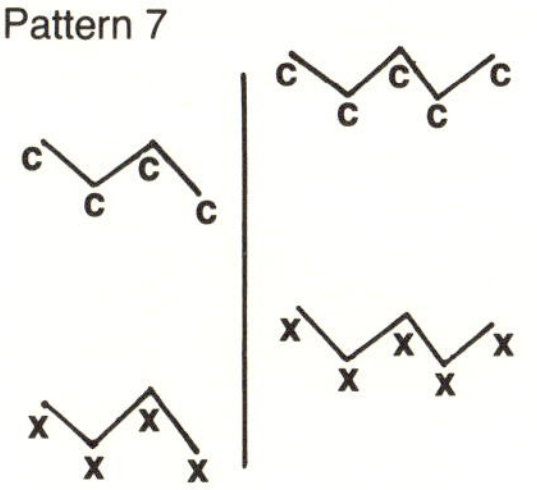	The pattern has not changed—just the frequencies, which are both higher. A change in program is needed.
Pattern 8	This pattern reveals different things, depending on the type of behavior being recorded. If it is academic, then a step up to the next academic level is warranted since limited learning takes place when no errors occur. If the behavior being recorded is inappropriate and appropriate behavioral responses, the pattern is very desirable.
Calendar Pattern Pattern 9	These are Monday through Friday data that indicate that the behavior increases sharply every Thursday. This may be for many reasons and needs close scrutiny. This is a *daily calendar pattern*—a significant change in behavior is observed on certain days of the week every week.

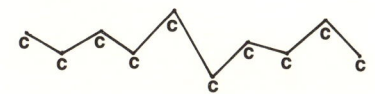

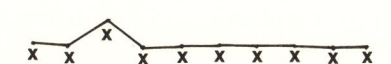

signs have been popularized within the ABA approach, their use is not limited to one approach; they may be used to evaluate psycholinguistic or perceptual-motor instruction.

The pre- and post-design is often referred to as an *AB design* and consists of a baseline period *(A)* and a treatment period *(B)*. Figure 14.7 shows a pre- and post-design. A primary problem with the AB design is that the teacher is not sure that the treatment accounts for the change in behavior.

The reversal design (ABAB) demonstrates causality and involves an initial baseline phase, a treatment phase, a second baseline phase, and a second treatment phase. This design is well suited for examining the effects of incentives on appropriate behavior, but difficulty is encountered in using this design with academic tasks. For example, if responses to multiplication facts are being charted and the child masters many facts during intervention, a return to a second baseline phase is not very practical or meaningful (i.e., learning influences learning, or memory of learned facts remains). Figure 14.8 presents a reversal design.

A multiple baseline is a good design for a teacher who does not wish to discontinue instructional activities. In this design she should chart two or more behaviors of a pupil or the same behavior across pupils. If instruc-

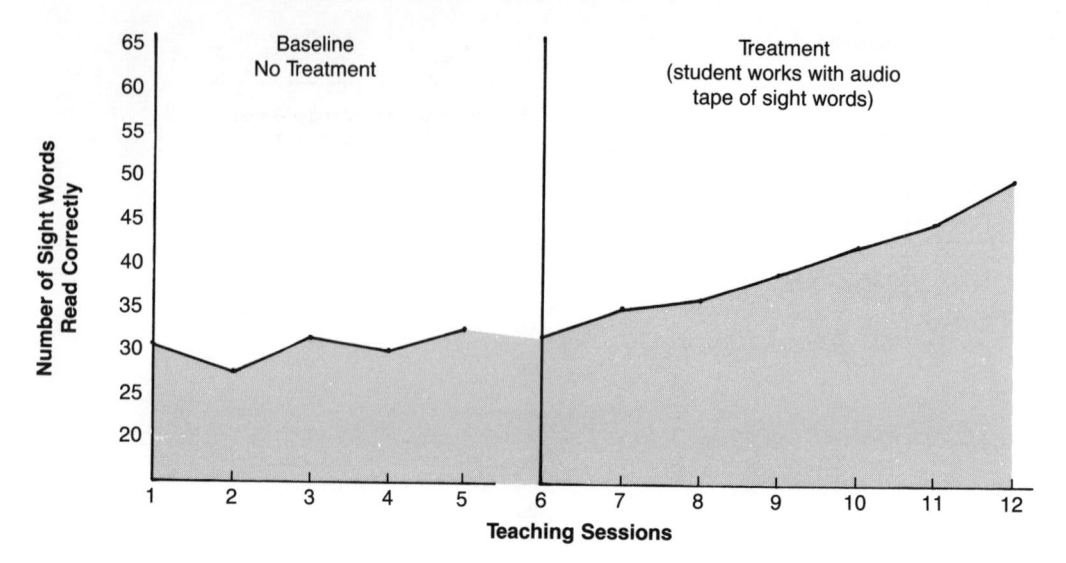

438 Educational services for the learning disabled

FIGURE 14.7

A pre- and post-design (AB).

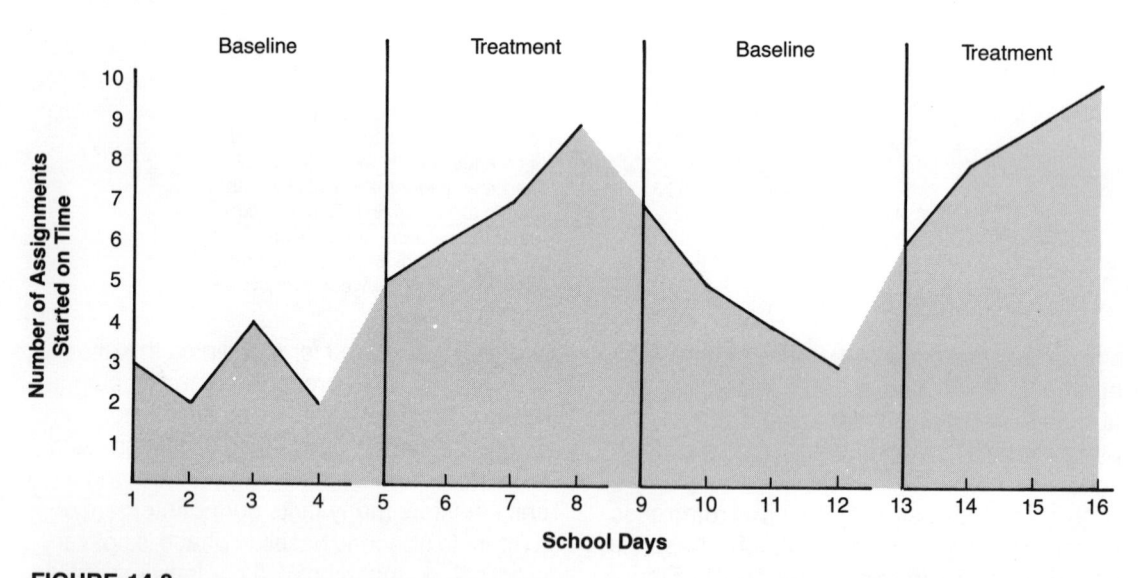

FIGURE 14.8

A reversal design (ABAB).

tion influences the targeted behavior and the untreated behavior remains unaffected, changes in the treated behavior can be attributed to the instruction. After an effect is demonstrated with the first behavior, she initiates intervention aimed at improving the second behavior. Figure 14.9 displays a multiple-baseline design.

For a more detailed description of evaluation designs the reader is referred to Hall (1974), Hallahan and Kauffman (1976), and White and Haring (1976). Lovitt's (1977)

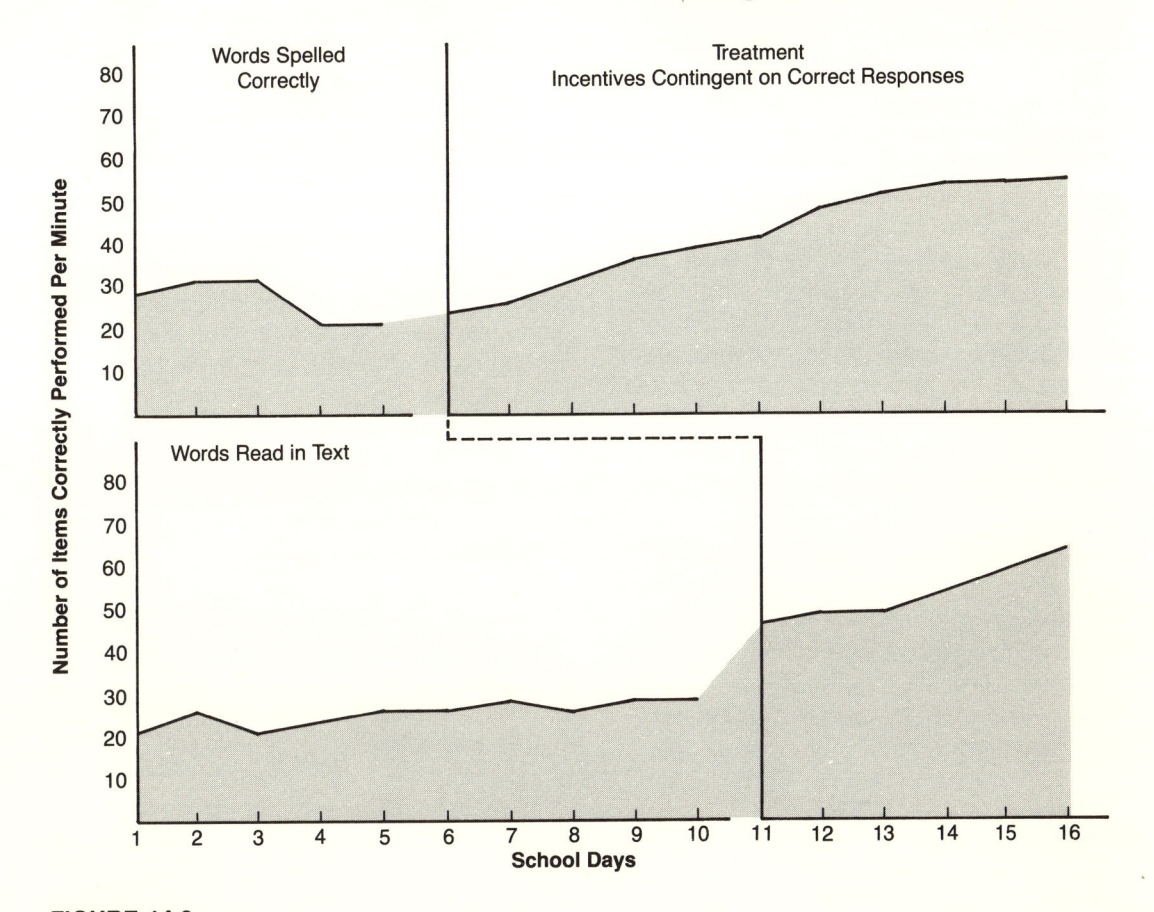

FIGURE 14.9

A multiple-baseline design.

statement, "We don't need to use expensive techniques to evaluate curriculum materials or teacher effectiveness; the data from kids will do these jobs for us" (p. 81), captures an important feature of evaluation.

Perspectives on Using Various Approaches

The instuctional approaches presented in this chapter are not mutually exclusive. Teachers often emphasize one of these approaches but actually use a combination of procedures and materials from several approaches. A myriad of different combinations is possible and a few are exemplified in the following examples.

1. The principles of operant conditioning (ABA) may be used by a teacher stressing the development of perceptual-motor skills or psycholinguistic skills.
2. Various academic skill hierarchies (content-developmental) may be used in the ABA approach or the materials approach.
3. Direct and continuous measurement (ABA) may be used in any approach as long as the target behavior can be observed and measured.
4. Some teachers use academic content in psycholinguistic and perceptual-motor instruction (e.g., use of letters to design visual discrimination activities).

5. Many teachers systematically examine learner variables (learner-developmental) and task variables (content-developmental) in planning instruction.

A teacher must foster the optimum growth of her students. To accomplish this, she should continuously review the research regarding teaching practices (i.e., which behaviors should be taught and how and when they should be taught). If the evidence supports approaches that are different from hers she should change. It is also possible for her to evaluate her effectiveness by continuous monitoring of pupil progress.

PLANNING INSTRUCTION

Once she has determined objectives for each child through assessment, the teacher plans instruction. Basically, this task means developing an instructional plan that includes the following components:

1. what is to be taught and to whom
2. where the instruction will occur
3. when the instruction will occur
4. what materials will be used
5. what activities or strategies will be used to accommodate children finishing their tasks at different rates
6. how instruction will occur

As mentioned earlier, *what* is to be taught and to *whom* are determined through an initial assessment and continuous monitoring of the pupil. It involves the prescriptive teaching cycle of test-teach-test-teach. *Where* the instruction will occur involves determining the exact location of the instructional activity (e.g., student's desk, classroom learning center, library, playground, classroom interest center, small-group instructional area, game area). *When* the activity will occur means specifying the time of the instruction, usually by making a schedule that sets up time for reading, math, spelling, recess, lunch, etc. The *materials* that are to be used in the instructional activity must be available to the teacher and accessible to the pupil at the scheduled times. Because so many materials are available, choosing the best can be time consuming. In addition, when resources are limited or noncommercial materials are needed for a specific activity, the teacher is faced with the task of constructing them. Making sure the materials are accessible to the pupils requires that the teacher organize the materials in the classroom. Furthermore, the child must understand the organization of the materials in order to obtain them and return them to their proper place.

How the instruction will occur involves selecting an instructional arrangement. In the classroom the teacher may choose one of five instructional arrangements:

1. large group with teacher
2. small group with teacher
3. one pupil with teacher
4. peer teaching
5. material with pupil

The *large group* is appropriate for numerous classroom activities, for example, show and tell, discussion of interesting events, taking a field trip, watching a play or movie, brainstorming, and playing a game.

The *small group* arrangement usually consists of three to five pupils and is the major vehicle for teaching academic skills. A teacher divides pupils into groups according to common skill needs. For example, groups may be based on placement in a basal or need for instruction in consonant sounds, vowel sounds, sight words, or specific math facts. The children usually sit in a semi-circle around the teacher, close enough for her to be able to touch their knees with her hands. *Distar* lessons work well in this arrangement.

One-to-one instruction or tutorial teaching allows for intensive instruction with a single pupil and can be used to help a pupil learn a new task. It must be spontaneously used to prevent or ameloriate frustration.

With the advent of mainstreaming, *peer teaching* has become more widely used. In

Teaching children and adolescents 441

This SLD teacher is working with a student on reading in a one-to-one setting.

this strategy one student who has mastered a skill teaches another student under the teacher's supervision. Peer teaching may involve demonstration, modeling, feedback, and giving instructions. Moreover, such materials as games, flash cards, and drill sheets lend themselves to this arrangement.

The last instructional arrangement does not require the teacher's presence. She simply presents the child with an *instructional material*. She can then work with other students in one-to-one or small-group sessions. Materials may include dittos, workbooks, games, flash cards, drill sheets, and commercial programs. Teachers need to be very careful with the material-to-child arrangement because inappropriate materials can lead to frustration, failure, and the practicing of errors. As noted by White and Haring (1976) and Stephens (1977), practice activities or seatwork should focus on tasks in which the student has acquired some mastery.

The last component of instructional planning consists of devising activites for students who finish their work early. Many teachers effectively handle this situation by allowing students to go to an interest or game center when they complete their work. Children can also start a new task when the previous task is completed.

Finally, the teacher must be able to adjust or modify plans during the day. Oftentimes interesting events or spontaneous happenings

After finishing his work, this youngster chooses to read the comics.

442 Educational services for the learning disabled

provide excellent on-the-spot instructional activities, and these situations should not be constantly omitted for the sake of a preplanned lesson.

Self-Correcting Materials

Since students spend much classroom time interacting with instructional materials, it is imperative that the types of materials used be thoroughly examined. To some extent the material serves as a teacher, and the more functions of the teacher that it can serve, the more useful it becomes. Realistically, the possible teaching functions of inexpensive materials include *(a)* providing instructions, *(b)* presenting a stimulus or task, and *(c)* providing correct-incorrect feedback regarding student responses. Ross (1976) believes that feedback is a factor in the learning paradigm that is often overlooked. As mentioned previously, immediate feedback is crucial to reducing frustration and minimizing the practicing of mistakes.

LD children usually bring a history of academic failure to the learning situation. They desperately need more success—and less failure in the presence of their peers. When the child makes a mistake with a self-correcting material (immediate feedback provided), no one else knows. The student can correct the errors immediately. If feedback is not immediately provided, the student may practice mistakes until corrected by the teacher at a later time.

In a single subject study (Olson & Mercer, 1977) at the University of Florida, the effects of self-correcting materials and nonfeedback materials on on-task behavior and rate of learning were examined. The data indicate that the self-correcting materials produced higher correct response rates and a higher percentage of on-task behavior. Furthermore, experiences with regular and special educa-

Math Man

flap

outside view

block of wood

inside view

stack of cards

tion teachers in Florida regarding teacher-made, self-correcting materials have been very positive. Although these preliminary findings are encouraging, replication with more data points is needed before making any definitive conclusions.

There are many ways to make these materials; Mercer and Mercer (1978) list 11 techniques that include materials using flaps, stylus, slots, matching cards, puzzles, balance scales, tabs, pockets, electricity, magnets, and calculators. Several self-correcting materials featuring various feedback procedures are presented next.

Math Man

Selected instructional pinpoints.
1. See math fact or problem—say answer.
2. See math fact or problem—write answer.

Feedback device.

A *flap* is placed over the mouth. When the flap is raised, the answer is revealed. Vinyl wallpaper is flexible and serves as a good flap.

Materials.
1. a cardboard box (e.g., cigar or school supply box)
2. 3" × 5" index cards
3. contact paper or lamination
4. a small wooden block, approximately 3" × 3½"

Construction.
1. Cut out three squares in the lid of the box so they form two eyes and a mouth.
2. Cut a section out of the right side of the box so the index cards can be fed into the box from the side.
3. Paint the box (inside and out).
4. Laminate a picture of a face on the box and place the eyes and the mouth over the squares.
5. Place a flexible flap over the mouth.
6. Prepare index cards with problems and answers so that the problem appears in the "eyes" and so that the flap over the mouth can be lifted to reveal the answer.

Math Man, a teacher-made material, reveals answers under a flap.

A student inserts cards into Math Man.

| 4   1
5
addition | 12   4
8
subtraction | 9   6
54
multiplication |

| 16   4
4
division | ⋰   ⋰
6
adding groups | ◔   ◔
1/2
adding fractions: pictorial |

| quarter   penny
26¢
money | are   not
aren't
contractions | ⋰   :
>
greater than less than |

| _at
bat
initial consonants | _irt
shirt
initial blends | ___coat
raincoat
compound words |

Poke Box

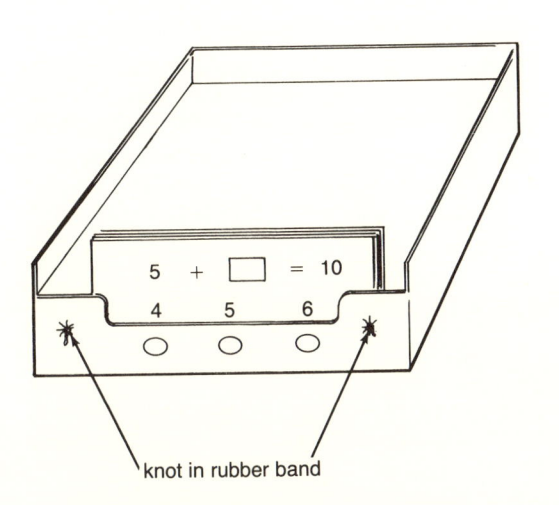

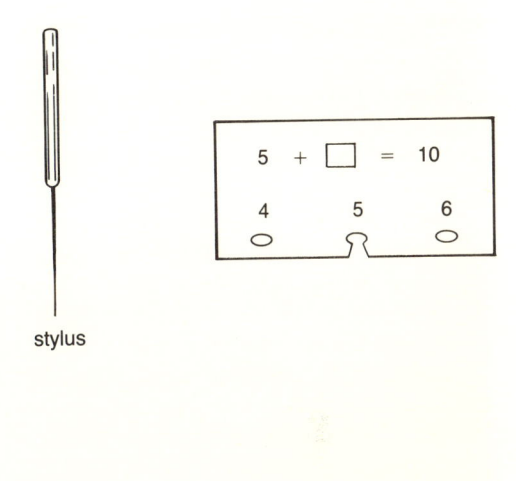

7. Use a grease (overhead projector) pencil to write the math operation (+, −, ÷, ×) in the space between the "eyes."

Modifications.

Vary the card formats; a variety of math problems and numerous reading tasks are thus available. Some possible card formats include those on p. 444.

Poke Box

Selected instructional pinpoints.

1. See math problem—choose answer.
2. See math problem—write answer.
3. See sentence—choose missing word.
4. See paragraph—choose title.
5. Any instructional pinpoint may be used with the Poke Box, which features a multiple-choice answer format.

Feedback device.

Insert a *stylus* in one of the holes below the respective answers. The student pulls the card to see if it comes out of the box. If the right hole is selected, the card is easily removed from the box because the area below the correct answer is cut out and offers no resistance to the stylus.

Materials.

1. a cardboard or wooden box big enough to hold 3″ × 5″ or 5″ × 8″ index cards
2. a large rubber band
3. a thin stick or poker
4. index cards

Construction.

1. Cut the front end of the box so the majority of the index card is visible, but leave a horizontal strip at the bottom of the box about 1″ high.
2. Using a hole-punch or drill, make three evenly spaced holes across the front of the box about ½″ from the bottom of the box.
3. Drill or punch a hole at each end of the front of the box that extends beyond the dimensions of the the index cards. Insert a broken rubber band from the inside of the box on both sides and tie the ends in knots on the outside of the box. The rubber band holds the cards and pushes them to the front of the box.

446 Educational services for the learning disabled

4. Paint the box inside and out.
5. Make holes in the index cards so they line up with the holes in the box.
6. Cut out one answer slot on each card.
7. Attach the stylus to the box.
8. Prepare index cards with problems or questions on top and possible answers beneath. Line up the answers with the appropriate holes.
9. Sometimes a student pulls too hard on the wrong choice and tears the card. To prevent this situation the holes may be strengthened with gummed reinforcers.

Directions.

The student says, writes, and/or chooses her answers. Then she pokes the stylus in the hole representing her answer. If the choice is correct, the problem card can be pulled up and out of the box, which allows the next problem card to be presented.

Modifications.

The size of the box may vary, thus allowing the use of large cards. Some poke boxes feature 8" × 11½" cardboard cards. The large space provides room for short stories and multiple-choice comprehension questions. The teacher may put the problem or story on a separate worksheet and put the answer selections on the cards.

Spinning Wheels

Selected instructional pinpoints.

Any pinpoint can be selected in which a matched pair can be devised (i.e., problems

Spinning Wheels

[Diagram showing front view of spinning wheels device with labels: problem, poster board, window, brass fastener, wheel, answer, with example "4 × 4" and "16" in windows]

front

[Diagram showing back view with labels: fastener back, symbols match when correct answer is selected]

back

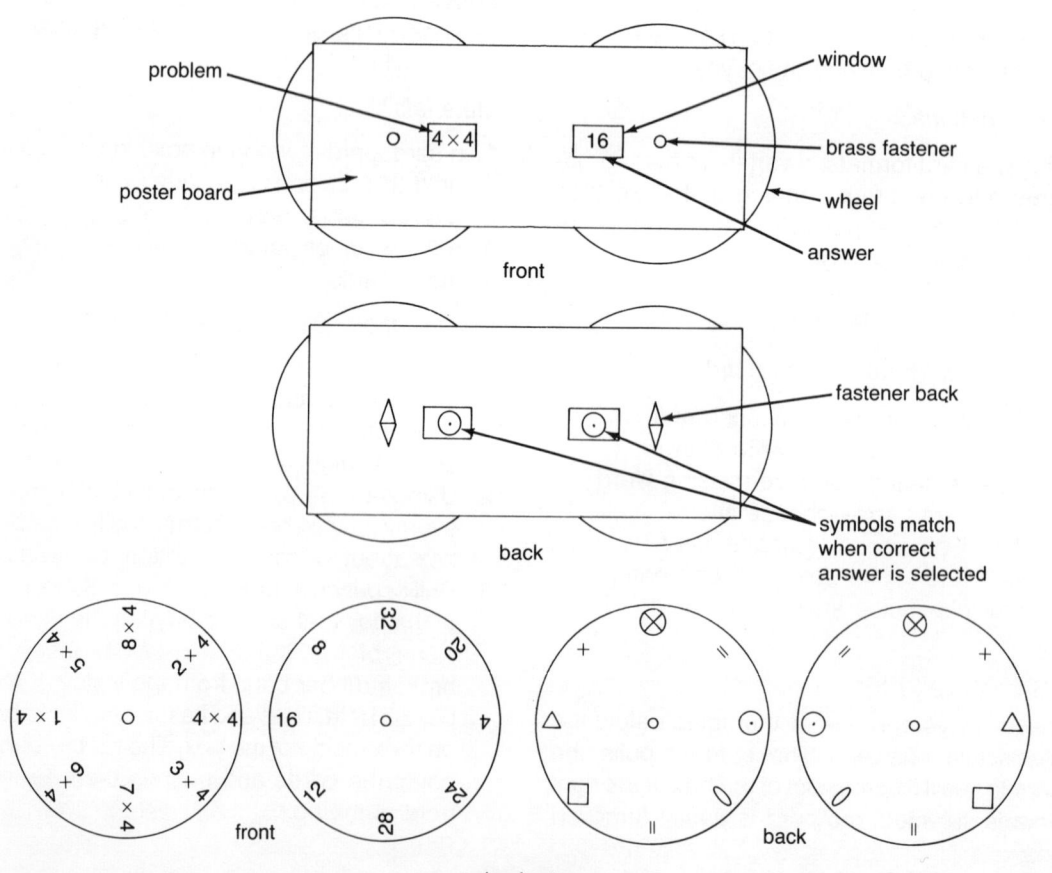

[Four wheel diagrams showing: front wheel with problems (5+4, 8×4, 2+4, 4×1, 4×4, 6+4, 7×4, 3+4); front wheel with answers (32, 8, 20, 16, 4, 12, 28, 24); back wheel with symbols (⊗, +, △, □, ○, ⊙, =); back wheel with symbols (⊗, +, △, □, ○, ⊙, =)]

front   back

wheel sets

on one wheel and the correct answers on another wheel). Fox example:

1. See math problem—select answer.
2. See picture—select word.
3. See picture—select initial sound.

Feedback device.

Windows provide feedback. When a correct match is obtained in the front windows, the objects, symbols, or numbers match in the back windows. Thus, to check an answer the student looks at the back windows.

Materials.

1. poster board
2. brass fasteners
3. small pictures or symbols

Construction.

1. Cut two horizontal pieces of poster board with matching dimensions.
2. Cut two windows on the same horizontal line in each piece. The windows should line up with each other when the pieces are placed together (back to back).
3. Decorate and laminate each piece and make the center holes for the fasteners.
4. Cut circles with dimensions that enable the outer 1" ridge to pass through the windows when the center of the wheel is lined up with the poster board hole.
5. Write, draw, or paste problems on one wheel and put answers on a corresponding wheel. Write, draw, or paste symbols, objects, or numbers on the back of each wheel set (see diagram).

Directions.

The student selects a wheel set that presents the task that the teacher wants her to work on. She places the wheels between the two rectangular pieces, lines up the holes, and inserts the brass fasteners. The student then rotates the task wheel until a problem is presented in the window. Next the student rotates the other wheel and selects one of the answers that passes through the window. Once an answer is selected, the student flips the material over and checks to see if her answer is correct. A correct answer yields matching objects in the two windows on the back.

Modifications.

Teachers can make many wheel sets and code them according to skill area. In addition, wheels that are to be used together (a wheel set) should have matching codes on them, (e.g., wheel set #1, #2, #3). The tasks that can be placed on the wheels are almost limitless. The size of the material can be varied to accommodate different size windows.

The Swinger

Selected instructional pinpoints.

Any pinpoint can be selected in which a problem is presented on one envelope and an answer on another envelope; for examples:

1. See words—select parts of speech.
2. See picture—select word.
3. See paragraph—select title.

Feedback device.

Weights placed on a balance scale are used to provide feedback. If a problem is placed on one side of the scale and the correct answer is placed on the other side of the scale, the two will balance.

Materials.

1. a block of wood (approximately $1\frac{1}{2}" \times 3" \times 4"$), a strip of wood (approximately $\frac{1}{2}" \times 1\frac{1}{2}" \times 12"$), and a piece of molding (approximately $\frac{1}{4}" \times \frac{1}{2}" \times 15"$)
2. a $\frac{1}{4}"$ bolt, $1\frac{1}{2}"$ long
3. a $\frac{3}{8}"$ pipe fastener
4. two small cup hooks
5. envelopes
6. index cards

Construction.

1. Nail the 12" strip of wood to the block of wood.
2. Drill a hole in the strip of wood about 1" from the top and equidistant from the sides.

448 Educational services for the learning disabled

The Swinger

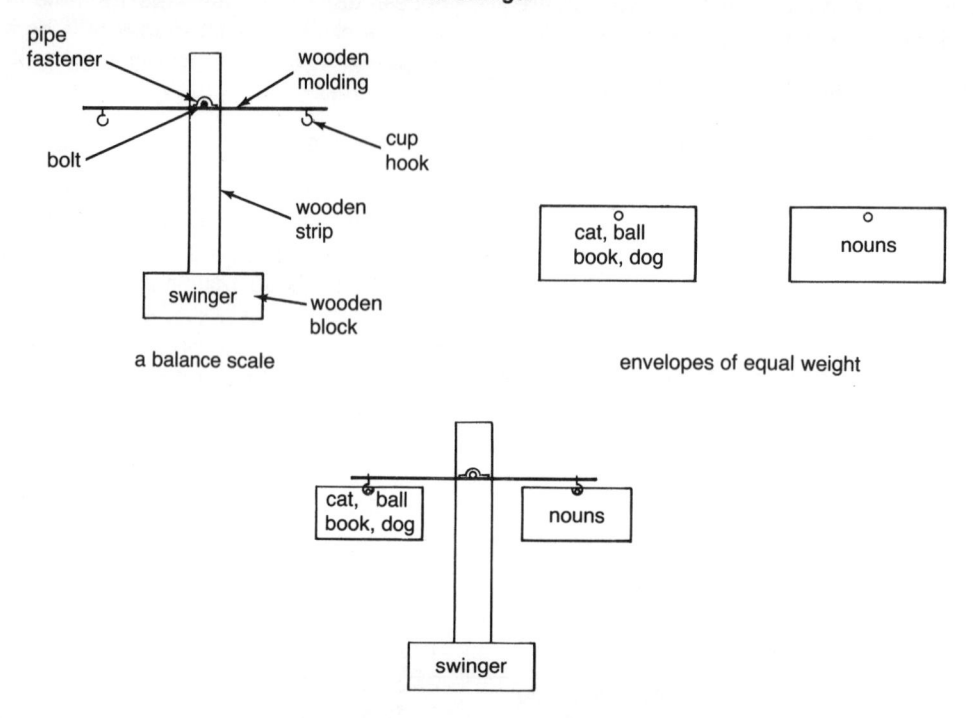

a balance scale

envelopes of equal weight

scale with problem envelope and correct answer envelope

3. Screw the bolt in the hole.
4. Fasten (nail, tack, or glue) the pipe fastener on top of the molding strip, equidistant from both ends.
5. Screw the cup hooks in the side of the molding about ½" from each end.
6. Slide the pipe fastener over the bolt and see if the scale is balanced. Balancing may be facilitated by moving the cup hooks or putting a rubber band on the light side.
7. Glue index cards together in sets of 2, 3, 4, 5, and 6.
8. Put problems and matching answers on sets of envelopes.
9. Insert an equal number of index cards in each matching set of envelopes and glue the cards to the inside of the envelope to prevent them from sliding.
10. Hang the matching envelopes on the scale to make sure they balance.

Directions.

The student selects an envelope with a problem on it. Next, the student selects an answer from the available answer envelopes. Both envelopes are hung on the scale and if a balance occurs, the answer is correct.

Modifications.

1. Make the envelopes plain and laminate them. Use a grease pencil to present different problems.
2. Make little buckets with handles on them to hang on the scales. Different numbers of objects can be placed in the buckets to teach less than, equal to, or greater than. Also, the buckets can be used to present any weighted problem-answer combination.

Other Types of Self-Correcting Materials

The scope of this book does not allow the inclusion of all the materials developed at the

University of Florida. However, some other devices that can be used for feedback include

1. *Pockets.* Pockets are easily made by stapling or gluing envelopes to a material. Pockets usually store an answer key.
2. *Puzzles.* In this type of feedback, pieces of material fit together to indicate a match or correct choice. For example:

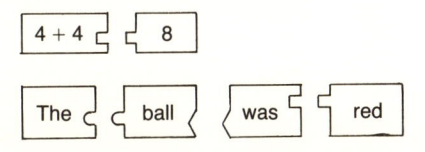

   [4 + 4] [8]

   [The] [ball] [was] [red]

3. *Tabs.* A tab may be pulled from a pocket to reveal an answer.

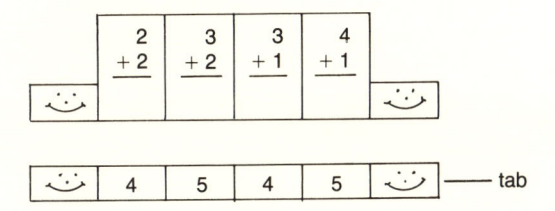

   | 2+2 | 3+2 | 3+1 | 4+1 |

   | 4 | 5 | 4 | 5 | — tab

4. *Electrical.* Electrical devices use lights, buzzers, and bells to signal a correct response. They range from fairly difficult to very difficult in construction but they usually compensate in durability.
5. *Magnets.* Magnets, by virtue of their ability to attract, repel, and spin to a certain position when confronted with another magnet, offer possibilities for self-correction. A paper clip may be hidden in the correct choice and tested against a magnet to prove itself. Tiny magnets may be properly positioned in the problem and each of the choices such that only the correct choice will attract and all the others will repel.
6. *Calculators.* The hand-held calculator may be designed into a self-correcting learning center for very young children. Simple math problems may be immediately corrected once the procedure is mastered.
7. *Matching or picture completion.* Matching or picture completion is used to provide feedback. A problem is presented on one card and the correct answer is presented on another card. When the correct answer is placed with the appropriate problem, the objects, numbers, colors, or picture on the backs of the respective cards will either match or fit together to complete a picture.

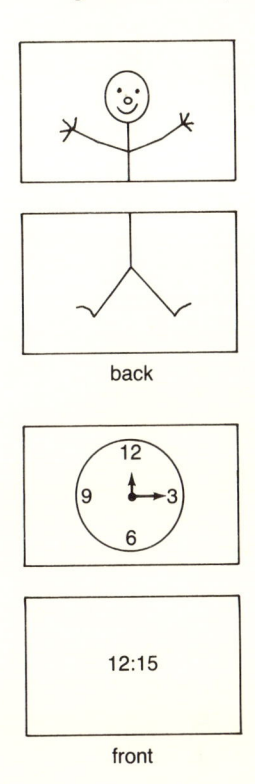

back

front

8. *Slot:* A slot is cut such that another item can fit into it or pass through it (p. 450).

One problem with self-correcting materials is that the students may not use the device correctly; they may misunderstand instructions or directions. Some students will look at the answer first without trying to solve the problem. It is important to show the student how to operate the material before beginning the initial task. It should be simply designed so that only a short demonstration is necessary. Furthermore, such materials probably work best with content that has already been introduced by the instructor.

Some initial cheating should be expected as exploratory behavior. Many students initially enjoy beating the system, but eventually it becomes more fun to select an answer and see if it is correct. If cheating persists, a check sheet or posttest may be administered on the content featured on the material. Usually it does not take long for the student to realize that cheating on the learning material will not help her on the check sheet.

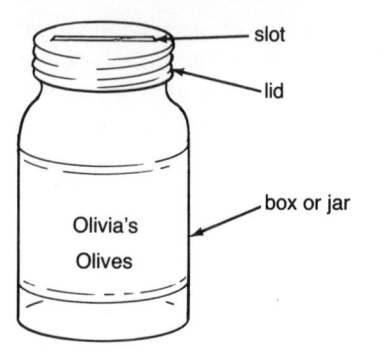

One final word concerning the use of self-correcting learning materials: *Don't fall in love with your material.* Change the content a few times, lend it to another teacher, or put it away for awhile. Children tire of anything.

Commercial Self-Correcting Materials

Commercial materials consist primarily of puzzle and window formats and electronic devices. They are usually expensive. This list provides a guide for examining some available materials and illustrates the use of self-correction.

1. *Locking Numbers* ($9.65) contains 10 two-piece jigsaw puzzles matching numerals to number groups. Each numeral fits only its corresponding group. *Ideal.*
2. *Noun Puzzles* ($4.75) contains 48 self-correcting puzzles that are printed on 24 double-sided cards made of heavy board. The top section of each puzzle shows an object, and the bottom section provides the printed name of the object. Top and bottom sections will interlock only if they belong together, so the puzzles are self-correcting. The reverse side of a properly assembled puzzle is also a properly assembled puzzle of another word or object. *Developmental Learning Materials.*
3. *Shapes Sorting Box* ($12.00) has five faces with one, two, three, four, and five holes, respectively. On the five-hole surface there is a square, circle, wide rectangle, narrow rectangle, and a triangle. There are two nesting boxes; the inner box is placed in the solid outer box with the chosen number of holes facing up. Ten colored blocks fit into the holes. Each shape comes in two colors. *Developmental Learning Materials.*
4. *Telor Learning System* ($49.95) consists of a hand-held instructional device that uses interchangeable teaching lessons in a visual cartridge format. The cartridges contain 40 frames (questions and answers). The student focuses on one fact at a time and selects a response by pushing up on the button corresponding to that answer. The choice of the correct answer advances the lesson to the next frame and provides the student with immediate reinforcement. For retention each fact is presented at least four times during a lesson. *Enrich.*
5. *Clock Puzzles* ($4.75) contains double-sided cards on which the two faces are color cued to separate the 48 puzzles into two 24-card categories of varying difficulty. One side shows the hours and half-hours, and the reverse side shows quarter hours and minutes before and after the hour. The cards are horizontally jig-cut into two sections. The top section shows a clock face and the bottom section states the time shown. Top and bottom sections will interlock only if they belong together so the puzzles are self-

These children are matching answer cards to stimulus cards, a self-correcting material.

correcting. *Developmental Learning Materials.*

6. *Key Word Self-Teaching Cards* ($7.95/set) contains self-correcting picture/word cards. The child matches one of 32 picture/word cards in each set to its position on one of four boards. To check her response, the child turns the picture over revealing the correct word, and the two words should match from card to board. *Childcraft.*

7. *Daigger Math Tutors* ($14.95/set) contains five sets, covering a range of skills from sorting and matching to multiplication and division. The child selects a work card (4–6 cards per set) and places it in the work tray. There are 49 exercises on each of the double-sided work cards. The answer chips are held in the chip storage tray provided in the box lid. The child answers the questions printed in each problem frame by selecting the correct answer chip and placing it over the question. Only the correct answer will fit; mistakes will be rejected. *Educational Teaching Aids.*

8. *Coin Puzzles* ($4.75) consists of 24 double-sided cards that are jig-cut to fit together exactly. The top part of each self-correcting puzzle shows an array of coins, and the interlocking bottom piece bears their printed money value. Matching combinations up to 50¢ are shown on one side of a card and 50¢ to $2 on the other side. Five different values of coins appear in money combinations, ranging from 1¢ to $2. *Development Learning Materials.*

9. *Number Worm* ($7.50) consists of a curvy red 18" worm with thick wooden pieces numbered from 1 to 12 in large, black numbers. The pieces fit together only in correct sequence, starting with the head of the worm and reading left to right. *Childcraft.*

10. *ETA Math Balance* ($12.50) includes 20 plastic weights and 88 labels and illustrates relationships between numbers and the processes of addition, subtraction, and multiplication. The child places light plastic strip weights on the weight hangers of each arm. Weight hangers are identified with numbers from 1 to 10 on the front of each arm. Combinations of weights placed on one arm that equal combinations of weights placed on the opposite arm will balance the arm, showing the child her combination is correct. Hangers can represent fractions, money, length, etc., by attaching labels provided. *Educational Teaching Aids.*

11. *Self-Correcting Action Learning Slates* ($4.95/set) contains 18 double-sided

problem/answer cards, blank cards for teacher-made problems, writing stylus, and erasable slate. The child selects slotted practice form and inserts it (problem side up) between the films of the slate. She answers the problems on the slate and removes and turns over the problem card, reinserting it with answer side facing up. The student gets immediate feedback on performance and can either rework the card or select another practice form. *Childcraft.*

12. *Rhyming Words Puzzles* ($4.75/set) contains 24 double-sided cards that are jig-cut into two pieces that interlock uniquely, thereby confirming the student's choice of pieces. Pictorial representation of the rhyming words appears on one side of the cards and the rhyming words themselves are printed on the other side. The self-correcting puzzles present long and short vowels as well as irregular vowel combinations. *Developmental Learning Materials.*

Instructional Games

LD children often need extensive practice and drill. Because drill can be tedious and boring, it calls for creative teaching in order to motivate students. Positive reinforcement, charting, self-correction, and high-interest formats (cartoon characters, etc.) are frequently used in drill. In addition, instructional games are a popular way of enriching practice. Such games feature feedback via peer response or an answer key. Some selected games are presented next.

Mystery Detective

Instructional objective.

Reading comprehension: See sentence clue card and select the meaning of underlined portion in terms of how, what, when, who, why, or where.

Feedback device.

Tabs with numbers that match those on the clue cards are used to provide feedback. For example, a number on a "What" card will be on the tab labeled "What." Thus, a correct response results in a number match between the card and the tab.

Materials.

1. poster board for game board, tabs, and clue cards
2. dice
3. pictures or drawings for decoration
4. objects to move from start to jail

Construction.

1. Cut a slot in the poster board and tape an additional piece of cardboard to the poster board in such a manner that a pocket is formed with the slot at the top of it.
2. Cut six tabs of a length that exposes the name of the tab but not the numbers when fully inserted in the pocket.
3. On the game side of the board draw a "start-to-jail" winding, segmented road.
4. Make a stack of sentence clue cards and underline a portion of each sentence that corresponds to one of the how, what, when, who, why, or where questions. Place a number in the right top corner of each clue card. Do not repeat the numbers.
5. Make six tabs, one for each of the questions. On each tab put the numbers that are on the respective clue cards that match the tab question. See diagram.
6. Lamination increases durability.

Directions.

1. A player rolls the dice and picks up a clue card.
2. The player determines if it is a how, what, when, who, why, or where clue and selects one of the tabs.
3. If the number on the sentence clue card is on the tab she chooses, the player gets to move her marker or object the number of spaces indicated on the dice.
4. If the number on the sentence clue card is not on the tab, the player does not move her marker.
5. The next player does the same thing and the first player to put the marker in jail wins.

Mystery Detective

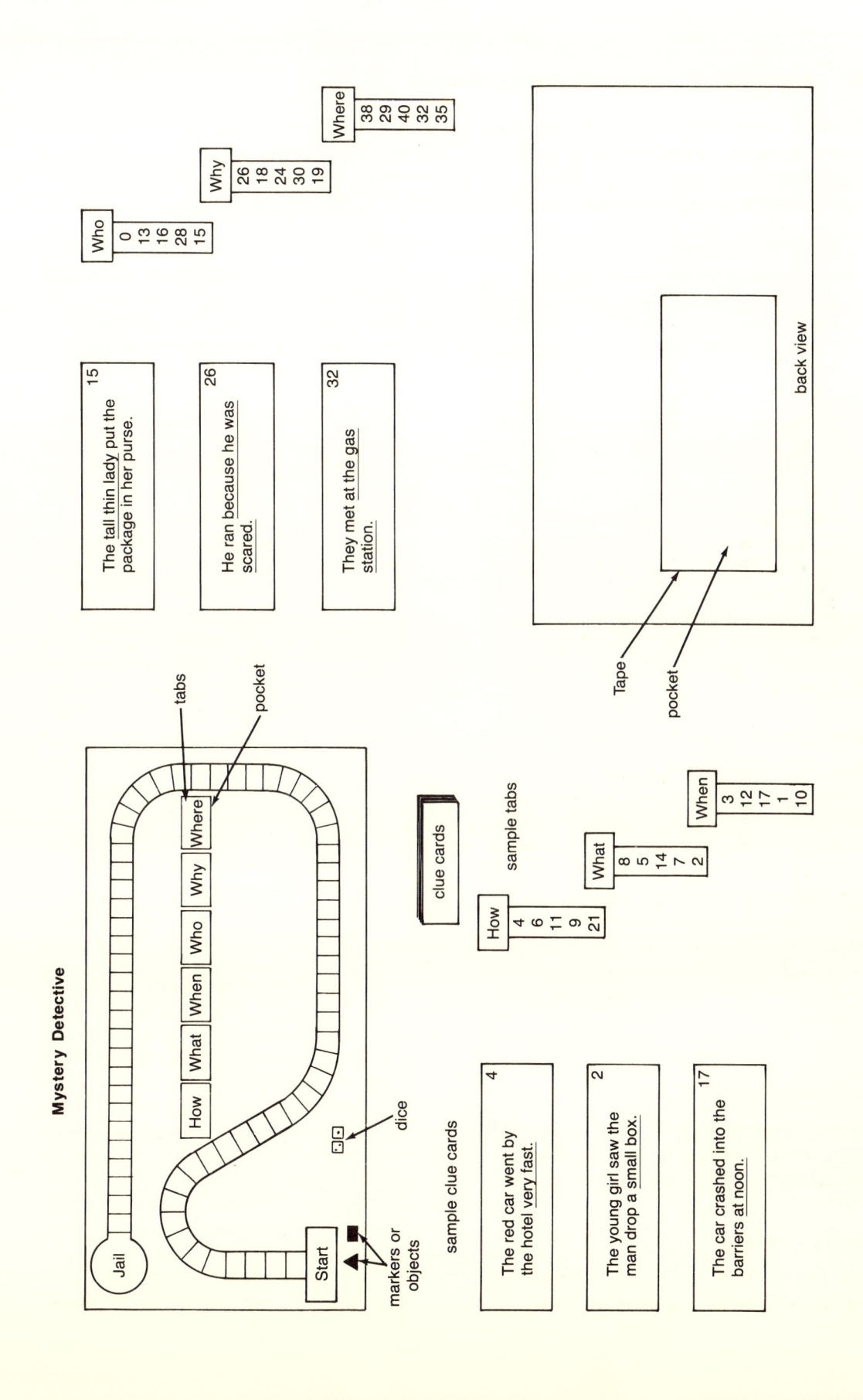

Who	Why	Where
0	26	38
13	18	29
16	24	40
28	30	32
15	19	35

15 The tall thin lady put the package in her purse.

26 He ran because he was scared.

32 They met at the gas station.

back view

Tape
pocket

tabs
pocket

Where | Why | Who | When | What | How

clue cards

sample tabs

How	What	When
4	8	3
6	5	12
11	14	17
9	7	1
21	2	10

dice

markers or objects

Start
Jail

sample clue cards

4 The red car went by the hotel very fast.

2 The young girl saw the man drop a small box.

17 The car crashed into the barriers at noon.

Modifications.

1. Use this game format to practice syllabication. Label each tab with a number to indicate the number of syllables on corresponding word cards.
2. Instead of using the pocket on the game board, put each tab in an envelope or in a separately constructed pocket (e.g., use a manila folder and staples).
3. To make the game more exciting, mark "Trouble" or "Good News" on certain squares. When a player lands on a marked square, a card is picked up and the player does the activity on the card (e.g., go ahead 3 spaces).

Simple Game Board Format

Instructional objective.

Any instructional task that can be presented on a card and performed in a few seconds is suitable.

Feedback device.

Answer key and peer correction provide feedback.

Materials.

1. poster board
2. index cards
3. golf tees
4. dice
5. tasks for the cards

Construction.

1. Draw a segmented road, race track, rocket path, football field, mountain path, or any other start-finish sequence on poster board.
2. Decorate the board to accent the game theme (e.g., racing cars, football, joggers, mountain climbers).
3. Make a stack of task cards with an accompanying answer key. For example, if the task card says $4 \times 4 = $ ___ the answer key would read $4 \times 4 = \underline{16}$.

Directions.

1. A player rolls the dice, picks up a task card, and says an answer.
2. If no player challenges this answer, she moves her marker the number on the dice.
3. If a player challenges her answer, it is looked up on the answer key. If it is correct, the player gets another turn. If it is incorrect, the marker is not moved and the challenger takes a turn.

Modifications.

1. The challenge factor may be omitted.
2. Certain spaces may be marked and a chance card is picked up when a player lands on one of them.

Simple Game Board Format

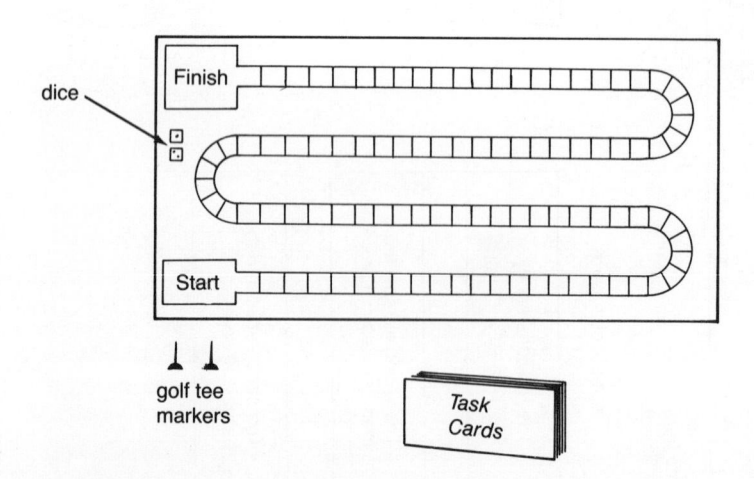

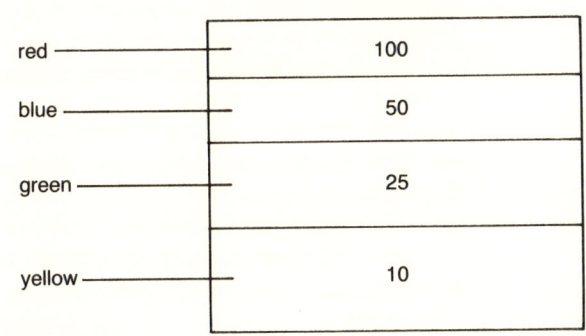

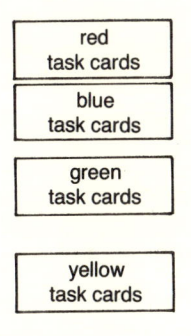

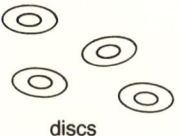

Toss A Disc

Instructional objective.

Any instructional task that can be presented on a card and performed in a few seconds is suitable.

Feedback device.

Answer key and peer correction provide feedback.

Materials.

1. poster board
2. colored index cards or color-coded index cards (e.g., colored dot in top corner)
3. discs (e.g., checkers, laminated circles of poster board or oak tag)
4. tasks for the cards

Construction.

1. Divide a piece of large poster board into color zones with the zones getting larger as the points decrease.
2. Put points for each zone in the center of the zone.
3. Use checkers as discs or make discs out of oak tag or poster board.
4. Decorate the poster board with a theme.
5. Laminate the poster board.

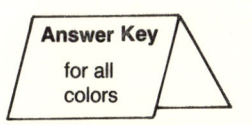

Directions.

1. Place the game board on the floor with the highest point zone flush against the wall.
2. Approximately 8–12 feet away, make a space for the player to stand behind while she is tossing the disc toward the game board.
3. If the tossed disc lands on red, the player picks up a red task card and answers the question on it. If the disc lands on blue, the player picks up a blue task card, etc.
4. The player checks her answer on the answer key. If she is correct, she gets the points indicated for the color zone her disc landed in; if she is incorrect, no points are awarded.
5. The first player to earn 500 (700, 1000, etc.) points wins.

Commercial Instructional Games

A perusal of the catalogues of major publishers of educational materials provides the reader with a descriptive resource of many games. In addition, several references serve as excellent resources of instructional games, such as the following:

The Kids' Stuff Series. Special Kids' Stuff—$9.95; Kids' Stuff Math—$9.95; Center Stuff for Nooks, Crannies and Corners—$9.95; More Center Stuff for Nooks, Crannies and

Corners—$9.95. *Incentive Publications,* Nashville, Tenn.

The Spice Series. ($5.25 each) Fifteen different books of activities for various academic areas. *Educational Service, Inc.,* Stevensville, Mich.

Helpful texts include Wallace & Kauffman (1978); Baratta-Lorton (1975); Bailey (1975); Hammill & Bartel (1978); Van Etten & Watson (1975); and Stephens (1977).

DEVELOPING AND MAINTAINING INTERACTION SKILLS

Teacher Attributes

Obviously teaching has only just begun when an instructional plan is readied. The plan then must be carried out in a positive and effective manner. The teacher begins to build a pleasant classroom environment that generates enthusiasm for learning.

How she accomplishes this atmosphere depends on her personal attributes. Unfortunately, the research on desirable teacher attributes is inconclusive. Rosenshine and Furst (1973) note that the research on teaching in natural settings "has tended to be chaotic, unorganized and self-serving" (p. 122). However, in a review of more than 50 correlational studies on teaching behavior and student achievement, Rosenshine and Furst acknowledge several variables that yield the most consistent results:

1. *Clarity* (as assessed on rating scales by students or observers) yielded significant positive results in all seven studies in which it was used. Rosenshine and Furst note that clarity generally refers to organization.
2. *Variability or flexibility* (as assessed by observer or student questionnaires) yielded positive results. Variability appears to be related to flexibility in procedure.
3. *Enthusiasm* (as assessed via observer ratings on paired adjectives [dull versus stimulating]) yielded positive results.
4. *Task oriented and/or businesslike* (as assessed via student and observer ratings) yielded positive results. This variable relates to whether or not the teacher is concerned that students learn something.
5. *Criticism* (as assessed by counting general and specific criticisms) consistently yielded negative results.
6. *Use of structuring comments* that provide an outline of what is about to happen or what has occurred yielded significant positive results.

In a study of teacher style on the behavior of children, Lovitt (1977) asked 60 students to list the behaviors they thought good teachers should exhibit. The children turned in 266 items, which were examined and reduced to a list of 15 behaviors that could be observed. The children agreed that this list fairly well described a good teacher: compliments children, enforces rules the same for all, lets children come to her for help, helps each child, listens to both sides of the story, gives homework, sets example by using good manners, does experiments, gives study time, shows trust for children, keeps room quiet, has children clean room, joins in class humor, explains more than once, and asks children for help. This list indicates that the children were concerned with fair play, inclusion in the action, getting work done in a quiet and orderly room, and they wanted the teacher to be a real person with a sense of humor. One of the findings revealed that when the teachers engaged in these behaviors more, the academic performance of the children improved. Lovitt notes that the most important message of this study is that "as the teacher did more things that pleased the students, they did more to please the teacher" (p. 94). An encouraging factor in Lovitt's study is that viable teacher behavior was identified, observed, and modified.

Lerner (1976) stresses the need for the clinical teacher to be aware of the pervasive effects of a learning disability on the child's world. The child's self-concept may be very poor and she may show little interest in school achievement. Such a learner needs a strong therapeutic relationship between herself and the teacher. To help develop this relationship, Lerner recommends the teaching principles of Roswell and Natchez (1971): *(a)* establish rapport, *(b)* colloborate with the learner by involving her in analyzing her problem and designing intervention, *(c)* provide structure via schedules of activities, etc., *(d)* be sincere with the learner, *(e)* provide realistic success, and *(f)* use materials that are interesting.

Although many characteristics of a good teacher have been offered, most remain nebulous. Hopefully the descriptions of the works of Lovitt (1977), Rosenshine and Furst (1971), and Roswell and Natchez (1971) reflect the essence of what is meant by desirable teacher behavior.

Responding to Correct Answers

Interaction skills are basic to managing and motivating pupils. In teacher education programs much effort is expended in getting teachers to praise students in a systematic manner. According to the principles of reinforcement, teachers are instructed to praise a student immediately following a correct or desirable response. One problem that beginning teachers frequently have involves "robot" praising. In robot praising the teacher gets in a praise "rut" that sounds something like: "good," "very good," "good work," "very good," "good, Tommy," "very good." This type of redundant praising may sound insincere. To correct this problem the teacher should develop and use a wide repetoire of praise phrases and techniques. For example, one can say "very good" in the following ways:

Excellent.
Super.
Great!
The best.
I knew you could do it.
That's better than ever.
Superior.
Spectacular performance.

Now you have it.
You can do two right. Let's try the others using the method that got them right.
That's coming along nicely.
You have just about mastered that.
One more time and you'll have it.
You're on the right track now.
You've really been working hard today.
That's quite an improvement.
That's the right way to do it.
Keep up the good work.
You're really going to town.
You're really improving.
Wow, you are hot today.
I like the way you _____.
That's really nice.
I think you've got it now.
That's what I call a fine job.
You've got your brain in gear today.
Nothing can stop you now.
Good work. Look at you go!

In giving out praise, be judicious. In paying a compliment to one child, it is easy to tear down the self-esteem or confidence of a less able child. It is frequently better to whisper your approval than to broadcast it to the whole room. These brief bits of praise can be whispered without a neighbor knowing:

Good thinking.
Perfect.
Good going!
That's it.
Tremendous.
Not bad.
That's good.
Fantastic.
Marvelous.
Sensational.

For older children, comments may include

You outdid yourself today.
This is not only a good paper—it is very neat.
You're getting better every day.
You must have been practicing to reach such perfection.
You haven't missed a thing.

Introduce the ways other people say "very good." Suggest that the class contribute to the list by asking family and friends who know other languages. For example:

Sehr gut. (German)
Muy Bueno! (Spanish)
Trés bien. (French)

Some other types of social reinforcement listed by Stephens (1977) include:

Positive Proximity

NEARNESS

eating with children
five minutes to discuss something with teacher
interacting with class at recess
pausing—while transferring objects
principal serves as personal tutor
sharing praise with outside person
sitting on desk near students
sitting within the student group
standing alongside

TOUCHING (social, positive proximity)

combing hair
dancing
gently raising chin
handshake
helping put on coat
hugging
kissing a hurt
touching
tying shoes

Positive Physical Expression

FACIAL EXPRESSION

cheering
forming kiss
laughing (happy)
nodding
raising eyebrows
rolling eyes enthusiastically
smiling
winking
whistling

BODILY EXPRESSION

bounding
circling hand through air (encouragement to continue)
clapping hands
high sign
jumping up and down
peace sign
raising arms
signaling OK
thumbs up
V for victory

Written Comments

Beautiful work.
Bravo!
Brilliant.
Congratulations.
Cool.
Delightful.

Stars are used to reinforce this student for progress.

Excellent.
Exciting.
Fabulous!
Fantastic!
Great!
Marvelous!
Outstanding.
Perfect.
Positively great work!
Show this to your parents.
Swell.
That shows hard work.
Wow!
Yeah!
You should be very proud of this.
For display.

Evaluation Marks

A-1
checkmarks
rubber stamps
stars
happy faces
percentages
+ (plus)
letter grades (pp. 304–306)

Responding to Incorrect Answers

Children with learning problems frequently get the wrong answers. However, teachers have little training in how to deal with incorrect responses; most efforts are aimed at responding to right answers.

How the teacher reacts to incorrect answers can easily influence the mood, motivation, and participation of the student. An insensitive reaction can discourage the student, promote frustration, and create behavior problems. On the other hand, a sensitive reaction helps maintain motivation and interest. The teacher should use a repetoire of responses to incorrect answers. These responses should avoid putting the student down and provide encouragement for effort. Some useful response methods include

1. *Develop sensitive responses.*
   Let's look at it together.
   That's close.
   You have almost mastered that.
   One more time and you'll have it.
   Nice try.
   Let me help you.
   I fooled you.
   Look again.
   Almost; let's try again.
2. *Delay feedback.* Some children answer before they have time to think. Simply pause and wait for a second response.
3. *Repeat the instructions with emphasis.* Example: "4 × 4 is what?"
4. *Use synonymous rephrasing.* Repeat the question or task using different words. For example: "Lift the box" can be rephrased as "Pick up the box."
5. *Partially complete the task.* For example: "Where did Bob hide the cookie? He hid the cookie under the ch___."
6. *Provide ridiculous alternatives and the right answer.* For example: "Did the dog bite the rock? Did the dog bite the bridge? Did the dog bite the stranger?"
7. *Model the correct answer and instruct the child to imitate.* For example: "4 × 4 is 16. What is 4 × 4?"

Preventing Frustration

Another important interaction skill is aimed at preventing frustration. The teacher should continuously scan the room for possible frustration signals (e.g., balling up paper, mumbling, breaking pencil points, continuous hand raising for help, general off-task behavior, muscle tenseness). Some techniques for reducing frustration include

1. Make sure the task is at the child's instructional or mastery level.
2. Provide hurdle help. Give the child cues or prompts.
3. Change tasks.
4. Put the task on a self-correcting material.
5. Make a statement that reflects an understanding of the situation. For example, "Those math problems are tough today, aren't they?"
6. Give the student a break.

SUMMARY

Diagnostic-prescriptive teaching consists of a four-step process: (a) identify skill to be taught via assessment, (b) provide instruction, (c) continuously evaluate the student's progress, and (d) depending on the progress of the student, select one of four alternatives—introduce new higher skill, introduce an easier skill, repeat instruction, or use a different teaching strategy. Individualized educational programs (IEP) as required by PL 94–142 incorporate many components of diagnostic-prescriptive teaching and influence the teaching practices with exceptional students. An IEP must include (a) a statement of the present levels of educational performance of the child, (b) a statement of annual and short-term instructional objectives, (c) a statement of what services are to be provided and how much the child will be able to participate in regular education, (d) the projected date for initiation and anticipated duration of such services, and (e) appropriate objective criteria and evaluation procedures and schedules for determining, on at least an annual basis, whether instructional objectives are being achieved.

Instructional Approaches

The content and teaching methods used in an instructional program are greatly influenced by the teacher's orientation regarding the numerous LD instructional approaches. Many writers dichotomize these approaches into a task-analysis or skill-training model and an ability-training model. The skill approaches focus on directly teaching academic skills and primarily emphasize an analysis of tasks. The ability approaches assume the learning problem is a result of impairments or dysfunctions in the learner. Instruction is aimed at correcting faulty processing problems. This approach is based on the rationale that correction of faulty learning processes results in improved academic learning. Another viewpoint (Smead, 1977) recommends combining components from both models.

Selected instructional approaches within the ability model include (a) perceptual motor, (b) psycholinguistic, and (c) learner developmental. The skill model instructional approaches include (a) academic materials, (b) content developmental, and (c) applied behavior analysis. The multisensory approach originated from the ability model, but it actually fits into either model. Teachers must combine the respective approaches into an individual style that is guided by research findings and/or pupil progress. The pre- and post-design, the reversal design, and the multiple-baseline design provide a framework for evaluating the effectiveness of teaching procedures.

Planning

Effective teaching often relies heavily on careful planning, which includes

1. what is to be taught, to whom
2. where the instruction will occur
3. when the instruction will occur
4. what materials will be used
5. what activities or strategies will be used to accommodate children finishing their tasks at different rates
6. how instruction will occur

Self-Correcting Materials and Instructional Games

Self-correcting materials offer numerous advantages (e.g., reduce practicing mistakes) over traditional worksheets and hold promise as an instructional procedure. Windows, flaps, weights, slots, magnets, puzzles, answer keys, and flip-side matches are some of the devices used to make materials self-correcting. Furthermore, instructional games provide children interesting practice in academic skill areas. Such games are easily made and are commercially available.

Interaction Skills

Developing a positive classroom atmosphere that facilitates social, emotional, and academic growth depends to a great extent on the teacher's interaction skills. Certain teacher at-

Success, structure, and support lead to mutual respect and appreciation between teacher and student.

tributes enhance effective and positive interaction. These attributes, although somewhat nebulous, are generally described with such terms as *fair, sincere, complimentary, structured or businesslike, provides clear instructions, has a sense of humor,* and *involves children.* Interaction skills are enhanced if the teacher uses a variety of ways to praise or reinforce children (e.g., different verbal phrases, touch, written comments, gestures). Moreover, it is important for the teacher to develop sensitive ways of replying to incorrect responses. Children with learning problems often respond incorrectly and caution must be used to avoid hurting their feelings or discouraging on-task efforts.

Preventing frustration or crisis situations frequently depends on skillful interaction. Through visual scanning of the classroom the teacher can notice frustration signals and intervene before disruptive or self-degrading behavior occurs. Some intervention procedures consist of hurdle help, changing the task, or counseling.

It is easy for the beginning teacher to get lost in the many details involved in the instructional process and lose sight of the major components of teaching. An experienced teacher once stated, "Teaching LD children is not complex. It simply involves providing each child with three things: success, structure, and support." Maybe she's on to something.

REFERENCES

Alper, T., Nowlin, L., Lemoine, K., Perine, M., & Bettencourt, B. The rated assessment of academic skills. *Academic Therapy,* 1974, *9,* 151–164.

Bailey, E.J. *Academic activities for adolescents with learning disabilities.* Evergreen, Colo.: Learning Pathways, P.O. Box 1407, 1975.

Baratta-Lorton, M. *Workjobs . . . for parents: Activity-centered learning in the home.* Menlo Park, Calif.: Addison-Wesley, 1975.

Barsch, R.H. *Achieving perceptual-motor efficiency* (Vol. 1). Seattle: Special Child Publications, 1967.

Bush, W.J., & Giles, M.T. *Aids to psycholinguistic teaching* (2nd ed.). Columbus, Ohio: Charles E. Merrill, 1977.

Cratty, B. *Active learning: Games to enhance academic abilities.* Englewood Cliffs, N.J.: Prentice-Hall, 1971.

Delacato, C.H. *Neurological organization and reading.* Springfield, Ill.: Charles C Thomas, 1966.

Dunn, L., & Smith, J.O. *Peabody language development kits.* Circle Pines, Minn.: American Guidance Services, 1966.

Durkin, D. Some questions about questionable instructional material. *Reading Teacher,* 1974, *28,* 13–17.

Ellis, D., & Prelander, J. *A program sequence of phonetic skills.* Annual Report for a Program Project for Investigation and Application of Procedures of Analysis and Modification of Behavior of Handicapped Children, University of Washington, Experimental Education Unit, 1973.

Fernald, G. *Remedial techniques in basic school subjects.* New York: McGraw-Hill, 1943.

Flavell, J.H. *The developmental psychology of Jean Piaget.* Princeton, N.J.: Van Nostrand, 1963.

Frostig, M., & Horne, D. *The Frostig program for the development of visual perception: Teacher's guide.* Chicago: Follett, 1964.

Getman, G.N. The visuomotor complex in the acquisition of learning skills. In J. Hellmuth (Ed.), *Learning disorders* (Vol. 1.). Seattle: Special Child Publications, 1965.

Gillingham, A., & Stillman, B. *Remedial training for children with specific disability in reading, spelling, and penmanship* (7th ed.). Cambridge, Mass.: Educators Publishing Service, 1966.

Glaser, R. Individuals and learning: The new aptitudes. *Educational Researcher,* 1972, *1,* 5–13.

Hall, R.V. *Managing behavior, Part I: The measurement of behavior.* Lawrence, Kans.: H & H Enterprises, 1974.

Hallahan, D.P., & Cruickshank, W.M. *Psychoeducational foundations of learning disabilities.* Englewood Cliffs, N.J.: Prentice-Hall, 1973.

Hallahan, D.P., & Kauffman, J.M. *Introduction to learning disabilities: A psycho-behavioral approach.* Englewood Cliffs, N.J.: Prentice-Hall, 1976.

Hammill, D.D., & Bartel, N.R. *Teaching children with learning and behavior problems* (2nd ed.). Boston: Allyn & Bacon, 1978.

Hammill, D.D., Goodman, L., & Wiederholt, J.L. Visual-motor processes: Can we train them? *Reading Teacher,* 1974, *27,* 469–478.

Haring, N.G., & Eaton, M.D. Systematic instructional procedures: An instructional hierarchy. In N.G. Haring, T.C. Lovitt, M.D. Eaton, & C.L. Hansen, *The fourth R: Research in the classroom.* Columbus, Ohio: Charles E. Merrill, 1978.

Haring, N.G., & Gentry, N.D. Direct and individualized instructional procedures. In N.G. Haring & R.L. Schiefelbusch (Eds.), *Teaching special children.* New York: McGraw-Hill, 1976.

Haring, N.G., & Schiefelbusch, R.L. (Eds.). *Teaching special children.* New York: McGraw-Hill, 1976.

Haughton, E. Correlation of say sounds to say words. *Behaviorgrams,* January 21, 1971, Article 061.

Haughton, E. Aims—Growing and sharing. In J.B. Jordon & L.S. Robbins (Eds.), *Let's try doing something else kind of thing.* Arlington, Va.: The Council for Exceptional Children, 1972.

Henderson, H.H., Clise, M., & Silverton, B. *Modification of reading behavior: A phonetic program utilizing rate acceleration.* Ellensburg, Wash.: H.H. Henderson, 1971.

Johnson, D., & Myklebust, H. *Learning disabilities: Educational principles and practices.* New York: Grune & Stratton, 1967.

Johnson, S.W., & Morasky, R.L. *Learning disabilities.* Boston: Allyn & Bacon, 1977.

Kephart, N.C. *The slow learner in the classroom.* Columbus, Ohio: Charles E. Merrill, 1971.

Kirk, S.A., & Kirk, W.D. *Psycholinguistic learning disabilities: Diagnosis and remediation.* Urbana, Ill.: University of Illinois Press, 1971.

Koorland, M.A., & Rose, T.L. *Consulting with classroom teachers: A behavioral approach for special educators.* Manuscript submitted for publication, 1978.

Kunzelmann, H. *Research and interpretation.* Paper presented at the Precision Teaching Workshop, Eugene, Oreg., August 1969.

Lerner, J.W. *Children with learning disabilities* (2nd ed.). Boston: Houghton Mifflin, 1976.

Lindsley, O.R. Direct measurement and prosthesis of retarded behavior. *Journal of Education,* 1964, *147,* 62–81.

Lovitt, T.C. Applied behavior analysis and learning disabilities—Part I: Characteristics of ABA, general recommendations, and methodological limitations. *Journal of Learning Disabilities,* 1975, *8,* 432–443. (a)

Lovitt, T.C. Applied behavior analysis and learning disabilities—Part II: Specific research recommendations and suggestions for practitioners. *Journal of Learning Disabilities,* 1975, *8,* 504–518. (b)

Lovitt, T.C. Thomas C. Lovitt. In J.M. Kauffman & D.P. Hallahan (Eds.), *Teaching children with learning disabilities: Personal perspectives.* Columbus, Ohio: Charles E. Merrill, 1976.

Lovitt, T.C. *In spite of my resistance: I've learned from children.* Columbus, Ohio: Charles E. Merrill, 1977.

Lovitt, T.C. Learning disabilities. In N.G. Haring (Ed.), *Behavior of exceptional children: An introduction to special education* (2nd ed.). Columbus, Ohio: Charles E. Merrill, 1978.

Lovitt, T.C., & Hansen, C.L. Round one—Placing the child in the right reader. *Journal of Learning Disabilities,* 1976, *9,* 347–353.

Mercer, C.D., & Mercer, A.R. The use and development of self correcting materials with exceptional children. *Teaching Exceptional Children,* 1978, *11* (1), 6–11.

Minskoff, E., Wiseman, D.E., & Minskoff, J. *The MWM program for developing language abilities.* Ridgefield, N.J.: Educational Performance Associates, 1972.

Myers, P.I., & Hammill, D.D. *Methods of learning disorders* (2nd ed.). New York: John Wiley & Sons, 1976.

Neisworth, J.T., & Smith, R.M. *Modifying retarded behavior.* Boston: Houghton Mifflin, 1973.

Newcomer, P.L., & Hammill, D.D. *Psycholinguistics in the schools.* Columbus, Ohio: Charles E. Merrill, 1976.

Olson, J., & Mercer, C.D. *The effects of self-correcting materials on academic performance and on-task behavior.* Unpublished manuscript, University of Florida, 1977.

Orton, S.T. *Reading, writing and speech problems in children.* New York: W.W. Norton, 1937.

Osgood, C.E. Motivational dynamics of language behavior. In M.R. Jones (Ed.), *Nebraska symposium on motivation.* Lincoln: University of Nebraska Press, 1957.

Quay, H.C. Special education: Assumptions, techniques, and evaluative criteria. *Exceptional Children,* 1973, *40,* 165–170.

Rosenshine, B., & Furst, N. The use of direct observation to study teaching. In R.M.W. Travers (Ed.), *Second handbook of research on teaching.* Chicago: Rand McNally, 1973.

Ross, A.O. *Psychological aspects of learning disabilities & reading disorders.* New York: McGraw-Hill, 1976.

Roswell, F., & Natchez, G. *Reading disability: Diagnosis and treatment.* New York: Basic Books, 1971.

Silverston, R.A., & Deichman, J.W. Sense modality research and the acquisition of reading skills. *Review of Education Research,* 1975, *45,* 149–172.

Slingerland, B.H. *A multisensory approach to language arts for specific language disability children: A guide for primary teachers.* Cambridge, Mass.: Educators Publishing Service, 1971.

Smead, V.S. Ability training and task analysis in diagnostic/prescriptive teaching. *The Journal of Special Education,* 1977, *11*(1), 113–125.

Starlin, C.M. Evaluating progress toward reading proficiency. In B. Bateman (Ed.), *Learning disorders* (Vol. 4). *Reading.* Seattle: Special Child Publications, 1971.

Starlin, C.M., & Starlin, A. *Guides to decision making in computational math.* Bemidji, Minn.: Unique Curriculums Unlimited, 1973. (a)

Starlin, C.M. & Starlin, A. *Guides to decision making in oral reading.* Bemidji, Minn.: Unique Curriculums Unlimited, 1973. (b)

Starlin, C.M., & Starlin, A. *Guides to decision making in spelling.* Bemidji, Minn.: Unique Curriculums Unlimited, 1973. (c)

Stephens, T.M. *Teaching skills to children with learning and behavior disorders.* Columbus, Ohio: Charles E. Merrill, 1977.

Tarver, S., & Hallahan, D.P. Children with learning disabilities: An overview. In J.M. Kauffman & D.P. Hallahan (Eds.), *Teaching children with learning disabilities: Personal perspectives.* Columbus, Ohio: Charles E. Merrill, 1976.

Turnbull, A.P., Strickland, B., & Hammer, S.E. The individualized education program—Part 1: Procedural guidelines. *Journal of Learning Disabilities,* 1978, *11,* 40–46. (a)

Turnbull, A.P., Strickland, B., & Hammer, S.E. The individualized education program—Part 2:

Translating law into practice. *Journal of Learning Disabilities,* 1978, *11,* 67–72. (b)

Van Etten, C., & Watson, B. (Eds.). Programs, materials, and techniques. *Journal of Learning Disabilities,* 1975, *9,* 541–549.

Wallace, G., & Kauffman, J.M. *Teaching children with learning problems* (2nd ed.). Columbus, Ohio: Charles E. Merrill, 1978.

White, O.R., & Haring, N.G. *Exceptional teaching: A multimedia training package.* Columbus, Ohio: Charles E. Merrill, 1976.

Wolking, W.D. *Rate of growth toward adult proficiency: Differences between high and low achievement children, grades 1–6.* Paper presented at the International Symposium of Learning Disabilities, Miami Beach, Florida, October 1973.

Worell, J., & Nelson, C.M. *Managing instructional problems: A case study workbook.* New York: McGraw-Hill, 1974.

Ysseldyke, J.E. & Salvia, J. Diagnostic-prescriptive teaching: Two models. *Exceptional Children,* 1974, *41,* 181–185.

Appendix a

Tests

The following selected tests help assess LD children. They are organized into these areas: academic achievement (general, math, and reading), auditory perception, information processing, intelligence, language, motor development, social-emotional, and visual perception. In addition, numerous tests in other areas are discussed within the chapters (e.g., early identification tests are presented in Chapter 12). An additional reference for tests is the *Mental Measurement Yearbook,* O.K. Buros (Ed.), Gryphon Press, Highland Park, New Jersey.

ACADEMIC ACHIEVEMENT

General

California Reading Tests. California Test Bureau, Monterey, Calif. Grade level: 1–12. Includes several subtests in vocabulary and comprehension.

Metropolitan Achievement Tests. Harcourt Brace Jovanovich, New York, N.Y. Grade level: K–9. Assesses several areas of academic achievement, including reading, arithmetic, and spelling.

Peabody Individual Achievement Test (PIAT). American Guidance Services, Circle Pines, Minn. Grade level: K and above. Includes subtests in mathematics, reading recognition, reading comprehension, spelling, and general information.

Stanford Achievement Test. Harcourt Brace Jovanovich. Grade level: early school–high school. Measures a child's cognitive abilities at various levels; includes subtests in reading, arithmetic, science, and social studies.

Wide Range Achievement Test (WRAT). Guidance Associates, Wilmington, Del. Age range: 5–adult. Measures reading, spelling, and computation.

Math

Diagnostic Tests and Self-Helps in Arithmetic. California Test Bureau. Grade level: 3–8. Determines diagnosis of arithmetic difficulties; is correlated with corrective self-help exercises.

Key Math Diagnostic Arithmetic Test. American Guidance Services. Grade level: K–6. Includes 14 subtests and measures math skills in content, operations, and applications.

Kraner Preschool Math Inventory. Learning Concepts, Austin, Texas. Grade level: preschool–1. Assesses ability to use quantitative concepts.

Prescriptive Math Inventory. McGraw-Hill, New York, N.Y. Grade level: 4–8. Diagnoses strengths and weaknesses in basic math skills.

Reading

Analytical Reading Inventory. Charles E. Merrill, Columbus, Ohio. Age range: 7–14. Tests five areas, including word recognition, word attack, comprehension, general reading potential, and potential growth.

Botel Reading Inventory. Follett, Chicago, Ill. Grade level: 1–12. Determines reading instructional levels through tests of word opposites, word recognition, and phonics.

Durrell Analysis of Reading Difficulty. Harcourt Brace Jovanovich. Grade level: K–6. Measures reading ability; tests oral reading, silent reading, listening comprehension, word recognition and word analysis, visual memory of word forms, auditory analysis of word elements, spelling, and handwriting tasks.

Gates-MacGinitie Reading Tests. Teachers College Press, New York, N.Y. Grade level: 1–9. Evaluates vocabulary, comprehension, speed, and accuracy.

Gates-McKillop Reading Diagnostic Test. Teachers College Press. Age range: nonreaders and above. Provides diagnostic information concerning reading skills.

Gilmore Oral Reading Test. Harcourt Brace Jovanovich. Grade level: 1–8. Measures accuracy of oral reading, comprehension of material read, and rate of reading.

Gray Oral Reading Tests. Bobbs-Merrill, Indianapolis, Ind. Grade level: 1–12. Contains oral reading passages and yields a grade level score that combines rate and accuracy.

Prescriptive Reading Inventory. McGraw-Hill. Grade level: 1–6. Pinpoints an individual's mastery or nonmastery of specific reading objectives.

Spache Diagnostic Reading Scales. California Test Bureau. Grade level: 1–8. Diagnoses reading difficulties and yields word recognition ability score as well as independent, instructional, and potential reading levels.

Woodcock Reading Mastery Tests. American Guidance Services. Grade level: K–12. Consists of five reading subtests (letter identification, word identification, word attack, word comprehension, and passage comprehension) and yields scores according to grade level and mastery level.

AUDITORY PERCEPTION

Goldman-Fristoe-Woodcock Auditory Skills Test Battery. American Guidance Services. Age range: 3–8. Consists of 12 tests of auditory skills.

Goldman-Fristoe-Woodcock Test of Auditory Discrimination. American Guidance Services. Age range: 4 and above. Measures auditory discrimination of phonemes under both quiet and noisy background conditions.

Wepman Auditory Discrimination Test. Language Research Associates, Chicago, Ill. Age range: 5–9. Measures auditory discrimination of phoneme sounds.

INFORMATION PROCESSING

Detroit Tests of Learning Aptitude. Bobbs-Merrill. Age range: 4–adult. Measures 19 various areas of mental processing.

Illinois Test of Psycholinguistic Abilities (ITPA). University of Illinois Press, Urbana, Ill. Age range: 2½–10. Contains 12 subtests in areas of mental processing skills.

Slingerland Screening Tests for Identifying Children with Specific Language Disability. Educator's Publishing Service, Cambridge, Mass. Grade level: 1–6. Contains tests in visual copying, memory, and discrimination: includes three auditory group tests and one individual auditory test.

Valett Developmental Survey of Basic Learning Abilities. Fearon, Belmont, Calif. Age range: 2–7. Consists of a survey of skill development in several areas of growth.

INTELLIGENCE

Boehm Test of Basic Concepts. Psychological Corporation, New York, N.Y. Age range: 5–6. Measures mastery of concepts considered necessary for achievement in school.

California Tests of Mental Maturity. California Test Bureau. Grade level: K–college. Includes five subtests (logical reasoning, spatial relations, numerical reasoning, verbal concepts, and memory) and measures the functional capacities deemed basic to learning, problem solving, and responding to new solutions.

Columbia Mental Maturity Scale. Harcourt Brace Jovanovich. Age range: 3½–9. Measures general reasoning.

Goodenough-Harris Drawing Test. Harcourt Brace Jovanovich. Age range: 3–15. Yields a nonverbal intelligence score obtained through standardized scoring of human figure drawings.

Otis-Lennon Mental Ability Test. Harcourt Brace Jovanovich. Grade level: K–12. Measures general mental ability.

Slosson Intelligence Test. Slosson Educational Publications, East Aurora, N.Y. Age range: 4 and over. Yields an estimate of mental ability.

Stanford-Binet Intelligence Scale. Houghton Mifflin, Boston, Mass. Age range: 2–adult. Measures general mental ability.

Weschler Adult Intelligence Scale (WAIS). Psychological Corporation. Age range: 16 and above. Consists of a basic psychological diagnostic instrument that yields verbal, performance, and full-scale scores.

Wechsler Intelligence Scale for Children (rev. ed.) (WISC-R). Psychological Corporation. Age range: 5–15. Yields verbal, performance, and full-scale IQ scores.

Wechsler Preschool and Primary Scale of Intelligence (WPPSI). Psychological Corporation. Age range: 4–6. Contains verbal and performance subtests and indicates intelligence potential.

LANGUAGE

Carrow Elicited Language Inventory. Learning Concepts. Age range: 3–8. Measures expressive language as the child imitates a sequence of sentences.

Goldman-Fristoe Test of Articulation. American Guidance Services. Age range: 2 and above. Measures articulation of speech sounds in words and sentences.

Houston Test of Language Development. Houston Test Company, Houston, Texas. Age range: 6 months–6 years. Focuses on measuring various aspects of language, including reception, expression, and comprehension.

Northwestern Syntax Screening Test. Northwestern University Press, Evanston, Ill. Age range: 3–8. Measures syntactic expression and comprehension.

Peabody Picture Vocabulary Test (PPVT). American Guidance Services. Age range:

2–adult. Assesses receptive language and includes 150 test plates and stimulus words.

Test for Auditory Comprehension of Language. Learning Concepts. Age range: 3–6. Measures auditory comprehension in the areas of vocabulary, morphology, and syntax.

Test of Oral Language Development (TOLD). Empiric Press, Austin, Texas. Age range: 4–9. Measures receptive and expressive aspects of vocabulary and grammar.

Utah Test of Language Development (UTLD). Communication Research Associates, Salt Lake City, Utah. Age range: 1.6–14.5. Measures expressive and receptive language skills and aspects of conceptual development.

MOTOR DEVELOPMENT

Lincoln-Oseretsky Motor Development Scale. Western Psychological Services, Los Angeles, Calif. Age range: 6–14. Measures overall motor ability.

Purdue Perceptual-Motor Survey. Charles E. Merrill. Age range: 6–10. Focuses on assessment of skills concerned with laterality, directionality, and perceptual-motor matching.

Southern California Sensory Integration Tests. Western Psychological Services. Age range: 3–10. Consists of the following separate tests: Southern California Kinesthesia and Tactile Perception Test, Southern California Motor Accuracy Test, Southern California Perceptual-Motor Tests, Figure-Ground Visual Perception Tests, Ayres Space Test, Position in Space, and Design Copying.

SOCIAL-EMOTIONAL

AAMD Adaptive Behavior Scales. American Association of Mental Deficiency, Washington, D.C. Age range: 3–adult. Consists of a behavior rating scale for emotionally maladjusted, mentally handicapped, and developmentally disabled persons.

Burk's Behavior Rating Scales. California Association for Neurologically Handicapped Children, Los Angeles, Calif. Grade level: 1–8. Identifies children with pathological behavior as seen by objective personnel.

Devereau Behavior Rating Scale. Devereau Foundation, Devon, Pa. Age range: children–adolescents. Provides a profile to measure 15 behavior dimensions.

Vineland Social Maturity Scale. American Guidance Services. Age range: preschool–adult. Provides an observation and interview scale for assessing personal-social competence.

Walker Problem Behavior Checklist. Western Psychological Services. Grade level: elementary grades. Provides a profile that measures behaviors that interfere with successful academic achievement.

VISUAL PERCEPTION

Bender Visual-Motor Gestalt Test. Western Psychological Services. Age range: 4–10. Tests child's ability to copy visual designs.

Developmental Test of Visual-Motor Integration. Follett Press. Age range: 5–20. Assesses visual-motor skills of the subject in copying designs.

Marianne Frostig Developmental Test of Visual Perception. Consulting Psychologists Press, Palo Alto, Calif. Age range: 3–8. Measures eye-hand coordination, figure-ground perception, constancy of form, position in space, and spatial relationships.

Motor-Free Test of Visual Perception. Academic Therapy, San Rafael, Calif. Age range: 5–8. Tests visual perception without integrating motor skills.

Appendix b
Films and filmstrips

These selected films and filmstrips present theories, diagnoses, and teaching strategies for learning disabilities.

Adolescence and Learning Disabilities. Describes adolescence and relates the period to the LD youngster. 40 minutes. Lawren Productions, Inc., P.O. Box 1542, Burlingame, Calif. 94010.

Albert Einstein: The Education of a Genius. Portrays Einstein's uniquely strong mode of thought; illustrates the importance of matching educational programming to individual differences. 44 minutes. Films For the Humanities, P.O. Box 2053, Princeton, N.J. 08540.

Anyone Can. Presents a teacher training guide for a program of motor development. 30 minutes. Bradley Wright Films, 309 N. Duane Ave., San Gabriel, Calif. 91775.

Bright Boy: Bad Scholar. Illustrates the diagnosis and treatment of LD children. 28 minutes. Contemporary Films, McGraw-Hill, 330 W. 42nd St., New York, N.Y. 10036.

Come On, Willy. You Can Do It. Depicts the program at the Child Study Center for treatment of children with emotional disturbance or learning disabilities. 40 minutes. Audiovisual Media Library, University of Ottawa, 65 Hastey Street, KIN 9A5.

Early Recognition of Learning Disabilities. Shows young LD pupils; interviews parents and teachers. 30 minutes. National Audiovisual Center, National Archives and Records Service, Washington, D.C. 20409.

Help in Auditory Perception. Presents an overview of problems in auditory perception and a description of materials and tasks assigned to students for independent study. 36 minutes. New York State Education Department, Division for Handicapped Children, Special Education Instructional Materials Center, 800 North Pearl Street, Albany, N.Y. 12204.

Help in Visual Perception. Presents the activities involved in increasing visual memory in a child whose "eyes play tricks" on him. 30 minutes. New York State Education Department, Division for Handicapped Children, Special Education Instructional Materials Center, 800 North Pearl Street, Albany, N.Y. 12204.

If a Boy Can't Learn. Deals with a 17-year-old high school student with a learning disability. 28 minutes. Lawren Productions, P.O. Box 1542, Burlingame, Calif. 94010.

I'm Not Too Famous At It. Shows the importance of knowing what children can and cannot do and discusses the varied behavioral problems associated with learning disabilities. 28 minutes. Contemporary Films, McGraw-Hill, 330 W. 42nd Street, New York, N.Y. 10036.

I'm Really Trying. Presents a segment of the "Marcus Welby, M.D." television show about a boy with learning disabilities. 52 minutes. ACLD, 220 Bownsville Road, Pittsburgh, Penn. 15210.

The Legacy of Learning. Discusses the three major learning theories and gives examples of each as they relate to teaching exceptional children. 22 minutes. Media Marketing, W-STAD, Brigham Young University, Provo, Utah 84602.

A Movigenic Curriculum. Explains an experimental motor curriculum and shows exercise for various areas of motor development. 41 minutes. Ray Barsch, SEIMC, 55 Elk Street, Albany, N.Y. 12224.

My Name is nevetS. Deals with learning disabilities—what they are and how they can be recognized in children in the classroom. 27 minutes. Media Marketing, W-STAD, Brigham Young University, Provo, Utah 85602.

Public School Program for Learning Disabilities. Shows a self-contained classroom of young children with various neurological learning disorders. 16 minutes. Office of Educational Service Region of Cook County, 33 W. Grand Avenue, Chicago, Ill. 60610.

Remediation of Learning. Presents a four-part method of remediation, including assessment of learning needs, determination of a prescription, implementation of the prescription, and evaluation of the child's progress. 20 minutes. Media Marketing, W-STAD, Brigham Young University, Provo, Utah 85602.

The School Daze of the Learning Disability Child. Explores and explains the basic handicaps of the LD child, how they create interpersonal problems at home and school, and what might be done to overcome their effects. 45 minutes. Alpern Communications, 220 Gulph Hills Road, Radnor, Penn. 19087.

The Sensitoric Readiness Program. Illustrates the academic implications of training in motor skills. 22 minutes. Pathway School Resource Center, Box 181, Norristown, Penn. 19404.

Specific Learning Disabilities in the Classroom. Presents the hierarchy of development of language in children and the characteristics portrayed by those with learning disabilities. 23 minutes. Davidson Films, 165 Tunstead Avenue, San Anselmo, Calif. 94960.

Specific Learning Disabilities: Evaluation. Graphically presents the specific tasks involved in the evaluation of two young LD children; depicts the team approach to evaluation and recommendations for remediation. 28 minutes. Davidson Films, 165 Tunstead Avenue, San Anselmo, Calif. 94960.

Specific Learning Disabilities: Remedial Programming. Presents the remedial programs designed for children based on the information gained through evaluation and observation of their learning problems. 31 minutes. Davidson Films, 165 Tunstead Avenue, San Anselmo, Calif. 94960.

Thursday's Children. Presents characteristics (especially sensory-motor problems), diagnostic evaluation, and educational programming. 32 minutes. Swank Motion Pictures, 201 South Jefferson Avenue, St. Louis, Mo. 63166.

Visual Perception and Failure to Learn. Uses the *Frostig Test of Visual Perception* to demonstrate the relationship between disabilities in visual perception and various difficulties in learning and behavior. 20 minutes. Churchill Films, 662 North Robertson Blvd., Los Angeles, Calif. 90069.

A Walk in Another Pair of Shoes. Narrator Tennessee Ernie Ford explains to children some of the problems encountered by children with learning disabilities. 18 minutes. CANHC Film Distribution, P.O. Box 1526, Vista, Calif. 92083.

Why Billy Couldn't Learn. Deals with problems, diagnosis, and education of children with neurological handicaps. 40 minutes. California Association for Neurologically Handicapped Children, 6742 Will Rogers Street, Los Angeles, Calif. 96405.

Name index

Abeson, A., 21, 33–34, 114, 116, 119
Abrams, J. C., 101, 116
Abt, I. A., 145
Ackerman, P. T., 44, 60, 199, 222
Adams, P. A., 118, 300, 314
Adams, R. M., 122, 143
Adelman, H., 351, 354, 362–63, 375
Agard, J. A., 320, 334, 395, 408
Aiello, B., 11, 30
Aldrich, R. A., 339, 374
Alexander, W. M., 385, 407
Algozzine, B., 51, 61, 63, 89, 302–3, 313–14, 340, 345, 374, 376
Algozzine, K., 302, 313
Allen, R. P., 137, 147, 301–2, 314
Allen, R. V., 215, 223
Allen, V. L., 326, 334
Alper, T., 431, 461
Alpern, G., 372, 374
Althaus, V., 227, 259–60
Anderson, E. A., 220, 222
Anderson, L., 386, 407, 409
Andrulonis, P. A., 141, 144
Arkans, J. R., 331, 335
Arnott, W., 129, 145
Arter, J. A. 66, 78, 88
Ashlock, R. B., 244, 255, 257, 259
Asperheim, M., 136, 143
Atkinson, J. W., 307, 313
Aymat, F., 138, 146
Ayres, A. J., 135–36, 143–44, 265–66, 271, 274, 293

Badian, N. A., 347, 355, 358–59, 365, 374
Baer, D., 102, 118
Bailey, B. L., 220, 222
Bailey, E. J., 219, 222, 456, 461
Baker, H. J., 173, 175, 191, 266, 293
Ballard, J., 33
Ban, T. A., 140, 144
Bandura, A., 24, 30
Bangs, T., 357–58, 376
Bannatyne, A., 66, 88, 256, 259
Baratta–Lorton, M., 456, 461
Barbe, W., 260
Barlow, C. F., 122, 144
Barnett, A., 219, 223
Barnett, H., 106, 117
Barnhart, C. L., 213, 222
Barr, E., 137, 147
Barr, M. L., 127, 144
Barrett, T. C., 375
Barry, H., 182, 191
Barsch, R. H., 29, 31, 48, 59, 94, 100, 104, 108–9, 116, 274–76, 279, 293, 419, 422, 461
Bartel, N. R., 61, 85, 89, 219, 223, 257, 260, 292, 294, 404, 408, 456, 462
Bastian, H. C., 13, 31
Bateman, B. D., 43, 48–49, 59–60, 66–67, 70, 88–89, 117, 123, 144, 197–99, 212, 218, 223, 401, 408, 463
Bauer, J. N., 53, 60
Baumeister, A. A., 119
Beck, L., 169, 194
Becker, L. D., 58, 60, 340, 362, 364, 376, 395, 408
Becker, W. C., 24, 31, 104, 117, 218, 222
Beery, K. F., 266, 293

Bell, A., 138, 144
Bell, B., 11, 31
Bell, R. A., 359, 378
Bellugi, U., 162, 192
Bender, L., 98, 117, 126, 144, 175, 191, 266, 293, 339, 374
Benger, K., 362, 374
Benthul, H. F., 220, 222
Benton, A., 377
Benton, C. D., 129–30, 144
Bentzen, F. A., 17, 23, 31, 39, 60, 330, 334
Bereiter, C., 254, 259
Berger, B. M., 382, 407
Berko, J., 156–57, 172, 191
Berman, A., 390, 407
Berman, S., 136, 139, 144
Bernstein, J. E., 139, 146
Bestor, A., 11, 31
Bettencourt, B., 431, 461
Betts, E. A., 129, 144
Biggy, M. V., 220, 222
Bijou, S. W., 24, 31, 67, 89
Bilovsky, D., 180, 191
Birch, H. G., 302, 313
Birch, J., 320, 334
Birch, J. W., 40, 61
Blackham, G. T., 104, 117
Blankenship, C. S., 248–49, 259
Bloom, F., 218, 224
Bloom, L., 153, 191
Bloomfield, L., 213, 222
Bluma, S., 372, 374
Boder, E., 123, 144
Boehm, A. E., 173, 191
Boll, T., 372, 374
Bonaventura, E., 365, 377
Bond, G., 72, 89
Bond, G. L., 202, 222
Book, R. M., 352, 354–55, 374
Bortner, M., 267, 293
Boshes, B., 58, 61, 300, 314
Botel, M., 173, 191
Bower, G., 18, 32
Bower, K. B., 139, 144
Brabner, G., Jr., 197, 222
Bradfield, R. H., 104, 117
Bradley, C., 88–89, 137, 144
Bradley, R. H., 343–44, 346, 354, 375
Brainard, S. G., 89
Braine, M., 152–53, 191
Bransome, E., 169, 194
Braud, L. W., 142, 144
Braud, W. G., 142, 144
Brazziel, W., 368, 374
Bridges, J. S., 355–56, 376
Bronfenbrenner, U., 370, 373–74
Brophy, J., 88–89
Brown, B. B., 34, 142, 144
Brown, D. G., 104, 117
Brown, L. F., 180, 191
Brown, R., 157, 162, 191–92
Brown, V., 219, 224, 244, 257, 261, 292, 295, 328–29, 335, 396, 398, 409
Bruner, E. S., 218, 222
Bruner, J. S., 151, 191

473

Name index

Brutten, M., 95–96, 99, 104–5, 108, 117, 390, 407
Bruyn, G. W., 147
Bryan, J. H., 29, 31, 38, 42, 60, 200, 222, 299, 301, 313, 401, 407
Bryan, T. H., 29, 31, 38, 42, 60, 200, 222, 299–301, 308–11, 313, 401, 407
Bryant, N. D., 233, 235, 259, 389, 407
Buchanan, C., 216, 222
Buck, R. D., 21, 34
Buktenica, N., 266, 293
Burns, P. C., 292–93
Buros, O. K., 85, 89
Buscaglia, L., 101, 117
Bush, W. J., 183, 191, 419, 423, 462
Buss, W., 114, 118
Buswell, G. T., 239

Caldwell, B. M., 366, 368, 374, 376
Camp, B. W., 122, 144
Campbell, S. B., 122, 144
Cantwell, D. P., 314
Carlson, J., 102, 112, 117
Carmichael, L., 193
Carnine, D., 24, 31
Carroll, J. B., 188, 191
Cartelli, L. M., 103, 117
Carter, J. L., 143–44
Cartledge, G., 298, 313
Cartwright, G. P., 187–91, 220–22, 284, 293
Cawley, J. F., 227, 259–60
Chaffee, J., Jr., 386, 407
Chalfant, J. C., 44, 49, 60, 233, 260, 265, 293
Chall, J., 202, 212, 222, 269, 295
Chambers, I., 279, 284, 293
Chomsky, C., 159, 191
Chomsky, N. A., 152–53, 191
Chow, S. H. L., 33
Christine, D., 270, 293
Christine, S., 270, 293
Chun, R., 141, 145
Church, A., 34
Church, R. L., 10, 20, 31
Cicirelli, V. G., 368, 374
Clark, E., 157, 191
Clark, G. M., 28, 31
Clark, J., 73, 90
Clark, J. P., 386, 407
Clarke, T. A., 343, 378
Claus, A., 220, 223
Cleeland, C. S., 141, 145
Clements, S. D., 21, 31, 40, 42, 43–44, 46, 54, 59, 60, 98, 117, 199, 222, 299, 313
Clise, M., 431, 462
Cloward, R., 326, 334
Cobb, J. A., 298, 313–14
Cohen, J. J., 359, 361, 374
Cohen, J. S., 21, 34
Cohen, S., 106, 118, 370, 373, 376
Cohen, S. A., 98, 117, 199, 222, 267, 293
Colarusso, R., 266, 293
Cole, C., 300, 314
Coleman, J. S., 367, 375, 383, 407
Coleman, R. W., 367, 375
Collins, N., 102, 118
Comrey, A., 366, 377, 406, 409
Conard, R. J., 392, 408
Conant, J. B., 11, 31, 385, 407
Conger, J. J., 383, 407
Conners, C. K., 137, 144–45
Connolly, A. J., 245, 260
Coppen, A., 301, 313
Cott, A., 98, 117, 140, 142, 144, 301, 313
Cottle, T. J., 382, 407

Coughran, L., 183, 192
Countermine, T., 340, 374
Coursin, D. B., 302, 313
Cowgill, M. L., 362, 375
Cox, L. S., 236, 260
Cratty, B., 48, 60, 274, 276–79, 293, 419, 422, 462
Crew, J. L., 69, 90, 364, 376
Crichton, J. UY., 351, 354, 375
Critchley, M., 200, 222
Cromwell, R. L., 138, 146
Crouse, M. A., 164, 172, 194
Crozier, J., 106, 117
Cruickshank, W. M., 16–18, 23–25, 27, 29, 31–32, 37–40, 56, 60–61, 114, 117, 131, 134–35, 143–45, 263, 277, 293–94, 302, 313–14, 321, 330, 334, 375, 401, 407, 422, 462
Crump, W. E., 235, 260
Curran, C. F., 139, 146
Curtis, B., 125, 141, 144
Curtiss, K. A., 248, 260
Czuchna, G., 102, 118

Danielson, L. C., 53, 60
Dardig, J., 104, 117
Davids, A., 139, 144
Davidson, K. S., 307, 314
Davison, R. G., 368, 377
Dechant, E. V., 218, 222
de Hirsch, K., 152, 192, 351, 353–54, 375–76
Deibert, A. A., 104, 117
Deichman, J. W., 69, 90, 421, 463
Delacato, C. H., 98, 117, 134–35, 144, 274, 293, 424, 462
de la Cruz, F., 222
Dembinski, R. J., 100, 117
DeMyer, M. K., 24, 31
Denckla, M. B., 127, 144
Denhoff, E., 123, 139, 144, 359, 365, 375
Dennis, W., 366, 375
Deno, E., 27, 31, 320, 334
DeRenzi, E., 175, 192
Deshler, D. D., 390, 407
Deutsch, A., 19, 31
Deutsch, C. P., 56, 61
DeYoung, H. G., 21, 34
Diner, H., 359, 361, 374
Dinkmeyer, D., 102, 112, 117
Divoky, D., 38, 60, 138, 147
Dolch, E. W., 188, 192
Doleys, D. M., 103, 117
Doll, E. A., 175, 192
Dolphin, J. E., 17, 31
Doman, G., 134, 144
Doman, R. J., 134, 144
Doster, J., 103, 117
Downing, J., 214, 222
Downs, M., 27, 34
Dreyer, P. H., 407–8
Dubnoff, B., 279, 284, 293
Duling, F., 391, 407
Duncan, L. W., 111, 117
Dunn, L. M., 27, 31, 42, 45, 49, 58, 61, 173, 192, 330, 334, 423, 462
Durkin, D., 423, 462
Dye, H. B., 367, 377
Dykman, R. A., 44, 60, 199, 222
Dykstra, R., 202, 222, 270, 293, 355, 375

Eaton, M. D., 260, 434, 462
Eaves, L. C., 351–52, 354, 375
Eddy, S., 391, 407
Edgington, R., 221–22
Edlund, C. V., 112, 117
Egan, R. A., 138, 146
Eichman, P., 141, 145

Eisenberg, L., 137, 144–45
Eisenhauer, L., 136, 143
Eisenson, J., 151, 162, 192
Elford, G., 221, 223
Eliasson, M., 169, 192
Elkind, D., 260, 384, 407
Elkins, J., 305, 308, 314
Ellis, D., 431, 462
Engelmann, S., 199, 218, 222
Epstein, M. H., 366, 377
Estes, R. E., 122, 143
Evans, J. W., 368, 374

Fairbanks, J. S., 279, 293
Fass, L. A., 85, 89
Feingold, B. F., 98, 117, 141, 145, 302, 313
Felcan, J., 308, 313
Fenton, K. S., 115, 119
Ferinden, W., 329, 334, 355–56, 359, 362, 375
Fernald, G. M., 16, 31, 216, 220, 222, 424, 462
Ferrier, E. E., 180, 192
Ferster, C. B., 24, 31, 303, 313
Feshback, S., 351, 354, 362–63, 375
Fisher, S., 118, 300, 314
Fitzgerald, P. W., 111, 117
Fitzmaurice, A. M., 227, 259–60
Flavell, J. H., 260, 424, 462
Flax, N., 128–29, 145
Fletcher, J., 344, 348, 377
Flye, M. E., 357, 359, 375
Forgnone, C., 43, 45–46, 49, 61, 70, 90
Forrest, T., 118, 300, 314
Foss, B. M., ⅜⅞⅞
Foster, C. R., 175, 192
Foster, G., 63, 89, 340, 375
Foster, G. E., 29, 33, 181, 193
Foster, S., 180, 192
Fowler, G., 137, 146
Fox, B., 222
Frankel, H., 123, 144
Fraser, C., 162, 192
Freeman, F. W., 284, 293
Freeman, R. D., 133, 138, 145
Friedland, S., 362, 375
Friedlander, B. Z., 376
Friel, J., 348–51, 353, 377
Frierson, E., 4, 30–31, 260, 393, 406–7
Fries, C. C., 214, 222
Fristoe, M., 170, 192, 269, 294
Frohman, A., 372, 374
Fromkin, V., 155–56, 158, 192
Frostig, M., 23–24, 31, 66, 89, 266–67, 274, 293–94, 419 422, 462
Fry, E., 215, 222
Fuller, W. W., 351, 354, 362–63, 375
Furst, N., 456–57, 463

Gage, N., 193
Gagne, R. M., 18, 32
Galante, M. B., 357, 359, 375
Gallagher, J., 48, 60, 99, 117, 339, 343–44, 346, 354, 375
Galloway, C., 106, 117
Galloway, K. C., 106, 117
Gantt, W., 302, 313
Garber, H., 338, 370–71, 373, 375–76
Gardner, E. F., 171, 192
Gardner, W., 304, 313
Garrard, S., 123, 145
Garrison, F. H., 123, 145
Gates, A. I., 202, 218, 222
Gattegno, C., 214, 223
Gay, W. D., 180, 194
Gayton, W. F., 106, 118
Gearheart, B. R., 27, 33, 59–60, 85, 89, 138, 140, 145, 212, 223, 257, 260, 338, 397–98, 401, 408–9
Gearheart, C. K., 27, 33, 388, 397–98, 401, 408
Geiger, S., 390, 407
Gentry, N. D., 431, 434, 462
Geschwind, N., 151, 192
Getman, G., 30, 32, 129, 145, 274, 279, 294, 424, 462
Getz, D. J., 129, 145
Giddan, J. J., 175, 192
Giles, M. T., 183, 191, 419, 423, 462
Gill, G., 102, 118
Gillespie, P., 87, 89
Gillingham, A., 15, 32, 217, 223, 292, 294, 424, 462
Glaser, R., 69, 89, 421, 462
Glass, G. V., 133, 135, 147
Glazzard, M., 362, 375
Goering, J. D., 359, 378
Goethals, G. W., 382, 407
Goins, J. T., 265, 294
Goldberg, H. K., 129, 145
Golden, N. E., 270, 294
Goldenberg, D., 365–66, 376
Goldman, R., 170, 192, 269, 294
Goldstein, E. H., 122, 145
Goldstein, K., 16, 32
Good, C. V., 4, 32
Good, T., 88–89
Goodman, L., 27, 32, 267, 294, 388, 397, 401, 404, 407, 409, 422, 462
Goodman, S. E., 377
Goodstein, H. A., 227, 259–60
Gordon, I. J., 106, 108, 117, 346, 370, 373, 375
Gordon, J. E., 313
Gordon, N., 122, 145
Gordon, T., 101, 112, 117
Gottlieb, J., 320, 334, 395, 408
Goyette, C. H., 141, 144
Grant, W. V., 27, 32, 389, 407
Gray, F., 136, 139, 145
Gray, S. W., 338, 375
Green, A., 142, 145
Green, E., 142, 145
Greenfield, P. M., 151, 191
Greenspan, S. B., 129, 145
Greenwood, G. E., 108, 117, 370, 375
Grinspoon, L., 136, 145
Groves, K., 256, 260
Grusec, J. E., 338, 366, 378
Guerney, B. G., Jr., 102, 117
Guilford, J. P., 173, 192
Gullion, M. E., 104, 118
Gussow, J. D., 302, 313
Guthrie, J. T., 377

Haan, N., 382, 407
Hackett, B. M., 382, 407
Hackett, L. C., 279, 294
Hagin, R. A., 390, 407
Hainsworth, M. L., 359, 365, 375
Hainsworth, P. K., 359, 365, 375
Hall, N. A., 219, 223
Hall, R. V., 104, 117, 438, 462
Hallahan, D. P., 16, 23–24, 29, 31–33, 44, 46, 57, 60–61, 114, 117, 122–23, 134–35, 143, 145, 152, 192, 267, 277, 293–94, 302, 313–14, 401, 407–8, 422, 427, 435, 438, 462–63
Halle, M., 155, 162, 192
Hallgren, B., 98, 118, 200, 223
Hallom, J. J., 180, 192
Hammer, S. E., 414, 418, 463
Hammerlynk, L. A., 314
Hammill, D. D., 14, 29, 32–33, 44–45, 56, 60–61, 66, 69, 85, 89–90, 133, 146, 172, 180–83, 192–93, 219–20, 223–24, 244, 257, 260–61, 266–67, 270, 277–78, 292–95, 299, 314,

Name index

328–29, 335, 388–89, 396, 398, 401, 404, 408–9, 422–23, 456, 462–63
Handy, L. C., 314
Hanes, M., 106, 117
Hansen, C. L., 260, 412, 462–63
Harding, C. J., 278, 295
Hare, B., 172, 193
Haring, N. G., 24–26, 32–34, 67, 88–89, 197–99, 212, 218, 223, 260, 334, 338, 362, 372–73, 375–76, 393, 401, 408–9, 427–28, 431, 434–35, 438, 441, 462–64
Harley, J. P., 141, 145
Harlow, H., 366, 375
Harmer, E. W., 28, 32
Harmon, A. J., 104, 117
Harris, A. J., 50, 60, 73, 89, 202, 223
Harris, D., 126, 145
Harris, I., 72, 89
Harris, S. P., 168, 194
Hart, J., 104, 108, 118
Hart, N. W. N., 307, 313
Hartman, A. S., 183, 192
Haughton, E., 210, 223, 247, 260, 431, 462
Havard, J., 142, 145
Havighurst, R. J., 382, 407–8
Hawkins, R., 139, 144
Hawthorne, N., 76, 89
Hayden, A. H., 338, 372–73, 375–76
Hayes, J., 320, 334
Hayes, M. L., 78, 89
Head, H., 13, 32
Hebb, D. O., 273, 294, 366, 376
Heber, R., 338, 370–71, 373, 375–76
Heckelman, R. G., 219, 223
Hegge, T. G., 15, 32, 213, 223
Heilman, A. W., 164, 192
Heins, E. D., 29, 32
Hellmuth, J., 60, 88, 147, 294, 462
Henderson, H. H., 431, 462
Henek, T., 308, 313
Henley, A., 390, 408
Hentoff, N., 136, 145
Herbert, K., 102, 118
Hermann, K., 200, 223
Heron, W., 366, 378
Herrick, V. E., 292, 294
Hess, R. D., 367, 376
Heward, W., 104, 117
Higgins, S. T., 320, 334
Hildreth, G., 282, 294
Hilgard, E., 18, 32
Hill, W. F., 18, 32
Hilliard, J., 372, 374
Hinshelwood, J., 14, 32, 198–200, 223
Hinton, G. G., 137, 146
Hobbs, N., 61, 116, 118
Hodges, L., 38, 61
Hodges, R. E., 219, 223
Hoffer, A., 140, 145
Hoffman, M. S., 359–60, 376
Hogan, G. R., 123, 145
Holliday, A., 339, 374
Holte, A., 391, 408
Homme, L. H., 18, 32
Hopkins, R. L., 392, 408
Hopper, R., 155, 157, 159, 192
Hops, H., 298, 313–15
Horn, E. A., 221, 223
Horn, T. D., 223
Horne, D., 24, 31, 267, 293, 419, 422, 462
Horowitz, F. D., 147, 191, 370, 374, 376
Hutchins, R., 11, 32
Hunt, J. McV., 377

Ikenberry, O. S., 4, 32

Irwin, J. V., 193

Jacobson, F. N., 390, 408
Jacobson, L., 340, 377, 388, 409
Jacobson, S., 125, 144, 355-56, 359, 362, 375
Jakobson, R., 155, 162, 192
Janicki, R. S., 139, 146
Jansky, J., 351, 353–54, 375–76
Jastak, J. F., 220, 223
Jenkins, J. J., 152–153, 192
Jenkins, J. R., 66, 78, 88
Jenson, R. C., 279, 294
Jobes, N., 76, 89
John, L., 239
Johnson, D., 22, 32, 42, 60, 66, 89, 164, 168, 182, 189–90, 192, 200, 223, 265, 282, 294, 301, 311, 313–14, 424, 462
Johnson, G. O., 27, 32, 131, 144
Johnson, M. S., 211, 223
Johnson, S. W., 424, 462
Johnson, W., 187, 192, 284, 294
Johnston, R., 21, 34
Jones, B., 104, 108, 118
Jones, L. V., 21–22, 34
Jones, M. R., 193, 463
Jones, R. L., 315
Jordon, J. B., 223, 260, 462
Junkala, J. B., 40, 60

Kaliski, L., 229, 233, 260
Kane, E. R., 279, 294
Kapelis, L., 362, 376
Karlsen, B., 171, 192
Karnes, M. B., 100, 118
Karp, E. E., 219, 224
Kaslow, F., 101, 116
Kass, C. E., 37, 58, 60, 233, 235, 259, 407
Kauffman, J. M., 24, 29, 31–33, 57, 60–61, 122–23, 145, 152, 192, 219, 224, 256–57, 261, 267, 292–95, 304, 315, 325, 328, 401, 408, 427, 435, 438, 456, 462–64
Kaufman, A., 73, 89
Kaufman, J., 63, 89
Kaufman, M. J., 115, 119, 320–32, 334, 395, 408
Keeney, A. H., 129, 145
Keldgord, R. E., 390, 408
Kelly, V. C., 146
Kendall, D. C., 351, 354, 375
Keniston, K., 382, 408
Kephart, N. C., 17, 32, 34, 48, 60, 274–75, 279, 294–95, 419, 422, 462
Keogh, B. K., 69, 89, 129–30, 145, 199, 223, 300, 314, 340, 357, 359, 362–64, 376, 395, 408
Kershner, J. R., 135, 146
Kessel, F., 159, 192
Kessler, J. W., 305, 314
Kimmell, G. M., 269, 294
King, F. S., 49, 60
Kirk, G., 376
Kirk, S. A., 15, 22, 26–27, 29, 32–33, 42, 48, 55, 57, 60, 66, 70, 89, 121, 127, 130–31, 146, 152, 172–73, 176, 180, 192, 197–98, 202–3, 211, 213–14, 216–17, 219, 223, 266, 269, 294, 305, 308, 314, 338, 367–68, 376, 419, 462
Kirk, W. D., 15, 32, 48, 60, 66, 89, 172–73, 176, 180, 192, 213, 223, 266, 269, 294, 419, 462
Kirp, D., 114, 118
Klaus, R. A., 338, 375
Kliebhan, J. M., 55, 57, 60, 197–98, 202–3, 211, 214, 216–17, 219, 223
Kneedler, R. D., 89, 408
Knights, R. M., 137, 146
Kocsis, J. J., 122, 143
Koenigsknecht, R. A., 183, 193
Konopka, G., 382, 408
Koorland, M. A., 435, 462
Koppitz, E. M., 266, 294, 359, 376

Name index

Kornetsky, E., 137, 146, 169, 192, 302, 314
Kottmeyer, W., 220, 223, 361–62, 376
Kovalinsky, T., 329, 334
Krakower, S. A., 284, 292, 295
Krasner, L., 24, 31, 34, 122, 147, 302, 315
Kratoville, B., 407
Kreinberg, N., 33
Kress, R. A., 211, 223
Krippner, S., 128, 146
Kronick, D., 96, 104, 106–8, 118
Kroth, R. L., 101, 106, 109–12, 114, 118
Kukic, M. B., 320, 334, 395, 408
Kunzelmann, H., 69, 90, 364, 376, 431, 462
Kuriloff, P., 114, 118
Kurtz, P. D., 139, 146
Kurtz, R. A., 102, 119
Kuska, A., 221, 223

Ladd, E. T., 136, 146
Lamme, L., 106, 117
Langford, K., 219, 223
Langford, W. S., 351, 353, 375
Lankford, F. G., Jr., 236, 260
Lapointe, C., 122, 146, 173, 175, 193–94
Larsen, S. C., 27, 29, 32, 66, 83, 87–90, 133, 146, 181–82, 192, 219–20, 223, 267, 270, 294, 333–34, 401, 408
Larson, K., 138, 146
Laurendeau, M., 229, 260
Laurie, T., 399–400, 409
LaVor, M. L., 11, 33
Lee, D. M., 183–84, 215, 223
Lee, L., 173, 175, 193
Lees, J. M., 141, 144
Lefever, D. W., 24, 31, 266–67, 294
Lehtinen, L. E., 17, 24, 34, 39, 42, 61, 263, 273, 283, 295
Leland, B., 173, 175, 191, 266, 293
Lemoine, K., 431, 461
Lenneberg, E. H., 152–53, 193
Lepore, A. V., 227, 259–60
Lerea, L., 172, 193
Lerner, J. W., 18–19, 29–30, 33, 37, 45, 55, 57–58, 60, 71, 85, 89, 105, 118, 133, 146, 197–98, 200–203, 211, 214, 216–17, 219, 223, 227, 260, 263, 265, 273, 284, 294, 301, 311, 313–14, 389, 408, 423, 456, 462
Lessen, E. I., 51, 61
Lessler, K., 355–56, 376
Levitt, E., 106, 118, 370, 373, 376
Levitt, M. L., 395, 408
Lewis, C. D., 32
Lewis, J., 87, 90
Liberman, R., 138, 146
Lighthall, F. F., 307, 314
Liles, B., 183, 192
Lilienfeld, A. M., 359, 377
Lillie, D. L., 93–94, 100, 118
Lilly, M. S., 27, 33
Lind, C. G., 27, 32, 389, 407
Lindsley, O. R., 25, 33, 372, 376, 414, 427, 462
Lobb, H., 138, 146
Logan, D. R., 78, 87, 89
London, P., 122, 146
Long, N. J., 32
Looney, P., 166, 193
Lord, F. E., 19, 33, 131
Lorenz, K., 382, 408
Lovitt, T. C., 25–26, 29–30, 32–33, 38, 61, 67–68, 89, 248–49, 259–60, 321, 332, 334, 412, 422, 424, 427, 434, 438, 456, 462–63
Lund, K. A., 29, 33, 181, 193
Lupin, M. N., 142, 144
Luria, A. R., 151, 193
Lynch, H. T., 302, 314
Lyon, R., 270, 294

Lyons, J. S., 357–58, 376

MacMillan, D., 122, 146, 315, 395, 408
Madden, R., 171, 192
Madle, R. A., 139, 146
Magliocca, L. A., 69, 90, 364, 376
Maietta, D. F., 390, 408
Maitland, S., 355, 376
Malone, J. R., 215, 223
Mandell, M., 142, 146
Mangel, C., 95–96, 99, 104–5, 108, 117, 390, 407
Mann, L., 27, 32, 35, 67, 90, 293–95, 388, 397, 401, 404, 407, 409
Manzo, A. V., 307, 314
Marcus, E., 125, 144
Mardell, C., 365–66, 376
Marge, M., 152, 193
Margolis, J., 199, 223
Marks, C. H., 188, 194
Marsh, G. E., 27, 33, 388, 397–98, 401, 408
Marshall, J. C., 167, 193
Mash, E. J., 314
Maslow, P., 24, 31, 267, 274, 294
Matthes, C., 212, 223
Matthews, C. G., 141, 145
Mauser, A. J., 100, 117, 390, 408
Maxwell, F. P., 115, 119
Mazurkiewicz, A. J., 214, 224
McCall-Perez, F., 29, 33, 181, 193
McCarron, L. T., 180, 193
McCarthy, D., 187, 193
McCarthy, J. J., 22, 33, 48, 60, 172–73, 176, 192, 266, 269, 294, 330, 335
McCarthy, J. M., 29, 33, 59, 61, 330, 335
McConnell, T. R., 138, 146
McCracken, G., 213, 223
McDaniels, G. L., 369, 373, 376
McDowell, R. L., 94, 100–102, 118
McGettigan, J., 172, 193
McGinnis, M. A., 182, 193
McGrady, H., 152, 193
McIntosh, D. K., 42, 45, 49, 58, 61
McKee, B. E., 69, 88, 90
McKee, G. W., 279, 294
McLeod, T. M., 235, 260
McLoughlin, J. A., 29, 34, 94, 106, 119, 189–90, 194, 199, 224, 267, 283, 295, 299, 304, 313, 315, 389, 407
McMenemy, R. A., 218, 224, 235, 260, 292, 295
McNeill, D., 151–53, 193
McNutt, G., 219, 223
McWhirter, J. J., 99–100, 118
Meadow, K. P., 112, 118
Meckel, H. C., 187, 193
Meehl, P. E., 344, 376
Meier, J. H., 58, 61, 166, 193
Meisgeier, C. H., 27, 33
Melcher, J. W., 12, 33
Menolascino, F. J., 119
Menyuk, P., 166, 193
Mercer, A. R., 443, 463
Mercer, C. D., 18, 33, 43, 45–46, 49, 51, 61, 70–71, 90, 139, 144, 325, 328, 340, 344–45, 359–61, 366, 368, 374, 376–77, 425, 442–43, 463
Mercer, J., 87, 90
Merenda, P. F., 365, 377
Michaels, J., 96, 118
Michelli, F. A., 139, 146
Milburn, J. F., 298, 313
Miller, D., 382, 408
Miller, G. A., 192–93
Millichap, J. G., 137–38, 146
Minskoff, E., 183, 193, 419, 423
Minskoff, J. G., 183, 193, 419, 423, 463

Name index

Mirel, E., 132, 146
Miron, M. S., 13, 33
Mirsky, A. F., 169, 194
Mittler, P., 180, 193
Molitch, M., 137, 146
Molloy, L., 27, 33
Money, J., 200, 224
Moneypenny, J., 21, 34
Monroe, M., 15, 33
Mooney, C., 303, 314
Morasky, R. L., 424, 462
Morency, A., 56, 61
Morris, P. R., 343, 378
Morse, W. C., 32
Moyer, S. C., 278, 295
Mulhern, S. T., 183, 193
Murphy, M. L., 43, 46, 61
Mussen, P. H., 191, 193, 378
Myers, P. I., 14, 33, 56, 61, 133, 146, 183, 193, 277–78, 295, 299, 314, 389, 408, 422–23, 463
Myklebust, H. R., 13–14, 22, 32–33, 42, 58, 60–61, 66, 72, 89–90, 147, 152, 164, 168, 182, 189–90, 192–93, 200, 222–23, 265, 282, 294, 298, 300–301, 311, 313–14, 347, 375–76, 408, 424, 462

Nachtman, W., 245, 260
Nadeau, G., 355, 376
Nadeau, J. B. E., 355, 376
Najarian, P., 366, 375
Naremore, R. C., 155, 157, 159, 192
Natchez, G., 457, 463
Neifert, J. T., 106, 118
Neisworth, J. T., 96–97, 119, 139, 146, 324, 335, 435, 463
Nelson, A. E., 143, 147
Nelson, C. M., 435, 464
Newcombe, F., 167, 193
Newcomer, P. L., 66, 69, 90, 172, 180–81, 193, 401, 408, 423, 463
Newland, T. E., 282, 295
Newman, R. G., 32
Niles, J. A., 278, 295
Noble, J. K., 284, 295
Norfleet, M. A., 359, 376
Novack, H. S., 365, 377
Nowlin, L., 431, 461

O'Betts, G., 102, 118
O'Donnell, P., 279, 295
Offer, D., 383, 408
Olmsted, P. P., 108, 117, 370, 375
Olson, D., 314
Olson, J., 442, 463
Olver, R. R., 151, 191
Oppe, T. E., 123, 146
Ort, L. L., 220, 224
Orton, S. T., 14, 33, 152, 193, 198–200, 217, 224, 283, 295, 424, 263
Osgood, C. E., 13, 33, 159, 176, 193, 423, 463
Osmond, H., 140, 145
Ott, J. N., 143, 146
Otto, W., 218, 224, 235, 260, 292, 295
Owen, R. W., 118, 300, 314

Paden, L. Y., 370, 374, 376
Page, B., 393, 408
Page, J. G., 139, 146
Palermo, D. S., 152–53, 192
Pasamanick, B., 359, 377
Patch, V. D., 146
Patterson, C., 102, 118
Patterson, G. R., 104, 118
Paul, J. L., 40, 60, 302–3, 314
Pauling, L. C., 140, 146, 301, 314

Pavlov, I. P., 302, 314
Payne, J. S., 79, 90, 321, 325, 328, 335, 366, 368, 377
Payne, R. A., 79, 90, 321, 335, 368, 377
Pearl, D., 377
Pedersen, F. A., 359, 378
Peniston, E., 372, 377
Perez, F. I., 27, 33
Perine, M., 431, 461
Peters, J. E., 44, 60, 199, 222, 299, 313
Phillips, E., 24–25, 32–33, 67, 89
Philpott, W. H., 142, 146
Piaget, J., 151, 153, 194, 273, 295
Pielstick, N. L., 135, 147
Pinard, A., 229, 260
Pinneau, S. A., 366, 377
Platts, M. E., 257, 260
Plunkett, M., 284, 295
Poling, D., 270, 295
Polloway, E. A., 79, 90, 321, 335
Poremba, C. D., 390, 408
Prelander, J., 431, 462
Pritchett, E. M., 245, 260
Provence, S., 367, 375
Purkey, W., 298, 305, 314
Pushaw, D., 102, 118

Quay, H. C., 29, 33, 67, 76, 90, 419–21, 463
Quinn, P. O., 360–61, 377

Randall, R., 139, 146
Ramp, E., 260
Rapoport, J. L., 360–61, 377
Rapoport, R., 382, 408
Rappaport, S., 298, 314
Rasmus, B., 171, 194
Ratzeburg, R. H., 17, 23, 31, 40, 60, 330, 334
Ray, R., 141, 145
Rayner, R., 302, 315
Reed, J. D., 141, 146
Reger, R., 292, 295
Resnick, L. B., 68, 90
Rheingold, H. L., 366, 377
Rhodes, W. C., 34, 302–3, 314
Ribble, M. A., 366, 377
Ricciuti, H. N., 376
Rice, J. A., 180, 191
Richardson, S. O., 95–96, 99, 104–5, 108, 117, 390, 407
Richmond, J., 123, 147
Rickover, H. G., 11, 34
Ridgway, R. W., 362, 375
Rinaldi, R. T., 69, 90, 364, 376
Risko, V., 391, 407
Ritvo, E. R., 301, 314
Roach, C., 275, 295
Roach, M. A., 165–67, 194
Roberts, R., 222
Robbins, L. S., 223, 260, 462
Robbins, M. P., 133, 135, 147
Roberts, G. H., 235, 260
Robinson, A., 295
Robinson, H. B., 94–95, 97–98, 118
Robinson, J., 279, 293, 295
Robinson, N. M., 94–95, 97–98, 118
Rodman, R., 155–56, 158, 192
Rogers, D., 382–83, 408
Rogers, D. C., 220, 224
Rogers, M. E., 359, 377
Rose, T. L., 141, 147, 302, 314, 435, 462
Rosen, A., 344, 376
Rosen, L., 95, 98, 100, 118
Rosenshine, B., 456–57, 463
Rosenthal, J. H., 166, 194, 305, 314
Rosenthal, R., 340, 377, 388, 409

Name index

Ross, A., 139, 146
Ross, A. O., 46, 61, 143, 147, 442, 463
Ross, R., 302, 315
Ross, S. L., 21, 34
Rosvold, H. E., 169, 194
Roswell, F., 269, 295, 457, 463
Rozynok, V., 143, 147
Rudegeair, F., 350, 353, 377
Rudorf, E. H., 219, 223
Ruebush, B. K., 307, 314
Russ, D. F., 24, 34
Russell, D. H., 219, 224
Russell, R. W., 390, 409
Ryan, N. J., 123, 145

Sabatino, D., 35, 90, 270, 293–95, 329, 335, 340, 375
Safer, D. J., 137, 147, 301–2, 314
Salvia, J., 29, 35, 67, 73, 78, 85, 90, 180, 195, 401, 409, 420–21, 464
Salzman, L., 383, 409
Samuels, S. J., 199, 224
Sandoval, J., 141, 147
Sarason, I., 169, 194
Sarason, S. B., 16, 34, 307, 314
Sartain, H. W., 333, 335
Satz, P., 344, 348–51, 353–54, 377
Saylor, J. G., 385, 407
Schaeffer, F., 279, 284, 293
Scheffelin, M., 44, 60, 233, 260, 265, 293
Schiefelbusch, R. L., 32, 393, 408–9, 427, 435, 462
Schiller, J. S., 368, 374
Schleichkorn, J., 365, 377
Schlenker, P., 106, 117
Schlesinger, H. S., 112, 118
Schloss, E., 34, 407, 409
Schlossman, S. L., 100, 118
Schmid, R. E., 21, 34
Schmidt, C., 340, 375
Schmitt, B., 279, 295
Scholes, R. S., 353, 377
Schoolfield, L., 213, 224
Schrag, P., 138, 147
Schroeder, W., 292, 295
Schucman, H., 96, 118
Scranton, T., 27, 34
Scrimshaw, N. S., 302, 313–14
Sedlak, M. W., 10, 20, 31
Sedlak, R., 227, 259–60
Segner, L., 102, 118
Selye, H., 12, 34
Semb, G., 260
Semel, E. M., 163–66, 168–69, 172–75, 184, 190, 194
Senf, G., 54, 61, 366, 377, 406, 409
Serra, M. C., 220, 224
Shapiro, R., 362, 375
Share, J., 180, 191
Sharp, F. A., 257, 260
Sharpe, L., 137, 145
Shaw, M. C., 305, 314
Shearer, D. E., 338, 371–72, 377
Shearer, M. S., 338, 371–72, 374, 377
Sherrington, C. S., 273, 295
Shipman, V. C., 267, 276
Siegel, E., 390, 409
Sievers, D. J., 22, 34
Silberman, A., 104, 117
Silva, W., 100, 118
Silver, L. B., 134, 140–41, 147, 360, 377
Silverman, R., 399–400, 409
Silverstein, A. B., 307, 315
Silverston, R. A., 69, 90, 421, 463
Silverton, B., 431, 462
Simches, R. F., 116, 188
Simpson, D. D., 143, 147

Simonson, G., 112, 118
Singer, S., 136, 145
Sitko, M., 87, 89
Skeels, H. M., 338, 367–68, 377
Skinner, B. F., 18–19, 34, 152–53, 194, 284, 292, 295, 302, 315
Slade, K., 219, 223
Slingerland, B. H., 218, 224, 424, 463
Slobin, D. I., 191, 194
Smead, V. S., 29, 34, 68–69, 88, 90, 182, 194, 420–21, 460, 463
Smith, A., 142, 147
Smith, C. E., 357, 359, 362–63, 376
Smith, D., 104, 119
Smith, D. A., 359–60, 378
Smith, D. D., 248–49, 260
Smith, F., 193
Smith, H. K., 295, 374
Smith, J., 104, 119
Smith, J. E., Jr., 79, 90, 321, 335
Smith, J. O., 331, 335, 423, 462
Smith, M., 11, 34
Smith, R. J., 218, 224, 235, 260, 292, 295
Smith, R. M., 70, 90, 96–97, 119, 191, 222, 244, 257, 260, 273–74, 293, 295, 324, 335, 435, 463
Smythies, J., 140, 145
Snell, M. E., 18, 33, 425
Solnit, A., 97, 119
Solomon, P., 132, 146
Southwick, D. A., 141, 144
Spache, E. B., 214, 219, 224
Spache, G. D., 214, 224
Spalding, R. B., 16, 34, 213, 224
Spalding, W. T., 16, 34, 213, 224
Spitz, E. B., 134, 144
Spitz, R. A., 366, 378
Spring, C., 141, 147
Sroufe, L. A., 138, 147
Staats, A., 152–53, 194
Stables, J. M., 106, 112, 118
Stahl, M., 102, 118
Stallings, J. A., 218, 224, 369–70, 373, 378
Stark, J., 97, 119, 175, 192
Starlin, A., 433–34, 463
Starlin, C. M., 431, 433–34, 463
Steger, B. M., 278, 295
Steiner, S., 270, 294
Stephens, L. S., 357, 359, 375
Stephens, T. M., 65, 67, 85–86, 90, 104, 106, 112, 119, 171, 194, 219, 224, 227, 244, 257, 261, 267, 270–71, 295, 326, 331, 334–35, 412, 420–21, 426–27, 434–35, 441, 456, 458, 463
Stephenson, B. L., 180, 194
Sterritt, G., 376
Stevens, G. D., 40, 61
Stick, S., 333, 335
Stillman, B., 15, 32, 217, 223, 292, 294, 424, 462
Stimbert, V. E., 338, 378
Stolz, L. M., 118, 300, 314
Stone, M., 135, 147
Strag, G. A., 300, 315
Strang, R., 212, 224
Strauss, A. A., 16–17, 24, 34, 39, 42, 61, 263, 273, 283, 295
Strickland, B., 414, 418, 463
Strother, C. R., 27, 34, 56, 61, 388, 390, 409
Stuart, R. B., 122, 147
Stuckless, E. R., 188, 194
Sturgis, L. H., 138, 146
Sullivan, J., 137, 146
Sulzbacher, S. I., 138, 147
Synolds, D., 143–44

Tanis, D., 353, 377
Tannhauser, M. T., 17, 23, 31, 40, 60, 330, 334
Tanyzer, H. J., 214, 224

Name index

Tarver, S. G., 89, 408, 422, 463
Taylor, H. G., 348, 377
Taylor, I., 157–59, 194
Tchir, C., 300, 314
Templin, M., 171, 194
Thomas, D. R., 24, 31
Thompson, A., 401, 409
Thompson, W. R., 338, 366, 378
Thoresen, C., 89
Timberlake, J., 213, 224
Tinker, M., 72, 89
Tjossem, T. D., 338–39, 370, 374, 376–78
Tomaro, M. S., 104, 199
Tomasi, L., 141, 145
Torgesen, J. K., 309, 312, 315
Trace, A. S., Jr., 213, 224
Tracy, M. L., 34, 302–3, 314
Traub, N., 218, 224
Travers, R. M. W., 463
Travis, L. E., 171, 194
Trifiletti, J. J., 345, 359–61, 376
Trippe, M. J., 122, 147
Trohanis, P. L., 118
True, R., 114, 118
Turnbull, A. P., 414, 418, 463
Turner, A., 353, 377
Tymchuk, A. J., 307, 315

Ullman, L. P., 24, 31, 34, 122, 147, 302, 315
Uschold, K., 292, 295
Utech, A. M., 220, 222

Vallett, R., 104, 119, 298, 315
Van Dyke, L. A., 386, 407
Van Etten, C., 82–82, 90, 94, 118–19, 175, 194, 456, 464
Van Etten, G., 82–83, 90
Van Handel, D., 329, 334
Van Pelt, D., 21, 34
Van Witsen, B., 279, 295
Vaughn, R. W., 38, 61
Vellutino, F. R., 278, 295
Venezky, R. L., 203, 224
Vignolo, L. A., 175, 192
Vinken, P. J., 147
Vogel, S. A., 55, 61, 164, 194
von Hilsheimer, G., 142, 146
Vuckovich, D. J., 125, 127, 147
Vygotsky, L. S., 151, 194

Wade, M. G., 137, 147
Wahl, J., 269, 294
Waite, R. R., 307, 314
Walcutt, C. C., 213, 223
Waldrop, M. F., 359, 378
Walker, H. M., 298, 315
Walker, S., 136, 147
Wallace, G., 29, 34, 85, 90, 94, 106, 119, 189–90, 194, 199, 219, 224, 256–57, 261, 267, 283, 295, 299, 304, 313, 315, 333, 335, 456, 464

Walton, J., 125, 147
Walzer, S., 124, 147
Ward, J., 180, 193
Ware, W. B., 108, 117, 370, 375
Watson, B. L., 94, 118–19, 175, 194, 456, 464
Watson, J. B., 302, 315
Webb, P. K., 180, 194
Weber, R. E., 108–9
Webster, E. J. D., 221, 223
Wechsler, D., 175, 194
Wedell, K., 271, 295
Weiner, L. H., 329, 335
Weintraub, F. J., 21, 33–34, 116, 119
Weiss, H. G., 95–96, 99–100. 103–4, 106, 108, 119, 393, 409
Weiss, M. S., 95–96, 99–100, 103–4, 106, 108, 119, 398, 409
Weithorn, C. J., 302, 315
Wender, P., 301, 315
Wepman, J. M., 21–22, 34, 56, 61, 264, 269, 295
Werner, H., 16, 34, 263, 273, 295
Wernicke, C., 13, 34
Wertlieb, E., 256, 261
Westerman, G. S., 220, 224
Wheeler, L. R., 270, 295
Wheeler, R., 299, 308, 310, 313
Wheeler, V. D., 270, 295
Whelan, R. J., 25, 32, 34, 106, 112, 118
White, O. R., 428, 434–35, 438, 441, 464
White, R. T., 68, 90
Whiting, H. T., 343, 378
Whittlesey, J. R. B., 24, 31, 266–67, 294
Wiederholt, J. L., 4, 12, 29, 35, 219, 244, 257, 261, 267, 292, 294–95, 328–29, 335, 396, 398, 409, 423, 462
Wiig, E. H., 163–69, 172–75, 184, 190, 194
Wilborn, B. L., 359–60, 378
Willenberg, E. P., 85, 89, 393, 409
Williams, E. L., 385, 407
Wilson, L., 103, 119
Windeguth-Behn, A., 300, 314
Wiseman, D. E., 183, 193, 419, 423
Wissink, J. F., 389, 409
Wolfensberger, W., 94, 102, 119, 391, 409
Wolking, W. D., 43, 45–46, 49, 61, 70, 90, 430–32, 464
Wolski, W., 172, 194
Wood, B. S., 155, 157–59, 195
Woodcock, R., 170, 192, 218, 224, 269, 294
Word, P., 143, 147
Worell, J., 435, 464
Wortis, J., 40, 61, 99, 119

Yoshida, R. K., 115–16, 119
Ysseldyke, J. E., 29, 35, 67, 73, 78, 85, 90, 180, 195, 340, 375, 401, 409, 420–21, 464

Zehrbach, R. R., 100, 118
Zigmond, N., 395, 399–400, 409
Zimmerman, E. H., 24, 35
Zimmerman, J., 24, 35
Zubek, J. P., 138, 144
Zucman, E., 134, 144
Zulch, K. J., 126, 147

Subject index

AB design, 435, 437–38
Ability model
   description, 66, 419–22
   functions, 68–70
   research, 66
Abstract level, 251–52, 254
Academic materials instructional approach, 423–424
Adolescence, 382–85
Adolescent, learning disabled
   characteristics, 389–90
   educational programs, 391–406
   prevalence, 389
Allergic reactions, 142
Alphabetic reading approach, 214–15
Anxiety
   activities, 307–8
   definition, 307
Applied behavior analysis
   evaluation of teaching procedures, 435–39
   learning principles, 435
   measurement system, 427
   precision teaching, 427–35
Arithmetic
   assessment, 237–47
   development, 228–32
   disabilities, 229, 233–37
   teaching activities, 248–59
     commercial, 258–59
     research, 248–49
     teacher-constructed, 249–57
   tests, 466
Assessment of Children's Language Comprehension, 175
Association for Children with Learning Disabilities (ACLD), 26–27, 114
Attention disorders, 46, 57
Audiologist, 130–32
Auditory
   association, 268–69
   attention, 169
   blending, 269
   discrimination, 170–71, 268
   figure-ground, 170
   memory, 269
Auditory Discrimination Test, 269
Auditory perception
   activities, 270–71
   description, 268–69
   diagnosis, 269–70
   research, 270
   tests, 466

Basal reading approach, 212
Basic Reading Series, 213
Behavior modification, 24–26
Behavioral theory, 302–3
Behavioristic language theory, 152–53
Bender Visual-Motor Gestalt Test, 266, 359
Biofeedback, 142–43
Biophysical theory, 301–2
Body image activities, 279
Boehm Test of Basic Concepts, 173
Botel Reading Inventory, 173, 207
Brain injured
   behavior criteria, 39

   biological criteria, 39
   definition, 39
   objections to term, 40

Cerebral dominance, 133
Characteristics of learning disabilities, 54–57, 389–90
Classical conditioning, 302
Concrete level, 250, 253
Content-developmental instructional approach, 426–27
Council for Exceptional Children (CEC), 19
Criterion-referenced tests, 208–11

Decibels, 130
Definition of learning disabilities
   adolescence, 388
   discrepancy, 42, 48, 53–54, 401
     diagnostic data, 71–73
   NACHC definition, 43–45
     academic component, 44
       diagnostic data, 71
     affective component, 45
     exclusion component, 44–45
       diagnostic data, 70–71
     intelligence component, 45
     neurological component, 45
     process component, 43–44
       diagnostic data, 71
   operationalization, 49–52
Deno's cascade system, 320
Detroit Tests of Learning Aptitude, 173, 175
Developmental Test of Visual-Motor Integration, 266
Diacritical marking system, 215
Diagnosis
   approaches, 65–70
     ability model, 66–70
     skill model, 67–70
   arithmetic problems, 237–47
   issues and directions, 87–88
   language disabilities, 169–82
   process, 70–83
   purposes, 64–65
   reading problems, 204, 206–12
   spelling problems, 220–21
Diagnostic-prescriptive teaching, 412–14
Diagnostic Spelling Test, 220
Direct measurement, 83
Directionality activities, 279
Distar
   arithmetic, 258
   reading program, 218
Division for Children with Learning Disabilities (DCLD), 26–27
Doman-Delacato theory, 23, 134–35
Doren Diagnostic Reading Test of Word Recognition, 20
Down's syndrome project, 372–73
Drugs
   action, 137
   definition, 136
   guidelines for teacher, 139–40
   nomenclature, 136–37
   research, 137–39
Durrell Analysis of Reading Difficulty, 75, 206
Dyslexia, 200, 202

481

Subject index

Early identification
  guidelines, 362, 364–65
  practices, 347–48
  prediction models, 341–47
  problems, 339–41
  rationale, 338
  single instruments as predictors, 355–61
  teacher perception as a predictor, 361–63
  test batteries as predictors, 348–55
Early intervention
  guidelines, 373–74
  Head Start, 368–70
  projects, 370–73
  rationale, 338, 366–68
Ecological theory, 303
Endogenous retarded, 16, 39
Etiological theories, 98
Exogenous retarded, 16, 39
Expectancy age, 50
Eye, 127–29

Federal Register (1976), 53
Federal Register (1977), 53–54, 58–59, 71, 264
Fernald method, 16, 216–17, 220, 424
Figure-ground discrimination, 266
Films and filmstrips, 469–71
Fine motor activities, 278–79
Food additives, 141
Frostig Developmental Test of Visual Perception, 24, 266–67
Frustration reading level, 211
Frustration tolerance
  activities, 306–7
  definition, 306

Game board format, 454
Gates-MacGinitie Reading Tests, 206
Gates-McKillop Reading Diagnostic Tests, 206
Gates-Russell Spelling Diagnostic Test, 220
Gillingham method, 217–18, 424
Goldman-Fristoe-Woodcock Test of Auditory Discrimination, 269
Graded word lists, 211–12
Gray Oral Reading Test, 207–8
Gross motor activities, 278

Handwriting
  activities, 284, 292
  common illegibilities, 282–83
  cursive and manuscript, 282–83
  diagnosis, 284–89
  left-handedness, 283–84
  objectives by grade level, 291
  problems, 282, 285–90
  programs, 285
  remediation, 285–89
Haptic perception
  activities, 271, 273
  description, 271
  diagnosis, 271
Harris method, 73
Head Start, 368–70
Hegge-Kirk-Kirk Remedial Reading Drills, 213
Hemisphere, 133
High school
  goals, 386–88
  types, 385–86
History of learning disabilities
  birth period, 8–9, 20–27
  genesis period, 4–8, 10–20
  growing pains period, 9, 27–30
Home management, 103–4
Hyperopia, 128
Hypoglycemia, 142

Illinois Test of Psycholinguistic Abilities (ITPA), 22, 69, 172–73, 176–82
Independent reading level, 211
Indirect measurement, 83
Individual Pupil Monitoring System — Reading, 211
Individualized educational program (IEP), 319–20, 324, 414–19
Individualized reading approach, 215–16
Informal reading inventory, 211
Informational counseling strategies, 100–101
Initial language programs, 182–83
Initial teaching alphabet, 214
Instructional approaches
  academic materials, 423–24
  applied behavior analysis, 427–39
  content developmental, 426–27
  learner developmental, 424–26
  multisensory, 424
  perceptual-motor, 422–23
  psycholinguistic, 423
Instructional arrangements, 440–42
Instructional games
  commercial, 455–56
  teacher-made, 452–55
Instructional reading level, 211
Interaction skills, 456–61
Interactionistic language theory, 153
Itinerant services, 327–28

Juvenile delinquency, 390–91

Kaiser-Permanente (K-P) diet, 141–42
Key Math Diagnostic Arithmetic Test, 75, 245
Kinesthetic perception, 271

Labeling, 340
Language
  assessment, 169–82
  components, 153–59
  development, 160–61
  disabilities, 159, 162–69
  disorders, 55
  programs, 182–84
  remediation, 182–87
  tests, 467–68
  theories of acquisition, 152–53
Language experience approach, 215
Learner-developmental instructional approach, 424–26
Learning disabilities
  characteristics, 54–57, 389–90
  definition, 43–54, 388
  diagnosis, 53–88
  incidence, 58–59
  prevalence, 49, 389
Learning disabilities specialist, 398–400
Learning quotient method, 72–73
Least restrictive environment, 320, 391–92
Legislation and litigation, 11–12, 21, 28–29
Linguistics
  language remediation approaches, 183–87
  reading approach, 213–14

Mainstreaming, 320–21
Math Man, 443, 45
Math War Game, 251–53
Medicine
  history, 122
  model, 122–23
  specialists, 123–33
  treatments, 133–43
Megavitamin therapy, 140–41
Memory problems, 57
Mental grade method, 72

Subject index

Metropolitan Achievement Tests — Reading, 206
Milwaukee project, 370–71
Minimal brain dysfunction
  characteristics, 41–42
  classification guide, 41
  criticisms, 42
  definition, 42
Morphology
  assessment, 172
  description, 156
  problems, 164
  remediation activities, 184–85
Motor
  disorders, 56
  generalization, 274–75
  learning, 276–77
  pattern, 274
  skill, 274
  tests, 468
Motor-Free Test of Visual Perception, 266
Movigenic
  curriculum, 276
  theory, 275–76
Multidisciplinary team, 54
Multiple-baseline design, 437–39
Multisensory instructional approach, 424
Myopia, 128
Mystery Detective Game, 452–54

National Advisory Committee on Handicapped Children
  (NACHC), 45–45
Nativistic language theory, 152–53
Nervous system, 124–25
Neural retraining, 133–36
Neurological impress method, 219, 424
Neurologist, 124–27
Norm-referenced tests, 204, 206–8
Northwestern Syntax Screening Test, 175

Open Court Basic Readers, 213
Operant conditioning, 303
Ophthalmologist, 129–30
Optometrist, 129–30
Organizations, 19, 26, 29
Orthomolecular medicine, 140–42
Osgood model, 13, 159, 162, 423
Otologist, 130–32

Parent training programs, 101–2
Parental adjustment
  acceptance of child, 98–100
  awareness of problem, 95–96
  recognition of problem, 96–97
  search for cause, 97–98
  search for cure, 98
Parents
  adjustment stages, 94–100
  cooperation with teacher, 109–11
  counseling, 100–2
  observation, 102–3
  PL 94-142, 114–16
  teacher conferences, 111–12
  tutoring, 104–8
Patterning, 134–35
Peabody Picture Vocabulary Test, 173
Peabody Rebus Reading Program, 218
Pediatrician, 123–24
Peer tutoring, 326–27, 440–41
Perception
  auditory, 268–71
  cross-modal, 265
  haptic, tactile, kinesthetic, 271, 273
  visual, 265–68
  whole-part, 265

Perceptual
  disabilities, 264–65
  disorders, 55–56
  modality, 264
Perceptual-motor
  activities, 278–81
  disabilities, 273–74
  history, 16–18, 23–24
  instructional approach, 422–23
  match, 275
  research, 277–78
  theory, 274–75
Pharmacology, 136–40
Phonic reading approach, 212–13
Phonology
  assessment, 169–71
  description, 155–56
  problems, 162–64
  remediation activities, 184
Phonovisual method, 213
Place value
  activities, 253–56
  problems, 236–37
Poke Box, 445–46
Portage project, 371–72
Pragmatics
  assessment, 175–76
  description, 159
  problems, 168–69
  remediation activities, 186–87
Precision teaching, 25, 114, 414, 427–35
Prediction models
  comprehensive evaluation, 344–47
  horizontal evaluation, 342–43
  vertical evaluation, 343–44
Prevalence of learning disabilities, 49, 389
Programmed reading approach, 216
Psychiatrist, 132
Psycholinguistics
  instructional approach, 423
  remediation approaches, 183
Psychologist, 132
Psychotherapeutic counseling strategies, 101
Public Law 91-230, 21, 43
Public Law 94-142, 28–29, 38, 51–53, 58–59, 94, 114–16, 320,
  338, 414
Purdue Perceptual-Motor Survey, 275

Reading
  approaches and materials, 212–19
  diagnosis, 204–12
  development, 202–4
  factors, 198–200
  problems, 200–202
  tests, 466
Rebus reading approach, 218
Referral, 322, 406
Regional Resource Center Diagnostic Inventories
  math, 245–47
  reading, 208–10
Regular class-based programs, 324–30
Reinforcement, 79–82, 457–59
Reinforcement theorists, 18–19, 24–26, 29
Reintegration of students, 331–32
Reporting pupil progress, 112–14
Representational level, 250–51, 254
Resource room, 328–30
Responding to correct answers, 457–59
Responding to incorrect answers, 459
Response modes, 79–80
Reversal design (ABAB), 437–38

Screening, 322

Subject index

Screening Test of Auditory Perception, 269
Secondary programs
  accommodation, 397–98
  factors, 393–95
  learning disabilities specialist, 398–400
  problems, 404, 406
  service delivery model, 395–97
  suggestions for development, 400–404
    curriculum, 402–4
    placement, 401–2
Self-concept
  activities, 305–6
  definitiion, 305
Self-correcting materials
  commercial, 450–52
  teacher-made, 442–50
Self-management skills
  activities, 311–12
  definition, 311
Semantics
  assessment, 172–74
  description, 156–58
  problems, 164–66
  remediation activities, 185
Sensory-integrative therapy, 135–36
Service delivery model, secondary level, 395–97
Services, special education
  placement selection process, 322–24
  procedural safeguards, 333–34
  regular class-based programs, 324–30
  special class-based programs, 330–31
  special school-based programs, 331
Single instruments as predictors
  intelligence tests, 355–56
  language tests, 355, 357–59
  perceptual-motor tests, 357, 359
  physical factors, 357, 359–61
  readiness tests, 355–56
Skill model
  description, 67, 419–22
  functions, 68–70
  research, 67–68
Slowness in work
  activities, 312
  definition, 312
Social-emotional problems
  anxiety, 307–8
  etiology and treatment, 301–3
  low frustration tolerance, 306–7
  poor self-concept, 305–6
  poor self-management, 311–12
  related to learning disabilities, 56–57, 298–99
  research, 299–301
  slowness in work, 312
  social withdrawal/rejection, 308–9
  task avoidance, 309–10
  task interference, 310–11
  tests, 468
Social withdrawal/rejection
  activities, 308–9
  definition, 308
Southern California Sensory Integration Tests, 271
Spache Diagnostic Reading Scales, 206–7
Spatial relations, 265
Special class-based programs, 330–31
Special school-based programs, 331
Spelling
  development, 219–20
  diagnosis, 220–21
Spinning Wheels, 446–47
Splinter skill, 274

Spoken language disorders, 12–14, 21–22
SRA Achievement Series — Reading, 206
Standard Behavior Chart, 428–29
Stanford Diagnostic Reading Test, 171
Stimulus events, 76–79
Strauss syndrome, 40
Subsequent events, 79–82
Sums to nine, 249–52
Swinger, 447–48
Syntax
  assessment, 174–75
  description, 158–59
  problems, 166–68
  remediation activities, 185–86

Tactile perception, 271
Task analysis, 419–22
Task avoidance
  activities, 309–10
  definition, 309
Task interference
  activities, 310–11
  definition, 310
Teacher attributes, 456–57
Teacher perception as a predictor, 361–63
Territorial rights issue, 332–33
Test batteries as predictors, 348–55
Test of Written Spelling, 220
Tests
  arithmetic, 239–47, 466
    informal measures, 239–44
    standardized, 244–47
  auditory perception, 466
  criterion-referenced, 208–11
  formal evaluation, 85
  general academic achievement, 465–66
  informal evaluation, 85–87
  information processing, 467
  intelligence, 467
  language, 169–181, 467–68
  motor development, 468
  norm-referenced, 204, 206–8, 244
  reading, 204, 206–12, 466
    informal measures, 211–12
  social-emotional, 468
  spelling, 220–21
  visual perception, 468
Token Test, 175
Toss A Disc Game, 455
Trace elements, 142
Tutoring
  parents, 104–8
  peer, 326–27

UNIFON, 215

Vineland Social Maturity Scale, 175
Visual
  closure, 266
  discrimination, 265–66
  memory, 266
Visual perception
  activities, 267–68
  description, 265–66
  diagnosis, 266
  research, 266–67
  tests, 468

Wechsler Intelligence Scale for Children (WISC), 72, 175
Woodcock Reading Mastery Tests, 207
Word blindness, 14

Words in Color, 214–15
Writing Road to Reading, 213
Written expression
   components, 187–88
   problems and remediation, 188–90
Written language disorders, 14–16, 22–23

Years-in-school method, 72

DISCHARGED
DISCHARGED
DISCHARGED
DISCHARGED
OCT 18 1985

DISCHARGED
DISCHARGED
FEB 28 1989

DISCHARGED
DISCHARGED

DISCHARGED
DISCHARGED

DISCHARGED
DISCHARGED
DISCHARGED 1989

DISCHARGED
AUG 22 1983
DISCHARGED
NOV 19 1992

DISCHARGED
DISCHARGED
MAR 15 1984

DISCHARGED

DISCHARGED
JAN 22 1991
DISCHARGED

OCT 4 1984

DISCHARGED
OCT 17 1984

APR 23 1987

MAR 29 1992

APR 08 1992